1850–1900

Small's maze learning study	**1900**	
	1899	Wilde: *The Importance of Being Earnest*
Thorndike's puzzle box research	1898	U.S. declares war on Spain over Cuba
Ellis: *Studies in the Psychology of Sex*	1897	
Dewey on reflex arc; Witmer's clinic founded	1896	Beginning of Klondike gold rush (Alaska)
Breuer and Freud: *Studies on Hysteria*	**1895**	Roentgen discovers X-rays
Washburn's PhD (first woman)	1894	
Külpe: *Outline of Psychology*	1893	Chicago's Columbian Exposition
Hall starts APA / Titchener and Münsterberg arrive	1892	New immigration center opens at Ellis Island
	1891	
James: *Principles of Psychology*	**1890**	First moving-picture film shows appear (New York)
	1889	London murders by "Jack the Ripper"
	1888	Rimsky-Korsakov symphony: Scheherazade
Hall starts *American Journal of Psychology*	1887	
	1886	Stevenson: *Dr. Jekyll and Mr. Hyde*
Ebbinghaus: *On Memory*	**1885**	Gilbert and Sullivan: *The Mikado*
Galton's anthropometric lab opens in London	1884	
First lab in U.S. opens (Johns Hopkins)	1883	Brooklyn Bridge opens in New York
	1882	Stevenson: *Treasure Island*
	1881	
Breuer begins treating Bertha Pappenheim (Anna O.)	**1880**	Rodin sculpts *The Thinker*
Official founding year for Wundt's lab at Leipzig	1879	Anti-Jesuit laws introduced in France
	1878	Gilbert and Sullivan: *H.M.S. Pinafore*
Darwin publishes biographical sketch of his infant son	1877	
The journal *Mind* established in England	1876	Bells invents telephone; Johns Hopkins opens
Galton publishes on twins	**1875**	Twain: *The Adventures of Tom Sawyer*
Wundt: *Principles of Physiological Psychology*	1874	First Impressionist art exhibit in Paris
	1873	
Darwin: *Expressions of the Emotions*	1872	
Darwin: *Descent of Man*	1871	The great fire in Chicago
Fritsch and Hitzig: first electrical stimulation of the brain	**1870**	J. D. Rockefeller founds Standard Oil Company
J. S. Mill: *The Subjection of Women*	1869	Clipper ship *Cutty Sark* launched
Donders publishes on reaction time	1868	
	1867	Russia sells Alaska to U.S. for $7,200,000
	1866	Nobel invents dynamite
James accompanies Aggassiz to the Amazon	**1865**	
	1864	"In God We Trust" first appears on U.S. coins
Wundt: *Lectures on Human and Animal Psychology*	1863	Lincoln's Gettysburg address
	1862	
Broca's autopsy on "Tan"	1861	U.S. Civil War begins (ends 1865)
Fechner: *Elements of Psychophysics*	**1860**	First British Open golf championship
Darwin: *Origin of Species*	1859	
Wundt becomes assistant to Helmholtz	1858	Burton and Speke explore the Nile
	1857	
	1856	Neanderthal skull found near Düsseldorf
Spencer: *Principles of Psychology*	**1855**	Florence Nightingale nurses in Crimean war
Helmholtz on the speed of neural impulse	1854	Pope declares Immaculate Conception as dogma
	1853	
Congress authorizes funds: first federal mental hospital	1852	Stowe: *Uncle Tom's Cabin*
	1851	Melville: *Moby Dick*
On October 22, Fechner's insight	**1850**	

FOURTH EDITION

A HISTORY OF MODERN PSYCHOLOGY

C. JAMES GOODWIN
Western Carolina University

WILEY

JOHN WILEY & SONS, INC.

To Susan

VP & Executive Publisher	Jay O'Callaghan
Executive Editor	Christopher Johnson
Associate Editor	Eileen McKeever
Editorial Assistant	Maura Gilligan
Marketing Manager	Margaret Barrett
Marketing Assistant	Patrick Flatley
Photo Researcher	Sheena Goldstein
Senior Media Editor	Lynn Pearlman
Senior Production Manager	Janis Soo
Assistant Production Editor	Yee Lyn Song
Cover Designer	Jerel Seah
Cover Photo Credit	Roy Botterell/Getty Images, Inc.

This book was set in 10/12 Times Roman by Laserwords Private Limited and was printed and bound by Malloy Lithographers. The cover was printed by Malloy Lithographers.

This book is printed on acid-free paper. ∞

Founded in 1807, John Wiley & Sons, Inc. has been a valued source of knowledge and understanding for more than 200 years, helping people around the world meet their needs and fulfill their aspirations. Our company is built on a foundation of principles that include responsibility to the communities we serve and where we live and work. In 2008, we launched a Corporate Citizenship Initiative, a global effort to address the environmental, social, economic, and ethical challenges we face in our business. Among the issues we are addressing are carbon impact, paper specifications and procurement, ethical conduct within our business and among our vendors, and community and charitable support. For more information, please visit our website: www.wiley.com/go/citizenship.

Evaluation copies are provided to qualified academics and professionals for review purposes only, for use in their courses during the next academic year. These copies are licensed and may not be sold or transferred to a third party. Upon completion of the review period, please return the evaluation copy to Wiley. Return instructions and a free-of-charge return mailing label are available at www.wiley.com/go/returnlabel. If you have chosen to adopt this textbook for use in your course, please accept this book as your complimentary desk copy. Outside of the United States, please contact your local sales representative.

Library of Congress Cataloging-in-Publication Data
Goodwin, C. James.
    A history of modern psychology / C. James Goodwin.—4th ed.
      p. cm.
    Includes bibliographical references and index.
    ISBN 978-1-118-01145-4 (hardback)
  1. Psychology—History—20th century. 2. Psychology—History—19th century. I. Title.
    BF105.G66 2012
    150.09'04—dc23

                                    2011032475

Printed in the United States of America

10 9 8 7 6 5 4 3 2

BRIEF CONTENTS

CONTENTS

KEY DATE BOXES—DATE SUMMARY

PREFACE

TO THE INSTRUCTOR

As you already know if you have taught the history and systems course, it can be a hard sell to students. They often come into the course with firm and long-standing negative preconceptions about studying history and prepared to agree that history is "just one d——d thing after another," as someone once said. And when they discover the last name of psychology's premier historian, E. G. Boring, they may nod their heads knowingly. This attitude is unfortunate, of course, because I can think of no more fascinating subject than the history of psychology. It is replete with extraordinary persons and events, and it yields insights into the basic questions still being asked in psychology today. More than any other course in the psychology curriculum, the history course gives students an overall perspective on their chosen field of study.

No one can be an informed psychologist without having some knowledge of the discipline's history. Our task as instructors is to show students how valuable a knowledge of psychology's history can be, help them connect psychology's present with its rich past, and get them to understand how exciting the journey from past to present has been. I hope that my textbook will aid in this process.

The book is titled a history of *modern* psychology, reflecting the decision about where to begin the course that faces everyone who teaches it. Psychology has deep roots in Western philosophical thought; hence, a full understanding of important and recurring themes requires some understanding of this heritage. Texts, however, differ in the depth of coverage given to our philosophical ancestors and tend to fall into two groups. Some books invest considerable effort in exploring philosophical issues and provide in-depth coverage dating back to the ancient Greeks. This certainly is a legitimate strategy, but not the one I have chosen to follow. Instead, my text belongs in the second grouping—that is, although not by any means ignoring philosophical roots, it devotes less space to them and more space to the recent history of psychology, especially that of the past 150 years. Like other "modern" histories of psychology, its treatment of philosophy begins in the vicinity of Descartes and the British empiricists.

The decision about a starting point is partly pragmatic—it has been my long experience as a teacher of this course, which typically has to fit into a 15-week semester, that extensive treatment of philosophical thought between the time of the Greeks and Descartes makes it impossible to get very far into the 20th century ("It's December and we've just started Watson!"). I always remind myself that the course is not just a history or a philosophy course, but part of the psychology curriculum, and that if I want students to make meaningful connections between my course and their other psychology classes (an important goal for me), it is necessary to get to the 19th and 20th centuries as quickly as possible. The history course must teach students about the ideas and research of pioneer psychologists, especially those who worked within the past 100 years or so. Students have heard about some of these people in other courses (e.g., Hall in adolescent psychology, Watson in the learning course, Freud in personality, Binet in tests and measurements, Münsterberg in industrial-organizational psychology). The history course serves to build on that rudimentary knowledge and interconnect it.

The book includes several pedagogical tools. For students, there is an online Study Guide that includes a guided concept review and several different forms of sample test material, with feedback. Students can reach it by going to the book's website (www.wiley.com/college/goodwin) and clicking on the "Student Companion Site." As for the text, all chapters begin with a *Preview* and a set of *Chapter Objectives*, which set the stage for what is to come, and end with a detailed *Summary* of the chapter's contents and a brief annotated list of articles and/or books in a *For Further Reading* section. The lists' journal articles in particular can be useful as additional reading assignments, providing insight into how historians of psychology do their work. The articles and books can also be useful starting points for research papers. Each chapter begins with a carefully selected quote that is also worked into the narrative at some point in the chapter. For each chapter, I have also identified a year that corresponds to some especially important event in psychology's history and have included a *Key Date* box that highlights events occurring both within and outside of psychology during that year. To further enable the student to make some links between psychology and the rest of the world, timelines are included on front and back endpapers of the book. A password-protected online Instructor's Manual (e.g., a variety of assignments that I have developed over the years and other assignments and activities culled from *Teaching of Psychology*) and Test Bank are available to instructors who use the text (go to the book's website, www.wiley.com/college/goodwin, and click on the "Instructor Companion Site").

New to the Fourth Edition

- The overall organization of the book remains about the same as in the third edition. However, adding material on the history of insane asylums lengthened an already long Chapter 12, so I have moved material on the history of clinical psychology in the United States (e.g., Witmer) from Chapter 12 to Chapter 13, where it works together smoothly with post–World War II developments in clinical psychology (e.g., the Boulder conference). I have also worked through every line of the book, clarifying points that appeared unclear and elaborating when necessary. The file that I keep as I go along, which documents specific changes from the prior edition, runs to nine pages.

- I have tried to keep up with scholarship in the history of psychology, and that is reflected in the addition of just over 70 new references in this edition.

- Although I have maintained a fair amount of biographical information, because it adds interest and helps situate historical characters in their times and places, I have reduced this information somewhat and replaced it with more information on psychology's important concepts, research, and theories.

- Coverage of the following topics has been added or elaborated from prior editions: archival researching, J. S. Mill's education, Broca and the discovery of the speech center, introspection as practiced in different labs, the effect of slavery on Darwin's thinking, sexual selection added to natural selection, De Candolle's argument with

Galton, effects of William James's Amazon trip, Hall's use of recapitulation, the psychology exhibit at the Columbian Exposition, E. W. Scripture and the application of laboratory procedures to sports, the fate of Little Albert, Scott's application of memory principles to advertising, applied psychology in Europe, the Brelands' IQ Zoo as an illustration of applied operant technology, the asylum movement and the attempt to improve mental health via architecture, British psychologist C. S. Myers and shell shock, James Gibson and ecological perception.

TO THE STUDENT

A primary theme of this book is that understanding the present requires knowing the past. You know something about psychology's present state by virtue of the other psychology courses you have taken, but you are probably not aware of the many interconnections that exist among the different areas of psychology you have studied. One goal of a history of psychology course is to make those connections. For example, although I am sure that you know something about the nature–nurture issue, you probably are not knowledgeable about how our current understanding of it has been affected by Darwinian theory, by the search for tests of mental ability, and by the behavior of rats in mazes. Presumably, this last sentence will have deeper meaning for you after you have finished the course than it does now.

You are about to meet some fascinating individuals who helped shape the psychology that you have been studying in other courses. While we tend to think of historical figures as being somehow remote and different from ordinary persons, I have tried to show that these individuals were real human beings, often struggling with the kinds of problems that affect the rest of us. In the pages that follow, you will be meeting some people whose efforts led to some extraordinary accomplishments, but who also dealt with some of the same issues that may be of concern to you. For example. . .

- Are you tired of school and ready to get out into the "real" world and learn things on your own?

    Read about René Descartes (Chapter 2).

- Are you fed up with the way things are, wish you could change them, and willing to take on the status quo?

    Learn about John B. Watson (Chapter 10), B. F. Skinner (Chapter 11), or Dorothea Dix (Chapter 12).

- Are you faced with major decisions about your future and worried about taking a big career risk?

    Refer to the discussion about E. B. Titchener (Chapter 7) or Wolfgang Köhler (Chapter 9).

- Are you fascinated by research and enjoy collecting and analyzing data?

    See Hermann Ebbinghaus (Chapter 4), Ivan Pavlov (Chapter 10), or Leon Festinger (Chapter 14).

- Do you have a strong desire to help others?

    Read about Mary Cover Jones (Chapter 10), William Tuke (Chapter 12), or Carl Rogers (Chapter 13).

- Do you have a strong desire to achieve but face a stacked deck because of racism or sexism?

    Learn about the determination of Francis Sumner, Mary Calkins (both in Chapter 6), or Eleanor Gibson (Chapter 15).

- Are you a slow starter, not doing well in school, and wondering if you have a future?

    Study the early life of Wilhelm Wundt (Chapter 4), Charles Darwin (Chapter 5) or Donald Hebb (Chapter 14).

- Are you concerned that health problems or a physical handicap will make it difficult for you to reach your goals?

    Read about Lewis Terman (Chapter 8) or Clark Hull (Chapter 11).

I hope that you will enjoy reading this book, that you will learn something about psychology's present by learning about its past, and that you will gain some insight into human behavior in the process. At the end of the course, I hope that you will want to continue learning more about psychology's fascinating history.

To help you master the material in this text, I have prepared an online Study Guide. You can find it by going to www.wiley.com/college/goodwin and clicking on "Student Companion Site" for this text. Among other things, it includes some practice tests that will help you ace the course.

ACKNOWLEDGMENTS

My graduate training was in the experimental psychology of memory and was typical in many ways: long hours in the lab, combined with joy whenever p was less than .05. The experience was a bit different for me, however, because my dissertation director, Darryl Bruce, was excited about psychology's history—and the feeling was infectious. While teaching me to be a good scientist, he was also convincing me of history's great truth: You cannot understand the present without knowing the past. So to Darryl, who recently passed away from complications following a stroke, I owe a debt that I will never be able to repay.

In Chapter 1, you will see a photo of John Popplestone and Marion White McPherson of the Archives of the History of American Psychology (AHAP) in Akron, Ohio. AHAP was about a 2-hour ride from my house for a number of years, so I benefited from their hospitality and their eagerness to help an aspiring psychologist-historian on numerous occasions. John has now retired, and Marion died in 2000. I think of them often. The new director of AHAP, David Baker, has also been immensely helpful to me and has become a good friend. Thanks also to my numerous colleagues in the Society for the History of Psychology (APA Division 26), especially Ludy Benjamin and Don Dewsbury, for their support and encouragement as I struggled to become knowledgeable as a historian of psychology.

The editors and staff at John Wiley continue to impress. Special thanks go to the psychology editor Chris Johnson, who has been consistently supportive of all three of my Wiley books, and assistant editor Eileen McKeever, whose enthusiasm, good cheer, and sharp mind has made this revision process considerably less burdensome than it otherwise would be. Thanks also go to production editor Yee Lyn Song, who efficiently coordinated the production process.

Finally, I am grateful for the many thoughtful comments of the stalwart reviewers for the text. They included, for this fourth edition,

Ronald B. McCarver, University of Alabama; Cathy A. Grover, Emporia State University; and Michael T. Scholes, University of Central Arkansas.

CHAPTER 1

INTRODUCING PSYCHOLOGY'S HISTORY

The seats on the train of progress all face backwards: you can see the past but only guess about the future. Yet a knowledge of history, although it can never be complete and fails miserably to foretell the future, has a huge capacity for adding significance to the understanding of the present.

—E. G. Boring, 1963a

PREVIEW AND CHAPTER OBJECTIVES

This chapter opens by describing the origins of psychology's interest in its history and the reasons why it is important to know and appreciate both history in general and psychology's history in particular. A contrast is drawn between traditional histories of psychology, which emphasized the contributions of distinguished psychologists, the outcomes of famous experiments, and the debates among adherents of different "schools" of psychology, and a newer approach, which tries to situate events and people into a broader historical context. This chapter also considers the methods used by historians to conduct research in history, and the problems they face when constructing historical narratives from available data. After you finish this chapter, you should be able to:

- Describe the events during the 1960s that led to a renewed interest in psychology's history among psychologists
- Explain why it is important for everyone to have some understanding of history
- Explain why it is especially important for students of psychology to understand psychology's history
- Distinguish between "old" and "new" history, as psychologist–historian Laurel Furumoto used the terms
- Distinguish between presentist and historicist views of history and articulate the dangers of presentist thinking
- Distinguish between internal and external histories of psychology and describe the benefits of examining each
- Explain the appeal of and the problems with a personalistic approach to history
- Describe a naturalistic approach to history, the kind of evidence used to support it (e.g., multiples), and its limitations
- Define historiography and describe the various selection and interpretation problems faced by historians when they do their work

- Distinguish between primary and secondary sources of historical information and describe the kinds of primary source information typically found by historians in archives
- Explain how the process of doing history can produce some degree of confidence that a measure of truth has been attained

PSYCHOLOGY AND ITS HISTORY

One hundred is a nice round number, and a 100th anniversary is ample cause for celebration. In the last 30 years or so, psychologists with a sense of history have celebrated often. The festivities began back in 1979, with the centennial of the founding of Wilhelm Wundt's famous laboratory at Leipzig, Germany. Then in 1992, the American Psychological Association (APA) created a yearlong series of events to commemorate the centennial of its founding in G. Stanley Hall's study at Clark University on July 8, 1892. During the centennial year, historical articles appeared in all of the APA's journals, a special issue of *American Psychologist* focused on history, and several books dealing with APA's history appeared (e.g., Evans, Sexton, & Cadwallader, 1992). Also, regional conventions had historical themes, and the annual APA convention in Washington featured events ranging from the usual symposia and invited addresses on history to a fancy dress ball at Union Station featuring period (1892) costumes and a huge birthday cake.

Interest in psychology's history has not been limited to centennial celebrations, of course. Histories of psychology were written soon after psychology itself appeared on the academic scene (e.g., Baldwin, 1913), and at least two of psychology's most famous books, E. G. Boring's *A History of Experimental Psychology* (1929; 1950) and Edna Heidbreder's *Seven Psychologies* (1933) are histories. It wasn't until the 1960s, however, that significant interest in the history of psychology as a specialized area of research began. During that decade, a number of individuals with training as psychologists and a keen interest in history came together and did the sorts of things that mark the creation of a new specialized discipline—they formed professional organizations, they created a journal, and they established institutional bases for the production of historical research.

Many people were involved, but the major impetus came from a clinical psychologist with a passion for history, Robert I. Watson (1909–1980). He began with a call to arms, a 1960 *American Psychologist* article entitled "The History of Psychology: A Neglected Area" (Watson, 1960), in which he documented a serious lack of interest in history among psychologists and a paucity of articles about history in psychology journals. Watson then mobilized a small group of like-minded psychologists within APA into a "History of Psychology Group," the eventual outcome being the creation of a new APA division (#26) of the APA in 1965 (Hilgard, 1982). Not surprisingly, Watson was first president of the division.[1] Also in 1965, (a) John Popplestone and Marion White McPherson (Figure 1.1), two more clinicians in love with history, established the Archives of the History of American Psychology at their school, The University of Akron, making Watson chair of the Archive's board of advisors; and (b) the first issue of a new scholarly journal, the *Journal of the History of the Behavioral Sciences*,

---

[1] Today, Division 26 is also known as the Society for the History of Psychology. Information can be found at http://historyofpsych.org/

FIGURE 1.1   Marion White McPherson and John Popplestone, cofounders of the Archives of the History of American Psychology, The University of Akron. From Cohen (1991).

appeared, edited by Watson. A few years later, as part of a reorganization of its graduate programs, the University of New Hampshire created the first doctoral program offering specialization in the history of psychology. Watson was its first director. Finally, also under the leadership of Watson, Joseph Brozek, and Barbara Ross, the National Science Foundation (NSF) sponsored a 6-week summer institute on the New Hampshire campus in 1968 that spawned Watson's final creation, the Cheiron Society, an interdisciplinary "International Society for the History of Behavioral and Social Sciences" (Brozek, Watson, & Ross, 1970). Within a decade, then, Watson was the prime mover in developing the history of psychology as a research specialty.

Since the 1960s, interest in psychology's history has grown. For example, membership in APA's Division 26 in 2010 stood at just under 500, compared with the 234 who joined as charter members in 1965. The story is the same for Cheiron. Psychologists also have become more likely to recognize the importance of the history course to the psychology curriculum. At a conference on the undergraduate curriculum, held at St. Mary's College in Maryland in 1991, one of the group's recommendations was for the curriculum to include a senior capstone course that integrated student experiences in other courses; the history and systems course was mentioned as a prime example of such a capstone (Lloyd & Brewer, 1992). And in a survey of the present status of the history of psychology course, circa 2000, Fuchs and Viney (2002) worried that course content and textbooks did not always reflect recent scholarship in psychology's history; however, the authors found that most psychology departments were teaching the course and that more than half required psychology majors to take it. On balance, they pronounced the history of psychology course to be "alive and well" (p. 12).

Despite some consensus among psychologists that studying the discipline's history is important, students majoring in psychology are often surprised to discover that a course in the history of psychology is offered in and perhaps required by their department. They check with their chemistry-major friends and find nothing comparable in that department. They examine the college catalog and discover that the closest course is one in the history of science, but the history department teaches it, not one of the science departments. What's going on? Why is there a history of psychology course taught by a psychologist, but not a history of chemistry course taught by a chemist?

The rationale for a history of psychology course is important, and it is considered shortly. First, however, let's examine the more general question of why it is important to study the history of anything. Is it true that "history is more or less bunk," as Henry Ford once said, or is it more likely, in the words of Abraham Lincoln, that "we cannot escape history" (both quotes from Simonton, 1994, p. 3), and that to "neglect history does not mean to escape from its influence," as Robert Watson (1960, p. 255) declared in his call for psychologists to become more involved in the history of their discipline?

WHY STUDY HISTORY?

Every history course you have taken has preached to you that knowing history helps avoid the mistakes of the past and provides a guide to the future. These well-worn platitudes may contain a germ of truth, but they are both simplistic. Concerning the "mistake" argument, rather than learning from the past, much of history appears to provide evidence that humans deliberately ignore the past. This possibility led the philosopher-historian G. W. F. Hegel to worry that the only true lesson of history is that people don't learn anything from history (Gilderhus, 2000). This overstates the case—it is also true that when trying to convince others of some course of action, part of our argument usually involves references to the past. Yet it is also true that knowing the past provides only a rough guide, for history never really repeats itself because all events are tied into the unique historical context in which they occur. History is also a less than reliable guide to the future (although it might help us *prepare* for the future), a fact that historians recognize, although the acknowledgement seldom prevents them from venturing forecasts. For instance, in his celebrated *What Is History?* the historian E. H. Carr wrote that "good historians, I suspect, whether they think about it or not, have the future in their bones. Besides the question why? The historian also asks the question: Whither?" (1961, pp. 142–143). This may be so, but it is worth noting that every paper I have ever read or listened to, for which the purpose was predicting the future, has begun with the same disclaimer. The writer or speaker always starts by going to great lengths to ensure the audience that predictions about the future are notoriously inaccurate. As psychology's eminent historian, E. G. Boring, once wrote, "The past is not a crystal ball. It has more whence than whither to it. The seats on the train of progress all face backwards: you can see the past but only guess about the future (1963a, p. 5)."

If knowing history is no guarantee that mistakes won't be repeated, and if history is an imperfect (at best) means of forecasting the future, then what is left? *The present.* In the sentence immediately following the one I just quoted from Boring, he wrote: "Yet a knowledge of history, although it can never be complete and fails miserably to foretell the future, has a huge capacity for adding significance to the understanding of the present" (1963a, p. 5). I believe the single most important reason to study history is that the present cannot be understood without knowing something about the past—how the present came to be. Popular historian David McCullough (1992) expressed this idea eloquently in a commencement address when he drew an analogy between knowing history and knowing someone we love:

> Imagine a man who professes over and over his unending love for a woman but who knows nothing of where she was born or who her parents were or where she went to school or what her life had been like until *he* came along—and furthermore, doesn't care to learn. What would you think of such a person? Yet we appear to have an unending supply of patriots who know nothing of the history of this country, nor are they interested. (p. 222, emphasis in the original)

Think of any current event, and you will recognize that it is impossible to understand the event adequately without knowing some of the history leading to it. For example, consider some recent history within psychology. I am sure that you have heard about APA, the American Psychological Association. You might also know about or at least have heard of APS—the Association for Psychological Science.[2] You might even know that the APS is a fairly recent creature—it was born in 1988 (and had its own set of celebrations in 2008, upon reaching age 20). Perhaps you also recognize that the APS seems more focused on scientific research than the APA, although maybe you are not quite so sure about that; and you might be wondering why there are two organizations for psychologists. Knowing some history would help you understand this. Specifically, your understanding of why APS exists and its purpose would be vastly enhanced if you knew of the long-standing tensions between research psychologists and psychologists whose prime interest is in the professional practice of psychology (e.g., psychotherapy). The problem traces to APA's very beginnings in the late 19th century and contributed to the formation of a separate group of "Experimentalists" in 1904 (the story of this remarkable group is elaborated in Chapter 7). Also, when the APA was reorganized after World War II, the divisional structure that exists today was designed in part to reconcile the conflicting goals of scientists and practitioners. The goodwill that accompanied the end of the war led those with different interests in psychology to unite, but the unity didn't last long. Without knowing something of this history, you could never have a clear understanding of the APS, why it exists today, or why there is lingering tension between APS leaders and the APA governing structure. And there are practical consequences. As a student, if you have an interest in becoming a psychologist, you will probably want to join one of these organizations as a student affiliate (at greatly reduced annual dues). Deciding which to join requires knowing something of the history I just described—someone aiming for a career in the professional practice of psychology might be more likely to affiliate with APA, but a future experimental psychologist might be better served by joining APS.

Another aspect of the importance of the past for understanding the present is that knowledge of history helps us put current events in a better perspective. In the same commencement address quoted earlier, David McCullough related the story of an encounter in Washington with a friend who had just visited the Vietnam Memorial and was visibly moved by it. She asked if McCullough had visited the site, and he said that he had, many times; his first visit was late on a day spent at the nearby Civil War battlefield of Antietam, in Maryland. McCullough was astounded to learn that his friend could not recall ever hearing of this battle, which included a day during which more American lives were lost than on any other day in history. McCullough pointed out that the Vietnam Memorial holds the names of about 57,000 Americans killed during 11 years, but at Antietam on September 17, 1862, there were 23,000

---

[2]In 2006, APS changed its name from the American Psychological Society to the Association for Psychological Science. The name change was designed to highlight the scientific focus of the organization, while at the same time making it international in scope.

casualties—on one day. Knowing about Antietam in no way lessens the importance of the Vietnam War, but an important perspective is gained by knowing about the battlefield just up the road. Knowledge of this kind adds an appreciation of the sacrifices of those from other times and yields an understanding of the idea that war and senseless death are not uniquely associated with just one period of recent history.

There is another way in which knowing history lends perspective to the present day. We sometimes believe that our current times are, as Charles Dickens wrote, "the worst of times." We complain about the seemingly insurmountable problems and the ever-present danger (e.g., from terrorism) that seems to accompany life at the beginning of the 21st century. We long for the "good old days," a simpler time when nobody locked their doors and a good house could be ordered from a Sears kit (this is true). We think that there really used to be places like Disney World's Main Street, USA. But knowing history is a good corrective here. Noted historian and former Librarian of Congress Daniel Boorstin, in an essay entitled "The Prison of the Present" (1971), described this fallacy:

> We sputter against the Polluted Environment—as if it had come with the age of the automobile. We compare our air not with the odor of horse dung and the plague of flies and the smells of garbage and human excrement which filled the cities of the past, but with the honeysuckle perfumes of some nonexistent City Beautiful. We forget that even if the water in many cities today is not spring-pure . . . , still for most of history the water of the cities (and of the countryside) was undrinkable. We reproach ourselves for the ills of disease and malnutrition, and forget that until recently, enteritis and measles and whooping cough, diphtheria and typhoid, were killing diseases of childhood, . . . [and] polio was a summer monster. (pp. 47–48)

Knowing history won't give us easy answers to current problems, but it certainly can immunize us against the belief that these problems are many times worse than they used to be. In fact, knowing the past can provide a comforting connection with it, and being aware of how others have wrestled with similar problems can provide us with some present-day guidance. There is at least the potential for learning from the past.

Besides making it possible for us to understand the present better, studying history provides other benefits. For example, it forces an attitude adjustment, keeping us humble in two ways. First, we occasionally delude ourselves into thinking we know a lot (especially true in my profession—university teaching). Studying history is a good antidote. For example, I grew up in southeastern New England, not far from Plymouth, and I thought I knew something about the Pilgrims. However, having read Nathaniel Philbrick's (2006) brilliant history of the Pilgrims, *Mayflower*, I am amazed by how little I knew—and by how much of what I thought I knew (e.g., about the Pilgrims' troubling relationships with local tribes) was dead wrong. Second, sometimes an ignorance of the past can lead us to a kind of arrogance; we believe that the present is the culmination of centuries of progress and that modern-day accomplishments and thinking are more sophisticated and far surpass those of a crude and uninformed past. Knowing history, however, forces an understanding that each age has its own marvelous accomplishments and its own creative geniuses. Modern-day neuroscientists seem to make fascinating discoveries every day, but the importance of their discoveries and the quality of their scientific thinking do not surpass the elegance of Pierre Flourens's 19th-century investigations of the brain (Chapter 3), which effectively disproved phrenology.

Finally, studying history ultimately means searching for answers to one of life's most fundamental yet perplexing questions: What does it mean to be human? Thus, to study the history of World War II is to delve into the basic nature of prejudice, aggression, and violence. To study the American Revolution is to examine the human desire for freedom and self-determination. To study the history of Renaissance art is to study the human passion for aesthetic pleasure. And to the extent that history involves people behaving in various situations, studying history means studying and trying to understand human behavior. For this reason alone, psychologists should be inherently attracted to the subject.

WHY STUDY PSYCHOLOGY'S HISTORY?

The preceding rationale for studying history is by itself sufficient justification for studying psychology's history, but there are additional reasons why psychologists should be interested in their ancestry. First, compared with other sciences, psychology is still in its infancy—not much more than 130 years old. Much of the content of the other psychology courses you have taken traces back through at least half of those years, and many of the so-called classic studies that you learned about (e.g., Pavlov's conditioning research) formed a major part of the first half of those years. Hence, modern psychology is closely tied to its past; being a literate psychologist necessarily requires knowing some history.

A second and related reason for an interest in psychology's history among psychologists is that the field is still grappling with many of the same topics that occupied it a century ago. Thus an important issue today is the heritability of traits ranging from intelligence to shyness to schizophrenia. This nature–nurture issue, first popularized more than 140 years ago by Sir Francis Galton (Chapter 5) and pondered by humans for centuries, reverberates through the history of psychology. Seeing the parallels between the arguments made now about the relative influence of heredity and environment, and comparing them with those made in earlier times, allows the psychologist a more informed understanding of the issue.

Earlier, a question was raised about the presence of a history of psychology course and the absence of a history of chemistry course. While an understanding of current research and related issues is essential in psychology, the situation is somewhat different in chemistry. Although the history of alchemy, with its stories of how people tried to transform lead into gold, is fascinating and can teach us a great deal about how science works and evolves, it doesn't inform today's students about the chemical properties of lead or of gold. Chemists, who tend to think (naively, as it happens) of their science as steadily progressing from the errors of the past to the truth of the present, aren't normally interested in cluttering their students' minds with "old" ideas. There is a small element of truth to this model of science as advancing through history (nobody tries to turn lead into gold anymore), but it is nonetheless unfortunate that many scientists don't see the value of studying the history of their discipline. At the very least, it would round out their education and teach them something about how scientific thinking has evolved. Indeed, there ought to be a history of chemistry course for chemistry students to take. Instead, they have to settle for history of science courses, typically taught in history rather than science departments.

A third reason why the history of psychology course exists is that it can provide some unity for what has become a diverse and highly specialized field. Despite its youth, psychology in the early 21st century is notable for its lack of unity. Indeed, some observers (e.g., Koch, 1992) have argued that a single field of psychology no longer exists, that a neuroscientist investigating the functioning of endorphins has virtually nothing in common with an industrial psychologist studying the effectiveness of various management styles. Yet all psychologists do have something in common—their history. For the student who has taken a seemingly disconnected variety of courses ranging from developmental to abnormal to social psychology, the history course can serve as a synthesizing experience. By the time you reach the final chapter of this text, where the issue of psychology's increased specialization is again addressed, you will have learned enough to begin understanding the interconnectedness among the different areas of psychology.

Fourth, an understanding of psychology's history makes one a more critical thinker. By being aware of the history of various treatments for psychological disorders, for example, the discerning psychologist is better able to evaluate modern claims for some "revolutionary breakthrough" in psychotherapy. A close examination of this allegedly unique therapy might reveal similarities to earlier approaches. The historically literate psychologist also is aware that on many other occasions, initial excitement over a flashy new therapy (e.g., lobotomy) is tempered by a later failure to find convincing evidence that it works. Furthermore, knowing about the developmental course of various historical pseudoscientific approaches to psychotherapy, and understanding their common features, enables the psychologist to spot the presence of a new one and be suitably skeptical.

Finally, the history of psychology course may be a history course, but it is also a psychology course. Thus one of its goals is to continue educating us about human behavior. Studying historical individuals as they helped develop the science of psychology can only increase our understanding of what makes people behave the way they do. For instance, our understanding of scientific creativity can be enhanced by studying the lives and works of historically creative individuals (Hermann Ebbinghaus is a good example; his work is highlighted in Chapter 4). Some insight into the psychology of controversy and the rigid, dogmatic adherence to one's beliefs can be gained by studying the behavior of scientists engaged in bitter debate with their peers (e.g., the Baldwin–Titchener controversy, described in Chapter 6). In general, if all human behavior reflects a complex interplay between individuals and the environments they inhabit, then studying the lives of historical characters being shaped by and in turn shaping their environments can only increase our understanding of the factors that affect human behavior.

KEY ISSUES IN PSYCHOLOGY'S HISTORY

A common misconception of history is that historians simply "find out what happened" and then write it down in chronological order. As you will learn in the next two sections of this chapter, the process is infinitely more complicated. When they are engaged in their craft, historians have to confront and take a stand on several important issues.

In 1980, APA created the G. Stanley Hall Lecture Series. Prominent psychologists deliver these talks, which are designed to aid undergraduate instruction by informing teachers of the latest developments in the various subfields of psychology. In 1988, Laurel Furumoto, a psychologist–historian from Wellesley College, delivered a lecture devoted to the teaching of psychology's history. The focus of her talk was on a distinction between what she referred to as "old" and "new" history.

The old history of psychology, according to Furumoto (1989), refers to an approach emphasizing the accomplishments of "great" psychologists and concentrates on celebrating "classic studies" and "breakthrough discoveries." Within psychology, the preservation and retelling of these "great events" helped psychology secure an identity as a respectable scientific discipline. The milestones, whether accurately described or not, are passed down from history text to history text as textbook authors rely heavily on secondary sources (e.g., earlier history texts). Furthermore, previous insights or achievements are valued only if they somehow "anticipated" or led up to some modern idea or research outcome. Old research or theory that is of no current relevance is considered erroneous or quaint and is either discarded or held up as an example of "how far we've come." Thus, from the standpoint of old history, the purpose of the history of psychology is to legitimize and even to glorify present-day psychology and to show how it has progressed from the murky depths of its unscientific past to its modern scientific eminence.

Old versus new approaches to psychology's history can be characterized in terms of three contrasts. Old history tends to be presentist, internal, and personalistic. New history, on the other hand, is more historicist, external, and naturalistic.

Presentism Versus Historicism

Earlier, I argued that a major reason for studying history is to better understand what is happening in the present. This is indeed a valid argument. On the other hand, to interpret and assess the past *only* in terms of present understanding is to be guilty of what George Stocking called **presentism**. In an editorial in the opening volume of the *Journal of the History of the Behavioral Sciences*, Stocking (1965) contrasted presentism with an approach called **historicism**. As Stocking described it, the presentist interprets historical events only with reference to modern knowledge and values, whereas the historicist tries to understand the same event in terms of the knowledge and values in existence at the time of the event. Because the historicist tries to place historical events within the overall context of their times, this approach is sometimes called a *contextual* approach to history.

The danger of presentist thinking is that it misleads us into thinking that individuals in the past should have known better and that they ought to have foreseen what was coming. Consequently, we tend to judge historical individuals more harshly than we ought to. "What were they thinking?" we say to ourselves. Consider, for instance, what happened one night at the Newport Folk Festival in 1965. Bob Dylan was a headliner at one of the evening performances, having begun to make a name for himself as a singer-songwriter. He and a small band came onto the stage, gave a vigorous performance of "Maggie's Farm," and were booed vociferously for their efforts. Dylan then played "Like a Rolling Stone," was booed again, and walked off the stage. Whenever I play the video of this event for students, their initial response is to question the intelligence of the audience—"What was wrong with them? This is Bob Dylan. How can anyone boo Bob Dylan?" I point out to them that from today's standpoint, we know how things worked out for him. Our current understanding of music history is that Dylan became famous, an iconic figure. But that outcome was not known in 1965. Even more important, to truly understand the audience reaction that night requires knowing the historical context, specifically, knowing about the Newport Folk Festival as it existed then. Briefly, the festival was designed to highlight "folk music," a very traditional form of music, often passed down in an oral tradition and typically performed with minimal instrumentation. The songs had messages—indeed many of those messages were of protest, common in the 1960s (and Dylan wrote several of them). What Bob Dylan did in 1965 was to challenge the conventions of the festival, in particular the unwritten rule that all instrumentation was to be acoustic. Instead, for the first time in public, Dylan presented what he had been toying with for a while—amplified music. So his performance, featuring loud electric guitars, was decidedly unwelcome at a Newport folk festival. The audience reaction—booing—makes perfect sense in that context.

To demonstrate the dangers of presentist thinking within psychology's history, consider some aspects of the history of intelligence testing. As you will learn in Chapter 8, in the years just before World War I, the American psychologist Henry Goddard was invited to Ellis Island in New York to help in the screening of immigrants. Immigrants deemed "unfit" for various reasons were returned to their country of origin. Goddard firmly believed that intelligence was an inherited trait and that it could be measured with a brand-new technology—something created in France and just beginning to be called an IQ test. Goddard used a version of an IQ test that he had translated from the French test to identify "feebleminded" immigrants. His work contributed to the deportation of untold numbers of people, and his conclusion that large percentages of immigrants were "morons" (a term he invented to describe a subcategory of feeblemindedness) might have contributed to the atmosphere that led Congress to pass restrictive immigration quotas in the 1920s. From today's standpoint, on the basis of an additional 75 years or so of research, we know about the problems with IQ testing and the need for caution when using and interpreting IQ tests. Hence, we find it difficult to believe that someone as smart as Goddard could have behaved with such obvious bias. "What was he thinking?" we might ask ourselves. But to understand Goddard's behavior, it is necessary to study it from the vantage point of the historical period in which it occurred instead of that of the present time. This means being knowledgeable about such things as (a) the powerful influence of Darwinian thinking and Mendelian genetics on the psychological testers of that day, which led easily to a belief that intelligence was a trait that had been naturally selected and enabled a physically weak species (humans) to adapt to their environment during the "struggle for existence" and was therefore inherited; (b) the nation's fears of being overrun with immigrants (large-scale immigration was a fairly new phenomenon at that time); and (c) the assumption, not yet brought into question by such things as atomic bombs and ozone-depleting aerosol cans, that any new technology (e.g., IQ tests) with the "scientific" seal of approval meant "progress" and was therefore good. The list could be continued, but the point is clear. Goddard's work cannot be fairly evaluated by what we now know; it can be understood only in the context of its times. On the other hand, his work does have relevance for us in the present. Knowing about it can (a) help us better understand modern concerns about immigration—it's not a new problem; (b) inform us of the subtle influence of racism and other forms of bigotry, even in intelligent people; and (c) make us properly cautious about the alleged wonders of new technologies that arrive in our own day. Furthermore, just because we attempt to understand Goddard within the context of his own time, this does not mean that we cannot judge his actions. Nonetheless, our criticisms should be made with some caution, taking the form of arguments that were also made by others during the period in question.

Both the Dylan and the Goddard episodes illustrate how difficult it is for us to avoid a presentist orientation. After all, we are the products of our own personal histories, and it is perhaps impossible to ask us to think like a person who doesn't know about the outcome of the Vietnam War, or never experienced Google or the events of 9/11. Nonetheless, for the historian and the reader of history, it is important to at least be aware of the dangers of a strictly presentist view of history and to constantly seek to understand historical episodes on their own terms. One must recognize, as pointed out by historian Bernard Bailyn (quoted in Lathem, 1994), that "the past is not only distant, but different" (p. 53). He went on to write that the major obstacle in overcoming presentism (or "anachronism," as historians often call it) is the problem of "overcoming the knowledge of the outcome. This is one of the great impediments to a truly contextualized history" (p. 53). As to how we might go beyond our knowledge of outcomes and overcome presentist thinking, Bailyn had this suggestion:

> Somehow one has to recapture, and build into the story, contemporaries' ignorance of the future.... One stresses the contingencies—looks for the accidents of the time and tries to avoid assigning the heroism or villainy that was unclear at the time but that was determined by later outcomes. And, if possible, one gives a sympathetic account of the losers. If one can, up to a certain point, work sympathetically with the losers, one can—in some small part at least—overcome the knowledge of the outcome. (pp. 53–54)

Let me close this section by giving you an example of presentist writing that I found while reading a biography of Sir Isaac Newton (White, 1997). Even good writers and historians can fall into the trap. One of Newton's strong avocations was alchemy, the quest to create gold from base metals. In describing the alchemy interests of one of Newton's predecessors, Paracelsus (otherwise famous in the history of medicine), the author wrote that "following many an alchemist in a stereotypical fixation with *finding the unattainable and achieving the impossible*, [Paracelsus] traveled Europe in search of the secrets of the ancients, squandering much of his talent and any money he earned along the way" (p. 120, emphasis added). This is a good example of writing from the standpoint of knowing the outcome (alchemy failed) while ignoring the importance of alchemy to the history of science and the historical context that made alchemy a respected endeavor for a time.

Internal Versus External History

Histories of psychology are often written by psychologists who wish to trace the development of the theories and research traditions held by various psychologists. This kind of approach is referred to as an **internal history**—what is written occurs entirely within ("internal to") the discipline of psychology. Such an approach has the value of providing detailed descriptions of the evolution of theory and research, but it ignores those influences outside of psychology that also influence the discipline. An **external history** considers those outside influences.

Internal histories are often referred to as histories of ideas. Typically, they are written by people trained in the specific discipline being analyzed, and they tend to be written by people with little or no expertise in history per se. They are inward looking, focusing on the development of ideas or the progression of research to the exclusion of the larger world. On the other hand, external histories take the broader view—they examine societal, economic, institutional, and extradisciplinary influences. An exclusively internal history is narrow and loses the richness of historical context, whereas an excessively external history can fail to convey an adequate understanding of the ideas and contributions of a discipline's key figures. A balance is needed.

The interplay between internal and external history is demonstrated nicely in the history of cognitive psychology, the study of such phenomena as perception, attention, memory, language, and thinking. The story of cognitive psychology's rise is told in Chapter 14, but for now a sketch of it provides a nice contrast between internal and external history. From the standpoint of internal history, cognitive psychology's rise in the United States is often seen in relation to the decline of behaviorism. Behaviorism was a major force in American psychology throughout the 1930s and 1940s, and well into the 1950s. Part of its attraction was its seeming ability to explain, by means of conditioning principles, all that was important about human behavior. Humans were a product of their conditioning history, so the argument went. One problem, however, became increasingly clear in the 1950s: Behaviorist accounts of human language were problematic. The nature of language and the learning of language by children seemed to be inconsistent with behaviorist doctrine. That is, *within psychology*, a shift began to occur from a behaviorist paradigm to one that emphasized cognitive factors.

External to psychology, there were several other forces at work that helped bring about what some called a cognitive revolution (*revolution* is probably too strong—see the Close-Up box in Chapter 14). First, it is no coincidence that interest in cognitive psychology occurred in parallel with the growth and development of computer science, because psychologists began to see the computer as an interesting metaphor for the human brain. In both cases, information was taken in from the environment, "processed" in various ways internally, and then put in the form of some output. In memory research, for example, diagrams of memory processes looked just like computer flowcharts, tracking the flow of information through a system (e.g., Figure 14.1). Second, the momentum for a shift from behaviorist to cognitive models grew significantly in the 1960s, a decade of great disruption and change in American society. The cultural climate embodied by the phrase "change is the only constant" made it easier for psychologists to embrace change within their discipline. In sum, then, understanding the development of cognitive psychology requires knowing not just about the difficulties encountered by behaviorism (e.g., language) but also about developments in the wider world (computer science, the '60s).

Personalistic Versus Naturalistic History

In addition to the presentist–historicist and internal–external distinctions, one additional contrast is worth noting. That distinction is between a personalistic history, one that sees the actions of individual historical characters as the prime movers in bringing about history, and a naturalistic history, one that emphasizes the overall intellectual and cultural climate of a particular historical era—what the German philosopher Hegel called the **zeitgeist**.

According to a **personalistic history**—or what used to be called the Great Man theory—the important events in history result from the heroic (or evil) actions of individuals, and without those individuals, history would be vastly different. Their actions are said to provide history's "turning points." This approach is often associated with the 19th-century historian and essayist Thomas Carlyle, whose "On Heroes, Hero Worship and the Heroic in History," written in 1840, is best remembered for this line: "The history of what man has accomplished in this world is at bottom the history of the great men who have worked here" (quoted in Boring, 1963a, p. 6). According to this view, people like Newton, Darwin, and Freud changed the course of the history of science. Without them, the history would have been completely different. From this standpoint, the preferred method of writing history is biography; as a consequence of this approach, what are sometimes called **eponyms** (Boring, 1963a) are created. That is, historical periods are identified with reference to the individuals whose actions are believed to be critical in shaping events. Thus we read of Newtonian physics, Darwinian biology, and Freudian psychology.

The personalistic approach has intuitive appeal. Although psychology's most famous historian, Edwin G. Boring (featured in the Close-Up), favored a naturalistic model of history and argued that "history is continuous and sleek," he recognized that great people "are the handles that you put on its smooth sides" (Boring, 1963b, p. 130). Boring argued that the persistence of a personalistic approach to history results from several factors, including a human need for heroes and the need of hardworking scientists for personal recognition. (Who would want to eliminate Nobel Prizes for science?) More important, if history is continuous and sleek, then it is also immensely complex. In seeking to understand it, we try to reduce the complexity to understandable dimensions—categorization is a universal cognitive process, essential for achieving understanding. Our recall of concepts like the Freudian unconscious and Pavlovian conditioning is easier when the eponyms serve as retrieval cues.

CLOSE-UP

EDWIN G. BORING (1886–1968)

It is unfortunate that psychology's most famous historian has a name that students often associate with the general topic of history. In fact, E. G. Boring's writings are lively and elegant. In recent years, his version of psychology's history has been criticized, but it is also true that historians of psychology owe a great debt to Boring's pioneering historical work.

While an engineering student at Cornell University, Boring first encountered psychology in the fall of 1905 by taking an elective course in elementary psychology, taught by the celebrated E. B. Titchener (Chapter 7). Boring described the lectures as "magic, so potent that even my roommates demanded, each lecture day, to be told what had been said" (Boring, 1961a, p. 18). He was not converted at that point, however; he continued his engineering studies and earned a master's degree in 1908. After two marginally successful years as an engineer for a steel company and as a high school teacher, he returned to Cornell and earned a PhD from Titchener in 1914. While at Cornell, Boring's research interests included (a) human maze learning, during which he met, fell in love with, and eventually married one of his research subjects, fellow doctoral student Lucy May (who died in 1996 at the age of 109); (b) nerve regeneration, studied firsthand and rather dramatically by severing a nerve in his arm and charting

its recovery; (c) the learning processes of schizophrenics; and (d) his dissertation topic, visceral sensitivity. Boring studied this last topic by learning to swallow a stomach tube to varying depths, then pouring different substances into the tube and noting the (often unpleasant) sensory effects (Jaynes, 1969b). Nobody could ever accuse Boring of not being involved in his work.

After finishing his degree at Cornell and staying on briefly as an instructor, Boring served in World War I in the Army mental testing program (Chapter 8), taught briefly at Clark University, and then went to Harvard in 1922. He remained there for the rest of his career. At Harvard, Boring spent the next decade building up the laboratory and trying to convince the authorities that psychology should be a separate department, not just part of the philosophy department. This did not occur until 1934. During the 1920s, he wrote his famous *A History of Experimental Psychology* (1929), partly to further his political fight with the philosophers and administrators at Harvard and partly to bolster basic research in experimental psychology at a time when most American psychologists seemed to be more interested in applied psychology (O'Donnell, 1979b).

In his years at Clark and Harvard, Boring's work habits, in imitation of Titchener, were legendary. In his words:

My friends, my children, and my students know how I have talked about the eighty-hour week in the fifty-week year (the 4,000-hour working year) and I have scorned those forty-hour academicians who take long summers off from work. I have no hobbies, except for a shop in my cellar. My vacations were never successful until I got a little study with a typewriter in it and could answer eight letters a day and write up the waiting papers. (Boring, 1961b, p. 14)

Also in the tradition of Titchener, Boring taught the introductory course in psychology, believing that a student's first encounter with psychology should be from the master. He even became a pioneer in the video course: 38 half-hour programs on Boston's educational TV channel WGBH in 1960 featured Boring demonstrating various phenomena, but mainly sitting "on the corner of a table and talk[ing] in a friendly, enthusiastic, paternal manner to the red lights on whatever camera was on the air" (Boring, 1961b, p. 77; see Figure 1.2).

We have seen that APA's Division 26, established in 1965, elected Robert Watson as its first president. According to Hilgard, this occurred after Boring refused to run for the office but agreed to be named "honorary president." Boring's increasing deafness kept him away from the division's inaugural meeting during the 1966 APA convention, but he sent a written introduction to Watson's presidential address, describing himself as the "ghost of History Past, when the interest in the history of psychology had not yet become as vigorous as it is now" (Hilgard, 1982, p. 310). Modern historians of psychology owe much to Boring's example.

FIGURE 1.2   Teaching to the masses: E. G. Boring on educational TV in 1957. From Boring (1961b).

The alternative to a personalistic history is a **naturalistic history**, an approach emphasizing the forces of history that act on individuals. The Russian novelist Leo Tolstoy was a famous advocate of this determinist approach. One of his goals in writing the massive *War and Peace* was to demonstrate that history is moved by forces beyond the control of individuals. For Tolstoy, so-called Great Men like Napoleon were in reality mere agents of historical causes larger than themselves. In Book IX of *War and Peace*, he refers to kings and generals as history's slaves: "Every act of theirs, which appears to them an act of their own will, is in a historical sense involuntary and is related to the whole course of history and predestined from eternity" (Tolstoy, 1942, p. 671).

Among psychologists, Boring has most vigorously promoted a naturalistic view of history. Especially in his later years, he championed the zeitgeist concept, both in the second edition of his famous *A History of Experimental Psychology* (1950) and in numerous essays. For Boring, understanding history meant understanding the historical forces that influenced the men and women living in a particular era. While not denying Darwin's genius, for example, Boring would argue that the concept of evolution was common in the 19th century and extended beyond just biology (to geology, for instance). Without Darwin, someone else would have produced a theory of biological evolution. Indeed, Darwin's theory might have been called the Darwin-Wallace theory, in recognition of Alfred Russel Wallace, a contemporary of Darwin's who independently developed virtually the identical theory (Chapter 5 tells this fascinating story). Great scientists can and do influence events, but simply focusing on individuals leaves unanswered the question of how those individuals were affected by the worlds they lived in.

In support of the zeitgeist concept, Boring pointed to two kinds of historical events. In the first, called a **multiple** by historian Robert Merton (1961), two or more individuals independently make the same discovery at about the same time. Darwin and Wallace codiscovering natural selection at a time when evolutionary thinking was "in the air" is an example. Darwin's grandfather, Erasmus Darwin, illustrates the second type of event, a discovery or a theory that is said to be "ahead of its time." Like his more famous grandson, Erasmus developed a theory of evolution, but he did so in the 18th century, when belief in the immutability of species (i.e., each species is created in its finished form by God and it doesn't change over time) was stronger than in the 19th century.

Relying on the zeitgeist as a way of explaining history can be problematic, however. For example, the uncritical observer might be tempted to *reify* (i.e., give a concrete and detached existence to an abstraction) the term *zeitgeist* and consider it a controlling force, independent of the historical persons who in fact give it meaning. That is, in answer to the question "Why did event *X* occur instead of event *Y* at time *Z*?" one might be tempted to answer, "Because of the zeitgeist." But such an answer hardly explains the event in question. The concept of the zeitgeist invites one to examine the attitudes, values, and theories in existence at the time of some event to be explained, but it cannot exist by itself as some mysterious directing agent. As historian Dorothy Ross (1969) pointed out with reference to the history of educational psychology:

> It has been stated, for example, that neither James, Dewey, Hall, Thorndike, Cattell, Galton, nor Darwin were necessary to the rapid development of educational psychology in America, for that was the trend of the "Zeitgeist." But certainly we only know what the Zeitgeist in fact *was* by the way in which James, Hall, Cattell, Darwin and others behaved. If they had not thought and acted the way they did, neither would the "Zeitgeist" they are said to embody. (p. 257, emphasis in the original)

Thus a balanced view of history recognizes the complex interrelationships between people and the environments in which they act. The historical characters you are about to encounter were all products of the world they lived in, but they also made decisions that helped form and transform the historical context that surrounded them. Wallace might have been inspired to write a paper proposing a theory of evolution that matched the essence of Darwin's, but it is no accident that the term *evolution* is associated with Darwin and not with Wallace. It was Darwin who invested the years of research examining the intricacies of numerous species, and it was Darwin who followed up his initial writings with the monumental texts that brought evolution into its fullest development.

This Book's Point of View

This section of the chapter began with a reference to Furumoto's distinction between old and new history. Presentist, internal, and personalistic approaches typically go together and comprise what she referred to as the old history of psychology. It is a history that interprets events only from the standpoint of the present, concentrates on the development of ideas within a specific discipline, and views progress as reflecting the accomplishments of important people. The new history of psychology, on the other hand, combines historicist, external, and naturalistic approaches. It tries to examine historical events on their own terms, with reference to the times in which they occurred, looks for the influence of extradisciplinary forces, and looks beyond great men and women to examine the contextual factors that helped to produce their ideas. Furumoto also pointed out that new history relies more on archival data and primary source materials than on secondary sources (e.g., textbooks), and it is more critically analytical than ceremonial and celebratory.

For historians of psychology conducting research, Furumoto's description of the new history of psychology provides a clear set of guidelines about how to proceed. The best historical research being published today is historicist, external, and naturalistic. For the author of a textbook and the teacher of the history of psychology course, however, the prescriptions about how to proceed are not quite as clear. As psychologist–historian Don Dewsbury (1990b) once pointed out in a review of several history of psychology texts, it is important to distinguish between "scholarly research directed at colleagues and . . . textbooks directed at introductory students" (p. 372). For the latter, the ideals of the new history need to be incorporated into the course, but they must be weighed against a need to inform students about content that is relevant to the psychology curriculum. This book presents a history of psychology that embraces the values espoused by Furumoto, but it is important to remember that the course for which this text is designed is a psychology course as well as a history course. Thus, while it is important to understand Pavlov's work within the historical climate of the early 20th century in Russia—especially the effects of the Russian Revolution of 1917—it is also important to understand the various classical conditioning phenomena that he investigated and how his work related to American behaviorism and influenced research on conditioning. It is important to understand the influence of computer science on the development of cognitive psychology, but it is also important for the psychology student to know about the difficulties that behaviorists experienced when trying to explain human language. Finally, although a purely personalistic history can degenerate into cute anecdotes and can overlook the complexities of historical events, it is also true that persons are interesting to study, and biographical information can increase the psychology student's understanding of human behavior and bring historical characters to life.

In this book, I try very hard to be historicist rather than presentist. On the second dimension, recognizing the need for psychology undergraduates to learn about research and theories that have occurred within their chosen area of study, I attempt to balance internal and external history, blending the various ideas, research, and theories that constitute psychology's internal history with the external historical context in which they developed. On the third dimension, I incorporate biographical information, especially when it is relevant to the person's contribution to psychology, but emphasize more heavily the ideas and the work completed by these individual psychologists, and the flavor of the times in which they did their work.

HISTORIOGRAPHY: DOING AND WRITING HISTORY

The simplest definition of **historiography** derives from the origins of the word itself—it means "to write history." But the term goes beyond the writing of historical narrative, referring also to theoretical issues like the ones just described and to the methods that historians use when doing the historical research that eventually leads to their written histories. Although the primary purpose of this book is to inform you about the history of psychology, a secondary goal is to give you some insight into the professional behavior of historians of psychology. That is, we will examine the kinds of data of interest to historians and the problems confronting historians as they do their work. At the outset, it is important to be aware of one crucial distinction. It might seem obvious, but accepting it allows one to realize that all history involves some degree of human interpretation. The distinction, pointed out by British historian Keith Jenkins (1991), is between "the past" and "history." They are not the same—"the past is gone and history is what historians make of it when they go to work" (p. 8). Hence, the past refers to the infinite number of events that have occurred before the present moment, and it can never be known because it is gone. What can be known is history—the manner in which *traces* of the past are selected, interpreted, and written into coherent narrative by professional historians. Whether those writings approach "truth" is an issue that is taken up at the end of the chapter. For now, let's examine these traces of history and what historians do with them.

Sources of Historical Data

Writers of psychology's history, especially textbook writers, have often relied on secondary sources to write their histories. A **secondary source** is a document that has been published and is typically an analysis or summary of some historical person, event, or period. These sources include books, articles published in journals, magazines, encyclopedias, and the like. Those doing research in the history of psychology, however, rely more heavily on **primary sources** of information, which are usually found in archives. An **archive** is normally an area within a university library that holds unpublished information. This primary source information includes university records, correspondence, diaries, speeches, minutes of the meetings of professional organizations, and documents donated by individuals connected in some way with the university. In addition to these separate university archives, historians of psychology often find primary source material at the Library of Congress archives in Washington, D.C., and, especially, at the Archives of the History of American Psychology (AHAP), part of the Center for the History of Psychology at The University of Akron in Ohio. In general, primary source materials are items written or created at or near the time of some historical event, while secondary sources are written at some time after a historical event and serve to summarize or analyze.

As mentioned earlier in the chapter, the founding of AHAP in 1965 by John Popplestone and Marion McPherson (Figure 1.1) was one of a series of events sparked by the efforts of Robert I. Watson to generate interest in psychology's history. As of its 40th anniversary in 2005, AHAP's collection included the following: the papers of more than 740 psychologists (e.g., Abraham Maslow, Henry Goddard) and organizations (e.g., APA's history division, #26); more than 1,000 pieces of original laboratory apparatus; approximately 20,000 photographs and 6,000 films; and over 15,000 psychological tests.

What can you expect to find in a place like AHAP? Just about anything. When looking into the records of a professional organization, for instance, you would probably find lists of officers and correspondence between them, minutes of meetings, early drafts of position papers, and the like. When examining the papers of an individual psychologist (as in Figure 1.3), you might find (a) letters between that person and other psychologists; (b) personal diaries and/or calendars; (c) course lecture notes and course schedules; (d) laboratory protocols, drawings of apparatus, data summaries, and other laboratory-related information; (e) early draft manuscripts of writings that eventually became secondary sources; (f) photographs and films of people, places, and research equipment; and (g) minutes of professional meetings attended by the psychologist. There will also be some surprises. For instance, AHAP holds the papers of the experimental psychologist Walter Miles. They include the usual materials, but when the papers first arrived at the archives, they also included a brick that Miles took from the building site of a new lab. A more startling example was reported in *Civilization*, a magazine published by the Library of Congress. A researcher was studying a 19th-century Viennese physician (Carl Koller) who was experimenting with the use of cocaine as an anesthetic in eye surgery. One of the folders contained a small pharmacist's packet containing, you guessed it, white powder. Federal authorities were called in to remove the drug, but the envelope remains in the archive collection, labeled as follows: "Remainder of the 1st dose of cocaine, which I used in my first cocaine experiments in August 1884. Dr. Koller" ("A Stash," 1996, p. 15).

How does a researcher interested in psychology's history know which archives to contact or visit when starting a project? Because their holdings are so extensive, AHAP is a good place to start. Even if it is not the primary repository for the papers of the person being studied, AHAP might hold some correspondence from that person in the papers it does have. Another good starting place is the university where the person in question worked. Third, bibliographic sources exist. The best known is *A Guide to Manuscript Collections in the History of Psychology and Selected Areas* (Sokal & Rafail, 1982). Suppose you are interested in the work of IQ researcher Henry Goddard, for instance. The guide briefly describes the contents of the Goddard papers, which happen to be held at AHAP. It also informs you of additional Goddard materials in the papers of Edgar Doll and Emily Stogdill at AHAP, and in the papers of developmental psychologist Arnold Gesell in the Library of Congress.

Historians also rely on their general knowledge to aid in their search. For example, some years ago I became interested in Edmund Clark Sanford (1859–1924), the first director of the psychology laboratory at Clark University (Goodwin, 1987). Naturally, Clark was the starting point for the search; through contact with the archivist there and two visits, I accumulated some information but not a great deal. Sanford didn't seem to save very much, or if he did, the information didn't find its way to Clark. Some of the university records were helpful, however, in determining such things as laboratory purchases, and the papers of psychologist–university president G. Stanley Hall yielded some additional data, including one exciting discovery—a series of photographs taken in the laboratory in 1892, several of which are to be found in later chapters of this book. Many of them showed (or simulated, most likely) experiments in progress, thus providing a glimpse of what it was like to be doing research in psychology then. By searching through secondary sources, I knew about other psychologists who were contemporaries of Sanford. I also knew from his obituaries that Sanford was very close to E. B. Titchener of Cornell and Mary Calkins of Wellesley (Sanford

FIGURE 1.3 Historians at work in the main reading room, Archives of the History of American Psychology, The University of Akron. Clockwise from left: this text's author; Jennifer Bazar, doctoral student at York University, Toronto and intern at the Archives; Sergio Cirino, psychologist–historian at the University of Minas Gerais, Pampulha, Brazil; Rodrigo Miranda, student at Minas Gerais (individual permissions granted).

died of a heart attack in 1924 on his way to give a talk at Wellesley). Visits to Wellesley and Cornell yielded more information. The Titchener papers were especially helpful—Titchener seemed to keep just about everything. I also wrote to about two dozen other archives that I guessed might be holding papers that Sanford might have written to his colleagues (this was before the days of e-mail). Copies of a few pieces trickled in. At the same time, I was reading everything that Sanford published (not much, actually) and everything else that could shed some light on him and the world he inhabited (e.g., histories of the decade of the 1890s, when Sanford was most productive at Clark).

Over the past decade, archival searching has been made considerably easier through electronic means. Archives frequently post "finding aids" (these are listings of the contents of a particular collection) online, and sought-after documents can often be transferred from an archive to a historian via PDF files. At AHAP, for example, as of early 2010, finding aids for more than 30 psychologists were online and searchable; that number undoubtedly will have increased by the time you read this. Other archival holdings can be discovered through a simple Google search. For example, as part of some research on Walter Miles, I was looking into his activities as a researcher at the Carnegie Nutrition Laboratory in Boston in the period from 1914 to 1922. From the Miles papers at AHAP, I knew that the laboratory's director was Francis Gano Benedict. A Google search for his name yielded a connection to his papers at the archives of the Harvard Medical School, which in turn led to e-mail correspondence with a helpful archivist there and, eventually, to some important information about Benedict and the Carnegie Lab (e.g., the details of three different trips made by Benedict to Russia, where he visited Pavlov's laboratory and reported on Pavlov's research).

Problems with the Writing of History

The journey from archive visits to a published paper or book is long, often tedious, occasionally exhilarating, but never easy. Along the way, the historian must confront two interrelated difficulties. First, there are problems associated with the collection of data. The historian must evaluate the validity of available data and select a subset of those data for inclusion in the historical narrative. The second problem concerns analysis. Historians are human, so their interpretations of the data will reflect their beliefs, their theories about the nature of history, and potentially, their unexamined biases.

Data Selection Problems Historians usually collect more information than will make its way into a historical narrative. Hence they must make judgments about the adequacy and relevance of the data at hand, and they must select a sample of the data while discarding the remainder. Sometimes, despite the large amount of data that might be collected during an archive visit, important pieces might be missing, further complicating the historian's life. For example, Titchener and Sanford wrote to each other frequently, but only Titchener saved his correspondence. The Titchener papers contain several hundred letters from Sanford to Titchener, but the Sanford papers include *none* from Titchener. In trying to piece together the Sanford–Titchener relationship, the historian gets only half the story.[3] Another example concerns Walter Miles again. He once wrote an article on the history of mazes in psychology (Miles, 1930) that included excerpts of letters he received from some of the early pioneers (e.g., Willard Small, who completed the first maze learning study with rats). The Miles papers at AHAP contain none of the correspondence related to the maze history paper, however. This is surprising, considering the size of the Miles collection. It fills 128 boxes, which occupy 70 linear feet on the shelves; the finding aid alone runs to 756 pages (Goodwin, 2003).

Sometimes information that could aid a historian can be lost through what insurance adjusters would call an act of God. For example, after painstakingly tracking down descendants of Mary Whiton Calkins (Chapter 6), the APA's first woman president, Laurel Furumoto discovered that many of Calkins's papers had been entrusted to her younger brother. Unfortunately, he put them in his cellar, where they were destroyed by flooding that accompanied a famous New England hurricane in 1938 (Furumoto, 1991).

Data might also be missing on purpose. In the last year of his life, John Watson, behaviorism's founder, burned all of his remaining notes, correspondence, and rough manuscripts. According to Watson's biographer, when "his secretary protested the loss to posterity and to history, Watson only replied: 'When you're dead, you're all dead'" (Buckley, 1989, p. 182). Similarly, on two separate occasions Sigmund Freud also destroyed his papers, partly to make it difficult for others to trace the sources of his ideas (Chapter 12 details one of these episodes).

In addition to missing data, some information might be restricted by the donor and inaccessible to the historian. Even someone with the status of E. G. Boring could be denied. In a letter to John Popplestone of AHAP, Boring wrote that even as a known historian and a faculty member at Harvard, he had been denied access to some papers at the Harvard archives. In his words:

> I trust the general atmosphere of the Archivists at Harvard. This is because I have been
> denied access to some things that are none of my business, graciously denied it because I

---

[3] More than half, actually. After about 1910, Titchener often made and kept carbon copies of the letters he sent.

am a Harvard professor. But, nevertheless, shut off from certain files of William James. (Popplestone, 1975, p. 21)

Beyond dealing with missing or incomplete information, the historian must make judgments about the adequacy of the available data. We know that eyewitness descriptions of everyday events can be quite wrong, that two witnesses can differ dramatically in their accounts. If eyewitness unreliability can be demonstrated easily in modern psychology laboratories, then it is safe to say that the same lack of reliability exists for eyewitness accounts of historical events. A good example of this was experienced by E. G. Boring. While preparing a history of Titchener's Experimentalists, Boring launched a massive letter-writing campaign to colleagues who had been to meetings, asking for their firsthand descriptions. There were numerous discrepancies among the letters, including one amusing example from a colleague who recounted to Boring in great detail a dinner conversation with Harvard's Hugo Münsterberg at the 1917 meeting at Harvard. Boring wrote back gently reminding his friend that Münsterberg had died in 1916 (Goodwin, 2005).

Information found in someone's correspondence or diary can also be of questionable value. Was the letter writer providing insight into the personality of a colleague or merely passing on cruel and unsubstantiated gossip? When the diarist described the meeting as meaningless and a waste of time, would others at the same meeting draw the same conclusion? Can letters and diaries be slanted by the writer's knowledge that historians might someday read his or her words? To what extent do the contents of letters and diaries reflect the personal prejudices of the writer? I think you can see the difficulty here.

Those who create the records that eventually occupy archives are human and therefore susceptible to the subtleties of human belief, preconception, and bias. Those who explore the archives and write the history are also human and subject to the same frailties. By virtue of their training, historians are certainly more disciplined than laypeople; nonetheless, when making decisions about what information to select for historical analyses and narratives, the historian is not a machine. E. G. Boring expressed the problem eloquently in the preface to his 1942 text on the history of research in sensation and perception:

> Indeed, so much a matter of selection is the preparation of an historical text, that I am sobered by the responsibility. The [history of psychology] text of 1929 has existed long enough for me to see how *the mood that determined the choice of an afternoon's exposition can fix the "truth" of a certain matter upon graduate students for years to come*. With industry and patience one may avoid the falsification of facts, but those virtues are not enough to make one wise in choosing what to ignore. For that one also needs the wisdom and the integrity of objectivity, and who knows for sure whether he commands such? (Boring 1942, p. viii; emphasis added)

As you will learn in a few paragraphs, this passage from Boring is ironic. One of the themes of modern historiography within psychology is that Boring's writings reflect a strong bias for a specific brand of psychology. It also appears that he was motivated at least partly by the political and institutional context that he occupied.

Interpretation Problems   Winston Churchill, who made history and also wrote it, is alleged to have said history would be kind to him because he was going to be the person writing it. Historians normally try to be objective though, while realizing that all historical narrative will necessarily reflect something about the writer. Decisions about selection and about writing history both involve interpreting the information at hand, and those interpretations are influenced by the individual characteristics of the historian and by the features of the historical context in which the historian is writing. That is, historians will be influenced by their preconceptions, by the amount of knowledge they already have, as well as by the theories they hold about the nature of history (e.g., personalistic versus naturalistic emphases). In addition, even without their necessarily being aware of it, historians can be influenced by the historical context in which their histories are being written. For example, you will discover in Chapter 4 that the work of Wilhelm Wundt has been reevaluated recently (e.g., Blumenthal, 1975), and many of his ideas have been found to be similar to those of modern cognitive psychologists. This similarity, of course, could not have been noticed before the advent of modern cognitive psychology—Blumenthal was writing at the height of the so-called cognitive revolution in psychology. Thus, historical characters are not the only ones influenced by the historical context in which they live; historians are affected as well.

The history written by E. G. Boring is a case in point. You know from this chapter's Close-Up that Boring was a devoted student of E. B. Titchener's and, in the 1920s, he was a vigorous advocate for the development of a separate psychology department at Harvard that would emphasize "pure" laboratory research rather than application. Both of those facts played a role in the way he wrote his 1929 history text. First, his training as an experimental psychologist in Titchener's laboratory at Cornell surely affected his overall conception of psychology. More specifically, it influenced what Boring thought about Wilhelm Wundt, in whose laboratory Titchener earned a PhD in 1892. In general, Boring believed that Titchener's brand of experimental psychology, called structuralism, was virtually identical to Wundt's psychology, and that Titchener had merely imported it to America. In fact, Wundt's system was quite different from Titchener's system (the details of Wundt's and Titchener's systems will become clear in Chapters 4 and 7, respectively). Because of Titchener's influence on Boring, however, combined with the fact that Titchener translated much of Wundt's work and that Boring was not fully knowledgeable about some of Wundt's nonexperimental writings, the distinctions were lost. Thus, when writing his history, Boring's description of Wundt was filtered through Titchener's version and was consequently flawed. Because most psychologists trained in the period 1950 to 1980 learned their history by reading Boring's *A History of Experimental Psychology* (1929; 1950), the mythological identification of Wundt's and Titchener's systems became conventional wisdom.

A second distortion in Boring's history relates to his emphasis on basic experimental psychology to the exclusion of applied psychology. As O'Donnell (1979b) has shown, Boring was disturbed by the growing status of applied psychology, especially mental testing. Believing basic laboratory research to be in jeopardy, he took several steps to restore its standing. One was writing the first edition of his history in 1929, which largely ignored the work of a substantial number of psychologists who were busily applying psychological principles to education, mental health, and the workplace. For instance, Boring (1929) began his brief section on mental testing by writing that "the history of mental tests can conveniently be excluded from the history of experimental psychology" (p. 545). The reader of his 1929 history could be excused for believing that applied psychology barely existed.

A common misconception of history goes like this: The events occurred in the past; now that they have been lined up chronologically and described in a historical narrative, that's the end of it. As the E. G. Boring case shows, however, historical analyses are in continual need of revision in the light of new information and new ways of examining old information. In recent years, for instance, scholars (e.g., Leahey, 1981) have taken a fresh look at (a) the relationship between Wundt's and Titchener's ideas and (b) the role of application in the development of psychology in America. As a result, newer histories describe the Wundt–Titchener differences more accurately and document the pervasive influence of applied psychology. Comparing different editions of a history text can illustrate this reexamination process. For example, one popular undergraduate history text, clearly influenced by Boring in its early editions, also shows the impact of the recent scholarship on Wundt in its later editions. In the book's third edition (Schultz, 1981), Wundt is described in a chapter that has *structuralism* in its title. The following chapter, on Titchener, refers to Wundtian psychology being "transplanted" to America by Titchener and includes this sentence: "A knowledge of Wundt's psychology provides a reasonably accurate picture of Titchener's system" (p. 87). Six years later, in the fourth edition, *structuralism* no longer appears in the title of the Wundt chapter, there is an explicit description of the problems with Boring's historical account, and the Titchener chapter opens by saying that the systems of Wundt and Titchener were "radically different," and that Titchener "altered Wundt's system dramatically while claiming to be a loyal follower" (Schultz & Schultz, 1987, p. 85).

The important lesson for the reader of history is to be alert to the dangers of assuming that if something is printed in black and white, it somehow must be true. Rather, it is important to read histories, including this one, with a healthy dose of skeptical awareness that other information might have been selected for inclusion in the narrative and that other ways of interpreting the historical record exist. As Bailyn (Lathem, 1994) put it, "there is no end to the writing of history—nor should there be, because new questions come up and new techniques develop, new data are discovered, and succeeding generations will and should tell the story differently" (p. 94). This raises an interesting question: Can history ever uncover the truth?

Approaching Historical Truth

From the foregoing discussion, you might be tempted to accept a version of historical relativism in which five different historians make five different claims for truth and there is no reasonable way to decide among them. A degree of relativism among historians is a postmodern outgrowth of a reaction against traditional history, which held that the job of the historian is to search out the facts of "what really happened" and place them into a narrative with enough style to attract readers. The outcome was a tendency to write history from the standpoint of what happened to those who happened to be in positions of power and influence, while ignoring the rich variety of alternative perspectives. Thus a traditional history of the American West, taught to American schoolchildren and grounded in a belief in the idea of Manifest Destiny, glorified the rugged pioneer who persevered in the face of daunting obstacles, including wild men who liked to shoot arrows. It is clear, though, that the very same history could be written from the standpoint of the Native American who valiantly defended the homeland against invasion by wild men who liked to shoot guns.

The postmodern critique of the narrowness and arbitrariness of traditional history has had the meritorious effect of enriching our knowledge of it. Thus we have come to recognize that history extends beyond the lives, deeds, and misdeeds of white males; it must be more inclusive. On the other hand, an unfortunate consequence of this broadening has been a relativism that, taken to extreme, can lead to absurd claims like the one made occasionally that the Jewish Holocaust in World War II never really happened but was merely "constructed" and exaggerated out of a few isolated events (said to have explanations other than genocide) by historians sympathetic to the Jewish movement who wished to encourage the creation of the nation of Israel following the war (Israel was created in 1948, three years after the close of World War II). Those arguing for the "myth" of the Holocaust claim that their version is as valid as any other. Yet this example makes it clear that some versions of history are indeed better (i.e., closer to truth) than others. How does one decide?

To reach the truth through historical analysis requires an objectivity that recognizes the limits of one historian's views but also has faith in the notion that meaningful historical narrative and analysis can emerge from the combined efforts of many scholars, according to historians Joyce Appleby, Lynn Hunt, and Margaret Jacob. In *Telling the Truth About History* (1994), they argue for a historiography in which truth about history emerges from a Darwinian-like struggle between competing ideas held by historians, that "knowledge-seeking involves a lively, contentious struggle among diverse groups of truth-seekers" (p. 254). Some measure of truth, then, evolves out of this struggle. Thus, just as individual variation within a species provides the basis for natural selection to operate, so do different versions of historical episodes exist, subject to competing critical analyses that determine which version adapts best to the scholarly environment. This does not mean that the goal is a single version of truth that is then "settled" and immune to change. Rather, historical truth continues to evolve as new information is discovered and brought to light and as old information is subjected to new interpretations. Also, evolving historical truth includes a variety of perspectives. Multiple eyewitnesses to an event might give different versions of it, but all agree that the event did indeed occur. From their combined information, a complex truth might emerge that would improve on a single description from one perspective. If one historian of the Civil War period "sees an event from a slave's point of view, that rendering does not obliterate the perspective of the slaveholder; it only complicates the task of interpretation" (p. 256).

Just as theories in science are temporary working truths that guide future research, their futures depending on the open and honest inquiry of scientists, so may historical truths be considered tentative yet valuable guides for further research by intellectually honest historians with open access to historical materials. And just as some theories in science are more durable than others, so are some historical truths: "All knowledge can be provisional, in theory, without eliminating the possibility of some truths prevailing for centuries, perhaps forever" (Appleby, Hunt, & Jacob, 1994, p. 284).[4]

Presumably, on the basis of the hard work of many historians of psychology, some degree of truth about the discipline's history has emerged over the past 100 years or so, and I will try my best to describe it to you in this book. Many disagreements among historians of psychology exist, but Appleby, Hunt, and Jacob (1994) would consider that to be a good thing, the basis for future historical truths to develop during psychology's next hundred years. By placing the word *A* in the title of this book, rather than *The*, I am recognizing that other histories exist now and more will exist in the future. Nonetheless, I believe that what you are about to read contains some truth about the discipline you have chosen to study. To the extent that some of the truth might be tentative, I hope it will motivate you to continue learning about psychology's history long after you have finished with this particular version of it.

---

[4]This is a more optimistic view of the chances of arriving at a degree of historical truth than the one held by Napoleon, who is said to have described history as "agreed upon fables."

SUMMARY

Psychology and Its History

- Recently, psychologists have celebrated several centennials, including the anniversary of the founding of Wilhelm Wundt's laboratory at Leipzig, Germany, in 1879 and the creation of the American Psychological Association in 1892.

- Interest in the history of psychology has grown steadily since the mid-1960s, primarily through the initiatives of Robert Watson. He helped establish professional organizations for historians of psychology (Division 26 of the APA; the Cheiron Society), a journal (*Journal of the History of the Behavioral Sciences*), an archive at The University of Akron (Archives of the History of American Psychology), and a doctoral program in the history of psychology at the University of New Hampshire.

Why Study History?

- Knowing history might occasionally help us to avoid mistakes of the past and to predict the future, but its most important value is that it helps us understand the present. Knowing history puts current events into a better perspective; without knowing some history, we cannot understand current events.

- Knowing history can immunize us against the belief that our current time has insurmountable problems, compared to the "good old days." Every age has its set of problems. Knowing history also reduces the tendency to think that modern-day accomplishments represent a culmination of the "progress" we have made from the inferior accomplishments of the past.

Why Study Psychology's History?

- Because psychology is a relatively young science, much of its history is recent and of relevance for understanding psychological concepts and theories. Also, many issues of concern to early psychologists (e.g., nature–nurture) are still important.

- The history of psychology course can provide a synthesizing experience, tying together the loose threads that comprise the diverse specialties of modern psychology.

- Knowing about historical examples of supposed breakthroughs in psychological research or practice, or new theories that were shown to be pseudoscientific, the student of history is able to evaluate modern claims more critically.

- Because the history of psychology course informs the student about people behaving within their historical context, the course provides further understanding of human behavior.

Key Issues in Psychology's History

- The traditional approach to the history of psychology has been presentist, internal, and personalistic. Recently, historians have tended to be more historicist, external, and naturalistic.

- The presentist evaluates the past in terms of present knowledge and values, often passing judgment unfairly. The historicist tries to avoid imposing modern values on the past and tries to understand the past from the standpoint of the knowledge and values existing in the past.

- An internal history of psychology is a history of the ideas, research, and theories that have existed within the discipline of psychology. An external history of psychology emphasizes the historical context—institutional, economic, social, political—and how this context influenced the history.

- A personalistic approach to history emphasizes the major historical characters and argues that history moves through the action of heroic individuals. When historical periods are labeled with reference to people, those labels are called eponyms (e.g., Darwinian biology). A naturalistic approach emphasizes the zeitgeist, the mood or spirit of the times, as the prime moving force in history. The existence of multiples, and of people with ideas said to be "ahead of their times," is consistent with a naturalistic view.

Historiography: Doing and Writing History

- Historiography refers to the process of doing research in history and writing historical narratives.

- Historians rely on both primary and secondary sources of information. A secondary source is a document that has been published and includes analysis. Primary source materials constitute the raw data for historians and include documents created at or near the time of the historical event in question (e.g., diaries, letters, photographs).

• Historical research often takes place in archives, which hold primary source information such as diaries, notes, original manuscripts, and correspondence as well as secondary source information. The major archive for historians is the Archives of the History of American Psychology, located at The University of Akron.

• Archival collections can be extensive, but they can also be incomplete and have important information missing for various reasons. The information that is available is subject to numerous sources of error (e.g., the biases of the diary writer; the vagaries of eyewitness memory).

• Historians are faced with two major problems: selection of information for their historical narratives and interpretation of the information at hand. These decisions can reflect bias on the part of the historian, and they can reflect the historical context within which the historian is writing. Nonetheless, most historians believe that some degree of truth can be reached through the open exchange of information and by examining historical events through a variety of perspectives.

STUDY QUESTIONS

1. During the 1960s, there was renewed interest in studying the history of psychology. Describe how Robert Watson contributed to this development.

2. Explain why "understanding the present" is a more compelling reason for studying history than the traditional arguments about avoiding the mistakes of the past and predicting the future.

3. Explain why it is important for (a) any educated person to understand and appreciate history, and (b) any student of psychology to understand psychology's history.

4. What is the point made by Boorstin in his essay "The Prison of the Present"?

5. Define presentism, give an example of presentist thinking, and explain the dangers of this manner of looking at history.

6. Explain why a historicist approach to history is sometimes called a contextualized history.

7. Distinguish between internal and external histories. Use the example from cognitive psychology to illustrate the point.

8. What is a personalistic history, how is it related to the concept of an eponym, and what are its limitations?

9. What is a naturalistic approach to history, and what kinds of evidence are used to support this approach?

10. Distinguish between primary and secondary sources of information, and describe some of the primary sources likely to be found in an archive.

11. Distinguish between "the past" and "history."

12. Give examples from psychology's history that illustrate the data selection problems that all historians face.

13. Use the example of Boring's famous text to illustrate the interpretation problems that face historians.

14. In their book *Telling the Truth About History*, Appleby, Hunt, and Jacob (1994) describe the process of arriving at historical truth in Darwinian terms. Explain what they mean, and explain why they would argue that while absolute truth might not be reachable, some historical accounts are "truer" than others.

FOR FURTHER READING

APPLEBY, J., HUNT, L., & JACOB, M. (1994). *Telling the truth about history.* New York: W. W. Norton.
Traces the rise of "intellectual absolutisms," such as the Enlightenment ideal of science and history as a purely objective chronicling of the facts, and their replacement with a post-modern relativism that questions the possibility of history ever achieving truth; proposes a "pragmatic" Darwinian approach to history in which working truths evolve through open scholarly research and debate.

BORING, E. G. (1963a). Eponym as placebo. In Robert I. Watson & Donald T. Campbell (Eds.), *History, psychology, and science: Selected papers by Edwin G. Boring, Harvard University* (pp. 5–25). New York: John Wiley & Sons.
A good example of Boring's erudition and his championing of the zeitgeist concept; argues that the effect of a "great man" theory is to create "eponyms" that give us an oversimplified and distorted view of history; given the complexity of history, however, eponyms serve as ways of classifying information,

and categorization is a natural and inevitable human cognitive process.

FANCHER, R. E. (1987). Henry Goddard and the Kallikak family photographs: "Conscious skullduggery" or "Whig history"? *American Psychologist, 42*, 585–590.
In addition to his work at Ellis Island, Goddard conducted a genealogical study of "feeblemindedness," attempting to bolster his claim that intelligence was inherited; focusing on a claim that photos in Goddard's study were doctored to make children appear feebleminded, this article provides a good illustration of how presentist thinking can distort historical interpretation.

FURUMOTO, L. (1989). The new history of psychology. In I. S. Cohen (Ed.), *The G. Stanley Hall lecture series: Vol. 9* (pp. 9–34). Washington, DC: American Psychological Association.
An excellent introduction to historiographic issues, written for teachers, but of interest to students as well; includes an example of old and new history by comparing early and more recent articles written by Furumoto about Mary Whiton Calkins, the APA's first woman president.

Lathem, E. C. (Ed.). (1994). *Bernard Bailyn on the teaching and writing of history: Responses to a series of questions.* Hanover, NH: University Press of New England.
A brief book summarizing a wide-ranging question and answer session with a noted historian, covering such topics as historiography, the reasons to study history, presentism (anachronism), the reasons why histories must continually be rewritten, and teaching history.

O'DONNELL, J. M. (1979b). The crisis of experimentalism in the 1920s: E. G. Boring and his uses of history. *American Psychologist, 34*, 289–295.
The best brief description of how Boring's concerns over applied psychology contributed to his efforts to reestablish the primacy of basic research through his behind-the-scenes APA activities and by constructing a history that emphasized experimental psychology.

CHAPTER 2

THE PHILOSOPHICAL CONTEXT

Psychology has a long past, yet its real history is short.

—Hermann Ebbinghaus, 1908

PREVIEW AND CHAPTER OBJECTIVES

This chapter introduces you to the major philosophical issues and concepts that have been and continue to be important for psychologists. A working knowledge of these ideas provides a necessary foundation for comprehending modern psychology. Although philosophers grapple with a wide range of problems, those especially relevant for psychology concern (a) whether mental and physical events are essentially the same or different and if the latter, how the two kinds of events relate to each other; (b) whether our knowledge of the world is derived primarily from our ability to reason or results from the cumulative effects of our sensory experiences; (c) the extent to which our heredity and our environment shape the way we are; (d) whether the things we think, feel, and do result from our own free choices or are the result of deterministic laws of nature; and (e) whether or not complex phenomena can best be understood by analyzing them into their component parts. These issues are explored by examining the ideas of several well-known philosophers, giving special attention to René Descartes, history's most famous rationalist and the father of modern philosophy; John Locke, the founder of British Empiricism; and John Stuart Mill, the 19th-century British empiricist– associationist. After finishing this chapter, you should be able to:

- Explain the meaning of the Ebbinghaus quote that opens the chapter
- Explain how the historical context shaped the ideas of Descartes (e.g., mechanism)
- Explain why Descartes is known as a rationalist and describe his arguments concerning the mind–body issue
- Describe how Descartes would explain an involuntary movement of the foot (reflex) and a voluntary movement of the foot (i.e., requiring the mind)
- Describe Locke's ideas about how we develop our knowledge of the world and how he applied these ideas to education
- Distinguish between Locke and Berkeley on the question of primary and secondary qualities of matter
- Describe how Berkeley's philosophical system attempted to counter materialism
- Distinguish between Hume and Hartley on the question of the basic laws of association
- Distinguish between J. S. Mill and his father on the issue of atomism versus holism
- Describe how Mill's rules for inductive logic provided an underpinning for modern conceptions of research in psychology
- Describe the alternative to Locke's white paper metaphor proposed by Leibniz

■ Describe the mind–body solution proposed by Leibniz and how his ideas relate to the psychological concepts of the unconscious and thresholds

■ Describe Kant's arguments about the origins of knowledge

A LONG PAST

Most psychology students know Hermann Ebbinghaus as the inventor of the "nonsense syllable" and as the first person to study human memory experimentally (you will learn of this in Chapter 4). One cannot get through the memory chapter of an introductory psychology text, even today, without encountering the famous Ebbinghaus curve of forgetting. Among historians of psychology, Ebbinghaus is also known for the opening sentence of a brief introductory textbook that he wrote in 1908. It is the "long past, short history" quote that opened this chapter.

By referring to psychology's "long past," Ebbinghaus was reminding readers that basic questions about human nature and the causes of human behavior are not new. Rather, they have been asked in some form or other since humans first started asking questions. More specifically, Ebbinghaus was pointing out that psychologists must recognize their deep roots in philosophy. All of the important issues that concern modern psychologists have been addressed by philosophers. In fact, you can notice the close association between psychology and philosophy the next time you go to the library—the place where you find the psychology books (BF...) is sandwiched between general philosophy, logic, and knowledge (B, BC, BD) on one side and by aesthetics and ethics on the other side (BH, BL).

Does this close connection mean that psychology is just another name for philosophy? No. In the last half of the 19th century, a number of converging forces produced an attempt to study human behavior and mental processes through the application of scientific methods rather than through philosophical analysis, logical reasoning, and speculation—by working in the laboratory rather than in the armchair. Thus what came to be called the New Psychology began to emerge as a separate discipline about 130 years ago—which led Ebbinghaus, just under 100 years ago, to proclaim that psychology's history as a new science had been quite brief.

A thorough analysis of the long past referred to by Ebbinghaus requires much more space than this chapter can offer. It would take us through ancient Greece, deep into the writings of Plato and Aristotle and others, through the great medieval church philosophers such as Thomas Aquinas, who united Christian faith with Aristotelian logic, and into the Renaissance. Instead, we will reach into the Renaissance for some historical context, and then begin with the 17th century and the multitalented René Descartes, sometimes considered the father of modern philosophy, mathematics, physiology, and psychology.

DESCARTES: THE BEGINNINGS OF MODERN PHILOSOPHY AND SCIENCE

Descartes appeared on the scene at the tail end of the Renaissance and thus benefited from the changes that occurred during that remarkable historical era. The Renaissance lasted for approximately 200 years, during the 15th and 16th centuries. It derives its name from the rediscovery of ancient Greek and Roman texts, especially those of Plato and Aristotle, which had been lost to the Western world for hundreds of years. The period was marked by tremendous advances in the arts, starting in northern Italy but quickly spreading throughout Europe. It was the time of Leonardo da Vinci (1452–1519), the prototypical "Renaissance Man," whose genius encompassed both art and science. His *Last Supper* and *Mona Lisa* are among the world's best-known paintings, and his scientific interests encompassed geology, astronomy, botany, anatomy, and the applied sciences of aeronautics, engineering, and weaponry. Another giant of the Renaissance was Michelangelo Buonarotti (1475–1564), who created artistic treasures ranging from a portrayal of the book of Genesis on the ceiling of the Sistine Chapel in the Vatican to the massive 17-foot-tall sculpture of David, now found in Michelangelo's home city of Florence.

In addition to rediscovering ancient texts and revolutionizing the arts, the Renaissance produced some notable advances in technology and science. In the 1450s, for instance, Johannes Gutenberg (c. 1394–1468) invented a new form of the printing press, enabling books to be created in larger numbers than ever thought possible, and at prices that brought literature, philosophy, and the Bible to more people than ever. Also during this time, clock makers improved upon simple medieval instruments to produce the elaborate mechanical displays mounted on the cathedrals and public buildings of Europe. On the hour at the Wells Cathedral in England, for instance, viewers would be treated to a performance that included lifelike figures of armored knights in combat, one of whom would unhorse the other as another uniformed character struck the hour with a hammer (Boorstin, 1983). Knowledge about the inner workings of the human body was advanced significantly in 1543, when the Belgian physician Andreas Vesalius established his reputation as the founder of modern anatomical studies with his *Fabric of the Human Body*, which featured incredibly detailed illustrations (Klein, 1970). In astronomy in the mid-1500s, the Polish astronomer Nicolas Copernicus challenged the traditional **geocentric** view of the universe, which placed the earth ("geo") at the center of the universe, and suggested instead a **heliocentric** theory, which proposed that the sun ("helio") was at the center and the earth moved around it just like the other planets. Well aware of the religious controversy sure to result from the idea that "God's planet" was not in the center of the cosmos after all, Copernicus delayed publication until just before his death in 1543. The appearance of classic scientific works by Vesalius and Copernicus in the same year led one historian of science to declare 1543 as the year when modern science was born (Singer, 1957).

The Copernican model of the universe, which appeared near the end of the Renaissance, is the clearest example of one of its evolving themes—a questioning of authority, especially the authority of the Church and the Church's official philosopher, Aristotle. The ancient geocentric model placed God's greatest creation, man, at the focal point of the universe. Copernicus questioned this notion. An even greater challenge soon arrived in the person of the renowned Italian scientist Galileo Galilei (1564–1642), who supported Copernican theory with empirical observations aided by a telescope (20× power) that he constructed in 1609.[1] Galileo's observations of things never seen before, such as the moons of Jupiter, further eroded traditional authority. How could Aristotle's view of the universe be correct when he was not capable of seeing what could now be seen? Galileo, a devout Catholic (his daughter

---

[1]The inventor of the telescope is a matter of some dispute, but it was not Galileo—he improved existing technology. Credit for inventing the telescope usually goes to Hans Lippershey (d. 1619), a lens maker from the Netherlands, primarily on the grounds of a 1608 letter that serves as a patent application (King, 1955).

was a nun), would eventually be charged with heresy by the Church's Inquisition and forced to recant his claim of a heliocentric universe, but he did so with his fingers crossed. Even though his writings were placed on the Catholic Church's *Index of Prohibited Books* and remained there for nearly 200 years, his works continued to be published and read widely (Sobel, 2000). By the end of the 17th century, the geocentric model was, as they say, history.

Another threat to established authority occurred in England, during the time of Galileo, in the person of Sir Francis Bacon (1561–1626). Bacon was a strong advocate of an **inductive** approach to science. That is, he argued that scientists must observe nature systematically as it presents itself, rather than follow the conclusions derived from a deductive analysis of Aristotle and other authorities. From many observations of individual cases, general statements about nature could be made. Bacon also believed that science should play an active role in controlling nature directly; indeed, for Bacon, a true understanding of nature follows from the ability to create and recreate its effects at will (Smith, 1992). This, of course, is a plea for direct experimentation on nature to supplement careful observation. Bacon's insistence on acquiring knowledge through experience makes him an ancestor of British empiricism; his emphasis on induction and the control of nature made him a hero in the eyes of the 20th-century behaviorist B. F. Skinner (Chapter 11), who explicitly adopted a Baconian value system.

Descartes and the Rationalist Argument

In the year that Galileo was observing the heavens with his telescope, René Descartes (1596–1650), a 13-year-old son of a prosperous French lawyer, was already in his third year of study at the College de la Flèche. The school was run by Jesuits, known for their skills as educators.[2] The education Descartes received was in the **scholastic** tradition, combining the received wisdom of Church authority with the careful use of reason. In particular, it relied on rational argument derived from the works of Aristotle to support the precepts of the Church. Descartes quickly established himself as a star pupil, so good that he was granted special privileges—a rare private room and exemption from regular class attendance and routine assignments.

Descartes left the college in 1614, not entirely satisfied with his Jesuit education. Like modern-day students surprised to learn that their formal education fails to give them clear answers to life's significant questions, he was dismayed to discover of philosophy that "it has been studied for many centuries by the most outstanding minds without having produced anything which is not in dispute" (Descartes, 1637/1960, p. 8). Consequently, he resolved to find things out for himself, rather than relying on authority. Reflecting a sentiment familiar to all senior-level college students, he was ready to abandon the classroom and get out into the real world, "resolved to seek no other knowledge than that which I might find within myself, or perhaps in the great book of nature" (p. 8).

Because Descartes tried to keep his personal life private, the next few years are not well documented, but it appears that he spent some time sampling all that Paris had to offer (Vrooman, 1970). In 1619 he experienced what can only be called a conversion experience,

---

[2]Descartes's birth date was March 31, 1596, a fact known only because it appeared below a portrait published after his death. During his lifetime, Descartes was secretive about his private life, refusing to disclose his birthday out of fear that it would lead to speculation by astrologers (Vrooman, 1970).

in which a series of dreams effectively told him to get serious about making a meaningful contribution to knowledge. He spent the next 10 years living in and around Paris, learning as much as he could about as many different topics as possible, especially the sciences. He firmly believed that he could produce a "unity of knowledge" that would be grounded in mathematics.

Descartes's time, the early 17th century, is known as an era of revolutionary developments in science. It was the time of Bacon, Galileo, and in the latter half of the century, the incomparable Sir Isaac Newton. It featured Galileo's telescope and the microscope of the Dutch lens maker Antoni van Leeuwenhoek, tools which made it possible to observe things never seen before both in the heavens and in a drop of water (Boorstin, 1983). In medicine, systematic observation in 1628 by the British physician William Harvey refuted a widely held belief that the heart creates blood to be consumed by other parts of the body, and demonstrated instead that it acts as a mechanical pump that recirculates blood throughout the body. A gradual weakening of Church authority, combined with an increasing faith in science, created optimism among thinkers like Descartes that everything about the world could be known, perhaps in one's lifetime.

During the early 1620s, Descartes resembled a scientist more than a philosopher, studying physics, optics, geometry, and physiology. For example, he combined his interests in optics and physiology by extracting the eye of an ox and examining the properties of the lens, showing that retinal images are inverted (Vrooman, 1970). By 1633 he had written *The World*, designed to summarize his life's work to that point, demonstrating how the various disciplines could be united through the careful use of reason and based on a foundation of mathematics. The section on astronomy, centering on a strong defense of the Copernican–Galilean heliocentric model of the universe, was a problem, however. Descartes was ready to publish *The World* when he learned that Galileo's work had been condemned by the Church. Fearing a similar fate, and desiring to avoid notoriety and remain in the good graces of the Catholic Church, Descartes suppressed publication so that the book did not appear until after he died. Portions of it, however, appeared in various forms in several treatises that Descartes published during his lifetime, including his *Discourse on Method*, to which we now turn.

The Cartesian System: Rationalism, Nativism, and Mechanistic Interactionism

Although skeptical of the scholasticism he encountered as a student, Descartes was always grateful to the Jesuits for teaching him to be precise and logical in his thinking. His belief that truth could emerge from the careful use of reason became his modus operandi and marks him as a **rationalist**. In his *Discourse on Method* (1637/1960), he explained how he would accept as truth only that which could not be doubted. Thus he rejected the evidence of the senses, because the senses can deceive; he also questioned the plausible arguments of philosophers, because equally plausible counterarguments existed. Yet he found that the one thing he was unable to doubt was that he was the one doing the doubting. As he put it in one of philosophy's most famous passages:

> I noticed that while I thus wished to think everything false, it was necessarily true that I who thought so was something. Since this truth, *"I think, therefore I am"* was so firm and so assured that all the most extravagant suppositions of the sceptics were unable to

shake it, I judged that I could safely accept it as the first principle of the philosophy I was seeking. (Descartes, 1637/1960, p. 24; emphasis added)

For Descartes, then, the way to truth was through the unique human capacity to reason. In his *Discourse on Method*, he described the four basic rules he used to arrive at the truth of some matter. First, he would accept nothing as true unless "it presented itself so clearly and distinctly to my mind that there was no reason to doubt it" (Descartes, 1637/1960, p. 15). Second, he would use a strategy of analysis, breaking problems into subproblems. Third, he would work from the simplest of these subproblems to the more complex ones; and fourth, he would carefully review his conclusions to be certain of omitting nothing. Now to our modern way of thinking, these rules of method may not appear to be extraordinary. Descartes seems to be saying not much more than to think clearly, logically, and without bias, to analyze problems carefully, to work systematically from the simple to the complex, and to check your work. Yet to conclude that these rules are ordinary is to fall prey to the kind of presentist thinking discussed in Chapter 1. In the context of Descartes's times, when the power of authority was weakening but still considerable, his rules of method were truly revolutionary. In effect, he was casting off authority completely. The only way to get to the certainty of truth is to *arrive at it oneself*, relying on the clear use of one's own reasoning powers. An indication of how unsettling this notion was to the authorities is the fact that after Descartes's death, the Catholic Church put his writings in the *Index*, their list of books to be avoided by right-thinking Catholics (Vrooman, 1970).

An implication of Cartesian rationalism was that the ability to reason is inborn or innate and that certain types of knowledge do not rely directly on sense experience, but result from our native ability to reason. For example, although we come to know the properties of wax (e.g., heat melts it) on the basis of our experience with it, there are certain things about wax that we know to be true simply as a result of a logical analysis, using our native reasoning powers. Thus Descartes would say that we can conclude, without doubt, that wax has the property of "extension"—it exists in space, and even though it may change form (e.g., through melting) it can never disappear. Because we can use our native reason to arrive at our knowledge of the concept of extension, Descartes considered this particular attribute to be an example of an **innate idea**. Similarly, he believed that we have other innate ideas. These included the ideas of God, the self, and some basic mathematical truths. On the other hand, many of our concepts result from our experiences. These Descartes called **derived ideas**. Knowing that a wax candle of a certain size will burn for about 10 hours would be an example of such an idea. Descartes's position on innate ideas means that he can be considered a **nativist** as well as a rationalist. His distinction between innate versus derived ideas foreshadows one of psychology's recurring issues, the relationship between nature and nurture.

Descartes was also history's best-known **dualist**, arguing for a clear separation between mind (or "soul") and body. They can be distinguished, according to Descartes, by the above-mentioned property of extension and by the additional property of movement—bodies take up space and move through it. Mind, on the other hand, possesses neither extension nor movement. The centerpiece of the unextended mind is the human ability to reason, while the body is in essence a machine. One implication of this dualism has come to be called the **Cartesian dichotomy**, which divides humans and animals. Descartes argued that animals were simple machines, incapable of reason and language, and therefore lacking a mind. Humans, on the other hand, combined a mechanical body with a mind that could reason. Thus animals consist only of bodies, whereas humans combine both bodies and minds. In addition to the labels rationalist and nativist, then, Descartes can also be considered a **mechanist**, for his belief that the body operates like a complicated machine. He was also an **interactionist**, believing that the mind could have a direct influence on the body (a decision to improve our health causes us to exercise) and the body could have a direct influence on the mind (a pulled hamstring causes us to redesign our exercise plan).

Descartes's use of the machine metaphor when describing the properties of bodies was no accident. We have seen that in the Renaissance, clock-building technology had advanced to the point where mechanical yet lifelike figures would put on an hourly show on the cathedrals and public buildings of Europe. Similarly, the wealthy of Europe created gardens that included elaborate mechanical fountains and statues that moved through the action of water-driven hydraulic systems. The unwary visitor to one of these 17th-century Disney Worlds might step on a hidden plate, thereby activating a system that caused a statue of Neptune to rise from the water in an adjacent pond. A less whimsical example of the mechanistic zeitgeist that infused Descartes's times was Harvey's demonstration of the heart as a mechanical pump.

Descartes on the Reflex and Mind–Body Interaction

In the year before his death, Descartes published *The Passions of the Soul* (1649/1969), which established his status as a pioneer psychologist and physiologist. Primarily a treatise on human emotions, it included an attempt to explain what we now call the **reflex**, an automatic stimulus–response reaction, and it provided a physiological model for Descartes's position on the mind–body question. Descartes opened the book with a characteristic attack on the traditional, authority-based approach to the study of the emotions, arguing in his opening sentence that "there is nothing in which the defective nature of the sciences which we have received from the ancients appears more clearly than in what they have written on the passions" (Descartes, 1649/1969, p. 331). He then introduced his mind–body distinction and began a discussion of the "bodily machine," which included a reference to William Harvey's discoveries about the mechanical heart, and a description of muscle action. Muscles, in turn, "depend on the nerves, which resemble . . . little tubes, which all proceed from the brain, and thus contain like it a certain very subtle air or wind which is called the animal spirits" (pp. 333–334).

The **animal spirits** referred to by Descartes, a notion that traces to the ancient Greeks, were said to be derived from the "heat" of the blood and were the driving forces behind movement. Descartes believed these spirits were tiny particles in constant motion and were found in the brain, the nerves, and the muscles. Muscle movement resulted from the action of animal spirits deriving from the brain, but what determined which muscles move? Two things, according to Descartes. First, the mind can initiate the movement of animal spirits in the brain by activating the nerves controlling certain muscles rather than others. That is, the mind can influence the body (more on this shortly). Second, certain muscles can move automatically in response to the results of certain sensory stimuli. That is, *reflexes* occur.[3]

Descartes explained reflexes by proposing the existence of thin, wirelike "filaments" that existed within the nerves and extended to the brain. When the senses are stimulated,

---

[3] Although Descartes was clearly describing reflex action, he did not invent or first use the term *reflex*. That distinction belongs to Thomas Willis (1621–1675), a British physiologist, who named the phenomenon "reflexion." Willis also coined the term *neurology* (Finger, 2000).

FIGURE 2.1 Descartes's illustration of reflex action. From Fearing (1930).

according to Descartes, these filaments move, causing "pores" in the brain to be opened. This in turn results in the flow of animal spirits that produces the reflex movement, as when we accidentally burn ourselves. Figure 2.1 shows a famous sketch by Descartes of this involuntary (i.e., reflexive) withdrawal of one's foot from a fire, taken from his *Treatise on Man*, published in 1637. The fire touches the foot, causing a tug on the filaments within the nerve there. These filaments extend all the way to the brain, where animal spirits are released into the nerve "tube." The spirits in turn are carried "partly to the muscles which pull back the foot from the fire, partly to those which turn the eyes and the head in order to regard it, and partly to those which serve to advance the hands and to bend the whole body in order to shield itself" (Descartes, 1637; quoted in Fearing, 1930, p. 24).

In addition to resulting in reflex action, sensations can also give rise to the movement of animal spirits in the brain that lead to deliberate decisions to act, and the mind by itself can initiate action. That is, the mind can intervene between sensory stimulus and motor response. How to explain the nature of this interaction between mind and body was a problem, however. It is one thing to say that the mind can directly affect bodily movement and vice versa, but it is quite another thing to demonstrate just how this occurs. After careful analysis, Descartes concluded that the interaction occurred in a part of the brain called the **pineal gland**, selected because he believed it was strategically located in a place where the flow of the animal spirits could be controlled. In Figure 2.2, Descartes showed how the pineal gland's movement could send animal spirits off in different directions (represented by the straight lines). The pineal gland was also a brain structure that was not duplicated on both the left and right side of the

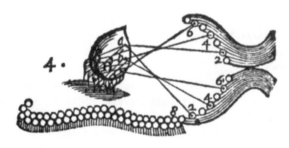

FIGURE 2.2 Descartes's illustration of the action of the pineal gland. From Finger (2000).

brain. Because the mind was considered to be unitary, Descartes reasoned, it must exert its effect through a structure that was also a single unit. Descartes was not arguing that the pineal gland had its special function because it was a part of the brain found only in humans—he was well aware, on the basis of some of his own dissections, that other animals possessed the structure (Finger, 2000). Instead, he was arguing that the gland had a function in humans that would not be found in animals—the locus for mind–body interaction.

Descartes was not asserting that the mind was *in* the pineal gland, only that the gland serves as the place where mind and body influence each other. Thus sensations produce a stretching of the small filaments that open pores in the brain, thereby moving the animal spirits. These movements are felt by the pineal gland and result in the mental event of a "sensation." The animal spirits also continue their movement back down the nerve fibers into the muscles, producing movement. Movement can also be created by the direct action of the will. The decision to move causes the pineal gland to move, which in turn produces the movements of the spirits that eventually move the muscles.

Of course, despite the noble effort, Descartes was wrong about the physiology. For example, the pineal gland, which secretes the hormone melatonin and remains poorly understood today (at least in mammals), is not a mind–body Grand Central Station. A more important problem, one pointed out almost immediately by critics in his own day, was that his proposal of the pineal gland as the point of mind–body interaction really did not explain *anything*, but merely restated the problem. If it is unclear how the unextended mind can influence and be influenced by an extended body in general, it is just as unclear how the unextended mind can influence, and be influenced by, the movements of a small, extended piece of the brain, the pineal gland (Cottingham, 1986). For psychology, the significance of Descartes's work is not that he made a serious yet flawed effort to solve the mind–body problem but that in so doing, he created the modern concept of reflex action with its explicit distinction between sensory stimulus and motor response, and he tried to explain psychological concepts (e.g., memory) by using a physiological model.

Shortly after publishing *The Passions of the Soul* in 1649, Descartes was persuaded by Queen Christina of Sweden to move to Stockholm to be her tutor. The queen had a keen mind, was fluent in five languages, and was determined to make Stockholm a center of learning in Europe. To that end she created a world-class library and began inviting scholars to her court, Descartes being among the first to be asked. He accepted with some misgivings and soon found himself conversing with and tutoring Christina for five hours a day, three days a week, beginning at 5 a.m., during a winter that was severe even by Swedish standards. For someone accustomed to lounging in bed until late morning while reflecting on the great issues of the day, the schedule was a killer. Sure enough, Descartes contracted pneumonia on February 1, 1650, and died 10 days later, just shy of his 54th birthday.

THE BRITISH EMPIRICIST ARGUMENT AND THE ASSOCIATIONISTS

Philosophy on the European continent has often been rationalist in spirit, especially after Descartes. In England, however, a different tradition arose at about the same time that Descartes's influence was spreading. This British tradition is strongly **empiricist**, based on the idea that our knowledge of the world is constructed from our experiences in it. Because this knowledge is woven together by the associations among our experiences and ideas, British empiricism is closely tied to the doctrines of **associationism**. Much of the history of British philosophy, from the 17th century on, has been concerned with the epistemological questions of how experience creates knowledge and how the rules of association work to organize that knowledge.

British empiricism has its roots in the inductive scientific thinking of Sir Francis Bacon and the social theories of Thomas Hobbes, a contemporary of Bacon and Descartes. We may conveniently begin with John Locke, however, usually considered the founder of this movement. We will then examine the work of other leading British empiricists and associationists, ending with the most important British philosopher of the 19th century, John Stuart Mill.

John Locke (1632–1704): The Origins of British Empiricism

John Locke was a reasonable man who lived during unreasonable times. He spent most of his adult life in the rational academic environment of Oxford as a lecturer and tutor, but he mixed the contemplative life of a philosopher with an active political and diplomatic career. He also was trained in medicine, but he was primarily interested in the scientific aspects of it, and he seldom practiced as a physician. In his lifetime, he witnessed (a) the English Civil War, which ousted the British monarchy in favor of a civilian Parliament; (b) the execution of one king and the overthrow of another (he might have been present at the former and had a hand in the latter); (c) several changes in England's official religion, each accompanied by varying degrees of persecution of those professing the "wrong" faith; (d) a fire that destroyed two thirds of London (he could see the smoke from Oxford); and (e) a political alliance that led him to flee England for a time and settle in the safety of Holland (Jeffreys, 1967). Out of these experiences, Locke developed a liberal political philosophy based on tolerance of dissent and the right of the people to determine how they would lead both their worldly and their more spiritual lives, and in particular, how they would be governed. In his best-known political work, *Two Treatises on Government* (1690/1960), he described a **social contract** between government and the people. The government would agree to govern wisely and protect the common good of its citizens; the citizens in turn would agree to support the government and participate in it. Citizens failing to do so could expect the government to act against them (e.g., throw them in jail for not paying taxes). On the other hand, governments failing their end of the bargain could expect to be overthrown by the people and replaced by a more just government. This concept should sound familiar—Thomas Jefferson modeled the Declaration of Independence on it.

Locke is important to psychology for the concepts expressed in two books, *An Essay Concerning Human Understanding* (1690/1963a) and *Some Thoughts Concerning Education* (1693/1963b). The former explains Locke's views on how knowledge is acquired, how we as humans come to understand our world. The latter is based on letters to a friend, showing how empiricist thinking could apply to a child's education.

Locke on Human Understanding   Like Descartes, Locke was enamored of the science that was such a prominent feature of the 17th century. While a student at Oxford, he was drawn to the ideas of Sir Francis Bacon, and he rejected the same scholasticism that Descartes questioned. While studying medicine, Locke befriended other scientists, including Robert Boyle (1627–1692), one of modern chemistry's pioneers and a founder of the British

Royal Society, established in 1662 to further the interests of science (Boorstin, 1983). Locke was also a contemporary of Sir Isaac Newton—his *Principia Mathematica* was published just three years before Locke's *Essay*. What Galileo, Harvey, Boyle, Newton, and others were doing for physical science, transforming it from the Aristotelian-based "natural philosophy" into an experimental discipline, Locke was determined to do for **epistemology**, the study of human knowledge and its acquisition.

As Locke noted in the book's opening "epistle to the reader," the ideas in his *Essay* derived from discussions with friends at Oxford and evolved into a series of notes, "written by incoherent parcels; and, after long intervals of neglect, resumed again, as my humor or occasions permitted" (Locke, 1690/1963a, p. xlvii). Twenty years after the originating discussions, it finally emerged in 1690 as *An Essay Concerning Human Understanding*.

Before describing how our ideas originate, Locke considered and rejected the existence of innate ideas. He granted that we have innate "faculties" such as the ability to think, but he did not accept Descartes's contention that ideas derived from reason (e.g., extension) could be considered innate ideas. Locke argued that there is no need to propose innate ideas, because it can be shown that ideas originate from other sources, requiring only the use of our basic mental abilities (faculties). For instance, while our reasoning ability enables us to conclude that all physical objects have the property of extension, the conclusion is based on the fact that we have experienced lots of extended objects during our lifetimes. In the absence of such experiences, Locke believed that we would not arrive at the conclusion about extension being a property of all matter; indeed, it would not even occur to us to think about it.

Another argument for innate ideas was the belief that some ideas were universal, found in all people. If all cultures include the concept of the Deity, for example, it could be said that the concept of God does not require specific experiences, but is innate. Locke would not buy it. A universal belief in God does not necessarily mean the idea of God is innate to us, he argued. Instead, it could be that because all people die (i.e., a universal experience), they all worry about death and whether there is an afterlife, and proposing the idea of a supreme being is a natural consequence of this line of thought.

A final argument for innate ideas was that some ideas seem to appear so early in life that they must be innate. Locke rejected this argument also, pointing out that even before children can use language, they are profiting from experience—by learning to recognize the difference between bitter and sweet, for instance. Furthermore, in a tone similar to that taken later by American behaviorists in the 20th century, Locke pointed out that we often overlook the fact that a child can have quite a few important experiences early in life.

Having rejected the concept of innate ideas, Locke turned to the question of how our minds develop ideas. In one of philosophy's most quoted passages, he declared that *all* of our knowledge about the world derives from experience:

> Let us then suppose the mind to be, as we say, white paper, void of all characters, without any ideas; how comes it to be furnished? Whence comes it by that vast store, which the busy and boundless fancy of man has painted on it with an almost endless variety? Whence has it all the materials of reason and knowledge? *To this I answer, in one word, from experience*; in that, all our knowledge is founded, and from that it ultimately derives itself. (Locke, 1690/1963a, pp. 82–83; emphasis added)

The mind at birth, then, is an empty sheet of **white paper** (Locke was renaming an old Aristotelian metaphor of the mind as a blank slate or wax tablet), ready to be written upon by the experiences of one's lifetime. Furthermore, the ideas that result from our experience and compose the mind have two and only two sources, according to Locke. He believed that every idea we have, without exception, originated from the two processes of sensation and reflection. *Sensation* refers to all of the information taken in by our senses from the environment, and *reflection* refers to the mental activities involved in processing information from both the senses and from memory. Thus our concept of green derives from all of our experiences with green objects and our further reflections about "greenness." The reflection process also can produce new ideas not encountered initially by our senses. Even without encountering the Dr. Seuss story directly, we can conceive of "green eggs and ham" by combining, through the reflective processes of memory and imagination, our learned ideas of green, eggs, and ham.

In another part of the *Essay*, Locke made a distinction between simple and complex ideas. **Simple ideas** resulted from experiencing basic sensory qualities such as yellow, white, heat, and so on, and from making simple reflections. A **complex idea** includes several other ideas, which can be a combination of simple and other complex ideas. The complex idea of a cold drink on a very hot day, for example, is composed of a number of simple ideas relating to color, temperature, shape, pleasantness, taste, and the additional complex idea of the good life. Complex ideas are compounds and can be ultimately reduced to simple ones, much as chemical compounds are composed of simple elements. This idea of the mind being an elaborate construction incorporating layers of ideas of varying complexity was a common feature of British empiricist thinking, and it reflects the influence of the other sciences, especially physics and chemistry. Just as water can be reduced to its elements and light can be broken down into the colors of the spectrum, so the mind could be analyzed into its fundamental units. The idea that complexity in nature can be understood by reducing objects to their most basic elements is sometimes referred to as **atomism**, and it is an assumption underlying many of the early systems of psychology, including E. B. Titchener's structuralism (Chapter 7) and John Watson's behaviorism (Chapter 10).

In the fourth edition of his *Essay*, Locke addressed the question of how simple ideas form compound ones, and in the process introduced the concept of **association** into the discussion. Just as gravity was the central concept of Newtonian physics, holding together the elements of the universe, so would association be the glue that held together one's experiences in life. But while Locke discussed the concept of association to some extent, it was for the other British philosophers we will meet shortly to develop it more fully. As will become evident, British empiricism and associationism went hand in hand.

A final distinction worth noting is between what Locke referred to as the primary and secondary qualities of matter. This was a distinction well known in the 17th century and first popularized by Galileo. **Primary qualities** were said to exist as an inherent property of an object. Extension, shape, and motion are examples. These were the features Descartes believed to be innate ideas. To Locke, there was nothing innate about them; the concepts might indeed result from the mind's reflection, but the data for that reflection came from one's sensory experiences with a range of objects. **Secondary qualities**, on the other hand, are not inherent attributes of objects, but depend on perception. The color, smell, warmth, and taste of objects are examples. Thus the redness of an object exists not in the object itself, but in the perceptual experience of the observer. As it gets darker, the tomato in the garden does not change its shape, but its color changes, gradually fading from red to almost black. The primary–secondary distinction raised questions that led naturally to a direct examination of how sensory systems actually work to create our "understandings." If "red" is not in the object but in the brain, how does it get there?

Locke's empiricist philosophy had several interesting implications. First, if our knowledge of the world is based on our experiences, and sensation is a major source of that experience, then defective senses should produce a distorted view of the world. This issue was posed to Locke in a letter from William Molyneux, a friend in Dublin. Molyneux asked what would happen if a man blind from birth, whose experience of objects like cubes and spheres would be limited to the sense of touch, would recognize the objects if his sight was suddenly restored. Molyneux answered his own question in the negative, and Locke agreed. Once sight had been restored, the man would have to learn to distinguish cube from sphere all over again, by relating the information from the visual and the tactile senses. As early as the 18th century, congenital cataracts were being removed surgically, thus providing a direct test (and support) for this empiricist claim (Morgan, 1977).

Another implication of Locke's theory connects his psychology with his political theory and illustrates how the turbulent times in which he lived helped shape his ideas. If human understanding results from experience, then people living in different environments will necessarily have different kinds of experiences. The result will be differences between people that range from food preferences to beliefs about the best way to live one's life to one's personal religious preferences. Locke did not believe in a total relativism—not all belief systems are of equal value, both intellectually and morally. But his commitment to the importance of the environment in shaping the mind, and the resulting differences between people, was tied closely to his political liberalism and in particular to his belief that individual differences, even differences in religious beliefs, should be tolerated. Having lived through several periods of extreme religious intolerance, Locke was aware of its destructive influence.

Locke on Education   A final implication of Locke's empiricist thinking concerned how to raise and educate children. If the mind is shaped by its experiences, then a deliberate program of education based on empiricist principles could be expected to produce the ideal citizen. Locke's contribution to the issue was *Some Thoughts Concerning Education* (1693/1963b), a brief volume based on letters written to a friend who was seeking advice about the education of his son. Locke's advice was wide-ranging and included the following:

1. Trained in medicine, Locke was a strong believer in the importance of physical health, and he began the book by advocating that a sound mind requires a sound body. His specific suggestions reflected his own strict Puritan upbringing, which fostered simplicity, individual initiative and effort, and the belief that good outcomes require some degree of suffering. Children should have hard rather than soft beds, for example; the former toughens the person, whereas "being buried every night in feathers, melts and dissolves the body, is often the cause of weakness, and the forerunner of an early grave" (Locke, 1693/1963b, p. 22).

2. Training must begin early, because young children are more malleable, and if they don't develop good habits early in life, they will develop bad ones. Locke believed that one of the greatest mistakes made by parents was that their child's "mind [had] not been made obedient to discipline, and pliant to reason, when at first it was most tender, most easy to be bowed" (Locke, 1693/1963b, p. 27). Good habits also require practice. Children learn such habits by doing things repeatedly, not by learning rules, "which will be always slipping out of their memories" (p. 46).

3. Locke argued against the use of punishment, especially as children get older. The child who is beaten for not doing lessons soon comes to dislike learning (and tutors). Further-more, while punishment might reduce unruly behavior, severe and repeated punishment carries the danger of "breaking the mind, and then, in place of a disorderly young fellow, you have a low-spirited moped creature" (Locke, 1693/1963b, p. 38).

4. Concrete rewards are to be avoided. Giving a child candy for good performance pro-duces a child interested only in obtaining candy. On the other hand, Locke recommended the use of rewards and punishments in the form of parental approval and disapproval. "If you can once get into children a love of credit, and an apprehension of shame and disgrace, you have put into them the true principle, which will constantly work, and incline them to the right" (Locke, 1693/1963b, p. 41).

Locke's views on education, and his empiricist philosophy in general, show a strong affinity with 20th-century behaviorism, as will be clear when you read Chapters 10 and 11. Although Locke was concerned with mental life and the behaviorists focused on overt action, strong resemblances exist. Like the modern behaviorists, Locke believed that complexity could be understood by analysis into component parts, that the environment directly shaped the mind and behavior, and that you can tell a great deal about a person if you know something of the person's experiences in life. Empiricism and behaviorism also share an emphasis on the importance of association, but as mentioned earlier, it was for empiricists subsequent to Locke to develop associationist doctrine to its fullest. It is to Locke's intellectual descendants that we now turn.

George Berkeley (1685–1753): Empiricism Applied to Vision

As the 17th century drew to a close, it was clear to the intelligentsia that the century had been marked by a steady decline in the authority of the Church and scholasticism. This was accompanied by, and to a large extent precipitated by, enormous advances in science. From Bacon to Galileo to Harvey to Boyle to Newton, a zeitgeist evolved that envisioned the universe as a large machine composed of material parts and operating according to laws that could be discovered only by combining scientific methods with mathematical rigor. Although it was not until the 19th century that the "ism" called **materialism** would reach its full development, its roots were in the 17th century. Materialists are monists on the mind–body question, believing that the only reality is a physical reality and that every event in the universe, including what we think of as mental events, involves measurable, material objects in motion in physical space. Materialism includes the above-mentioned atomism, the idea that complex entities can be understood by reducing them to their component parts. Materialism also poses a threat to the concept of free will by implying **determinism**, the belief that all events have prior causes. If we are not free to choose, then perhaps we cannot be held responsible for our actions.

Such a materialistic and scientific worldview does not necessarily rule out religion (e.g., Boyle thought that to do science was to discover God's will), but it threatens the concepts of free will and moral responsibility and so it was seen by some as a danger. One thinker who was especially concerned about the materialistic implications of 17th-century science was George Berkeley, a bishop of the Anglican Church in Ireland.

Berkeley (pronounced *BARK-lee*) is important for psychology because of two books that he published when he was in his mid-twenties: *An Essay Towards a New Theory of Vision* (1709) and *Treatise Concerning the Principles of Human Knowledge* (1710). Both were strongly empiricist and focused on analyzing sensory processes. Legend has it that Berkeley's interest in sensation had its roots in a hanging that he witnessed while a student. Curious about the sensations accompanying being hung, he arranged to have *himself* hung from the rafters in the company of friends who were instructed to cut him down after a few minutes. Evidently, Berkeley lost consciousness and almost died from the incident, which contributed to his reputation for being a bit eccentric (Klein, 1970).[4]

Berkeley's work on vision was the first systematic example of how empiricist thinking could be applied to the study of perception. It was timely, written when advances in optics were producing new and improved telescopes, microscopes, and eyeglasses. In his book, Berkeley tried to show that perceptions of distance, size, and location are judgments depending entirely on *experience*. When judging distance, for example, Berkeley made use of what your general psychology book referred to as the monocular (only one eye needed) cues of overlap, relative clarity, and relative size:

> The estimate we make of the distance of objects considerably remote is rather an act of judgment grounded on experience than of sens[ation]. For example, when I perceive a great number of intermediate objects, such as houses, fields, rivers, and the like, which I have experienced to take up considerable space, I thence form a judgment or conclusion that the object that I see beyond them is at a great distance. Again, when an object appears faint and small, which at a near distance I have experienced to make a vigorous and large appearance, I instantly conclude it to be far off. (Berkeley, 1709/1948, p. 171)

Berkeley also examined the question of judging depth for relatively close objects and provided clear descriptions of phenomena today referred to as convergence, a binocular (two eyes needed) cue, and accommodation. In **convergence**, when objects move closer to us or farther away, "we alter the disposition of our eyes, by lessening or widening the interval between the pupils" (Berkeley, 1709/1948, p. 174). These eye movements are the result of muscle movements, which in turn create sensations that we come to associate with various distances. Similarly, objects are perceived clearly through **accommodation**, in which changes in the shape of the lens serve to keep objects focused on the retina. Closer objects produce a greater bulging of the lens than objects farther away. Again, these changes are accompanied by muscle action and sensations to be associated with different distances.

The basic principles of optics had been known for some time, and it had been common knowledge since Descartes that the retinal image was inverted (as shown in Figure 2.3, taken from Berkeley's book). The question was how we manage to see an upright world. Berkeley rejected as oversimplified the notion that our brain simply makes a correction and proposed instead that once again, the key lies in our experience with the world. Specifically, we learn to relate what we see with what we experience using our other senses, especially touch and the senses related to physical movement. We develop concepts of up and down through our sense of touch, according to Berkeley, by learning that "up" is farther away from the earth than "down." When we touch the top and the bottom of the cross in Figure 2.3, we learn to make the connection between the lower portion of the retinal image and the top of the cross,

---

[4]The reputation was enhanced when Berkeley died. He believed that noticeable decay was the only sure sign of death, so he gave instructions that he not be buried until his body became offensive to the senses.

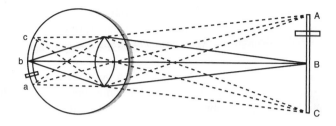

FIGURE 2.3 The inverted retinal image. From Berkeley (1709/1948).

and we come to "see" the top of the cross as being farther away from the earth (i.e., higher) than the bottom of the cross. Again, all depends on experience.

An important theme of Berkeley's theory of vision, made clear from the opening sentence of the monocular cues quote, is that we do not see objects directly; rather, we make judgments about them based on visual information and our experiences. The theme was carried into his other major work, *Treatise Concerning the Principles of Human Knowledge* (1710/1957), and provided the basis for Berkeley's attack on materialism. Just as we do not see "distance" directly, so it is the case that we do not see "material objects" directly. In both cases, they are "judged" on the basis of perception. Thus we cannot be entirely certain of the reality of material objects; the only certainty is that we are perceiving them. This position of Berkeley's is known as **subjective idealism** (sometimes "immaterialism"). It is in the empiricist tradition because experience is the source of all knowledge, but it denied Locke's distinction between primary and secondary qualities of matter. For Berkeley, everything was a secondary quality. Just as color depends on the perceiving person, so does extension. The only thing that has reality for us is our own perception.

Does this mean that we can never be sure about the reality of the world? Does a tree falling in the forest exist only if we hear it? No. Reality exists, according to Berkeley, because objects, including the tree in the forest, are *always* perceived by God, who Berkeley referred to as the Permanent Perceiver. We can be sure of the permanence of reality, but only through our faith in God. In this way, Berkeley sought to attack what he saw as a Godless materialism. Instead, faith in God becomes essential to our understanding of the world.

Berkeley was not successful in countering the trend toward materialism, as will be clear in the next chapter. By emphasizing the importance of perception in one's understanding of reality, however, and by directly attacking the question of how visual perception actually works, he furthered the cause of British empiricism while at the same time turning the issue of *how knowledge is acquired* from a purely philosophical question to a more psychological one. As historian of psychology Daniel Robinson put it, Berkeley "rendered epistemology a branch of psychology, and the two have never been divorced since" (1981, p. 228). Once the problem of human knowledge became a psychological one, people began asking different questions. Rather than asking a philosophical question like "How much can be known about the nature of reality?" thinkers now began asking questions like "Just exactly how does visual perception work to produce what we know?" This shift would eventually bring about a scientific psychology.

British Associationism

Like John Locke, Berkeley had little to say about how our sensory experiences and our reflections combine to produce the more complicated forms of our knowledge. That is, while both addressed the issue of association of ideas, neither carefully examined the phenomenon. Association would soon occupy center stage for British philosophers, however, and be seen as a force controlling the events of mental life. Associationism is the doctrine that the mind can be understood as a complex set of ideas, related to each other by the force of the associations among them. Things become associated in our minds through our experiences in the world; thus, associationism is grounded in empiricism. The British philosophers David Hume and David Hartley both made important contributions to the understanding of how association operated.

David Hume (1711–1776): The Rules of Association   Hume was born near Edinburgh, Scotland, and entered the university there at age 12; he left after three years without finishing a degree. He tried studying law, hated it, then decided on a business career and hated it as well. Determined to become a scholar, he retreated to the French countryside[5] for three years and wrote his first book, *A Treatise of Human Nature* (1739–1740/1969). Unfortunately, the book did not sell well, disappointing the ambitious Hume, who later said of the book: "It fell deadborn from the press, without reaching such distinction, as even to excite a murmur from the zealots" (quoted in Klein, 1970, p. 552). He later wrote shortened versions of the *Treatise* under different titles, but as a writer he was best known for writing a massive, five-volume history of England. Still highly regarded, Hume's history went beyond the usual military and political history and incorporated social and literary history into the narrative. Hume's exalted stature among the Scots is clear from Figure 2.4.

FIGURE 2.4   Statue of Scotland's David Hume, portrayed as a heroic figure, found on Edinburgh's Royal Mile.

[5]He chose the quiet town of La Flèche, known for the Jesuit school that trained Descartes.

Never modest, Hume believed that his *Treatise* would do for philosophy what Newton had accomplished for physics. Indeed, the subtitle of the treatise is "Being an Attempt to Introduce the Experimental Method of Reasoning into Moral Subjects." By *experimental method*, Hume did not mean the use of experiments as we understand the term today, but the careful and systematic observation of human thinking and behavior, mainly his own, accompanied by a logical analysis of the process to uncover basic laws of the mind.

In good British empiricist tradition, Hume built his system on the basic premise that all of our understanding is rooted in experience. To dissect human experience, Hume first tried to discover the mind's basic elements, analogous to the physicist's atoms. Upon reflection, Hume believed these elements were two in number: impressions and ideas. **Impressions** are basic sensations, the raw data of experience. We feel pleasure, we see red, we taste sweetness, and so on. **Ideas**, on the other hand, are "faint copies" of impressions. That is, while similar to impressions, and deriving from them, ideas are not as vivid. To support his contention that ideas derived from impressions, Hume noted that it is possible to reduce all of our ideas to impressions, even complex ideas that have never been experienced directly. Thus, even if we have never found a real four-leaf clover, we can have a complex idea of it by combining simple ideas (e.g., "four" and "clover" and "green") that can be traced to impressions.

Note that Hume's analysis of impressions and ideas is mainstream British empiricism. If all ideas are faint copies of impressions, then all ideas derive from the impressions we experience in life. Hence, there are no innate ideas. Also, Hume included the Lockean distinction between simple and complex ideas. But how do impressions connect with ideas, and how are complex ideas formed? How does one idea lead to another? In a word, from the process of association, the analysis of which Hume considered perhaps his major philosophical achievement.

Hume proposed three laws of association: resemblance, contiguity, and cause–effect. Sometimes an object reminds us of another because it is similar to or has a **resemblance** to it. Thus a photo of the Yosemite's Half Dome resembles the actual piece of granite and brings to mind memories (ideas), perhaps of a visit to Yosemite Valley. **Contiguity** means experiencing things together. Thus, because purists eat lobster only in Maine, reading about lobster brings to mind the Maine coast. Hume's third law of association concerned the relationship between **cause and effect**. If one event follows another with some regularity, we will develop an association between the two. Hume's example was a healed wound. The original wound "caused" us to experience pain; thus, when we now examine the old wound, we are reminded of the pain and the circumstances that produced it. But what determines causes and effects? Hume's answer made him a controversial figure in his day but might have been his most important contribution to modern psychology.

Hume believed that we can never be absolutely certain about the causes of events. Rather, all we can know is that events occur together with some predictable regularity. To conclude that A causes B, he argued, it is necessary to know that (a) when A occurs, B occurs regularly; (b) A occurs before B does; and (c) B does not occur unless A does. Invoking empiricist thinking and aware of the basic problem of induction, Hume pointed out that we know about these regularities only because of our experience. Furthermore, because our experiences are limited, we can never be completely certain about the causes of events. Hume's conclusion that absolute certainty was unattainable labeled him a "skeptic" and brought him into conflict with sources of authority such as the Church, which naturally took offense at the implication that the existence of God could be questioned.

It is important to note, however, that Hume did not deny the existence of reality, God, or the possibility of there being absolute causes of events. His point was that we as humans could never arrive at them with certainty. From the practical standpoint of day-to-day living, what is important, Hume believed, is to be able to accumulate enough experience to make the best possible predictions. If events occur together reliably in the past, we have every reason to expect that they will covary in the future. Thus Hume was not denying causality; he was merely shifting it from a search for absolute causes to a search for greater-than-chance regularities. Modern psychologists searching for the "causes" of behavior are essentially following Hume's lead in this regard. They recognize that multiple factors contribute to all behaviors; the best one can hope for is to identify the factors that predict behaviors with probabilities greater than chance.

David Hartley (1705–1757): A Physiological Associationism   Hume paid heed to the process of association, but the topic commanded an even greater share of David Hartley's attention. His *Observations on Man, His Frame, His Duty, and His Expectations* (1749/1971) summarized the essentials of British empiricist thought with great clarity and added a forceful description of how association could be the guiding principle for a theory of how the human mind was organized. The book also attempted to describe the neurological correlates of the association process.

Hartley was a contemporary of Hume, but not influenced by him. He began preliminary drafts of his *Observations* in the early 1630s, before Hume's 1639 *Treatise*, and he seemed to be unaware of Hume's work (not surprising, considering the poor sales of Hume's book). Three years before producing the final *Observations*, Hartley published a version of the book as an appendix to a medical book on kidney and bladder stones. The appendix was written in Latin, under the tentative-sounding title of *Conjecturae*. Apparently, Hartley wished to preview his ideas to a restricted group of scholars before going public with it (Webb, 1988).

Hartley made it clear in the book's opening sentence that he was a dualist on the mind–body question: "Man consists of two parts, body and mind" (Hartley, 1749/1971, p. i). Unlike Descartes's interactionism, however, Hartley took a stance known as psychophysical **parallelism**. That is, he considered psychological and physical (physiological) events separately, but operating in parallel; he even structured the book as a series of propositions that alternated between the mind and the body. The widely quoted propositions 10 and 11 outline the core of his associationism, first on the mental side and then on the physical. Proposition 10 reads, in part:

> Any Sensations A, B, C, &c. by being associated with one another a sufficient Number of Times, get such Power over the corresponding Ideas a, b, c, &c. that any one of the Sensations A, when impressed alone, shall be able to excite in the Mind b, c, &c. the ideas of the rest.
>
>   Sensations may be said to be associated together, when their Impressions are either made precisely at the same Instant of Time, or in the contiguous successive Instants. We may therefore distinguish Association into two sorts, the synchronous, and the successive. (Hartley, 1749/1971, p. 65)

For Hartley, then, the main law of association is contiguity, the experiencing of events together. If we repeatedly see Adam (A), Brent (B), and Charlie (C) together, and each sensory experience produces the corresponding ideas of them (a, b, and c), then in the future if we see Adam (A), the ideas of Brent (b) and Charlie (c) will occur to us. The chances of this happening relate to how often we have seen the three of them together. Thus the strength of association relies on repetition. Furthermore, contiguity occurs either for events experienced simultaneously or in quick succession. Although Hartley used the terms *synchronous* and *successive*, these concepts are commonly referred to as **spatial contiguity** and **temporal contiguity**, respectively. Thinking of your house might lead you to think of your dog sitting by the front door (synchronous or spatial), while your dog's drooling might be the result of him associating your smiling face with the presentation of food (successive or temporal).[6]

There is no need to quote Hartley's Proposition 11, because it is identical to Proposition 10, except that the word *Vibrations* substitutes for *Sensations* and the phrase *miniature Vibrations* replaces *Ideas*. This was Hartley's version of nervous system activity, taken from Newton, who suggested that all matter could be conceptualized as vibrating particles in space. Hartley had the advantage over Descartes in knowing that the nerves were not hollow; hence, there was no space for animal spirits to be flowing back and forth. Rather, nerves were tightly packed fibers, and he believed they conveyed sensory information by vibrating. In the brain, smaller nerves produced even smaller vibrations, which Hartley called "miniature vibrations." These correspond to ideas. Like Hume, who referred to ideas as "faint copies" of impressions, Hartley thought of ideas (miniature vibrations) as less "vigorous" than sensations (vibrations).

Hartley's model of the mind was a kind of building-block structure in which complex ideas were constructed from the individual component parts. He used the complex idea of a horse as an example, writing that "we could have no proper idea of the Horse, unless the particular Ideas of the Head, Neck, Body, Legs, and Tail, peculiar to this Animal, stuck to each other in the Fancy [i.e., occurred to us], from frequent joint Impression" (Hartley, 1749/1971, p. 71). These subparts can also be divisible into even simpler ideas (e.g., legs include hoofs, etc.). If we experience all these atomistic elements frequently enough, then seeing a part of a horse (e.g., a hoof) will make us think of the horse as a whole.

Hartley's analysis brings the issue of atomism versus "holism" into focus. Most of the British philosophers took an atomistic approach, and Hartley was perhaps the most explicit of the philosophers considered thus far. One problem with this approach is that it requires knowledge of the parts before one can know the whole. That is, complex ideas are built up from simpler ones. In his horse example, Hartley wrote of the parts "coalescing" into the whole animal. The whole is equal to the sum of its parts. **Holism**, on the other hand, argues for the primacy of the whole over its constituent elements, that the parts have no meaning without first knowing the whole. The psychologist G. F. Stout once used the example of a pyramid constructed of oval stones (Klein, 1970). Each element of the pyramid may be perfectly round, but the whole figure has an overall triangular shape not found in any of its parts. The holistic approach would eventually find a voice within psychology through the work of the Gestalt psychologists (Chapter 9).

Hartley, who was clearly in the atomist camp, had a direct influence on James Mill (1773–1836), another in the long line of British empiricists and associationists. The influence

---

[6]As you can guess from the latter example, contiguity was an important concept for the Russian physiologist Ivan Pavlov, who you will encounter in Chapter 10.

is clear from this often-quoted example provided by Mill in his *Analysis of the Phenomena of the Human Mind* (1829/1948):

> Brick is one complex idea, mortar is another complex idea; these ideas, with ideas of position and quantity, compose my idea of a wall. My idea of a plank is a complex idea, my idea of a rafter is a complex idea, my idea of a nail is a complex idea.
>
> These, united with the same ideas of position and quantity, compose my duplex idea of a floor. In the same manner, my complex idea of glass, wood, and others, compose my duplex idea of a window; and these duplex ideas, united together, compose my idea of a house....How many complex, or duplex ideas, are all united in the idea of furniture? How many more in the idea of merchandise? How many more in the idea called Every Thing? (p. 154)

Mill was another important character in British philosophy and, like Hume, was also well known as a historian; his *History of British India*, written in 1817, helped him to become financially secure. James Mill was not as important as his son, however—an outcome that Mill, Senior, deliberately set out to produce. Read the Close-Up for more on the deliberate shaping of a philosopher.

CLOSE-UP

RAISING A PHILOSOPHER

James Mill was not content simply to write about the importance of experience for developing the mind. When his son was born, he was determined to put empiricism into action by filling the empty white paper of his son's mind with as much information as possible. John Stuart Mill experienced (endured might be a better term) an unusual childhood and described it later in a brief yet remarkable autobiography (Mill, 1873/1989).

Mill, Junior, never went to school with other children, but by his 12th birthday, he could match the intellectual accomplishments of any university graduate. Under his father's stern tutelage, he started learning Greek vocabulary at age 3, Latin at age 8, and by the time he was 10 had read most of the classic Greek and Roman texts, ranging from *Aesop's Fables* to Plato's *Dialogues* to the Greek histories of Herodotus to Aristotle's *Rhetoric*. He also devoured art and literature and mastered algebra and geometry. For fun he read books like *Robinson Crusoe*, the *Arabian Nights*, and Shakespeare's history plays. The latter might have reflected a minor rebellion against his father, who "never was a great admirer of Shakespeare, the English idolatry of whom he used to attack with some severity" (Mill, 1873/1989, p. 35).

Young Mill spent the better part of each day in his lessons. His father tutored him directly, but he was also expected to learn a great deal on his own. A typical routine was for Mill to read a portion of some book, take notes, and then report on it to his father the following day, during prebreakfast walks through the countryside. Mill later wrote that "my earliest recollections of green fields and wild flowers [were] mingled [with] the account I gave him daily of what I had read the day before" (p. 29). During the walks, his father would also lecture to him on "civilization, government, morality, [and] mental cultivation, which he required me afterwards to restate to him in my own words" (p. 30). But the education was not simply drill and practice. Mill came to value the fact that his father often challenged him with difficult material and forced him to learn as much as he could on his own. Concerning Mill's education in logic and political economy, for instance, he wrote:

> Striving...to call forth the activity of my faculties, by making me find out everything for myself, he gave his explanations not before, but after, I had felt the full force of the difficulties; and not only gave me an accurate knowledge of

these two great subjects, as far as they were then understood, but made me a thinker on both.... Anything which could be found out by thinking, I was never told, until I had exhausted my efforts to find it out for myself.... A pupil from whom nothing is ever demanded which he cannot do, never does all he can. (pp. 44–45)

John Stuart Mill is often cited as an example of a brilliant child prodigy, one whose native intellectual gifts enabled him to learn so much so early in life. There is probably some truth in this, but Mill never believed it for a minute. Because he was not allowed to play with other children as he was growing up, he had no point of comparison except for his father.

In fact, throughout his childhood he was under the impression, as he put it, that "I was rather backward in my studies, since I always found myself so, in comparison with what my father expected from me" (Mill, 1873/1989, p. 46). When he eventually realized how far advanced he was, he showed the empiricist spirit by crediting it to his experiences rather than to any innate ability. Indeed, he believed his "natural gifts [to be] rather below than above par" (p. 44) and that his advantages over others resulted from their inferior educations. In his self-effacing words, his accomplishments "could not be ascribed to any merit in me, but to the very unusual advantage which had fallen to my lot, of having a father who was able to teach me" (pp. 46–47).

John Stuart Mill (1806–1873): On the Verge of Psychological Science

Mill's adult life was no less extraordinary than his childhood. Following in his father's footsteps, he supported himself through Foreign Service work with the British East India Company, starting as a clerk at age 17 and gradually rising through the ranks to an executive position. Royalties from the sales of his books eventually assured him a comfortable living. In his later years, he was elected to Parliament's House of Commons and served for 3 years. Very little else about his life was conventional. Raised by his father to be a "reasoning machine," he became a committed activist for political and social reform by age 15, but 5 years later, he suffered a mental collapse that today we would call an existential crisis—he wondered about the meaning of his life.

After several lethargic years, Mill emerged from this depression, partly as a result of discovering Wordsworth. The beauty of the Lake poet's words awakened an emotional life in Mill for the first time, showing him there was more to life than cold rationality. His feelings were further developed when he met and fell in love with Harriet Taylor, a remarkable woman who combined beauty with intellect. Unfortunately for Mill, Taylor was married—and happily, it appears. Despite the impediment, a relationship between the two developed; Mill even lived with the Taylors for a brief time and tagged along on vacations. The alliance was evidently platonic, but it created a minor scandal nonetheless. They finally married in 1851, waiting a respectful 2 years after John Taylor's death. Harriet contributed significantly to Mill's work while she lived, especially to his most important political work, *On Liberty*, published in 1858. After she died unexpectedly in 1858, her daughter carried on the intellectual partnership with Mill. Helen Taylor (with Mill in Figure 2.5) contributed to Mill's classic feminist essay, *The Subjection of Women* (1869).[7] The book was written at a

[7] Helen Taylor was more of an activist than her mother; she helped create Britain's first women's suffrage organization (the National Society for Women's Suffrage) and recruited such notable women as Florence Nightingale into the group.

FIGURE 2.5   John Stuart Mill and stepdaughter Helen Taylor. From Mazlish (1975).

time when married women had almost no rights—they could not own property, they could not inherit, they could not vote, divorce was virtually impossible, and, if they managed to get a divorce, they had no child custody rights (Capaldi, 2004). Mill's essay challenged the prevailing mores and contributed a small step in increasing the rights of women. A year after the essay was published, Parliament (and Mill was a member at the time) passed the Married Women's Property Bill, which gave married women the right to own and to inherit property.

Mill's politics derived from and contributed to his psychology. As an empiricist, he believed that all knowledge came through experience and that under the proper circumstances, anyone could become knowledgeable. Thus he favored government support for universal education and was appalled at the traditional English system that favored the landed gentry, an elite minority. At the same time, he endorsed a meritocracy in which the vote would be given only to those men and women who had reached a certain level of education. In short, he aimed for a society that endeavored to fill everyone's blank slates to the maximum.

Mill's Psychology   Mill's views on psychology can be found scattered in several places, including his *System of Logic* (1843/1987), which we will examine shortly; in the extensive notes that he wrote for a republication of his father's *Analysis*, published in 1869; and in his *Examination of Sir William Hamilton's Philosophy* (1865). His attack on Hamilton is another illustration of the strong connection between Mill's reforming zeal and his empiricist views. Mill criticized Hamilton's rationalism and his belief in innate ideas, arguing that the result was an antireform philosophy. As Mill put it:

> I have long felt that the prevailing tendency to regard all the marked distinctions of human character as innate, and in the main indelible, and to ignore the irresistible proofs that by far the greater part of those differences, whether between individuals, races, or sexes, are . . . produced by differences in circumstances, is one of the chief hindrances to the rational treatment of great social questions and one of the greatest stumbling blocks to human improvement. (Mill, 1873/1989, p. 203)

KEY DATE—1843

This year marked the publication of John Stuart Mill's *Logic*, which included the foundational rules for conducting empirical research.

These events also occurred that year:

- Daniel M'Naughton tried to assassinate the British Prime Minister, Sir Robert Peel, but killed Peel's private secretary by mistake; he was later acquitted because he was judged to be incapable of distinguishing right from wrong; the subsequent "M'Naughton rule" became the basis for the modern defense of not guilty by reason of insanity
- The first large wave of Western migration occurred along the legendary Oregon Trail; approximately one-half million made the journey over the next 25 years
- The S.S. Great Britain, first propeller-driven ship to cross the Atlantic, was launched
- Congress granted Samuel Morse $30,000 to build first telegraph line (Washington to Baltimore)

- Charles Dickens published *Martin Chuzzlewit* and *A Christmas Carol*
- William Wordsworth was appointed poet laureate of England
- The Mormon leader Joseph Smith proclaimed that God approves of polygamy

These people were born:

- William McKinley, U.S. President (assassinated in 1901, at the start of his second term in office)
- Henry James, novelist (e.g., *The Turn of the Screw*) and brother of psychologist William James

These people died:

- John Trumbull, American painter, known for his portraits of the leaders of the American revolution
- Noah Webster, American lexicographer (*Webster's Dictionary*)

Mill subscribed to the basic tenets of British empiricism and associationism, but he extended the ideas of his father and others (especially Hartley) by using a chemical rather than a mechanical metaphor in his description of how complex ideas are built from simple ones. The earlier quote from James Mill ("Brick is one complex idea, mortar is another complex idea," etc.) portrays the mind as passively accumulating experiences in which the elements combine mechanically to form larger wholes. John Stuart Mill, however, believed the mind to be a more active force in synthesizing our experiences; he argued the holistic position that complex ideas are more than a passive combination of elements:

> When many impressions or ideas are operating in the mind together, there sometimes takes place a process of a similar kind to chemical combination. When impressions have been so often experienced in conjunction that each of them calls up readily and instantaneously the ideas of the whole group, those ideas sometimes melt and coalesce into one another, and appear not several ideas, but one.... [So] it appears to me that the Complex Idea, formed by blending together of several simpler ones, should, when it really appears simple (that is, when the separate elements are not consciously distinguishable in it), be said to *result from*, or be *generated by*, the simple ideas, not to *consist* of them. (Mill, 1843/1987, p. 39–40; emphasis in the original)

A wall, then, derives from the simple ideas of our experiences, but goes beyond the simple combination of brick and mortar and has properties all its own, just as water has its own properties even though it results from the simple elements of hydrogen and oxygen. To use the phrase later popularized by gestaltists, the whole is more than the sum of its parts.

Mill's Logic   In 1843, Mill published *A System of Logic, Ratiocinative and Inductive, Being a Connected View of the Principles of Evidence, and the Methods of Scientific*

Investigation. It described some of his beliefs about association and mental chemistry, and it included an argument for the creation of a scientific approach to the study of psychology, on the grounds that although it might not reach the level of precision of physics, it could do as well as some disciplines that were considered scientific at the time (meteorology was an example he used). The *Logic* also outlined a methodology for applying inductive logic while trying to determine causality in science. He called the methods Agreement, Difference, and Concomitant Variation. Descriptions of these methods remain popular today in modern research methods texts (although the labels are no longer used).

In the **Method of Agreement**, one looks for a common element in several instances of an event. For example, suppose a researcher suspects that a particular gene causes depression. Let X symbolize the proposed cause (the gene) and Y symbolize the effect (depression). To use the method of agreement, the researcher studies a sample of depressed people and looks to see if they all have gene X. If they do, then it can be said that X is sufficient for Y to occur: "If X, then Y." Does this mean that X caused Y? Not necessarily, and the example illustrates the problem with induction. Every depressed person in the sample might have X, but it is possible that some yet undiscovered person is depressed but does not have gene X. The method of agreement can both support some hypothesis and call it into question, but it cannot establish cause by itself.

Neither can the **Method of Difference**, in which one looks for evidence that the absence of an effect is always accompanied by the absence of a proposed cause: "If not X, then not Y." To stay with the depression example, this would mean examining nondepressed people and looking for gene X, hoping *not* to find it. If this outcome occurs, then one can say that gene X is necessary for depression to occur, because without X (the gene), nobody is Y (depressed). Again, there are problems. A sample of nondepressed people, none of whom have the gene, does not prove the case; there still could be some nondepressed people out there with gene X.

Combined, in what Mill called the **Joint Method**, the methods of agreement and difference have the potential for identifying cause, within the limits of induction (i.e., you will never study every case). Thus if it could be determined that every person with gene X is depressed, and that every person without gene X is not depressed, then it could be concluded that gene X is both sufficient and necessary for depression to occur (i.e., the gene causes depression). Of course, the conclusion about cause would be tentative, subject to potential disproof in the future.

The logic of the methods of agreement and difference underlie the use of the modern-day experimental method in psychology: The method of agreement corresponds to an experimental group, and the method of difference corresponds to a control group (Rosnow & Rosenthal, 1993). Thus a hypothetical experiment on the effect of gene (X) on depression (Y) would involve identifying two equal groups and implanting the gene in the experimental group but not in the control group. If everyone in the experimental group comes down with depression (if X, then Y), and if nobody in the control group gets depressed (if not X, then not Y), then you have evidence that X causes Y (again, within the limits of your study). Of course, you would have a hard time finding volunteers for this study. Mill recognized this ethical limitation and, along with a concern about precision of measurement and control, it made him skeptical of psychology becoming as rigorously scientific as physics:

> Are the laws of the formation of character [i.e., personality] susceptible of a satisfactory investigation by the method of experimentation? Evidently not, because, even if we

suppose unlimited power of varying the experiment (which is abstractly possible, but no one but [a] despot has that power . . .), a still more essential condition is wanting—the power of performing any of the experiments with scientific accuracy. (Mill, 1843/1987, pp. 50–51)

Mill's third method, **Concomitant Variation**, is reminiscent of Hume and underlies today's correlational method. Using this approach, one looks to see if changes in X are associated with predictable changes in Y. The method is especially useful when either X or Y (or both) can be found in every person to some degree. For example, everyone gets at least some exercise, and everyone is more or less healthy. Using the method of concomitant variation, a researcher could see if those who exercise a great deal are healthier than those who exercise infrequently.

Unlike any of the philosophers considered thus far, John Stuart Mill did not attempt to write anything like an essay on human understanding (Locke), a treatise on human knowledge (Berkeley) or human nature (Hume), a series of observations on man (Hartley), or an analysis of the mind (his father). That is, none of his books can be pointed to and labeled as "J. S. Mill's psychology." Because he saw himself above all as a political and economic philosopher, this is not too surprising. Yet Mill is as important for modern psychology as any of those philosophers who did write a "psychology." He brought British associationism to its zenith, and he provided an analysis of scientific thinking that guides psychological research to this day. He was a key transition figure in the shift from the philosophy of the mind to the science of the mind.

RATIONALIST RESPONSES TO EMPIRICISM

Except for the section on Descartes, this chapter has focused on British empiricist and associationist philosophy. But other strong voices were heard during the times that have been described, and those voices also resonate with aspects of modern psychology. In particular, two German philosophers make a notable contrast to British empiricism and associationism. Gottfried Leibniz was a contemporary of Locke and responded directly to Locke's *Essay Concerning Human Understanding* with his own *New Essays on Human Understanding*, published posthumously in 1765. Immanuel Kant (1724–1804) lived during the same time as Hume and Hartley and wrote in response to them (especially Hume).

Gottfried Wilhelm Leibniz (1646–1716)

Leibniz had a remarkably wide range of interests, from politics to math to engineering to alchemy to philosophy. As a mathematician, he is best known as the coinventor (with Newton) of calculus; the event was celebrated in the German stamp in Figure 2.6. His importance for psychology rests with his reply to Locke, his approach to the mind–body problem, and his "monadology." He was a great admirer of Locke, agreeing that experience is essential to the formation of knowledge. However, he disagreed with Locke's "mind at birth = white paper" metaphor, proposing instead that the mind be seen as analogous to veined marble (Leibniz, 1765/1982). The sculptor can take a block of marble and shape it in many different ways, but the way the marble is veined limits the number of shapes that are possible. The veins in essence represent the innate properties of the marble, to be revealed by the artist's

FIGURE 2.6 German stamp commemorating Leibniz and the discovery of calculus.

skill. Similarly, according to Leibniz, the mind has innate properties that help determine the limits and shape the effects of experience. The innate properties, such as reason, enable the individual to arrive at what Leibniz called "necessary truths," truths that are proven with reason and logic and not by direct experience. The fundamental principles of mathematics (e.g., the three angles of a triangle will always add up to 180°) are examples of necessary truths, he thought. In response to the empiricist claim that there was nothing in the intellect that was not first in the senses, Leibniz replied, "except the intellect itself!" Like Descartes, Leibniz agreed that animals lacked the innate properties found in humans, and thus could be considered pure "empirics."

On the mind–body question, Leibniz could not accept the Cartesian notion of direct and mutual influence, because it led inevitably to a search for the manner of interaction and resulted in a fruitless hunt for things like pineal glands. Instead, Leibniz proposed a psychophysical *parallelism* solution to the mind–body problem, similar to Hartley's idea. Thus he proposed that mind ("psycho") and body ("physical") work in parallel to each other, kept in a "pre-established harmony," as Leibniz put it, by the hand of God. He illustrated his parallelism with a metaphor of two clocks that are constructed to be in perfect harmony. Like mind and body, they operate independently of each other, but in agreement. By implication, parallelism legitimizes the separate study of mental (psychological) and physical (biological) events, thus providing a philosophical basis for "the eventual emergence of psychology as a separate science as distinct from physiology as a separate science" (Klein, 1970, p. 353).

The elements of both mental and physical reality were called **monads** by Leibniz. These were infinite in number and more like energy forces than material atoms. They were said to be arranged in a hierarchy, from rational to sentient to simple. Rational monads, according to Leibniz, form the essence of the human mind; sentient monads are found in all living beings that are not human, and simple monads make up physical reality. Rational monads account for consciousness, but Leibniz believed that awareness is not an all-or-nothing affair. Rather, he proposed a continuum of awareness, thus laying a foundation for two important developments in psychology. First, the continuum implies a level of unawareness, an idea leading directly to the concept of the unconscious, which was later to become the centerpiece of Freud's theories. Leibniz distinguished between what he called apperception, perception, and petites perceptions. **Apperception** is the highest level of awareness, in which we focus our attention on some information, apprehend it fully, and make it personally meaningful. Perception is an awareness of something, but it is not as sharp as in apperception. **Petites**

perceptions are below the level of awareness, but ultimately essential for enabling higher levels of perception to occur. To illustrate the latter, Leibniz used the example of an ocean wave or a waterfall. Petite perceptions are created by individual drops of water, which we never hear. Yet all of the drops, taken together, are necessary for us to perceive or apperceive the larger reality of the ocean wave or the waterfall.

The second implication of the proposal about different levels of awareness is that there must exist points on the continuum of consciousness where one goes from unawareness to awareness. These points can be called **thresholds**; as we will learn in the next chapter, identifying and measuring thresholds became an important feature of the earliest experiments in psychology.

Immanuel Kant (1724–1804)

In his role as a diplomat, Leibniz traveled throughout Europe. In contrast, Immanuel Kant evidently never ventured more than 40 miles from his home in the eastern German city of Königsberg. He was born there, went to school there, eventually taught at the university there, and is buried there. Despite the apparent provincialism, Kant was a towering intellect in 18th-century German philosophy, doing for the rationalist view what Leibniz had done in the 17th century. Kant is best known to psychologists for three books published in his later years: *Critique of Pure Reason* (1781/1965), *Critique of Judgment* (1788/1952), and *Critique of Practical Reason* (1790/1959).

Kant agreed with the empiricists that our knowledge is built from experience, but, like Leibniz, he argued that the more important question was how the process occurs. That is, he wondered how experience itself was possible, and he concluded that it required the existence of some a priori (prior to experience) knowledge that helps shape the experiences we have. For instance, Kant pointed out that whenever we experience events in the world, we organize them with reference to space and time. Thus we water the garden, which occupies space, and which takes X amount of time to complete. Our understanding of the concept "water the garden" is not possible without the a priori knowledge of space and time. The concepts of space and time, then, we know "intuitively," according to Kant; we don't have to "learn" about the concepts. To contrast Hume's view that we can never be certain of causality, Kant argued that the mind inevitably thinks in terms of cause and effect—everyone's experience of the world is that it operates according to causal laws (water poured on earth always goes down). Like space and time, cause and effect were considered by Kant to be innate properties of the mind.

Kant argued that psychology could never become a science like the physical sciences. He pointed out that compared with physical objects, mental phenomena could not be observed directly by an independent observer, nor could they be defined or measured with the precision of mathematics. As we shall learn, when German psychologists such as Wilhelm Wundt declared psychology a science in the 19th century, they had to disavow specifically their countryman's argument about the feasibility of the endeavor.

IN PERSPECTIVE: PHILOSOPHICAL FOUNDATIONS

This chapter only scratches the surface of psychology's "long past." Nonetheless, you should emerge from your reading with a basic understanding of some of the philosophical underpinnings of modern psychology. Furthermore, you should be starting to develop a sense of the continuity of ideas in our discipline's history. Psychology did not just pop out of the ground in the late 19th century. Rather, psychology's founders were wrestling with the same issues that concerned the people highlighted in this chapter. They chose to attack the questions from a slightly different angle than the philosophers, that of direct experimentation, but they were trying to answer the same questions: How do we accumulate our knowledge of the world? How is the mind organized? How do the senses work? Is any of our knowledge built into the system (i.e., innate)? The founders of 19th-century psychology also had an ever-increasing knowledge of how the brain and the rest of the nervous system worked, and they were beginning to develop objective methods for studying the mind. In Chapter 3, we encounter these developments in physiology and methods.

Before closing this chapter, however, an important point must be made about presentism. From the standpoint of the early 21st century, knowing that psychology evolved into a scientific discipline, it is easy to look back at the early philosophers and wonder why they "failed" to take what might appear to us now to be an easy step—the one from careful observations and a close logical analysis of some mental phenomenon to the experimental investigation of it. That is, when we first read of people like Descartes and Locke and Mill, we tend to see them as gradually approaching but not quite reaching the "holy grail" of scientific psychology. It is a serious mistake, however, to think of these individuals as somehow falling short. In fact, they were clearly the best and the brightest of their day, going far beyond their peers in the brilliance of their insights. The proper way to view the philosophers in this chapter is to think of them as people living in the context of their times and grappling as best they could with the issues of their day. That these philosophers wrestled with the same questions that exist today is not an indication of steady progress upward from then to now, but of the universality of the issues. It is futile and simply wrong to criticize them for not doing what others did later.

SUMMARY

A Long Past

• The Ebbinghaus statement that psychology has a long past but a short history is a reminder that the issues that concern psychologists have been addressed by serious thinkers for thousands of years, even though psychology as a self-defined discipline is just over 130 years old. The "new psychology" that emerged in the late 19th century differed from philosophy in that the questions about human behavior and mental life were taken into the laboratory for the first time.

Descartes: The Beginnings of Modern Philosophy and Science

• Descartes lived during years of great advances in science and technology. It was a time when the authority of the Church and of Aristotle came to be questioned, by

Galileo's support for the Copernican heliocentric model of the universe instead of the traditional geocentric model, for example. Descartes's life also overlapped that of Sir Francis Bacon, who argued for an inductive scientific strategy for understanding the universe.

• Descartes was a rationalist, believing that the way to true knowledge was through the systematic use of his reasoning abilities. Because he believed that some truths were universal and could be arrived at through reason and without the necessity of sensory experience, he was also a nativist. In addition, he was a dualist and an interactionist, believing that mind and body were distinct essences but had direct influence on each other.

• To explain mind–body interactionism, Descartes developed a model of nervous system activity that included the first model of reflex action. His concept of bodily action was a mechanistic one—the body was like a machine. According to the Cartesian dichotomy, animals are pure machines, but humans have a rational mind (soul) to complement their machinelike bodies.

The British Empiricist Argument and the Associationists

• The founder of British empiricism was John Locke, who rejected the nativist belief in innate ideas and argued that the mind was analogous to a blank piece of paper, to be written on by our experiences. Ideas that result from our experiences have two sources: sensation and reflection. Locke used an atomistic model, assuming that complex ideas were built from the basic elements of simple ideas. Primary qualities (e.g., extension) exist independently of the perceiver, but secondary qualities (e.g., the perception of color) depend on perception. Locke's beliefs led him to recommend that parents take an active role in educating their children, that children be encouraged with praise rather than concrete rewards, and that punishment be avoided as an educational strategy.

• George Berkeley wrote a detailed analysis of visual perception based on empiricist arguments, in the process describing visual phenomena such as convergence, accommodation, and depth perception. He rejected Locke's distinction between primary and secondary qualities; to counter materialism, he proposed (subjective idealism) that we cannot be sure of the reality of objects except through our belief in God, the Permanent Perceiver.

• David Hume was an empiricist-associationist known for making a distinction between impressions, which result from sensation, and ideas, which he said were faint copies of impressions. He also identified the rules of association as resemblance, contiguity, and cause and effect. He believed that we cannot know causality absolutely; we know only that certain events occur together regularly.

• David Hartley is considered the founder of associationism because of his systematic attempt to summarize all that was known about it and his argument that the essence of association was contiguity (both spatial and temporal) and repetition. He developed a model of nervous system action based on the Newtonian concept of vibrations, and his position on the mind–body issue was that of psychophysical parallelism.

• John Stuart Mill, a child prodigy, was the leading British philosopher of the 19th century. Compared with others (including his father, the empiricist philosopher James Mill) who described the mind in mechanical, atomistic, building-block terms, J. S. Mill used a more holistic chemical metaphor, arguing that complex ideas are greater than the sum of their individual simple ideas. Mill analyzed the logic of science and described several methods for trying to arrive at scientific truth: the method of agreement and the method of difference, which underlie today's experimental method; and the method of concomitant variation, which is similar to the modern correlational method.

Rationalist Responses to Empiricism

• Gottfried Leibniz challenged Locke's white paper analogy and said the mind was more like veined marble, in which the veins were analogous to innate abilities that shape our experiences. He also challenged Descartes's interactionism, arguing for a parallelist position and using the metaphor of two synchronous clocks to make his point. His monadology provided a basis for the concepts of the unconscious and sensory thresholds.

• Immanuel Kant recognized the importance of our experiences for developing our understanding of the world, but he argued that experience itself was not possible without a basis in some a priori knowledge to provide the framework for our experiences. Kant believed that psychology could not achieve the status of a science, because psychological events could not be observed objectively.

STUDY QUESTIONS

1. What did Ebbinghaus mean when he said that psychology had a long past but a short history?

2. How did a "mechanistic" zeitgeist influence Descartes's thinking?

3. Distinguish between a heliocentric and a geocentric model of the universe, and explain why advocating the former earned Galileo a charge of heresy.

4. Explain what it means to advocate a Baconian inductive strategy for gaining knowledge of human behavior.

5. Explain why Descartes is considered (a) a rationalist and (b) a nativist.

6. According to Descartes, how does a reflex work? Use the example of the boy putting his foot in a fire.

7. In Descartes's model of the nervous system, how did mind and body interact, and why was the pineal gland chosen as the point of interaction? What was the essential flaw in the logic of identifying a part of the brain (pineal gland) as the point of mutual influence of mind and body?

8. What is meant by the "Cartesian dichotomy"?

9. Compare rationalist and empiricist explanations for how we arrive at our knowledge of widely held concepts (e.g., God).

10. Compare Locke's white paper and Leibniz's veined model metaphors, and relate them to fundamental epistemological questions.

11. Distinguish between primary and secondary qualities of matter, and compare the views of Locke and Berkeley with regard to these qualities.

12. Define materialism, and explain how Berkeley's subjective idealism attacked the concept.

13. Using Berkeley's depth perception examples, show how British empiricists applied their concepts to visual perception.

14. Compare Hume's and Hartley's laws of association. Explain why Hume's concept of cause and effect resonates with modern research psychologists.

15. Describe J. S. Mill's mental chemistry, and contrast it with his father's more mechanical view.

16. Show how Mill's rules for inductive logic relate to modern conceptions of the experimental and correlational methods.

17. Show how Leibniz's monadology relates to the concepts of the unconscious and thresholds.

18. Describe Kant's rationalist response to empiricist thinking.

FOR FURTHER READING

VROOMAN, J. R. (1970). *René Descartes: A biography*. New York: G. P. Putnam's Sons.
A brief and very readable biography of Descartes, especially descriptive of the times in which Descartes lived; provides a good summary of Descartes's ideas and how he developed them from his varied experiences.

BOORSTIN, D. J. (1983). *The discoverers*. New York: Vintage Books.
A substantial treatment of many of the scientists briefly mentioned in this chapter, including Vesalius, Galileo, Bacon, Boyle, Newton, and Harvey; written in a style that makes Boorstin one of the more popular modern historians.

MILL, J. S. (1989). *Autobiography*. London: Penguin Books. (Original work published 1873)
A fascinating account of Mill's childhood and relationship with his father, his mental crisis and how he overcame it, his relationship with Harriet Taylor, and the development of his ideas; can be occasionally confusing without some knowledge of British political history during Mill's time.

SOBEL, D. (2000). *Galileo's daughter: A historical memoir of science, faith, and love*. New York: Penguin.
A lively account of Galileo's research and how it landed him in hot water with the Catholic Church; elegant description of the historical context of Galileo's (and therefore Descartes's) time; part of the story is told through a remarkable set of letters between Galileo and his daughter, a cloistered nun.

CHAPTER 3

THE PHYSIOLOGICAL CONTEXT: EARLY RESEARCH ON THE NERVOUS SYSTEM

> The entire doctrine of [phrenology] is contained in two fundamental propositions, of which the first is, that understanding resides exclusively in the brain, and the second, that each particular faculty of the understanding is provided in the brain with an organ proper to itself. Now, of these two propositions, there is certainly nothing new in the first one, and perhaps nothing true in the second one.
>
> —Pierre Flourens, 1846

PREVIEW AND CHAPTER OBJECTIVES

Partitioning the philosophical and neurophysiological antecedents to psychology into two chapters implies the presence of two nonoverlapping paths that eventually merged to form the new psychology during the late 19th century. There is a grain of truth to this—the British empiricists did not spend their time cutting into spinal cords or stimulating nerves connected to frog legs, and the scientists to be encountered in this chapter did not write long philosophical treatises on "human understanding." But the distinction between philosophical and physiological antecedents to psychology is artificial, brought about by the decisions made when structuring a textbook. In fact, developments in philosophy and in the natural sciences proceeded apace, especially in the 18th and 19th centuries. The physiologists and other natural scientists were deeply concerned with philosophical issues, especially the epistemological questions about human understanding and the problem of the relationship between mental and physical reality (the mind–body problem). In turn, philosophers were well aware of, and in some instances contributed to, developments in physiology (e.g., Berkeley's work on vision), and they proposed theories that led naturally to physiological research.

This chapter focuses on 19th- and early 20th-century studies of the nature and functioning of the nervous system. In particular, we examine research that explored (a) the physiology of reflexes and basic sensory-motor processes, (b) the issue of whether specific functions could be "localized" in different areas of the brain, and (c) the nature of the basic unit of the nervous system, the neuron. The chapter closes with a brief description of Karl Lashley's research on the role of the cortex in learning. Lashley was the 20th century's first prominent physiological psychologist. After you finish this chapter, you should be able to:

■ Show how Enlightenment thinking contributed to the idea that psychology could become scientific

- Describe and explain the importance of Whytt's research on reflex action
- Describe Magendie's research on sensory-motor function in the spinal cord, and explain why the Bell-Magendie law might have been misnamed
- Describe the doctrine of the specific energies of nerves
- Describe Helmholtz's research on nerve impulse speed and relate it to the vitalism–materialism issue
- Describe the contributions of Helmholtz to vision and hearing, and understand the issue that he referred to as the "problem of perception"
- Describe the essential tenets of phrenology and explain why it ultimately failed scientifically
- Explain phrenology's widespread popularity, especially in America
- Understand the differences between phrenology and physiognomy
- Describe the logic of the method of ablation and show how Flourens used it to dispute phrenology
- Describe the clinical method and two different examples (Phineas Gage, Broca's "Tan") of how it shed light on brain function
- Describe the method of electrical stimulation ("scientific phrenology") and the results it produced
- Describe neuron theory and Sherrington's research leading to the conclusion that synapses exist
- Describe Lashley's research on learning and the brain, his principles of mass action and equipotentiality, and the similarities with the conclusions drawn by Flourens

HEROIC SCIENCE IN THE AGE OF ENLIGHTENMENT

As discussed in the last chapter, the years marking the end of the Renaissance were characterized by a gradual change from a reliance on authority as the source of truth to a belief that science and human reasoning could lead to an understanding of the natural world. Bacon, Galileo, Harvey, and Descartes exemplified this shift in the beginning of the 17th century. Sir Isaac Newton solidified the change in the second half of the century. With the publication of his *Principia Mathematica* in 1687, serious thinkers began to take for granted the idea that objective truth could be gained through the methods of science and the unbiased use of reason. Because science and reason came to be seen as the only sure way to shed light on the darkness of ignorance, this period became known as the **Enlightenment** (Appleby, Hunt, & Jacob, 1994). Scientists like Newton became heroic figures, searching for "objective" truth about the universe by applying scientific methodology to its study. Newton's influence on the philosophers was mentioned in the last chapter—his analysis of light into basic components and his theory of gravitation influenced the British empiricists, who tried to produce a similar analysis of the mind and conceived of association as a force analogous to gravity.

Enlightenment thinking even spread into the political arena. America's founding fathers were passionate and knowledgeable about science, and Benjamin Franklin made substantial contributions to the theory of electricity, including the invention of the lightning rod. The Constitution itself borrowed from the Newtonian concept of equilibrium when developing the notion of a balance of powers among the executive, legislative, and judicial elements of government (Cohen, 1995).

The Enlightenment reached the height of its influence in the second half of the 18th century, but its ideals remained strong throughout the 19th century and even into the 20th. By the early 19th century, faith in science seemed to be paying dividends in the form of techno-logical innovations that eventually produced the industrial revolution. Thus science seemed to lead inevitably to progress, and scientists were viewed as being totally objective—simply looking for the truth without imposing their values, and improving society through the inven-tions that derived from their science. It wasn't until such technological innovations as the poison gas that spread ominously over the battlefields of World War I, and the atom bomb of World War II that hinted at the end of civilization, that serious questions began to be raised: Could science be objective and value free, and did scientific discoveries always mean progress? Nonetheless, during the period when the idea of a scientific approach to psychology began to take shape in the minds of such philosophers as the British empiricists, the model of scientist as hero held sway. If scientific thinking and human reason could enlighten the world about physics and chemistry, why not biology? If biology, why not psychology?

In the middle of the 19th century, scientific psychology evolved out of the philosophical questions examined in Chapter 2 and the research on the nervous system to be described in this chapter. Physiologists trying to "shed light" on how the senses and the nervous system actually worked developed methods and made discoveries that were directly relevant to the epistemological questions about the nature and origins of human knowledge being raised by philosophers such as John Stuart Mill. This dynamic convergence of philosophy and physiological science created an atmosphere out of which a "scientific" approach to psychology was perhaps inevitable.

FUNCTIONING OF THE NERVOUS SYSTEM

In Chapter 2, we saw how Descartes developed a model of nervous system functioning as he sought answers to the mind–body question. His ideas fired the imaginations of others, and during the course of the next few centuries our understanding of the nervous system gradually improved. Many of the advances resulted from the medical community trying to deal with the problem of brain and nervous system damage, which was quite common in the context of two European wars in the middle of the 18th century and both the American and French revolutions during the second half of that century. At a time long before the development of antiseptic surgical procedures and antibiotic drugs, the vast majority of those suffering head wounds died from infection. Many of those who lived, however, became case studies that increased our knowledge of the brain and nervous system.

One issue of interest was whether the brain was the center of consciousness and the controller of voluntary action. Decapitated soldiers often showed arm and leg movements for a brief time. How did this happen? The issue was directly investigated with reference to executions during the French Revolution at the end of the 1700s that used the invention of noted a French physician, Joseph Guillotin. The device, which bears his name, was said to be a marvelous improvement over large, hairy (and often intoxicated) men with axes, who some-times required several tries before completing their gruesome task of separating head from body. Although the guillotine was clean and quick and therefore considered humane, bodies continued to twitch for a brief time after execution. Eye movements and quivering facial muscles could also be seen. Did some level of awareness, and perhaps some perception of extreme pain, remain after a beheading? If so, then perhaps the instrument was not so humane after all. The problem was investigated in the early 19th century by Theodor Bischoff, who arranged to conduct tests on the decapitated head of a criminal immediately after execution. If consciousness remained, Bischoff reasoned, then the head should react predictably to having fingers thrust toward its eyes, having smelling salts placed under its nose, or, cruelly, having the word "Pardon!" spoken in its ear. Bischoff tried all of these tests, but the unfortunate head showed no reaction (Fearing, 1930). He concluded that consciousness ended with the moment of execution, thereby reinforcing the theory that consciousness resides in the brain, while at the same time reassuring investors in guillotines. The muscle twitches that occurred after death were therefore involuntary actions unrelated to consciousness. The question of why they occurred at all still remained, however, resulting in intensive research into the nature of basic reflex action and the role of the brain and spinal cord in these movements.

Reflex Action

As we have seen, Descartes was the first to develop a model of reflex action as part of his attempt to show that the body operated like a machine. After Descartes, and before the 19th century, the most significant scientific contribution to the study of reflexes was made by Robert Whytt (1714–1766; pronounced *white*) of Edinburgh, Scotland. The leading neurologist of his day, Whytt is known primarily by historians of psychology for his research into the physiology of the reflex, but he is also justly famous in the history of pediatric medicine for being the first person to adequately describe tuberculous meningitis (Radbill, 1972). With regard to reflexes, in 1751 Whytt published *The Vital and Other Involuntary Motions of Animals*, the outcome of years of research on the role of the spinal cord in mediating reflex action. It was the first extensive treatment of reflexes to be based on experimental research (Fearing, 1930). Studying decapitated animals (mainly frogs), Whytt was able to show that leg muscles responded in predictable ways to physical stimulation. Pinching the leg of a recently decapitated frog reliably produced a muscle contraction. On the other hand, if the connection between the nerve in the leg and the spinal cord was severed, these "involuntary motions" of the leg failed to occur. Hence, Whytt demonstrated that the spinal cord played a crucial role in reflexive behavior.

Whytt distinguished between voluntary and involuntary actions, the former under the control of the "will" with the action originating in and requiring an intact brain, and the latter controlled through the spinal cord. In between voluntary and involuntary control, and serving to link them, was habit formation. Thus actions that begin as voluntary, and under the deliberate control of the will, become similar to reflexes when they have been sufficiently practiced. As Whytt put it:

> We not only acquire, through custom and habit, a faculty of performing certain motions with greater ease than we are wont to do them, but also, in proportion as this facility is increased, we become less sensible of any share or concern the mind has in them.
> (quoted in Fearing, 1930, p. 79)

Whytt also pointed out a consequence of the formation of habits—that the mere idea of a stimulus was sometimes sufficient to bring about a response. In a passage that will make you think of Ivan Pavlov (Chapter 10), Whytt illustrated the point with two everyday examples of what would eventually come to be called conditioned reflexes: "Thus the sight, or even the recalled idea of grateful food, causes an uncommon flow of spittle into the mouth of a hungry person; and the seeing of a lemon cut produces the same effect in many people" (quoted in Fearing, 1930, p. 80).

The existence of the kinds of reflexes documented by Whytt demands that a distinction be made between the sensory and motor components of the reaction, which in turn implies that some nerves may be for the purpose of conveying sensory information and others designed to pass messages along to the muscles, telling them to move. This distinction between sensory and motor nerves became established through the work of two scientists working at about the same time in different countries.

The Bell-Magendie Law

As you recall from Chapter 1, a *multiple* refers to a case in which two or more people make the same discovery during the same historical era, but do so independently of each other. E. G. Boring (1950) used the concept to support his idea that the zeitgeist helped to determine the activities and ways of thinking of scientists during a particular historical era. The Bell-Magendie law is sometimes used as an example of a multiple—two scientists, working in different laboratories (different countries, in this case) at about the same time and neither aware of the other's research, arrive at similar results. The situation was not quite that simple in the case of Bell and Magendie, however; during the years following their work, there was a nasty fight over priority. The judgment of history is that Magendie should have been credited with the discovery; his research was more systematic, and he published it in the public forum of a journal. Bell's research, while occurring a few years earlier than Magendie's, was published in a private pamphlet with limited distribution and was based more on inference from anatomy than actual experimentation (Sechzer, 1983). Furthermore, Magendie got it right; Bell didn't. That Bell's name became paired with Magendie's is more of a tribute to the public clamoring of the politically influential Bell and his equally vociferous friends than to the quality of his research.

François Magendie (1783–1855), the son of a surgeon, grew up during the turbulent years of the French Revolution. Lacking much in the way of formal education, François used his father's influence to become an apprentice at a Paris hospital, where, at the tender age of 16, he was entrusted with the task of doing anatomical dissections (Grmek, 1972). After becoming a medical student and completing a degree in 1808, he quickly earned a reputation as a gifted scientist who distrusted theorizing in favor of inductively collecting "facts." This Baconian attitude he once described in this way: "I compare myself to a ragpicker: with my spiked stick in my hand and my basket on my back, I traverse the field of science and gather what I find" (quoted in Grmek, 1972, p. 7).

In 1822, Magendie published a three-page article summarizing the results of a study on the posterior and anterior roots of the spinal cord. From his earlier dissections, he knew that nerve fibers exited the spinal cord in pairs before joining together: One type of fiber, the posterior root, was closer to the surface of the skin; the other (anterior root) was closer to the interior of the body. Different structures suggest different functions, and Magendie's research aimed at identifying these functions. Using a 6-week-old puppy as a subject,[1] Magendie exposed its spinal cord and cut the posterior fibers (i.e., those closer to the surface) while leaving the spinal cord intact. He sutured up the wound and observed the animal after it recovered. As he described it:

> I did not know what would result from this operation.... At first I believed the limb corresponding to the cut nerves to be completely paralyzed; it was insensitive to pricking and the hardest pressures and, further, it seemed immobile; but soon, to my very great surprise, I clearly saw it move, although sensibility remained completely absent. (Magendie, 1822/1965, p. 20)

Hence, the posterior roots controlled sensation. When this root was destroyed, the animal could still move the limb but had no sensation in it. Next, Magendie severed the anterior root in another animal, a task that required all of his considerable surgical skills. Because the anterior root lies below the posterior one, it is difficult to get to the former without damaging the latter. Nonetheless, Magendie worked out a successful procedure and managed to sever an anterior root cleanly (Bell, on the other hand, was never able to accomplish this). The results were clear: "There could be no doubt whatsoever; the limb was completely immobile and flaccid, although it retained an unequivocal sensibility. Finally, for completeness' sake, I cut both the anterior and the posterior roots; there was an absolute loss of feeling and movement" (Magendie, 1822/1965, p. 20). In summary, then, Magendie's finding, now known as the **Bell-Magendie law**, was that the posterior roots of the spinal cord controlled sensation, while anterior roots controlled motor responses. This was a major discovery, for it provided anatomical foundation for further study of the two sides of the reflex: sensation and movement. Furthermore, the distinction implied that nerves send messages in a single direction and that there are different sensory and motor tracts within the spinal cord and perhaps different sensory and motor regions within the brain.

As for Sir Charles Bell (1774–1842), his *Idea of a New Anatomy of the Brain: Submitted for the Observation of His Friends* had been written 11 years before the publication of Magendie's work, but it had been sent privately to about 100 colleagues. Bell was a prominent English anatomist with influential friends, however, and together they launched a campaign against Magendie when the latter's work was published. They accused the Frenchman of everything from unnecessary replication of Bell's original finding to animal cruelty (ether had not been discovered when Magendie did his experiments, so his surgery must have been brutally painful to the young dogs). Bell went as far as to alter the wording of some of his later work and republish it to make it appear that he had anticipated Magendie by a decade (Gallistel, 1981). Yet Magendie was unaware of Bell's work, which involved an analysis of anatomy of the spinal cord and an experiment on a "stunned rabbit." Bell deserves some credit for concluding that the posterior and anterior roots had different functions, but he mistakenly concluded that both roots had some sensory and motor function and that they were differentiated primarily by virtue of their connections to the cerebellum (posterior roots) and the cerebrum (anterior roots) (Sechzer, 1983).

---

[1]Magendie used these immature animals after having difficulty cutting through the tough protective covering of the spinal cord in older dogs. "A litter of eight puppies, six weeks old, ... seemed to me to be eminently suited for a new attempt at opening the vertebral canal. And, in fact, by using a very sharp scalpel, I was able with a single stroke ... to lay bare the posterior half of the spinal cord" (Magendie, 1822/1965, p. 19).

Magendie, personally affronted by the attacks from across the English Channel, recognized the value of Bell's research once he learned of it; but he refused to concede priority for discovering the critical (and correct) distinction between sensory and motor functions. In particular, while acknowledging Bell's priority concerning the strategy of segregating the spinal roots and the discovery that the anterior root influenced "muscular contractility" more than the posterior root did, Magendie vigorously asserted that "as for having established that these roots have distinct properties, distinct functions, that the anterior ones control movement, and posterior ones sensation, *this discovery belongs to me*" (quoted in Grmek, 1972; emphasis added).

The Specific Energies of Nerves

Another feature of Bell's 1811 pamphlet was his argument that different sensory nerves have different "qualities." Thus, "an impression made on two different nerves of sense, though with the same instrument, will produce two distinct sensations" (Bell, 1811/1965, p. 24). As an example, Bell pointed to the "papillae" on the tongue, some of which convey the sense of taste, others the sense of touch. When touching these latter papillae with a sharp steel pin, the resulting sensation is one of "sharpness." When touching one of the taste papillae with the same pin, however, the resulting sensation is one of a "metallic taste." Similarly, if two different types of stimuli affect a single type of nerve, then the sensation experienced will be determined by the type of sensory nerve stimulated. Thus light waves stimulate the optic nerve to produce a visual sensation, but pressing on the side of the eyeball also results in the sensation of a flash of light. Further, according to Bell, cataract patients often reported seeing a "spark of fire" when the surgeon's needle pierced their eye.

This idea of Bell's eventually became known as the doctrine of the **specific energies of nerves**, and although Bell's 1811 paper once again had chronological priority, credit went elsewhere, this time to the leading German physiologist of the first half of the 19th century, Johannes Müller (1801–1858). Müller, whose manic pace of work alternated with long periods of severe depression, was the first person ever named a professor of "physiology" at the University of Berlin, Germany's premier university. Müller elaborated on the specific energies doctrine and developed it more fully than Bell. In addition to making the point about different sensory qualities, Müller pointed out that in perception, we are not directly aware of the external world; rather, we are only aware of the action of our nervous system, which conveys information of the world to us. Thus our knowledge of the world is filtered through the physiology of the nervous system.

The doctrine of specific energies of nerves eventually became associated more with Müller than with Bell, mainly because Müller named it as such and presented it as a series of 10 related principles in his massive (eight books totaling more than 1,600 pages) *Handbook of Human Physiology*, which first appeared in 1840. This was the authoritative physiology text of the mid-19th century, and its stature guaranteed that Müller's name, not Bell's, would become attached to the doctrine (Boring, 1950).[2]

[2]After producing his famous handbook, Müller was less productive as a scientist and fell into a severe depression. Few of his friends believed that his death in 1858 was anything but a deliberate overdose of morphine (Steudel, 1972).

Helmholtz: The Physiologist's Physiologist

If Müller was the leading German physiologist of the first half of the 19th century, the honor for the second half goes to one of his followers—Hermann von Helmholtz (1821–1894), shown in Figure 3.1. Shortly after he died, Helmholtz was eulogized by Carl Stumpf, another well-known German physiologist, as the person most responsible for building the "bridge between physiology and psychology that thousands of workers today go back and forth upon" (quoted in Turner, 1972). Helmholtz became *the* 19th-century authority on the sensory systems for vision and audition, developing theories still considered to be at least partly correct. He also provided a simple demonstration of nerve impulse speed that paved the way for one of psychology's most enduring methods, reaction time. And despite accomplishing more than any other 19th-century physiologist, his true love actually was physics, to which he also made original contributions.

Helmholtz was born in 1821 into a family of modest means in Potsdam, Germany. He quickly emerged as an academic star at the local gymnasium (high school), where he developed his lifelong love for physics, but financial straits prevented him from attending a university. The government was offering full scholarships for students to attend medical school in Berlin, however, and Helmholtz jumped at the opportunity, even though it meant committing himself to 8 years of service in the army's medical corps. He left for Berlin in 1838, where he completed the 5-year program in 4 years. While enrolled at the medical institute, he also studied informally at the University of Berlin with the great Johannes Müller. Helmholtz quickly moved into Müller's inner circle and developed lifelong friendships with three other students destined to become leaders in the world of German science: Ernst Brücke (who will appear in Chapter 12 as Freud's mentor), Emil du Bois Reymond, and Karl Ludwig.

Although he was the leading physiologist of his day, Müller was already being challenged by his students in the 1840s, especially on the issue of **vitalism** versus **materialism**.

FIGURE 3.1 Hermann von Helmholtz (1821–1894).

Müller believed that in addition to the physical and chemical properties of physiological systems, there also existed a "vital force," a life force that could not be reduced further. It was an idea with deep roots and obvious theological connotations. Opposed to vitalism was a position that also had a long history but was becoming especially prominent in the 19th century—*materialism* (Chapter 2). According to this view, the vital force was a myth: Physical matter was the only reality, and all living organisms could be reduced to physical, mechanical, and chemical processes that eventually would be understood by applying scientific methods. Müller's students were committed materialists with all the enthusiasm and confidence of youth (all were under 30), and they all made important contributions to physiology that supported the materialist position.

After finishing his medical degree in 1842, Helmholtz began his stint as an army surgeon, while at the same time maintaining his Berlin connections. During this time he made the first of his lasting contributions, one that simultaneously reflected his love of physics and his desire to support a materialist philosophy. It was a paper on the mathematical basis for a law of **conservation of energy**, first read to a scientific society in Berlin in 1847 and then published privately after being rejected for publication by a leading journal (Warren, 1984). Helmholtz is today considered one of the originators of this important principle in physics, which states that the total energy within a system remains constant, even if changes occur within the system. For Helmholtz, the principle was an important weapon in the fight against vitalism. He argued that body heat and muscle force could be explained by chemical energy accumulated during the oxidation process that accompanied digestion—there was no need to propose a special life force that could create its own energy. He supported his argument by showing that muscle contractions generated measurable amounts of heat (Turner, 1972).

Measuring the Speed of Neural Impulses After being released early from his army commitment, Helmholtz was hired by the University of Königsberg in 1849, where he stayed for 6 years.[3] During this time, he completed a series of studies that had important implications for the study of the reflex as well as laid the groundwork for the reaction time methodology that would become a key feature of every laboratory of experimental psychology.

When Helmholtz began studying the problem of nerve impulse speed in the early 1850s, it was already known that the impulse had electrical properties. A theory of electricity had arisen in the 18th century, and several scientists, including Helmholtz's colleague Du Bois Reymond, had demonstrated that nerves could conduct electricity to make muscles twitch. Authorities such as Müller believed that the nerve impulse might be instantaneous—or at the very least, it occurred too rapidly to be measured—but a study by Du Bois Reymond in 1850 suggested that the impulse was propagated along the nerve by an electrochemical process that would be slower than a pure electrical transmission. If so, then perhaps impulse speed could be measured. Helmholtz succeeded in doing so by isolating a motor nerve and a connected muscle from a frog's leg. He then stimulated the nerve electrically at several different distances from the muscle and recorded the time from stimulus to response. Knowing distance and time, the calculation of rate was easy (rate = distance/time). It averaged about

---

[3]Having well-connected friends never hurts. The position at Königsberg opened when Brücke, one of Helmholtz's Berlin friends, left a position there to take one at Vienna (where his prize student would be Sigmund Freud). The Königsberg job was first offered to Du Bois Reymond, who turned it down but apparently recommended Helmholtz, who accepted (Turner, 1972).

90 feet per second (or just over 60 miles per hour), which was quite sluggish compared with estimates that placed it near the speed of light. Helmholtz also roughly estimated impulse speed in sensory nerves by showing that human subjects took longer to respond to stimulation of their toe than their thigh.

For Helmholtz, the implications of the research were obvious. Here was more evidence that vitalism was wrong and materialism was right. Vitalists argued that the conscious decision to move an arm and the arm's movement were simultaneous, but Helmholtz had shown that the event took a measurable amount of time, a conclusion consistent with the idea that nervous action involved the movement of physical, material entities. For Helmholtz, this conclusion was enough: He was not interested in any further applications of the concept of reaction time. It would be for others to develop the idea into a technique for measuring the time of various mental activities. That story is told in the next chapter.

Helmholtz on Vision and Audition   During the Königsberg years, Helmholtz also began investigating the physiology of vision and audition and invented a tool that made him famous among eye doctors—the **ophthalmoscope**, a device for directly examining the retina. His research on vision culminated in a massive three-volume *Handbook of Physiological Optics*, published over an 11-year period from 1856 to 1867. During this same time he moved twice, first to Bonn and then to Heidelberg, where he spent 13 of the most productive years of his career (1858–1871).

Helmholtz is perhaps best remembered for elaborating a theory of color vision first proposed by the English scientist Thomas Young at the beginning of the 19th century. Sometimes considered an example of a multiple, it has come to be called either the Young-Helmholtz theory or, as Helmholtz called it, the **trichromatic theory**. It is based on the facts of color-matching experiments. If you shine a red spotlight against a wall and then shine a green light so that it overlaps the red, the colors in the area of overlap will "mix" and be seen as a new color, yellow. Both Young and Helmholtz demonstrated that by mixing various combinations of three colors (red, green, and blue) together, the resulting color could be made to match any other single color. On this basis, they concluded that the eye must contain three different kinds of color receptors, one for each of these so-called primary colors, red, green, and blue (or violet). Incoming light of a particular wavelength was said to stimulate these receptors to different degrees, resulting in the perception of a certain color. In Helmholtz's words:

> Suppose that the colors of the spectrum are plotted horizontally in Fig. [3.2] in their natural sequence, from red to violet, the three curves may be taken to indicate something like the degree of excitation of the three kinds of fibres, No. 1 for the red-sensitive fibres, No. 2 for the green-sensitive fibres, and No. 3 for the violet-sensitive fibres.
>
> Pure *red* light stimulates the red-sensitive fibres strongly and the two other kinds of fibres feebly; giving the sensation red.
>
> Pure *yellow* light stimulates the red-sensitive and green-sensitive fibres moderately and the violet-sensitive fibres feebly; giving the sensation yellow.
>
> Pure *green* light stimulates the green-sensitive fibres strongly and the two other kinds much more feebly; giving the sensation green.
>
> . . . When all the fibres are stimulated about equally, the sensation is that of *white* or pale hues. (Helmholtz, 1860/1965, p. 42; emphasis in the original)

Although Helmholtz's Figure 3.2 was hypothetical, it is similar to modern-day data plotted in spectral sensitivity curves. Thus the trichromatic theory has held up over the years, at

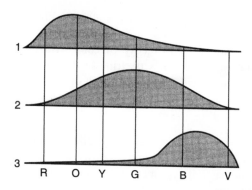

FIGURE 3.2 Relative sensitivity of the three color receptors proposed by Helmholtz. From his *Handbook of Physiological Optics* (1860/1965).

least in part. It failed to account for certain color phenomena that were better explained by other theories, however—most notably Ewald Hering's theory, which came to be called **opponent process theory**. Hering proposed that color-sensitive cells were designed to respond to opposing pairs of colors (i.e., red-green, yellow-blue, black-white). When seeing red, for instance, Hering proposed a chemical breakdown in the receptor for red-green, what he called a "catabolic" process. Seeing green resulted in an "anabolic" or building-up process. If red and green were mixed together, Hering believed the two processes would cancel each other, resulting in the perception of a neutral gray color. One problem with the trichromatic theory was its prediction that someone with severe red-green color blindness would not be able to see yellow properly. Yellow, according to Helmholtz, relies on the stimulation of properly functioning red and green fibers, both of which would be defective for someone with red-green color blindness. Such persons do see yellow, however. Also, the phenomenon of color afterimages seemed to fit Hering's model better than the Helmholtz model. After staring at a red square for a minute or so and then shifting one's gaze to a white surface, an afterimage in the form of a green square appears briefly. Yellow and blue complement each other in a similar manner. Today, theories of color vision include elements of both theories. The Young-Helmholtz version applies well at the retinal level; there do seem to be three different kinds of cones, each maximally responsive to the three colors of trichromatic theory—red, green, and blue. As for Hering's theory, his notions of anabolic and catabolic processes within individual receptors have not held up, but there are indeed opposing pairs of cells (i.e., red-green pairs, blue-yellow pairs) located along the visual pathway (Goldstein, 1996).

Color vision was only a small portion of Helmholtz's work on the visual sense. His love of physics, for example, led him to examine the basic question of optics: How does light become focused on the retina? Thus he provided a systematic analysis of how light rays are bent, both by the cornea and through the process of *accommodation* that Berkeley had described (Chapter 2), in which the lens changes shape to alter the focus of objects at different distances. He also examined the perception of depth through the operation of **binocular vision**, and in the spirit of Bishop Berkeley, took a strong empiricist stance on the question of how we come to perceive objects in space.

Helmholtz would be justly famous even if he had restricted his expertise to vision. In 1863, between the publication of volumes II and III of his *Optics*, however, he also published what quickly became the authoritative text on the sense of hearing, *The Theory of the Sensation of Tone as a Physiological Basis for the Theory of Music*. In it, Helmholtz presented his famous **resonance theory** of hearing, which proposed that different frequencies of sound were detected by receptors located in different places along the basilar membrane of the cochlea.

It is worth noting that both the trichromatic theory of color vision and the resonance theory of hearing were elaborations of Müller's doctrine of the specific energies of nerves. Whereas Müller proposed a single specific energy for each of the five basic senses, Helmholtz's theories amounted to proposing more than one specific energy for each sense: three for color vision and many for hearing.

Helmholtz and the Problem of Perception

As a physicist, Helmholtz was accustomed to look for precision in nature. Hence, he was perplexed by what he thought of as the **problem of perception**. On the one hand, it appears that the human sensory systems for seeing and for hearing are remarkably capable. On the other hand, the structures designed to deliver this sensory information seemed to him to be terribly flawed. In vision, for example, Helmholtz noted that aberrations in the cornea often distorted light waves; that the fluids within the eye distorted the perceptions of shape, motion, and color; and worst of all, that when light reached the retina, it had to pass through several layers of blood vessels and nerve fibers before reaching the receptors. Helmholtz once wrote that "if an optician wanted to sell me an instrument which had all these defects, I should think myself quite justified in blaming his carelessness in the strongest terms, and giving him back his instrument" (quoted in Warren, 1984, p. 257). Similar problems occurred for hearing with the structure of the ear.

Given such design flaws, Helmholtz asked, what accounts for the quality of our perception? The answer, he believed, could be found in the doctrine of the specific energies of nerves and in British empiricist philosophy. Thus, because our nervous system mediates between reality and the mind, we are only indirectly aware of the external world. As a result, the role of experience is central to perception, he argued. The raw information processed by the sensory systems is meaningless by itself, but takes on meaning only when a particular combination of sensory events becomes associated with specific consequences. Consider, for example, perceiving objects located at different distances. According to Helmholtz, we make what he called an **unconscious inference** about distance, based on our past experiences of various cues that are associated with distance (this should remind you of Berkeley). As a person gets closer to us, for example, the retinal image enlarges, but we perceive the person getting closer, not doubling or tripling in size. Helmholtz would say that because we know *through experience* that people don't actually grow as they approach, we conclude logically (i.e., unconsciously infer) that the person must be getting closer. All of this occurs quickly and without our awareness, hence the term *unconscious inference*.

Despite being sickly as a youth, Helmholtz was strong and energetic in his later years. His favorite hobby was mountain climbing, for example, and he could often be found hiking through the Alps (Wade, 1994). The experience gave him a metaphor that summed up his approach to science. The elegance of his final theorizing contrasted with the messy and unpredictable day-to-day process of doing research. To explain how he proceeded, he compared himself to

> an Alpine climber who, not knowing the way, ascends slowly and with toil, and is often compelled to retrace his steps because his progress is stopped; sometimes by reasoning, and sometimes by accident, he hits upon traces of a fresh path, which again leads him a little further; and finally, when he has reached the goal, he finds to his annoyance a royal road on which he might have ridden up if he had been clever enough to find the right starting-point at the outset. In my memoirs I have, of course, not given the reader an

account of my wanderings, but I have described the beaten path on which he can now reach the summit without trouble. (quoted in Warren, 1984, p. 256)

In 1871, at age 50, Helmholtz left Heidelberg for Berlin when he was offered a prestigious professorship in physics. Thus, in the last stage of his career, he returned to his first love—physics. He traveled widely, even visiting the United States in 1893 to represent German science at the famous Columbian Exposition in Chicago (Chapter 7). On the return voyage, he suffered a severe concussion and prolonged double vision from a fall down a flight of stairs. He died of a cerebral hemorrhage the following year.

LOCALIZATION OF BRAIN FUNCTION

In addition to the advances in knowledge about sensory physiology, 19th-century scientists explored the nature of the brain and argued over the issue of localization. Even a superficial visual inspection of the brain reveals some obvious structural differences. There are clearly two hemispheres, the cortex subdivides further into a number of ridges (convolutions), the cerebellum is separate from the cerebrum, and the lower brain areas, an extension of the spinal cord, have their own distinct shapes and features. It is only natural to suppose that there are functional differences corresponding to these structures, and this raises the question of **localization of function**. To what extent do the different structural locations in the brain correspond to different physiological and psychological attributes?

The Phrenology of Gall and Spurzheim

The phrenologists proposed the first important theory of localization. According to advocates of **phrenology**, distinct human "faculties" could be identified and located in precisely defined areas of the brain.[4] Phrenology began as a legitimate scientific attempt to study the brain, but it eventually degenerated into the 19th century's best example of pseudoscience. When portrayed in today's introductory psychology texts, it is usually caricatured as a bizarre scientific dead end in which charlatans read a person's character by looking at the bumps on his or her head (i.e., lots of presentist thinking here). Actually, the story is considerably more complex, and much that is of importance to American psychology has its roots in the phrenological movement (e.g., the importance of practical application).

The origins of phrenology can be traced to a respected but eccentric Viennese physician and comparative anatomist, Franz Josef Gall (1758–1828). Gall was born in Tiefenbronn, Germany, into an intensely devout Catholic family—his parents assumed that he would one day become a priest. Instead, his theory about the brain came to be considered antireligious, his books were banned by the Church, and upon his death in 1828 he was denied a religious burial (Young, 1972). Gall decided on a career in medicine early in life, earning an MD in Vienna in 1785. There he developed a successful practice and became a skilled anatomist. After his public lectures and surgical demonstrations were banned for promoting materialism

---

[4]Phrenology is often confused with the related doctrine of physiognomy, which also proposed a relationship between one's physical attributes (in particular, facial features) and character or personality. Physiognomy has a long history, dating to the ancient Greeks; it was most clearly spelled out in the work of Johann Kaspar Lavater (1741–1801), who published lavishly illustrated volumes on physiognomy in the mid-1770s. Lavater's physiognomy related facial features (e.g., chins, noses, width between eyes, forehead height, etc.) to personality and character.

(and by implication, immorality and atheism), he took the show on the road and lectured throughout Europe before settling in Paris in 1807, where he remained until his death.

Gall secured a place in the history of medicine with his careful anatomical work. He identified the fibers connecting the cerebral hemispheres (corpus callosum) and confirmed earlier speculation that some fibers crossed from one side of the brain to the opposite side of the spinal cord. Thus Gall confirmed the concept of **contralateral function**, the notion that each side of the brain controls the opposite side of the body. Gall also compared the brain structures of different species and made a convincing argument that the mental abilities of different species correlated with the size and complexity of the brain, especially the cortex. He was also the first to argue that the brain's convolutions formed the same pattern within a given species; hence, the surface of the brain was not a random jumble of ridges and valleys, but had a reliable structure. His anatomical research was impeccable—the great French physiologist Pierre Flourens, phrenology's harshest critic (discussed later), nonetheless reported that when he saw Gall dissect a brain, it was like seeing the organ for the first time. Unlike most anatomists, including Flourens, who dissected brains by slicing off segments from the top down, Gall worked from the brain stem up, removing structures one by one and thereby tracing the interconnections between structures with a precision not possible when starting at the top (Temkin, 1947).

Despite these notable accomplishments, Gall is best known for originating phrenology. He began developing his ideas about localization early—as a youth, he thought he detected a relationship between the shape of a person's head and certain behavioral characteristics of that person. He noticed, for example, that schoolmates with protruding eyes seemed to have better memories than he did. This early experience began a lifelong pursuit of inductive evidence to support his theories. For example, Gall claimed that the impulse to steal resulted from an overdevelopment of the faculty of "Property" (later called "Acquisitiveness"), located in the temporal lobe of the cortex about an inch above and in front of the ear. According to Gall:

> When these cerebral parts are very much developed, they produce a prominence on the head and skull....I have constantly found this prominence, in all inveterate thieves confined in prison, in all idiots with an irresistible propensity to steal, and in all those who, otherwise well endowed with intellect, take an inconceivable pleasure in stealing, and even feel incapable of resisting the passion which forces them to theft. One of my friends...has this organ very large. When he sees scissors, knives, or other similar trifles, he feels a certain uneasiness...until he has put those objects in his pockets. (Gall, 1825/1965, p. 218)

This quote hints at Gall's typical modus operandi, which was to study the skull shapes of people with especially notable attributes. By examining exceptional cases, Gall believed it would be easy to relate skull contour with the person's special talent. The principles could then be generalized to others. By 1802, according to Finger (2000), Gall had collected more than "300 skulls from individuals with well-documented mental traits ranging from literary talent to murderous tendencies [and] 120 casts from living persons who had distinguished themselves" (p. 127).

Gall's beliefs eventually developed into the theory that his followers came to call phrenology, a term that derives from the Greek words for the study of ("–ology") the mind ("phrenos"). The term was coined by Johann Spurzheim (1776–1832), who collaborated with Gall for a time but later broke with him. Spurzheim is the person most responsible for popularizing the theory, both in Europe and in America. As described in his *Outlines of Phrenology* (1832/1978) and elsewhere, phrenology's main principles reduced to five:

a. The brain is the organ of the mind.

b. The mind is composed of a large number (about three dozen) of abilities or attributes called "faculties"; some of these faculties are intellectual (cognitive) and some are affective (emotional).

c. Each faculty is located in a specific area of the brain and that location is the same for everyone.

d. For a given faculty, some people have more than others, and those with more of a particular faculty will have more brain tissue in the corresponding location than those with less of that same faculty.

e. Because the skull corresponds roughly to the shape of the brain, the strength of various faculties can be inferred from the shape of the skull.

This last point came to be known as the **doctrine of the skull**, and for the phrenologists it was the key to measurement. If the size and shape of various brain locations reflected the strength of faculties, and if brain shape affected skull shape, then measuring the skull would yield a measurement of faculties. In short, everything of importance about people could be known by examining the shapes of their skulls. Figure 3.3 shows a typical phrenological skull with its faculties labeled.

In the first two decades of the 19th century, phrenology was a legitimate attempt to identify the localized functions of the brain. By the time Spurzheim produced his *Outlines of Phrenology*, in the year he died while on an American lecture tour (1832), thousands of skulls had been examined with an eye toward correlating skull shape with ability and character. The *Outlines* includes detailed analyses of the faculties: Each description identifies the faculty's location in the brain and describes some of the supporting evidence. On close examination, however, it is clear that there were serious weaknesses with the evidence. As indicated earlier in connection with the faculty of Property (Acquisitiveness), the phrenologists

FIGURE 3.3 A phrenological skull with faculties identified.

relied heavily on **anecdotal evidence**. That is, they looked for specific case examples to support their theory. This approach is not necessarily flawed; gathering lots of data and then looking for generalizations is a standard inductive strategy. The problem, however, is that the phrenologists tended to ignore or discount examples that did not support their case. Furthermore, their theory failed an important criterion of any viable scientific theory: It must be stated precisely enough to be capable of disproof. But the phrenologists would not do this. A thief with a small area of Property would be ignored, described as a potential thief ("he will start stealing any day now"), or explained away by referring to combinations of other faculties that would be said to offset the lack of Property. For instance, the thief might be described as having large faculties of Imitation and Self-Esteem, causing him to maintain his self-image by copying his pickpocket older brother, despite his lack of "natural" Property faculty. Perhaps the ultimate example of phrenological refusal to consider disproof was a comment attributed to Spurzheim upon learning that Descartes's skull was rather small in the areas related to some of the intellectual faculties. Spurzheim was said to have suggested that perhaps Descartes wasn't so smart after all (Finger, 2000).

The failure of phrenology as a theory did not seem to bother phrenologists, but other scientists quickly recognized the flaws; by the middle of the 19th century, phrenology was relegated to the status of pseudoscience. Unfortunately, it shared an important feature with other pseudosciences—the general public loved it. Phrenology became enormously popular throughout the rest of the 19th century. Gall and Spurzheim spread the faith throughout Europe, and Spurzheim and others exported it to the United States.

Phrenology reached its zenith of popularity in America. The version that was imported by Spurzheim and spread by him and others fit perfectly with the American culture of the "common man," especially during the middle and last half of the 19th century (Bakan, 1966). Although Gall believed the size of a person's faculties was an indication of native traits, Spurzheim argued that faculties could be affected by nurture. To Spurzheim, the brain was analogous to a muscle—its faculties could be exercised and strengthened through education and self-help. Thus phrenology provided a seemingly scientific basis for the traditional American belief that anyone, regardless of heritage, could "pull oneself up by one's bootstraps" and accomplish anything in life. The hopeful notion that children's brains and therefore their futures could be shaped by controlling their environments and improving their educations resonated with Americans. That same optimism would make behaviorism just as fashionable with the public in the 1920s. Phrenology also was consistent with the American idea that everyone is a unique person, possessing his or her own special talents. In phrenological terms, this translated into everyone having his or her own distinctive configuration of faculties, to be measured with proper phrenological tools. Thus phrenology was an important early example of a major theme of research in psychology that continues today: the search for ways to identify and gauge individual differences (Bakan, 1966). And if individual differences could be identified and measured, then a person's strengths and weaknesses could be known and he or she could be counseled about careers, mate selection, and so on. A final reason for phrenology's appeal, then, was in its promise to deliver practical applications to improve daily living.

Phrenology's popularity with the masses was enhanced through the energetic marketing efforts of the firm of Fowler and Wells. Although the scientific and more educated community rejected phrenology rather quickly, the public never seemed to tire of it. As you can see from this chapter's Close-Up, phrenology was big business in late 19th-century America.

CLOSE-UP

THE MARKETING OF PHRENOLOGY

When Orson Fowler was a student at Amherst College in the early 1830s, he made pocket money by examining the heads of classmates for two cents a head (Joynt, 1973). Upon graduation, he joined with his brother Lorenzo and sister Charlotte in forming a museum of phrenology in New York City that featured a large collection of skulls, casts of heads, and other phrenological tools of the trade. Admission was free, but once the museum goers were in the door, the Fowlers tempted them with a phrenological assessment that cost from one to three dollars. When Charlotte married a medical student named Samuel Wells, the firm of Fowler and Wells was born. Located at 753 Broadway, with branches in Boston and Philadelphia, it dominated the phrenology business from its inception in 1844 to the turn of the 20th century.

Fowler and Wells, Inc. published a seemingly endless list of pamphlets designed to bring phrenological insights into every home. They also began the popular *Phrenological Journal* (Figure 3.4), trained and "certified" phrenologists, and during an era when the public lecture was a primary means of communication, maintained a list of accomplished public speakers ready to spread the phrenological faith. To give you some idea of the range of topics addressed by the firm, consider the following titles of pamphlets and books that could be ordered from Fowler and Wells, as advertised in the October 1881 issue of the *Phrenological Journal*:

> *The Indications of Character*, as manifested in the general shape of the head and the form of the face. Illustrated. 15 cents.
>
> *Wedlock*; or, The Right Relations of the Sexes. A Scientific Treatise disclosing the Laws of Conjugal Selection, Pre-natal Influences, and showing Who Ought and Who Ought Not to Marry. $1.50; in fancy guilt, $2.00.
>
> *Choice of Pursuits*; or, What to do and Why. Describing Seventy-five Trades and Professions, and the Temperaments and Talents required for each. 508 pp. $1.75.

As for the journal itself, each issue contained phrenological sketches of well-known individuals, articles on other hot topics of the day (e.g., hypnotism, spiritualism, physiognomy), and short pieces covering just about anything (e.g., "Why Bees Work in Darkness"). Although nothing quite like the *Phrenological Journal* exists today, the *Old Farmer's Almanac*, with its Down East commonsense wisdom, bears some similarity.

A typical phrenological article in the journal featured some well-known person and showed how a phrenological assessment could "explain" that person's character and behavior. For example, the September 1873 issue included a piece about a notorious murderer. Here's how a phrenologist who interviewed the killer described him:

> I found his head to be 22 inches in circumference, 13.5 inches from Individuality to the occipital spine, and 14 inches from Destructiveness to Destructiveness, over the top of the head at Firmness. The animal portion of the brain predominates over all others. Destructiveness is the largest organ in his brain, the head swelling out enormously over the ears. The organ of Conscientiousness is, I think, the smallest I ever saw.... All the spiritual organs are small and inactive, while Cautiousness and Secretiveness are both below the average.

You will not be surprised to learn that the phrenologist knew that the person he was assessing was a murderer—knowledge that almost certainly biased his report. That biased reporting was a serious liability for phrenology is evident from an often-reported account of the famous American humorist Mark Twain, who apparently went to a phrenologist, did not reveal who he was, and received a report indicating that he was completely lacking in sense of humor.

The firm of Fowler and Wells had a long run, but interest in phrenology finally began to wane near the end of the 19th century as the general public became more informed about the workings of the brain and as other approaches to measurement (e.g., IQ testing) began to be popularized. In 1911, the *Phrenological Journal* published its last issue.

FIGURE 3.4 The October 1881 cover of Fowler and Wells's popular *Phrenological Journal*.

Flourens and the Method of Ablation

Phrenology might have seemed like good science to Main Street America, but the real scientists were not fooled. As mentioned earlier, the scientific community rejected the Gall-Spurzheim theory well before the middle of the 19th century. Phrenology's worst enemy was the distinguished French physiologist and surgeon Pierre Flourens (1794–1867), who deliberately set out to disprove phrenology. He reduced the doctrine to two main points: The mind is centered in the brain, and the mind is composed of numerous faculties, each located in specific places in the brain. In his sharply worded *Examination of Phrenology*, first published in 1843, he sarcastically observed that "of these two propositions, there is certainly nothing new in the first one, and perhaps nothing true in the second one" (Flourens, 1846/1978, p. 18). Flourens also reported an embarrassing example of the phrenologists' susceptibility to bias, describing a case in which Magendie presented a skull to Spurzheim for examination. Magendie told Spurzheim that the skull belonged to a famous French scientist (Simon-Pierre Laplace), but in fact the skull belonged to a severely retarded man. As Flourens reported, "Spurzheim, who had already worked up his enthusiasm, admired the brain of the imbecile as he would have admired that of Laplace" (quoted in Finger, 2000, p. 134).

To falsify the phrenologists' claims directly, Flourens took an experimental approach to the problem of localization, using the method of **ablation**. Although he did not create the procedure, he raised it to such a level of refinement that it is now associated with his name. Rather than wait for natural experiments to occur, in the form of accidental brain damage, Flourens created brain damage surgically by destroying specific sections of the brain and observing the effects (*ablation* derives from the Latin words for "carry away" or "remove"). If the result of an ablation was an inability to see, then presumably the area of the removed portion had something to do with vision. Clearly, the method required animals as research subjects, and Flourens experimented on numerous species ranging from dogs to pigeons.

Flourens's attack on phrenology took the form of showing that specific areas of the brain that were alleged by the phrenologists to serve function X in fact served function Y, and that the cerebral cortex operated as an integrated whole rather than as a large collection of faculties located in specific places. One focus of his research was the cerebellum. To the phrenologists, this portion of the brain controlled sexual behavior and was the center of the faculty of "amativeness." Flourens had little trouble disproving this and demonstrating instead that the cerebellum is the center of motor coordination. Thus pigeons deprived of the organ were unable to coordinate wing movements to fly, and dogs were unable to walk properly and would be observed staggering, falling down, and bumping into objects they could normally avoid. Also, the degree of abnormality in movement was directly proportional to the amount of cerebellum ablated.

Through his experiments in removing varying amounts of the cerebral cortex, Flourens found a similar relationship between the amount removed and the seriousness of the ensuing problem. He could find no indication of distinct functions residing in specific areas of the cortex, however, so he concluded that it operated as a whole and served the general functions of perception, intelligence, and will. Thus pigeons without a cortex or with most of it removed maintained some basic sensory functioning, but they showed no indication of the ability to learn from their experiences and did not seem capable of doing anything except vegetating. The difference between a pigeon without a cerebellum and one without a cortex was that the first bird would attempt to fly but could not coordinate the movements, while it would never occur to the second bird that flying was an option in life.

The general principles that the cortex acts as a whole and that the amount of disability is proportional to the extent of ablation were verified and extended by the discoveries of the great American physiological psychologist Karl Lashley, who referred to them as the principles of equipotentiality and mass action, respectively (Lashley's work is considered briefly at the end of the chapter). Yet while Flourens was able to use these principles to attack phrenology in such a way that it never recovered, at least in the eyes of the scientific community, he overstated his case. He argued against any degree of localization in the cortex, a position soon to be shown inadequate by other brain scientists using other methods.

The Clinical Method

The results of ablation studies are not always easy to interpret, mainly because destroying one portion of a brain also influences connections to that portion, producing outcomes that are not always predictable or consistent. Also, ablation studies are sometimes impossible to do, as in the case of human subjects. It is one thing to systematically ablate portions of a person's brain for certain beneficial medical reasons (e.g., severing the corpus callosum to treat epilepsy), but destroying human brain tissue simply for the purpose of observing what happens is difficult to justify.[5] An alternative way to study human brain function is called the **clinical method**. This involves either (a) studying the behavioral and mental consequences of brain injury, events such as strokes, or illness; or (b) identifying people with some behavioral or mental disorder and examining their brains for structural abnormalities after death. The person generally credited with developing the clinical method is Paul Broca, who we meet shortly, but there are numerous examples of famous clinical cases in the mid-19th century. Perhaps the best known concerned a well-respected Vermont railroad worker, Phineas Gage.

The Remarkable Phineas Gage   While blasting rock in preparation for a new railway line near Cavendish, Vermont, in 1848, Gage survived an accident that seemed certain to be fatal. After pouring gunpowder and placing a fuse into a hole drilled in rock that was about to be blasted, Gage accidentally ignited the powder while using a "tamping iron" (metal rod a little over three feet long, about an inch in diameter, flat at one end, and tapered at the other) to compress the powder. The explosion converted the tamping iron into a missile that flew into the air and landed 30 meters away. Unfortunately for Gage, his head was in the flight path. The tapered end of the missile entered just below his left eye and exited from the top left of his forehead, taking a healthy portion of his left frontal cortex with it (Figure 3.5). Miraculously, Gage only briefly lost consciousness; once he arrived back in town, he was able to walk with assistance to a doctor's office for treatment. Within 2 months, he was sufficiently recovered to live independently;[6] but he had difficulty working productively again, and his personality changed. From a dependable, conscientious, respected community leader (he was foreman of the railroad crew), Gage degenerated into an obstinate, profane, irresponsible embarrassment to the community (MacMillan, 1986).

[5]This ethical point was lost on Dr. Roberts Bartholow of Cincinnati. In 1874, he inserted electrodes into the cortex of an unwitting immigrant domestic worker who had come to him for treatment of an ulcerous scalp wound that had exposed a portion of her brain. Mild stimulation produced some muscular contractions; but when the curious Bartholow inserted the electrodes deeper and increased the strength of the current, the unfortunate woman went into severe convulsions and soon died (Hothersall, 1995).

[6]That Gage survived at a time before the use of antibiotics to treat infection was nothing short of amazing. His recovery was probably aided because the entry wound provided a natural drainage area that prevented him from developing the kind of abscess that would almost certainly be fatal (MacMillan, 1986).

FIGURE 3.5 Sketch of Gage's skull, showing position of tamping iron. From the original medical report by Harlow (1868).

One of Gage's doctors, John Harlow, was amenable to phrenology and thought the case supported the phrenologist's localization beliefs. Harlow kept meticulous notes on the case and published accounts of it in 1848 and 1868. He described this case of frontal lobe damage as one in which

> the equilibrium or balance ... between his intellectual faculties and animal propensities seems to have been destroyed. He is fitful, irreverent, indulging at times in the grossest profanity (which was not previously his custom), manifesting but little deference for his fellows, impatient of restraint or advice when it conflicts with his desires, at times pertinaciously obstinate, yet capricious and vacillating, devising many plans of future operation, which are no sooner arranged than they are abandoned. ... In this regard his mind was radically changed, so decidedly that his friends and acquaintances said he was "no longer Gage." (Harlow, 1868, quoted in MacMillan, 1986, p. 85)

Thus, while Gage survived the injury, he was radically altered by it—the brain damage resulted in changes to his personality and behavior. In terms of localization, the Gage case seemed to indicate that the brain's frontal lobes served the function of rationality, helping to maintain control over the emotions. As for Gage, he died young (37), 12 years following the accident, after experiencing a number of increasingly severe convulsions. The tamping iron and Gage's skull can be seen today at Harvard's Warren Anatomical Medical Museum.

Broca and the Speech Center   In the Gage case, it was possible for Harlow to trace events from the initial brain injury to the resulting psychological outcome. Another type of clinical case occurs when a patient manifests some specific mental or behavioral problem, but it cannot be correlated with brain damage until a postmortem analysis. Such was the situation facing the French neurologist Paul Broca (1824–1880) in April of 1861 when treating a very unusual patient—known to history as "Tan," for reasons that will soon be apparent.

The patient had been in the Bicêtre hospital in Paris for a remarkable 21 years, and had been incapacitated and in bed for the 7 years before 1861, when a severe case of gangrene brought him to Broca's attention. He first came to the hospital when, at the age of 30, he had lost the ability to speak coherently. In Broca's (1861/1965) account, the patient was

> quite healthy and intelligent and differed from a normal person only in his loss of articulate language. He came and went at the hospice, where he was known by the name of "Tan." He understood all that was said to him. His hearing was actually very good,

but whenever one questioned him he always answered, "Tan, tan," accompanying his utterance with varied gestures by which he succeeded in expressing most of his ideas. If one did not understand his gestures, he was apt to get irate and added to his vocabulary a gross oath ("Sacré nom de Dieu!"). (p. 224)

After 10 years (!) in the hospital, "Tan" began to lose control of the right side of his body, and over the next 11 years (!), his condition deteriorated. By the time he was brought to Broca's attention, he was near death. Broca reported that he hesitated to examine Tan because his general state "was so grave that it would have been cruel" (p. 225). Nonetheless, Broca proceeded with a physical exam that confirmed the paralysis of the right arm and leg as well as with an examination of Tan's mental capacities:

> His numerical responses, made by opening or closing his fingers, were best. . . . How many years had he been at Bicêtre? He opened his hand four times and then added one finger. That made 21 years, the correct answer. The next day I repeated the question and received the same answer. . . . Two days in succession I showed him my watch . . . [and] after having looked at the watch for a few seconds, he could each time indicate the time correctly. It cannot be doubted, therefore, that the man was intelligent, that he could think, that he had to a certain extent retained the memory of old habits. He could understand even quite complicated ideas. For instance, I asked him about the order in which his paralyses had developed. First he made a short horizontal gesture with his left index finger, meaning that he had understood; then he showed successively his tongue, his right arm, and his right leg. That was perfectly correct, for quite naturally he attributed his loss of language to paralysis of his tongue. (p. 226)

Broca guessed that Tan had a cerebral lesion that for the first 10 years of the illness remained confined to a fairly limited area in the left side of the brain, but then had spread. He did not have long to wait to confirm the diagnosis—Tan died 6 days after Broca first examined him. Broca immediately performed an autopsy and removed the brain (which still resides in Paris's Musée Depuytren). As you can see from Figure 3.6, the damage is clear. The disorder suffered by Tan is known as expressive or **motor aphasia**, and it is characterized by an inability to articulate ideas verbally, even though the vocal apparatus is intact and general intelligence is normal. Over the next few years, Broca encountered several other aphasic patients like Tan, found the same general pattern of left frontal lobe (third frontal convolution) damage, and concluded that the ability to produce speech was localized in the left frontal lobe. Although others with a strong belief in localization of function had argued

FIGURE 3.6 Tan's brain—note damage in lower left.

KEY DATE—1861

This was the year that Paul Broca studied the aphasic patient "Tan" and confirmed the location of the brain's speech center.

These events also occurred that year:

- Wilhelm Wundt (Chapter 4), then an assistant in the laboratory of Hermann Helmholtz (this chapter) read a paper on reaction time at a conference of German scientists in Speyer; it was his first public presentation of research that would eventually become part of his work in experimental psychology

- Louis Pasteur proposed a germ theory of fermentation

- Daily weather forecasts began appearing in Great Britain

- The Pony Express, created to deliver mail in the American west in 1860, was discontinued after just a year of operation, following development of a transcontinental telegram service

- The skeleton of a link between reptile and bird (archaeopteryx) was discovered in Germany

- The United States introduced the passport system

- Russian Tsar Alexander II abolished serfdom

- The U.S. Civil War began with Confederate victories at Fort Sumter in South Carolina and Bull Run in Virginia

- In Wheeling, a convention adopted a constitution for a new state, to be called West Virginia

These people were born:

- Alfred North Whitehead, English mathematician and philosopher

- Frederick Remington, artist/sculptor of the American West

- James Naismith, inventor of basketball

These people died:

- Elizabeth Barrett Browning, English poet (e.g., *Sonnets from the Portuguese*)

- Albert, prince consort of England and husband of Queen Victoria

---

that speech production resided in the frontal lobe (e.g., Jean-Baptiste Bouillaud, a student of Magendie, as early as 1825), Broca generally gets credit for the discovery on the grounds of the level of detail of his description of the Tan case (Finger, 2000). In his honor, this part of the cortex is now called Broca's area.

Broca's research challenged Flourens's conclusions about the degree of localization to be found in the cortex. Broca joined a growing number of physiologists who were willing to argue for localization, even while they were rejecting the specific claims of the phrenologists. Additional evidence for localized language function came from clinical studies by the German neurologist Carl Wernicke (1848–1905). He studied a group of patients who had the ability to produce articulate speech, but the speech tended to be nonsensical; they also had difficulty comprehending the speech of others. He named the disorder **sensory aphasia**, to distinguish it from motor aphasia, and discovered consistent brain damage to an area of the left temporal lobe of the brain, several centimeters behind Broca's area.

Mapping the Brain: Electrical Stimulation

We have seen that in the 19th century, discoveries about the nature of electricity were being applied to research on sensory physiology, and the idea was evolving that neural activity was electrochemical in nature. In that context, two young German physiologists, Eduard Fritsch (1838–1927) and Edward Hitzig (1838–1907), both lecturers at the University of Berlin, wondered whether the surface of the cortex would respond to mild electrical current. Hitzig had observed muscle movements when the exposed brain of a wounded soldier had been mechanically stimulated, but it was generally believed that touching the surface of the brain did not produce reliable effects. Using dogs as their subjects, Hitzig and Fritsch exposed the cortex and probed different surfaces. The stimulus was an electric current of "an intensity that just barely evoked a sensation of feeling on the tongue" (Fritsch & Hitzig, 1870/1965, p. 230). It was delivered across two thin platinum wires that could be placed anywhere from 2 to 3 millimeters (mm) apart. Despite the relative crudeness of their procedures—the experiments were done in Fritsch's home—they contributed evidence of localization by identifying several motor centers in the front half of the brain. Stimulation of the areas marked in Figure 3.7 produced consistent movements in the right side of the dog's body, as follows:

   Area 1: neck

   Areas 2 and 3: anterior leg (extension and flexion, respectively)

   Area 4: posterior leg

   Area 5: face

The Fritsch and Hitzig research motivated a number of physiologists, who proceeded to map out motor areas in other species and with more precision. This activity became known as the "new" phrenology or "scientific phrenology": Localization was the goal, but now the brain's functions would be identified scientifically, rather than through the selected anecdotes of Gall and Spurzheim. Just a few years after Fritsch and Hitzig published their work, the Scottish neurologist David Ferrier (1843–1928) wrote *Functions of the Brain* (1876), which included the map of a monkey's brain shown in Figure 3.8. Comparing this with Figure 3.7 makes it clear

FIGURE 3.7 Motor centers of a dog's brain, identified via electrical stimulation by Fritsch and Hitzig (1870/1965).

(a)   (b)

FIGURE 3.8 David Ferrier's map of the cortex of a monkey. From Boring (1950).

how rapidly brain science was advancing. Ferrier also extended the localization search beyond motor functions, identifying several sensory areas. Using both electrical stimulation and ablation, Ferrier was able to identify the occipital lobe as the primary sensory area for vision, and a portion of the temporal lobe as the center for hearing. It began to look like sensory nerves differed more in terms of their destinations in the cortex than in terms of "specific energies."

EARLY 20TH-CENTURY STUDIES OF THE NERVOUS SYSTEM AND BEHAVIOR

As the 19th century drew to a close, knowledge of the nervous system in general and of the brain in particular was increasing rapidly. In addition to research on sensory physiology and the localization of brain function, however, another line of research developed toward the end of the century and spilled over into the 20th. This concerned the nature of the basic unit of the nervous system itself, the neuron. This is a long and complicated history, but a few of the highlights can be sketched here.

Neuron Theory

Identifying the neuron as the nervous system's basic element did not occur until the second half of the 19th century, when several important developments occurred in histology (the study of the microscopic structure of plant and animal tissue). Microscopes became more powerful, for instance, and techniques for studying brain tissue were perfected. Before it was discovered that the brain could be solidified by soaking it in alcohol, precise dissection was virtually impossible. Once it was known how to harden the brain, however, its nerve pathways could be traced with some precision. For example, in 1857, Louis Gratiolet was able to trace the optic nerve from the retina all the way to the back of the brain, where it radiated like a fan into the occipital cortex (Diamond, 1985).

It was also discovered that the brain could be immersed in paraffin, hardened, then cut into very thin slices via a procedure called sectioning. Furthermore, if these sections were stained with various chemicals, identifiable structures could be observed in a microscope because the chemicals would collect within these structures. The Italian Camillo Golgi (1844–1926; Figure 3.9) produced the first clear pictures of nerve cells in the 1870s when he immersed sections of brain tissue in silver nitrate. The silver stained about 3% of the cells in the section, which appeared as black images against a yellow background under the microscope (Finger, 2000). The silver staining technique earned Golgi a share of the 1906 Nobel Prize for medicine. He believed the nervous system was composed of these neurons, but he also argued that the cells were physically connected to each other in a "nerve network"—this position was eventually discarded in favor of the theory proposed by the other winner of the 1906 Nobel Prize for medicine.

Santiago Ramón y Cajal (1852–1934; Figure 3.10) was a gifted and passionate Spanish neuroanatomist with a love of art; his research laid the foundation for the modern theory of the neuron (Taylor, 1972). Ramón y Cajal's artistic side can be seen in his eloquent description of the neuron as the "aristocrat among the structures of the body, with its giant arms stretched out like the tentacles of an octopus to the provinces on the frontier of the outside world" (quoted in Restak, 1984, p. 26). His passion for science can be seen in his comment that "all outstanding work, in art as well as in science, results from immense zeal applied to a

FIGURE 3.9 Camillo Golgi (1844–1926).

FIGURE 3.10 Santiago Ramón y Cajal (1852–1934).

great idea" (Ramón y Cajal, 1999, p. 7). Like Golgi, Cajal believed the neuron to be the nervous system's basic unit. In contrast with Golgi, however, he argued that each neuron was a separate unit, not physically connected with other units but merely in contact with them. Ironically, when he first proposed his neuron theory in 1889, he used a modification of Golgi's own staining techniques to make his case. The modification produced sharper images, and Cajal could find no evidence of neurons being directly connected with each other.

Thus the cowinners of the 1906 Nobel Prize for medicine were at odds over the nature of neuron structure. To complicate matters further, Golgi the Italian and Cajal the Spaniard were both fiercely patriotic and convinced of the inaccuracy of each other's research. Hence, there was a certain amount of tension at the 1906 Nobel Prize ceremony, where they met for the first time. Golgi vigorously defended his nerve network theory (which, by 1906, had been discredited by the scientific community for years) and sarcastically declared Cajal's neuron theory to be a fad (Finger, 2000). When it was Cajal's turn, he graciously credited Golgi for his pioneering work with staining technique while firmly asserting that Golgi's nerve network theory was of historical interest only.

Sir Charles Sherrington: The Synapse

Direct photographic evidence supporting Ramón y Cajal's neuron theory and refuting Golgi's would have to await the discovery of the electron microscope, but empirical evidence supporting the existence of gaps between neurons was provided by a British contemporary of both men and a close colleague of Ramón y Cajal: Sir Charles Sherrington (1857–1952).[7] It was Sherrington who coined the term **synapse** (from the Greek word meaning "to join together") for this hypothesized space between neurons. He did not observe its existence directly; rather, he deduced it from a brilliant series of studies on spinal reflexes. The research was presented as part of a prestigious series of lectures at Yale University in 1904 and then published as *The Integrative Action of the Nervous System* in 1906 (dedicated to David Ferrier), the same year that Golgi and Ramón y Cajal shared the Nobel Prize. Sherrington would eventually win a Nobel Prize of his own, in 1932 (Swazey, 1972). Figure 3.11 shows him at work in his Oxford laboratory in 1920.

In the tradition of Robert Whytt, but with the advantages of improved technology, Sherrington examined reflex action in "spinal dogs," dogs with spinal cords surgically severed from their brains. As all dog owners know, stimulating a dog's side in the area of the rib cage will cause the dog's hind leg to produce a rapid and repetitive scratching reflex. The fact that Sherrington found these reflexes in spinal dogs replicated Whytt's basic finding about the role of the spinal cord in reflex action. Furthermore, the reflex was even more pronounced in spinal dogs than in intact dogs, which led Sherrington to conclude that the cortex has an *inhibitory* effect on reflex action. He also showed that excitatory and inhibitory action in the nervous system are closely coordinated with each other, producing **reciprocal innervation**, one of his most important discoveries. Although the concept had been known since the time of Descartes, Sherrington was able to demonstrate directly that pairs of muscles worked in conjunction with each other under the control of the nervous system—when one flexed, another extended. This action allowed such complex and coordinated actions as walking and balance (Finger, 2000).

[7]Both contemporary descriptions and obituary accounts of Sherrington describe him as a genial and mild-mannered scientist. On a visit to Sherrington's lab in 1920, for example, Walter Miles reported that "one cannot help but be impressed with the genuineness and kindly eagerness of Sherrington. He is the very antithesis of self assertion and so ready to point out things of interest in your own work rather than discussing the importance of his own" (Goodwin & Royer, 2010, p. 109). Sherrington was eulogized as being "gentle in criticism, whole hearted in admiration and appreciation of the work of others, embod[ying] the intellectual and physical serenity which appears so characteristic of the Victorian era" (Denny-Brown, 1952, p. 477). Yet this "serenity" did not keep him from his favorite sport during his youth—while a lecturer in physiology at St. Thomas's Hospital in London, he spent his Sunday mornings parachute jumping from the hospital's tower (Swazey, 1972).

FIGURE 3.11 Sir Charles Sherrington (center) in his Oxford laboratory (photo by Walter Miles).

Sherrington made several observations with his spinal dogs that led him to infer that synapses exist. First, the reaction time of the reflexes he observed was much slower than predicted from what was known of the speed of neural transmission. This slowing would presumably not happen if the neurons were directly connected with each other, so something must have been slowing down the impulse. A second line of evidence came from the phenomena of temporal and spatial summation. Sherrington discovered that a single stimulation at a certain point on the skin might fail to elicit a scratch reflex, but if the point was stimulated many times in succession (at a rate of about 18 per second), the reflex occurred (Sherrington, 1906). This is **temporal summation**—stimuli separated in time combine to produce a response. **Spatial summation** occurred when two or more adjacent points on the skin were stimulated at the same time. Again, responses occurred only to the combined stimulation. Sherrington concluded that summation must occur where the end points of neurons met each other, the synapse. Each subthreshold stimulus caused some unspecified action at the end of neuron A that was by itself insufficient to fire the separate neuron B, but the combined action of information coming many times from A (temporal) or from other locations (spatial) triggered the firing of B. In effect, Sherrington predicted the later discovery of neurotransmitters, chemicals that we now know cross the synapse to promote (or inhibit) neuron firing. After Golgi, Ramón y Cajal, and Sherrington, then, the neuron was established as the fundamental unit of the nervous system, interrelated with other neurons through synaptic activity.

Karl Lashley: Learning and the Cortex

A brief consideration of the life and work of Karl Spencer Lashley (1890–1958) is a fitting way to end this chapter. Like the 19th-century physiologists, neurologists, and physicists encountered thus far, his training was not in psychology. Unlike anyone else in the chapter, however, he eventually came to think of himself primarily as a psychologist. Thus Lashley provides a transition between the physiologists of the 19th century and the physiological psychologists of the 20th. You will encounter him again in Chapter 10, as a research colleague of behaviorism's founder, John B. Watson, and yet again in Chapter 14, where his paper on "serial order" attacked simplistic S-R (stimulus–response) models of behavior and helped set the stage for the shift from behaviorism to cognitive psychology.

Karl Lashley was born in rural West Virginia. He earned a bachelor's degree in zoology from West Virginia University and a master's degree in bacteriology from the University of Pittsburgh, before enrolling in a doctoral program in zoology at Johns Hopkins University in 1911. There he completed the PhD under the tutelage of noted zoologist H. S. Jennings. More important for psychology's history, Lashley also came under the influence of the behaviorist Watson and S. I. Franz, a psychologist at a psychiatric hospital (St. Elizabeth's in Washington, DC), who was interested in the effects of brain damage on behavior. With Watson, Lashley conducted field studies of animal behavior, laboratory experiments on the sensory abilities of various species, and research on the conditioning of salivary and motor responses, adapting the procedures of two Russian physiologists who were just beginning to be known to Americans: Vladimir Bekhterev and Ivan Pavlov. The conditioning research is especially noteworthy because it marked the point at which Lashley decided that his future would be not in biology, but in the intersection between biology and psychology (Bruce, 1986). This decision was cemented when he completed postdoctoral research on the effects of brain injury on behavior with Franz. By 1920, Lashley knew he would be an experimental psychologist specializing in how learning and memory affect the brain.

Lashley's distinguished academic career included stops at the University of Minnesota, the University of Chicago, and Harvard University. In 1942, he became director of the Yerkes Laboratories of Primate Biology in Florida, where his research on animal behavior bridged the laboratory-based comparative psychology favored by American scientists and the field-based, naturalistic approach of European ethologists (Bruce, 1991). He died of heart failure in 1958, while on holiday in France. Among psychologists, Lashley is best known for the research he completed in the 1920s while at Chicago; this series of experiments was characterized at the time of his death as being "without equal in recent experimental psychology" (Hebb, 1959, p. 142).

Equipotentiality and Mass Action   The year 1929 was an important one for Lashley. His peers elected him president of the American Psychological Association, recognizing the value of the research he had been engaged in during the decade of the 1920s. That research was summarized in his *Brain Mechanisms and Intelligence*, which also appeared in 1929. Lashley defined intelligence in an animal learning context, using it to cover the behavior of rats learning to negotiate mazes and solve simple discrimination and puzzle box problems. He readily admitted that his choice of tests could be criticized: "They all deal with some aspect of the learning process, [but their] relation to the problem of intelligence is not yet clearly established" (Lashley, 1929, p. 14). Nonetheless, he argued that simple mechanical or reflexive explanations of learning, such as the ones proposed by Watson and Pavlov, were inadequate to capture the complexity of how animals went about solving the kinds of problems that enabled them to survive in their environments. Thus he considered the tasks presented to his rats to be sufficiently intricate to bear at least some relation to the intelligent, adaptive behavior found in the animals' real-world environments.

Lashley's procedures were in the tradition of the great French physiologist Flourens—he observed the effects of brain ablations on behavior, systematically destroying different amounts of cortex and observing the effects on learning and retention. One of Lashley's

FIGURE 3.12 Mazes used by Lashley (1929) in his studies of equipotentiality and mass action (S = start box; F = food).

procedures was maze learning; Figure 3.12 shows three of the four mazes he used. Maze I was a simple T-maze in which the animal had to make a single left–right choice. Maze II had three possible dead ends, while Maze III had eight.[8] During training, each brain-damaged rat negotiated one of the mazes five times per day, and learning was defined as 10 consecutive errorless trials. The relationship between the extent of cortical damage and performance for each of these mazes can be seen in Lashley's graph (Figure 3.13). For simple mazes such as Maze I, performance was quite good even after large amounts of cortical destruction. With Maze II, the performance deteriorated slightly but was still only marginally affected by the brain lesions. It is only with a more difficult problem, Maze III, that the rat's performance was dramatically affected by the extent of the damage. As the percent of destruction increased, performance declined precipitously. Hence, for simple tasks, the extent of destruction had little effect; but on difficult tasks, performance was directly related to the amount of destruction.

On the basis of his maze studies and similar experiments with other procedures, Lashley reached two related conclusions very similar to the ones arrived at by Flourens nearly a century earlier. First was the principle that Lashley called **equipotentiality**, a term

> used to designate the apparent capacity of any intact part of a functional area to carry out, with or without reduction in efficiency, the functions which are lost by destruction of the whole. This capacity varies from one area to another and with the character of the functions involved. It probably holds only for the association areas and for functions more complex than simple sensitivity or motor coordination. (Lashley, 1929, p. 25)

[8]Maze IV had the same design as Maze III, but with the pattern reversed. In addition, while Mazes I–III were alley mazes (i.e., they had walls), Maze IV was an elevated maze, which required the rat to run on the edges of boards (only 3/16 inch wide) that were placed vertically on a table.

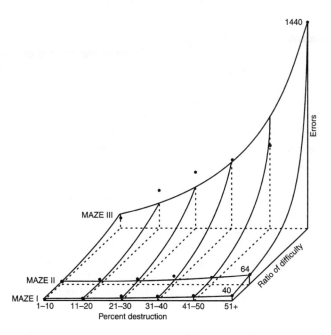

FIGURE 3.13 The effects of maze difficulty and degree of cortical destruction on maze learning. From Lashley (1929).

Equipotentiality—different parts of the cortex had "equal potential" to control learning—was a strong argument against cerebral localization of function, at least within the broad area of learning and in those cortical areas not known to govern specific sensory-motor functions. It was supplemented by the law of **mass action**:

> Equipotentiality is not absolute but is subject to a law of mass action whereby the efficiency of performance of an entire complex function may be reduced in proportion to the extent of brain injury within an area whose parts are not more specialized for one component of the function than for another. (Lashley, 1929, p. 25)

Thus, although the process of learning does not seem to be localized in any specific area of the cortex (equipotentiality), learning efficiency is proportional to the amount of cortical destruction (mass action).

The principles of equipotentiality and mass action were Lashley's key findings, but he was also interested in the general process of maze learning. He was well aware of the maze research of his former colleague John Watson, for example, and disagreed with Watson's belief that maze learning involved the kinesthetic sense and the conditioning of a chain of specific motor responses (Watson's ideas about maze learning are elaborated in Chapter 10). Lashley argued that Watson's model could not account for the strange behavior of those animals with lesions affecting their motor movements. They could still make it through the maze, even if their motor movements were considerably altered:

> One drags himself through with his forepaws; another falls at every step but gets through by a series of lunges; a third rolls over completely in making each turn, yet manages to avoid rolling into a cul-de-sac and makes an errorless run.... If the customary sequence of movements employed in reaching the food is rendered impossible, another set, not previously used in the habit, and constituting an entirely different pattern, may be directly and efficiently substituted without any random activity. (Lashley, 1929, p. 136)

Lashley's conclusions about how the rat learned the maze were similar to those soon to be drawn by the neobehaviorist Edward Tolman (Chapter 11), who argued that rats developed an overall "cognitive map" of the maze and were thus aware of the general direction of the goal. When describing such maps, Tolman (1948, p. 203) referred specifically to Lashley's work for support. Although Lashley did not use the term *map*, he clearly had the concept of directionality in mind when planning the following variation with Maze III. When he removed the mesh cover normally on top of the maze, a few of Lashley's rats (5 out of 20 tested) climbed on top of the maze and went straight across the top of it to the point where the goal was located. Lashley noted that "the behavior of the 5 that followed the direct course to the food suggested that they were perfectly oriented with respect to its direction, although they had never before reached it save by the indirect path of the maze" (Lashley, 1929, p. 137).

Lashley's sophisticated research on the relationship between brain and behavior was a natural culmination of the developments in nervous system physiology that occurred in the 19th century and a link to the physiological psychology of the 20th century. We are now a bit ahead of the story, however, and must return to the 19th century to examine how psychology emerged as a "new science," especially in Germany (Chapter 4), and how it was influenced by the theory of evolution, the 19th century's most important intellectual event (Chapter 5). As you are beginning to discover, psychology in America has deep roots.

IN PERSPECTIVE: THE NERVOUS SYSTEM AND BEHAVIOR

During the 19th century, scientists made exciting discoveries about the nature of the brain and the nervous system. At the start of the century, reflexes were generally understood (at least the fact that they could operate without requiring the brain), thanks to the work of Robert Whytt and others. But there was no understanding of how nerves actually worked, the concept of a "neuron" did not exist, and the most sophisticated notion about brain function was an emerging phrenological theory. Within 100 years, dramatic changes had occurred. Sensory and motor nerves were found to be distinct; neurons themselves had been identified and even seen, thanks to new staining techniques; the concept of a synapse was coming to be accepted; the physiology of nervous system function was starting to be understood; and knowledge of brain function had gone far beyond phrenology and identified areas responsible for language comprehension and production as well as areas responsible for various sensory and motor functions. A remarkable century indeed.

In the last 30 years of the 19th century, as you are about to discover, several scientists who had been studying the physiology of the nervous system began to think that the scientific methods they were using could be applied to questions that were distinctly psychological in nature. Could science shed light on how we perceive the world? On how we come to understand things? On the very nature of human conscious experience? One such person was Wilhelm Wundt, who served an important apprenticeship with the 19th century's most important physiologist, Hermann Helmholtz. By the early 1870s, Wundt was thinking that it was time for a brand new science—the science of psychology. This remarkable German is the central figure in the next chapter.

SUMMARY

Heroic Science in the Age of Enlightenment

• The Enlightenment was a period during the 18th and 19th centuries when great faith existed in the ability of science and human reason to produce truthful knowledge about the natural world. Scientists were heroes, considered to be objective and value free, and Newton was the prime exemplar. Science was thought to lead inevitably to progress through technological innovation. In this context, the belief that psychology could become scientific began to take hold.

Functioning of the Nervous System

• From the time of Descartes, scientists had been interested in the nature of the simple reflex. In the 18th century, Whytt completed the first systematic studies, showing conclusively that the spinal cord was sufficient for reflexes to occur. Whytt also pointed out that stimulus–response connections could develop through habit, an idea similar to modern behaviorist accounts of conditioning.

• When Magendie severed the posterior root of a dog's spinal cord, the affected area could move but was insensitive to stimulation. When the anterior root was severed, no movement occurred. Magendie concluded that the posterior root controlled sensation, while the anterior root controlled motor movements. Bell made similar observations, but was not as systematic as Magendie. The distinction between the functions of the two roots is now known as the Bell-Magendie law.

• According to Müller's doctrine of the specific energies of nerves, (a) we are directly aware of our nervous systems, not the world; and (b) each of the basic sensory systems has nerve fibers designed for that specific sense.

• Helmholtz was opposed to vitalism and fought it through his doctrine of conservation of energy and by measuring the speed of the neural impulse. He was without peer as an expert on visual and auditory perception. He was known for the trichromatic theory of color vision, the resonance theory of audition, and his empiricist approach to perception, which emphasized unconscious inference.

Localization of Brain Function

• Phrenology, developed by Gall and promoted by Spurzheim, was the first serious theory of localization of brain function. Phrenologists believed that different parts of the brain served different faculties, that the portion of brain allocated to a faculty was proportional to the strength of the faculty, and that faculties and their strengths could be determined by measuring skull shape.

• Because it relied too heavily on anecdotal evidence and faulty logic, phrenology lost scientific credibility. It remained popular with the general public, however, being consistent with the American ideals of individuality, self-improvement, and the value of practical application.

• By developing the ablation method, Flourens was able to disprove phrenological doctrine while at the same time showing that the cortex operates as an integrated system.

• Evidence for localization came from clinical studies, in which those suffering from various forms of brain disease or damage were studied. The Phineas Gage case illustrated the effects of severe frontal lobe damage on judgment and personality. Broca's study of "Tan," who suffered from motor aphasia, showed that the ability to produce articulate speech depended on a fairly circumscribed area of the left frontal cortex.

• By developing the procedure of electrically stimulating the surface of the cortex, Fritsch and Hitzig in Germany and Ferrier in Scotland began to map the functions of the surface of the brain with a "scientific phrenology."

Early 20th-Century Studies of the Nervous System and Behavior

• The identification of neurons as the basic units of the nervous system was made by Golgi, who thought they were physically connected to each other, and Ramón y Cajal, who thought they were physically separate from each other. Cajal's theory hinted at the presence of synapses.

• Ramón y Cajal's theory was verified by Sherrington, who is credited with naming the synapse and demonstrating its existence in his research on spinal reflexes and through the phenomena of temporal and spatial summation.

• Lashley's research on the brain and learning showed that maze learning was not localized in any particular area of the cortex. Rather, the cortex operated as a system and was characterized by equipotentiality and mass action.

STUDY QUESTIONS

1. What was the Enlightenment attitude toward science, and how did this influence psychology's history?

2. Robert Whytt was able to demonstrate that reflexes required a spinal cord but not a brain. What was the research that led him to this conclusion?

3. What is the Bell-Magendie law? Explain why it probably should be called the Magendie law.

4. What was the vitalism–materialism issue, and how did Helmholtz provide support for the latter?

5. How did Helmholtz measure the speed of neural impulses, and what was the significance of this work?

6. Compare the color vision theories of Helmholtz and Hering.

7. According to Helmholtz, what is the "problem of perception?" Explain how his concept of unconscious inference was congenial to British empiricist thinking.

8. Describe the essential principles of phrenology, and explain why it eventually failed as science.

9. Explain why phrenology was highly popular in America. Why would the Spurzheim version be more popular with Americans than the Gall version?

10. Describe the method of ablation and how Flourens used it to assess phrenology.

11. Show how the two varieties of the clinical method for studying the brain are illustrated by (a) Phineas Gage and (b) Tan.

12. How did Broca establish that Tan had relatively normal mental capacity? What did Broca conclude on the basis of his postmortem examination of Tan?

13. Describe the importance of the late 19th-century research that came to be known as scientific phrenology.

14. What was neuron theory, and what were the two versions proposed by the cowinners of the 1906 Nobel Prize for medicine?

15. Describe the work of Sherrington that led to the idea of the synapse.

16. Describe Lashley's research, list his two principles, and relate the work to that of Flourens.

FOR FURTHER READING

BAKAN, D. (1966). The influence of phrenology on American psychology. *Journal of the History of the Behavioral Sciences*, *2*, 200–220.

A close analysis of the development of phrenology, its rejection by the scientific community, and its popularity with the American public; shows how phrenology fit in with the temperament of progressivism and was an early example of the approach to psychology that emphasizes individual differences.

BRUCE, D. B. (1986). Lashley's shift from bacteriology to neuropsychology, 1910–1917, and the influence of Jennings, Watson, and Franz. *Journal of the History of the Behavioral Sciences*, *22*, 27–44.

A description of Lashley's formative years and how his eventual self-identification as a physiological psychologist was affected by his doctoral studies with Jennings, his collaboration with Watson, and his postdoctoral work with Franz.

FINGER, S. (2000). *Minds behind the brain: A history of the pioneers and their discoveries.* New York: Oxford University Press.

Using a biographical approach, Finger chronicles the life and work of the major pioneers in the study of the brain, starting with the ancient Egyptians, continuing with many of the scientists featured in this chapter (e.g., Gall, Broca, Ferrier, Sherrington); includes more than 100 photos and drawings.

MACMILLAN, M. B. (1986). A wonderful journey through skull and brain: The travels of Mr. Gage's tamping iron. *Brain and Cognition*, *5*, 67–107.

Despite the odd title, this scholarly and detailed account of the case of Phineas Gage includes a description of his medical treatment by Harlow and an analysis of how the case bears on the localization issue.

RAMÓN Y CAJAL, S. (1999). *Advice for a young investigator.* (N. Swanson & L. W. Swanson, Trans.). Cambridge, MA: MIT Press.

A translation of a brief book by Ramón y Cajal that, in the guise of offering advice for budding scientists, reveals the author's depth of thinking on philosophy of science issues and his passion for science.

CHAPTER 4

WUNDT AND GERMAN PSYCHOLOGY

The book which I here present to the public is an attempt to mark out a new domain of science.

—Wilhelm Wundt, 1874

PREVIEW AND CHAPTER OBJECTIVES

Chapters 2 and 3 describe the context out of which modern psychology began to emerge in the 19th century. Philosophers, interested in the same fundamental questions about the human mind and behavior that occupy psychologists today, began to speculate about the need to examine these issues scientifically. At least one 19th-century British philosopher, John Stuart Mill, even proposed the development of a scientific approach to psychology. Meanwhile, European scientists made great strides in furthering our understanding of the physiology of the nervous system and, in particular, of the brain. This chapter examines how this experimental physiology combined with philosophical inquiry to create a new experimental psychology in Germany in the late 19th century. The chapter opens with a brief discussion of some aspects of German education that made it attractive to American students and then continues with a look at how Gustav Fechner's psychophysics provided a standardized set of methods for studying sensory thresholds. The creation of the "New Psychology" and its first laboratory by Leipzig's Wilhelm Wundt forms the focus of the middle of the chapter. The chapter ends with consideration of three other important German researchers, Hermann Ebbinghaus, G. E. Müller, and Oswald Külpe. After you finish this chapter, you should be able to:

■ Describe the philosophy of education in Germany that facilitated the development of the sciences, including psychology

■ Describe the early history of psychophysics, through the work of Weber

■ Describe the methods of psychophysics developed by Fechner, and how his work related to the philosophical position of materialism

■ Explain why Wundt, not Fechner, is considered the founder of modern psychology

■ Describe Wundt's vision for his New Psychology, distinguishing between his laboratory and his nonlaboratory approaches to psychology

■ Describe the kinds of research typically completed in Wundt's laboratory at Leipzig

■ Describe the logic of the complication experiment, and explain why it was valued so highly

■ Compare the traditional description of Wundt and his work with more recent revisions, and explain why the discrepancies occurred

■ Describe the methods developed by Hermann Ebbinghaus to study memory, his findings, and the importance of his research

■ Describe the contributions to early experimental psychology made by G. E. Müller, and contrast his approach to memory with that of Ebbinghaus

■ Describe the contributions of Oswald Külpe and his students at Würzburg, especially their elaboration of the concept of introspection

AN EDUCATION IN GERMANY

American students have always looked to European universities as a way to further their educations. Even today, a semester abroad is a valued experience. In the 19th century, Germany was an especially attractive location for young scholars; it has been estimated that in the 100-year span beginning in 1820, at least 9,000 American students enrolled in one German university or another (Sahakian, 1975), usually to study medicine or one of the sciences. By the end of that century, they were going there to study psychology.

One reason for the popularity of German universities was mere quantity. Between the time of the 1815 Congress of Vienna and the unification of Germany under Bismarck in 1871, Germany did not exist as a "country," but was a loosely organized federation of 38 autonomous "principalities" (e.g., Bavaria, Hanover, Saxony; Palmer, 1964). Each ministate wanted to keep up with its neighbors, of course, and one means of accomplishing this goal was to have its own university. Hence, universities proliferated throughout the federation, although some of them were little more than a building with some classrooms and a few professors. Several gained international stature, however, and drew students from all over Europe as well as from America.

Circumstances in 19th-century Germany were especially conducive to the development of a new and more scientific approach to psychology. Beginning in the middle of the century, and originating at the University of Berlin, German universities developed a distinctive philosophy of education known as *Wissenschaft*. The term roughly translates as "scientific," and the philosophy encouraged scholars to take a scientific approach to the examination of nature. In addition, an academic culture developed that established academic freedom for professors to pursue their research interests without fear of administrative or political censure. Students were free to wander from one university to another, and earning a degree resulted more from passing special exams and defending a research thesis than from completing a specific curriculum.

For the professors who would create a new scientific psychology, many of whom you will meet in this chapter, the timing was perfect. The success of the physiologists (Chapter 3) reinforced the *Wissenschaft* emphasis on a research-based atmosphere and contributed directly to the growth of the new experimental approach to psychology throughout Germany, especially at Leipzig. As Blumenthal (1980) pointed out, the methods being developed by the physiologists "involving measurement, replicability, public data, and controlled tests" (p. 29) were being applied to the study of the nervous system, but they might just as well be applied to other aspects of human behavior. Gradually, the term *physiological* in German came to mean "experimental." When Wilhelm Wundt referred to the new psychology as a "physiological psychology," he meant it in this broader sense of psychology being a discipline based on experimental methodology. He used the term *physiological* to refer to the fact that most of the methods in this new laboratory approach to psychology derived from the techniques first developed by the 19th-century physiologists (Greenwood, 2003).

FIGURE 4.1 Map of Germany, showing locations of the universities relevant for psychology's history.

For the American student of the 1880s who desired to learn about this new field of study firsthand, several choices were available (e.g., Göttingen, Heidelberg, Berlin; see map in Figure 4.1). Because Wundt's laboratory was well equipped and was the first to appear, traveling to Leipzig became fashionable. During Wundt's tenure, approximately three dozen Americans completed doctorates under his supervision, and a number of others at least sampled the Leipzig environment (Benjamin, Durkin, Link, Vestal, & Accord, 1992). Before we consider Wundt and his influence on the development of experimental psychology, however, some important preliminaries are in order.

ON THE THRESHOLD OF EXPERIMENTAL PSYCHOLOGY: PSYCHOPHYSICS

A strong case can be made that scientific research on psychological topics began as a natural extension of the physiological research being done in the 19th century. Later in this chapter, you will encounter one example of this in the connection between Helmholtz's physiological studies of nerve impulse speed and the psychological method of reaction time. In this section, we examine an association between physiological research on sensory processes and the development of **psychophysics**, the study of the relationship between the perception of a stimulus event ("psycho") and the physical dimensions of the stimulus being perceived ("physics"). Psychophysics originated in the sensory research of Ernst Weber and became clearly defined with the enigmatic Gustav Fechner.

Ernst Weber (1795–1878)

Weber spent most of his academic career at the University of Leipzig, first as a student and then as a professor of anatomy and physiology from 1821 until his retirement in 1871. In the 1820s physiologists were beginning to learn a great deal about vision and hearing, but little was known of the other senses. Weber set out to correct the imbalance by becoming the leading authority on the tactile senses (Dorn, 1972). He made two major contributions: mapping the relative sensitivity of various locations on the skin, and demonstrating a mathematical relationship between the psychological and the physical that would later be known as Weber's law.

Two-Point Thresholds   To examine tactile sensitivity, Weber used a technique in which he touched the skin's surface with a simple device resembling a two-point drawing compass. The distance between the points could be varied, and the blindfolded observer's task was to judge whether one or two points were being felt. For any specific area of the skin, there exists a **two-point threshold**—the point where the perception changes from feeling "one" point to feeling "two." For skin areas of great sensitivity, the thumb for instance, Weber found the threshold to be quite small. That is, the points didn't have to be very far apart before being noticed as two distinct points rather than one. On the other hand, for areas of less sensitivity—the upper arm, for instance—the points would have to be placed farther apart before they were perceived as being two separate ones. Figure 4.2 shows a series of

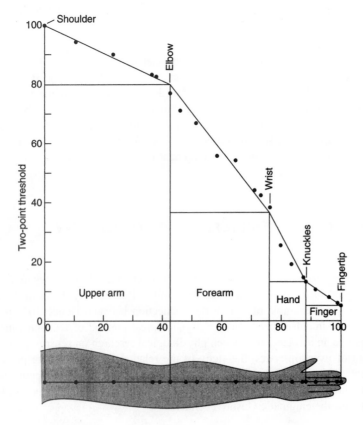

FIGURE 4.2 Two-point thresholds for various locations between shoulder and fingertip. From Boring (1942).

two-point thresholds from shoulder to fingertip, taken from a later study by Karl von Vierordt (cited in Boring, 1942, p. 478).

Weber's Law   Weber's second contribution derived from his interest in the "muscle sense," what we would today call kinesthesis. He wanted to know how important this sense was for making judgments about the comparative weights of objects (Heidbreder, 1933). Picture two tasks: (a) Your hand is resting on a table, and first one and then another weighted cylinder is placed in your palm. Your task is to judge which cylinder is heavier. (b) The two cylinders are on the table, and this time you lift each one before making the same judgment. In performing such an experiment, Weber found that he and other observers could make finer discriminations when they lifted the weights than when the weights were just placed in the hand—that is, lifting brings the muscle sense into play to a greater extent. More important for the history of psychology, Weber also discovered that the ability to discriminate between two weights did not depend on the absolute difference between them in weight, but on a proportional relationship that became known as Weber's law.

In his weight-lifting experiments, Weber was dealing with thresholds again. For example, if observers could not distinguish between 30 and 31 grams, and between 30 and 32 grams (they judge them to be the same weight), but *could* distinguish between 30 and 33 grams, then clearly some kind of threshold had been passed at 33 grams. Weber referred to the discrimination between 30 and 33 grams as a "just noticeable difference" or **jnd**. He discovered that the jnd depended not on the absolute size of the difference between the weights, but on the relationship between this jnd and the smaller of the two weights (called the "standard stimulus," or S). As the standard stimulus became heavier, a greater difference between it and the comparison weight was necessary before the difference was noticed. That is, **Weber's law** was this: $jnd/S = k$. So observers would notice a difference between 30 and 33 grams, but not between 60 and 63 grams. If the standard stimulus is 60 grams instead of 30, no difference can be detected until the second weight is at least 66 grams ($3/30 = 6/60$). Similarly, if S = 90 grams, the jnd will be 9 grams. Hence, the jnd was proportional to the size of S.

The importance of Weber's law is threefold. First, as with the two-point threshold research, Weber was subjecting mental events (sensations) to measurement and mathematical formulation. This would eventually make psychophysics a key element of Wilhelm Wundt's new psychology, which claimed to be a science. Science demands objective measurement, and threshold research seemed to fit the bill. Second, Weber showed that there was not a one-to-one relationship between changes in the physical world and the psychological experience of those changes. Increasing a weight by 3 grams does not always produce the same sensation. Sometimes differences are perceived (if S = 30), sometimes not (if S = 60). Consequently, understanding how the mind organizes its experiences requires knowing more than just the physical dimensions of the stimuli we are exposed to; it also requires an attempt to determine how the mind interprets those physical stimuli. Third, Weber's law showed that mental and physical events could be related mathematically. That insight would be developed more fully by another Leipzig scientist.

Gustav Fechner (1801–1889)

Weber's goal as a physiologist was to understand the tactile and muscle senses, and to do so he used methods that would eventually be known as psychophysical. His younger

Leipzig colleague Gustav Fechner (Figure 4.3) had an even more ambitious goal, however. Fechner was obsessed with the idea of resolving the ageless mind–body problem in a way that would defeat materialism, which he considered nothing short of evil, and he thought that psychophysics was the way to do it. A case can be made for calling Fechner the first experimental psychologist, even though he was trained as a physician, made his reputation as a physicist, and, when he was in the midst of his pioneering research in psychophysics, thought of himself as a philosopher.

Fechner was born in a Lutheran parsonage in southern Germany in 1801; he was a precocious child, familiar with Latin by age 5. At 16 he entered the University of Leipzig to study medicine, and his education included a dose of physiology with Weber. Though Fechner earned an MD in 1822, he never practiced medicine. In the 1820s, his interests centered on math and physics; during this time, he lectured in these areas (without pay), earning a living by translating physics and chemistry texts from French to German. He also made original research contributions in the new physics of electricity.[1] His research was notable enough to earn him a position at Leipzig as professor of physics in 1834, the same year that Weber published his research on the sensation of touch.

Fechner's interests in science broadened in the 1830s to include the study of visual afterimages, the kind that occurs after a bright light is flashed on and off. He discovered a relationship between the brightness of the light and the strength of the afterimage, which led him to consider the quality of afterimages resulting from a quick glance at the brightest of all lights, the sun. Quick glances become longer glances and, even though he wore filters to reduce the effects of looking at the sun, Fechner damaged his eyesight severely. The problem was serious enough to force him to resign his professorship in 1839 and accept a disability pension from the university.

Long before the afterimage episode, Fechner suffered from headaches and an occasional inability to control his thoughts, but the blindness triggered a descent into neurosis that lasted several years (Balance & Bringmann, 1987). Fechner became an invalid, forced to spend long periods of time in total darkness and plagued by a variety of anxiety, depressive, and somatic symptoms. His ascent to normality began in 1842 and was complete by the mid-1840s. It was accomplished largely through his efforts at regaining control over his life, but was facilitated by a steady improvement in his vision. After recovering, he turned his attention to philosophical matters and in 1851 was reappointed to the Leipzig faculty. During this period, he became immersed in the question of the relationship of mind to body and consumed with the idea of defeating materialism. As you recall from the last chapter, materialism, the belief that all events have causes that can be traced to physical and chemical changes, was favored by most of the younger physiologists of the day (e.g., Helmholtz).

Fechner referred to materialism as the *Nachtansicht*, or "night view," and he hoped to replace it with a contrasting *Tagesansicht*, or "day view." This day view derived from an idealism movement then popular in German philosophy, which held that the universe as a

---

[1] Fechner's research on electricity reveals an interesting connection with his father, a Lutheran minister whose faith extended into the realm of science. The elder Fechner was aware of the famous electricity experiments of Benjamin Franklin, and of Franklin's invention of the lightning rod in 1787. Knowing that church steeples were favorite targets of lightning bolts, he prudently installed one of Franklin's devices on his church steeple. Members of the church felt that their pastor was not showing much faith in God's ability to protect the church, but Pastor Fechner commented that the laws of physics also had to be considered (Boring, 1950). Pastor Fechner died when his son was only 5, but young Gustav apparently inherited his father's love of and respect for science.

FIGURE 4.3 Gustav Fechner.

whole had a form of consciousness to it that went beyond the individual consciousnesses of the organisms within it. Upon death, one's personal consciousness merged with this cosmic consciousness. For Fechner, this meant that although mind and body could be considered two aspects of the same fundamental reality, the mind was the primary and ultimate feature of that reality. In searching for a way to conceptualize the exact mind–body relationship, he created psychophysics. He later claimed that he achieved the insight suddenly, upon waking on the morning of October 22, 1850.[2] It occurred to him that mind and body could be united harmoniously and with mathematical precision by measuring psychological sensations and the physical stimuli that produced the sensations. The resulting field of psychophysics he defined as "an exact theory about the functional relationships between body and soul and between the bodily, mental, somatic, and psychological world" (quoted in Meischner-Metge & Meischner, 1997, p. 102). Fechner's insight triggered a decade of intense work on sensory thresholds, resulting in the publication in 1860 of the *Elements of Psychophysics*, often considered the first book of experimental psychology.

Fechner's Elements of Psychophysics Fechner was aware of Weber's research on thresholds, but did not realize its significance until after his insight of 1850. The breakthrough for Fechner was the conviction that sensations could be subjected to exact measurement by assuming that jnd's were subjectively equal in magnitude. Thus weights of 30 and 33 grams are just noticeably different, as are weights of 60 and 66 grams. The differences in weight between the two pairs of stimuli are 3 and 6 grams, respectively. Psychologically, however,

[2]If you want to impress your professor, send him or her a "Happy Fechner Day" card on October 22. To this day, experimental psychologists, especially those who study sensation and perception, take some time out on that day to raise a glass in honor of Fechner's insight, and modern psychophysicists plan an annual conference around the date.

the difference between 30 and 33 *feels* the same as (i.e., is subjectively equal to) the difference between 60 and 66, according to Fechner.

By assuming that jnd's could be the unit of psychological measurement, Fechner was able to conceive of a scale that began at the point where sensation was first noticed. This point he called the **absolute threshold**. As stimulus intensity increases above this threshold, the person eventually experiences a just noticeable difference, then another, and so on. These jnd's above the absolute threshold are **difference thresholds**. Consider the familiar example of a light with a dimmer switch. With the light completely off, there is of course no stimulation and no sensation of light. As the dimmer switch is slowly turned, the zero sensation continues briefly, but soon we just barely notice the first glimmerings of light. This is the absolute threshold. If the dimmer switch continues to be turned, a point is reached where the light is now just noticeably brighter than a second ago. This is a difference threshold. Difference thresholds can also be determined by examining pairs of lights.

Fechner's assumption of equal jnd's was challenged almost immediately, and the mathematical relationship he developed was shown to be true only under limited circumstances. No matter. The enduring legacy of his *Elements of Psychophysics* was his systematization of the methods used to establish thresholds, which are still in use both in the laboratory and in such applications as vision and hearing tests. These are known today as the methods of limits, constant stimuli, and adjustment.[3] Consider them in the context of a hearing test designed to establish absolute thresholds. In the **Method of Limits**, a stimulus is presented that is well above threshold and then gradually reduced in intensity until the subject reports that it can no longer be heard. This is called a *descending trial*, and it is followed by an *ascending trial*, in which the stimulus is first presented below threshold and then increased until the subject hears it for the first time. Descending and ascending trials are alternated many times, and the threshold is calculated as an average of all trials. In the **Method of Constant Stimuli**, sounds of varying intensities are presented in a random order and the subject's task is to indicate whether or not they are heard. This method solves a problem with the method of limits, which is a tendency for the listener to anticipate the place where the threshold lies. In the **Method of Adjustment**, the subject directly varies the intensity of the stimulus until it seems to be at threshold. Ascending and descending trials can be used. Of the three techniques, a study using the method of adjustment takes the least amount of time, but is the least accurate; the method of constant stimuli is the most accurate, but takes the longest time (Goldstein, 1996). In an actual hearing test, the method of limits with descending trials is normally used; "catch trials" are inserted to prevent subjects from signaling ("I hear it") when there is in fact no stimulus presented.

Boring (1963b) referred to Fechner as the "inadvertent founder of psychophysics." He believed that Fechner's main purpose was philosophical—to establish his day view while defeating materialism (the night view). Unfortunately for Fechner, that goal was not reached and the philosophical implications of his work were largely ignored. Fortunately for psychology, though, Fechner's efforts resulted in the creation of a research program and a set of methods that enabled others to see what Fechner did not—that psychological phenomena could be subjected to scientific methodology. By inadvertently creating psychophysics in 1860, Fechner paved the way for another German physiologist, Wilhelm Wundt, to proclaim a New Psychology a few years later.

---

[3]Fechner referred to them as the methods of just noticeable differences, right and wrong cases, and average error, respectively.

WUNDT ESTABLISHES A NEW PSYCHOLOGY AT LEIPZIG

The brief quote that opens this chapter comes from the preface of the epoch-making two-volume *Principles of Physiological Psychology*, published in 1873–1874. It was written by the German most often described as the "founder" of experimental psychology, Wilhelm Wundt. To claim, as Wundt did, that one is making an "attempt to mark out a new domain of science" is the kind of statement that separates founders from their contemporaries. Clearly, Fechner's work on psychophysics entitles him to a claim as the first experimental psychologist. We've seen, however, that Fechner had other, more philosophical, purposes. Thus, as Boring (1950) pointed out, founders are promoters. They might not be the first to accomplish something, but they are the first to proclaim loudly that their accomplishment breaks dramatically new ground. They make important scientific contributions, but they also have a talent for propaganda. Wundt had that talent.

Wilhelm Wundt (1832–1920): Creating a New Science

Experimental psychology's founder had a childhood of modest accomplishment. Marginal performance characterized his early school years, and it wasn't until his late teens that he began to show any interest in education. Despite a dismal academic record, family connections enabled him to begin medical studies at the University of Tübingen at the age of 19; after a year he switched to Heidelberg, where he finally began to show promise. By 1855, he had earned an MD from the University of Heidelberg and had finished first on a certifying exam (Bringmann, Balance, & Evans, 1975).

The Heidelberg years also saw the blossoming of Wundt's interests in science. The famous chemist Robert Bunsen (inventor of the Bunsen burner) made a lasting impression: When Wundt eventually became a professor himself, he copied Bunsen's technique of illustrating points in class through the use of visual displays and demonstrations. Bunsen also inspired Wundt's first independent research project, an examination of the effects of restricting salt input on the chemical composition of his urine. Wundt also conducted an experiment on the touch sensitivity of hysteric patients, using Weber's two-point threshold technique; this study served as his MD dissertation research.

Following completion of his MD in November of 1855, Wundt practiced medicine for a brief 6 months as a clinical assistant at Heidelberg's university hospital, but he was already beginning to think that a life of research was more appealing than a life of writing prescriptions and setting bones. He spent a semester in Berlin studying experimental physiology with the great Johannes Müller (Chapter 3), resolving to become a professor of physiology upon his return to Heidelberg. In February 1857 he was given a position of *Privatdozent*, which in the German system meant that he was entitled to offer courses but that his salary depended on student fees. Wundt's first course attracted only four students; and near the completion of the course he fell seriously ill, probably with tuberculosis (Bringmann, Bringmann, & Balance, 1980). After a yearlong recovery period, he applied for an opening as the assistant in the laboratory of the esteemed Hermann Helmholtz (Chapter 3), who had just begun his tenure at Heidelberg. Wundt got the job, a major boost for his career.

Wundt worked in Helmholtz's lab for 6 years (1858 to 1864), but he did much more with his time than just run the laboratory. He continued to offer courses as *Privatdozent*, and he began writing. In addition to several papers, Wundt published two important books that marked him as an emerging experimental psychologist. *Contributions to a Theory of Sensory Perception* appeared in 1862, followed a year later by *Lectures on Human and Animal Psychology*. The first book is noteworthy because it marks the first time that Wundt called for an explicitly experimental approach to basic psychological questions. Thus he was thinking about the possibility that psychology could be a science well before his famous pronouncement of 1873–1874. The second book repeated the call and described some of the early research in psychophysics and reaction time. Two full books in a short period of time was just the beginning of what became a remarkably prodigious output. Boring (1950) estimated that Wundt published 53,735 pages in his lifetime, for an average of 2.2 pages per day.

Wundt left Helmholtz's laboratory in 1864 but remained at Heidelberg for another decade, setting up a private laboratory and earning a living through teaching fees and book royalties. In 1871 his efforts were rewarded by the university, which appointed him to the rank of Extraordinary Professor (similar to the associate professor level in American universities). This meant that for the first time in his life, Wundt had full faculty status and a salary that was not tied to student enrollment. Nearing the age of 40, he was finally secure enough to marry his fiancée of many years. During this time he wrote his famous two-volume *Principles of Physiological Psychology* (1873–1874/1910), which included this chapter's opening quote in its Preface. The book, which eventually went through six editions, earned him a professorship in "inductive philosophy" at the University of Zurich (academic year 1874–1875). And then, after just a year in Switzerland, Wundt was offered a similar position at the more prestigious University of Leipzig, which he accepted immediately. There he remained until his retirement in 1917. He died three years later.

We tend to associate Wundt only with his Leipzig years, but it is important to realize that when he arrived there in 1875, he was already in his mid-forties and had been an active scientist at Heidelberg for 17 years. He had already written three important books and numerous papers, more than most professors produce in a lifetime. Furthermore, he had announced that at least some aspects of psychology could become scientific, and he had set out a plan for establishing what quickly came to be called the New Psychology. Thus he had accomplished what would be a life's work for many. Yet Wundt still had more than 40 highly productive years left in him during his time at Leipzig.

During his years at Heidelberg, Wundt had accumulated a private collection of laboratory apparatus, both for his own research and for demonstrating various phenomena during his lectures (in the spirit of his old chemistry professor, Robert Bunsen). Soon after his arrival at Leipzig, the university gave him some space to store the equipment. This modest space, a room with approximately 400 square feet, eventually became experimental psychology's first laboratory and the model for dozens of imitators. Wundt used the lab for demonstration purposes initially, but by 1879 he and his students were conducting original research in what he now called the *Psychologisches Institut*. Of course, calling 1879 the "official" founding date for experimental psychology's first laboratory is a bit arbitrary—the room and its equipment were there before 1879. The designation is probably another reflection of the pervasive influence of Boring's 1929 history, which includes this sentence: "In 1879, four years after he had come to Leipzig, Wundt founded, as almost every psychologist knows, the first psychological laboratory in the world" (Boring, 1929, p. 318).[4]

---

[4] The identical wording appears on page 323 of the second edition of Boring's book (Boring, 1950).

FIGURE 4.4 An elderly Wilhelm Wundt (center) in his laboratory at Leipzig.

Regardless of when it actually began, Wundt's laboratory quickly became a magnet, attracting curious students from all over Europe and from America. Additional rooms were added over the years, and in 1897 a new and more elaborate laboratory was built to Wundt's specifications. It was destroyed by an Allied bombing raid in 1943. An inside look at the workings of Wundt's laboratory, a glimpse of which can be seen in Figure 4.4, follows shortly. First, however, it is necessary to examine Wundt's vision for his new science.

Wundt's Conception of the New Psychology

The "new domain of science" that Wundt attempted to "mark out" in his *Principles of Physiological Psychology* was a vision first outlined 12 years earlier in his 1862 book on perception. This new psychology called for the scientific examination of human conscious experience, using methods borrowed from experimental physiology and supplemented by new strategies. Today, when we see a book with the label "physiological psychology," we are inclined to think the book will focus on the relationship between biology and behavior. Wundt, however, used the label *physiological* only in referring to the fact that many of the methods for his New Psychology (e.g., reaction time) had been developed in physiology laboratories (Greenwood, 2003). As he put it:

> The introduction of the experimental method into psychology was originally due to the modes of procedure in physiology, especially in the physiology of the sense-organs and the nervous system. For this reason experimental psychology is also commonly called "physiological psychology." (Wundt, 1897, p. 1)

Wundt's new psychology included two major programs: the examination of "immediate" conscious experience using the experimental methods of the laboratory and the study of higher mental processes, using nonlaboratory methods.

Studying Immediate Conscious Experience To understand the contrast that Wundt drew between immediate experience and "mediate" experience, consider a simple example. If you look out the window at a thermometer and it reads 15°F, you are not experiencing the phenomenon of temperature directly. Rather, temperature is being *mediated* by a scientific instrument. On the other hand, if you then step outside without a coat, you have a direct experience of coldness. It is an immediate conscious experience. That is, there is no thermometer standing between you and the weather; you are encountering it firsthand. For Wundt, this immediate conscious experience was to be the subject matter of his laboratory psychology.

Wundt recognized the fundamental problem with studying immediate consciousness. To examine mediate experience objectively is simple. Because the temperature reading is a public event, two or more observers can agree on it; thus, it is a straightforward matter to apply scientific methods. Various aspects of the environment can be manipulated systematically, and the resulting effects on temperature can be assessed with some precision. Describing immediate experience is more difficult, however. How can you be sure that your experience of coldness compares with mine? Here Wundt made a critical distinction between *self-observation* and *internal perception*. The distinction has been blurred over the years, according to Danziger (1980), and both terms have been called **introspection**. Self-observation is the traditional philosophical attempt to analyze life's experiences through introspective reflection. This was unsystematic; and because such observations by definition take place some time after the experienced event has occurred, they rely heavily on faulty memory. Wundt rejected self-observation as nothing better than philosophical speculation. **Internal perception**, on the other hand, was like self-observation but was a much narrower process of responding immediately to precisely controlled stimuli. The problem of memory was reduced by the immediacy of the response and by using observers (Wundt and his students) trained to respond automatically and without bias. Such precision came with a price, however. Internal perception could yield valid scientific data only if its results could be replicated. For Wundt, this meant that laboratory research had to be limited to a narrow range of experiences. In practice, this amounted to basic sensory/perceptual/attentional ones. Such experiences could be controlled by means of sophisticated apparatus used to present stimuli to observers, who in turn would give simple responses to these stimuli. In Wundt's lab, these types of introspective responses were "largely limited to judgments of size, intensity, and duration of physical stimuli, supplemented at times by judgments of their simultaneity and succession" (Danziger, 1980, p. 247). These, of course, are the kinds of judgments made in psychophysics experiments, which comprised a significant portion of the research in Wundt's laboratory. As we will learn, Wundt's conception of introspection as internal perception differed sharply from the "systematic experimental introspection" used by two of his better-known students, Oswald Külpe (this chapter) and Edward B. Titchener (Chapter 7).

Studying Higher Mental Processes Although Wundt believed that laboratory investigation was necessarily limited to the immediate conscious experience of basic mental processes, he also had a broader aim for his psychology. He wished to examine other mental processes such as learning, thinking, language, and the effects of culture, but he believed that such processes could not be studied in the laboratory. Because they were closely tied to an individual's personal history, cultural background, and social environment, these higher mental processes could not be controlled sufficiently to be examined in a laboratory context.

KEY DATE—1879

This year marks the date normally associated with the establishment of Wundt's laboratory of experimental psychology in Leipzig.

These events also occurred that year:

- Thomas Edison patented the electric light
- London established its first telephone exchange
- Ferdinand de Lesseps formed the Panama Canal Company
- In South Africa, England extended its empire by provoking a brief war and eventually defeating the Zulus
- The American novelist Henry James, brother of psychologist William James, published *Daisy Miller*
- In Utica, New York, Frank Woolworth opened a store with no item costing more than 5 cents; it failed almost immediately, leading him to try again in Lancaster, Pennsylvania, this time adding items costing 10 cents, thus creating the 5 and 10-cent Woolworth stores

- Mary Baker Eddy became pastor of the Church of Christ, Scientist, in Boston
- The first Madison Square Garden (there have been four different ones) opened in New York City

These people were born:

- Joseph Stalin, Soviet dictator
- Albert Einstein, German physicist
- Will Rogers, American humorist and social commentator (allegedly, never met a man he didn't like)

These persons died:

- William Lloyd Garrison, American abolitionist, who formed the American Anti-Slavery Society in 1833
- Sir Rowland Hill, knighted in England for inventing the first adhesive postage stamp in 1837

Instead, they could be studied only through inductive observational techniques, cross-cultural comparisons, historical analysis, and case study.

These higher mental processes were a lifelong interest of Wundt's, first outlined in detail in his second major book (*Lectures on Human and Animal Psychology*, 1863/1907). They fully occupied the last two decades of his life; and during this time, he enhanced his reputation as a prodigious writer by publishing the massive 10-volume *Völkerpsychologie* (*volker* translates roughly as a combination of "cultural," "ethnic," "social," and/or "communal"). The books include detailed analyses of language and culture, and they encompass topics that would today be considered under the headings of psycholinguistics, the psychology of religion and myth, social psychology, forensic psychology, and anthropology. There were three volumes on myth and religion, two on language, two on society, and one each on culture and history, law, and art (Blumenthal, 1975).

Wundt, like other thinkers of his time, believed that an implication of evolutionary theory was that cultures could be arranged on a continuum, from "primitive" (e.g., Australian aboriginal) to "advanced" (German, presumably). By studying the social customs, myths, religions, and languages of cultures differing in their level of sophistication, Wundt thought that an understanding of the evolution of human mental processes could be attained (Farr, 1983). He was especially interested in language. Much of what he wrote about language was ignored at the time, only to be rediscovered in the 1950s and 1960s, when psycholinguistics became a key element in the rise of cognitive psychology (Blumenthal, 1975). For example, Wundt distinguished between the idea that was to be conveyed by a sentence, the actual structure of the sentence itself, and the manner in which the listener took the sentence structure and inferred the speaker's meaning from it. The relationship between the idea to be conveyed and the sentence structure is similar to the distinction later made by linguist Noam Chomsky between the deep and surface structures of a grammar, and Wundt's belief that the listener would not recall the actual sentence but the meaning of it is similar to later research on memory for the "gist" of communicated messages.

Inside Wundt's Laboratory

Once Wundt's students began producing original research at Leipzig, the need for a way to publicize the work became apparent. Wundt solved the problem in 1881 by creating the journal *Philosophische Studien* (*Philosophical Studies*). It was the first journal designed to report the results of experimental research in psychology, and Wundt served as editor for its first two decades (1881–1903). The journal became a mouthpiece for the work done by Wundt and his students, so a look at its contents reveals the kind of research done at Leipzig during the last two decades of the 19th century. According to Boring (1950), who examined the 100 or so experimental studies published in the journal during this time, at least half of the research was in the area of sensation and perception. Of the remaining half, reaction time studies were the most popular, followed by studies on attention, feeling, and association.

Sensation and Perception Most of the basic information about sensory systems encountered in today's courses in sensation and perception was known by the turn of the century, and some of the research was carried out in Wundt's laboratory. As mentioned earlier, most of these "internal perception" studies were psychophysical in nature, examining such topics as the abilities to distinguish colors presented to different areas of the retina and tones presented in various combinations of pitch and loudness. In perception, Wundtians studied such topics as positive and negative afterimages, visual contrast, illusions, and the perception of size, depth, and motion (Boring, 1950).

Mental Chronometry When Helmholtz measured the duration of a nerve impulse and found it to be more leisurely than expected (Chapter 3), he provided the impetus for a method that came to be known as **mental chronometry** in Wundt's lab. Today we call it reaction time. Wundt was aware of this research long before he arrived in Leipzig. He became Helmholtz's assistant at Heidelberg shortly after the nerve impulse studies had been carried out, and he became very interested in the problem of measuring mental speed in the 1860s. The problem had also been around for a number of years in the form of a practical difficulty faced by astronomers. The creation of tables for calculating longitude required knowing the precise positions of various stars and planets at specific times of a lunar cycle (Sobel, 1995). Identifying these positions involved a complicated procedure that measured the time taken for a planet to make a "transit" from one side of the crosshair of a telescope lens to the other. Humans were making the judgments, of course. Even though the astronomers were highly trained, their judgments of transit times were inevitably affected by small individual differences in reaction times. To solve the problem, an attempt was made to calibrate one astronomer against another by determining each one's **personal equation**. Thus, if astronomer A was regularly 0.12 second slower than astronomer B, their transit times could be made comparable through a personal equation: A = B + 0.12 second.

The individual who developed the reaction time procedure as it came to be used by the Wundtians was F. C. Donders (1818–1889), a Dutch physiologist. Donders reasoned that if nerve impulses take a measurable amount of time, and if mental activity is composed of nerve impulses, then the times taken by various mental events could be determined with some precision. Assuming that mental events could be combined in an additive fashion, Donders developed the **subtractive method** in the late 1860s. First, he would measure the time taken for a simple reaction, for example, by holding down a telegraph key and then releasing it as soon as possible after perceiving a light. The procedure would then be "complicated" by adding other mental tasks. For instance, the observer might be asked to respond only if a red light came on; if the light was another color, no response was to be made. This "discrimination reaction time" (DRT) was composed of everything involved in simple reaction time (SRT), *plus* the mental event of discriminating between the colors. Thus:

$$DRT = SRT + \text{discrimination time}$$
$$\text{discrimination time} = DRT - SRT$$

Similarly, "choice reaction time" (CRT) involved releasing one key if the light was one color and another key if the light was a second color. In addition to simple reaction time and the time taken to discriminate between the two colors, the observer had to choose which key to release. Thus:

$$CRT = SRT + \text{discrimination time} + \text{choice time}$$
$$\text{choice time} = CRT - (SRT + \text{discrimination time})$$
$$\text{choice time} = CRT - DRT$$

For reasons that are apparent, this procedure was also called the **complication experiment**, and studies using it flourished in Wundt's laboratory, especially in the 1880s. The procedure was eventually discarded, however, when it became clear that the subtractive assumptions underlying the method were simplistic. In the above procedures, for instance, more complicated reactions should always be longer than less complicated ones; in actual experiments, however, this outcome did not always occur. Wundt's student Oswald Külpe (discussed in more detail later) pointed out that complicating the procedure by adding discrimination and/or choice does not simply add elements; rather, it changes the entire psychological experience.

James McKeen Cattell (look ahead to Figure 8.2), perhaps the best known of the American students who studied with Wundt, was an enthusiastic advocate of the reaction time method (Garrett, 1951). An examination of one of his studies (Cattell, 1885/1948a) nicely illustrates the logic of the reaction time method and the close attention to detail needed to carry out such research. In the article, Cattell described some research on simple, discrimination, and choice reaction times that were completed with his German colleague Gustav Berger. The research formed the basis for Berger's doctoral dissertation for Wundt on the effects of stimulus intensity on reaction time (Sokal, 1981a).

In the first experiment, Cattell and Berger gave simple reaction times to lights that varied in intensity. The experimental setup probably looked something like the one in Figure 4.5 (photo taken at Clark University in 1892). As Cattell described it, "The observer sat in the dark, and looked through a telescopic tube at the point where the light was to appear" (1885/1948a, p. 323–325). Cattell and Berger each made 150 reactions for each of 8 intensity levels, finding that reaction time generally was faster as the light brightened. They also found individual differences—Cattell was consistently quicker. Table 4.1 summarizes some

FIGURE 4.5 Reaction time experiment in progress at Clark University, 1892.

TABLE 4.1 The Results of a Complication Experiment

	B[erger]			C[attell]		
	V	III	I	V	III	I
Reaction Time	189	218	273	189	209	303
Reaction with Perception Time	238	293	373	274	328	417
Reaction with Perception and Will Time	287	320	393	356	388	495
Perception Time	49	75	100	85	119	114
Will Time	49	27	20	82	60	78

of their data. Note that there are just two participants in the study, Berger and Cattell. This was common practice in early experimental psychology—very few participants, each person contributing a great deal of data, and no clear distinction between what in later years would be called the *experimenter* and the *subject* or *participant* (Danziger, 1988). Furthermore, data from several participants would not be averaged together. Rather, all data from each subject would be reported, and additional participants served the purpose of replication.

Table 4.1 reports data for three of the eight light intensities (labeled V, III and I), for simple RT (Cattell called it "reaction time"), discrimination RT ("reaction with perception time"), and choice RT ("reaction with perception and will time"). Here is his description of the complication rationale and the data:

> The time is longer when it is necessary to distinguish the colours before the reaction is made. We can determine this time, if instead of always reacting as quickly as possible, we react if it is red, but not at all if it is blue.... We can further let the subject lift his right hand if the light is red, his left hand if it is blue; we then have, besides the time necessary for the simple reaction and for distinguishing the colour, the time it takes to make a choice between two motions. (Cattell, 1885/1948a, p. 325)

As you can see, Cattell used the Donders system to arrive at his "perception" (i.e., discrimination) and "will" (i.e., choice) times. For example, with Cattell as the participant and the stimulus intensity at V:

$$\text{discrimination ("perception") time} = \text{DRT} - \text{SRT}$$
$$= 274 - 189$$
$$= 85 \text{ (i.e., } 0.85 \text{ sec)}$$

$$\text{choice ("will") time} = \text{CRT} - (\text{SRT} + \text{discrimination time})$$
$$= 356 - (189 + 85)$$
$$= 356 - 274$$
$$= 82 \text{ (i.e., } 0.82 \text{ sec)}$$

Like Külpe, Cattell eventually became a critic of the complication experiment while continuing to see the usefulness of reaction time to test various hypotheses about mental processing. This led him to study individual differences in reaction time and such phenomena as recognition times for different letters of the alphabet and reaction times for verbal associations (e.g., Cattell, 1886). Cattell also left an intriguing account of day-to-day life in Wundt's laboratory, some of which is described in the following Close-Up.

CLOSE-UP

AN AMERICAN IN LEIPZIG

In 1886, James McKeen Cattell (1860–1944) became the first American to earn a Leipzig PhD in experimental psychology under Wundt's supervision (Benjamin, Durkin, Link, Vestal, & Accord, 1992). While at Leipzig, he kept a detailed journal and corresponded frequently with his parents in America. These materials were compiled and annotated with great care by historian of science Michael Sokal, who published the letters in *An Education in Psychology: James McKeen Cattell's Journal and Letters from Germany and England, 1880–1888* (Sokal, 1981a). The book is a rich source of information about life in the early years of Wundt's laboratory at Leipzig.

Cattell first went to Leipzig as part of a European tour in 1881–1882. He then spent the 1882–1883 academic year at Johns Hopkins University in Baltimore, studying in the lab created by G. Stanley Hall (Chapter 6). He returned to Leipzig in the fall of 1883 and emerged with his doctorate 3 years later. Here are some of the observations he made about working in Wundt's laboratory.

Most of Cattell's research concerned the problem of reaction time. In a letter to his parents in 1884, he briefly described this research. Like others immersed in basic research that might seem trivial to outsiders, Cattell apparently felt a bit defensive and believed it necessary to convince his parents that his reaction time work had value:

Letter to Parents, 8 October 1884 In [my research] I determine the time required by simple mental processes—how long it takes us to see, hear or feel something—to understand, to will, to think. You may not consider this so very interesting or important. But if we wish to describe the world—which is the end of science—surely an accurate knowledge of our mind is more important than anything else.... [I]f one thinks that knowledge for its own sake is worth the pursuit, then surely a knowledge of mind is best of all. Not only is the mind of man of infinitely more worth and importance than anything else, but on its nature the whole world depends.

As to my special work—it is surely...in itself interesting to know how fast a man thinks—for on this, not on the number of years he lives depends the length of his life. (Sokal, 1981a, p. 125)

Cattell's parents were apparently concerned that their son might overwork himself in the Leipzig lab. To reassure them, Cattell described a typical research day with his colleague, Gustav Berger. Only a portion of it required the kind of focused attention that would be fatiguing, Cattell reported:

Letter to Parents, 26 November 1884 Berger began work with me again this morning. I do not think I shall hurt myself in working, if I keep taking...constant exercise. It is undoubtedly true that making experiments on one's self is trying, but I do not do this continuously. If I spend six hours a day at this work, perhaps two must be given to looking after apparatus, preparing things &c. This is very easy work indeed. Then in two of the other four hours the other man is the subject and my work is not especially difficult. So you see I only spend two hours in work that strains. It were a pity if at twenty-five I could not stand that. (p. 141)

Cattell's observation about the 2 hours set aside for the apparatus illustrates the difficulty of developing a new science. Most of the apparatus had to be either adopted from the physics or physiology lab or invented on the spot. Apparatus maintenance was a constant irritant:

Letter to Parents, 5 January 1885 You have no idea how much one must fuss over apparatus. The trouble is not that one must know physics, but that he must be an original investigator in physics. For example Prof. Wundt thought that when a magnet was made by passing a current around a piece of soft iron, it was made instantaneously. I find with the current he used it takes over a tenth of a second. All the times he measured were that much too long. Now the time required for magnetism to be developed in soft iron has nothing on earth to do with psychology, yet if I had not spent a great deal of time on this subject all my work would have been wrong.... All this, getting the apparatus and running it, is very aggravating when one is in a hurry. (pp. 151–152)

Throughout his career, Cattell never hesitated to speak his mind and was not known for modesty or discretion. In the following comment, made near the end of his time at Leipzig, he made it clear what he thought of Wundt's laboratory.

Letter to Parents, 22 January 1885 I worked in Wundt's laboratory this afternoon probably for the last time.... Wundt's laboratory has a reputation greater than it deserves—the work done is decidedly amateurish. Work has only been done in two departments—the relation of the internal stimulus to the sensation [i.e., psychophysics], and the time of mental process [i.e., reaction time]. The latter is my subject—I started working on it at Baltimore [at Johns Hopkins] before I had read a word written by Wundt—what I did there was decidedly original. I'm quite sure my work is worth more than all done by Wundt & his pupils in this department, and as I have said it is one of the two departments on which they have worked. Mind I do not consider my work of any special importance—I only consider Wundt's of still less. (p. 156)

Rewriting History: The New and Improved Wilhelm Wundt

In Chapter 1, you learned that histories are continually being rewritten in light of new information, new ways of interpreting information, and so on. Wundt's psychology is a perfect illustration. If you had taken a history of psychology course about 40 years ago, you would have learned this about Wundt:

- He founded the first "school" of psychology, called structuralism.

- The main goal of Wundt's structuralist school was to analyze the contents of the mind into its basic structural components or elements, using a highly complex form of *introspection* of mental contents as the chief method.

- He was not really interested in cultural psychology; the 10-volume *Völkerpsychologie* was just a secondary hobby for an old man.

- Wundt's intellectual son was E. B. Titchener, who spread the Wundtian gospel of structuralism in America.

- His model of the mind was similar to that of the British empiricists; that is, he did not believe in the concept of the mind as an active agent, but as the result of the buildup of passive associative experiences.

Today, the only time you read descriptions like this will be in narratives pointing out that each of these points is either a serious distortion or just plain wrong. In the 1970s, historians of psychology began taking a closer look at Wundt (e.g., Blumenthal, 1975; Danziger, 1980; Leahey, 1979), as part of the resurgence of interest in psychology's history prompted by Robert Watson (Chapter 1), and they discovered that the traditional accounts were erroneous. Since that time, histories have begun to include more accurate descriptions of Wundt's life and work. Three questions arise: How did the distortions occur? Why were they not uncovered until the 1970s? What did Wundt really say?

The Source of the Problem Part of the difficulty derives from the fact that Wundt wrote more in his lifetime than most people read in theirs. Also, much of his work is either very difficult to read or has not been translated from German. Hence, there is a tendency for non-German speakers to rely on what others have written about Wundt, rather than on what Wundt said himself. Most psychologists before 1980 learned their history from E. G. Boring, Boring learned most of his from Titchener, and therein lies the root of the problem. As you will learn in Chapter 7, Titchener studied with Wundt for 2 years and earned a Leipzig PhD in 1892. He then spent his entire academic career at Cornell, where he spread the gospel of *structuralism*—his school of thought, not Wundt's. Titchener also translated several of Wundt's books and wrote a long obituary shortly after Wundt's death (Titchener, 1921b). In essence, Titchener took a portion of Wundt's work and exaggerated its importance while downplaying or ignoring other parts of Wundt's work. The distortions were reflected in the way he taught about Wundt and in his translations of Wundt's writings. This was not a deliberate attempt to distort—Titchener was simply emphasizing what was most congenial to his own way of thinking. For example, Titchener's lack of interest in nonexperimental psychology led him to shrug off Wundt's interest in cultural and social psychology, making the remarkable comment in the obituary for his mentor that Wundt's 20-years-in-the-making, 10-volume *Völkerpsychologie* was little more than "a grateful occupation for his old age" (Titchener, 1921b, p. 175) and that "the dominant idea of Wundt's life ... [was] the idea of an experimental psychology" (p. 175).

Boring was Titchener's best known student and psychology's most venerable historian (see Close-Up in Chapter 1). Boring's *A History of Experimental Psychology*, written in 1929 and revised in 1950, was the book that informed several generations of psychologists and until recently provided the model for other history texts. It was dedicated to Titchener (both editions), and the chapter on Wundt contains many of the distortions that originated with Titchener. The *Völkerpsychologie*, for instance, is barely mentioned. As for whether Boring might have probed more deeply and revised his treatment of Wundt in his second edition, "The chapter on Wundt...was republished unchanged in 1950," according to Blumenthal (2001, p. 124).

The Rediscovery of Wundt

For two reasons, Wundt's ideas began to be reexamined in the 1970s. First, as you recall from Chapter 1, during the late 1960s and early 1970s the history of psychology as a discipline gathered new momentum under the leadership of Robert Watson and others. To some extent, new scholarship directed at Wundt's history reflects the increased interest in psychology's history. The second reason is more subtle and provides another justification for the continual rewriting of history. As you will learn in Chapter 14, during the 1960s, cognitive psychology happened. That is, psychologists became increasingly interested in the experimental study of mental processes, a topic that had languished in America between 1930 and 1960 due to the influence of behaviorism. Some scholars versed in the new cognitive research, most notably Arthur Blumenthal and Thomas Leahey, saw connections between the cognitive psychology of the 1960s and the earlier Wundtian psychology. Indeed, some of the cognitive research methods essentially duplicated research completed at Leipzig, even though modern researchers seemed unaware of it. Blumenthal and Leahey began examining Wundt's work in light of the new cognitive psychology, producing papers that showed the connections between the two (Blumenthal, 1975; Leahey, 1979). The broader lesson is that histories can be strongly influenced by the context within which they are written. One effect of modern cognitive psychology was to view Wundt in a new light. In the days of behaviorism's dominance, such a reexamination of Wundt would not have occurred.

The Real Wundt

The traditional but erroneous view of Wundt is that he was a structuralist. Now there is no question that one of Wundt's goals for his laboratory work was to identify the elements of immediate conscious experience. After all, he was originally trained in medicine and physiology and had a natural penchant for classification. Thus his experimental papers include descriptions of the basic elements of consciousness, which he decided were sensations and feelings. Moreover, each of these elements could be further categorized along certain dimensions. Sensations, for instance, were classified according to such dimensions as quality (e.g., different colors), intensity, and duration.

Analysis and classification, however, were only minor aspects of Wundt's overall system, and he was relatively uninterested in them. He was more concerned with the manner in which the mind actively organized its experiences through an act of will. He labeled his system **voluntarism** to reflect the active nature of the mind. A central concept of his voluntaristic system was the phenomenon of **apperception**, a term borrowed from the German philosopher Leibniz (Chapter 2). To apperceive some event is to perceive it with full clarity and have it in the focus of one's attention. As you are reading this page, for example, your full attention and focus (let's hope) is on this sentence and its meaning. It is being apperceived. Other information (e.g., perhaps some music in the background) is in the periphery of your attention—Wundt would say that it is being apprehended, but not apperceived.[5] Thus, at any given time, there is information in the focus of attention and other information in

---

[5]The association–apperception difference was the key component of an important theory proposed by one of Wundt's more famous students, the psychiatrist Emil Kraepelin (1856–1926). Kraepelin devised a classification scheme for mental illness that produced the first clear description of what we call schizophrenia today. For more on Kraepelin and his system for diagnosing mental illness, see the Close-Up in Chapter 12.

the margins. Furthermore, apperception is a process that actively and vigorously organizes information into meaningful wholes. When we see the word *dog,* we do not perceive three separate letters; we perceive a single concept that has meaning for us. Our visual sense might be initially processing meaningless lines and symbols, but our mind creates a meaningful whole. Wundt referred to the apperceptive process as a "creative synthesis."

Wundt's concept of apperception is a far cry from a more passive associationism. Yet Wundt did recognize that some elements of conscious experience do combine as passive associations. As the British associationists said, if you see John and Mary together often enough, you will soon come to think of one when you see the other. This happens automatically because of a passively formed association. On the other hand, apperception is occurring if, when you see John and Mary, you bring them into the focus of your attention and perceive them as a special couple, or perhaps as two people who seem completely ill suited for one another. That is, you are going beyond the information given and perceiving them clearly, distinctly, and meaningfully.

One final point about the historical misperception of Wundt concerns introspection. As described earlier, Wundt restricted verbal reports in the laboratory to simple responses to carefully controlled stimuli (e.g., "object A is heavier than object B"), a process he called *internal perception*. Titchener's approach to self-report, called *systematic experimental introspection*, was much more elaborate (see Chapter 7), involving detailed descriptions of mental experiences after some experimental task had been completed. From these descriptions, inferences would be made about human mental processing. Accounts of introspection based on Boring's history failed to distinguish between the two approaches, assuming that Wundt's strategy for self-report was the same as Titchener's (Danziger, 1980). It wasn't, and Wundt in fact was highly critical of Titchener's version, once writing that the method

> relies either on arbitrary observations that go astray or on a withdrawal to a lonely sitting room where it becomes lost in self-absorption. The unreliability of this method is universally recognized. . . . Clearly, Titchener has himself come under the influence of the deceptions of this method. (quoted in Blumenthal, 2001, p. 125)

The Wundtian Legacy

Because it was his intention to create a new way of conceptualizing psychology, Wundt is justifiably considered the first true experimental psychologist of the modern era. Although it is difficult to identify a single Wundtian among the early American psychologists, he had a strong influence on the origins of American psychology. The Americans who studied with Wundt may not have returned as disciples, and Blumenthal (1980) suggested that most came back with little more than a laboratory floor plan and an equipment list. Nonetheless, they emerged from Leipzig convinced that something new and exciting was in the air, and they wanted to be a part of it. American psychology quickly established its own distinctive and non-Wundtian shape, but much of the motivation for it derived from Wundt's example.

THE NEW PSYCHOLOGY SPREADS

It should not be surprising to learn that Wundt did not hold a monopoly on the New Psychology. As you recall from the opening of the chapter, the *Wissenschaft* environment created an atmosphere conducive to the creation of a scientifically based examination of psychological phenomena. Sure enough, several German·contemporaries of Wundt were actively engaged in exploring this new approach to understanding the human mind. We will examine the work of three investigators: Hermann Ebbinghaus, G. E. Müller, and Oswald Külpe.

Hermann Ebbinghaus (1850–1909): The Experimental Study of Memory

One indirect effect of Fechner's *Elements of Psychophysics* is that it helped launch the experimental study of human memory. This occurred sometime in the mid-1870s, when a young German philosopher named Hermann Ebbinghaus (Figure 4.6) stumbled on an English translation of Fechner's book while browsing in a used bookstore in Paris. Fechner's demonstration that the mind could be subjected to scientific methods inspired Ebbinghaus, who was wrestling with the philosophical problem of the association of ideas at the time.

Not much is known about the formative years of Hermann Ebbinghaus. After finishing a gymnasium education, he studied at several universities and fought briefly for the German side in the Franco-Prussian War in the early 1870s. His academic interests shifted from history to philology (the historical study of language) to philosophy, and he eventually earned a doctorate in the latter from the University of Bonn in 1873. During the mid-1870s he traveled in England and in France, discovered Fechner's *Elements* along the way, and evidently began to think about how to study the manner in which associations were first created in the mind.

As a philosopher, Ebbinghaus was thoroughly familiar with the British empiricist-associationists and their analysis of association processes. As you recall from Chapter 2, they considered association to be analogous to gravity as a force that attracted and bound together ideas. The British philosophers all considered association to be an essential component of the mind's organizational structure, but they argued over the basic laws of association—for

FIGURE 4.6   Hermann Ebbinghaus.

example, is contiguity sufficient to explain associations (Hartley), or are other principles necessary (Hume)? For Ebbinghaus, Fechner's scientific approach to the mind's sensory processes apparently triggered a creative leap. If sensations could be measured, why not other mental processes? Why not association? Sometime during the late 1870s, Ebbinghaus became resolved to study the formation and retention of associations scientifically. By the middle of the next decade, he had produced *Memory: A Contribution to Experimental Psychology* (1885/1964). This brief book (123 pages in a 1964 reprinting) inaugurated a research tradition that continues today and includes results that are still described in textbooks of general psychology. As Ernest Hilgard pointed out in an introduction to the 1964 reprinting, "For the experimental study of learning and memory there is one source that is pre-eminent over all others: this small monograph by Ebbinghaus" (Hilgard, 1964, p. vii).

Ebbinghaus (1885/1964) opened his memory book by considering the various forms of memory and the difficulty of studying the process experimentally. He pointed out that what little was known about memory was known through common sense and from anecdotes about "extreme and especially striking cases" (p. 4). As for more fundamental questions about the exact relationships between our experiences and our memories, however, he wrote that "these and similar questions no one can answer" (p. 5). He also recognized that studying the initial formation of associations required materials that would not be familiar. Ebbinghaus realized that memorizing meaningful materials like poems or prose would be a problem, for these materials already carried with them innumerable meaningful associations that could affect how quickly they could be learned. In one of psychology's more notable acts of creativity, he hit upon the idea of using materials that did not meaningfully relate to each other and were not especially meaningful themselves. That is, he created **nonsense syllables** or CVCs, three-letter units comprised of two consonants with a vowel in the middle. He created about 2,300 of them.

Ebbinghaus recognized that some of the syllables would have meaning (i.e., would sound like words), but he was not overly concerned. Keep in mind that his main interest was in how associations *between* syllables were first formed, not the relative meaningfulness of individual syllables. Individual syllables might have some meaning, but the chances were quite remote that two successive syllables would be meaningfully related to each other. Gundlach (1986) has pointed out that one of Ebbinghaus's phrases was translated as a "series of nonsense syllables"[6] when a better translation might have been "meaningless series of syllables." That Ebbinghaus chose **serial learning** as his memory task is a further indication of his intent to analyze the buildup of associations between elements of a fixed sequence. Serial learning, in which correct recall includes accurately reproducing a set of stimuli in the exact order of their presentation, is well suited for examining associations between a "meaningless series of syllables."

How Ebbinghaus actually hit upon the idea to use nonsense syllables is not clear, but Hilgard's (1964) analysis makes the most sense. Familiar with the mechanistic and atomistic assumptions of British empiricism-associationism, Ebbinghaus would have looked for the simplest possible unit that would still yield a large number of stimuli. Individual letters or numbers were too few, words too meaningful. Syllables of words comprise the simplest pronounceable unit in the language, so they would be a logical choice. The fact that Ebbinghaus called his stimuli nonsense "syllables" suggests that he was deliberately thinking of this reduction to a small functional unit.

---

[6]The phrase appears at the bottom of page 23, in the context of a comparison with memorizing poetry.

Once he had created the stimulus materials, Ebbinghaus (1885/1964) set about creating lists of them and then memorizing the lists. He would read the lists to himself at a constant rate, aided by a metronome set to 150 strokes per minute (he later switched to a ticking watch), and he would consider a list to be learned "when, the initial syllable being given, a series could be recited at the first attempt, without hesitation" (p. 23). He also made "no attempt to connect the nonsense syllables by the invention of special associations of the mnemonotechnik type; learning was carried on solely by the influence of the mere repetitions upon the natural memory" (p. 25).

As you might have suspected, an important feature of this project was that Ebbinghaus was the *only* subject. He completed the research during two yearlong periods: 1879–1880 and 1883–1884, and used the second set of experiments primarily to replicate those of the first. Also, to become proficient at the task, he spent an unspecified "long time" (Ebbinghaus, 1885/1964, p. 33) practicing before he began the 1879–1880 studies. Thus, for more than two separate yearlong periods, he devoted a significant portion of his time to memorizing lists of nonsense syllables (about an hour or two per day), by his own admission a task tedious enough to occasionally produce "exhaustion, headache, and other symptoms" (p. 55). On just one set of experiments, the ones that produced his famous forgetting curve (see Figure 4.7), Ebbinghaus memorized just over 1,300 different lists. One attribute said to characterize famous scientists is a total passion for their research. Ebbinghaus was certainly a case in point.

Ebbinghaus described the results of his research in several different chapters. For example, he examined how quickly a series of syllables could be learned as a function of the number of syllables per list. "Quickly" meant the number of repetitions needed before the list could be produced without errors. He reported the results in this table (p. 47):

Number of syllables in a series	Number of repetitions necessary for first errorless reproduction	Probable error
7	1	
12	16.6	+/−1.1
16	30.0	+/−0.4
24	44.0	+/−1.7
36	55.0	+/−2.8

There are two things to note here. First, although it might not be surprising that it takes more repetitions to learn longer lists, this marks the first time that anyone had documented, with precision, the exact relationship between the length of material to be learned and the amount of effort required to learn it. Second, very little effort was needed when the list had just seven syllables. This result has recurred frequently during the history of experimental psychology, and George Miller's (1956) systematic investigation of this "magic number seven" became a landmark paper in the rise of cognitive psychology (see Chapter 14). You probably recall learning about the number 7 ± 2 in your general psychology course in the memory chapter under the heading "capacity of short-term memory."

After showing that it took more repetitions to learn longer lists, Ebbinghaus wondered whether increasing the number of *original* repetitions in a list of fixed length would strengthen memory. Thus he repeated lists of 16 syllables 8, 16, 24, 32, 42, 53, or 64 times and discovered that the ease of relearning the list 24 hours later was proportional to the number of original repetitions (he also discovered that 64 repetitions gave him headaches). Ebbinghaus also studied what today is called distribution of practice, finding that his memory performance was better if he spread his study over a period of time rather than cramming in all the study at once. He even provided a calibration of the advantage of distributed over massed practice—it took 68 repetitions on one day to equal the effects of just 38 repetitions spread over 3 days.

The most famous of the studies completed by Ebbinghaus concerned the rate of forgetting for information that had already been learned. Here, Ebbinghaus relied on an ingenious measure of recall that he called the **savings method**, which enabled him to measure memory after the passage of time, even if, initially, nothing could be recalled after the interval. He described the logic of it early in the book:

> A poem is learned by heart and then not again repeated. We will suppose that after a half year it has been forgotten: no effort at recollection is able to call it back into consciousness. At best only isolated fragments return. Suppose that the poem is again learned by heart. It then becomes evident that, although to all appearances totally forgotten, it still in a certain sense exists and in a way to be effective. The second learning requires noticeably less time or a noticeably smaller number of repetitions than the first. (Ebbinghaus, 1885/1964, p. 8)

To examine the effects of time on memory, Ebbinghaus memorized lists of syllables, tried to relearn them after the passage of a fixed amount of time, and applied his savings method to assess the outcome. Ebbinghaus recorded the total time for the original learning of the lists, which was typically about 20 minutes, and the time for relearning. Original learning minus relearning yielded a measure of savings, which was converted to a percentage by dividing by the time of original learning. Thus, if original learning took 20 minutes and relearning took 5 minutes, 15 minutes or 75% ($15/20 \times 100$) of the original learning time was saved.

Ebbinghaus reported the results for each of the 163 separate experiments (i.e., "double tests") that he completed over the different retention intervals. The results of this study have made their way into almost every introductory psychology textbook. They are normally shown in a graph like the one in Figure 4.7 (in the book, Ebbinghaus presented these results in a table). The results are clear—the rate of forgetting was rapid at first and then slowed. Thus, after just 20 minutes (0.33 hour), Ebbinghaus's savings score was 60%. After an hour, 45% was saved, and after just a day, only about 33% was saved.

A final example of the Ebbinghaus memory project is his investigation of **remote associations**. When the sequence of syllables A, B, and C is to be learned in order, direct associations are formed between A and B and between B and C, but are they also formed (remotely) between A and C? If so, then the association concept extends beyond the idea of two immediately contiguous events. Ebbinghaus devised a clever procedure to test for these potential remote associations. He first learned a list of 16 syllables in the usual serial order:

LIST A 1 2 3 4 5 6 7 8 9 10 11 12 13 14 15 16

Next he would relearn the list in an order that skipped a syllable:

LIST B 1 3 5 7 9 11 13 15 2 4 6 8 10 12 14 16

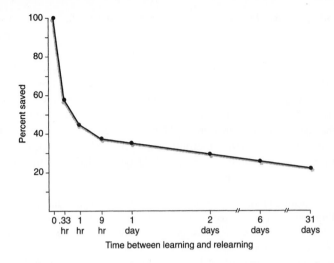

FIGURE 4.7 The Ebbinghaus forgetting curve, constructed from data he presented in table form.

Similarly, for other lists he would relearn a list that skipped two syllables:

LIST C 1 4 7 10 13 16 2 5 8 11 14 3 6 9 12 15

If remote associations had been forming during the original learning of syllables 1 through 16 (list A), then the relearning of lists B and C would be faster than learning a new list of 16 syllables, and this is exactly what Ebbinghaus found. Furthermore, there was a direct relationship between the ease of relearning and the degree of remoteness of the associations (list B was relearned faster than list C).

In Chapter 14, you will learn about the development of modern cognitive psychology. One of its recent trends is a tendency to criticize the narrowness and artificiality of the "Ebbinghaus tradition." For modern cognitive psychologists, the memorizer is actively processing information, not passively strengthening associations through mindless repetition. Also, there is more emphasis today on **ecological memory**: memory for more realistic everyday events rather than for abstract lists. One prominent contemporary researcher lamented the "terrible struggle our field has had just to overcome the nonsense syllable" (Kintsch, 1985, p. 461). The criticism has some merit, but for the historian it clearly has the ring of presentism. Considering the Ebbinghaus memory research in the context of its time, a more apt evaluation of its importance comes from a retrospective review of *On Memory* by Roediger, written 100 years after the original publication:

> Considering that [Ebbinghaus] only began his research in the same year that Wundt founded his psychology lab and that he performed all experiments on himself and still produced such regular and compelling results, his achievement is nearly incredible. (Roediger, 1985, p. 522)

Other Contributions by Ebbinghaus The memory research was Ebbinghaus's greatest accomplishment, but not his only one. He was also a pioneer in the field of mental testing; he invented a sentence completion test in 1895 that was similar in spirit to the intelligence test soon to be developed in France by Binet (Chapter 8). Ebbinghaus held academic positions in the German universities at Berlin and Breslau and created the psychology laboratories at each university; he also worked at the university in Halle, where he rebuilt a lab. In 1890, he started the *Zeitschrift für Psychologie und Physiologie der Sunnesorgane* (*Journal of Psychology and Physiology of the Sense Organs*). While Wundt's *Philosophische Studien* was primarily a means for publishing the work completed in his Leipzig laboratory, Ebbinghaus's *Zeitschrift* filled its pages with research from laboratories throughout Germany. The journal's catholicity of interests and the prestige of its contributing authors (e.g., Helmholtz, G. E. Müller) led one historian to describe it as "the most important psychological organ in Germany" (Shakow, 1930, p. 509). Ebbinghaus also wrote two popular introductory psychology texts, including a brief version (just before his sudden death from pneumonia in 1909) that included the famous opening sentence, quoted at the start of this book's Chapter 2: "Psychology has a long past, yet its real history is short" (Ebbinghaus, 1908, p. 3).

G. E. Müller (1850–1934): The Experimentalist Prototype

Although Wundt is rightly given credit as the founder of experimental psychology, the psychology of the laboratory occupied only a portion of his interest. This is a theme that will be repeated: Many of the early pioneers of laboratory psychology actually spent little time in the laboratory. An exception was G. E. Müller,[7] an experimenter's experimenter, who devoted 40 years of his professional life to the psychology laboratory at the University of Göttingen. From 1881 to his retirement in 1921, Müller's laboratory rivaled the other German facilities in the quality of research produced. Studies completed in Müller's lab were known for their precision, experimental control, and meticulous attention to detail. That Müller is not well known today is primarily because little of his work was translated into English. Also, much of his research did not break radically new ground; rather, it systematically replicated and extended the research of others. Thus he made important contributions in extending Fechner's work in psychophysics,[8] Hering's work on color vision, and Ebbinghaus's work on memory. In this last area, Müller was a worthy successor to the venerable Ebbinghaus (Haupt, 1998).

During the decade of the 1890s, Müller and his students replicated and elaborated on many of the Ebbinghaus findings, developed a number of methodological refinements, and reached different conclusions about the formation of associations. Whereas Ebbinghaus concluded that associations were formed automatically and mechanically as a result of stimulus factors such as the number of repetitions and list length, and that the memorizer played a relatively *passive* role in the process, Müller believed that the individual forming the associations played a more *active* role. The conclusion resulted from a procedural modification—Müller added introspection to the memory process, and his observers reported that they engaged in a number of active strategies to learn the nonsense syllables. For example, they found themselves grouping nonsense syllables in clusters, organizing them by different degrees of

---

[7]No relation to Johannes Müller, the famous physiologist you met in Chapter 3. Müller is a common name in Germany, a bit like the German version of "Smith."

[8]According to Boring (1950), E. B. Titchener held up publication of the second volume of his famous laboratory manual (Chapter 7) until Müller had published a handbook of psychophysics in 1903. Titchener had to rewrite the psychophysics portions of his manual after Müller's book appeared, and the second volume of the lab manual was not published until 1905, four years after volume 1. Margaret Washburn, Titchener's first graduate student, told experimental psychologist Walter Miles that Titchener was awed by Müller's research, and that Titchener "was always playing to an audience, usually G. E. Müller. T said that a postcard from G. E. M. was his best reward" (quoted in Goodwin, 2003, p. 74).

meaning, and in general doing much more than just associating them by contiguity. This outcome foreshadows the modern view of memory, which assumes that the learner is actively involved in the memorizing process.

Müller and his students also made some discoveries that went beyond what Ebbinghaus had found. For example, with Alfons Pilzecker he discovered that if a second list is learned between the learning of list 1 and the subsequent attempt to relearn list 1, the second list interferes with the relearning of list 1. They named the phenomenon **retroactive inhibition**, thus initiating a long line of research that eventually produced the interference theory of forgetting in the 1960s. With another student, Adolph Jost, Müller discovered that if two associations have equal strength, further practice will strengthen the older of the associations more than the recent one. This phenomenon, later called **Jost's law**, was based on rather meager evidence but was considered important as part of the explanation for the advantage of distributed practice over massed practice, another phenomenon studied extensively in Müller's lab (Woodworth, 1938).

Another of Müller's contributions to the experimental study of memory was the invention of the **memory drum**, which automated the presentation of stimulus materials. Müller and his assistant Friedrich Schumann cleverly altered a kymograph, a rotating drum normally used to record data (as shown in the reaction time photo of Figure 4.5). Stimuli were mounted on the drum, which revolved at a fixed speed, displaying stimuli through a small window for measured amounts of time and thereby adding precision to the procedure (Popplestone, 1987). Memory drums were standard laboratory equipment until 1990s, when computer presentation of stimuli became more efficient. Figure 4.8 shows an early version of a memory drum.

One final point is that although the University of Göttingen did not award advanced degrees to women, Müller welcomed several notable American women psychologists into

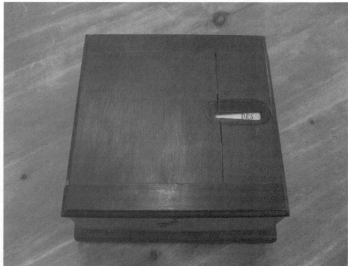

FIGURE 4.8 An early memory drum developed in G.E. Müller's lab, with the cover open (left) and closed (as a subject would see it).

his laboratory, including Christine Ladd-Franklin of Columbia (Chapter 6), Lillien Martin of Stanford, and Eleanor Gamble of Wellesley. As you will learn in Chapter 6, women faced numerous obstacles when trying to obtain graduate-level training. This was especially true in the United States, but it was also the case in Europe. Müller was ahead of his time in recognizing that women could be capable laboratory workers.

Oswald Külpe (1862–1915): The Würzburg School

After flirting with history and philosophy, Oswald Külpe became interested in psychology while taking a course from Wundt in the early 1880s. He then went to Berlin to study history and to Göttingen, where a year and a half in G. E. Müller's lab convinced him that psychology was to be his career. He eventually returned to Leipzig and earned a doctorate under Wundt's supervision in 1887; he remained with his mentor for another 7 years, earning a living as a *Privatdozent* and as Wundt's assistant in the laboratory (he succeeded Cattell). Külpe befriended E. B. Titchener (Chapter 7), who was at Leipzig for part of this time. In 1894 Külpe was called to Würzburg, where he created a laboratory sometimes considered second only to Wundt's and a match for Müller's at Göttingen. At Würzburg, Külpe created a brand of experimental psychology distinctive enough to earn the label "Würzburg school." It investigated topics and produced outcomes that put Külpe at odds with both his mentor Wundt and his friend Titchener.

Wundt had declared higher mental processes (e.g., memory, thinking) off limits for laboratory research, deeming them too complex and too heavily influenced by language and culture to be controlled adequately. Instead, such topics needed to be investigated with nonlaboratory methods while the lab was to be restricted to such topics as sensation and perception as well as mental chronometry. Yet Ebbinghaus and Müller had managed to control conditions reasonably well in their studies of memory. It was up to Külpe, however, to challenge his former mentor directly by studying thought processes in the lab and by significantly elaborating upon the Wundtian introspective procedure.

Külpe exercised close but congenial supervision over his students; he published little research under his own name, preferring instead to give his students the credit. In the words of his American student, Robert Ogden:

> [Külpe] was intimately engaged in all that went on in his laboratory. It was a matter of principle to him to act as observer in the experimental work of his students. In the instance of my own study . . . he came almost daily to the laboratory for what must have been weary hours of committing nonsense syllables to memory. His influence upon his students was never dominating. Instead, they were engaged together in a joint enterprise of scientific discovery. (Ogden, 1951, p. 9)

To study thought processes in the laboratory, Külpe found it necessary to expand what he thought of as the Wundtian limitations on introspection. Recall that Wundt distinguished between self-observation, in which someone experiences some event and then from memory describes the mental processes that occurred during the event, and inner perception, a more controlled introspective procedure in which simple stimuli are presented many times and responses are given immediately after stimulus presentation. For Wundt, only the latter procedure was appropriate in the laboratory. In Külpe's laboratory, however, introspection was more like what Wundt called self-observation. It came to be called **systematic**

experimental introspection. Observers would experience more complicated events than in Wundt's laboratory and then give a full description of the mental processes involved. This created a potential memory problem, because as Woodworth (1938) later pointed out, the mental experience of a 10-second event might take 10 minutes to describe. To deal with the fact that giving an introspective account of a complicated event might be distorted by memory, Külpe and his students developed a procedure called **fractionation**, a separation of the task into its components, each of which could be introspected many times. For example, in a study on word association by Watt (i.e., given a stimulus word, say the first word that comes to mind), the task was fractionated into "the preparation for the experiment, the appearance of the stimulus-word, the search for the reaction-word (if such search occurred), and finally the cropping up of the reaction-word" (Watt, 1904, quoted in Sahakian, 1975, p. 162).

Külpe believed he was improving the introspective procedure, enabling it to be applied to higher mental processes, but Wundt rejected the Würzburg technique, calling it nothing but the unsystematic self-observation he had denounced years earlier. Thus, because he believed them to be built on unsound methods, Wundt dismissed the results of the Würzburg research. What were those results?

Mental Sets and Imageless Thoughts The Würzburg research on thinking produced several interesting outcomes. For example, in a study by Narziss Ach, observers were shown pairs of numbers after first being instructed that they would be performing some specific operation (e.g., add them, subtract them). Ach measured reaction time and also asked for introspections. He found that reaction time was the same, regardless of the type of operation asked of subjects, and that observers reported no conscious awareness of the instructions themselves once the task had begun. In other words, after receiving the instructions, their mind was "prepared" to function in a specific way (e.g., adding), so that once the number pair was presented, the addition occurred automatically and without further thought. Thus the instructions created what the Würzburgers called a determining tendency or **mental set**. This concept would eventually become important for the German Gestalt psychologists (Chapter 9). The absence of a difference in reaction time was also significant, because Külpe used it to question the validity of the subtractive assumption underlying the mental chronography experiments that were such an important part of the Leipzig laboratory. Because instructions create a mental set, he argued, discrimination reaction time cannot be equal to simple reaction time plus the mental event of discrimination. Rather, DRT results from a different kind of "set" than SRT.

A second important finding of the Würzburg lab, and a controversial one, concerned the phenomenon of **imageless thought**. According to Titchener (and Wundt), a close analysis of thought processes reveals that the essential element in all thinking is an image of some form. In a psychophysics weight-lifting experiment, for example, the standard description was that the observer would lift one weight, form a kinesthetic image of it, and then lift the second weight and compare the sensation of it with the image of the first one to decide if the weights were the same or different. The judgment process was composed of sensory and image components from the two weights. In a weight-lifting study by Karl Marbe at Würzburg, however, no sensations or images occurred at the moment of judgment. Observers reported sensations and images while lifting the weights, but the judgment seemed to occur automatically and without images. That is, the judgment was an imageless thought. Furthermore, Marbe's observers reported other mental processes occurring just before the judgment, and these didn't seem reducible to sensations and images either. These processes included things like hesitation, doubt, and vacillation; collectively they were referred to as **conscious attitudes**.

The potential existence of imageless thoughts, mental sets, and conscious attitudes posed an especially serious threat to Külpe's colleague E. B. Titchener, who believed that all mental content under analysis would be found to contain the basic elements of conscious experience (more on Titchener and the imageless thought issue in Chapter 7). If some thoughts occur without images, however, then not all thinking can be reduced to such basic elements. This imageless thought controversy was never resolved; its most notable side effect, however, was to raise questions about the validity of introspection as a method and to help pave the way for a radical new movement in psychology that you will learn about in Chapters 10 and 11: behaviorism.

IN PERSPECTIVE: A NEW SCIENCE

The new laboratory psychology that emerged in Germany quickly caught the attention of a number of American intellectuals, most notably William James, G. Stanley Hall, and James McKeen Cattell. All three either toured German labs, or, in Cattell's case, earned a PhD from one. You will learn more about these pioneers in Chapters 6 through 8. A number of other Americans followed in their footsteps, earning doctorates from Leipzig and other labs and then returning home enthusiastic about the idea of making psychology scientific. In addition, several American universities (e.g., Johns Hopkins, Clark, Chicago), with the German spirit of *Wissenschaft* clearly in mind, opened in the last third of the 19th century and developed laboratories in imitation of the German labs. American psychology, then, derives from the movement that started with Wundt. More generally, one could say that the new discipline of psychology had two clear sets of parents—the philosophers you learned about in Chapter 2 and the physiologists of Chapter 3. But parentage is sometimes a tricky business, and in the case of psychology, there was also a third parent—Darwinian biology. Darwin and his influence on modern psychology is the focus of Chapter 5.

SUMMARY

An Education in Germany

• In the 19th century, a large number of American students studied the sciences in Europe, especially in Germany. In the latter half of the century, many students went to Germany, in particular to Leipzig, to study a new approach to psychology that was developing there.

• The German educational system promoted a philosophy of *Wissenschaft*, which emphasized original research and the academic freedom to pursue that research. This created an environment conducive to new ideas, including the idea of a new scientific approach to the study of psychology.

On the Threshold of Experimental Psychology: Psychophysics

• Psychophysics is the study of the relationship between physical stimuli and the psychological reaction to them. The first research in this tradition was completed by Ernst Weber, who investigated the relative sensitivity of various areas on the surface of the body using the two-point threshold. In experiments in which observers made comparisons between two weights, Weber discovered that the ability to distinguish between them depended on the relative rather than the absolute differences in their weights (Weber's law).

• Gustav Fechner elaborated Weber's research, and his *Elements of Psychophysics* (1860) is considered experimental psychology's first text. Although more interested in using his research to defeat materialism, Fechner is known for developing several important psychophysics methods in use today (limits, constant stimuli, adjustment) and for the precision of his work in measuring absolute and difference thresholds.

Wundt Establishes a New Psychology at Leipzig

• Wilhelm Wundt is generally known as the founder of experimental psychology. He explicitly set out to create a new psychology that emphasized the experimental methods borrowed from physiology, and he created the first laboratory of experimental psychology and the first journal devoted to describing the results of scientific research in psychology.

• Wundt's new science involved studying immediate conscious experience under controlled laboratory conditions. Because they could not be subjected to experimental control and replication, higher mental processes (e.g., language), as well as social and cultural phenomena, had to be studied through nonlaboratory methods (e.g., observation).

• In Wundt's laboratory, most of the research concerned basic sensory and perceptual processes. The lab also produced a large number of "mental chronometry" studies, which attempted to measure the amount of time taken for various mental processes. James McKeen Cattell, an American student and Wundt's first official lab assistant, completed a number of these "complication" studies, which utilized a subtraction procedure developed by the Dutch physiologist F. C. Donders.

• Recent historical scholarship has uncovered serious distortions in the traditional accounts of Wundt's ideas.

Rather than being a structuralist, seeking to reduce consciousness to its basic elements, Wundt was more interested in the mind's ability to actively organize information. One of his main interests was the process of apperception—an active, meaningful, and attentive perception of some event. He called his system voluntarism to reflect the active nature of mental processing. The distortions stem from Boring's famous history text.

The New Psychology Spreads

• One of the most important programs of research carried out in psychology's history involved the study of memory by Hermann Ebbinghaus. To investigate the development of new associations between unassociated stimuli, he invented nonsense syllables. Ebbinghaus measured retention in terms of the amount of effort "saved" in relearning. His famous forgetting curve showed that forgetting occurs at a very rapid rate shortly after initial learning and then tapers off.

• G. E. Müller and his students significantly extended contemporary research on color vision, the psychophysics research of Fechner, and the memory research of Ebbinghaus. By adding introspection to the nonsense syllable experiments, he argued that memory was an active process, not the passive buildup of associative strength. He was the first to identify retroactive inhibition (i.e., forgetting results from interference from events occurring between initial learning and recall), and he invented the memory drum.

• Oswald Külpe and his students created the Würzburg school of psychology, which defied Wundt by studying the higher mental process of thinking under laboratory conditions and liberalizing the method of introspection. In their research they found evidence for mental sets, imageless thought, and conscious attitudes.

STUDY QUESTIONS

1. Describe the *Wissenschaft* philosophy of education that developed in Germany in the 19th century. What were the implications for psychology?

2. Show how Fechner's three psychophysics methods could be used to determine a two-point threshold.

3. Describe Weber's law and the concept of a jnd.

4. Wundt, rather than Fechner, is considered to be the founder of modern experimental psychology. Why?

5. Describe Wundt's contributions to psychology before his arrival at Leipzig.

6. Wundt's concept of psychology involved two major programs. Describe each of them.

7. Describe how Wundt (and others) used reaction time to measure the duration of various mental events. In what way was the method flawed?

8. Describe and criticize the traditional description of Wundt's "system." How did the misconceptions develop?

9. Explain why Wundt called his system voluntarism, and show how the concept of apperception was important to him.

10. What were nonsense syllables, why did Ebbinghaus use them, and what was the overall goal of his research project?

11. What was the method of savings, and why was it such a creative way to study memory?

12. Describe any three of the findings from the Ebbinghaus research.

13. Describe how G. E. Müller's view of memory differed from that of Ebbinghaus. Why was Müller described as the "prototype" experimentalist?

14. Describe Külpe's version of introspection and how introspection would occur for a complex mental process.

15. How was mental set investigated in Külpe's lab, and what were the implications of the findings for the complication experiment?

16. What was an imageless thought, and how was it studied in Külpe's lab?

FOR FURTHER READING

BLUMENTHAL, A. L. (1975). A reappraisal of Wilhelm Wundt. *American Psychologist*, *30*, 1081–1086.

Probably the most frequently cited of the articles appearing in the 1970s that pointed out the errors in the traditional accounts of Wundt; draws comparisons between Wundt's research and theorizing and modern concepts from cognitive psychology.

EBBINGHAUS, H. (1964). *Memory: A contribution to experimental psychology* (H. A. Ruger & C. A. Bussenius, Trans.). New York: Dover. (Original work published 1885)

A very readable, and brief (123 pages), account of the famous experiments by Ebbinghaus; the Dover republication includes a helpful foreword by Hilgard; a good retrospective review of the book can be found in Roediger (1985).

LEAHEY, T. H. (1981). The mistaken mirror: On Wundt's and Titchener's psychologies. *Journal of the History of the Behavioral Sciences*, *17*, 273–282.

A clear description of Wundt's and Titchener's systems of psychology, highlighting their differences and drawing attention to the misconceptions that have developed over the years; shows how Wundt and Titchener had radically different philosophies of science (emphasis on causality for Wundt and on description for Titchener).

SOKAL, M. M. (Ed.). (1981a). *An education in psychology: James McKeen Cattell's journal and letters from Germany and England, 1880–1888.* Cambridge, MA: MIT Press.

A fascinating and highly detailed account of Cattell's years with Wundt at Leipzig, Hall at Johns Hopkins, and Galton in England. The entries are from letters written by Cattell, usually to his parents, and from a diary; the annotations by Sokal are as informative as Cattell's firsthand accounts.

BRINGMANN, W. G., & TWENEY, R. D. (Eds.). (1980). *Wundt studies: A centennial collection.* Toronto: C. J. Hogrefe.

A collection of 21 articles about Wundt's life and work, ranging from biographical treatment to interpretation; main sections are the Heidelberg years, the Leipzig period, and impact and assessment.

CHAPTER 5

DARWIN'S CENTURY: EVOLUTIONARY THINKING

This preservation of favorable individual differences and variations, and the destruction of those which are injurious, I have called Natural Selection.

—Charles Darwin, 1859

PREVIEW AND CHAPTER OBJECTIVES

Chapter 4 described the rise of scientific psychology in Germany in the 19th century. Preceding chapters examined the explosive growth of knowledge about the brain and nervous system in that same century, and the maturation of British empiricist and associationist thought during that time. As remarkable as these 19th-century developments were, they were overshadowed by the impact of one man's theory about the nature of life itself. Biologists appropriately claim Charles Darwin as their most eminent historical figure, but his ideas also shaped the direction of psychology's history. This chapter examines Darwin's life and the development of his theory and then considers the impact of his ideas on psychology's history. His argument for continuity among species challenged the Cartesian distinction between humans and animals and led to comparative psychology, the systematic study of animal behavior. His emphasis on the variability within species led to the study of individual differences, most clearly manifested in the work of his cousin, Sir Francis Galton. In later chapters, we examine how Darwinian thinking resonated with the functionalist school of thought in American psychology. After you finish this chapter, you should be able to:

- Describe the species problem and how the British theological community responded to it in the 19th century
- Describe how the concept of "evolutionary change" came to permeate 19th-century thinking in both geology and biology, thereby creating a zeitgeist conducive to Darwin's ideas
- Trace the influence of his education and the *Beagle* voyage on Darwin's developing ideas about evolution
- Show the effects of Malthusian population ideas and the artificial selection principles of pigeon breeders on Darwin's thinking
- Describe the basic principles of Darwin's theory of evolution and explain why he delayed publishing them for almost 20 years
- Explain how Darwin studied and interpreted the expressions of emotions in humans and animals

- Describe the work of Douglas Spalding and show how it connects with modern ethology
- Describe and evaluate the comparative psychology of George Romanes
- Explain the importance of Lloyd Morgan's canon for the subsequent study of animal behavior
- Describe Sir Francis Galton's beliefs about the nature of intelligence, how he arrived at them, and how they led to his interest in eugenics
- Describe the logic of Galton's approach to mental testing
- Describe Galton's work on the psychological topics of association and mental imagery
- Show how Darwin's ideas have influenced modern psychology

THE SPECIES PROBLEM

From the time that Newtonian physics burst on the scene in the late 17th century, intellectuals became increasingly convinced that the scientific approach was the way to attain truth, that it would shed light on our ignorance of the laws of nature, and that it would lead to the improvement of life through technological advancement. Thus, as we discussed in Chapter 3, the 18th and 19th centuries became known as an era of Enlightenment in which science became religion and scientists seemed heroic.

One manifestation of Enlightenment science was a questioning of the literal truth of the Bible's version of the origin of the earth's plants and animals. Global exploration was uncovering new species of plants and animals by the thousands. How did the earth come to be populated by such diversity? Why did some species seem to disappear, their existence known only from fossils? Why did some living species seem so similar to (but usually smaller than) species suggested by fossils? And for those accepting the literal truth of the Bible, how did all these species fit on Noah's ark? Collectively, these questions became known as the **species problem**, sometimes referred to as the "mystery of mysteries."

The problem created great stress within the academic community in Great Britain, where those in the intellectual elite were also leaders of the Anglican Church, the Church of England. One solution was to turn the problem into an argument for the supreme power of the deity. This **argument from design**[1] is normally associated with the Reverend William Paley's 1802 *Natural Theology*, but it is also recognizable as one of the proofs for the existence of God suggested by the great medieval philosopher Thomas Aquinas (Scott-Kakures, Castagnetto, Benson, Taschek, & Hurley, 1993). The argument held that the very existence of precision and complexity in nature required a supreme being to create and oversee it. Paley drew an analogy between the complex design of a watch, which necessitates a watchmaker to make it, and that of the infinitely more complicated human eye, which requires an "eyemaker" who is infinitely superior to the humans using those eyes (Ruse, 1979). The argument from design enabled a minister-scientist to study the workings of nature while maintaining a belief in the Supreme Designer. There was no need to speculate about how species might develop; it was simpler to assume that God in his infinite wisdom had created each species and designed each one to fit

---

[1]The modern version of this idea, in no way substantially different from it, is called intelligent design.

into its place in the world. Hence, the orderliness to be found in nature derived from explicit design, which in turn came from a mind greater than any found in nature—that is, from God.

Despite the power of this argument from design, several evolutionary ideas developed in the 18th and early 19th centuries. Two pre-Darwinian examples are worthy of note. First, Darwin was not even the first person in his family to propose an evolutionary solution to the species problem. A century earlier, his grandfather, Erasmus Darwin (1731–1802), a physician, rejected the biblical account of creation and proposed that all organic life evolved from a single living filament. Over time, new species developed from old ones, and later species were more "advanced" than earlier ones. The human species represented the culmination of evolution, but there was no reason to assume that humans would not continue to improve.

The best-known pre-Darwinian theory of evolution belonged not to Darwin's grandfather, however, but to a prominent French naturalist, Jean Baptiste de Lamarck (1744–1829). Like Erasmus Darwin, Lamarck believed that all the species on earth could be arranged on a linear scale with reference to their complexity; the idea is sometimes referred to as the **chain of being** (Ruse, 1979). Furthermore, each species is constantly evolving into a species that is more complex, he believed, and new life at the bottom of the scale is continually being created from inorganic life. Thus, at any one point in time, a variety of species exists that could be ranked in terms of how much they had evolved from the first spark of life. Lamarck also believed that an important mechanism of evolution was the idea that changes occurring during the lifetime of an organism could be passed on to offspring. For instance, if during the course of its life an animal developed the ability to use simple tools, that new ability would be inherited by the next generation. This concept became known as the **inheritance of acquired characteristics**. It was taken seriously throughout most of the 19th century before being discarded, and it was included as part of Darwin's original theory. But we are getting ahead of the story.

CHARLES DARWIN (1809–1882) AND THE THEORY OF EVOLUTION

Little in the early life of Charles Robert Darwin (Figure 5.1) predicted the greatness to come—he appeared to be just an aimless, spoiled child of wealthy parents. He was born and raised in the rural west of England, in Shrewsbury. His father, Robert, was a successful and affluent country doctor; his mother, Susannah Wedgwood, was heir to a fortune from the family that created the renowned Wedgwood china. Like most successful and ambitious men, Robert Darwin expected great things of his son and was frustrated by the boy's indifferent school performance and his apparent lack of purpose. By early adolescence, Darwin's wayward behavior drove his father to distraction. "You care for nothing but shooting, dogs, and rat-catching, and you will be a disgrace to yourself and all your family," he exclaimed (quoted in Desmond & Moore, 1991, p. 20), in a scene easily imagined by many parents of an adolescent boy.

The Shaping of a Naturalist

Determined that his son would follow in his footsteps, Robert Darwin sent Charles to study medicine at Edinburgh, Scotland, one of Europe's best medical schools. The experiment

1840

1881

1854

FIGURE 5.1 Darwin at three stages of his life: In 1840, four years after the *Beagle* voyage ended; in 1881, a year before his death; in 1854, when fully immersed in the research that would produce *Origin of Species* five years later.

failed—Darwin's academic performance did not improve, and he was nauseated by the clinical procedures of the day. Anesthesia did not exist then, nor was the importance of a sterile environment widely recognized. Thus surgery was a gruesome experience in which the most important skill was speed. For young Charles, medicine would not do. He left Edinburgh in 1827.

The next stop was Cambridge University, where Darwin studied for the clergy. The Cambridge that he encountered in the period 1828 to 1831 was not the fine academic university we think of today. Rather, it was an institution under the firm control of the Church of England, its professors were Anglican priests who normally expected little scholarship on the part of their students, and its students (all male) tended to meet those expectations.[2] Most students were there to prepare for the clergy, but they were primarily concerned with learning how to become proper gentlemen. Studying to be a clergyman in the Anglican Church was a common vocation for sons of wealthy Britishers, an activity described as a "safety net to stop second sons [from] becoming wastrels" (Desmond & Moore, 1991, p. 47). Honors programs for serious students did exist in classics and mathematics, but at a time when England was the most powerful nation on earth and was leading the industrial revolution, the university was strangely deficient in the study of science and technology (Ruse, 1979). Darwin never

[2]The same could be said at this time of England's other famous university, Oxford.

became a minister, of course. Nonetheless, he entertained the notion for several years, even after he had found his true vocation.[3]

Although he was not destined for the clergy, Darwin found his calling at Cambridge. Young people growing up in rural areas often develop a love for the natural world, and Darwin was no exception. From his earliest youth, he recalled being a collector of natural objects ranging from rocks to beetles to butterflies. While at Cambridge, he realized for the first time that his love of the natural world could become a life's work. Darwin's model and mentor was the Reverend John Henslow (1796–1871), a professor of botany. In the minister-scientist Henslow, Darwin saw his future—he could become an Anglican clergyman, use his wealth to acquire a quiet rural parish, and devote all of his spare time to natural science. Darwin sat in on Henslow's classes, and his fervor quickly caught the botanist's attention. Before long, Henslow began including Darwin in weekly meetings in his home, at which a small group of like-minded enthusiasts, including some of Cambridge's leading scientists, debated the scientific issues of the day (including evolution). Between 1828 and 1831, Darwin continued to be an average student in his formal preparation for the ministry, but he was in regular contact with some of the leading scientific minds of the day, and he was making a favorable impression on them (Ruse, 1979).

One of those scientific minds belonged to a noted geologist, the Reverend Adam Sedgwick (1785–1873). Sedgwick became a second mentor to Darwin, teaching him the basic methods of geology and sharpening his ability to make precise observations by taking him on a long geological field trip through the mountains of Wales in the summer of 1831. Darwin eventually rejected Sedgwick's views about the earth's formation, but he profited immensely from the experience. Darwin began thinking of himself as a geologist.

After Darwin returned from the walk through Wales, opportunity knocked. A voyage to South America was being planned, and the captain, 26-year-old Robert FitzRoy, was advertising for an onboard dinner companion. FitzRoy tended to depression and was looking for intelligent conversation to relieve the long hours of tedium at sea. It would also help if this person had some training in science, for there would be opportunities to collect specimens of South America's fauna and flora. Henslow recommended Darwin, Darwin's father eventually approved the plan, and Darwin undertook the voyage of a lifetime aboard the HMS *Beagle*. It lasted 5 years and took him around the globe. In his autobiography, Darwin had this to say about the trip:

> The voyage of the *Beagle* has been by far the most important event in my life, and has determined my whole career....I have always felt that I owe to the voyage the first real training or education of my mind; I was led to attend closely to several branches of natural history, and thus my powers of observation were improved. (Darwin, 1892/1958a, p. 28)

The Voyage of the *Beagle*

Darwin's home away from home for 5 years was a small (90 feet long and 24 feet wide) three-masted brig that carried just over 70 officers, marines, geographer-surveyors, and crew.

---

[3]In his autobiography, Darwin reported that later in his life, a German phrenological society requested a photograph of his head. He complied, the photo was carefully examined, and a member of the society proclaimed that Charles had "the bump of reverence developed enough for ten priests" (Darwin, 1892/1958a, p. 18).

H. M. S. Beagle 1832

1. Mr. Darwin's seat in Captain's Cabin   2. Mr. Darwin's seat in Poop Cabin
3. Mr. Darwin's drawers in Poop Cabin   4. Azimuth Compass   5. Captain's skylight   6. Gunroom skylight

FIGURE 5.2   Cross-section of the HMS *Beagle*.

Darwin shared a small cabin at the rear of the ship with two of the survey officers, sleeping in a hammock with his face 2 feet from the underside of the main deck and contending with the surveyors for workspace on the small charting table during the day (Thomson, 1975). Some idea of the cramped living arrangements can be seen in Figure 5.2.

The primary purpose of the *Beagle*'s voyage was to survey the southern coasts of South America, especially its port areas, thus allowing the powerful British merchant fleet to retain its edge in the competition for trade with developing South American countries; the ship would also circumnavigate the globe, using its 24 chronometers to check the precise longitude of various locations on the globe (Desmond & Moore, 1991). Once the *Beagle* reached South America, much of its time was spent going back and forth from one coastal region to another.[4] This procedure enabled Darwin to spend months at a time ashore, exploring the continent, observing nature, and collecting. According to Desmond and Moore (2009), these periods ashore also exposed Darwin to the harsh realities of slavery, an experience that greatly affected him, and contributed eventually to his motivation to develop an evolutionary theory that featured descent from a common origin. If everyone descended from a common species, it questioned the logical basis for slavery, he believed. Long periods away from the ship also benefited Darwin for a practical reason—he suffered from seasickness that lasted the entire trip. When aboard ship, he was ill practically every day.

Darwin the Geologist   At the outset of the voyage, Darwin had a strong interest in geology. The field trip with Sedgwick was still fresh in his mind, and just off the press and among his possessions was the first volume of a book destined to have the same effect on geology that his own book eventually would have on biology. Its simple title, *Principles of Geology*, belied its revolutionary nature. Its Scottish author, Charles Lyell (1797–1875), took issue with the prevailing theory of geological change, called **catastrophism**. Much

[4]The *Beagle* spent 57 months at sea. Of these months, 42 were spent in South American waters, 27 on the east coast and 15 on the west coast (Browne, 1995).

like the argument from design, catastrophism was an attempt to maintain the supremacy of God and the Bible while accounting for what scientists were discovering about nature. Catastrophists, including Darwin's geologist-mentor Sedgwick, argued that geological change occurred abruptly and dramatically as the result of major catastrophic events under the control of God. The flood in the Book of Genesis was the standard example. Lyell, on the other hand, argued that geological change occurred more slowly and involved forces that are constantly at work. These forces included such things as volcanic action, earthquakes, erosion, and the cumulative effects of weather. This view came to be called **uniformitarianism**, because of the assumption that uniform laws of nature operated to produce gradual geologic change. The Swiss Alps were not thrust up overnight in some cataclysmic upheaval; they arose only gradually, over vast amounts of time, Lyell believed.[5]

Lyell's ideas about the origins and development of the earth's structures were never far from Darwin's thoughts. Indeed, while we now think of the trip as the event that gave Darwin the raw material for his theory of evolution of species, he also made important contributions to geology. For instance, he experienced, firsthand, the landscape-altering effects of an earthquake in Chile; he observed fossilized seashells high in the Andes Mountains; and, during the Pacific portion of the trip, he was able to demonstrate that coral reefs were built on the rims of slowly sinking volcanoes. Darwin's immersion in Lyellian geology also convinced him that the earth had to be much older than previously thought. This idea would eventually be critical for Darwin's ideas about evolution, because slow changes in species required vast amounts of time. Lyell's new geology supplied an earth that was sufficiently ancient for evolution to do its work.

Darwin the Zoologist With the *Beagle* in South American waters completing its surveying work, Darwin collected specimens in earnest and kept encyclopedic notes. By the end of the voyage, he had compiled a 770-page diary, 1,383 pages of notes on geology, and 368 more pages on zoology. He also wrote a specimen catalog that included 1,529 species of animals that had been preserved in spirits and another 3,907 labeled items that were either bones, fossils, skins, or dried specimens (Desmond & Moore, 1991).

For at least a year into the voyage, Darwin firmly believed that he would return to England and become the Anglican priest–amateur scientist that he so admired in Henslow. He also assumed that his work would have no bearing on the biblical account of creation; he was initially a believer in the argument from design. Yet his zoological observations gradually led to him to wonder about the species problem. It began to occur to him that just as the earth evolved slowly, gradually, and according to uniform laws, perhaps the same was true for the organisms populating the earth.

The Galápagos Islands On September 7, 1835, more than 3 years into the voyage, the *Beagle* left South America and headed across the Pacific. A week later, it made landfall at a remote series of about 20 volcanic islands owned by Ecuador and located on the equator about 600 miles west of South America. The islands featured a variety of unusual species,

---

[5]A modern form of catastrophism, minus the theological element, has gained adherents since the accumulation of evidence that comets or large meteors have occasionally struck the earth. It is estimated that one such meteor destroyed 95% of all marine species when it landed about 250 million years ago. More recently (a mere 65 million years ago), a huge meteor produced effects leading to the rapid extinction of about 70% of the earth's species, including the dinosaurs (Monastersky, 1997).

including oversized, dinosaur-like lizards, and tortoises with shells up to 5 feet in diameter. The islands were named for the Spanish word for the giant tortoise, *galápagos*. They had little practical value, being used primarily as an Ecuadorian penal colony and as a stopping point for whaling vessels to replenish their stocks of food and water.[6]

The Galápagos were to give Darwin significant clues to evolution, although at the time of the visit and for some time thereafter, he had little idea of the importance of what he encountered there. During the 5 weeks spent on the islands, Darwin did some hiking and specimen collecting; but he was not as systematic as he had been in South America. Nor did he pay much attention to the claim, made by the vice governor of the penal colony, that it was possible to tell the home island of a tortoise merely by observing the design of its shell. He did notice differences from one island to another in the various bird populations, however, especially in what he thought were mockingbirds. And it appeared that many of the species of birds and plants resembled those from the mainland, while having their own unique qualities. He later discovered that the shapes of the beaks of several species of finch provided a clue to his theory, but while in the Galápagos he failed to notice these differences by mislabeling some of the finches as warblers, wrens, and "gross-beaks," and he was more intrigued by their coloration than their beaks (Sulloway, 1982). These birds, now known as Darwin's finches, became an important source of data for naturalists who followed Darwin to the Galápagos, and they still contribute to evolutionary theory.[7]

After leaving the Galápagos, the *Beagle* sailed west across the Pacific, around Africa, and finally returned to England in October 1836. Upon his return, Darwin was a changed man. He now seriously doubted that life as an Anglican priest was for him; a full-time devotion to science seemed more in the cards. During the voyage, he routinely shipped crates of specimens home to Henslow, and they had made a strong impression on the scientific community during his absence. By the time he returned, he was already a celebrity among zoologists and geologists and viewed as a rising young star. Darwin's reputation even impressed his father, who rewarded his son with a generous allowance and a healthy stock portfolio to enable him to continue his scientific work (Desmond & Moore, 1991).

The Evolution of Darwin's Theory

During the first few years after his return, Darwin set out to organize and classify his enormous collection of specimens, enlisting the help of other scientists and museum curators. In 1837 he moved to London, and 2 years later he married his cousin, Emma Wedgwood. Their union was a long and happy one, even though Emma's strong religious beliefs eventually conflicted with her husband's gradual loss of faith. Emma was destined to become the family's source of strength, caring for the 10 children she would bear and for Darwin, who became ill soon after his return. Darwin was a partial invalid for the remainder of his life, suffering from a variety of chronic digestive, headache, and cardiac symptoms. For months at a time, he spent a significant portion of the day either in bed or being violently ill. The Darwins remained in

---

[6]While accumulating the experiences that would eventually yield his classic novel *Moby Dick*, Herman Melville was aboard a whaling vessel that reached the Galápagos shortly after the *Beagle*'s visit. Of the islands, Melville wrote, "Little but reptile life is here found; the chief sound of life is a hiss" (quoted in Moorehead, 1969, p. 187).

[7]From 1905 to 1906, for instance, a project sponsored by the California Academy of Sciences collected 8,691 finch specimens (Weiner, 1994).

(a)

(b)

FIGURE 5.3 (*a*) Darwin's home at Down; (*b*) Darwin's study at Down House.

London for 3 years, but the unrelenting street noise, coal-generated smog, and stench from the polluted Thames seemed to contribute to Darwin's declining health, so in 1842 they bought a country house at Down, about 15 miles south of London. Down became their permanent home and Darwin's laboratory. Today, Down House (Figure 5.3) serves as the Darwin Museum.

Despite his illnesses, Darwin produced. Within 10 years of his return to England, he published a journal of the voyage (Darwin, 1839), books on the geology of coral reefs, volcanic islands, and South America, and several technical reports that were read to various scientific societies in London. During this time, he also formulated his theory on the evolution of species and wrote a brief abstract of it in 1842. Two years later he elaborated the sketch into a 200-page document, instructing his wife to publish it in the event that his ailments proved fatal (Desmond & Moore, 1991).

Darwin's theory developed out of his reflections on the *Beagle* voyage, aided by hints that came from two distinct sources. First, in 1838 he read an essay on population by political economist Thomas Malthus (1766–1834), who championed the idea that government welfare for the poor would only increase their number, thereby decreasing Britain's overall standard of living. Instead, Malthus argued, society must recognize that life is a constant "struggle for existence" and only those best suited for survival will do so. He pointed out that while food supplies grow at a relatively constant rate, population growth, if unchecked, occurs much more rapidly. Eventually, a population would outgrow its resources and its members would begin to die until a level of stability occurred. For Darwin, this idea provided a model to be applied to species change. For any species, the time would come when unchecked population growth would result in food shortages, especially when growth combined with environmental change such as a prolonged drought. Under such circumstances, *only those best suited to survive would do so*. If those characteristics enabling survival could be passed on to offspring, the next generation would be better suited for survival and would be different from previous generations. Over time, might these changes be sufficient to create a new species? Darwin began to think so.

Darwin's second clue came from his reflections on what he knew of breeding by farmers and hobbyists. For instance, pigeon breeders had been able to produce breeds of pigeons that hardly resembled each other (see Figure 5.4 for a sample). The breeders accomplished this by observing tiny variations that occurred naturally within a breed of pigeons and then developing

FIGURE 5.4 The variety of pigeons that could result from selection breeding. Darwin saw an analogy between this "artificial" selection and what he termed "natural" selection.

those differences through generations of selective breeding. The results were such that if these pigeon varieties had been encountered in the wild, zoologists would have judged them to be different species! If such differences can be created artificially by pigeon breeders, could they not also be created naturally? Could there be a *natural* selection that was analogous to this *artificial* selection? Darwin began to think so.

In the midst of these ruminations about population and selective breeding, Darwin learned from the famous ornithologist John Gould, who was classifying some of his *Beagle* specimens, that there was something very interesting about the Galápagos birds. The birds that Darwin thought were finches, warblers, wrens, and "gross-beaks" were in fact all finches. Furthermore, Gould was "induced to regard them as constituting an entirely new group containing 14 species, and appearing to be strictly confined to the Galápagos islands" (Gould, quoted in Weiner, 1994, p. 28). These finch species were distinguished by their size and by clear differences in the shapes of their beaks. Wondering about these differences, Darwin reexamined his sketchy notes on the islands of origin for the birds and saw a pattern—finches with specific beak shapes tended to cluster on islands that differed in terms of available food sources. For instance, finches living on islands with a large supply of certain types of hard-shelled nuts and seeds had tough, blunted beaks, ideally suited for cracking open this food source. Other birds had thinner beaks, nicely designed to spear the insects that populated their islands (Figure 5.5).

Darwin's Delay   Much has been made of the fact that Darwin had outlined the essential features of his theory of evolution by the early 1840s, yet it took him almost 20 years to publish his *Origin of Species* in 1859 (Richards, 1983). Part of the reason was health—he was often incapacitated for months at a time. A second reason for the delay was that he was concerned about the reactions of his peers. When the anonymously authored and highly speculative *Vestiges of Creation* appeared in 1844, the same year that Darwin was entrusting his 200-page manuscript to his wife's care, it was ridiculed by the British community of zoologists, geologists, and botanists (including Lyell, who was now a close friend of Darwin's). Some of the reaction was to the vagueness of the proposed mechanism for evolutionary change in *Vestiges*. Darwin knew his model was better, but much of the negative response to

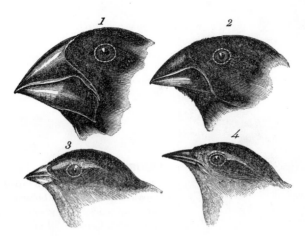

FIGURE 5.5   Darwin's finches—note the differences in beak size and shape.

Vestiges was to the idea of evolution itself. In a letter to the botanist Joseph Hooker, a close friend to whom he was confiding about his theory, Darwin wrote that proposing a theory of evolution was like "confessing a murder" (Colp, 1986). If he published in 1844, Darwin feared that his theory would be confused with *Vestiges* and condemned by association.

A third reason for Darwin's delay was his conservative scientific nature. He knew he had a good theory and some data to support it, but he also knew that he needed more evidence before he would be willing to go public. Thus he spent years carefully gathering evidence to flesh out the theory. For instance, in 1846 he began an intensive 8-year study of the evolutionary history of barnacles, eventually publishing the results in four volumes. He also joined a local pigeon fanciers club and did some of his own pigeon breeding. And at Down House, one could always find a dozen experiments going on at the same time. For example, to determine how seeds could be spread over large distances, he tested the idea that undigested seeds might be carried in the stomachs of birds. So he collected bird droppings, poking through them until he came across the occasional seed, which he planted. To his pleasant surprise, the seeds often germinated and grew.

Darwin's delay in publishing would have been even longer if not for a letter he received on June 18, 1858. It was from a fellow naturalist with an interest in evolution, Alfred Russel Wallace (1823–1913), who was at the time on the other side of the world in Malaysia. Wallace (Figure 5.6) asked Darwin's opinion on a brief paper that he enclosed with the letter—the paper outlined a theory of evolution that was remarkably similar to Darwin's. Darwin was

FIGURE 5.6 Alfred Russel Wallace (1823–1913).

KEY DATE—1859

This year marked the publication of Darwin's revolutionary *Origin of Species*, perhaps the most important book published in the 19th century.

These events also occurred that year:

- Hermann Helmholtz (Chapter 3) published important research on color blindness
- America's first oil well was drilled in Titusville, Pennsylvania
- The steamroller was invented
- Abolitionist John Brown attacked the federal arsenal at Harper's Ferry in October; he was captured, tried, and hung
- German chemist Albert Niemann successfully isolated the drug cocaine from the leaves of the coca plant
- The French acrobat Charles Blondin crossed Niagara Falls on a tightrope

- Samuel Smiles published *Self-Help*, a manual on how to succeed in life
- Daniel Emmett composed the song "Dixie"

These people were born:

- Arthur Conan Doyle, British creator of Sherlock Holmes
- Georges Seurat, French neo-impressionist painter (e.g., *Sunday Afternoon on the Island of La Grande Jatte*)

These people died:

- Washington Irving, American author (e.g., *The Legend of Sleepy Hollow*)
- Alexander von Humboldt, German astronomer, geologist, and explorer

shaken, writing to Lyell that "If Wallace had my MS. sketch written out in 1842, he could not have made a better short abstract!" (quoted in Desmond & Moore, 1991, p. 467).

After seeking the advice of Hooker and Lyell, Darwin agreed to a joint presentation at the July 1, 1858, meeting of the Linnean Society. Thus it occurred that the first public disclosure of Darwin's theory of evolution came at a professional meeting of botanists. The secretary of the society read Wallace's paper and an abstract of Darwin's 1844 essay. Neither Darwin (distraught—his youngest child had died 2 days before the meeting) nor Wallace (still on the other side of the world) attended the meeting, and neither paper attracted much attention at the time. The Wallace letter sent a clear message to Darwin, however. To establish his legitimate priority, he needed to publish his theory, along with the supporting evidence that he had accumulated over the years. Despite continuing ill health, Darwin completed the work over the next 15 months, and *On the Origin of Species by Means of Natural Selection or the Preservation of Favoured Races in the Struggle for Life* appeared in bookshops on November 22, 1859. The initial printing of 1,250 copies sold out on the first day.

Elements of the Theory of Evolution After a brief introduction, in which Darwin emphasized the importance of the *Beagle* voyage and gave credit to Wallace, the *Origin of Species* opens with two chapters establishing the fact that members of a given species vary from each other. In the first chapter, "Variation Under Domestication," Darwin showed how individual differences within a species could be accentuated through deliberate breeding—artificial selection. This chapter prepared the way for him to argue later that just as there is deliberate selection by human breeders, there is also a "natural" selection by the conditions of everyday existence. In Chapter 2, "Variation Under Nature," Darwin noted the universality of individual differences within species found in nature. He made the connection to Chapter 1 by pointing out that these differences "thus afford materials for natural selection to act on and accumulate, in the same manner as man accumulates individual differences in his domesticated products" (Darwin, 1859/1958b, p. 59).

Because the science of genetics was yet to be born, Darwin had no concept of the phenomenon of genetic mutation, the primary means of creating individual differences within a species. Thus he had to guess about the causes of variation. He believed that some variation was spontaneous and random, much like mutation, but he also allowed for the Lamarckian idea that characteristics acquired during one's lifetime could be passed on to offspring.

Darwin's third and fourth chapters, the "Struggle for Existence" and "Natural Selection," contain the core of the theory. Citing Malthus, Darwin first argued that in nature, species face an inevitable struggle to survive because they produce offspring at a rate that outpaces the food supply. If that is the case, then those individuals having a variation that puts them at a slight advantage in the struggle will be "selected" by nature and live long enough to reproduce; those without the advantage will die. Over several generations, the "adaptive" variation will become more common. In Darwin's words:

> Owing to this struggle [for life], variations, however slight and from whatever cause proceeding, if they be in any degree profitable to the individuals of a species, . . . will tend to the preservation of such individuals, and will generally be inherited by the offspring. . . .
>
> This preservation of favorable individual differences and variations, and the destruction of those which are injurious, I have called Natural Selection, or the Survival of the Fittest (Darwin, 1859/1958b, pp. 74, 88)

Darwin's finches illustrate the manner in which the struggle for existence and **natural selection** combine to alter species. Darwin believed that the original finches arrived as a single species from the mainland and settled in the various islands of the Galápagos. Because there is variation among members of a species in the wild, slight differences from one finch to another existed, including variations in the shapes of the birds' beaks. Suppose some of the birds happened to land on islands rich in certain types of seeds that are encased in hard shells. Those finches with slightly tougher and more blunted beaks would have an advantage in the hunt for these seeds. Finches with slightly thinner beaks would have a more difficult time getting at the seeds and would be more likely to die. Hence, the finches with the more "adaptive variation" would be "naturally selected" in the "struggle for existence." They would survive and pass on the advantage to their offspring. Over time, finches on that particular island would form a new species characterized by the specific beak shape. Similarly, on another island rich in insects, a species of finch with beaks thin enough to reach into small spaces would evolve.

Darwin believed that evolution by natural selection also explained extinction and the reason why modern species resemble fossils of extinct species found in the same geographical region. In South America, for example, Darwin had uncovered fossilized bones of animals similar to modern llamas but two to three times as large. Over time, he argued, the larger species had encountered environmental events (e.g., droughts) that reduced the food supply and favored the survival of smaller variations that did not need to eat as much.

In the remaining 11 chapters of the *Origin*, Darwin described evidence in support of his theory and tried to answer the objections he knew would be forthcoming. He recognized that most people believed in the divine creation of every single species, but asked his readers to consider the evidence he had placed before them.

After the Origin of Species Reaction to Darwin's theory was not long in coming. Although he did not discuss humans in the *Origin*, the implications were clear and directly threatening to the Church of England. It might have been declining in power during the second half of the 19th century, but the Anglican Church was still capable of making its presence felt and Darwin was denounced from pulpits throughout England. In the debates over evolution, Darwin himself stayed above the fray, preferring to have his case argued by others. One such ardent Darwinian was Thomas Huxley (1825–1895), who became known as "Darwin's bulldog" (Browne, 2002). In a famous debate at Oxford, during a meeting of the British Association for the Advancement of Science, Huxley defended Darwin against Samuel Wilberforce, an Anglican bishop and vocal opponent of evolution. Each made a series of complex arguments, but what is remembered is that at the end of his talk, Wilberforce, in jest, asked whether Huxley was related to an ape on his grandmother's or his grandfather's side of the family. Before beginning his reply, Huxley is said to have muttered, "The Lord hath delivered him into my hands." He then began a point-by-point rebuttal of Wilberforce's arguments, ending with this response to the question about his lineage:

> If I would rather have a miserable ape for a grandfather or a man highly endowed by
> nature and possessed of great means and influence, and yet who employs those faculties
> for the mere purpose of introducing ridicule into a grave scientific discussion—
> I unhesitatingly affirm my preference for the ape. (quoted in Browne, 2002, p. 122)

Darwin's theory caused considerable consternation in the religious community, but the reaction in the scientific community was quite different. In his autobiography, Darwin argued that although there had been some initial resistance among some scientists (e.g., Lyell), general acceptance of the idea of evolution by natural selection came rather quickly. While rejecting the idea that the success of his book demonstrated that the topic of evolution was "in the air," Darwin nonetheless recognized the importance of the zeitgeist: "What I believe was strictly true is that innumerable well-observed facts were stored in the minds of naturalists ready to take their proper places as soon as any theory which would receive them was sufficiently explained" (Darwin, 1892/1958a, p. 45).

As you recall from Chapter 1, one issue that pervades historical analysis is the extent to which people either move history or are themselves moved by historical forces—the personalistic versus naturalistic issue. The theory of evolution is a good illustration. From a personalistic standpoint, there is no question that Darwin had enormous influence. Regardless of whether the topic was in the air, Darwin was the one who marshaled the massive amounts of evidence, developed a workable theory, and produced the book that made a compelling case for evolution. Indeed, the importance of Darwin's ideas eventually led some observers to begin using the phrase Darwinian evolution, an example of what Chapter 1 called an *eponym*—identifying an idea with a person's name. The title of this chapter, borrowed from the title of a well-known book by Loren Eiseley (1958) on Darwin and evolution (*Darwin's Century: Evolution and the Men Who Discovered It*), emphasizes the personalistic. Yet it is also clear that Darwin was not the only intellectual who was thinking in evolutionary terms. Note that the title of Eiseley's book suggests the involvement of more people than just Darwin. We have already seen that Lyell proposed an evolutionary theory for geology, that several earlier evolutionary models of biological change had appeared before Darwin's (Erasmus Darwin, Lamarck, *Vestiges*), and that the Wallace theory featured natural selection. There were others. For example, William Wells, an American physician, delivered an address to the Royal Society of London in 1813 in which he explicitly drew the same comparison that Darwin later made between artificial and natural selection, although he didn't use the same terms. And in 1831, the Scottish botanist Patrick Matthew described what amounted to natural selection in an obscure book on trees. Much to Darwin's chagrin, shortly after the publication of his *Origin of Species* in 1859, the belligerent Matthews publicly challenged Darwin on priority, going as far as to print and distribute cards proclaiming himself the originator of the theory (Eiseley, 1958). Neither Wells nor Matthews followed their writings with sustained research on evolutionary change, however, so their primary importance is to provide additional evidence that the idea of evolutionary change was not uncommon in the 19th century.

As for Darwin, despite his ever-present illnesses, and in the face of public criticism and religious condemnation, he worked vigilantly during his remaining years. He continued to collect evidence for his theory, publishing important works on topics ranging from orchids to earthworms. Although he avoided discussing human evolution in the *Origin of Species*, he addressed the topic head on in *The Descent of Man, and Selection in Relation to Sex* (1871) and *Expressions of the Emotions in Man and Animals* (1872). In *Descent of Man*, Darwin added the idea of **sexual selection** to accompany his core idea of natural selection. Sexual selection entails the complementary processes of same-sex competition and female mate preference—the basic idea is that when males compete for female attention, any advantage they might have (e.g., larger antlers) will favor them in establishing dominance over other males and in the likelihood of being selected by females (Buss, 2009). Traits resulting from sexual selection are those that seem, by themselves, to have no direct survival benefit for the individual (e.g., a peacock's feathers) but do seem to favor the individual when competing for mates.

The end for Darwin came on April 19, 1882. Although he wished to be buried quietly at Down, his cousin Francis Galton organized a successful campaign to have him interred among other British heroes at London's Westminster Abbey, just across the street from the Houses of Parliament. Today, the large rectangular stone marking Darwin's burial place can be found on the floor of the north side of the Abbey, just below the bust of Sir Isaac Newton.

Darwin and Psychology's History

In 1877 Darwin contributed directly to the history of developmental psychology by publishing, in the British journal *Mind*, an article called a "Biographical Sketch of an Infant." It was based on extensive notes written years before on the physical and psychological development of his firstborn son, William. But Darwin's main contribution to psychology was his theory of evolution, which promoted a way of thinking among American psychologists that eventually became known as **functionalism**. This school of thought is examined in Chapters 7 and 8; for now, it is enough to say that the functionalists were interested in studying human behaviors and mental processes in terms of how they helped the individual adapt to an ever-changing environment (Green, 2009). Consciousness, for instance, was said to serve the adaptive function of enabling the individual to assess a problem situation and solve it quickly. Similarly, habits served to free the individual's limited consciousness to concentrate on unsolved problems.

Two specific aspects of the theory also have strongly influenced psychology's history (Boring, 1963c). First, an obvious implication of the theory, which Darwin made explicit in *The Descent of Man* (1871), was that a continuity of mental processes existed between humans and other species. This led to an increased interest in what came to be called **comparative psychology**, the systematic study of similarities and differences among all animal species. Second, the emphasis on individual variation led to the systematic study of **individual differences**, a research tradition that eventually led to the measurement of differences via intelligence and personality tests. These developments need some elaboration.

THE ORIGINS OF COMPARATIVE PSYCHOLOGY

Studies of animal behavior preceded Darwin, but comparative research accelerated in the wake of Darwin's argument for continuity among species. Darwin himself may be considered one of the earliest comparative psychologists—many of the observations of animal behavior in his *Beagle* notebooks were comparative in nature (Armstrong, 1993). Comparisons among species also appear frequently in his book on emotions. Originally intended as a chapter in *The Descent of Man* (1871), the topic of the origins of emotional expression took on a life of its own, and Darwin published it separately as the *Expressions of the Emotions in Man and Animals* (1872). As the first scientific attempt to study emotional expressions, the book is Darwin's most important direct contribution to psychology's history. It includes accounts of the circumstances producing the various types of emotional responses, detailed descriptions of how these emotions are expressed by the facial musculature, and a theory of how the expressions might have evolved.

Darwin on the Evolution of Emotional Expressions

Darwin opened his book by arguing for an evolutionary approach to the study of emotional expressions, pointing out that for humans, things such as "the bristling of the hair under the influence of extreme terror...can hardly be understood, except on the belief that man once existed in a much lower and animal-like condition" (Darwin, 1872, p. 12). He then described the problems encountered when studying emotions in normal adults. First, while strong emotions certainly occur, most emotional expressions are muted. Studying one's own emotions is not easy either, because the experience of a strong emotion is incompatible with a rational analysis of it. One cannot feel terror and dispassionately observe it in oneself at the same time. Investigating the forms and the causes of emotional expressions required a more creative strategy, and Darwin met the challenge by proposing several methods. For instance, he suggested studying children and the insane as a way to classify the patterns of emotional expression. Their expressions of such emotions as anger, joy, and fear, not restricted by normal adult inhibitions, would be more intense and their features more easily classified as a result. Another method was to use a technique called galvanization. As shown in Figure 5.7, electrodes touched the surface of the skin and stimulation produced recognizable muscle contractions. The idea was to establish exactly which muscles were involved in each emotional expression. Hence, Figure 5.7a shows an elderly man with a normal smile, whereas Figure 5.7b shows the result of stimulating the muscles to the sides of the mouth. Darwin used the example to show that laughter involves specific sets of muscles.

Darwin also reasoned that if emotional expressions were the result of evolution, then the same basic expressions would be found around the world. By using a large network

(a)   *(b)*

FIGURE 5.7 Expressing emotions: natural versus "galvanized" smiles. From Darwin (1872).

of correspondents, including many encountered on the *Beagle* voyage, Darwin conducted the first cross-cultural study of emotional expressions. Darwin asked his correspondents to examine the facial expressions displayed in cultures far and wide and answer questions like the following:

> Is astonishment expressed by the eyes and mouth being opened wide, and by the eyebrows being raised?...
>
> When a man sneers or snarls at another, is the corner of the upper lip over the canine or eye tooth raised on the side facing the man whom he addresses?...
>
> Is the head nodded vertically in affirmation, and shaken laterally in negation? (Darwin, 1872, pp. 15–16)

Darwin's final method, studying the emotional expressions of animals, gave him clues for a theory about the origins of emotional expressions. His theory involved three basic principles. He devoted a chapter to each principle and then filled the bulk of the 366-page book with chapters devoted to detailed descriptions of the various emotions.

Principle one, the principle of **serviceable associated habits**, was the most important. Incorporating the Lamarckian idea of the inheritance of acquired characteristics, Darwin argued that some emotional expressions were initially serviceable, or useful (Hess & Thibault, 2009). That is, they originated in bodily actions that served some adaptive function, helping the organism to survive the struggle for existence. Those actions then became associated with situations similar to the ones in which they originally occurred. These acquired expressions were then inherited. Consider the expression of contempt. In exaggerated form, it includes a pronounced intake of air through the nose, accompanied by a lifting and turning away of the head. According to Darwin, the characteristic expression of this emotion derived from a situation in which our evolutionary ancestors reacted to a physically offensive odor. Through habit and inheritance, the same reaction now occurs whenever a person is confronted with a person or situation judged to be offensive: "We seem thus to say to the despised person that he smells offensively, in nearly the same manner as we express to him by half-closing our eyelids, or turning away our faces, that he is not worth looking at" (p. 255). Similarly, the emotion of surprise includes raising one's eyebrows, which is a "serviceable habit." We wish to determine quickly the cause of that which surprises us, according to Darwin, "and we consequently open our eyes fully, so that the field of vision may be increased, and the eyeballs moved easily in any direction" (p. 281).

Darwin's second principle for explaining the form of emotional expression was based on the idea that emotions that are just the opposite of each other are expressed in bodily reactions that are similarly opposed. He called it the principle of **antithesis**. As examples, Darwin pointed to numerous animal expressions. When faced with a perceived threat, for instance, a dog will strike a pose designed to make it look bigger and more of a danger to a potential enemy (e.g., the hair on its back bristles). The opposite of this threat gesture, however, is a gesture of submission. While a stranger might elicit the dog's threat gesture, the dog's master would elicit the gesture of submission.

Darwin's third principle concerned what he called the **direct action of the nervous system**. In effect, these expressions are side effects of the physiological arousal that accompanies strongly felt emotions. As an example of direct action, Darwin cited the tendency to tremble, which could accompany any strong emotion and would therefore not be associated with any specific one.

A theme throughout Darwin's book is the universality of emotional expression. His questionnaire results, similar to the findings of modern cross-cultural studies, showed that all over the world, basic emotions were expressed in the same manner. A smile means the same thing everywhere. If emotional expressions are universal, the implication is that they are instinctive; and consequently, human emotional behavior can be understood only by knowing its evolutionary past.

Along with Darwin's *Descent of Man*, the emotions book made it clear that humans shared traits with animals and that continuity in mental and emotional processes existed. Almost immediately, other naturalists began exploring this continuum. Many people were involved, but the best known were two Englishmen, George Romanes and Lloyd Morgan. Before reading about them, however, read the Close-Up; it describes the contributions of a third Briton, Douglas Spalding, who is normally ignored in histories of psychology but worthy of special note.

CLOSE-UP

DOUGLAS SPALDING AND THE EXPERIMENTAL STUDY OF INSTINCT

An important but typically overlooked pioneer in the study of animal behavior was Douglas Spalding. Had he lived a full life, he almost certainly would be known today as the founder of modern **ethology**, the study of instinctive animal behavior. Born in London to working-class parents in 1840, he did not have the luxuries of inherited wealth and an Oxford or Cambridge education to support his scientific work. Instead he earned his keep by repairing slate roofs, and he was mostly self-educated. He did manage to complete a law degree in London in his early twenties, however, and during this time he contracted the tuberculosis that eventually would kill him. While traveling for health reasons in southern Europe in the late 1860s, he met and came under the influence of the famous British philosopher John Stuart Mill (Chapter 2), who by then had retired to Avignon in the south of France. Mill recommended Spalding as a tutor for the two young sons of Lord and Lady Amberly, two ardent followers of Mill's liberal political philosophy. The younger son would become one of the best-known philosophers of the 20th century, Bertrand Russell.

Spalding apparently began his animal research in the 1860s, influenced by the evolutionary fervor that swept through the intelligentsia of the day. Although he never wrote a book and his studies were scattered throughout several popular magazines of the day, his research was noteworthy enough to catch the attention of the famous American psychologist-philosopher William James (Chapter 6). In a chapter on instinct in Volume II of his famous *Principles of Psychology*, James (1890/1950b) described "Mr. Spalding's wonderful article on instinct" (p. 396). He was referring to a piece that Spalding wrote for *Macmillan's Magazine* in 1873.

In that article, Spalding addressed the British empiricists' claim that such skills as depth perception and sound localization were learned very early in life as the result of direct sensory experience. Spalding's observations showed that experience was irrelevant, however—certain perceptual abilities, at least in animals, did not result from practice but were the result of **instinct**. He also demonstrated several "species-specific" phenomena that later became associated with the work of 20th-century ethologists Konrad Lorenz and Niko Tinbergen.

Instinct

To determine whether experience is necessary for depth perception in baby chicks, Spalding developed a clever procedure. In his words, "Taking eggs just when the little prisoners had begun to break their way out, I removed a piece of the shell, and before they had opened their eyes drew over their heads little hoods" (Spalding, 1873; reprinted in Haldane, 1954, p. 3). The hoods remained intact for several days, preventing the chicks from having any visual experiences. Other hatchlings had "gum paper" inserted into their ears to eliminate auditory experiences. When the hoods were removed, the chicks showed no ill effects. For example, after spending just a minute or two adjusting to light, they had no difficulty pecking accurately at the insects provided by Spalding. Those with plugged ears responded similarly—when the obstruction was removed, they responded immediately to the call from an unseen mother hen and ran in the proper direction. Spalding concluded that raw instinct played an important role in animal behavior and that the British empiricists had overstated the importance of experience.

Imprinting

A famous picture, found in virtually all general psychology texts, shows a fatherly Konrad Lorenz, the modern-day founder of ethology, walking through a field followed by a string of young goslings. Lorenz showed that the young birds would follow the first object that they were able to detect moving, and he called the phenomenon **imprinting**. Although he did not label it, Spalding observed the same behavior.

> Chickens as soon as they are able to walk will follow any moving object. And, when guided by sight alone, they seem to have no more disposition to follow a hen than to follow a duck, or a human being.
>
> Unreflecting onlookers, when they saw chickens a day old running after me, and older ones following me miles and answering to my whistle, imagined that I must have some occult power over the creatures, whereas I simply allowed them to follow me from the first. (Spalding, 1873; reprinted in Haldane, 1954, p. 6)

Critical Periods

Spalding also described behavior illustrating the modern ethological concept of a **critical period** —certain behaviors must develop within a specific time frame, if they are to develop at all. For example, Spalding found that if chicks were prevented from hearing the call of the mother hen for 8–10 days, they would never recognize the mother. Also, while the chicks became attached to him when they were hooded for up to 3 days, those hooded for 4 days were afraid of him.

Spalding continued his animal studies when he began tutoring the children of Lord and Lady Amberly in 1873. The sprawling country house in England's Wye Valley was soon filled with a variety of species. The unconventional Lady Amberly, a strong advocate for women's equality, served as Spalding's research assistant and, according to some accounts (e.g., Boakes, 1984), she also tutored the naive Spalding in the human instinct of love. During this time, Spalding studied the flight instinct, demonstrating that birds did not have to learn how to fly. After they hatched, he placed swallows and other nesting birds in wire mesh enclosures that prevented them from using their wings. Once released, they nonetheless flew immediately if sufficiently mature.

Spalding's idyllic life with the Amberlys came to an abrupt end in 1874, when both Lady Amberly and a young daughter died of diphtheria. A dispirited Lord Amberly also died within 2 years, naming Spalding as guardian to his two sons. Amberly's parents successfully contested the will, however, and Spalding was on his own (Gray, 1962). He soon left England, and his tuberculosis reappeared. He was 37 when he died in France in 1877.

George Romanes (1848–1894) and the Anecdotal Method

Like Darwin, George Romanes (Figure 5.8) was wealthy, stumbled through an adolescence of minimal accomplishment, appeared headed for the ministry but didn't get there, and became devoted to science as a result of his experiences at Cambridge (Lesch, 1972). A skilled researcher in physiology, Romanes became caught up in the prevailing excitement over Darwin's theory and decided to investigate the levels of mental ability that could be found in other species. Darwin apparently considered the younger man to be his protégé; he often entertained Romanes at Down House and turned over some of his notes on animal behavior to the young scholar (Desmond & Moore, 1991).

Romanes combined Darwin's data with information he had been collecting on his own and in 1882, shortly after Darwin's death, he published *Animal Intelligence* (Romanes, 1882/1886), a detailed catalog of animal behavior, from insects to primates. The book has earned Romanes the title of founder of comparative psychology, even though the term was introduced by Pierre Flourens (Chapter 3) in 1864 (Jaynes, 1969b), and several books similar to Romanes's effort preceded him or appeared about the same time (Johnston, 2003). Romanes gets credit because he made an effort to define the new field in a systematic fashion, doing so by drawing a parallel between comparative psychology and comparative anatomy. Romanes argued that just as the specialist in anatomy made comparisons among the anatomical features of various species, to examine the evolution of physical structure, so the comparative

FIGURE 5.8 George Romanes (1848–1894).

psychologist would study differences among the psychological (i.e., mental) features of different species, to examine mental evolution.

Traditional accounts of Romanes's work focus on his overuse of uncritical stories about animal behavior supplied by others. **Anecdotal evidence**, as we have already seen in the discussion of phrenology (Chapter 3), has great potential for introducing bias and, in the case of comparative psychology, exaggerating the abilities of animals. Thus Romanes's work has sometimes been discredited. This is unfortunate, because Romanes was well aware of the problems with anecdotal evidence and took some care to include reliable reports of behavior in his book. For example, he tried to include accounts from observers known to be competent (e.g., Darwin), and he accepted unusual accounts of behavior only if they were reported independently by two or more persons. Nonetheless, Romanes himself recognized that the book, considered by itself, might seem to be little more than a collection of unusual animal stories. He expected that his subsequent books, outlining a theory of mental evolution, would be more important, and that this initial "fact" book would come to be viewed as a preliminary step to the more systematic treatises (Boakes, 1984). Romanes indeed published his theory books, but they were largely ignored; his reputation, somewhat tainted, rests on the fact book.

Romanes took more precautions in his accounts of animal behavior than are usually attributed to him, but *Animal Intelligence* does nonetheless rely mainly on stories told by others and not on direct observation by Romanes. It also tends toward **anthropomorphism**, the attribution of human faculties to nonhuman entities. For instance, he argued that spiders have a "fondness" for music (p. 205), that scorpions feel despair and commit suicide when surrounded by fire or intense heat (p. 222), that birds show sympathy and conjugal fidelity (pp. 271–273), that beavers show "sagacity and forethought" when selecting sites for their lodges (p. 371) and have an intellectual appreciation for the architectural principles involved in dam building (p. 376). Romanes was especially impressed with the intellectual capacity of dogs, arguing that they were capable of planning, bartering, recognizing information in pictures, and in this example, logical inference:

> Coming now to cases more distinctly indicative of reason . . . , dogs indisputably show that they possess this faculty. Thus, for instance, Livingstone [the African explorer] gives the following observation. A dog tracking his master along a road came to a place where three roads diverged. Scenting along two of the roads and not finding the trail, he ran off on the third without waiting to smell. Here, therefore, is a true act of inference. If the track is not on A or B, it must be on C, there being no other alternative. (Romanes, 1882/1886, p. 457)

Conwy Lloyd Morgan (1852–1936) and his "Canon"

The problems with Romanes's first book on animal behavior, with its emphasis on anecdotes and its excessive anthropomorphism, were noted by another British naturalist, C. Lloyd Morgan (Figure 5.9). Son of a lawyer, Morgan attended the School of Mines at the Royal College of Science in London to be trained as a mining engineer. At the School of Mines, he came under the influence of the evolutionist Thomas Huxley (Darwin's "bulldog"). This led Morgan to an interest in zoology and geology, and eventually to a lifetime position as a professor of these topics at University College, Bristol, starting in 1883. He published several books on geology, but he is best known for his work in comparative psychology, reflected in

FIGURE 5.9 C. Lloyd Morgan (1852–1936).

books with titles like *Animal Life and Intelligence* (1890) and *An Introduction to Comparative Psychology* (1895). Just as Romanes was a protégé of Darwin, Morgan was a follower and admirer of Romanes, but he eventually developed a more systematic comparative psychology than his mentor, based more on direct observation than the compiling of anecdotes.

Morgan is known today for arguing that explanations for animal behavior should be no more complex than observational evidence allowed. This appeal came to be called **Lloyd Morgan's canon**. As he put it: "In no case may we interpret an action as the outcome of the exercise of a higher psychical faculty, if it can be interpreted as the outcome of the exercise of one which stands lower in the psychological scale" (Morgan, 1895/1903, p. 59). In response to the account you just read of a dog apparently using inference (a "higher psychical faculty"), for example, Morgan would have noted that just because the dog chose the third path quickly does not rule out the use of scent ("lower on the psychological scale") as determining the choice.

Morgan did not rule out the use of anecdotes—after all, they often amount to careful observations. Yet Morgan believed that anecdotes needed to be interpreted with caution, and he had greater confidence in systematic observation, especially if he was the one doing the observing. Two examples illustrate the point. First, before beginning his tenure at Bristol, Morgan taught for 5 years in South Africa, where he had the opportunity to observe scorpion behavior firsthand. Thus he had the opportunity to examine Romanes's anthropomorphic claim about scorpions feeling despair and committing suicide when surrounded by fire. Could there be a simpler explanation of the fact that scorpions occasionally sting themselves to death? Morgan thought so. He observed that scorpions regularly used their tails to remove foreign substances and other irritants (e.g., smoke) from the surface of their bodies. It was a simple reflex action, not a deliberate, calculated response arising out of "despair." Every once in a while, Morgan observed, the reflex action would be just a bit too vigorous, resulting in the demise of a scorpion. There was no need to propose a "higher psychical faculty" (a decision to commit suicide) when the behavior could be seen as the result of some factor "lower in the psychological scale" (a functional reflex action).

A second example used by Morgan is a famous one. Romanes had credited cats and dogs with the mental ability to understand simple mechanical principles and to plan, based on anecdotal examples of dogs opening gates and escaping from yards. Morgan, however, believed that such behavior had a simpler explanation, and he used his fox terrier, Tony, as a case in point. Tony could place his head through an opening in a gate and open the latch by lifting upward. The gate then swung open and Tony was free to leave the yard and "get out into the road, where there was often much to interest him; cats to be worried, other dogs with whom to establish a sniffing acquaintance, and so forth" (Morgan, 1895/1903, p. 292). To a naive observer, it might appear that the dog rationally "understood" the mechanics of the gate operation and the concept of lifting the latch as a planned means to a desired end. To Morgan, however, the behavior was simply the result of a 3-week series of trial-and-error actions prompted by the dog's attempts to escape the yard for the romance of the road. He noted that before hitting on the correct solution, Tony had tried just about everything else, running back and forth along the fence, sticking his head between the bars at numerous locations, and eventually hitting upon the correct action by accident. After he had escaped one time, he soon abandoned the unsuccessful behaviors and learned to repeat the successful one.

Morgan's canon is sometimes used to highlight an important shift in how comparative psychologists thought about animal behavior and Darwin's notion of the continuity among species. It is often argued that before Morgan, naturalists were overly anthropomorphic and searched for evidence of varying amounts of cognition in virtually all species. After Morgan, so the story goes, researchers looked for simpler (i.e., more "parsimonious") processes to explain an animal's actions, gradually resulting in the behaviorist dictum that behaviors, even human ones, are best understood in terms of simple conditioning processes. Thus B. F. Skinner wrote in the opening pages of his first book, *The Behavior of Organisms* (1938), that "Lloyd Morgan, with his principle of parsimony, dispensed with [mental faculties in animals] in a reasonably successful attempt to account for characteristic animal behavior without them" (p. 4). And in a well-known book on "theories of learning," Hilgard (1948) stated that the canon "which had seriously undercut the attributing of higher mental processes to animals had fairly well succeeded via behaviorism in excising them from humans as well" (p. 179). In short, Morgan is often seen as a pivotal figure in the "progress" from cute animal stories implying animal cognition to sophisticated experimental research and a mechanical conception of animal behavior (including human animals) that eliminates the need for mental processes as explanations for behavior. Such an interpretation is mistaken, however. Morgan can indeed be credited for arguing that an understanding of animal behavior must go beyond the collection of anecdotes and embrace more systematic observational strategies. Yet to say that Morgan wished to rule out the existence of animal consciousness and intelligence is wrong. As Morgan himself said, in the sentence immediately following the canon:

> To this, however, it should be added, lest the range of the principle be misunderstood, that the canon *by no means excludes the interpretation of a particular activity in terms of the higher processes*, if we already have some independent evidence of the occurrence of these higher processes in the animal under observation. (Morgan, 1895/1903, p. 59; emphasis added)

Thus Morgan did not intend for his canon to be a prohibition against the idea of higher mental processes in animals—he was merely urging methodological caution. According to Costall (1993), Morgan's true purpose was to broaden the range of criteria on which to base continuity among species. Rather than relying exclusively on a search for sophisticated rational reflection on the part of a variety of species, other types of mental processes, differing in degrees of complexity, could be included. Put in evolutionary terms, Morgan's proposal was that animals exhibited many levels of cognition, reaching a level of complexity just sufficient to enable them to survive their own unique struggle for existence. The point of the canon was to argue that there was no reason to suggest levels of mental capability *beyond* that needed to survive. It is also wrong to say that Morgan rejected anthropomorphism as a means for understanding animal behavior. Although he thought Romanes might have been overgenerous in his anthropomorphic attributions, Morgan saw no problem with the basic logic of trying to understand animal cognition by looking for parallels in human cognition.

Comparative Psychology in America

It is not surprising that comparative psychology developed a firm foothold in Great Britain in the mid to late 19th century, as reflected in the work of Darwin, Romanes, Spalding, and Morgan. Interest in the topic developed quickly in the United States as well, and you will learn about two prime examples in later chapters: first, an animal laboratory developed at Clark University in the mid-1890s, under the leadership of Linus Kline, Willard Small, and Edmund Sanford, the laboratory director there. As you will discover in the Close-Up for Chapter 6, these researchers can be credited with creating one of psychology's enduring methods—maze learning. Also, Kline wrote an article entitled "Suggestions Toward a Laboratory Course in Comparative Psychology" (1899) that influenced instruction in comparative psychology for years. The second example occurs in Chapter 7—E. L. Thorndike's work on puzzle box learning. It is also worth noting that several American researchers developed interests in animal behavior and studied it in the British naturalist tradition. One, John Bascom, even wrote a textbook with *comparative psychology* in the title as early as 1878 (Johnston, 2003).

STUDYING INDIVIDUAL DIFFERENCES

A cornerstone of Darwin's theory, the raw material for natural selection, was the idea that individual members of a species varied from each other. For psychology, this fact led to the systematic study of *individual differences*, a research tradition that includes the creation of techniques to measure those differences. Today's intelligence and personality tests are just two outcomes of this tradition. The person most directly responsible for initiating the study of individual differences was Darwin's half-cousin, Francis Galton, whose obsession with measurement led one scientist to refer to him as the 19th century's "apostle of quantification" (Gould, 1981, p. 75).

Francis Galton (1822–1911): Jack of All Sciences

Like his more famous relative, Galton (Figure 5.10) thought for a time that his future was in medicine; but he was likewise put off by the experience of witnessing "grisly postmortems and

FIGURE 5.10 The ever-curious Francis Galton.

assist[ing] at live operations performed without anesthetics" (quoted in Fancher, 2009, p. 86). Fortunately for his future prospects, though, inherited wealth enabled him to indulge a wide range of interests. His insatiable curiosity, combined with a brilliant intellect that manifested itself at an early age,[8] resulted in a diverse set of accomplishments, only a small portion of which relates directly to psychology. For example, he became one of a number of famous British explorers of Africa during the Victorian era. His exploits won him a gold medal from the Royal Geographical Society, and he became a recognized public figure after publishing an account of his explorations and a popular (eight editions) travel guide for the inexperienced explorer. The latter included suggestions on everything from shelter to navigation to hunting to cooking, along with paternalistic advice on dealing with native populations: "A frank, joking but determined manner joined with an air of showing more confidence in the good faith of the natives than you really feel, is the best" (Galton, 1855; quoted in Forrest, 1974, p. 64).

In addition to geography and exploration, Galton made original contributions to several other fields. By gathering weather information from various locations at the same times during the day, for instance, he created the first systematic weather maps, and he was the first to observe the relationships between high- and low-pressure systems and how they influenced the weather. By measuring the patterns of swirls on the fingertips of hundreds of people, he demonstrated that every person had a unique pattern. Scotland Yard eventually started using this "fingerprinting" technique for identification purposes. This procedure, of course, is an example of looking for individual differences. Indeed, Galton's work in fingerprinting was just a small piece of his overall strategy of quantifying differences between people over a range of variables. And this leads to Galton's importance for psychology.

---

[8]Galton resembled another child prodigy, John Stuart Mill, in this regard. Like Mill, Galton displayed adultlike abilities at a tender age. He could read and write English by age 3, translate some Latin by age 5, and quote from Shakespeare by his 6th birthday.

The Nature of Intelligence As a wealthy, upper-class, British white male living in the Victorian era, when England was the most powerful nation on earth, Galton had little difficulty believing that he and his peers were superior to those from other classes, countries, races, or the other gender. Furthermore, Galton was more a product of his environment than he cared to admit; he shared the widespread assumption among his peers that this preeminence was no accident, but based on an inherited superiority. When his cousin published on evolution in 1859, humans were not discussed, but Galton immediately saw the ramifications. If inherited individual variation, acted upon by natural selection, influenced the evolution of animal and plant species, it must have influenced humans as well. If human intelligence was a key trait enabling physically weak humans to survive the struggle for existence, then the more intelligent humans would naturally rise to the top of society. From this it was not hard for Galton to conclude that he and others of his class had achieved their lofty positions in society by virtue of their highly evolved and superior intellectual ability, rather than by the accident of being born to the right parents. He set out to collect evidence in support of his belief that intelligence was innate, producing *Hereditary Genius* in 1869 (Galton, 1869/1950).

To examine the question of whether intelligence was inherited, Galton relied on his penchant for quantification and statistical analysis. First, by examining the contents of biographical dictionaries, which profiled people who had achieved eminence in some field, and comparing the numbers therein with overall population data, he estimated that the "rate of eminence" in Great Britain was about 1 person in 4,000. He then looked at the family trees of these highly capable people and discovered that talent tended to run in families. Of those noted in the dictionaries, about 10% had at least one relative who was also so noted, a rate much higher than could be expected by the one in 4,000 probability for the general population. And talent within a family tended to be similar—lawyers related to lawyers, doctors related to doctors, and so on. Furthermore, if two relatives appeared in the dictionaries, they were four times more likely to be directly related (e.g., father–son) than related at a secondary level (e.g., uncle–nephew). Today, of course, we recognize that these patterns are just as likely to reflect environmental factors as genetic ones, but Galton was operating within the context of a social environment that was biased toward an assumption of inherited differences in ability and an intellectual environment that was dominated by the evolution discussion.

It is not that Galton failed to consider the effects of environmental circumstances. In fact, in *Hereditary Genius*, he granted that they played a small role, but he also went to great lengths to argue their overall irrelevance. Drawing an analogy between mental and physical prowess, for example, he pointed out that no matter how much one exercises, there is an upper limit to "the muscular powers of every man, which he cannot by any education or exertion overpass" (Galton, 1869/1950, p. 13). Similarly, a student learns to accept mental limits: "He knows he can beat such and such of his competitors; that there are some with whom he runs on equal terms, and others whose intellectual feats he cannot even approach" (p. 14). Galton also pointed out that many people manage, through their natural ability, to overcome the effects of an impoverished environment. Conversely, he argued that an enriched environment could not overcome limited natural ability. He even used the United States to bolster his case, arguing that opportunity "is more widely spread in America, than with us, and the education of their middle and lower classes far more advanced; but, for all that, America certainly does not beat us in world-class works of literature, philosophy, or art" (p. 34). For Galton, then, all the signs pointed to the same conclusion—intelligence was part of human nature, the product of evolutionary forces.

Darwin responded enthusiastically to his cousin's work on natural ability, but not all of Galton's contemporaries agreed. In particular, there was dissent from Alphonse de Candolle (1806–1893), a distinguished Swiss botanist. He responded to Galton with a study of his own, which he believed showed the importance of environmental factors in paving the way for someone to achieve eminence. Candolle examined the lives of 300 European scientists, finding that a number of social, political, and economic factors were associated with scientific fame (Fancher, 1983). For instance, he found that eminence in science was more likely to occur in democratic than totalitarian countries (more academic freedom), and more likely to occur in countries with higher standards of living (greater opportunity, more funding for labs, etc.).

Following *Hereditary Genius*, and in response to Candolle, Galton sought to strengthen his argument about the inheritance of talent by pioneering two methodological techniques in use today: surveys and twin studies. Although his cousin was using a similar technique to study emotional expressions at about the same time, Galton is credited with being the first person to use the **survey method**. Right from the start, he had a good understanding of the difficulties involved in writing a good questionnaire: "There is hardly any more difficult task than that of framing questions which are not likely to be misunderstood, which admit of an easy reply, and which cover the ground of inquiry" (Galton, 1883; quoted in Dennis, 1948, p. 279).

Sometime in the early 1870s, Galton wrote a questionnaire and distributed it to 180 fellows of the Royal Society, the scientific elite of England. The survey asked its respondents to describe their personalities, physical attributes, family characteristics, and the details of their upbringing; it also asked them to describe the origins of their scientific interests and to indicate "How far do your scientific tastes appear innate?" (quoted in Forrest, 1974, p. 126). Galton received about 100 usable replies, and they formed the basis of his next book, which included a subtitle that popularized two words destined to become catchwords in the continuing debate over the origins of intelligence. The book was called *English Men of Science: Their Nature and Nurture* (Galton, 1874).[9] While granting that some of the replies demonstrated that the environment (nurture) helped to shape the scientists, Galton believed that his respondents overwhelmingly supported the idea that talent in science was inherited (nature). This he concluded from making the questionable assumption that scientific ability could be considered innate if a subject reported being interested in science very early in life and could not point to any particular set of circumstances bringing about such an interest. It just seemed to be there from the start. As one of his respondents put it: "As far back as I remember, I loved nature and desired to learn her secrets" (quoted in Forrest, 1974, p. 126).

Galton's second methodological innovation, **twin studies**, was on firmer scientific ground. He sent questionnaires to twins known to him, asking them to supply names of other twins; he eventually surveyed 94 pairs about their physical and psychological attributes. As might be expected, he found support for his hereditarian beliefs—many similarities between pairs of twins, even in their later years, after they had been living in different environments. He reported the data anecdotally, and both his questionnaire wording and his interpretation of the results were affected by his preconceptions about intelligence. Still, the twin studies

---

[9]Galton is sometimes credited with inventing the label "nature–nurture issue," by virtue of the subtitle to his 1874 book. He had numerous predecessors, however, including Shakespeare (Conley, 1984), who described the notorious Caliban in the *Tempest* (Act IV, Scene 1) in these terms:

A devil, a born devil, on whose nature
Nurture can never stick.

method itself has proven effective over the years as a way to assess the interactive influence of nature and nurture.

The general conclusion that Galton reached on the basis of all these studies is clear from the opening sentence of *Hereditary Genius*: "I propose to show in this book that a man's natural abilities are derived by inheritance" (Galton, 1869/1950, p. 1). One implication of this statement, resulting from Galton's reading of Darwin's parallels between the artificial selection of the breeder and the natural selection of the wild, is spelled out in the book's second sentence. He wrote that just as it is possible "to obtain by careful selection a permanent breed of dogs or horses gifted with peculiar powers of running, . . . so it would be quite practicable to produce a highly-gifted race of men by judicious marriages during several consecutive generations" (Galton, 1869/1950, p. 1). This suggestion eventually led Galton to coin the term **eugenics** to promote the idea that society should take active steps toward improving its genetic material. This would include encouraging certain people to reproduce, known as "positive" eugenics. These individuals presumably would be those with great talent, people like Galton (ironically, Galton and his wife were childless). He founded a Eugenics Society in 1908, a journal a year later, and spent his remaining years promoting a eugenics-based society. Indeed, he came to think of eugenics as a new religion, as evidenced by this comment from his autobiography: "I take Eugenics very seriously, feeling that its principles ought to become one of the dominant motives in a civilized nation, much as if they were one of its religious tenets" (Galton, 1908, p. 232). As will be seen in the chapter on mental testing (Chapter 8), Galton found a sympathetic audience for his eugenicist views, both in Great Britain and in the United States.

The Anthropometric Laboratory To breed selectively for the intelligence that would keep Great Britain in its position as a world power, Galton knew he needed a way to identify those best suited to improve the race. This meant developing ways to measure talent, a task close to Galton's quantitative heart. The measurement of ability was a natural outgrowth of his obsession with measuring all possible differences between people. His efforts reached their peak in the 1880s, when he established an Anthropometric Laboratory, initially as part of an international health fair held in South Kensington in 1884. It later moved to a nearby museum, where Galton collected data for another 10 years. Nearly 10,000 fairgoers were tested in 1884; about 17,000 were tested altogether (Forrest, 1974).

Each person entering the laboratory completed several tests, and many of the measuring instruments were created by Galton. One famous example was the Galton whistle (Figure 5.11), which measured the ability to distinguish small differences in tone frequency (i.e., measured auditory thresholds). Many of Galton's measures were simple physical ones: height, weight, arm span, and breathing capacity. Others tested basic sensory-motor capacities: reaction time, auditory and visual acuity, color naming, judgment of line lengths, and grip strength. After the lab moved from the health fair, head size was added as a measure. Although these might not appear to be valid measures of intelligence to us today, Galton argued that superior mental capacity was related to neural efficiency and sensory ability:

> The only information that reaches us concerning outward events appears to pass through the avenue of our senses; and the more perceptible our senses are of difference, the larger is the field upon which our judgment and intelligence can act. (Galton, 1883/1965, p. 421)

FIGURE 5.11   A Galton whistle.

Galton also argued that women were intellectually inferior to men (a widely held 19th-century belief) and traced the deficiency to their inadequate sensory capacity. He noted that professions requiring sharp senses, such as piano tuners, wine tasters, and wool sorters, were all populated by men. Deeply immersed in his times, of course, he failed to consider that women would never be given the opportunity to learn these skills or the chance to be employed in these trades.

Galton's measures never proved to be useful indexes of intelligence, and they were soon replaced by tests like those devised in France at the turn of the century by Alfred Binet (Chapter 8). Galton's effort is noteworthy, however, as the first serious attempt to measure individual differences in human ability. It is also important for the history of statistics—in his attempts to determine whether scores on his various measures were associated with each other, he invented the statistical concept of **correlation**. In an 1888 paper entitled "Co-relations and their Measurement, Chiefly from Anthropometric Data," Galton argued that the strength of association between any two measures could be stated mathematically. This idea was soon refined into the modern concept of the correlation coefficient by one of his followers, the mathematician Karl Pearson, whose name is associated with the most common expression of a correlation coefficient, Pearson's r.

Investigating Imagery and Association   Galton's major interest in psychological phenomena might have been in the area of mental ability, but he also studied two other psychological topics—mental imagery and association. As he had done for his project on the inheritance of intelligence, Galton turned to the survey to examine the use of visual imagery and the quality of the images seen. Respondents were asked to imagine their breakfast table and were asked these questions:

1. *Illumination*. Is the image dim or fairly clear? Is its brightness comparable to the actual scene?

2. *Definition*. Are all the objects pretty well defined at the same time, or is the place of sharpest definition at any one moment more contracted than it is in a real scene?

3. *Colouring*. Are the colours of the china, of the toast, bread-crust, mustard, meat, parsley, or whatever may have been on the table, quite distinct and natural? (Galton, 1883, quoted in Dennis, 1948, p. 279; emphasis in the original)

Galton's long-standing interest in scientists led him to survey a number of his scientist friends, but he also distributed the survey more widely (e.g., to schoolchildren). He was surprised by the results. Compared to the general public, which reported imagery of varying degrees of vividness, most of his scientist friends appeared to report a virtual absence of imagery. As he described it:

> To my astonishment, I found that the great majority of the men of science to whom I first applied protested that mental imagery was unknown to them....They had no more notion of its true character than a colour-blind man, who has not discerned his defect, has of the nature of colour. (Galton, 1883; quoted in Dennis, 1948, p. 279)

To the 21st-century observer, the lack of imagery among scientists seems like an odd result. This unusual finding led William Brewer and his colleagues to attempt a replication of Galton's study (Brewer & Schommer-Aikens, 2006). They found that in fact modern scientists tended to show a relatively large amount of imagery. Intrigued, Brewer went back to Galton's original data and discovered that Galton had not reported his own results accurately. Perhaps overly influenced by some early questionnaire returns from a few prominent scientists who indeed reported a lack of imagery (Romanes was apparently one of them), Galton evidently failed to carefully summarize the data as a whole.

Concerning association, we have already seen that the topic was of great importance to philosophers and scientists in the 18th and 19th centuries, and Galton was no exception. He was aware of the long history of philosophical speculation about the nature of association, of course, but he was unaware of the work that Hermann Ebbinghaus (Chapter 4) was doing at about the same time. To examine associations systematically, Galton developed a **word association test**. He generated a list of 75 words and then looked at each one for a measured amount of time, noting any associations that occurred to him. He also tried to date his associations. Of the 124 associations the 75 words generated for him, 48 (39%) were from his "boyhood and youth," 57 (46%) from "subsequent manhood," and the remaining 19 (15%) from "quite recent events" (data and category labels from Forrest, 1974, p. 146). Galton's results also showed a tendency for associations to repeat themselves in one's mind. For example, after going through his list of 75 words four times, he found that in about 25% of the cases, the word gave rise to exactly the same association on all four trials. This led him to conclude that there was "much less variety in the mental stock of ideas than I had expected, and makes [me] feel that the roadways of our minds are worn into very deep ruts" (Galton, 1883; quoted in Dennis, 1948, p. 288). Galton also observed that we are only dimly aware of the course of our mental life, hinting at the unconscious mind that would shortly become the focus of another famous 19th-century mind, Sigmund Freud (Chapter 12):

> Perhaps the strongest of the impressions left by these experiments regards the multifariousness of the work done by the mind in a state of half-consciousness, and the valid reason they afford for believing in the existence of still deeper strata of mental operations, sunk wholly below the level of consciousness. (Galton, 1883; quoted in Dennis, 1948, p. 289)

It has been estimated that a mere 25% of Galton's research and writings were of direct concern to psychology (Forrest, 1974). Yet his contribution to our discipline is impressive: He pioneered the study of individual differences in human ability, he introduced research methods and statistical tools still in use, and he made some astute observations about human cognition. Galton's lifelong devotion to British science earned him a knighthood in 1909. He died 2 years later.

IN PERSPECTIVE: DARWIN'S CENTURY

Although Darwin's major influence has been on the biological sciences, modern psychology cannot be properly understood without knowing about his theory and its implications. The study of individual differences derives from his observation about individual variation within a species, and comparative psychology has its origins in an attempt to evaluate the claim of an evolutionary continuum. As will be seen in Chapter 12, Darwin's theory also directly influenced Freud's thinking about the importance of sexual motivation in directing the course of human behavior. Finally, functionalism (to be encountered in Chapters 7 and 8), which examined behaviors and mental processes in terms of their capacity for adapting the organism to the environment, also had its roots in evolutionary thinking. Darwin, in effect, naturalized the mind, causing it to be seen as the means by which the human animal survives in the struggle for existence.

In recent years, some psychologists have become even more explicit in looking toward evolution as a means to explain human behavior, and the result is a new field of study called **evolutionary psychology**. Advocates (e.g., Wright, 1994) argue that if evolutionary forces have been powerful enough to create the physical characteristics that make us human, then why not behavioral and mental characteristics as well? Evolutionary psychologists have paid special attention to social behaviors and to sexuality and sex differences in behavior, relying heavily on Darwin's theory of sexual selection. The general strategy is to describe some behavior that occurred regularly, then look for an evolutionary explanation for it, and then develop testable predictions about behavior. Evolutionary psychologists believe, for example, that much of the behavior that surrounds male–female relations reduces to an attempt to ensure that one's genetic material makes it to the next generation. Many of their ideas have been controversial, especially among psychologists who tend to emphasize the importance of the environment in shaping human behavior. Yet their increasing presence in the discussion about the causes of human behavior is just another indication of the lasting power of Darwin's ideas.

SUMMARY

The Species Problem

• During the Enlightenment, some scientists began questioning the biblical account of how species were created. The species problem concerned the question of how species originated, why there were so many, and how extinction could be explained. The argument from design enabled scientists to continue to examine nature scientifically while maintaining religious beliefs.

• An early theory of evolution that omitted reference to the deity was proposed by Charles Darwin's grandfather, Erasmus. A more important theory was proposed by the French naturalist, Lamarck. His theory included the concept of the inheritance of acquired characteristics.

Charles Darwin (1809–1882) and the Theory of Evolution

• After several false starts, Charles Darwin found a vocation in science while a student at Cambridge. He initially thought of himself as a geologist, but he was also greatly interested in zoology. Two important mentors were the botanist John Henslow and the geologist Adam Sedgwick.

• During a 5-year voyage aboard the *Beagle*, Darwin collected evidence that made contributions to both geology and zoology. He made discoveries that supported Charles Lyell's uniformitarian model of geological change (the earth changes gradually according to known principles, rather than as a result of periodic geological catastrophes), and he collected data that would eventually provide evidence for his theory of evolution. Evidence from the Galápagos Islands (e.g., finches) was especially important.

• In developing his theory, Darwin was influenced by the views of Thomas Malthus, who pointed out that because populations tend to grow faster than food supplies, a struggle for existence occurs among members of those populations. Darwin also observed that hobbyists (e.g., pigeon breeders) and farmers were able to bring about dramatic changes in species by selective breeding.

• Darwin created the essence of his theory in the early 1840s but did not publish for nearly 20 years. He was slowed by poor health, a concern over how his theory would be received by the scientific community, and a scientific cautiousness that led him to accumulate as much evidence as possible to support his theory. He was motivated to publish in 1859 by the appearance of a similar theory by Alfred Russel Wallace.

• Darwin's theory proposed that individual members of every species vary from each other; that some variations are more favorable in the struggle for existence than others, enabling the organism to adapt to the environment; and that nature "selects" (natural selection) those with the most favorable variations for survival.

The Origins of Comparative Psychology

• An implication of Darwin's theory was that continuity existed among species. This led to the development of comparative psychology, the study of differences and similarities among species on various traits (e.g., ability). Darwin was an early pioneer, examining the evolutionary history of emotional expressions and demonstrating that human expressions had evolutionary roots.

• George Romanes is considered the founder of comparative psychology, and he provided extensive descriptions of the behavior of many species. He relied on anecdotal observations and was too anthropomorphic in his interpretations of the behaviors he described. A more empirical approach was taken by Douglas Spalding, who demonstrated that certain behaviors were the result of instinct, not experience. C. Lloyd Morgan took issue with the excessive anthropomorphism shown by other comparative psychologists, favored empirical observations over anecdotal data, and argued that explanations of animal behavior could involve cognition processes, but only those processes just complex enough to enable survival. For example, some behaviors (e.g., dogs opening gates) were better explained as being examples of trial-and-error learning than rational planning.

Studying Individual Differences

• Individual variation is a cornerstone of evolutionary theory, and Francis Galton was the first to carefully examine these individual differences in humans. He examined individual differences in visual imagery, studying it through the first systematic use of the survey method (questionnaire). He also invented the word association method to study the nature of associations.

• Galton believed that intelligence was an inherited ability; nurture played a minimal role at best. As evidence, he pointed to the fact that certain abilities tended to run in families. He argued for a eugenics-based society—only those who are fit should be encouraged to reproduce. To identify those who were most fit, he set out to measure individual differences in ability. This resulted in the first widespread attempt to measure and classify human abilities. His measures relied heavily on basic sensory-motor processes and did not prove very useful.

STUDY QUESTIONS

1. What was the species problem, and how did the argument from design propose to answer the problem?

2. Describe Lamarck's ideas about evolution.

3. What were the important events leading to Darwin's appointment on the *Beagle*, and why did he consider himself as much a geologist as a naturalist at this time?

4. Distinguish between catastrophist and uniformitarian views of geology, and describe the evidence that Darwin collected relating to the issue.

5. Describe the example of Darwin's finches as a way of summarizing the essential features of his theory of evolution.

6. In developing his theory of evolution, what was the lesson that Darwin learned from (a) Malthus and (b) his pigeon-breeder friends?

7. Darwin had his theory worked out in the early 1840s. Why did he delay publication, and why did he eventually publish in 1859?

8. Concerning the issue of whether his theory was in line with the zeitgeist, what were Darwin's thoughts?

9. Describe Darwin's contribution to comparative psychology. In particular, show how he applied evolutionary thinking to the concept of emotional expression.

10. Describe Spalding's research on instinct. How did his work demonstrate the phenomena that later came to be called imprinting and critical periods?

11. Describe and criticize the comparative psychology of Romanes. In what way has the criticism been unfair to him?

12. Describe Lloyd Morgan's canon, and apply it to the example of Morgan's terrier. Explain the important misconception about Morgan's canon that has developed over the years.

13. According to Galton, why is one person more intelligent than another? What kinds of evidence did he use to support his claim?

14. What is the connection between Galton's beliefs about intelligence and (a) eugenics, and (b) mental testing?

15. Describe Candolle's research on eminent scientists, and explain how it favored a nurture explanation.

16. Describe how Galton used the questionnaire method to study the mental imagery of scientists and others. What did he find that surprised him? What has recent research suggested about Galton's conclusions?

17. Describe the two different methods that Galton used to study the nature of his own associations. What did he discover and conclude?

18. Summarize the overall impact of Darwinian thinking on psychology.

FOR FURTHER READING

BOAKES, R. (1984). *From Darwin to behaviourism: Psychology and the minds of animals.* New York: Cambridge University Press.
Detailed yet highly readable treatment of the rise of comparative psychology, from its evolutionary roots to its connection with behaviorism; notable for its collection of unique photos.

DESMOND, A., & MOORE, J. (1991). *Darwin: The life of a tormented evolutionist.* New York: W. W. Norton.
One of several biographies of Darwin; as the subtitle suggests, the book deals extensively with Darwin's struggle to create and provide supporting evidence for his great theory; highly detailed account of the Beagle trip.

RUSE, M. (1979). *The Darwinian revolution: Science red in tooth and claw.* Chicago: University of Chicago Press.
Fits the development of Darwin's theory within the framework of 19th-century science and religion and within the historical context of Victorian England.

WEINER, J. (1994). *The beak of the finch.* New York: Vintage Books.
A scientific page-turner, and winner of a Pulitzer Prize; recounts the story of Darwin's finches and focuses on recent finch research, which provides direct evidence of evolutionary changes occurring in a relatively brief period of time.

CHAPTER 6

AMERICAN PIONEERS

Psychology is the Science of Mental Life, both of its phenomena and their conditions.

—William James, 1890

PREVIEW AND CHAPTER OBJECTIVES

Having considered the philosophical and scientific contexts out of which modern psychology emerged, its origins and early development in Germany, and the far-reaching importance of Darwin's ideas, we are ready to shift our focus to the development of psychology in the United States. The chapter opens with a discussion of the influence of faculty psychology in pre–Civil War America and a description of the development of higher education in America in the latter half of the 19th century. Considered in this section are the limited opportunities available to women and minority students during this era. The chapter then examines the life and work of America's first major psychologist: William James. Although he eventually thought of himself more as a philosopher than a psychologist, his 1890 *Principles of Psychology* is arguably the most important book written in psychology's brief history. The chapter also examines the careers and contributions of several other members of the first generation of American psychologists, especially G. Stanley Hall and Mary Whiton Calkins. Hall exemplified the pioneering spirit said to characterize Americans: He spread the gospel of the New Psychology by founding laboratories, journals, and the American Psychological Association. Mary Calkins was the best known of a handful of pioneering women psychologists who made their presence felt despite daunting odds. After you finish this chapter, you should be able to:

- Explain what it was like to study psychology in America before the arrival of the New Psychology and the writings of William James
- Describe the rise of the modern university and how the German model influenced education in America
- Enumerate the obstacles facing women and minority students who tried to obtain higher education and graduate education in the late 19th and early 20th centuries
- Describe the formative influences on William James, especially the development of his pragmatic philosophy
- Describe James's definition of psychology and his attitude about the new laboratory approach to psychology
- Provide a Jamesian description of consciousness and its attributes, and describe the functions of consciousness and habit, according to James
- Describe the James-Lange theory of emotion and the arguments James used to support it

- Explain why spiritualism was popular in late 19th-century America, and explain James's attitude about the investigation of spiritualism
- Describe the contributions of G. Stanley Hall to the professionalization of psychology in America
- Explain why Hall thought of himself as a "genetic" psychologist, and describe the importance of the idea of recapitulation to his thinking
- Describe the significance of the work of Hall's student Francis Sumner and the obstacles he faced
- Explain why Mary Calkins is considered an important pioneer in memory research, and describe the difficulties she had in obtaining graduate education
- Describe the contributions of Margaret Washburn, Christine Ladd-Franklin, George Trumbull Ladd, and James Mark Baldwin to American psychology in its formative years

PSYCHOLOGY IN 19TH-CENTURY AMERICA

E. G. Boring (1929) once described American psychology as the offspring of the new psychology created in Germany (i.e., Wundt) and of British biology (i.e., Darwin), and he asserted that American psychology did not really begin until William James appeared on the scene. In his words, "James began psychology in America with his recognition of the significance of the new experimental physiological psychology in Germany" (p. 493).[1] Boring influenced a whole generation of psychologists, of course, and one consequence has been the neglect of pre-Jamesian psychology. Although James was a towering figure during the formative years of modern scientific psychology in the United States, he was not the first American thinker to write about psychological issues or to teach psychology in an American university (Fuchs, 2000). Before James, psychology was taught in courses typically called "intellectual" or "mental" philosophy, and it was dominated by **faculty psychology**, which derived from a Scottish philosophical movement called Scottish Realism.

Faculty Psychology

As you recall from Chapter 2, empiricism and associationism, represented in the philosophies of Locke, Berkeley, Hume, Hartley, and Mill, were dominant intellectual forces in Great Britain during the 18th and 19th centuries. Empiricists argued that knowledge resulted from our experiences in the world, and the structure of our minds was organized through the laws of association. The empiricists also addressed the concept of reality: Locke distinguished between primary and secondary qualities of matter, Berkeley argued that only the secondary qualities were real, and Hume extended the argument by contending that we cannot be absolutely certain about the reality of anything. Thus, when we look at a tree, Locke would say that its basic shape and mass ("extension") are primary qualities that have existence independent of our observations; its color is a secondary quality, depending for its existence on the perceiving person. Berkeley would deny the distinction and say that all aspects of the tree rely on the subjective perception of the observer and we can be sure of its existence only by

---

[1]The identical wording appears on page 505 of the second edition of Boring's book (Boring, 1950).

believing in God, the Permanent Perceiver. Hume would argue that we cannot even be 100% sure about the reality of our perception of the tree—rather, we make our best guesses based on probability estimates.

The Scottish Realist philosophers, most notably Thomas Reid (1710–1792) in the 18th century and Thomas Brown (1778–1820) in the 19th, took issue with the extreme Humean view of reality on the grounds that such an idea simply violates common sense. They believed that humans have an intuitive understanding that a real world truly exists—daily human life would have no foundation otherwise. They also rejected the implication that the mind is little more than a collection of associated ideas based on experience. Instead, the Scots argued that the mind had an independent existence in reality, was active rather than passive, and was composed of various interacting attributes that they called *faculties*. Reid divided these faculties into two broad categories—intellectual and active (Evans, 1984). Intellectual faculties included such things as memory, reasoning, and judgment, whereas active faculties concerned the emotions and the will. Understanding faculties required observation and inductive logic (i.e., a number of similar observations about how people memorize yields a general principle about the faculty of memory), making faculty psychology, in the words of one historian, "the first fully empirical psychology in history" (Albrecht, 1970, p. 36). If the concept of faculty sounds familiar, it is because you encountered it in Chapter 3; the phrenologists borrowed the concept of faculty and used it in their localization theory.

The Scottish influence in early American psychology arrived in the form of a wave of Scottish immigration in the 18th century. Many of the immigrants were educated—doctors, teachers, and ministers—and many played a role in the explosive growth of higher education in the United States in the years between the American Revolution and the Civil War. In the 140 years between the founding of Harvard in 1636 and the American Revolution of 1776, 9 colleges had been created; by the start of the Civil War in 1861, 85 years later, students could choose from 182 colleges. Faculty psychology dominated the curriculum of most of them.

American Psychology's First Textbook   Thomas Upham (1799–1872) of Bowdoin College in Maine is usually credited with authoring the first American psychology textbook when he organized his lecture notes and published them in 1827 as *Elements of Intellectual Philosophy*. The text eventually grew to three volumes and was given the broader title of *Elements of Mental Philosophy*. It quickly became the principal text in American colleges and universities for courses that today would be called introductory psychology (Evans, 1984). The book was organized along the lines of the Scottish faculty approach, although it included a healthy dose of associationism as well. It also made references to the deity, and morality was a recurring theme. This is hardly surprising, given the fact that before the Civil War, most professors at American colleges (including Upham) were Protestant ministers. As we see shortly, the postwar rise of universities like Johns Hopkins, with its emphasis on the German model of research, created a need for a new type of textbook.

Upham organized his book into three main divisions: the intellect (cognition), the sensibilities (emotion), and the will (action). This "trilogy of mind" (Hilgard, 1980) was not unique to Upham, but represented a theme that can be traced back to the Greeks and ahead to the present day. For Upham, the mind that he described in his book was an active one, and the book had a distinctly functional tone to it, emphasizing the purposes and uses of the various faculties (Fuchs, 2000). Here is a sample of topics found under each of Upham's main divisions (from Evans, 1984, pp. 40–41):

Division I: The Intellect

–Sensation, perception, consciousness, imagination

–Concepts, abstraction, reasoning

–Primary and secondary laws of association, memory

–Disordered intellectual action: insanity (later expanded by Upham in 1849 into abnormal psychology's first textbook: *Outlines of Disordered Mental Action*)

Division II: The Sensibilities

–Instincts, appetites, propensities

–The malevolent affections (e.g., anger, jealousy, revenge)

–The benevolent affections (e.g., love, patriotism, pity)

–The moral sensibilities or conscience

Division III: The Will

–Laws of the will

–Freedom of the will implied in man's moral nature

–On the power of the will

Upham's text was a best seller on campuses well into the 1870s. By the end of the century, however, American psychology had changed dramatically, reflecting the mid-century influences identified by Boring: German psychology and British biology. The American system of higher education changed as well.

The Modern University

The impressive growth of colleges before the Civil War was nothing compared with the revolution in higher education that occurred between the war and the turn of the 20th century. During this time, the modern university was created, the result of a complex interplay of forces. One factor was the emergence of the public high school and the heightened expectation that education was a key to success. An increase in high school graduates in turn meant a greater number of students eligible to attend college, and attend they did. An estimated 67,000 students attended college in 1870, 157,000 in 1890, and 335,000 in 1910 (Hofstadter & Hardy, 1952). This expanding college student population produced a need for teachers who had degrees beyond the bachelor's level, thereby creating a demand for graduate education. The initial lack of it in the United States was one reason students went to Germany. There they encountered an approach to education that emphasized graduate training, independent research, and a variety of courses to choose from—the *Wissenschaft* philosophy that you read about in Chapter 4. The decade of the 1880s was the high point for Americans studying in Germany. By the 1890s, several good American universities were available, and some of the second-level German universities were developing the reputation of being mere diploma mills (two semesters for a PhD at the University of Halle, for example; Veysey, 1965).

The modern American university began to develop shortly after the end of the Civil War. One major catalyst was the Morrill Land Grant Act of 1862, which gave every state a minimum of 30,000 acres of federal land. If the state built a university on the land within 5 years, it could keep the land; otherwise, it reverted to the government. This produced the great state universities, run by laypeople rather than clergy and emphasizing science and practical applications (e.g., applying science to improve agriculture and mining). Also during this time, several of the Ivy League schools developed graduate training: Yale in 1860 and Harvard in 1872, for instance. Another impetus was due to the accumulation of great wealth by a handful of business tycoons in the second half of the 19th century. Several of them donated large amounts of money to found universities, motivated partly by a philanthropic desire to give something back to society, partly to blunt criticism of the exploitive manner in which they became wealthy, and partly to have their names associated with an enterprise that was universally valued. Four of the better-known schools created in this way were Johns Hopkins University (1876), Clark University (1887), Stanford University (1891), and the University of Chicago (1891). All but the last, which was created with Rockefeller money, was named for the major benefactor.

Johns Hopkins University in Baltimore became the prototype of the new university in America. It was explicitly modeled on the German example that emphasized research and the creation of new knowledge and, although it had a small undergraduate division from the start, its main focus was on graduate education. Endowed with $3.5 million by its founder, wealthy Baltimore merchant Johns Hopkins, it quickly became the most important American university of the 1880s, the only legitimate competitor to the German universities (Hawkins, 1960). Its innovative president, Daniel Coit Gilman, attracted good students by creating the concept of the competitive "university fellowship," which included a $500 stipend plus free tuition, and by encouraging the development of laboratory training and the seminar, to supplement the traditional lecture course. Gilman also recognized the growing need to train educators, and Johns Hopkins became a leader in this area—during the school's first 10 years, 56 of its doctoral graduates were employed as professors in 32 different colleges and universities (Ryan, 1939).

Education for Women and Minorities The growth of opportunity for higher education that I just described was not equally available to all Americans; rather, it was mostly limited to middle- and upper-class white males. Women and minority group students faced significant barriers when trying to become educated.

Women in search of an education faced an entrenched set of beliefs about "the women's sphere"—an integrated set of concepts centering on the idea of woman as wife and mother. Nineteenth-century women were socialized to believe they were created for the purpose of perpetuating the family. This meant getting married, having and raising children, and being content with those roles. Women who wanted to pursue higher education or to have a career were discouraged from doing so. For one thing, it was believed that pursuing a degree beyond high school would have adverse medical consequences. One Harvard medical school professor urged women to abandon education after reaching puberty; too much mental activity after that stage could retard the development of their reproductive organs, he warned (Scarborough & Furumoto, 1987). If education could reduce the chances of bearing children, then what would happen to the human species if too many women pursued higher education? And if undergraduate education could have such dangerous effects, education at the graduate level presumably would be much worse for a woman's health. As for pursuing a career, there was a zero-sum choice—it was considered out of the question for women to be married *and* have a career. It was one or the other. Furthermore, the unmarried woman, whether or not she had a career of some kind, had another family claim. She, not the brothers in the family, was the one expected to care for elderly parents.

In addition to the women's sphere, another impediment was the widespread belief that women were intellectually inferior to men. The belief had deep roots, even reflected in the biblical legend of women's creation—built from a piece of a man (a rib). The belief was maintained in part by the argument that women were intellectually incapacitated every month during menstruation—this handicap was referred to as the **periodic function**. Evolutionary theory provided additional fuel, producing what was called the **variability hypothesis**. You recall from Chapter 5 that a cornerstone of Darwin's theory was the idea that individual members of a species differed from each other, and this variability provided the material for natural selection to do its work. Nature "selected" those individuals whose variations had high survival value. It follows that the greater the degree of variability for a particular trait, the better off a species will be. According to the variability hypothesis, men had a greater degree of variability than women on a number of traits, including intelligence. Although this presumably meant a higher proportion of retarded men than women, it also meant that the brightest men would be more intelligent than the brightest women. One implication of the difference at the high end of intelligence was the belief that men were thought to be better suited for higher education than women.

Despite these barriers to women's education, some opportunities arose in the second half of the 19th century. At the land grant universities, for instance, women were admitted, although they tended to be enrolled in programs of study that "suited" them—home economics, for instance. But they also began to be trained to meet the increasing need for teachers, both at land grant schools and at colleges created for the purpose of teacher training, the so-called normal schools. Ivy League schools such as Harvard and Yale resisted efforts to have women enrolled, but attempted to achieve something of a compromise by creating women's schools affiliated with the men's school. At Harvard, for example, a "Harvard Annex" was created in 1879 and renamed Radcliffe College in 1894. The best opportunities for women to pursue a high-quality college education came with the creation of a new educational phenomenon—elite colleges created for women only. One of the first, Vassar College, was created in 1865 with a gift from Matthew Vassar, a man with ideas well ahead of his time. He endowed the college, he wrote, because "it occurred to [him] that woman, having received from the Creator the same intellectual constitution as man, has the same right as man to intellectual culture and development" (quoted in Brubacher & Rudy, 1976, p. 66). Other women's colleges—Smith in 1871, Wellesley in 1875, and Bryn Mawr in 1885—soon followed; by 1901, there were 119 of them in the United States (Brubaker & Rudy, 1976). These colleges produced the three important women psychologists highlighted in this chapter, and many others.

If educational opportunities for women were limited, they were even worse for minorities, especially African Americans in the wake of the Civil War. The slavery era had created a widespread belief among whites of the essential inferiority of blacks. This belief in the intellectual superiority of whites was so strong that it even colored the interpretation of research that might have suggested otherwise. For example, an early study by Bache (1895) comparing the reaction times of whites, blacks, and Native Americans found that whites had the slowest times. Ignoring the Galtonian idea that reaction time was assumed to be related to mental quickness and therefore to intelligence, the author concluded that the results provided evidence for the mental superiority of whites because it showed that whites, a "higher" human form, could be characterized as "reflective," while the swifter reactions of the more "primitive" blacks and Native Americans showed an immature and intellectually backward impulsiveness. Similarly, in a study comparing 500 white children with a like number of black children, Stetson (1897) found no differences in their ability to memorize poetry. Rather than drawing the reasonable conclusion that the groups were similar in this type of cognitive skill, Stetson decided that his study simply showed that memorization was useless as a test of intelligence. In short, strongly held prejudices rendered some scientists immune to data that might have called their beliefs into question.

One consequence of the prejudice against African Americans was inferior education and reduced opportunities for higher education. On the assumption that education would put ridiculous ideas like "freedom" into their heads, black slaves in the South were barred from formal education by "black codes" in the pre–Civil War years. After the war, conditions improved only marginally. Blacks were segregated into schools that were supposedly separate, but equal, and higher education was limited mostly to whites. Colleges and universities designed for African Americans began to be created in the second half of the 19th century, however, mainly in the South. By 1940, there were more than 100 such schools. They focused on training teachers, who usually returned to their communities to teach in the segregated schools there (Guthrie, 1976).

Psychology, especially as it applied to education, was typically part of the curriculum in the black colleges, but few of these schools offered a concentration in psychology. A 1936 survey on psychology at black colleges by Herman Canady (1901–1970), a psychologist at West Virginia's black college (West Virginia State College at Institute, West Virginia), found that only 14 of the 50 schools he surveyed had psychology departments. Of those 14, only 4 offered majors in psychology (data from Guthrie, 1976, p. 105). Very few laboratory courses were offered and, aside from introductory psychology, the most popular courses were educational, child, social, and adolescent psychology. Thus few black students had the background necessary to pursue graduate degrees in psychology. Those who did faced further obstacles. They were denied admission to graduate programs in the South and, although a handful of graduate programs in the North were more accommodating (Clark University, for instance), few African Americans could afford to travel that far from home.

For the African American who did manage to persevere and earn an advanced degree, the prospects for employment following graduate school were not good. About the only opportunity for a black psychologist with an advanced degree was to return to a black college to teach, where conditions typically included a heavy teaching load, minimal salary, no benefits, and poor research facilities, if any (Guthrie, 1976). Nonetheless, many bright young African Americans took this path, significantly enhancing the educations of countless black college students.

The best known of these pioneers was Francis Sumner (1895–1954), shown in Figure 6.1 in his graduate student days at Clark. Sumner was born in Arkansas, but his family soon moved east, where he received his early education in New Jersey, Washington, DC, and Virginia. During his high school years, he was taught at home by his father, who distrusted the quality of Virginia's segregated schools. In 1911, the 16-year-old Sumner was accepted "by examination" into Pennsylvania's Lincoln University, which had been founded in 1854 as the country's first black college. He earned a bachelor's degree in 1915, then a second bachelor's from Clark College in Massachusetts, the undergraduate counterpart of Clark University (both located in the same building on the Worcester campus). He then returned to Lincoln to teach psychology and German, while also completing the requirements for a master's degree. Sumner returned to Clark (the university this time) in 1917 to

FIGURE 6.1 Francis Sumner as a graduate student at Clark University.

study "race psychology" with G. Stanley Hall (discussed later), financed by a university fellowship and strong moral support from Hall (Hicks & Ridley, 1979). Although Hall held stereotypical views about racial differences in intelligence, he welcomed "exceptionally talented" blacks at Clark. During Hall's years at Clark, three African American scholars earned master's degrees, and two, Sumner and Thomas Brown, earned doctorates (Guthrie, 1976). Sumner's doctorate came in 1920, and he was the first African American to complete a PhD in psychology. His dissertation was a critical interpretation of Freudian and Adlerian psychoanalysis, which Hall praised by writing that Sumner had "shown unusual facility in mastering and even pointing out the limitations and defects of the great authorities in the field" (quoted in Guthrie, 1976, p. 182).

Like a handful of other black scholars, Sumner found his opportunities limited to teaching at black colleges, and he spent time at Wilberforce College in Ohio and West Virginia State College before finding his way to Howard University in Washington, D.C., in 1928. Sumner remained at Howard as psychology department chair until his untimely death from a heart attack while shoveling snow in the winter of 1954. At Howard he established the country's leading psychology department at a black institution, offering both bachelor's and master's degrees in psychology. An indication of Howard's importance, and by extension Sumner's influence, is that of the 300 African Americans who held doctorates in 1975, 60 had earned their bachelor's and/or master's degrees at Howard (Bayton, 1975).

The explosive growth of higher education at the end of the 19th century, accompanied by a willingness to experiment with new ideas, teaching methods, and the curriculum itself, made the new universities fertile ground for the creation of novel approaches to old problems. This was advantageous for psychology, which was of course undergoing a change from traditional faculty psychology to the new laboratory psychology. A major agent of this change was a troubled young man from a talented and wealthy Boston family.

WILLIAM JAMES (1842–1910): AMERICA'S FIRST "NEW" PSYCHOLOGIST

William James did not establish a "school" of thought in psychology, produced no meaningful experimental research, and did not leave behind a dedicated group of students to carry on his work. Indeed, near the end of his life, he insisted on being referred to as a philosopher rather than as a psychologist. When delivering an invited address at Princeton in 1896, for instance, he was adamant about not being introduced as a psychologist (O'Donnell, 1985). In the closing pages of *Psychology: The Briefer Course* (James, 1892), a condensed version of his monumental *Principles of Psychology*, James made it clear that in his opinion at least, psychology had a way to go before it could claim the status of a genuine science—it was "no science, it is only the hope of a science" (p. 468). And when he was just finishing the briefer version of the *Principles*, he expressed his disenchantment with psychology in a letter to his Wellesley colleague and former student Mary Whiton Calkins, writing that he was "sick of the association of ideas and all things connected with psychology. The result of too unending an application to . . . the 'Briefer Course' of which the miserable proofs are not yet finished! . . . Treadmill work seems preferable" (James, 1891).

On the other hand, it is quite clear that James was crucial to the development of modern psychology in the United States and that his role was recognized not just by historians but also by his contemporaries. When James McKeen Cattell (Chapter 8) asked psychologists to rank their peers for eminence in 1903, James was ranked first. In fact, he was ranked first on *every* return (Hothersall, 1995). His peers also elected him to the presidency of the American Psychological Association (APA) twice, in 1894 and again in 1904. Later, when second-generation psychologists wrote chapters for the series *A History of Psychology in Autobiography*, at least a dozen explicitly mentioned James and/or his *Principles* as the main reason for their initial interest in psychology (King, 1992). Today, James's star continues to shine brightly. Several biographies have appeared (e.g., Croce, 1995; Lewis, 1991; Richardson, 2007; Simon, 1998), and the 1990s saw the publication of two edited books celebrating the centennial of the *Principles* (Donnelly, 1992; Johnson & Henley, 1990). In a 1991 poll of historians, he ranked second (just behind Wundt) on a list of the most important contributors to psychology (Korn, Davis, & Davis, 1991). Who was this person who did not want to be called a psychologist, yet is high on everyone's list of "most important psychologists of all time?"

The Formative Years

William James was raised in an unusual family. His father, Henry James Sr., had sufficient income from an inheritance to avoid working,[2] and he devoted himself to controlling the

---

[2]Henry's father lived the stereotypical American success story; an Irish immigrant who rose from store clerk to business tycoon, he was one of the wealthiest men in 19th-century America (Croce, 1995).

education and moral development of his five children, who were born within 6 years of each other in the 1840s. In addition to William, the oldest, there was Henry Jr., the celebrated American novelist, two younger brothers, and a sister, Alice. Although the intellectual equal of her brothers, she was unable to develop her creativity into a professional career due to prevailing 19th-century beliefs about the proper role for women (the women's sphere described earlier in this chapter). Henry James Sr., who had been raised by a domineering father who demanded strict obedience, was determined to raise his own children in a more liberal fashion, but he was controlling in his own way. On the surface it appeared that he indulged his children, allowing them to study whatever they wanted whenever they wanted to, taking them to Europe frequently to expand their horizons, and caring little about their formal education. However, he insisted on being perceived as their primary educator, and some of the family's moving back and forth between America and Europe was motivated by Henry Sr.'s desire to maintain control (Simon, 1998). His primary expectation was that his children learn foreign languages; he believed that "to learn a language was not to enforce particular points of view, but to gain access to another realm of culture and thought; to be fluent was to see the world from another perspective" (Croce, 1995, pp. 43–44). Young William did not attend school formally before the age of 10 and attended only sporadically through adolescence. He made three trips to Europe before the age of 21, though, and spent at least a year there each time. By age 18, he knew the essentials of Latin, had a reading knowledge of German, and was fluent in French. He would later add Greek and Italian to the list.

As he neared the end of adolescence, however, one other fact characterized William James—he was utterly at a loss about what to do with his life. He had a strong interest in art and some talent for it (Figure 6.2 is a self-portrait), but after lessons in Paris and a brief stint under the tutelage of the American artist William Morris Hunt, he realized that he would not achieve greatness (Simon, 1998). Despite abandoning a career in art, James

FIGURE 6.2 Self-portrait sketch of William James, completed in the early 1860s.

never lost interest in it, and in some ways he remained an artist in temperament for the rest of his life (Bjork, 1983). Psychologist–historian David Leary (1992) has pointed to James's recurring use of artistic metaphors in the *Principles*. For instance, he used the metaphor of a sculptor creating one result from the multitude of possibilities in a piece of stone to make the point that individual minds create different realities out of the varying experiences of life: "Other sculptors, other statues from the same stone! Other minds, other worlds from the same monotonous and inexpressive chaos" (James, 1890/1950a, p. 289).

A Life at Harvard

In the fall of 1861, James (then 19) enrolled in the Lawrence Scientific School of Harvard University, much to his father's delight. Although his philosophy of child rearing prevented him from forcing careers on his children, Henry Sr. had always hoped that his oldest son would become a "scientist."[3] At the Lawrence school, William first studied chemistry with Charles W. Eliot, soon to be one of Harvard's most innovative presidents. He quickly learned to hate the subject, especially what he viewed as the tedium and obsession with detail that characterized laboratory work. It was an attitude that would later lead him to disparage much of the laboratory work of the new experimental psychology.

After abandoning chemistry, James sampled several of the other sciences at Lawrence. One of his biology professors there was the famed Swiss naturalist Louis Agassiz, a fervent believer in a close relationship between science and religion and in the use of science to confirm religious truths. Thus he was a strong advocate of the argument by design (Chapter 5) and an anti-Darwinian who believed that all species were created separately by God. James, of course, was a student during the height of the debates about Darwin's theory, which had been published in 1859. Although awed by Agassiz, James eventually became a firm Darwinian and realized that history would judge his professor to be on the wrong side of the argument over evolution. Accompanying Agassiz on a collecting expedition to the Amazon in 1865, James traveled 2,000 miles up the river (and 2,000 back), much of the journey in small boats and canoes. Agassiz was hoping to discover markedly different species of fish in different parts of the river; he thought this would support an argument from design (instead, although he refused to acknowledge it, he found similarities in species that would comfort a Darwinian). For James the trip was exhilarating, but he eventually found the precise details of collecting and categorizing fish about as enjoyable as chemistry lab. So he would not become a professional naturalist; as he wrote to his brother, "When I get home I'm going to study philosophy all my days" (quoted in Simon, 1998, p. 93).

James enrolled in the Harvard Medical School in 1864 and completed his medical training in 1869, but not before taking another trip to Europe to (a) try to recover his health—he was afflicted with a bad back, severe headaches, and chronic gastritis after the Amazon trip; and (b) to investigate the new experimental physiology that had been developing in Germany. In addition to health spas, his trip included stops at Heidelberg, where he met Helmholtz and learned of Wundt, and Berlin, where he attended lectures by the noted physiologist Emil du

---

[3]He was also pleased that his son was able to avoid the Civil War, which began that same year. Henry Jr., the novelist, also avoided the war, but the two younger brothers both fought for the North. One brother was severely wounded in the attack on Fort Wagner, near Charleston, South Carolina (the battle was dramatized in the 1990 film *Glory*).

Bois Reymond. The experience was educational, but it also deepened a profound depression that had been lingering at the edges of his psyche for several years. He was completing a medical degree, but had no desire to actually practice medicine. He was trained in science, but hated the details. And as a reflective person, he was disturbed by the overwhelming determinism and materialism of the science that he was learning. If all life reduces to physical matter moving through space according to predictable laws, then what happens to free will? If freedom of choice is an illusion, then what is the basis for personal responsibility and morality? James was driven to the point of despair, and he even contemplated suicide (Croce, 1995).

Salvation (temporary, at least—he continued to suffer periodic bouts of depression throughout his life) came when James read an essay by the French philosopher Charles Renouvier. In an often-quoted diary entry from April 1870, James noted that his life had reached a crisis point when he encountered an essay by Renouvier and "saw no reason why [Renouvier's] definition of free will—the sustaining of thought *because I choose to* when I might have other thoughts—need be the definition of an illusion. At any rate I will assume for the present . . . that it is no illusion. My first act of free will shall be to believe in free will" (quoted in Simon, 1998, p. 126; emphasis in the extract). James later wrote to Renouvier, expressing his gratitude: "Thanks to you I have for the first time an intelligible and reasonable conception of freedom" (quoted in Richardson, 2007, p. 145).

The insight from Renouvier enabled James to continue studying physiology and psychology without being worn down by the materialist implications. Free will might be an illusion, but by choosing to believe in it, James found that the concept became *useful* for him, enabling him to continue his scientific work without despair. This "pragmatic" approach to the concept of free will, in which the truth-value of the idea was a consequence of its functional value or usefulness, became a cornerstone of James's philosophical position of **pragmatism** and established him as a forerunner among those American psychologists who came to be known as functionalists.

In 1873, James accepted an offer from Charles Eliot, his old chemistry professor and now president of Harvard, to teach a course in physiology. Two years later, he taught his first psychology course, a class on the relationship between physiology and psychology. By incorporating the latest research from Germany, it differed radically from the typical mental philosophy course based on faculty psychology, thus inaugurating a new approach to the teaching of psychology in America. To help students understand some of the research he was describing, James set up some apparatus in a small room, thus creating in 1875 what eventually became Harvard's laboratory of experimental psychology.[4] James remained at Harvard until his retirement in 1907. He died 3 years later of heart disease, 2 days after a return from one final trip to Europe.

Creating American Psychology's Most Famous Textbook

In July of 1878, a 36-year-old William James married Alice Howe Gibbens, a 29-year-old teacher at Miss Sanger's School for Girls in Boston. Alice was a stabilizing force in William's life and had a mind sharp enough to make her an intellectual colleague. Indeed, on

---

[4]This event has led some to argue that James created psychology's first laboratory, beating Wundt by 4 years. The lab was no more than a demonstrational adjunct to his lectures, however—Wundt's laboratory produced original research.

KEY DATE—1890

This year marked the publication of psychology's most famous textbook, *The Principles of Psychology* by William James.

These events also occurred that year:

- James Mark Baldwin (this chapter) established a laboratory at the University of Toronto, the first experimental psychology laboratory in Canada
- Rubber gloves were used in surgery for the first time, at the Johns Hopkins Hospital, Baltimore
- The first entirely steel-framed skyscraper was built in Chicago by Louis Sullivan, mentor of Frank Lloyd Wright
- The Daughters of American Revolution was founded in Washington, DC
- Oscar Wilde wrote *The Picture of Dorian Gray*

- Japan held its first general elections
- Idaho and Wyoming achieved statehood

These people were born:

- Dwight David Eisenhower, American general and president
- Julius "Groucho" Marx, American comedic actor
- Agatha Christie, English mystery writer (creator of Hercule Poirot)

These people died:

- Vincent Van Gogh, Dutch post-impressionist painter (e.g., *Starry Night*)
- Sitting Bull, Sioux chief on the winning side at the Battle of Little Big Horn

---

their honeymoon in New York's Adirondacks, she helped him begin writing *The Principles of Psychology*, a book destined to become the classic among classics in psychology's history (Lewis, 1991). A month before the wedding, James had signed a contract with an aggressive young Bostonian publisher named Henry Holt for a "manual" of psychology. Holt wanted the completed manuscript from James within a year, but the book took on a life of its own and finally appeared 12 years later, in 1890. It was encyclopedic, encompassing two volumes totaling nearly 1,400 pages. It was an immediate best seller, in part because the academic public knew what was coming—James published numerous articles based on it during the 1880s, and Holt began advertising it in 1881 (King, 1992). Shortly after its publication, James agreed to write a smaller version (referred to earlier in the letter to Calkins), which appeared in 1892 as *Psychology: The Briefer Course*.

In the opening sentence of *Principles of Psychology*, James (1890/1950a) defined psychology as "the Science of Mental Life, both of its phenomena and their conditions" (p. 1). These phenomena of mental life included "such things as we call feelings, desires, cognitions, reasonings, decisions, and the like" (p. 1). By "their conditions" he was referring to the physiological processes that accompany these phenomena, as well as the social, personal, and environmental circumstances in which they occur.

On Methodology James was an eclectic, willing to include in his book the results of research using any methodological approach that could shed light on mental life. He was quite clear about what he believed to be the primary means of studying mental life, however: "Introspective Observation is what we have to rely on first and foremost and always" (James, 1890/1950a, p. 185). By **introspection** he meant careful self-observation, an examination and reflection on the states of consciousness that characterize one's mental life. He recognized the difficulties with the method—it was open to bias; one person's introspections could not be verified by a second person; and because it is impossible to experience a mental process and introspect to it at the same time, all introspection must rely on memory. Nonetheless, he believed that careful self-reflection was essential to gain insight into the workings of the human mind. One consequence of this belief was that the book was reviewed harshly by psychologists enamored of the new laboratory approach that had emerged from Leipzig. Thus Wundt thought it was more like literature than science, and G. Stanley Hall (discussed later), after writing that one's overall reaction to the book must be "gratitude and admiration" (Hall, 1890–1891, p. 578), criticized what he viewed as its "inconsistencies and incoherencies" (p. 589) and referred to James as an "*impressionist* in psychology" (p. 585, emphasis in the original).

James did not ignore the new experimental methods. He gave a thorough description of reaction time methodology, for example, and he referred to the results of psychophysics research in numerous places. Nonetheless, his personal dislike of the tedium of laboratory work led him to declare that the German psychophysics and reaction time research "taxes patience to the utmost, and could hardly have arisen in a country whose natives could be *bored*" (James, 1890/1950a, p. 192; emphasis in the original). He later created a phrase that came to sum up this laboratory approach, with its emphasis on precise laboratory apparatus often constructed using brass, when he referred to it sarcastically as a **brass instrument psychology**.

In addition to introspective and experimental methods, James listed the "comparative method" as a third approach. This involved learning about mental life by comparing normal human consciousness with that of "bees and ants,... savages, infants, madmen, idiots, the deaf and blind, criminals, and eccentrics" (James, 1890/1950a, p. 194), and included the use of data derived from the kinds of questionnaires pioneered by Darwin and Galton. While James recognized the value of this kind of information, he once again disliked the tediousness of the survey method, suspecting that the next generation of psychologists might rank these questionnaires "among the common pests of life" (p. 194).

Consciousness The chapter on **consciousness** shows James at his most eloquent. It is a central chapter, one in which James made it clear that he vehemently opposed the analytic approach that presumed to understand consciousness by reducing it to its basic elements. That strategy characterized "structuralism," which you will learn about in the next chapter; it also formed the basis for the reaction time and psychophysics research imported from Germany, and it was an integral part of most British empiricist-associationist thinking. James believed that trying to identify the individual elements of consciousness and then seeing how they could be constructed to form "mind" was a meaningless, artificial exercise. In one of psychology's more frequently quoted passages, he argued that consciousness is not a set of interconnected units:

> Consciousness, then, does not appear to itself chopped up in bits. Such words as "chain" or "train" do not describe it fitly as it presents itself in the first instance. It is nothing jointed; it flows. A "river" or a "stream" are the metaphors by which it is most naturally described. *In talking of it hereafter, let us call it the stream of thought, of consciousness, or of subjective life.* (James, 1890/1950a p. 239; emphasis in the original)

This quote appears in the chapter titled "The Stream of Thought," which is the first of several dealing with the nature of consciousness. Using an artistic metaphor, James told the reader that the chapter was introductory, with more detail to follow, and described it as being "like a painter's first charcoal sketch upon his canvas" (James, 1890/1950a, p. 225). His preliminary sketch included these additional attributes of consciousness:

- It is *personal*; all consciousness includes an element of self-consciousness; thoughts don't exist independently of the person having them ("Consciousness of Self" was elaborated in a complete chapter).

- It is *constantly changing*, as implied by the stream metaphor; no two states of consciousness are ever quite the same; once a state has disappeared, there will never be another one identical to it.

- It is *sensibly continuous*; our perception of consciousness is that it is one continuous stream of thoughts; the stream may be temporarily interrupted, as in sleep, but upon awaking, the sleeper immediately reenters the same stream.

- It is *selective*; out of the mass of sensory information available to it, it selects some for closer attention (James elaborated this in a chapter on "Attention").

- It is *active*, rather than a passive collection of associated elements; it is goal directed and purposive.

In elaborating on this last attribute, James used an example that provides a compelling description of what has come to be known as the "tip-of-the-tongue phenomenon," investigated later by Brown and McNeill (1966):

> Suppose we try to recall a forgotten name. The state of our consciousness is peculiar. There is a gap therein; but no mere gap. It is a gap that is intensely active. A sort of wraith of the name is in it, beckoning us in a given direction, making us at moments tingle with the sense of our closeness, and then letting us sink back without the longed-for term. If wrong names are proposed to us, this singularly definite gap acts immediately so as to negate them. They do not fit into its mold. (James, 1890/1950a, p. 251)

One final point about consciousness shows how James was affected by Darwinian thinking. In addition to describing the features of consciousness, he was interested in understanding the *function* of consciousness. How did it enable us to adapt to our environment? What was its survival value? For James, the answer was that consciousness served individuals by enabling them to adapt quickly to new environments, to learn new things, and to solve new problems that present themselves. Furthermore, in keeping with James's belief in free will, he argued that consciousness serves the function of selection—it enables us to choose one course of action over another (Richardson, 2007). And those making the best, most functional choices adapt most efficiently to the environment.

Habit Habits also had an adaptive function, according to James. Because they occurred more or less automatically, they enabled the consciousness to focus attention on other, more important (i.e., survival-related) problems. On a broader scale, habit serves as:

> the enormous flywheel of society, its most precious conservative agent.... It alone prevents the hardest and most repulsive walks of life from being deserted by those brought up to tread therein. It keeps the fisherman ... at sea through the winter; it holds the miner in his darkness, and nails the countryman to his log-cabin and his lonely farm through all the months of snow.... It dooms us all to fight out the battle of life upon the lines of our nurture or our early choice. (James, 1890/1950a, p. 121)

In his typical pragmatic fashion, James also had some advice on forming good habits. The first was motivational, an admonition to "launch ourselves with as strong and decided an initiative as possible" (James, 1890/1950a, p. 123). For instance, he recommended making a public pledge about the habit to be developed. Second, we must not allow for any lapses to occur: "Never suffer an exception to occur till the new habit is securely rooted in your life" (p. 123). Third, he urged readers to arrange their lives to increase the opportunities to act on the new habit; mere good intentions are not sufficient.

Emotion   James's theory about emotion is the idea most likely to be familiar to modern students. He acknowledged borrowing the theory from a Dutch physiologist, Carl Lange, and today it is known as the **James-Lange theory of emotion**. It can be found in the emotion chapter of every modern introductory psychology text. James criticized contemporary thinking about emotion, which described emotions as following the sequence: perception of some emotion-arousing event (e.g., a bear) → subjective experience of the emotion (e.g., fear) → bodily reaction (e.g., trembling, heart pounding). James reversed the sequence, as he described it in one of psychology's most famous passages:

> Our natural way of thinking about . . . emotions is that the mental perception of some fact excites the mental affection called the emotion, and that this latter state of mind gives rise to the bodily expression. My theory, on the contrary, is that *the bodily changes follow directly the perception of the exciting fact, and that our feeling of the same changes as they occur IS the emotion.* Common-sense says, we lose our fortune, are sorry and weep, we meet a bear, are frightened and run; we are insulted by a rival, are angry and strike. The hypothesis here to be defended says that this order of sequence is incorrect, that the one mental state is not immediately induced by the other, that the bodily manifestations must first be interposed between, and that the more rational statement is that we feel sorry because we cry, angry because we strike, afraid because we tremble, and not that we cry, strike, or tremble because we are sorry, angry, or fearful, as the case may be. (James, 1892/1961, pp. 242–243; emphasis in the original)

James's argument was that the bodily changes that are the emotions are felt immediately upon the perception of an emotion-arousing stimulus, prior to the awareness of a cognitively recognizable emotion: Our heart pounds before we feel fearful. He also argued that we recognize different emotions because each one is associated with a unique pattern of bodily action. Thus, for the James-Lange theory to work, each emotion must have its own unique pattern of bodily reaction, and be recognized as such. We now know that although there are some physiological differences between emotions, most strong emotions are accompanied by similar patterns of physiological arousal in the autonomic nervous system. Of course, there was no way for James to be aware of the flaw, given the state of knowledge about the physiology of emotion in the 1890s.

As always, James was pragmatic. In the case of emotions, practical application was a natural consequence of his theory. If the emotion is, in essence, the physiological arousal, then a corollary is that if we could deliberately bring about the "bodily changes" associated with an emotion, we would experience the emotion. As he put it:

> There is no more valuable precept in moral education than this: . . . if we wish to conquer undesirable emotional tendencies in ourselves, we must assiduously, and in the first instance cold-bloodedly, go through the *outward movements* of those contrary dispositions which we prefer to cultivate. The reward of persistency will infallibly come,

in the fading out of the sullenness or depression, and the advent of real cheerfulness and kindliness in the stead. Smooth the brow, brighten the eye, contract the dorsal rather than the ventral aspect of the frame, and speak in a major key, pass the genial compliment, and your heart must be frigid indeed if it do not gradually thaw. (James, 1892/1961, pp. 249–250; emphasis in the original)

The idea that forcing emotions to occur by deliberately producing specific bodily reactions, which might seem a bit far-fetched, has been supported by 20th-century research on emotions. People whose facial muscles have been arranged to match certain emotions, for instance, tend to experience those very emotions, at least to a degree (e.g., Izard, 1977).

James's Later Years

After completing the *Principles* in 1890 and the abridged version 2 years later, James (Figure 6.3) began to turn away from psychology and toward philosophy. In 1892, he convinced the research psychologist Hugo Münsterberg (Chapter 8) to emigrate from Germany to America and run the psychology lab at Harvard, thereby separating James from the tedium of laboratory work. Although he continued to be involved in the APA and was elected its president in 1894 and 1902, James also supported the formation of the American Philosophical Association shortly after the turn of the century, and his publications after 1900 were mainly devoted to philosophy (e.g., *Pragmatism* in 1907) and religion (e.g., *Varieties of Religious Experience* in 1902).

FIGURE 6.3 A healthy-looking William James in New York's Adirondack Mountains, taken in the 1890s when James was shifting his focus from psychology to philosophy. From Lewis (1991).

Spiritualism In addition to the shift from psychology to philosophy during his final two decades, James also became fascinated with **spiritualism**, a popular movement in the late 19th century. Spiritualists believed that consciousness survived death and that those who died could be contacted by mediums, who in turn could convey messages from the dead to the living. Mediums were also said to be able to predict the future and to know details of people's lives through telepathic means. The movement began at mid-century, but gained momentum after the Civil War—the war's appalling death toll dramatically increased the number of people desiring to contact deceased relatives and acquaintances.[5] Spiritualism was also fueled by 19th-century technological advances such as the wireless telegraph. If living people could communicate over great distances via some mysterious invisible process, and if there was life after death, then why not a communication channel from the dead to the living (Coon, 1992)? Of course, not everyone was enthralled. The tough-minded British scientist Thomas Huxley (Darwin's "bulldog"—see Chapter 5) sarcastically commented that it would be "better to live a crossing-sweeper than to die and be made to talk twaddle by a medium hired at a guinea a séance" (quoted in Blum, 2006, p. 44).

The more open-minded James became seriously interested in spiritualism in the 1880s, after discovering the Society for Psychical Research while on a trip to London (Benjamin, 1993). He helped establish a similar organization in the United States and became a promoter of research into the phenomenon. He believed that psychologists, with their expertise in the powers of the mind and their training in scientific methodology, would be ideally suited for such investigations. And reflecting his pragmatic philosophy, in which the value of something is a consequence of its usefulness, he insisted on keeping an open mind about psychic phenomena—they might prove to be beneficial if they could be shown to be valid.

Starting in 1885, James began an extended study of Mrs. Leonore Piper, a popular Boston medium. Although most mediums, even in the 19th century, were easily shown to be frauds on careful investigation, James (and others) could find no trickery in Mrs. Piper's seances. In an article for the *Proceedings of the British Society for Psychical Research*, James wrote that he could not avoid concluding that in her seances, "knowledge appears which she has never gained by the ordinary waking use of her eyes and ears and wits. What the source of this knowledge may be, I know not, and have not the glimmer of an explanatory suggestion to make" (cited in Lewis, 1991, p. 494). On the other hand, James was somewhat skeptical about messages from the dead that Mrs. Piper received during seances. If the dead were truly communicating, surely they would have some rather important things to say—they might be expected to describe the afterlife, for example. Instead, they tended to communicate inconsequential bits of information. In a letter to a colleague, James questioned Mrs. Piper's ability to reach the dead, pointing to the "extreme triviality of most of the communications. What real spirit, at last able to revisit his wife on this earth, [wouldn't] find something better to say than that she had changed the place of his photograph?" (quoted in Benjamin, 1993, p. 83). Furthermore, Mrs. Piper's spirit-control (the intermediary between her and the dead

---

[5]The death toll of the Civil War was greater than in any other war fought by Americans, based on the percentage of the overall population who perished. The 620,000 who died would be the equivalent of 6 million in today's population. To convince survivors of the possibility of communication with dead loved ones, the spiritualist newspaper *Banner of Life* often carried stories that were *supposedly* (the names did not appear on military lists) from dead soldiers giving "firsthand" accounts of their deaths. These stories appeared in the newspaper for at least 10 years after the end of the war (Faust, 2008).

spirits) was supposed to be a French doctor, yet he was unable to respond when James asked questions in French (Murphy & Ballou, 1960).

James was not rewarded for open-mindedness by his scientific peers. At a time when there was no formal licensure procedure for accrediting doctors, the medical community roundly criticized him for opposing legislation to create such rules. His reason? The guidelines would prohibit mediums and "mental healers" from practicing without a license (Murphy & Ballou, 1960). The censure from psychologists was equally strong. Psychology was trying to establish its identity as a legitimate scientific discipline, and it was embarrassing for one of its stars to be attending séances and publicly expressing confidence in a medium (Coon, 1992). In a letter to James published in his journal *Science*, for example, James McKeen Cattell wrote that the "Society for Psychical Research is doing much to injure psychology" (quoted in Benjamin, 1993, p. 88); concerning James, Cattell pointed out that the psychological community "all acknowledge his leadership, but we cannot follow him into quagmires" (p. 88). Always independent, James was unmoved by the criticism, and in turn accused his critics of narrow and unscientific prejudgment. He continued to be fascinated by psychic phenomena for all of his remaining years.

Summing Up William James

In his lifetime, William James experienced the vast changes that characterized late 19th-century America. In his youth, America was an agricultural society, the western frontier was east of the Rocky Mountains, the possibility that Americans would kill each other in a Civil War was unthinkable, and higher education was limited mainly to the undergraduate college, which was aimed primarily at the training of ministers. In his last decade, America had entered the 20th century an industrialized power, the western frontier had been declared closed, the trauma of the Civil War was becoming a memory, and higher education, which now included universities devoted to graduate studies, was producing professionals and PhDs in a variety of disciplines.

Psychology in America also changed significantly during this time; the mental philosophy of Upham's day was becoming an independent discipline with aspirations to be a science. Despite his reservations about the New Psychology, William James was a prime mover in bringing about its emergence. With his training in physiology, he saw how advances in that field could make a new laboratory psychology possible. At heart an artist and philosopher, he could see the problems inherent in a purely scientific attack on the human mind. His monumental *Principles of Psychology* stands at the transition point, artfully blending physiology, philosophy, and the new laboratory psychology. James was the acknowledged leader of the first generation of American psychologists, but he was not alone.

G. STANLEY HALL (1844–1924): PROFESSIONALIZING THE NEW PSYCHOLOGY

G. Stanley Hall had none of William James's reluctance about psychology. Rather, he was a vigorous promoter of the new field; more than any other American psychologist, he was responsible for its evolving identity as a distinct academic discipline. Like Wundt did in Germany, Hall professionalized psychology in the United States by founding laboratories and journals. In addition, he institutionalized psychology's professional status by creating the

American Psychological Association (APA). As a psychologist, Hall was a man of diverse interests, careening from one enthusiasm to another throughout his career. His biographer aptly described him as a "prophet" for his zeal in promoting new ideas (Ross, 1972). He could be characterized as either creative and visionary or unsystematic and capricious. On the one hand, he pioneered the child study movement and the study of adolescence and aging; he demonstrated the importance of psychology to education; and he introduced Freud and psychoanalysis (Chapter 12) to America. On the other hand, his catholicity of interests resulted in failure to contribute a substantial body of knowledge to any one of them. He also alienated his peers, including James, and some questioned the value of his work. In a letter to Clark University librarian L. N. Wilson in 1906, for instance, Cornell's E. B. Titchener (Chapter 7) commented on Hall's ability to prepare graduate students:

> You probably have no idea of the sort of contempt in which Hall's methods and the men trained solely by him are in general held in psychology, whether here or on the continent. Whenever his questionary papers get reviewed, they get slightingly reviewed.... He has made no impression on the men of scientific training. (Titchener, 1906)

You will discover in the next chapter that Titchener had a rather narrow concept of what scientific training should be like; the criticism of Hall might be overstated, but it was not far from the mark.

If there was a common thread and guiding principle to Hall's various interests, it was evolution. In his autobiography, Hall (1923, p. 357) wrote, "As soon as I first heard it in my youth I think I must have been almost hypnotized by the word 'evolution,' which was music to my ear." Most of his work can be classified under the heading of **genetic psychology**—which in his day meant the study of the evolution and development of the human mind—and included comparative, abnormal, and, especially, developmental psychology.

Hall's Early Life and Education

Hall was born in western Massachusetts in 1844. His mother was a teacher and stern taskmaster; his father, who also had experience teaching, was mainly a farmer. For Hall, the primary benefit of being raised on a farm seemed to be the creation of a strong urge to leave it. He went to nearby Williams College and graduated in 1867 with an interest in philosophy and history and a desire to imitate many of his peers by studying for an advanced degree in Europe. Money was a problem, however; the most reasonable postgraduate option for a young man interested in philosophy, and unable to cross the ocean, was to study for the clergy, so Hall enrolled in New York's Union Theological Seminary shortly after graduation from Williams (Ross, 1972).

New York was daunting for the farm boy from rural Massachusetts, but Hall took advantage of the cultural, educational, artistic, and social opportunities available to him. After a year at Union, he was able to borrow enough money to go to Europe. There he stayed until 1871, studying theology and philosophy but also encountering scientific physiology. He then returned to New York and finished his education at Union. He was just going through the motions, however, and felt stifled by religious orthodoxy.[6] So the ministry was

---

[6]Hall (1923) probably embellished the story he told about how Union's president reacted to Hall's trial sermon, supposedly the culmination of one's theological development at Union. According to Hall (1923, p. 178), rather than critique the sermon, the president simply knelt on the floor and prayed for Hall's soul.

out—Hall wanted to teach philosophy. After doing some private tutoring, he taught for 4 years at Antioch College in Ohio, where he encountered Wundt's *Principles of Physiological Psychology* and resolved to return to Germany to study this new laboratory psychology. First, however, he moved to Cambridge to study at Harvard, feeding himself by teaching English composition to Harvard sophomores. He met William James, took several courses with him, and completed a doctoral thesis on "the muscular perception of space" in 1878. It was primarily a philosophical piece, but it also included some experimental work in perception, conducted in the physiology laboratory of H. P. Bowditch. Harvard had just begun offering the doctorate in philosophy, and Hall was the first person to complete one. Because the topic was in the area that would eventually become known as experimental psychology, Hall's doctorate is sometimes considered to be the first one in psychology.

Doctorate in hand, Hall returned to Germany and found himself in Leipzig in 1879, the "official" year of the founding of Wundt's laboratory. He later claimed to be Wundt's first American student, but he actually had very little contact with Wundt, completed no publishable research, and was in fact preceded by at least one other American (Benjamin, Durkin, Link, Vestal, & Accord, 1992). Hall was disappointed with his experience in Leipzig and was later critical of Wundt, writing to James that he considered Wundt's experiments "utterly unreliable and defective in method" (quoted in Ross, 1972, p. 85). After Leipzig, Hall went to Berlin to study briefly with Helmholtz. While there, he became reacquainted with a young woman he knew from his days at Antioch; she was in Berlin to study art. They were married in Germany.

The Halls returned to Boston in the fall of 1880. Hall was 36 years old, highly educated, and devoted to his new bride. He was also poor and unemployed. Yet within 10 years, he would be a university president and one of the acknowledged leaders of psychology in America. His big break was an invitation from President Eliot of Harvard to lecture on education. Hall had already given considerable thought to how psychology might contribute to the educational reform that was occurring in the late 19th century. His lectures, given on Saturday mornings so that local teachers could attend, were highly successful. The publicity caught the attention of President Gilman of Johns Hopkins and eventually led to Hall's being asked to give a similar series of talks in Baltimore in January of 1882. Their success led to a job as part-time lecturer in philosophy. In 1884, Hall was hired as a professor at Hopkins at the generous (for the time) annual salary of $4,000 (Ross, 1972). His apparent expertise at using psychological principles to make recommendations about education was reflected in his title—Professor of Psychology and Pedagogy. At age 40, then, Hall had his first full-time job!

From Johns Hopkins to Clark

Hall did not stay long at Johns Hopkins, but while he was there, he significantly advanced the cause of psychology in America. In 1883, when still a part-time instructor, he created the first true research laboratory of experimental psychology in America. With the help of talented students such as Cattell and John Dewey (Chapter 7), Hall began to produce experimental research. In 1887, he founded the *American Journal of Psychology*, the first journal for the new psychology published in the United States. It served partly as a mechanism for publishing original research from Hall's lab and elsewhere, but it also included summaries and reviews of the psychological literature and sections devoted to "Notes and News" about psychology and psychologists. Journal finances were aided by a $500 donation from an advocate of spiritualism, who apparently thought the journal would be devoted to "psychic" research. This was an understandable confusion—the terms *psychic* and *psychological* were used interchangeably in those days. Hall did not correct the donor's misperception and took his money. Over the years, articles on spiritualism occasionally appeared in the journal, but only to ridicule the scientific basis for it. For example, Hall argued that what passed for telepathy, clairvoyance, and the like was nothing more than magic tricks and other forms of deception. Indeed, he became an accomplished magician and used his skills to demonstrate how easily people could be fooled by deception (Ross, 1972).

Hall's journal was a bold and risky venture, undertaken at a time when nobody could have predicted psychology's future. In an opening editorial, he made it clear that the purpose of the *American Journal of Psychology* would be "to record the psychological work of a scientific, as distinct from a speculative character [and to] record the progress of scientific psychology" (Hall, 1887, pp. 3–4). The opening number included research articles on "The Variations of the Normal Knee-Jerk," "Dermal Sensitiveness to Gradual Pressure Changes," and "The Psycho-Physic Law and Star Magnitudes."

In the late 1880s, an economic slowdown created financial difficulties for Hopkins (Hawkins, 1960). Facing dwindling resources, Hall began to look for greener pastures and found them in Worcester, Massachusetts. Jonas Clark, a merchant made wealthy by selling supplies at inflated prices to prospectors during the California gold rush, had decided to buy respectability in his hometown by opening a college to educate its youth. Hall seemed the perfect choice for president—ambitious, knowledgeable about higher education, and with a record of accomplishment in his brief time at Johns Hopkins—and Clark hired him in April of 1888. Clark wished to create a school for the youth of Worcester, but Hall had a grander vision. He managed to convince Clark that the school should offer graduate education in the mold of Johns Hopkins, and that it should focus on science. An undergraduate division could be added later. Thus, when Clark University opened its doors in the fall of 1889, it offered graduate training in five areas: psychology, biology, chemistry, physics, and mathematics. The initial group included 18 faculty members and 34 graduate students, and almost all of the instruction took place by means of directed research; the teaching load was just two lectures per week (Ross, 1972).

For three years, Clark University approached Hall's vision of a true university. Faculty produced cutting-edge research, students came from as far away as Japan to join the elite group of scholars, and Hall developed an international reputation as a visionary leader in education. All was not well, however. At the end of the first year, Hall suffered a personal tragedy when his wife and 8-year-old daughter died in an accident. In the second year, faculty began to hear about new opportunities and larger salaries being offered at another new university being created in Chicago with Rockefeller money. And throughout these early years, Hall was constantly in conflict with his faculty. Things came to a head in 1892, when a combination of financial problems (severe economic depression), faculty unrest, and the lure of the University of Chicago almost closed the university. Approximately two thirds of the faculty and students left Clark that year, leaving psychology as the only viable graduate department (Ross, 1972).

Psychology at Clark

Psychology survived after the fiasco of 1892, in part because Hall was deeply involved in the work of the department and in part due to the loyalty of its two faculty members, Edmund Sanford and William Burnham. Both had been students of Hall at Johns Hopkins. In Clark's

FIGURE 6.4 Edmund Sanford, Clark's first laboratory director, serving as the subject in an experiment that measured hand–eye coordination and "steadiness." From the Clark University Archives.

department of "psychology and pedagogy," Burnham was in charge of educational psychology and Sanford was in charge of the research laboratory (see Figure 6.4). Hall was clearly the leader of the department, however, and dictated its general direction. He also directed the doctoral dissertations of most of the students, and his Monday evening seminars became legendary among Clark alumni. Held in the parlor of his home, the seminars began at 7:30 and often lasted 3 hours. Students would make presentations, other students would contribute, and then Hall would have the final word:

> For a half-hour or longer, depending on the importance he attached to the theme, he presented from his armchair in the central archway a masterly critique of the research just reported and added to it new illumination from fresh angles that sometimes left the [students] gasping....
>
> After the intellectually provocative evening was ended, many of the graduate students set off for their boarding-places but found themselves so moved by the galvanism of their emotions that only a long walk near midnight and a warm bath before retiring could relax them enough to permit them to sleep. (Averill, 1982, p. 342)

Implied in this quote is that Hall possessed an impressive awareness of the psychological literature of the day. Indeed, his knowledge was encyclopedic, based on a rigorous system he developed of voraciously reading everything available (in several languages) and then summarizing the material in a set of bound notebooks. As early as 1900, long before the end of his career, he had accumulated 30 volumes of these notebooks (Leary, 2006).

During the early 1890s, the laboratory at Clark was a state-of-the-art facility, in part because when Hall left Johns Hopkins, he took most of the research equipment with him. As a result, the Hopkins laboratory disappeared; it reopened in 1903, under the leadership of James Mark Baldwin (discussed later). The Clark lab, meanwhile, was off to a flying start. Hall was generous with expenditures in the early years, giving Sanford all he needed to equip the laboratory; the abundance of costly "brass instrument" technology is evident from Figure 6.5a. Figure 6.5b provides an inside look at the experimental psychology of the day—it illustrates an actual research project (voice reaction time) in action. Sanford gave students considerable leeway in the Clark laboratory; in addition, Hall was constantly suggesting ideas to students. Hence, although the experimental research from Clark was unsystematic and scattered, it reflected the wide range of topics that interested American psychologists in the 1890s.

(a)

(b)

FIGURE 6.5   The Clark Lab in 1892: (*a*) "brass instruments," including timing devices and reaction time apparatus; (*b*) a voice reaction time study. From the Clark University Archives.

In the mid-1890s, as part of his deep interest in evolution, Hall began supporting research in comparative psychology. One consequence was the creation of the first studies using what later became a standard piece of laboratory equipment—the maze. For details on the origins of the venerable rats-in-mazes tradition, read this chapter's Close-Up.

CLOSE-UP

CREATING MAZE LEARNING

Ask psychologists to name famous pieces of apparatus in experimental psychology, and mazes will be at or near the top of the list. The maze reached its peak of popularity from about 1920 to 1950, especially in the research of behaviorists Edward Tolman and Clark Hull (Chapter 11), and the apparatus remains in use today. Hundreds of maze studies have been completed over the years, and one might ask how it all started. Credit is sometimes given to the Darwinian Sir John Lubbock, who used crude Y-shaped mazes in the 1870s to study how ants followed scent trails, or to E. L. Thorndike (Chapter 7), who observed chicks escaping from simple mazes created by placing books on end. The research that launched the systematic study of rats in mazes, however, was completed by Willard Small of Clark University at the turn of the 20th century.

Small arrived in Worcester in 1897 as a 27-year-old graduate student and was soon doing animal research with another student, Linus Kline. Kline completed the first general study of the abilities of rats (Dewsbury, 1984), and one of his interests concerned the rat's

"home-finding" capacities. He discussed the problem with the lab's director, Sanford, who gave him the idea for a maze study and suggested a specific maze design. As Kline later told the story:

> I . . . described to [Sanford] runways which I had observed several years ago made by large feral rats to their nests under the porch of an old cabin on my father's farm in Virginia. These runways were from three to six inches below the surface of the ground and when exposed during excavation presented a veritable maze. Sanford at once suggested the possibility of using the pattern of the Hampton Court maze for purposes of constructing a "home-finding" apparatus. (Miles, 1930, p. 331)

One can only speculate about why the Hampton maze occurred to Sanford. That it was on his mind is clear from Kline's comment that "the readiness with which he directed my attention to the Hampton maze is presumptive evidence that he had thought of its use before" (Miles, 1930, p. 331). One possibility is that Sanford may have been in the Hampton Court maze himself just before the conversation with Kline. He was on sabbatical in the spring of 1898 and visited a number of laboratories in Europe (Goodwin, 1987). His last stop was in England; it is at least conceivable that he visited Hampton Court, a favorite tourist stop, which is just outside of London and includes England's most famous hedge maze.

It is not clear why Small did the first maze study and not Kline. Kline reported that other work prevented him from pursuing the idea, and it was perhaps natural for his friend and laboratory coworker to take up the project. At any rate, in January of 1899, Small constructed three 6×8 foot mazes with wire mesh walls, using the Hampton Court design but adjusting it to a rectangular pattern, as shown in Figure 6.6. He then began his historic research on the manner in which rats learn mazes.

Sanford reported on Small's study at the December 1899 APA meeting, and Small published a more detailed report in 1901. Modern accounts, perhaps inspired by Thorndike's rather caustic review (Thorndike, 1900), usually dismiss Small's description of the maze studies as a series of overly anthropomorphic comments about such things as the rat's alleged "disgust" over reaching a dead end. The criticism has some merit, but Small's report also gives a trial-and-error description of maze learning similar to other contemporary accounts by Thorndike (Chapter 7)

and Lloyd Morgan (Chapter 5). Small also commented extensively on what he believed to be the mental processes involved, and he used blind rats to investigate the effects of sensory capacity on learning. These blind rats seemed to learn the maze as well as their sighted peers, leading Small to conclude that "tactile motor sensations furnish the essential data for the recognition and discrimination involved in forming the special associations" (Small, 1901, p. 237).

Small's work is less important for its conclusions than for the fact that it initiated a flood of similar research. In the next few years, comparative psychologists used versions of the Hampton Court maze to study species ranging from rhesus monkeys (Kinnaman, 1902) to English sparrows (Porter, 1904). With the white rat, research followed up on Small's ideas about the influence of the various senses on learning. The most famous of these were the studies by Watson and Carr at the University of Chicago (Chapter 10), who concluded, like Small, that the kinesthetic sense was most critical. Subsequent research, and dozens of such studies were completed by 1920, showed the process to be much more complicated. It is worth noting that the animal maze literature began by investigating the sensory and mental processes involved in maze learning and by investigating how organisms adapted to their environment. These of course were topics clearly in tune with the psychology of the early 1900s: the psychology of mental life, which reflected the pervasiveness of evolutionary theory.

(a)   (b)

FIGURE 6.6 (a) Design of England's Hampton Court maze; (b) Small's readjustment of the Hampton Court maze design to a rectangular configuration.

In his remaining years at Clark University, Hall left his stamp on psychology in several ways. First, he continued to professionalize psychology by creating its first formal organization, the American Psychological Association (APA). He and about a dozen other psychologists held an organizational meeting in his study in July 1892, at which time 31 charter members were named (Sokal, 1992). As you might expect, Hall was elected the association's first president. Eighteen of the charter members convened in December 1892, at the University of Pennsylvania, for the APA's first annual meeting. The organization grew rapidly: It had 74 members after 4 years, and 127 by the turn of the century (Ross, 1972). It adopted a constitution in 1894, making clear its role in creating disciplinary identity for a scientific psychology. The purpose of the organization was to be "the advancement of Psychology as a science. Those are eligible for membership who are engaged in this work" (Cattell, 1895, p. 150). The APA also enhanced psychology's professional and scientific status by affiliating with older, more recognized associations, such as the American Association for the Advancement of Science (Camfield, 1973).

Hall and Developmental Psychology In addition to activities connected with the journal and the APA, Hall contributed to American psychology by advancing his genetic psychology. He was a pioneer in developmental psychology, promoting the child study movement, writing the first textbook on adolescent psychology, and near the end of his career, writing a book on aging. He also continued to champion the importance of psychology for education, in part by establishing summer schools for the training of educators but also by founding a second journal, *Pedagogical Seminary* (now the *Journal of Genetic Psychology*) in 1891.

Hall became interested in child study while at Johns Hopkins, where he published the first in a series of studies about children. He used the results from questionnaires filled out by children, teachers, and parents (these were the "questionary" studies that Titchener disparaged in his letter to Wilson). His overall goal was identified in the title of his first research paper: "The Contents of Children's Minds" (Hall, 1883/1948). In this survey, Hall accumulated data from more than 200 Boston children who were just beginning school. They were questioned by about 60 different teachers, who asked what they knew about a wide range of objects. The level of knowledge was not high. For instance, 75.5% could not identify what season of the year it was, 87.5% didn't know what an island was, and 90.5% couldn't locate their ribs. Hall also discovered that children reared in the country did much better than those raised in the city. As a farm boy himself, Hall did not find this surprising:

> As our methods of teaching grow natural we realize that city life is unnatural, and that those who grow up without knowing the country are defrauded of that without which childhood can never be complete or normal. On the whole the material of the city is no doubt inferior in pedagogic value to country experience. A few days in the country at this age has raised the level of many a city child's intelligence more than a term or two of school training could do without it. (Hall, 1883/1948, pp. 261–262)

This quote contains strong hints of Hall's philosophy of education. He ridiculed rote memorization and the rigid discipline of the classroom. Instead, he favored a more permissive approach that took for granted the child's "natural" curiosity about the world and encouraged what would be called "active learning" today—giving children problems to solve or activities to complete that would have some specific pedagogical value.

Hall was not only interested in children. Some of his questionnaire studies collected data from teenagers, and he reported the results, along with everything else then known about that age group, in his encyclopedic two-volume *Adolescence* (1904). It was the first book devoted to the study of teenagers, and Hall is the person most responsible for identifying adolescence as a distinct stage of development. The description of adolescence as a period of "storm and stress" has its origins in Hall's book. The book also contains the most thorough description of Hall's use of the theory of **recapitulation**. The theory originated with the German evolutionary biologist Ernst Haeckel, who proposed that an organism's stages of development, from cell to a fully formed individual, can be seen as a recapitulation of the evolution of the species.[7] Thus, at one stage of development the human fetus resembles a fish, reflecting that point in evolutionary history where the human species had aquatic ancestors. Hall and others extended the idea beyond biological development and into the area of psychological development, arguing that the psychological development of the individual reflected evolutionary history (Arnett & Cravens, 2006). For example, Hall believed that the high level of recklessness and impulsiveness found in adolescence reflected a time in evolutionary history when humans were less "civilized" than they were in more modern times.

Hall has been criticized for his reliance on recapitulation theory, and some have dismissed the adolescence book on the grounds that it is tied to a failed theory. Yet Leary (2006) has argued that such criticism is unfair to Hall and shows a lack of understanding of historical context. According to Leary, although recapitulation was under attack in the early 20th century, the scientific community did not wholly abandon it until 1930. Also, Hall was cautious in his use of recapitulation, relying on it merely as a general framework. He was also aware of and open to criticism of the theory—one of the scientists he invited to the 1909 twentieth anniversary celebration at Clark (discussed later) was August Weismann, the fiercest critic of recapitulation (Weismann declined the invitation). The key point is that recapitulation theory had the beneficial effect of stimulating Hall's interest in *all* stages of development, for testing the implications of recapitulation demands close attention to development across the life span (Youniss, 2006).

Toward the end of his life, Hall became interested in the middle and final stages of life and eventually wrote about aging in *Senescence: The Last Half of Life* (1922). He once again relied on questionnaire data, asking the elderly their opinions about such topics as their fear of death and their ability to recognize the signs of aging. He also criticized the lack of retirement pension programs and recommended that the elderly organize politically (long before the advent of today's AARP).

Hall and Psychoanalysis A significant portion of Hall's *Adolescence* concerned sexual behavior, including an entire 50-page chapter entitled "Adolescent Love." Hall also offered a course at Clark entitled "The Psychology of Sex" (Rosenzweig, 1992) and, consistent with his ideas on education, he believed that the natural expression of sexual behavior should not be inhibited. This attitude raised eyebrows among his peers, leading one of them to wonder: "Is there no turning Hall away from this d—d sexual rut? I really think it is a bad thing

---

[7]Haeckel's theory had been highly visible and heavily debated during Hall's first visit to Germany from 1868 to 1871 (Ross, 1972).

morally and intellectually to harp so much on the sexual string, unless one is a neurologist" (letter from F. Angell to E. B. Titchener on March 19, 1990; quoted in Ross, 1972, p. 385).

Hall's preoccupation with sex, combined with an interest in abnormal behavior, led him to become fascinated by Freud's theories. In 1909, to celebrate the university's 20th anniversary, Hall organized the Clark Conference, a series of public lectures by prominent psychologists. The centerpiece was a series of five talks given by none other than Freud himself.[8] Accompanied by his younger colleague Carl Jung, who lectured on his new word association technique, Freud made his first and only visit to America and delivered five lectures that were published in the *American Journal of Psychology* in 1910 and then separately in book form. The American psychologists in attendance had mixed reactions to Freud. William James, for example, while characteristically open to Freud's new ideas, was skeptical about Freud's dream theory and wrote to Mary Calkins that Freud seemed to be "a man obsessed with fixed ideas" (quoted in Evans & Koelsch, 1985, p. 847). Nonetheless, a grateful Freud later said that the Clark Conference was an important point in the history of psychoanalysis and constituted the first international recognition of his theories. Figure 6.7 shows one of psychology's most famous pictures. In the front row, Hall is sixth from the left, Freud seventh, and Jung eighth; Ernest Jones, Freud's biographer, is in the second row, between Hall and Freud (also in the front row, Titchener is second from the left and James is third; Cattell is just over the left shoulder of James).

Hall retired from the presidency of Clark in 1920 but remained active in his remaining 4 years of life. He published his book on aging in 1922 and an autobiography, *Life and Confessions of a Psychologist*, a year later (Hall, 1923). In 1924, he was elected to a second

FIGURE 6.7 Psychologists at the 1909 Clark Conference.

[8]Hall originally hoped for an all-star cast of international psychologists, including not just Freud, but Wundt, Binet, and Ebbinghaus. Wundt and Binet declined, however; Ebbinghaus accepted the invitation, but he died just before the conference began (Evans & Koelsch, 1985).

term as president of the APA; he was only the second person ever to be elected twice (William James was the other). He died before he could assume his duties, however.

MARY WHITON CALKINS (1863–1930): CHALLENGING THE MALE MONOPOLY

Professional women in the early 21st century often face discrimination in the workplace and find themselves unable to rise above the proverbial "glass ceiling." As frustrating as the problem is for modern women, it was many times worse in psychology's early years. As described earlier in the chapter, women were widely believed to be intellectually inferior to men in the 1890s, and they had little standing in society (e.g., they could not vote until 1920). Combining marriage and a career was virtually impossible—marriage was assumed to be a woman's career. Even if they didn't marry, they were expected to care for other members of their family, especially aging parents. Although women began attending college in increasing numbers in the late 19th century, higher education for women was looked on with skepticism by a male-dominated society. It was even believed that an education could harm women; their weak constitutions could be permanently damaged by the cerebral demands of college. Hence, in the 1890s it was almost impossible for a woman to obtain a doctorate in psychology—a dilemma faced by Mary Whiton Calkins.

Calkins's Life and Work

Mary Calkins grew up in Buffalo, New York, the oldest of five children in a close-knit family headed by her Congregationalist minister father. He shared with William James's father a belief in the educational value of travel to Europe and in the importance of being multilingual. In fact, Mary's parents spoke only German in her presence during her first few years; by adulthood, Mary was fluent in English, German, and French (Furumoto, 1979). The Calkins family moved to the Boston area when Mary was 17, and soon after that she entered Smith College (one of the new women's colleges) in western Massachusetts. She graduated in 1885 and then went to Europe with her family for 16 months; there, among other things, she added Greek to her list of language competencies. Upon her return, she took a position teaching Greek at Wellesley College. Calkins (Figure 6.8) remained at Wellesley for the rest of her career.

By the late 1880s, Wellesley's leaders decided that to keep up with trends in modern science, the college needed to offer the new laboratory approach to psychology. Calkins had expressed some interest in teaching philosophy and had impressed her superiors in her first few years as a teacher, so she was given the opportunity to develop a course in laboratory psychology. It was understood, however, that she would take a year off to learn about this new field. Thus began her frustrating search for graduate education in psychology.

Graduate Education for Females   Calkins quickly learned that opportunities for advanced training were quite limited for women. After considering Europe and a few American schools (e.g., Yale, Michigan), she attempted to become a student at Harvard—it had William James to offer, and it was close to home. She also looked into Clark University, 30 miles to the west of Boston. At Harvard, she was grudgingly allowed to attend

FIGURE 6.8 Mary Whiton Calkins as a young instructor at Wellesley College. From Scarborough and Furumoto (1987).

seminars with James and the philosopher Josiah Royce, both of whom supported her application vigorously. Harvard officials made it clear that she was merely an unofficial "guest" of the university, however. It was the same story at Clark. Women were not allowed in officially, but Edmund Sanford welcomed her into his new laboratory. Calkins later credited Sanford, who contributed time, advice, and apparatus, with being the true founder of the psychology laboratory at Wellesley (Calkins, 1930).

Calkins entered Harvard in the fall of 1890 and immediately encountered the educational opportunity of a lifetime. She and four male students were enrolled in Philosophy 20a, Physiological Psychology, with William James; the males, perhaps unnerved by the presence of a woman, dropped out within a few days. As Calkins (1930) later recalled:

> James and I were left ... quite literally at either side of a library fire. *The Principles of Psychology* was warm from the press; and my absorbed study of those brilliant, erudite, and provocative volumes, as interpreted by their writer, was my introduction to psychology. (p. 31)

After her year of study at Harvard and Clark, Calkins returned to Wellesley. But her appetite for the new psychology had been whetted, and she was soon looking into further training. In 1892, when William James recruited Hugo Münsterberg (Chapter 8) from Germany to run the Harvard lab, Calkins returned to Cambridge, once more as an unofficial guest. Again the timing was perfect for Calkins—Münsterberg's English was poor, but she was fluent in German. They became colleagues immediately. For the next 2 years, Calkins worked in Münsterberg's lab part-time while continuing to teach 10 miles away at Wellesley. In the academic year 1894 to 1895, she took a leave from the college to complete her studies.

Calkins's Research on Association Münsterberg treated Calkins just like any other doctoral student. For her thesis, she completed a brilliant series of experimental studies on association, publishing the research in two parts (Calkins, 1894; Calkins 1896) and then writing an extended account as a *Psychological Review Monograph* paper in 1896. Traditional philosophical and introspective accounts often described how the strength of associations could be influenced by such factors as frequency, recency, vividness, and primacy. In the spirit of Ebbinghaus, Calkins was determined to go beyond "ordinary self-observation" and examine these factors experimentally. The procedure she developed is an important one historically—although she did not use the term, she invented **paired-associate learning**, later to become a standard method in memory research. Her subjects first studied stimulus–response pairs comprised of sequentially presented color patches and numbers (each shown for 4 seconds) and then tried to recall the number responses when shown the color stimuli. Calkins manipulated frequency by presenting the same color several times, once with one number, then either two or three times with a second number. Here's how she described series #89:

> I. Medium gray, 29; blue, 82; violet, 61 (n); red, 23; violet, 12 (f); peacock, 79; violet, 12 (f); strawberry, 47; violet, 12 (f); light brown, 53; dark gray, 34; light green, 72.

> II. Peacock, red, green, violet, medium gray, brown, strawberry, dark gray, blue. (Calkins, 1894, p. 478)

Thus, during presentation (I.), violet was first paired with 61 (referred to by her as the "normal" pairing, or n), then three times (f = frequency) with the number 12. During recall (II.), violet was the fourth color presented and the question was whether subjects would recall the number 61 or 12. In like manner, Calkins studied recency by comparing the recall of two numbers paired with the same color, one pairing in the middle of the sequence and one at the very end. Vividness was examined by presenting a critical pair in some way that made it stand out from the other pairs, such as by altering the size of the numbers. Primacy was studied by looking at performance for the first pair in a series. In general, her results showed that recall was enhanced by each of the four factors: frequency, vividness, recency, and primacy. In subsequent trials in which she directly compared these factors by combining them within the same list, Calkins found that frequency was the most critical factor. She also ran some trials in which the colors and numbers were presented together on the same card. This enabled her to compare "simultaneous" associations with the earlier "successive" ones, thus examining the old British empiricist distinction between simultaneous and successive forms of contiguity. She found no major differences.

Calkins did not mention the Ebbinghaus memory research (Chapter 4) published in 1885, but she was clearly aware of it. She was fluent in German and very familiar with James's *Principles*, which includes a thorough description of the Ebbinghaus research in its chapter on "Memory." The Ebbinghaus influence is also apparent in Calkins's choice of materials when she altered her procedure to use auditory presentation. The stimuli in this case (and she used the term) were "nonsense syllables" instead of colors. Calkins found about the same outcome for both visual and auditory presentation, except that the recency effects were more striking with the latter (years later, this finding was rediscovered by cognitive psychologists and called the modality effect).

Calkins (1896) summed up her overall results by emphasizing the importance of the frequency variable, but adding a caution that the laboratory results might not be completely "representative of ordinary trains of association" (p. 49). She even added a statement about the practical implications of her findings, referring to frequency as a "corrective influence.... The prominence of frequency is of course of grave importance, for it means the possibility of exercising some control over the life of the imagination and of definitely combating harmful or troublesome associations" (p. 49). Calkins was thinking along the same pragmatic lines as her teacher, William James, and her research can be seen as providing some empirical evidence for James's suggestions (discussed earlier) about how to firmly entrench a habit. Practice makes perfect.

Madigan and O'Hara (1992) closely examined Calkins's research on memory, including some studies completed after her dissertation research. They found clear indications that Calkins discovered a number of effects that would be rediscovered half a century later, when psychologists once again became interested in studying cognitive psychology (Chapter 14). These included such immediate memory phenomena as the primacy, recency, and negative recency effects, the aforementioned modality effect, and the effects of interference.

Although it was unofficial, Calkins completed a defense of her thesis and a PhD examination in May of 1895. Münsterberg, James, and other examiners appealed to the Harvard authorities to grant her the PhD; Münsterberg described her as "superior...to all candidates of the philosophical Ph.D. during the last years" and "surely one of the strongest professors of psychology in the country" (quoted in Scarborough & Furumoto, 1987, pp. 44–45). Harvard refused, though—after all, Calkins was a woman. Later, when Radcliffe College was created as a Harvard for women, Calkins was offered a Radcliffe PhD. This time it was Calkins who refused. She would have a doctorate from the school where she earned it or none at all. Although she would earn several honorary degrees, Harvard never did change its mind, and Calkins was never awarded the PhD.

From Psychology to Philosophy

After completing her nondoctorate from Harvard, Calkins returned to Wellesley, continued building her lab with Sanford's help, and produced a string of research publications with her students through the turn of the century. In 1898, she turned over the laboratory to Eleanor Gamble, a new PhD from Titchener's lab at Cornell (one of the few institutions that admitted women doctoral students). From about 1900 on, her publications became less research oriented as she developed her major theoretical contribution to psychology, **self-psychology**. It was a system that clearly showed the influence of her mentor, William James. Calkins argued that psychology could be the study of mental life, as James had said, but the central fact of psychology must be that all consciousness contains an element of the self (Strunk, 1972).

At a time when strong disagreements were developing over the proper direction for the New Psychology, Calkins saw her self-psychology as a means of resolving disputes. For example, as will be clear from the next chapter, one conflict was between structuralism, which emphasized analyzing consciousness into its basic elements, and functionalism, which focused on how consciousness served to adapt the individual to the environment. When her peers elected her the 14th president of the APA in 1905, the first female so honored, Calkins (1906) delivered a presidential address called "A Reconciliation between Structural and Functional Psychology." In it, she argued that both views could be accommodated within a system that recognized the self as the fundamental starting point.

Like James, Mary Calkins gradually shifted her interests over the years from psychology to philosophy. Shortly after her APA presidency, for instance, she wrote *The Persistent Problems of Philosophy* (1907), perhaps her most important work. In 1918, the American

Philosophical Association elected her president of that organization, making her the first woman to be elected to the presidency of both APAs. Calkins retired from Wellesley in 1929 and died of cancer a year later.

Other Women Pioneers: Untold Lives

Calkins wasn't the only woman struggling against a male-oriented discipline at the turn of the century. In *Untold Lives: The First Generation of American Women Psychologists*, Elizabeth Scarborough and Laurel Furumoto (1987) have thoroughly documented the experiences of Calkins and several other pioneering women psychologists. Two of the better known were Christine Ladd-Franklin and Margaret Washburn.

Christine Ladd-Franklin (1847–1930) Like Calkins, Ladd-Franklin was educated at one of the new women's colleges. She entered Vassar College (Poughkeepsie, New York) in 1866, a year after it had been founded. There she excelled in science and math and was inspired by the example of the astronomer Maria Mitchell, said to be the most eminent woman scientist in America at that time (Furumoto, 1992). She graduated in 1869 and taught in secondary schools for about 10 years before deciding to pursue a graduate education in math at Johns Hopkins. There she encountered the same roadblock that Calkins faced later—Hopkins did not admit women as official students. Nonetheless, she was allowed to attend classes and, by 1882, she had completed all the requirements for a doctorate in math. It was 1926, however, before Johns Hopkins officially awarded her the degree, which she accepted in person at age 79 (Scarborough & Furumoto, 1987).

While at Johns Hopkins, Christine Ladd met, fell in love with, and married a faculty member in the math department. Upon marrying Fabian Franklin, she became Christine Ladd-Franklin. With her husband's active support, she was able to continue her interests in math and published several scholarly papers. In the mid-1880s she became interested in visual perception, a shift that led her to the new psychology. Her first publication, on binocular vision ("A Method for the Experimental Determination of the Horopter"), appeared in 1887 in the inaugural issue of Hall's *American Journal of Psychology*. During her husband's 1891–1892 sabbatical in Europe, she was able to conduct research on vision in the Gottingen lab of G. E. Müller. As you recall from Chapter 4, Müller's lab was one of the best in Germany. She also spent time with Helmholtz in Berlin. While in Germany, she developed a theory of color vision that was grounded in evolutionary theory; it was influential for several decades.

Of the three pioneer women considered here, Ladd-Franklin was the most outspoken about the lack of professional opportunities for women. For example, she directly challenged the "men only" rule of a group of psychologists known as the Experimentalists. Organized in 1904 by Titchener (Chapter 7) of Cornell, this select group met annually at various labs to discuss their current research. After being refused permission to attend in 1912, she wrote to Titchener that she was "shocked to know that you are still—at this year—excluding women from your meeting of experimental psychologists. It is such a very old-fashioned standpoint" (quoted in Furumoto, 1988, p. 107). Two years later her persistence had worn Titchener down somewhat, and she presented her work on color vision at one of the Experimentalists' meetings. It was the only time a woman participated in a meeting during Titchener's lifetime.

Ladd-Franklin also vigorously campaigned for a faculty position at a research university, but she never managed to obtain more than part-time lectureships, first at Johns

Hopkins and then at Columbia when she and her husband moved to New York. Failure to land a university position also meant failure to gain access to laboratory facilities. According to Furumoto, this explained why Ladd-Franklin's contributions to psychology were more theoretical than data based. Despite the obstacles, Ladd-Franklin persevered in her work as a mathematician and expert on visual perception, never giving in to the prevailing belief that science was for men only.

Margaret Floy Washburn (1871–1939) In addition to Ladd-Franklin, Vassar College produced Margaret Washburn and then later reclaimed her. Washburn graduated from Vassar in 1890 with her interests divided between science and philosophy. She decided to pursue "the wonderful new science of experimental psychology" (Washburn, 1932, p. 338) because it seemed to combine her interests. She applied for graduate studies at Columbia University, where she ran into the same problems faced by Calkins and Ladd-Franklin. Cattell welcomed her as a serious student, but (sound familiar?) she was permitted to attend his classes only unofficially. Cattell saw her potential and encouraged her to apply to Cornell, which accepted women graduate students. There she encountered Titchener, who had just finished his doctorate with Wundt at Leipzig. Women might have been excluded from Titchener's Experimentalists, but they were accepted into his laboratory; and Washburn was Titchener's first PhD student. She became the first woman to earn a doctorate in psychology when she completed the degree in 1894 with a study of the effects of visual imagery on tactile sensitivity. It was one of the few studies published in Wundt's journal (*Philosophische Studien*) that was not completed at the Leipzig laboratory.

After leaving Cornell, Washburn held several teaching positions and then returned to her alma mater, Vassar, in 1903. She spent her remaining professional career there. Despite the heavy teaching load and inadequate research facilities that invariably accompany faculty life at small colleges, Washburn fashioned a remarkable career that included an APA presidency in 1921, coeditorship of the *American Journal of Psychology* for more than a decade, and election to the prestigious National Academy of Sciences in 1931. When the Experimentalists reorganized after Titchener's death in 1927, she was one of two women elected as a charter member of the new group, and she hosted a meeting of the reconstituted "Society of Experimental Psychologists" at Vassar in 1931 (Goodwin, 2005).

As a psychologist, Washburn published in the areas of perception, imagery, "social consciousness" (empathy and helping behavior), and developed a motor theory of consciousness, but she is best known for her work in comparative psychology. She contributed some original research (e.g., on the perception of color in fish) and summarized the field in her well-known text, *The Animal Mind*. First published in 1908, it went through four editions (1917, 1926, 1936) and became the standard textbook of its day (Dewsbury, 1992). It was notable for its exclusion of evidence based solely on anecdotal data; Washburn included only the results of experimental research. As implied by its title, her book focused on the cognitive processes of perception, attention, and consciousness as exhibited by the behaviors of various species.

OTHER PIONEERS: LADD AND BALDWIN

Figures such as James, Hall, and Calkins stand out among other early American psychologists, but of course there were others. Two notables were George Trumbull Ladd of Yale and James Mark Baldwin, who spent his most productive years at Princeton.

George Trumbull Ladd (1842–1921)

Ladd was a transitional figure who bridged the chasm between the old mental philosophy and faculty psychology of the early and mid-19th century and the modern laboratory-based psychology that took hold toward the end of the century. He was trained for the ministry and worked as a minister for 10 years before taking a position, in 1879, as professor of psychology at Bowdoin College (where Thomas Upham had written the popular pre-Jamesian psychology text described earlier in this chapter). Two years later, Ladd was hired at Yale, where he remained for the rest of his career. He was the second person elected president of the APA, after Hall.

Ladd's reputation and his importance for early psychology rest on his work as a textbook writer. His best-known book, *Elements of Physiological Psychology*, appeared in 1887 and was an immediate hit. It was the first detailed description of the Wundtian laboratory psychology to appear in English; hence, it provided the introduction to the New Psychology for most English-speaking psychologists (Mills, 1974). Cornell's Titchener, a student at Oxford when the book first appeared, recalled his "excitement on finding this book in the library of the Oxford Union" (Titchener, 1921a), and argued that the book

> helped toward the establishment of laboratories and the recognition of experimental
> psychology as an academic study. Coming, as it did, from a professor of philosophy at
> Yale who had been a Congregational minister, it gave the young science an air of
> respectability . . . which was of high advantage in its struggle for life." (p. 600)

Ironically, although he provided a faithful rendition of Wundtian laboratory psychology, full of the requisite descriptions of such topics as psychophysics and reaction time, Ladd was never a "laboratory man" himself. He preferred a more philosophically based psychology that relied on reflective introspection to study the mind. He never quite outgrew his early training in faculty psychology. In his APA presidential address, Ladd expressed concern over the direction psychology was taking, that an introspective strategy for understanding the mind was being replaced by experiments with their quantitative measurements. His fears, of course, were realized.

The *Elements of Physiological Psychology* went through 10 printings and then was revised in 1911 by Ladd and Robert Woodworth (Chapter 7). During the 1890s, Ladd wrote no fewer than four other psychology textbooks, but by then James's *Principles*, along with its briefer version, was dominating the field. Although uninterested in laboratory work himself, Ladd established a state-of-the-art psychology lab at Yale in 1892 and brought in Edward Scripture (with a newly minted PhD from Wundt's lab in Leipzig) to run it. For the remainder of the 1890s, Scripture produced a steady stream of laboratory research. Unfortunately, Ladd and Scripture were equally strong willed and often at odds over the direction that psychology at Yale should take; the conflict eventually cost both of them their jobs shortly after the turn of the century (Sokal, 1980).

James Mark Baldwin (1861–1934)

Like Ladd, Baldwin made important contributions to the new experimental psychology without being much of a laboratory researcher himself. Although he founded two laboratories and resurrected another, for example, his publications were primarily theoretical and seldom empirical. In the words of E. G. Boring (1950), "while he was one of the 'new' psychologists, his skill was the philosopher's ability in speculative theorizing" (p. 529). Baldwin was among the leaders in American psychology from about 1890 until 1909, when scandal forced him out of academia and, in effect, into exile.

Baldwin earned his PhD in philosophy from Princeton University (then called the College of New Jersey) in 1889 and, that same year, joined the faculty at the University of Toronto. The appointment produced some controversy, because another candidate for the position was a Canadian, and Toronto newspapers and university alumnae could not understand why an American would be favored over a native son (Green, 2004). Yet Baldwin was hired (to soothe Canadian interests, the other candidate, a philosopher, was also hired) and quickly made an impact; shortly after his tenure began, he founded Canada's first psychology laboratory. Four years later he returned to Princeton, founded his second lab, and began his most productive period as a psychologist. He staked a claim as pioneer developmental psychologist by writing *Mental Development in the Child and the Race* (Baldwin, 1895) and *Social and Ethical Interpretations in Mental Development* (Baldwin, 1897). As would be the case for Hall's 1904 book on adolescence, these books by Baldwin were much influenced by evolutionary thinking. The books had little in the way of empirical evidence, being based mostly on Baldwin's application of evolutionary theory and the observations he made of his two daughters. Contemporary reviews of the books were mixed. In an obituary for Baldwin, Washburn (1935) noted that the lack of empirical evidence to support his claims about development "accounts for the fact that the name of this brilliant thinker seldom if ever appears in present-day volumes on child psychology" (p. 169). Yet Baldwin's ideas about the origins of cognition later directly influenced the developmental theorizing of the famous Swiss psychologist Jean Piaget (Chapter 14; Cairns, 1994). For example, Baldwin used the terms *assimilation* (relating new concepts to already known concepts) and *accommodation* (developing new concepts) to refer to the processes involved in developing new ideas; Piaget used the same terms, and in the same manner. Along with Hall, Baldwin can justifiably be considered a founder of developmental psychology.

Although Baldwin's research output was meager, he did contribute some important reaction-time research that produced a brief, yet somewhat rancorous debate with Titchener. At issue were some reaction time findings, with the main issue coming down to who was best able to provide data on reaction time (RT). As you will learn in the next chapter, Titchener believed that to avoid making errors and to avoid bias, subjects (usually referred to as "observers" then) in experiments had to be highly trained. With his highly trained observers, Titchener was able to demonstrate a distinction between what was called a sensory reaction time (when attention was focused on the stimulus) and a motor reaction time (when attention was focused on the response). Baldwin could not replicate the finding when using relatively untrained observers, but he identified what he thought were individual differences in RT performance (Krantz, 1969). Some people were "imagery types" and responded faster when given sensory RT instructions rather than motor RT instructions. Others, "motor types," would do the opposite. Because Baldwin's observers were not highly trained, Titchener considered the results meaningless. As is the case with many scientific controversies, neither side "won," although a study by Angell and Moore (1896) provided a reasonable resolution—early in RT training, results like Baldwin's occurred; later, after more training, results like Titchener's occurred. As for Baldwin and Titchener, as the controversy played out in print, their exchanges became increasingly acrimonious. It is easy to see why they never became friends, and why

Baldwin often had difficulty developing close professional relationships. In print, for example, Baldwin wrote that he could not "help thinking that Professor Titchener sometimes allows the dust of his machinery to obscure his vision" (quoted in Krantz, 1969, p. 11). Titchener replied that he had "no wish to emulate Professor Baldwin in the matter of name calling," and he chastised Baldwin's attitude as being neither "scientifically or ethically defensible" (p. 11).

During his Princeton years, in addition to his theoretical and occasional empirical work, Baldwin contributed to the professionalization of psychology. He was a charter member of the APA and its sixth president in 1897. With Cattell, he founded *Psychological Review* in 1894; the journal quickly began to compete successfully with Hall's *American Journal of Psychology* and remains an important journal of theoretical psychology. *Psychological Index*, an important reference source identifying publications in psychology, accompanied the *Review*. Its first issue, listing everything published in psychology for 1894, had 1,312 entries; the *Index* lasted until the 1930s, at which time it was publishing about 6,000 references per year (Benjamin & VandenBos, 2006). It was replaced and improved upon (i.e., brief summaries rather than just a reference listing) by *Psychological Abstracts*, the forerunner to today's PsycINFO. In 1904, Baldwin helped launch another journal that continues to be prominent today, *Psychological Bulletin*. And shortly after the turn of the century, with the help of up to 60 different contributors, he began a huge project to create the definitive dictionary of psychology and philosophy. The final product, which appeared in 1901–1902 and was soon referred to as "Baldwin's Dictionary," occupied two volumes and had more than 1,500 entries (Wozniak, 2009). As a measure of Baldwin's eminence, he was ranked fifth on Cattell's 1903 survey of psychology's most prominent persons.[9]

In 1903, Baldwin accepted a new challenge. He left Princeton for Johns Hopkins University, where he reestablished the laboratory that essentially had been moribund since Hall departed (with his suitcase full of laboratory apparatus) in 1888. There Baldwin remained until 1909, when he resigned abruptly and under pressure after being arrested in a raid on a Baltimore house of prostitution. Baldwin claimed it was all a misunderstanding, but he was sufficiently embarrassed about it that he gave police a phony name at first. His career effectively over, Baldwin spent his remaining years in Mexico and in Europe. Based on a series of lectures delivered at the National University in Mexico City, his last substantial publication was a brief history of psychology that appeared in 1913 (Horley, 2001).

IN PERSPECTIVE: THE NEW PSYCHOLOGY AT THE MILLENNIUM

During the last 20 years of the 19th century, psychology in America changed dramatically. Before that time, it was dominated by traditional faculty psychology and taught as "intellectual" or "mental" philosophy. By the end of the century, it was still being taught in philosophy departments for the most part, but it now reflected the influence of the New Psychology of Germany and the revolutionary ideas of Charles Darwin. In the early 1880s there were no research laboratories of psychology in the United States, and most American psychologists

---

[9] As mentioned earlier, James headed the list. Rounding out the "top 10" were, in order, Cattell, Münsterberg, Hall, Baldwin, Titchener, Royce, Ladd, Dewey, and Jastrow.

wishing to study the new laboratory psychology had to travel to Germany. By 1890, laboratories had been established at 9 American universities; by the end of the century, at least 41 universities had laboratories (Hilgard, 1987). Although in the early 1890s a German PhD in psychology held higher status than one earned in the United States, this was no longer true by the end of the decade. The shift is reflected in the numbers: Between 1884 and 1892, the number of Americans earning PhDs in America (9) and Germany (8) was about equal, but from 1893 to 1899, 63 American psychologists earned their doctorates in the United States, whereas only 10 earned theirs in Germany (O'Donnell, 1985).

Hall's Clark University was a leader in the production of PhDs in psychology in the 1890s, but other young psychologists were being trained at several other up-and-coming universities. Foremost among them were Cornell, where students would find Titchener and a school of thought known as structuralism, and Columbia and Chicago, two leading centers of a uniquely American movement that became known as functionalism. The story of these "isms" occupies the next chapter.

SUMMARY

Psychology in 19th-Century America

• Before the Civil War, psychology in America was taught as mental or intellectual philosophy. It was taught following the precepts of faculty psychology, which was based on Scottish Realist philosophy. Faculties were separate subdivisions of the mind, normally falling into three categories: cognitive, affective (emotional), and behavioral.

• Thomas Upham's *Elements of Intellectual (Mental) Philosophy* is considered to be the first textbook of psychology, and it was organized around the concepts of faculty psychology.

• The post–Civil War period was one of great expansion in higher education. The modern university (e.g., Johns Hopkins), based on the German model that emphasized graduate education and independent research, began during this time.

• In the second half of the 19th century, educational opportunities multiplied for white males but were limited for women and minorities. Although higher education was believed to harm women and keep them from their traditional roles, opportunities existed at newly founded women's colleges. Opportunities for minorities were limited by entrenched beliefs about their abilities. Nonetheless, some persevered, including Francis Sumner—the first African American to earn a PhD (in 1920)—who developed a highly successful psychology department at Howard University.

William James (1842–1910): America's First "New" Psychologist

• Although he was an artist by temperament, was trained in medicine, and ultimately thought of himself as a philosopher, William James is considered America's first modern psychologist. He brought the new laboratory psychology to Harvard, and in 1890 he wrote what is considered the most important book in all of psychology's history, *The Principles of Psychology*.

• Disturbed by 19th-century materialism and determinism, James decided to believe in free will because it was a useful belief for him to hold. Out of this emerged his general approach to philosophy, called pragmatism.

• In the *Principles*, James took issue with those who would dissect consciousness into its elements. Instead, he argued that it was more appropriately conceived of as analogous to a stream. Consciousness was personal, constantly changing, continuous, selective, and active, and it served individuals by enabling them to adapt quickly to new environments and solve problems. Habit also had survival value, allowing individuals to avoid having to think about some activities so they could save their consciousness for more difficult and novel problems.

• According to the James-Lange theory of emotions, emotional responses were identified with the bodily reactions that accompanied the perception of some emotion-generating event. When trying to conceive of emotions without the physiological arousal, James argued, nothing remains. A problem with the theory is that it requires a recognizably different pattern of arousal to be associated with each different emotion.

• In his later years, James became interested in the possibility that there could be some validity to spiritualism. Despite criticism that he was harming the fragile scientific status of the new psychology, he believed that spiritualists and mediums should be investigated with an open mind.

G. Stanley Hall (1844–1924): Professionalizing the New Psychology

• Hall is best known for his efforts in professionalizing psychology. He founded the first psychology laboratory in America (at Johns Hopkins in 1883), America's first academic journal (the *American Journal of Psychology* in 1887), and the American Psychological Association (in 1892).

• As the first president of Clark University, Hall copied the German ideal of graduate education that he first encountered at Johns Hopkins. For several years, Clark was a leader in graduate education in several scientific fields. After 1892, however, only psychology remained as a prominent field of study at Clark.

• Hall was interested in a wide range of topics, which fell under the broad heading of genetic psychology, the study of the origins and development of consciousness and behavior. The importance of evolution was a consistent theme in Hall's work. At Clark, Hall encouraged research in developmental, abnormal, and comparative psychology. Under the direction of Edmund Sanford, Clark's laboratory produced important research throughout the 1890s, including the first maze-learning studies.

• As a developmental psychologist, Hall pioneered the child study movement and is responsible for identifying adolescence as a distinct stage of development. He characterized adolescence as a time of "storm and stress." Later in life he wrote about the developmental changes associated with adulthood and aging. He used the theory of recapitulation (the development of the individual organism is a mirror of the evolution of the species) as an overarching framework for his work.

• Hall's interests in development, sexuality, and abnormality led him to invite Freud to America for Clark's 20th anniversary in 1909. It was Freud's only trip to America,

and he viewed the invitation as the first sign that his ideas were developing an international reputation.

Mary Whiton Calkins (1863–1930): Challenging the Male Monopoly

• Mary Calkins was barred from being an official student at Harvard. Nonetheless, she completed an important experimental dissertation on association, during which she invented a memory procedure still in use: paired associate learning. In her thesis, Calkins investigated frequency, recency, vividness, and primacy as conditions that could strengthen associations; she found that frequency was the most important for developing associative strength.

• In 1905, Calkins became the first woman elected president of the American Psychological Association; as her interests shifted to philosophy, she became (in 1918) the first woman elected president of the other APA, the American Philosophical Association.

• Calkins's major theoretical contribution was her self-psychology, which was centered on the idea that all consciousness is personal. She used it as a way to reconcile competing theoretical schools of thought (e.g., structuralism and functionalism).

• Two other important women psychologists during this era were Christine Ladd-Franklin and Margaret Washburn. Both faced the exclusionary practices that made it difficult for women to become professional psychologists. Ladd-Franklin was a skilled mathematician who developed an evolutionary theory of color vision. Washburn was best known for her work in comparative psychology.

Other Pioneers: Ladd and Baldwin

• George Trumbull Ladd, the second president of APA, was a transitional figure who bridged the gap between the old faculty psychology and the new psychology of the laboratory. He is best known as a textbook writer, and his *Elements of Physiological Psychology,* the first clear summary of Wundtian psychology in English, introduced the English-speaking world to Wundt's ideas.

• James Mark Baldwin founded two laboratories of psychology, resurrected a third, and was active in creating and developing important journals of psychology. He was also a pioneer in developmental psychology, publishing two well-known books on child development in the 1890s; his ideas later influenced Jean Piaget.

STUDY QUESTIONS

1. Describe the Scottish Realists' objection to British empiricism and what they proposed instead.

2. Describe the barriers that made it difficult for women to obtain higher education, and describe what opportunities were available to them.

3. What were the barriers that made it difficult for African Americans to obtain higher education?

4. Describe the career and accomplishments of Francis Sumner.

5. Describe how William James overcame his concerns about materialism and developed a "pragmatic" philosophy.

6. What did James think of the "New Psychology"? What did he propose as appropriate methodologies for psychology?

7. According to James, what is the best metaphor for consciousness? What did he believe to be the main functions of (a) consciousness and (b) habit?

8. Briefly state the essence of the James-Lange theory of emotions, using the example of meeting a bear in the woods to illustrate. What was the theory's fatal flaw? How did James use his theory to make some practical suggestions to improve one's life?

9. Why was spiritualism popular in the late 19th century? What was James's opinion about the phenomenon, and why was his view a cause for concern among his peers?

10. What does it mean to say that G. Stanley Hall was a genetic psychologist?

11. Describe Hall's contributions to the professionalization of psychology in America.

12. Describe the origins and importance of maze-learning research in psychology's history.

13. Describe Hall's contributions to the study of human development throughout the life span, but especially during adolescence.

14. Describe the difficulties Calkins encountered when trying to attain graduate training. What training was she able to accomplish?

15. How did Calkins study memory and association, and what did she conclude about the nature of the association process?

16. Describe the accomplishments of (a) Christine Ladd-Franklin and (b) Margaret Washburn.

17. What was Ladd's most important contribution to the New Psychology? Why is he sometimes considered a transitional figure?

18. Describe the ways that Baldwin contributed to (a) the professionalization of psychology and (b) developmental psychology.

FOR FURTHER READING

CROCE, P. J. (1995). *Science and religion in the era of William James: Eclipse of certainty, 1820–1880.* Chapel Hill: University of North Carolina Press.
Documents the early intellectual development of William James; shows how James was at the center of the debate about the relationship between science and religion and how the debate was affected by evolutionary thinking; first of a two-part biography.

ROSS, D. (1972). *G. Stanley Hall: The psychologist as prophet.* Chicago: University of Chicago Press.
The definitive intellectual biography of American psychology's premier entrepreneur; also documents the development of psychology during Hall's time and provides its social and institutional context.

SCARBOROUGH, E., & FURUMOTO, L. (1987). *Untold lives: The first generation of American women psychologists.* New York: Columbia University Press.
Examines the lives, struggles, and contributions of several pioneering women psychologists; includes detailed treatment of Mary Calkins, Milicent Shinn, Ethel Puffer, Margaret Washburn, and Christine Ladd-Franklin.

Special issue: The history of American psychology. (1992). *American Psychologist, 47*(2), 109–368.
Includes articles on the early years of the APA (Sokal), the founding of early laboratories (Capshew), spiritualism (Coon), William James (Leary), Mary Calkins's memory research (Madigan & O'Hara), Christine Ladd-Franklin (Furumoto), and G. Stanley Hall (Bringmann, Bringmann, & Early; Vande Kemp).

CHAPTER 7

STRUCTURALISM AND FUNCTIONALISM

The first object of the psychologist.... is to ascertain the nature and number of the mental elements. He takes up mental experience, bit by bit, dividing and subdividing, until the division can go no further. When that point is reached, he has found a conscious element.

—E. B. Titchener, 1896

If you adopt as your material for psychological analysis the isolated "moment of consciousness," it is very easy to become so absorbed in determining its constitution as to be rendered somewhat oblivious to its artificial character. The most essential quarrel which the functionalist has with structuralism arises from this fact.

—James R. Angell, 1907

PREVIEW AND CHAPTER OBJECTIVES

This chapter begins with the story of a remarkable Englishman who came to a remote new university in America in 1892 and fashioned a unique and powerful but ultimately sterile system of psychology called structuralism. Cornell's E. B. Titchener was trained by Wundt at Leipzig but had his own ideas about the proper definition of a scientific psychology. Its main goal was to analyze the adult mind into its fundamental structural elements, using a precise form of introspection that required extensive training. For Titchener, psychology was a pure positivist science that was centered in the laboratory; he was not interested in applications. Titchener was an influential and commanding presence in academic psychology's early years in America, but most American psychologists rejected structuralist doctrine. Reflecting the influence of Darwin and traditional Yankee pragmatism, they were more interested in how the mind functioned than in its structure, and they knew that for psychology to succeed in America, it had to be applicable to everyday life. While Titchener believed that the structure of mind had to be clarified before its functions could be studied, most American psychologists disagreed and adopted what came to be called functionalism. Functional psychologists were scattered throughout the academic landscape, but two schools became closely associated with the movement—Chicago and Columbia. The second half of the chapter examines how functionalism "evolved" at these locations, through the efforts of James Angell, John Dewey, and Harvey Carr at Chicago and James McKeen Cattell, E. L. Thorndike, and Robert Woodworth at Columbia. After you finish this chapter, you should be able to:

- Distinguish between a structuralist and a functionalist approach to psychology
- Describe the general contents and the overall importance of Titchener's Manuals, and the content of a typical "drill course"

▓ Describe the impact of the Experimentalists and the effect of the group on opportunities for women in experimental psychology

▓ Articulate psychology's three main goals, as Titchener saw them

▓ Explain Titchener's version of introspection and explain how he believed the limitations of introspection could be overcome

▓ Describe the elements of human conscious experience, and their attributes, according to Titchener

▓ Show how the controversies over imageless thought and between Titchener and Baldwin pointed out the limitations of Titchenerian introspection as a methodology

▓ Evaluate Titchener's overall contributions to experimental psychology

▓ Describe the link between evolutionary theory, social Darwinism, and functionalism

▓ Describe contributions to functionalist thought made by the Chicago functionalists Dewey, Angell, and Carr

▓ Describe Thorndike's puzzle box research and his conclusions about animal learning, and understand the significance of the research

▓ Describe Woodworth's dynamic psychology and his reasons for proposing an S-O-R model for psychology

▓ Explain the importance of the "Columbia bible" for the training of psychologists

TITCHENER'S PSYCHOLOGY: STRUCTURALISM

In 1898, a paper appeared in the new journal *Psychological Review* entitled "The Postulates of a Structural Psychology" (Titchener, 1898b). Its author, E. B. Titchener, was a young professor from Cornell University who had been in the United States for just 6 years but already had a reputation as a talented laboratory psychologist with some clear and uncompromising ideas about the new psychology. In the article, he named his approach a "structural" psychology and contrasted it with what he saw all around him at other American universities, which he labeled a "functional" psychology. Drawing a parallel to biology, he wrote that **structuralism** is just like anatomy—the purpose is analysis. Just as the anatomist organizes knowledge about the body into component structures, so would a structural psychologist analyze the human mind and organize it into its elementary units—basic sensations, for example. **Functionalism**, on the other hand, is like physiology. The physiologist examines how the various parts of the body operate and the functions they serve to help keep the individual alive; similarly, the functional psychologist studies how the mind serves to adapt the individual to the environment. Although not rejecting a functional approach outright, Titchener used the biology metaphor to argue that it was futile to study function before structure had been fully understood. Anatomy provides the foundation for physiology, Titchener contended. Similarly, a thorough understanding of the structure of the human mind was a necessary prerequisite to the study of its function. As Titchener had written 2 years earlier in his first text, *An Outline of Psychology*, the psychologist's goal "is to ascertain the nature and number of the mental elements. He takes up mental experience, bit by bit, dividing and subdividing, until the division can go no further. When that point is reached, he has found a conscious element" (Titchener, 1896/1899, p. 16). Titchener's system was never widely popular in America, but as we shall see, Titchener had an undeniable impact.

From Oxford to Leipzig to Cornell

Such a position of prominence in American psychology was a long journey from relatively humble beginnings in southern England. Edward Bradford Titchener (1867–1927) was born in Chicester, an hour's drive southwest of London and a few miles from the English Channel. His early years were unsettling—his father, only marginally capable in business, died when Titchener was 13; Edward was raised mainly by his paternal grandfather. Titchener's grandfather, a lawyer and stereotypical British country "gentleman," gave Titchener the set of attitudes and values that he never lost. Even after residing in America for many years, Titchener never stopped living according to the strict code of the behavior of a proper upper-middle-class English gentleman (Leys & Evans, 1990).

Young Titchener was a talented student, good enough to win scholarships to attend Malvern (one of England's better "public" schools) and then Brasenose College of Oxford University.[1] Titchener remained at Oxford from 1885 to 1890, where he excelled in the classics and philosophy. He also became fascinated with evolutionary biology, Darwinism, and through the acquaintance of George Romanes (Chapter 5), comparative psychology. To strengthen what he perceived was a weak background in science, he spent most of his final year at Oxford in the physiology laboratory of John Scott Burdon-Sanderson. In that setting, Titchener showed himself to be just the opposite of William James in at least one respect—he discovered that he loved the precisely detailed work of the laboratory. For the rest of his life, he judged the quality of his peers by their standing as "lab men," which accounts for his derogatory comments about Hall (Chapter 6) and his paradoxically close friendship with John Watson (Chapter 10). Watson derided Titchener's structuralism, and Titchener disliked everything about Watson's behaviorism, but Watson was a true laboratory scientist in Titchener's eyes and that was sufficient grounds for respect and friendship. After first meeting Watson, Titchener wrote to a colleague: "I think that he has a big career, and I like him very much personally" (quoted in Larson & Sullivan, 1965, p. 340).

While at Oxford, Titchener learned of the new "physiological" psychology that was developing at Leipzig. Fluent in German and enamored of Germanic culture, Titchener was accepted for study in Wundt's new laboratory. There he encountered a group of like-minded laboratory devotees, including Oswald Külpe (Chapter 4), who was Wundt's assistant at the time (i.e., in charge of day-to-day operation at the lab), and several Americans. Titchener completed a doctorate with Wundt in 2 years and returned to Oxford to teach a summer course in biology. He hoped to remain at Oxford or move to Cambridge, but neither school seemed interested in the New Psychology. Fate intervened on Titchener's behalf, however, in the form of an offer to cross the Atlantic and teach at Cornell University. Titchener was recommended to Cornell's president by Frank Angell, one of the American psychologists Titchener had befriended at Leipzig. Angell had created a small lab at Cornell on his return from Leipzig in 1891, but was now leaving for the just-created Stanford University in California. Angell recommended his British friend as his replacement, the offer was made, and Titchener accepted.

---

[1] In England, *public school* actually refers to a highly selective and expensive private high school. Malvern was not among the top tier of public schools like Eton, Harrow, or Rugby, but it had a solid academic reputation. Only a small percentage of British schoolchildren attended public schools, but most of the students at England's prestigious universities, Oxford and Cambridge (sometimes referred to collectively as Oxbridge), came from the public schools. Oxbridge graduates thus represented a small, elite group of the British upper middle class. Brasenose is one of several independent colleges that constitute Oxford University.

Cornell University sits high on a hill in Ithaca, New York, overlooking the southern end of Lake Cayuga, in the beautiful Finger Lakes region. In 1892 it was in the middle of nowhere, barely accessible by the occasional train. Even today, residents refer to their town as "centrally isolated." If you can imagine finishing your education and deciding to take a job somewhere in a remote area of Australia, then you have some idea of what the decision must have been like for the young Britisher with his new doctorate. Yet he took the risk, arrived in 1892, and never left.[2] Over the years, *Titchenerian psychology*, *structuralism*, and *the Cornell school of psychology* became interchangeable terms.

Promoting Experimental Psychology at Cornell

Titchener (Figure 7.1) moved quickly upon his arrival at Cornell, expanding the laboratory (Figure 7.2), attracting students, and starting a research program. By the turn of the century, he and his students had published more than 60 research articles (Boring, 1961a).[3] To ensure

FIGURE 7.1 E. B. Titchener of Cornell, with ever-present cigar. From Popplestone and McPherson (1994).

[2]Titchener initially thought he would go to Cornell for a few years and then return to Oxford when it came to its senses about laboratory psychology. Oxford didn't, and Titchener never returned to England, even to visit. He later considered offers from Clark University and Harvard but turned down both.

[3]Titchener developed very close mentoring relationships with his students and continued to advise them even after they left Cornell. For example, in a letter to Walter Pillsbury, who had just started a new position at the University of Michigan, Titchener cautioned him about writing a book too soon in his career. Instead he urged Pillsbury to focus on perfecting his teaching and getting students involved in research: "Give your investigations to your students, and let them work out your ideas. Forget, so far as you can, that YOU have any part or lot in the work; let the students feel that they are making psychology" (Titchener, 1897; emphasis in the original).

FIGURE 7.2 Floor plan of Titchener's domain in the top floor of Cornell's Morrill Hall, as of 1898 (Titchener, 1898b).

a forum for the research from the Cornell laboratory, he signed on with Hall in 1895 as editor of the *American Journal of Psychology*, thus gaining control over one third of the journal's pages (Hall and Sanford, the other editors, controlled the remaining two thirds). In addition, Titchener spread the word about German psychology by translating books by Wundt and Külpe into English, and he began producing texts of his own. His *Outline of Psychology*, first published in 1896, went through several revisions and was rewritten and expanded as *A Text-Book of Psychology* in 1909. It was the clearest overall statement of his structuralist system. By 1900, Titchener was firmly established as a major player on the American psychological scene. His status was confirmed when he published "the Manuals."

The Manuals In German laboratories, students learned laboratory procedures mainly on their own, by participating in and running studies and by observing and questioning their more experienced peers. In American universities, the instructors developed what came to be known as **drill courses**. Students in these courses did not produce original research but would repeat the classic studies, learn how to set up and work the "brass instruments," and in general become acclimated to the laboratory (Titchener, 1898a). At Cornell, for example, Titchener taught a yearlong drill course to undergraduates ("laboratory work and occasional lectures," p. 314), typically juniors, after they had completed his introductory course. As the new laboratory psychology expanded, these drill courses proliferated, but Titchener worried about the quality of instruction. Although some drill course instructors were adequately trained, either in Germany or in one of the new American laboratories, many were not so knowledgeable about the new psychology. Thus a need developed for a text that could explain how to train students in basic laboratory procedures. Edmund Sanford of Clark wrote the first one in the early 1890s, and it started the process of standardizing laboratory instruction in the drill course (Goodwin, 1987). Titchener recognized the value of his close friend's manual, but he also knew that it was just a beginning and that it had some weaknesses. For instance, Stanford's manual was not always clear about how the instructor should proceed in the laboratory, and it seemed to assume more expertise than many instructors possessed. To remedy the problem, Titchener set to work on his own manuals and published them under the title of *Experimental Psychology: A Manual of Laboratory Practice*. They became his best-known work, serving for years as the guide into the complexities of laboratory investigation.

FIGURE 7.3 Sketch of an olfactometer, from Titchener's manual of qualitative experiments.

The Manuals, as they came to be known, were published in two volumes, in 1901 and 1905, each containing separate texts for students and instructors. Because of Titchener's concern that teachers might need to have procedures worked out step-by-step, the instructor manuals for both volumes were almost twice the length of the student manuals. The 1901 volume was subtitled *Qualitative Experiments*, and it included experiments on basic sensory, perceptual, and affective processes (Titchener, 1901). *Quantitative Experiments* filled the 1905 volume; these dealt mainly with psychophysics and reaction-time procedures (Titchener, 1905a).

Students in drill courses worked in pairs, alternating between the roles of experimenter and **observer**, the latter being the person we would call the research subject or participant today. Observers were so called because while they were participating in the experiment, they would be observing their own mental processes and would give a description of these processes at the close of the experiment. This introspective procedure is described more fully later.

In the qualitative experiments, observers would experience some sensory, perceptual, or affective event, give an introspective account of it, and then answer some specific questions about it in their notebooks. For example, olfactory sensations were studied with the use of the double olfactometer sketched in Figure 7.3. The two thin glass tubes were bent at a 40° angle for insertion into the nostrils. Over their other ends were fitted slightly larger enclosed glass cylinders holding various odorous substances. These cylinders could be moved back and forth over the narrow tubes to vary the intensity of the smell. In a typical experiment, observers smelled pairs of substances (e.g., iodine, beeswax, various herbs) with differing degrees of intensity, described the experience introspectively, and responded in their notebooks to questions about "compensation" (did one smell overwhelm the other?) and "smell mixture" (did the smells mix to form a new odor?).

The quantitative experiments involved numerical data, such as stimulus intensities identified as just noticeably different in psychophysics experiments or response times in reaction-time studies. Figure 7.4 shows two different ways of responding in a reaction-time experiment. The most common device was an ordinary telegraph key (Figure 7.4a); it would be held down, and then released when the observer detected a stimulus. The right hand of the observer in Figure 4.5 is using this type of key. The second device (Figure 7.4b) was a lip key, used in voice reaction-time experiments. It is probably the same one shown in the Clark photo in Chapter 6 (Figure 6.5b). The right side of the key would be inserted into the closed mouth, and when observers opened their mouths to respond to a stimulus, the contacts separated from each other, breaking a circuit and stopping a clock.

FIGURE 7.4 Reaction-time apparatus, from Titchener's manual of quantitative experiments. From Titchener (1905a).

Titchener's system of psychology faded rapidly after his death, but his encyclopedic manuals provided a lasting contribution to laboratory psychology. They remained in use well into the 1930s and trained several generations of experimental psychologists. Even today, they can provide excellent demonstrations of sensory and perceptual phenomena. One final aspect of their timelessness is illustrated in Table 7.1. Titchener's half-serious recommendations to students about "how to fail" the drill course might remind you of some of your student friends.

TABLE 7.1 How to Fail in Laboratory Psychology

In the Instructor's Manual for the *Qualitative Experiments* (1901, pp. xxvii–xxviii), Titchener described a program on how to fail that he routinely gave to students at the start of the drill course. He obviously hoped for students to avoid each point and he told instructors that students wouldn't take offense at the list as long as it was presented "tactfully and good-naturedly." In Titchener's words, here are some ways to fail in lab:

- Do not accept any general explanation, under any circumstances. Cherish the belief that your mind is different, in its ways of working, from all other minds. . . .
- See yourself in everything. If the Instructor begins an explanation, interrupt him with a story of your childhood which seems to illustrate the point he is making.
- Call upon the Instructor at the slightest provocation. If he is busy, stroll about the laboratory until he can attend to you. Do not hesitate to offer advice to other students, who are already at work.
- Tell the Instructor that the science is very young, and that what holds of one mind does not necessarily hold of another. Support your statement by anecdotes.
- Work as noisily as possible. Converse with your partner, in the pauses of the experiment, upon current politics or athletic records.
- Explain when you enter the laboratory, that you have long been interested in experimental psychology. . . . Describe the telepathic experiences or accounts that aroused your interest.
- Make it a rule always to be a quarter of an hour late for the laboratory exercises. In this way you throw the drudgery of preliminary work upon your partner, while you can still take credit to yourself for the regularity of your class attendance.

The Experimentalists   Titchener was a charter member of the American Psychological Association; and though he was not at Hall's organizational meeting at Clark, he did attend the first annual meeting in the winter of 1892. He quickly became disillusioned with the organization, however, and resigned his membership (he rejoined the organization on two later occasions, only to resign twice more). Part of the problem was personal. The British Titchener felt like an outsider in an "American" Psychological Association, and the organization violated his strict code of proper behavior when it refused to censure an APA member (E. W. Scripture of Yale) accused by Titchener (with good cause) of plagiarizing portions of his translation of one of Wundt's books. More important, Titchener believed the organization did not represent his vision for experimental psychology, and the format of its meetings did not advance psychology. In 1895, in a note for the *American Journal of Psychology*, he complained that the presentations of research were "hardly possible to follow intelligently.... when method and results are thrown in lecture form and the lecture reduced to a compass of twenty minutes" (Titchener, 1895, p. 448). Instead, he suggested that "the meetings [be] allowed to take the form of a conversazione, the apparatus employed shown in their working, and the results made to speak for themselves in charts and diagrams arranged near the apparatus" (p. 448).

By 1904, Titchener was ready to fix the problem himself, and he proposed the creation of an informal "club" of experimental psychologists. He did not intend to compete with APA, but to provide a better means for researchers to present their work to peers. Thus was born a group that came to be known as the Experimentalists (Boring, 1967; Goodwin, 1985). They met for 3 days every spring, rotating from one laboratory to another. They discussed research in progress, tinkered with apparatus, and in general tried to keep the spirit of pure laboratory psychology alive. No formal papers were allowed, and published descriptions of the meetings were discouraged. Titchener generally dominated the group—for instance, hosts would often check with him about whom to invite. Figure 7.5 shows a group photo taken at the 1926 meeting at the University of Pennsylvania.

FIGURE 7.5   The Experimentalists at Penn in 1926. Note the similarity (posture, cigar) between Titchener (front and center) and Boring (first row, far right), Titchener's most famous student.

Those invited to the spring meetings included laboratory directors and other researchers deemed satisfactory by Titchener. That is, they had to be committed to the laboratory, but it wasn't necessary that they be strict followers of Titchenerian structuralism. Also, to help ensure continuation of the ideal of a "pure" psychological science, talented graduate students often accompanied their mentors to meetings. The group was small but influential beyond its size. For instance, correspondence among its members frequently resulted in the placement of Experimentalist colleagues or their students in good academic positions (Goodwin, 1985).

One other important feature of the group was gender—all the Experimentalists were men. Part of the reason was the prevailing cultural norms of the day, as described in Chapter 6. In Titchener's mind, however, the prohibition followed from his ingrained code of gentlemanly conduct. His desire was to have something like an English club, where men could converse freely on any subject without being concerned about behaving "properly" in the presence of women. This meant being able to argue vociferously about some issue without either party taking offense; Titchener and other males of his time took it for granted that women would take such arguments personally (i.e., they would be too emotional). The club atmosphere also included smoking, and the social mores of the day usually excluded women from rooms where men smoked. These sentiments were summed up in a letter from Sanford to Titchener just before the group was formed. Probably thinking of Calkins, Washburn, and Ladd-Franklin (Chapter 6), he pointed out that several women

> on scientific grounds have full right to be there and might feel hurt (in a general impersonal way) if women are not asked. On the other hand they would undoubtedly interfere with the smoking and to a certain extent with the general freedom of a purely masculine assembly. (quoted in Furumoto, 1988, p. 104)

Similarly, Lightner Witmer of the University of Pennsylvania (Chapter 13) wrote to Titchener that it would be impossible to have

> an informal meeting of men and women. . . . We want a small vigorous association where we can speak our minds with perfect freedom. . . . I think that the presence of women. . . . adds greatly to this danger [of mistaking argument for attack], owing to the personal attitude which they usually take even in scientific discussions. (quoted in Furumoto, 1988, p. 105)

In defense of the charge that Titchener was antifemale, it has been pointed out that almost half of his graduate students were women (26 of 60), his first doctoral student was Margaret Washburn (Chapter 6), and on at least one occasion he argued for the hiring of a particular woman psychologist at Cornell over the objections of the administration (Leys & Evans, 1990). On the other hand, part of the reason for there being women in Titchener's laboratory was institutional—Cornell for years was about the only place for a woman to go to be an "official" student. At any rate, the exclusion of women from Titchener's club created a barrier to advancement and contributed to their difficulty in securing major academic positions. Even after the group reorganized following Titchener's death and technically included women, few were ever nominated for membership until the latter part of the 20th century (Furumoto, 1988).[4]

---

[4]The noted physiological psychologist Donald Hebb (Chapter 14) resigned from the Society in 1953, mainly on the grounds that it seemed more like an exclusionary social club than a true honor society. His resignation letter included a handwritten note asking, "Why no women? Charter admits them" (quoted in Glickman, 1996, p. 243).

Titchener's Structuralist System

At the opening of the chapter, I pointed out that for Titchener, a prime goal for psychology was to analyze human consciousness into its basic elements or structural components. Hence, Titchener's psychology was the science of the structure of the human mind, and a primary purpose of research was to determine this structure through experimental research. Analysis was not the sole purpose, however. Psychology must also understand the process of *synthesis*, how the mental elements combine and connect into more complex phenomena. In Titchener's words, the observer in an experiment

> learns to formulate the laws of connection of the elementary mental processes. If sensations of tone occur together, they blend or fuse; if sensations of colour occur side by side, they enhance one another: and all this takes place in a perfectly regular way, so that we can write out laws of tonal fusion and laws of colour contrast. (Titchener, 1909, pp. 37–38)

In addition to the goals of analysis and synthesis, both of which resulted in detailed descriptions of mental phenomena, Titchener argued that a third goal for psychology was explanation, by which he meant an understanding of how the nervous system produced the various sensory, perceptual, and cognitive phenomena that interested him. Very little of his research focused on this third goal.

To accomplish a thorough description of the analysis and synthesis of mental phenomena, Titchener developed a research program involving the kinds of qualitative and quantitative research described in the Manuals. To get a good idea of the topics that Titchener considered essential in an introductory course, examine Table 7.2, which summarizes the chapter organization for his *Text-Book of Psychology*, a text you might have used had you taken Titchener's introductory psychology course in 1909. As you can see, the topics of sensation and perception dominated the book. There is very little about the nervous system in it, but a great deal concerning the descriptive goals of analysis and synthesis. Note that fully one third of the book is devoted to describing basic sensory processes.

Titchener accompanied these research topics with a methodology that is often associated with his name—introspection. As you recall from Chapter 4, introspection was important in the Leipzig laboratory, but Wundt called it *internal perception* and limited it to simple verbal reports of the results of psychophysics ("this weight is heavier than this other one") and other sensory studies. Wundt's student (and Titchener's friend) Oswald Külpe, however, elaborated the procedure into **systematic experimental introspection**, in which observers would give detailed reports of the conscious events occurring while completing some task (e.g., word association). Titchener took this latter approach and developed it to a high level of sophistication.

Titchener was well aware of the fundamental problem of introspection: It is impossible to have a conscious experience and reflect on it at the same time. To deal with the problem, he suggested three solutions. The first was to rely on memory, delaying the introspective "observation until the process to be described has run its course, and then to call it back and describe it from memory. Introspection thus becomes retrospection; introspective examination becomes post mortem examination" (Titchener, 1909, p. 22). Titchener's second suggestion for reducing the memory load was to break the experience into stages, using the

TABLE 7.2 The Contents of Titchener's *Text-Book of Psychology* (1909)

Chapter Heading	No. of Pages	Percent
Subject-Matter, Method and Problem of Psychology	43	8
Sensation, subdivided into:	179	33
vision		
audition		
smell		
taste		
cutaneous senses		
kinesthetic senses		
other organic sensations		
synaesthesia		
the intensity of sensation (psychophysics)		
Affection	39	7
Attention	38	7
Perception, subdivided into:	71	13
spatial perceptions		
temporal perceptions		
qualitative perceptions		
composite perceptions		
the psychology of perception		
Association	22	4
Memory and Imagination	31	6
Action	42	8
Emotion	33	6
Thought	43	8
Conclusion—The Status of Psychology	3	<1

fractionation method associated with Külpe's laboratory (Chapter 4). His third, and most important technique, was to acquire what he called the **introspective habit**:

> The practiced observer gets into an introspective habit, has the introspective attitude ingrained in his system; so that it is possible for him, not only to take mental notes while the observation is in progress, without interfering with consciousness, but even to jot down written notes, as the histologist does while his eye is still held to the ocular of the microscope. (1909, p. 23)

This is an important passage, for it is the main reason Titchener insisted that his observers be highly trained (recall from Chapter 6 that the issue of training was at the heart of the Baldwin-Titchener controversy). In effect, the observers were to become introspecting machines, behaving so automatically that problems of memory and any biasing influences would presumably disappear. Training was also important to avoid what Titchener referred to as the **stimulus error**. This was a tendency to report events by describing the stimuli presented rather than the conscious experiences resulting from those stimuli. For instance, when observing a tree, a proper introspective description would include statements about the sensory elements present: shapes, colors, textures, and movement, along with the affective dimensions of pleasantness–unpleasantness and any accompanying images that came to mind. To commit the stimulus error would be to report simply that you were observing a large "tree." The introspective habit is difficult for us to grasp today, because this type of laboratory training no longer exists. This chapter's Close-Up, however, should give you some insight into what the habit was like.

CLOSE-UP

THE INTROSPECTIVE HABIT

The absence of Titchenerian introspection in contemporary psychology makes it difficult for us to grasp what an introspective description was really like. One way to find out is to read articles summarizing this kind of research, because they often include verbatim introspective accounts. For example, consider the following study on attention. It was the doctoral thesis of Karl Dallenbach, one of Titchener's students and later a colleague on the Cornell faculty. Using procedures similar to those found in modern research on attention, Dallenbach (1913) was interested in what happens to consciousness when attention is divided and overloaded. In the early, training portion of his study, observers listened to two metronomes set at different speeds and tried to count the number of beats occurring between coincident beats. At the same time, they completed a second mental task, such as continually adding numbers, singing, or saying the alphabet backward. Each "experiment" lasted 90 seconds. Here is one observer's introspective account:

> The sounds of the metronomes, as a series of discontinuous clicks, were clear in consciousness only four or five times during the experiment, and they were especially bothersome at first. They were accompanied by strain sensations and unpleasantness. The rest of the experiment my attention was on the adding, which was composed of.... visual images of the numbers, sometimes on a dark grey scale which was directly ahead and about three feet in front of me. This was accompanied by kinaesthesis of eyes and strains in chest and arms. When

these processes were clear in consciousness the sounds of the metronomes were very vague or obscure. (Dallenbach, 1913, p. 467)

Reading articles full of introspective accounts like this can be revealing, but they tend to be long, repetitive, and boring enough to make one understand why psychologists eventually abandoned the method. A more interesting way to gain insight into the introspective attitude is to read the letters that experimental psychologists wrote to each other during this era (Goodwin, 1991b). Introspective thinking was so much a part of their everyday thinking that their correspondence is liberally sprinkled with informal introspections relating to their experiences. After returning from a holiday in New Hampshire, for instance, Edmund Sanford of Clark wrote to Titchener about his fear of thunderstorms. He wrote that he had

> observed enough this summer to find that I cannot find anything in it but organic and other sensations unpleasantly colored and, on the cognitive side, a cramp of apperception towards a small group of ideas related to the thing dreaded with certain resultants in instinctive act and thought.... When the storm became imminent there would be cardiac and visceral symptoms to describe, etc. etc.—though when the thing was actually present these were as a general thing not so marked as in anticipation. (Sanford, 1910)

A more dramatic example of how introspection was never far from the thoughts of turn-of-the-century psychologists comes from an 1893 letter from Lightner Witmer of the University of Pennsylvania to Hugo Münsterberg of Harvard. Witmer had been studying the psychology of pain firsthand in a rather unusual manner.

I let a horse throw me from his back, allowing me to drop on my shoulder and head. I showed a beautiful case of loss of consciousness before the act....I not only do not remember mounting and the horse running, but I forgot almost everything that happened....[F]rom the time I got up in the morning till I regained complete consciousness...., I can form no continuous series of events. My head was bad for a while but is all right now, but my arm has served the purpose of quite a number of experiments as it still continues quite painful at times....The psychological side of my afflictions will form the basis of at least three lectures next fall. (Witmer, 1893)

The Structural Elements of Human Conscious Experience   Based on his introspective analyses, Titchener identified three types of elementary mental processes: sensations, images, and affections. Sensations were the basic elements of the more complex process of perception, images were the elementary components of ideas, and affections (feelings) were the building blocks of our emotions. You should be able to detect all three elements in Dallenbach's sample introspective account. The basic elements could not be reduced further, but they did have various features or **attributes**. All sensations, for instance, had the attributes of quality, intensity, duration, and clearness. *Quality* is what distinguishes one sensation from another: red from green, cold from warm, a high-pitched tone from a low-pitched tone. *Intensity* refers to the strength of the stimulus, decibel level for example. *Duration* is self-evident—all sensations last for some measurable period of time. And *clearness* "is the attribute which gives a sensation its place in a consciousness: the clearer sensation is dominant, independent, outstanding, the less clear sensation is subordinate, undistinguished in the background of consciousness" (Titchener, 1909, p. 53). According to Titchener, attention essentially reduced to this attribute of sensory clearness.

Images have the same four attributes, according to Titchener, but compared with sensations, the qualities are "relatively pale, faded, washed out, misty" (1909, p. 198).[5] In addition, he argued that the intensity and duration of images were "markedly less" (p. 198) than sensations. Affective states, the elements of our emotional life, differ from sensations and images in two important ways. First, although there are literally thousands of different sensorial and imaginal qualities, Titchener believed that affect had only two fundamental qualities—pleasantness and unpleasantness. Second, affect had the attributes of quality, intensity, and duration, but they lacked clearness. If we want to experience pleasure at a concert, for example, we must attend to the sensory elements (i.e., the music), not to the feeling of pleasure itself; if we focus on the feeling, the pleasure disappears. Titchener rejected the James-Lange theory of emotion on the grounds that by equating emotions with bodily reaction, James was

---

[5]Recall from Chapter 4 that Wundt identified two elements: sensations and affections. He believed, like Hume, that images were merely faint copies of sensations and ultimately reducible to them. Titchener was thinking along similar lines, and expressed some uncertainty about calling them separate elements, but he nonetheless felt that sensations and images were sufficiently distinct to justify separate elementary status, at least at that stage of his thinking (Hindeland, 1971).

reducing affect to sensation (Heidbreder, 1933). For Titchener, on the other hand, pleasantness and unpleasantness were different from and could not be reduced to sensory qualities.

Titchener's structuralism continued to evolve over the years, and in the 1920s he moved away from an emphasis on elements and developed a more phenomenological model that described sensory processes in terms of dimensions. Thus sensation shifted "from an observable entity to a classificatory term" (Evans, 1972, p. 172). Titchener also moved away from the idea that affects were separate elements after one of his students completed a dissertation that seemed to reduce the affective qualities of pleasantness and unpleasantness to the sensations of "bright pressure" and "dull pressure," respectively (Henle, 1974). Titchener was working on a major revision of his system along these lines; but his productivity dropped during the 1920s, possibly showing the early effects of the brain tumor that would kill him in 1927, and the final system was never completed. Some introductory chapters were published posthumously (1929) as *Systematic Psychology: Prolegomena*.

Evaluating Titchener's Contributions to Psychology

Psychology for Titchener was a pure laboratory science aimed at discovering the basic structure of human consciousness. Systematic experimental introspection was its prime method; and because this form of introspection required extensive training, it was limited to highly motivated adult observers. Thus, according to Titchener, psychology was the science of the "generalized adult mind." Two immediate consequences of this rather limited definition of the field were that (a) Titchener was uninterested in individual differences between one mind and another; and (b) he excluded from his definition of psychology all research using children, animals, and the insane—they could never introspect properly. Also, because the discipline was to retain the purity of the laboratory, Titchener omitted such applied concerns as industrial and educational psychology from his definition of the field. Although his vision of psychology was therefore extremely narrow, it also led directly to his major lasting contribution—the promotion of an experimental psychology that featured the tight controls found in the laboratory. Although his particular introspective methodology passed from the scene, his insistence on the value of basic laboratory research as the way to provide the foundation for psychological knowledge created a place for the laboratory in all colleges and universities with programs in psychology. As one historian put it, Titchener was "responsible for making psychology scientific—for setting psychology up in the laboratory and reaching his conclusions through experiment, under controlled conditions" (Hindeland, 1971, p. 28).

On the other hand, Titchener's narrow brand of psychology became as isolated from American psychology as Ithaca was from other centers of learning. Structuralism ultimately failed as a system, primarily due to the shortcomings of introspection as a method but also because of Titchener's uncompromising insistence that his way was the only way. Despite Titchener's belief that highly trained observers gained the "introspective habit," thereby avoiding bias and allowing for replication of experiments to occur, it soon became apparent that serious problems existed with the method. The difficulty is illustrated in the controversies that surrounded Titchener. One was the conflict with Baldwin over reaction time (Chapter 6), which featured Titchener's rejection of the use of untrained observers and his belief that studying individual differences was of little value. The second was the imageless thought problem, described briefly in Chapter 4. As you recall, introspectors in Külpe's lab at Wurzburg discovered situations in which conscious thoughts occurred in the absence of images. In a psychophysics weight-judging study, for instance, images occurred at various points in the process but not at the exact moment of judgment. The judgment itself seemed to be an "imageless" thought. This was a direct threat to Titchener's system, which held as dogma that images were the underlying elements of *all* ideas. To counter the assault, Titchener dismissed the Wurzburg outcome as a failure of experimental control and found that in *his* laboratory, observers were indeed able to detect images at all stages of the weight-judging experiment. Due to the inherently subjective nature of introspection, however, there was no independent means of determining who was right. It began to appear that introspection could not produce objective data.

Thus psychologists started to suspect that the extensive training insisted on by Titchener produced bias rather than eliminated it—the training began to look like indoctrination. In a 1913 paper that launched behaviorism, John Watson summarized introspection's essential problem:

> Take the case of sensation. A sensation is defined in terms of its attributes. One psychologist will state with readiness that the attributes of a visual sensation are *quality, extension, duration*, and *intensity*. Another will add *clearness*. Still another that of *order*. I doubt if any one psychologist can draw up a set of statements describing what he means by sensation which will be agreed to by three other psychologists of different training. . . . I firmly believe that two hundred years from now, unless the introspective method is discarded, psychology will still be divided on the question as to whether auditory sensations have the quality of "extension," whether intensity is an attribute which can be applied to color, whether there is a difference in "texture" between image and sensation and upon many hundreds of others of like character. (Watson, 1913, p. 164; emphasis in the original)

The failure of introspection signaled the ultimate demise of structuralism, but the force of Titchener's personality provided one final contribution to psychology. As suggested by Boring's obituary (see p. 232), Titchener's death deprived American psychology of a focal point of opposition. Titchener, who lectured in his academic gown and said that the attire conferred on him the right to be dogmatic, insisted on the validity of introspective psychology and was a persistent and articulate critic of those who deviated from it. By so doing, he made it necessary for opponents to be intelligible about their own systems. If schools of thought in psychology gain momentum by virtue of their opposition to some established force, then Titchener's structuralism served the valuable purpose of giving movements such as functionalism and behaviorism a clear target.

AMERICA'S PSYCHOLOGY: FUNCTIONALISM

Titchener might not have been interested in applied psychology, in the examination of individual differences, or in studying animals, children, or the insane, but practically every other psychologist in America was. Part of the reason for this derives from the historical context of late 19th-century America. During the final three decades of the century, following the Civil War, the United States entered a period of sustained growth. It was a time of reconstruction in the South, westward expansion, railroad building, technological innovation (e.g., telephone, typewriter), industrialization on a massive scale, and the amassing of great wealth by Gilded Age entrepreneurs with names like Rockefeller, Vanderbilt, Carnegie, and Mellon.

The evidence of this "progress" was put on display at a world's fair in Chicago in 1893—the Columbian Exposition. Timed to celebrate the 400th anniversary of the arrival of Columbus (but opened a year late because of construction delays), the Exposition was a massive undertaking. About 200 buildings were constructed, scattered over 600 acres near Lake Michigan and housing exhibits depicting business, industry, science, and the arts.[6] An estimated 27 million attended during the Exposition's 6 months—about one in four Americans (Brands, 1995). Of course, this period in American history was also a time when Native American populations were uprooted from their land and decimated, workers endured long hours and unsafe working conditions for pitiful wages, women and minorities were considered mentally inferior to white males, and an enormous gap developed between the very few rich and the very many poor. Nonetheless, most (white, male) Americans came to develop a concept of their national character that placed a high value on taking individual responsibility for success or failure, making something of oneself regardless of one's background, competing and winning in the marketplace, and—of importance for our story—always thinking of the usefulness or practical value of objects and ideas.

This emerging prototype of American pragmatic individuality was consistent with evolutionary thinking, although most Americans would have strongly denied that they were Darwinians. Nonetheless, Americans were attracted by the views of the British popularizer of evolution, Herbert Spencer (1820–1903), who promoted a brand of evolution congenial to Americans on the "winning" side of things. Spencer, not Darwin, invented the phrase "survival of the fittest," but Spencer's idea of fitness was not the same as Darwin's.[7] Whereas any attribute that furthered the cause of survival (e.g., camouflage) would constitute fitness for Darwin, Spencer's use of the term implied that survivors were winners of fierce battles for limited resources. As Spencer used the phrase, survival of the fittest blended with and contributed to the developing American character of the 19th century. Spencer's system has come to be known as **social Darwinism**.

Social Darwinists believed that evolutionary forces were natural and inevitable and that any attempt on the part of humans to alter these forces was misdirected and harmful. Evolution must be left unchecked, Spencer argued, an attitude that had direct social, political, and economic implications. It meant, for example, that government should not interfere with business practices—losers in business failed simply because they weren't "fit." Those who accumulated enormous wealth, on the other hand, should not in any way be regulated or penalized (e.g., taxed)—their wealth was simply a sign of their fitness. Government also should not provide services to the poor—their poverty was believed to result from a lack of fitness. If supported by the government, their lack of fitness would spread as they produced similarly unfit children. Social Darwinists took the Darwinian notion "if fit, therefore successful," and made the logically flawed reversal "if successful, therefore fit." Thus evolutionary

---

[6]Two rooms in a science building were set aside to exhibit apparatus and mental testing materials from the "new" science of psychology. The exhibit was organized by Joseph Jastrow, one of Hall's first students at Johns Hopkins (Perloff & Perloff, 1977). Clark University sent a set of photos of its lab, several of which appear in this text (Figures 4.5, 6.4, and 6.5).

[7]Another important difference between the men was that Darwin was scientifically conservative, unwilling to speculate in the absence of a large database. As discussed in Chapter 5, this unwillingness to go far beyond the data was one reason for his delay in publishing the *Origin of Species*. Spencer, on the other hand, did not hesitate to speculate far beyond available evidence. It was once said of Spencer that his "idea of a tragedy was a deduction killed by a fact" (quoted in Boakes, 1984, p. 10).

fitness became a means of rationalizing the huge gap between rich and poor and of maintaining a belief in the superiority of the white male over all others (e.g., women, blacks, Native Americans). Most American psychologists, especially those interested in mental testing (see Chapter 8), were generally agreeable to social Darwinist thinking.

As we shall see, the evolutionary mind-set that psychologists found congenial led naturally to interests in studying individual differences, animal behavior, development, and abnormal behavior as well as to the search for practical applications of psychological principles. This trend toward a more diverse psychology than Titchener's structuralism was clear from the work of James and Hall (Chapter 6), both of whom made important contributions before Titchener arrived from Leipzig. The movement came to be called functionalism. Although it shared some common ground with structuralism (interested in studying human consciousness, willingness to use introspection), it represented a fundamental break with the structuralist goal of studying the "generalized adult mind." Instead, it was firmly grounded in evolutionary theory, which led functionalists to ask questions that either would not have occurred to Titchener or would not have interested him (Green, 2009). These questions, as we shall see, led American psychologists to study the diverse range of topics that eventually formed the chapter titles of modern psychology textbooks.

Although functionalist thinking was widespread enough to be considered "America's psychology," it was especially associated with two universities, Chicago and Columbia. The remainder of the chapter describes the work of several psychologists at these two schools. Chapter 8 elaborates on the theme of application, a central component of functionalist thinking.

The Chicago Functionalists

In May 1889, John D. Rockefeller, pockets bulging with Standard Oil profits, donated $600,000 to establish a Baptist university, contingent on the Baptists pledging an additional $400,000 (Ryan, 1939). The university would be located in Chicago, a city already developing the reputation that led the poet Carl Sandburg to call it the "City of the Big Shoulders." Nearly destroyed by the famous fire of 1871 that burned 1,688 acres, consumed buildings valued at $192 million, and bankrupted 64 insurance companies (Cashman, 1993), Chicago was one of America's fastest-growing cities in the late 1800s. Its hundreds of acres of cattle and hog pens, slaughterhouses, and packinghouses made it the center of the beef and pork industry, and its location made it a natural hub for railroads and a key location for industries (e.g., lumber, steel, agriculture) relying on transportation via rail and Great Lakes steamers. The new university was a bold enterprise, far removed from the East Coast academic community. Its success was entrusted to President William Rainey Harper, a biblical scholar who had earned a doctorate from Yale at age 18. Harper's main challenge was to hire a quality faculty—a task made easier by the troubles at Clark University. As you recall from Chapter 6, Harper filled a number of his faculty positions with disgruntled Clark University faculty and graduate students when financial problems and Hall's capriciousness as president led them to look for greener pastures.

The University of Chicago opened in 1892 and quickly became a leader in higher education, despite its remoteness from the East. It included separate colleges of liberal arts, practical arts, literature, and science, as well as a graduate school and a school of divinity. It began with a large staff of 120 faculty, who within 3 years were teaching 534 graduate students—more than Johns Hopkins and Clark combined (Ryan, 1939).

Two years after the opening, Harper hired a young instructor from the University of Michigan to chair Chicago's philosophy department. Although he became better known for his philosophical writings on democracy and his innovative approach to education, John Dewey also wrote a paper that is often considered the starting point for functionalism in America.

John Dewey (1859–1952): The Reflex Arc   John Dewey was born in Burlington, a small city in western Vermont. There he was raised in a setting that shaped in him the traditional Yankee values of hard work, respect for others, thrift, simplicity, and a love of democracy. After completing high school at age 15, Dewey enrolled in the nearby University of Vermont, whose 8 faculty members taught just a few dozen students; along with 16 peers, Dewey graduated in 1879 (Barone, 1996). While at Vermont, he studied the traditional curriculum of the classics and humanities, but he also sampled evolutionary thinking by studying the new sciences of geology and zoology.

After graduating, Dewey taught high school for several years and then decided to continue his education. Johns Hopkins was the rising star in academia, and Dewey enrolled there to study philosophy in 1882. The new psychology was included in the Hopkins philosophy curriculum, so Dewey's schedule included work in G. Stanley Hall's brand new laboratory. After earning his doctorate in philosophy in 1884, Dewey's next stop was Michigan. There he taught both philosophy and psychology, working his notes into a text, *Psychology*, in 1886. The book was used on numerous campuses for several years and was the standard text at Michigan for a decade (Raphelson, 1973), but it met its demise upon the 1890 publication of William James's instant classic. Dewey himself readily acknowledged *The Principles of Psychology* to be superior to his own effort.

Dewey went to Chicago in 1894. His new department included traditional philosophy, laboratory psychology, and another area of great interest to Dewey—pedagogy. During his 10 years there, Dewey established Chicago as a center of functionalism, partly through recruiting colleagues sympathetic to the movement but also through an article published in 1896 and entitled "The Reflex Arc Concept in Psychology." In it, he took issue with the traditional manner of thinking about reflexes. Dating from Bell and Magendie's separation of the reflex into separate sensory and motor pathways (Chapter 3), physiologists thought of the **reflex arc** in terms of three separate elementary components: the stimulus producing sensation, central processing producing an idea, and the act or motor response. Dewey believed that dividing the reflex into these "elements" was artificial, however, resulting in a reflex concept that was "not a comprehensive, or organic unity, but a patchwork of disjointed parts" (Dewey, 1896/1948, p. 356). Instead, Dewey proposed a model of the reflex that substituted a functional for a structural approach.

The reflex, Dewey argued, is best conceived of as an integrated, coordinated whole that serves the function of adapting the organism to its environment. Also, it is more like a continuous circuit than an "arc," the latter implying distinct starting and ending points. Consider a child reaching for a candle flame, to use Dewey's example. Those using the traditional reflex arc model would analyze the event into a series of stimulus–response elements: seeing the flame, reaching for it, feeling the heat, and reflexively withdrawing. For Dewey, though, such an analysis oversimplified a complex action. Reaching for something after seeing it, for example, can make sense only in the larger context of the child's learning history: "Seeing and grasping have been so often bound together to reinforce each other, to help each other out, that each may be considered practically a subordinate member of a bigger coordination" (p. 356). The second part of the event, being seared by the flame and withdrawing the hand, is also part of the larger coordination that produces a learning event; the flame now takes on new meaning for the child. From that point on, seeing a burning candle is "no longer mere seeing; it is the seeing-of-a-light-that-means-pain-when-contact-occurs" (p. 357). Hence, the child has adapted to the environment as a result of experience. Furthermore, the sight of a burning candle now has a specific meaning that differs from the same sight viewed by a different child with different experiences. Dewey argued forcefully that psychologists studying human action should not be concerned with microscopic analysis into elements, but with how the act functions to promote the organism's well-being in the struggle to adapt to its ever-changing world. That is, Dewey was proposing a change in emphasis about reflex behavior, a shift in thinking from an emphasis on "what?" to a focus on "what for?"

America at the turn of the century was just entering the Progressive era, a time of sweeping reform and the beginning of a reaction against social Darwinism. During this time, business monopolies were being attacked and their leaders were as likely to be called robber barons as heroes of the struggle for existence. Labor unions made significant gains on behalf of workers, the federal government enacted regulations to protect ordinary Americans from a variety of abuses (e.g., child labor, unsanitary conditions in food production industries), and social reformers set out to improve the welfare of those who used to be written off as "unfit." John Dewey fit perfectly into this context, making significant contributions to educational reform and launching the movement that came to be known as **progressive education**.

As a schoolteacher, Dewey developed a strong dislike for the conventional approach to education, which emphasized rote learning, drill and practice, and strict discipline. Such an atmosphere made the classroom a place to avoid rather than a place to learn. Yet education was the key to an effective democracy, Dewey believed, because it offered everyone an equal opportunity to advance. At a time when public education was growing by leaps and bounds,[8] educational reform was essential. Dewey responded by creating a "Laboratory School" at Chicago in 1896 to study how children learned best in the classroom. He wrote *The School and Society* (1899), which established his reputation as a leading philosopher of education. Using his presidential address to the American Psychological Association in 1899 as a forum, he also implored psychologists to use their new knowledge of the mind to improve education (Dewey, 1900). According to Dewey, children learn by interacting with their environment—they learn by doing. Consequently, the school must create an atmosphere that encourages children to explore on their own, to think critically and creatively, and to be actively involved in learning.

Dewey left Chicago for Columbia University in 1904, turning over departmental leadership to James Angell. At Columbia, he made no further contributions to psychology, but he continued to agitate for educational and social reform within the context of his democratic philosophy. He was a strong supporter of teachers' unions, helped found the American Association of University Professors, became a member of the American Civil Liberties Union, and actively campaigned for women's suffrage (Hilgard, 1987). He remained a committed activist for liberal causes well into his eighth decade.

James R. Angell (1869–1949): The Province of Functional Psychology

Like Dewey, James Rowland Angell was born in Burlington, Vermont, the son of the president

---

[8]Attending school was compulsory in just six states in 1871, but by 1900 virtually every state had compulsory education laws. Between 1890 and 1910, the number of students in public schools increased by a factor of four (Cashman, 1993).

KEY DATE—1906

This year marked the publication date of James Angell's APA presidential address ("The Province of Functional Psychology") that brought functional psychology into clear focus.

These events also happened that year:

- A famous exchange of letters began between Sigmund Freud (Chapter 12) and Carl Jung; it started as a thank you note to Jung for sending Freud a set of papers on word association
- The first U.S. Pure Food and Drugs Act was passed, after Upton Sinclair's description of the Chicago stockyards and slaughterhouses in the novel *The Jungle*
- China and Britain agreed to a reduction in the production of opium
- The San Francisco earthquake killed 700 people and produced $400 million in property loss
- Teddy Roosevelt visited the Panama Canal, the first trip outside the U.S. by a president in office

- U.S. troops occupied Cuba, remaining for three years
- The first running of the French Grand Prix motor race occurred

These people were born:

- Greta Garbo, Swedish film actress (in *Grand Hotel*, Academy Award winner for Best Picture in 1932, she delivered her most famous line → "I want to be alone.")
- Dmitri Shostakovich, Russian composer
- Gracie Allen, comedic actor and wife of George Burns

These people died:

- Henrik Ibsen, Norwegian playwright (e.g., *A Doll's House*)
- Paul Cezanne, French impressionist painter (e.g., *Still Life with Apples*)

---

of the University of Vermont. When his father took the same job at the University of Michigan in 1871, the Angells moved to the Midwest and James was raised in the academic environment of Ann Arbor. He went to school at his father's university, studying philosophy, the classics, and the natural sciences. His introduction to psychology came in a course with Dewey, using the professor's new textbook. Angell graduated from Michigan in 1890 and then stayed another year to earn a master's degree in philosophy. During this last year, his courses included a seminar with Dewey that used James's new *Principles of Psychology* as the text. As he later recalled, the text "unquestionably affected my thinking for the next 20 years more profoundly than any other" (quoted in Raphelson, 1973, p. 120). To experience William James firsthand, Angell went to Cambridge and spent a year under James's tutelage. He then decided to earn a German doctorate. By this time doctoral training in America was as good as if not superior to training in Germany, but there was still a high prestige value to a doctorate from the Continent. That Angell was aware of this status benefit is clear—his cousin Frank, with Leipzig credentials paving the way, had just been lured from Cornell to Stanford by an outstanding offer of $3,000 annually (O'Donnell, 1985).

Angell intended to follow his cousin to Leipzig, but Wundt's laboratory was full, so he studied briefly with Ebbinghaus in Berlin before settling into the University at Halle. There he completed the work for his doctorate but never finished the final version of it (he was asked to improve the German) after receiving an offer to teach at the University of Minnesota. The salary and the stability of real employment enabled him to marry the woman he had known since his Michigan days, and for the 24-year-old Angell, love and a new job were sufficient to offset the loss of what seemed to be a mere piece of paper. Thus, although he would go on to direct the doctoral projects of many prominent American psychologists, he never quite finished his own.

After Angell (Figure 7.6) had spent a year at Minnesota, Dewey hired the young instructor to be in charge of the psychology portion of the philosophy curriculum; the Angells moved to Chicago in 1894. When Dewey moved on to Columbia a decade later, psychology became its own department, separate from philosophy, and Angell was made department chair. He moved further toward administration and away from psychology by being named dean of the faculty in 1911. He eventually followed in his father's footsteps and became a university president, leading Yale University for most of the 1920s and 1930s. His stellar work as president (e.g., he quadrupled the endowment) landed him on the cover of *Time* in 1936, just before his retirement the following year.

Angell's importance to psychology derives from his work in the period from 1894 to 1911. During this time he contributed valuable research in areas such as reaction time, imagery, and sound localization,[9] and he built one of the top two or three departments in the country. He also became the most visible spokesperson for functionalism by writing a popular introductory textbook (Angell, 1904) and by delivering a memorable address after

FIGURE 7.6 James R. Angell.

[9]Sound localization depends in part on sound waves reaching our ears at slightly different times. Angell, who was deaf in one ear, served as his own observer in a study on how localization was accomplished monaurally (Hunter, 1949).

being elected to the presidency of the American Psychological Association in 1906 (Angell, 1907/1948). Dewey's reflex arc paper might have been the foundation paper for functionalist thinking, but it was not a "Here is what functionalism means" type of paper. Angell's was—he called it "The Province of Functional Psychology." In part, it was a response to Titchener's 1898 paper, "The Postulates of a Structural Psychology."

Angell opened the paper with the modest disclaimer that functional psychology was not a dogmatic "school" of psychology, but rather "little more than a point of view, a program, an ambition" (Angell, 1907/1948, p. 439). He then drew a sharp contrast between functional and structural psychologies. Whereas a structuralist is interested in mental contents, the "what?" of conscious experience, Angell stated, the functional psychologist wants to study mental operations, the "how?" and "why?" of consciousness. If the structuralist is asking *what is consciousness?* the functionalist is asking *what is consciousness for?* Furthermore, with a dig at what he considered to be the highly artificial nature of the results from Titchenerian-style research, Angell argued that a minute analysis of some hypothetical "moment of conscious-ness" fails to capture the importance of consciousness for everyday life:

> If you adopt as your material for psychological analysis the isolated "moment of consciousness," it is very easy to become so absorbed in determining its constitution as to be rendered somewhat oblivious to its artificial character. The most essential quarrel which the functionalist has with structuralism arises from this fact and touches the feasibility and worth of the effort to get at mental process as it is under the conditions of actual experience rather than as it appears to a merely postmortem [introspective] analysis. (1907/1948, p. 441)

Angell then explicitly rejected the analogy between psychology and biology that Titchener had used to argue for the primacy of a structuralist approach. As you recall, Titchener had likened structuralism to anatomy and argued that just as anatomy provides the basis for physiology, so must structuralism precede functionalism. But Angell would have none of it. Anatomy involves material objects that can be manipulated, observed, and measured with some precision, but mental contents are "evanescent" and "fleeting." We can attempt to isolate them, but they are fundamentally different from the materials being studied by anatomists. With the analogy between anatomy and structuralism shown to be faulty, Angell believed the supposed primacy of structuralism over functionalism to be meaningless.

Angell's functionalist approach to consciousness had the same evolutionary flavor found in James. Like James, Angell described the function of consciousness to be in allowing the individual to solve problems and therefore to adapt to novel situations. Near the close of his article, he pointed out the connections between functionalist thinking and the interests of American psychologists. If the psychologist is interested in the functions of consciousness, then it is important to understand how those functions develop, both ontogenetically and phylogenetically. Therefore, the psychologist has legitimate interests in developmental and comparative psychology. Similarly, an interest in failures to adapt leads naturally to the study of abnormal psychology; an interest in how some individuals adapt better than others leads one to study individual differences and develop mental tests to measure those differences; and an interest in how the individual learns to adapt and can be best trained to do so leads to the study of educational psychology and of learning in general. In short, virtually every topic of interest to American psychologists could be gathered under the umbrella of functionalism. Furthermore, studying these diverse areas requires a liberal attitude about appropriate methods.

FIGURE 7.7 Designs for two Carr mazes.

Angell had no quarrel with introspection, but he believed that it had to be defined more broadly than Titchener would allow and that it must be supplemented with more direct observational methods.

In his productive years at Chicago, Angell mentored several individuals destined to become key figures in psychology's story. One was John Watson, normally considered the founder of behaviorism as a school of psychology (Chapter 10); another was Harvey Carr, Angell's successor as department head.

Harvey Carr (1873–1954): The Maturing of Functionalism

Carr found his way to Chicago in 1902, after completing both a bachelor's and a master's degree in psychology at the University of Colorado. At Colorado, he learned of the new laboratory psychology from Arthur Allin, a former student of Hall and Sanford at Clark. While at Chicago, Carr developed lifelong interests in two diverse topics, the perception of space and maze learning. His doctoral dissertation in 1905 was on the former topic and eventually led to a book (Carr, 1935). Most of his research publications concerned maze learning, however, and a famous study with behaviorist John Watson is featured in Chapter 10. He was also interested in the general problem of maze standardization. In the early years of maze-learning research, results often failed to replicate because the mazes used from one study to the next varied considerably. Carr improved the situation substantially by inventing a type of maze that came to be called the "Carr maze" (Warner & Warden, 1927). Two examples are shown in Figure 7.7. Although each maze had a different solution, the number of choices per maze was constant, as was the length of each pathway and dead end.

After earning his doctorate in 1905, Carr taught elsewhere for several years and then returned to Chicago in 1908. When Watson left for Johns Hopkins that year, Angell hired Carr to run the psychology laboratory. Carr remained at Chicago until his retirement in 1938, chairing the department for the second half of his years there. He contributed to the evolution of Chicago functionalism through his influence on students and by publishing a popular textbook in the mid-1920s—*Psychology: A Study of Mental Activity* (Carr, 1925). In his years at Chicago, Carr had a hand in the doctoral work of no fewer than 131 students; he directed 53 dissertations, 18 in comparative psychology, 6 in space perception, and 29 in learning (Pillsbury, 1955). The 1925 text can be considered a statement of the "mature" functionalism, with the understanding that functionalism always remained more of an attitude than a systematic theoretical position.

The Columbia Functionalists

Because functionalism was more of a state of mind than a rigorous system, it existed well beyond Chicago. Indeed, elements of functional thinking could be found throughout the academic landscape, with the possible exception of Cornell. Even there, however, Titchenerian orthodoxy occasionally relaxed. For instance, E. G. Boring once ran a human maze-learning study that featured blindfolded humans navigating an outdoor maze, their pathways marked by trails of flour leaking from sacks attached to their backs; Boring reported that the only significant outcome of the study was that he became infatuated with one of the maze runners, eventually marrying her (Jaynes, 1969a). Beyond Chicago, however, functionalism at the turn of the century was associated with Columbia University in New York. In its formative years, James McKeen Cattell headed the psychology program. You met him in the Chapter 4 discussion of reaction time, and you will learn more extensively of his work on mental testing in the next chapter. While at Columbia from 1891 to 1917, Cattell created a vibrant graduate department, possibly the best in the country. Under his tutelage, dozens of historically important psychologists earned their doctoral stripes, and Cattell personally directed more than 50 dissertations (Jonçich, 1968). His two of best-known students were Edward Thorndike and Robert Woodworth.

Edward L. Thorndike (1874–1949): Connectionism Most of Thorndike's impact was in the fields of educational psychology and psychological testing, but he is most often remembered among research psychologists for studying how cats learned to escape from puzzle boxes. For this reason he is considered a pioneer in comparative psychology, an example of what Lloyd Morgan had in mind as the proper way to do animal research. He also appears occasionally in chapters on behaviorism as a precursor to the conditioning work of Pavlov and Watson. In a certain sense, then, he was a transition figure from the early comparative psychologists to the later behaviorists. More important, he was a leader of the functionalist movement, interested in studying how individuals adapted to their environments and how this knowledge could be applied to improve the human condition.

Thorndike's early life was nomadic; his father was a Methodist minister who moved his family from one New England town to another as he was frequently reassigned to different congregations. Always the new kid in town, young Thorndike became terribly shy. Yet he also developed self-reliance and, under the stern eye of his puritanical and demanding mother, he became an excellent student. He gained easy acceptance to the Methodist-run Wesleyan University in Connecticut, graduating with honors in 1895. While there, he found his vocation by discovering James's *Principles of Psychology*, which electrified him as it had James Angell and countless others of that generation. Thorndike (1936) later described the book as more stimulating "than any book that I had read before, and possibly more so than any book read since" (p. 263). As Angell had done 4 years earlier, Thorndike entered Harvard's graduate program to experience James directly.

It is not clear exactly how Thorndike's interests in animal behavior developed, but a seminar taken with James used Wundt's *Lectures on Human and Animal Psychology*, and he might have attended public lectures given by the visiting Lloyd Morgan, Britain's premier comparative psychologist (Chapter 5). Like every educated person of his day, Thorndike was thoroughly familiar with evolutionary thinking. With a characteristic self-confidence bordering on arrogance, Thorndike's explanation for his choice of research topic was simple: "My first research was in animal psychology, not because I knew animals or cared much for them, but because I thought I could do better than had been done" (quoted in Jonçich, 1968, p. 89).

Thorndike first studied instinct and intelligence in baby chicks by requiring them to escape from simple mazes formed by placing books on end. Figure 7.8 shows three of the patterns he used. Chicks would be placed in the maze at location A and then observed to see if they could find the exit. Thorndike reported that they initially jumped at the walls, made a lot of noise, and were just as likely to go more deeply into the maze as to escape from it. After several trials, however, they eliminated the useless behaviors and found their way out. Incidentally, some of this research was completed in the cellar of the William James household. Thorndike's landlord had evicted the animals, and James had taken them in after being unable to secure space for them on campus. Thorndike believed that the "nuisance to Mrs. James was...somewhat mitigated by the entertainment to the two youngest children" (Thorndike, 1936, p. 264).

For reasons partly financial and partly because of a romantic relationship that seemed to be going nowhere (with the woman who would become his wife, as it turned out), Thorndike applied for and received a fellowship to Columbia. Cattell was impressed with the young psychologist, and Thorndike was awarded $700 a year in aid, more than the average annual income for most families at that time (Jonçich, 1968). At Columbia, he expanded his animal research to several different species, but his most famous work was done with cats in puzzle boxes. He published his findings as "Animal Intelligence: An Experimental Study of the Associative Processes in Animals" in 1898. Later, in 1911, Thorndike wrote *Animal Intelligence: Experimental Studies* (1911/2000); it included the 1898 monograph and some additional chapters.

Thorndike on Puzzle Box Learning   Thorndike was a strong critic of contemporary comparative psychologists, especially when they relied on anecdotal data to support claims of higher mental powers for a variety of animals. As he put it, rather sarcastically:

> Dogs get lost hundreds of times and no one ever notices it or sends an account of it to scientific magazines. But let one find his way from Brooklyn to Yonkers and the fact immediately becomes a circulating anecdote. Thousands of cats on thousands of occasions sit helplessly yowling, and no one takes thought of it or writes to his friend, the professor; but let one cat claw at the knob of a door supposedly as a signal to be let out, and straightaway this cat becomes the representative of the cat-mind in all the books. (Thorndike, 1911/2000, p. 24)

FIGURE 7.8 Maze designs for baby chicks that Thorndike created by placing books vertically on a table.

Thorndike knew he could do better, and the most important aspect of the puzzle box studies was the methodological rigor that he brought to the project (Galef, 1998). Disdaining anecdotes, Thorndike instead developed more systematic procedures to test claims for animal intelligence—he would study more than a single case, he would repeat the experiments, and he would control the learning history and the environments of the animals he studied. The method he decided upon was "to put animals when hungry in inclosures from which they could escape by some simple act, such as pulling at a loop of cord, pressing a lever, or stepping on a platform" (Thorndike, 1911/2000, p. 26). Their behavior, and the amount of time it took to escape, would be recorded.

Although Thorndike's research strategy was clear and logical, he was the exception to the rule that the early research psychologists were talented and creative apparatus builders. His books-on-end mazes for chicks hinted at a lack of mechanical aptitude, and his puzzle boxes confirmed the handicap.[10] Thorndike included a sketch of one of the 15 boxes he built (Figure 7.9). Although the drawing suggests a neat, clean design, his actual boxes were crudely built (Burnham, 1972). Nonetheless, there was a method to the apparent chaos in the box construction. Figure 7.9 ("Box K") was actually one of the more complex boxes, designed to combine responses that had been the only ones necessary in each of three other boxes. Box K was used with cats that had learned each of the individual responses, to see if they could combine the information and escape quickly. Thorndike used 13 different cats in his puzzle boxes. It is not clear from his description exactly how many cats were tested in each of the boxes, but it appears that each cat was tested in at least several of the boxes.

And how did the cats behave when placed in the boxes? At first, their behavior seemed random—a series of attempts to escape by any means possible (e.g., clawing at or biting the wood slats). Eventually, the correct response occurred, by accident at first. From trial to trial,

FIGURE 7.9 One of Thorndike's puzzle boxes: K (complex, requiring three responses, sketched by Thorndike). From Burnham (1972).

[10]Also, Thorndike never learned how to use a typewriter or how to drive a car, and his son could never recall seeing his father "fix" anything (Thorndike, 1991).

the ineffective responses dropped out and the successful one occurred sooner. In Thorndike's (1911/2000) words:

> The other nonsuccessful impulses will be stamped out and the particular impulse leading to the successful act will be stamped in by the resulting pleasure, until, after many trials, the cat will, when put in the box, immediately claw the button or loop in a definite way. (p. 36)

Thorndike's explanation for this behavior, which also applied to his chicks-in-mazes experiments, was the same as that given by Morgan to explain the behavior of dogs opening gates to escape from yards—**trial-and-error learning** (Thorndike preferred the phrase "trial and accidental success"). Because he believed that the cat learned to make *connections* between stimuli in the boxes and successful escape responses during this trial-and-error learning, Thorndike's learning model is sometimes called **connectionism**. When first placed in the puzzle box, the cat exhibits behavior that is a random sequence of acts—clawing, biting, pushing, screeching, and so on. Eventually, the animal hits upon the correct response (e.g., claws a loop), but its first solution is accidental. Nonetheless, that behavior has been successful, and such behaviors tend to be repeated, "stamped in" by their pleasurable consequences (escape). On subsequent trials, the failed behaviors are gradually eliminated and the successful one occurs earlier and earlier in the sequence. Before long, the animal is in and out of the box in a few seconds. Figure 7.10 charts the gradually improving, if erratic progress of one of Thorndike's cats. Also, to account for the fact that every situation encountered in life is somewhat unique, Thorndike applied the results of some research on transfer that he completed with Woodworth (discussed later). He proposed that if a new situation had some elements in common with an old situation, then transfer would occur. For example, he found that some of his cats, after learning to escape from one box and then being put into a box

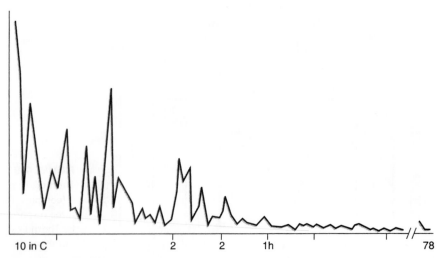

FIGURE 7.10   Performance of cat 10 in puzzle box C. On the x-axis, the unlabeled vertical dash meant a day, 2 meant two days, 1h meant an hour, and 78 meant 78 hours. From Thorndike (1911/2000).

with a similar but not identical escape mechanism, learned more quickly than a cat without such an experience.

While allowing for transfer, Thorndike rejected the idea that cats are capable of complex reasoning or able to benefit from imitation when escaping from the boxes, however. For instance, in Box K (Figure 7.9), which combined three responses that had been learned earlier, the cats showed no evidence of combining what they had learned into a more complex sequence of behaviors. He also tested for imitation directly—a box D had two chambers separated by wire mesh. One side had an escape mechanism and other did not. Thorndike would put two cats in the box, one on either side of the wire partition, and record instances when the "observer" cat was watching the other cat escape successfully. There was no evidence of observational learning—when put to test, the observer cat behaved exactly like other, naive cats, prompting Thorndike (1911/2000) to conclude, "No one, I am sure, who had seen them, would have claimed that their conduct was at all influenced by what they had seen" (p. 89).

Thorndike proposed two general principles as a result of the puzzle box studies, a **Law of Effect** and a **Law of Exercise**. According to the former:

> *Of several responses made to the same situation, those which are accompanied or closely followed by satisfaction to the animal will, other things being equal, be more firmly connected with the situation, so that, when it recurs, they will be more likely to recur; those which are accompanied or closely followed by discomfort to the animal will, other things being equal, have their connections with that situation weakened, so that, when it recurs, they will be less likely to recur.* (Thorndike, 1911/2000, p. 244; emphasis in the original)

Thorndike's Law of Exercise stated simply that the connection between stimulus situation and response would be strengthened with practice. As discussed in Chapter 11, Thorndike's Law of Effect bears a close resemblance to B. F. Skinner's concept of operant conditioning; Skinner recognized his debt to Thorndike, referring to the Columbia psychologist's work as "one of the first serious attempts to study changes brought about by the consequences of behavior" (Skinner, 1953, p. 59).

The Thorndike-Mills Controversy   Thorndike was excited about his dissertation research and willing to take on critics, writing to his future wife that his 1898 thesis was "a beauty....I've got some theories which knock the old authorities into a grease spot" (quoted in Jonçich, 1968, p. 146). One authority who was not amused by Thorndike's youthful exuberance was Wesley Mills, a comparative psychologist who criticized Thorndike's research at the 1898 meeting of the American Psychological Association and followed it up with an article in *Psychological Review*. Mills started by faulting Thorndike's lack of respect for his "elders," noting that "Dr. Thorndike has not been hampered in his researches by any of that respect for workers of the past. . . . which usually causes men to pause before differing radically from them, not to say gleefully consigning them to the psychological flames" (Mills, 1899, p. 263). More important, Mills rejected the study's conclusions because of the *artificiality* of the environment created by Thorndike. Cats placed in small enclosures, Mills argued, cannot be expected to act naturally. Thus nothing about their normal behavior can be determined from their behavior in highly artificial, abnormal surroundings. Mills concluded that one might as well "enclose a living man in a coffin, lower him, against his will, into the earth, and attempt to deduce normal psychology from his conduct" (p. 266).

Far from being chastened, Thorndike (1899) offered a point-by-point rebuttal. He admitted to being unimpressed with animal research based on uncritical observation and anecdote and made no apology for it. He denied Mill's claim that his cats had been in a panic, pointing out caustically that if Mills had acted like a genuine scientist and bothered to repeat the puzzle box studies, he would have discovered that little if any panic occurred. Furthermore, those cats that did show a higher "fury of activity" (p. 412) did not differ in learning speed from their more sanguine peers. As for the charge of artificiality, Thorndike simply asked what Mills could mean by a natural environment. Animals constantly face new situations; who is to say one is more "natural" than another? To drive home the point, Thorndike turned around an example that Mills had used, a cat navigating a bookshelf: "The situation here coped with is as 'unnatural' as that in.... my experiments" (Thorndike, 1899, p. 414).

The Mills-Thorndike exchange is a good illustration of a difference of opinion about the appropriateness of laboratory methods that continues to this day. On the one hand are those who argue that understanding animal behavior requires the precision afforded by a controlled laboratory environment. In such a setting, the effects of various influences on behavior can be studied systematically. As will be seen, this approach was taken by most of the American animal researchers who came to be known as behaviorists (e.g., Skinner). In contrast, other psychologists followed Mills and argued that animal behavior can be understood only if it is studied outside the artificial confines of the laboratory. Most 20th-century European researchers took this route, producing a field known as **ethology**—the study of animal behavior in its "natural" surroundings. The best known of these scientists are Konrad Lorenz, Karl von Frisch, and Niko Tinbergen, who shared the 1973 Nobel Prize in Biology for their work on instinctive animal behavior. Lorenz is familiar to most students from a photo of him being followed by ducklings.

After earning his doctorate, Thorndike taught for a year at Case Western Reserve in Cleveland. He then returned to Columbia's Teachers College, where he remained for the rest of his professional career. There he extended his research on learning to humans and became a leading educational psychologist. He also developed a series of aptitude tests for schoolchildren, thereby contributing to the psychological testing movement as well. Honors came his way in the form of an APA presidency in 1912, election to the National Academy of Sciences in 1917, and the presidency of the American Association for the Advancement of Science in 1934 (Figure 7.11 shows Thorndike at the ceremony marking the end of his AAAS presidency; in the center of the photo is his successor, the noted physicist Karl Compton; Thorndike's mentor James McKeen Cattell, who had been the first psychologist to be elected president of the AAAS in 1924, is on the right). He was a prolific writer, averaging about a dozen articles a year. He also wrote numerous textbooks, including a three-volume *Educational Psychology* in 1913, that made his name "practically synonymous with the field of educational psychology for many years to come" (Goodenough, 1950, p. 295). Like James, he followed this multivolume effort with a single-volume "briefer course" the following year (Thorndike, 1914). Most of Thorndike's texts were compilations of lecture notes, and as Titchener pointed out in a scathing review, publishing "lecture courses as soon as the lectures have been delivered.... must inevitably show marks of hasty preparation and of immaturity of judgment" (Titchener, 1905b). The criticism didn't slow Thorndike down for a minute, however, and by the 1920s his royalty earnings far exceeded his Columbia salary. In 1924, for instance, his royalty income of $68,000 was five times his faculty salary (Jončich, 1968). Thorndike retired from Columbia in 1940 and died 9 years later.

FIGURE 7.11 E. L. Thorndike (left) as retiring president of the American Academy for the Advancement of Science.

Robert S. Woodworth (1869–1962): A Dynamic Psychology Woodworth (Figure 7.12), named Robert Sessions after an ancestor who participated in the Boston Tea Party, was born in the small western Massachusetts town of Belchertown. Like Thorndike, he was the son of a minister; his mother was an educator, a graduate of Mt. Holyoke College and the founder of the Lake Erie Female Seminary in Ohio (Poffenberger, 1962). Woodworth considered the ministry, but emerged from Amherst College with an interest in teaching. After a few years of teaching high school science and math, he discovered (who else?) William James and *The Principles* and decided to pursue a career in either philosophy or psychology. Like Angell and Thorndike, Woodworth wanted to experience the master directly, so off he went to Harvard in the fall of 1895. Woodworth stayed in Cambridge for 3 academic years, earning a second bachelor's degree, a master's degree, and serving as assistant in physiology at the Harvard Medical School. During this time, he developed two lifelong friendships: one with the noted physiologist Walter B. Cannon, whose work eventually yielded a theory of emotion to rival the James-Lange theory (the Cannon-Bard theory), and a second with Thorndike. This latter friendship contributed to Woodworth's next stop after Harvard—partly because Thorndike pestered him to do so, Cattell offered Woodworth a fellowship to Columbia (Jonçich, 1968).

Woodworth completed his doctorate at Columbia in 1899 and was immediately appointed instructor in physiology there. After spending a productive year in England in the laboratory of the esteemed physiologist Charles Sherrington (Chapter 3), he accepted Cattell's invitation in 1903 to join the psychology department. He remained there until his retirement in 1939 at age 70. Retirement barely slowed him down, however, for Woodworth continued to teach part-time until he was 89 and to write until he was 91.

Woodworth was a modest man who once wrote this to a friend: "I rate my achievement very low, believing that I am one of the sort whose name will soon be forgotten, though of service during his lifetime" (quoted in Poffenberger, 1962, p. 687). It was true that he did not

FIGURE 7.12 Robert S. Woodworth, author of the "Columbia bible." Woodworth is also in Figure 7.5, at the far left of the front row.

contribute much in the way of original research, and he did not create a school of thought that produced "Woodworthians," but he was quite wrong about his influence. He is remembered for (a) his research with Thorndike on transfer of training; (b) his "dynamic" psychology, with its emphasis on drives and organismic variables; and (c) his impact on students, both directly and through textbook writing, especially the so-called Columbia bible. This latter achievement, by itself, was sufficient to ensure his lasting importance to 20th-century experimental psychology.

The research on **transfer** derived from a fundamental problem in higher education—the validity of claims made on behalf of the doctrine of "formal discipline." Rooted in faculty psychology, it was the mid-19th-century belief that the curriculum for higher education should be designed to "exercise" and strengthen the intellectual faculties. This was to be accomplished through the study of such disciplines as Latin, Greek, and classical literature. Once the faculties were "in shape," the skills that had been developed were assumed to transfer to other disciplines to be learned later. The doctrine came under fire near the end of the century, when several schools copied Harvard's radical concept of an "elective" curriculum, which enabled students to avoid Latin and Greek if they wished. The debate generated much rhetoric, but little evidence accumulated for or against the idea that learning topic A (e.g., Greek) made it easier to learn topic B (e.g., zoology). Thorndike and Woodworth, in a series of coauthored publications (e.g., 1901), set out to find direct evidence for transfer of training. Their subjects practiced one simple task and then tried other tasks that varied in the degree of resemblance to the original task. After estimating the areas of rectangles, for instance, they estimated the areas of triangles (high resemblance) or the weight of objects (low). Briefly, what they found was that the amount of transfer occurring was directly proportional to the number of elements shared by the tasks. Although their tasks were quite different from curricular topics, Thorndike and Woodworth generalized their results to the issue of formal discipline, concluding that the doctrine had little merit. Because subjects like Greek bore minimal relationship to subjects like zoology, Thorndike and Woodworth predicted very little benefit to zoologists from studying Greek (except for some word origin information). As mentioned earlier, Thorndike also used the transfer concept to explain how cats that escaped from one box would find it easier to escape from a new box, assuming the two boxes shared similar escape elements.

Woodworth is often described as an *eclectic* when it came to theorizing; he was willing to incorporate the features of various diverse systems. In his popular introductory text, for example, he defined psychology as the study of both mental processes *and* behavior, thus blending the new behaviorism (Chapter 10) with the traditional psychology of consciousness. This definition continues to be found in virtually all general psychology texts. Woodworth also believed that psychologists should use a variety of methods, ranging from introspection to mental testing to the objective observation of behavior. He disliked those who would define psychology narrowly, naming both Titchener (structuralism) and Watson (behaviorism) as examples, and he revealed his basic philosophy by ending his popular history of psychology, *Contemporary Schools of Psychology*, with a chapter called "The Middle of the Road" (Woodworth, 1931, pp. 205–219). He was especially critical of a simple mechanistic, stimulus–response psychology, arguing for what he referred to as an **S-O-R model**. That is, he insisted that psychologists must understand not just the stimulus and response but also the organism (O) that responds to the stimuli and produces the behaviors. This includes studying what motivates or drives the organism. In his *Dynamic Psychology* (1918) and *Dynamics of Behavior* (1958), Woodworth argued for the importance of studying motivational factors influencing behavior. As he put it in a later autobiography, "Motivation has always seemed to me a field of study worthy to be placed alongside of performance. That is, we need to know not only what the individual can do and how he does it, but also what induces him to do one thing rather than another" (Woodworth, 1932, p. 371).

Like his best friend Thorndike, Woodworth became wealthy by writing textbooks. His *Psychology* (editions appeared in 1921, 1929, 1934, and 1940) introduced thousands of students to the field for over two decades. More important for research psychologists, his *Experimental Psychology* shaped the very definition of the term *experiment*. When the book made its initial appearance in 1938, it was already so well known that no psychologist was perplexed when the publisher announced, "The Bible is out" (Estes, 1981). As early as 1909, Woodworth had been distributing mimeographed handouts for his course in experimental methods, and by 1920 these had grown into a 285-page handout called "A Textbook in Experimental Psychology" (Winston, 1990). Columbia students who became professors used the materials in their own classes. By 1938, the eagerly anticipated volume finally appeared and was an immediate success. More than 44,000 copies were sold by 1954, when it was revised and a coauthor added (Woodworth & Schlosberg, 1954). Psychologist-historian Andrew Winston (1990) estimated that between 1938 and 1959, more than 100,000 psychology majors learned about research in psychology from Woodworth.

Woodworth's 1938 text was encyclopedic; it included more than 823 pages of text and another 36 pages of references. After an introductory chapter, it was organized into 29 different research topics, including such diverse topics as memory, transfer of training, maze learning, reaction time, hearing, visual perception, and thinking. Students using the text learned about the procedures related to each content area as well as virtually everything there was to know in 1938 about each topic. They also learned some distinctions that were to have important ramifications for future psychologists.

Before Woodworth, the term *experiment* had been used broadly as a label for procedures ranging from the introspection of a mental event to a mental test to an observation under controlled circumstances. Woodworth, however, narrowed the definition and contrasted experimental research with what he referred to as correlational research. The defining feature of the experimental method was to be the manipulation of a factor that was the main focus of study, what Woodworth called an **independent variable**, and this variable would have its effects on some measure of behavior—or as he called it, the **dependent variable**. Woodworth did not invent the terms, but he was the first psychologist to use them in this way. While the experimental method manipulates independent variables, Woodworth wrote, the correlational method "measures two or more characteristics of the same individuals [and] computes the correlation of these characteristics. This method....has no 'independent variable' but treats all the measured variables alike" (Woodworth, 1938, p. 3). Furthermore, Woodworth originated the argument, now found in the methodology chapter of every introductory text but not widely accepted during his time, that the experimental method was the only technique allowing causal conclusions; no causation could be inferred from correlations. Although Woodworth argued that correlational research should have the same overall status as experimental research, he omitted correlational findings from the remainder of the text. The reader could be excused for thinking that the experimental approach was superior. Indeed, the consequences of Woodworth's distinction were sufficient to become the focus of a cautionary APA presidential address in 1957. In "The Two Disciplines of Scientific Psychology," Lee Cronbach argued for reestablishing the status of correlational research to that of the controlled experiment.

IN PERSPECTIVE: STRUCTURALISM AND FUNCTIONALISM

Traditionally, internal histories of psychology have been organized around the concept of "schools of psychology," which referred to a broad conceptual framework that includes statements about psychology's definition, its preferred methods, and its important concepts. Thus structuralism, functionalism, Gestalt psychology (Chapter 9), behaviorism (Chapters 10 and 11), and psychoanalysis (Chapter 12) are normally considered to have been the predominant schools in psychology's history. This chapter has examined structuralism and functionalism, the former associated primarily with one man (Titchener) and the latter associated with just about everyone else in American psychology, at least during the period from 1890 to 1930, when behaviorism came to be the dominant force in American psychology.

Structuralism essentially died with Titchener, but it continues to command a substantial portion of all modern history texts and thus indicates the strength of Titchener's influence and the importance of his work. When Titchener died in 1927, E. G. Boring wrote this in an obituary for his mentor:

The death of no other psychologist could so alter the psychological picture in America. Not only was he unique among American psychologists as a personality and in his scientific attitude, but he was a cardinal point in the national systematic orientation. The clear-cut opposition between behaviorism and its allies, on the one hand, and something else, on the other, remains clear only when the opposition is between behaviorism and

Titchener, mental tests and Titchener, or applied psychology and Titchener. (Boring, 1961a, p. 246)

Boring's claim is inflated, the kind of thing likely to be found in obituaries, yet it has a ring of truth to it. As you will learn in Chapter 10, for example, John B. Watson described the advantages of behaviorism by contrasting them directly with Titchener's structuralism.

Throughout psychology's history, psychologists have been less likely to call themselves structuralists or functionalists or behaviorists and more likely to refer to themselves simply as psychologists. The "functionalists" illustrate this point perfectly. Angell, Woodworth, Thorndike, and others show why functionalism was not a dogmatic *school* of psychology but rather a set of attitudes about psychology, attitudes rooted in American pragmatic thinking and firmly grounded in evolutionary logic. These pioneers would be surprised to find themselves in a chapter on "functionalism"—like most of their peers, they considered themselves simply "psychologists" or "experimental psychologists." The same can said for those functionalists who extended their laboratory research interests into the areas of applied psychology. Their work occupies the next chapter.

SUMMARY

Titchener's Psychology: Structuralism

• E. B. Titchener earned a PhD with Wundt at Leipzig and then came to Cornell University, where he established an approach to psychology called structuralism. Its main goals were to analyze human conscious experience into its elemental units and then show how these units could be synthesized into mental processes.

• Titchener promoted an experimental laboratory approach to psychology by writing a series of highly detailed training manuals that introduced students and instructors to precise laboratory work and by forming a close-knit group of fellow male researchers called the Experimentalists, who met annually to share the details of their ongoing research.

• The main goals for a structuralist psychology, according to Titchener, were to achieve a complete analysis of the "generalized adult mind," show how elements could be combined into more complex phenomena (synthesis), and provide an explanation of mental processes by understanding the workings of the brain and nervous system.

• Titchener identified introspection as psychology's primary method and believed that introspections could yield valid data only if introspectors were highly trained and capable of the introspective habit. Training was also needed to avoid the stimulus error, a tendency to describe

a meaningful stimulus instead of the direct conscious experience of that stimulus.

• The main elements of conscious experience, according to Titchener, are sensations, images, and affects. Sensations and images have the attributes of quality, intensity, duration, and clearness, but images aren't as clear as sensations. Affects have but two qualities—pleasantness and unpleasantness—and they lack clarity.

• Titchener's primary contribution was to promote laboratory psychology. But his system omitted major topics of interest to most American psychologists, and his method of introspection was shown to be fundamentally flawed due to its lack of objectivity.

America's Psychology: Functionalism

• Most American psychologists, influenced by evolutionary theory and a generally pragmatic attitude, were interested more in the functions of consciousness than in its structure. Functionalism was widespread but mainly associated with the University of Chicago and Columbia University.

• The origins of functionalism are often traced to a paper on the reflex arc by John Dewey of Chicago. Dewey argued against the analytic strategy of reducing the reflex to its elements; instead, he said the reflex needed to be seen in its broader context as a coordinated system that served to adapt the organism to its environment. Dewey was known primarily for his progressive views on education (e.g., that students should be active learners) and for his philosophical writings on democracy.

• The earliest clear statement of the functionalist philosophy came from the 1906 APA presidential address of James Angell, who succeeded Dewey at Chicago. Angell explicitly compared structuralism and functionalism, pointing out that structuralists were more likely to ask the question "What is consciousness?" whereas functionalists were more concerned with the question "What is consciousness for?" This led the functionalists to study topics ranging from developmental to abnormal psychology and led them to be interested in individual differences and how psychology could be used to solve everyday problems.

• Angell's successor at Chicago was Harvey Carr, who brought functionalism to its maturity there. He was known for his maze-learning research and for developing Chicago into one of the country's best graduate programs.

• Functionalism at Columbia was led by James McKeen Cattell and associated with two of his students, Edward

Thorndike and Robert Woodworth. Thorndike became a leading educational psychologist, but in his early years he was known for his studies of cats in puzzle boxes. He was highly critical of contemporary comparative psychology, which relied on anecdotal evidence and was overly anthropomorphic. He studied trial-and-error learning and proposed that learning occurred through the creation of connections between situations and responses that were successful in those situations (Law of Effect) and that connections were strengthened with repetition (Law of Exercise). His debate with Mills reflected a fundamental disagreement between those advocating laboratory methods and those who preferred to study animals in their daily environments.

• Woodworth is remembered for his research with Thorndike on transfer, which called traditional educational practices into question; his dynamic psychology, which replaced an S-R model with an S-O-R framework and emphasized motivational influences on behavior; and his textbook writing, especially on methodology. His "Columbia bible" institutionalized the distinctions between experimental and correlational research and between independent and dependent variables in experimental research.

STUDY QUESTIONS

1. In his 1898 paper on structural psychology, what was the argument that Titchener made for studying structure before function?

2. Distinguish between German and American (drill course) methods for training students how to be experimental psychologists.

3. Describe the contents of Titchener's Manuals, distinguish between the qualitative and quantitative manuals, and explain the significance of the work.

4. What were the Experimentalists, why were they formed, what did they do, and why did they exclude women?

5. According to Titchener, what were psychology's three main goals?

6. Describe Titchener's version of introspection, and explain why it was so important for introspectors to be highly trained. Be sure to work the concept of the stimulus error into your answer.

7. What did Titchener conclude were the elements of human conscious experience? And what were the attributes of those elements?

8. Why did Titchener exclude the study of children, animals, and the insane from his definition of psychology?

9. Describe the imageless thought controversy, and show how it was a good illustration of the problems with introspection.

10. Show how the school of functionalism is related to evolutionary thinking.

11. Describe the main points of Dewey's reflex arc article, and discuss the significance of the article.

12. Use Angell's APA presidential address of 1906 to provide a comparison of structuralist and functionalist ways of thinking about psychology.

13. What was a "Carr maze," and what was the importance of this apparatus?

14. How did Thorndike describe the process by which cats escaped from his puzzle boxes? How did this illustrate the laws of effect and exercise?

15. Explain how Thorndike ruled out the idea that cats could learn the escape process through reasoning and imitation.

16. What was the substance of the Thorndike-Mills controversy, and what was its significance?

17. How did Thorndike and Woodworth study transfer, what did they conclude, and what were the implications of their research for the educational philosophy of the day?

18. What was the importance of Woodworth inserting an *O* between the *S* and the *R*, when describing behavior?

19. What was the significance of Woodworth's "Columbia bible"? What distinctions did he make in the book that continue to be in use today?

FOR FURTHER READING

DEWSBURY, D. A. (Ed.) (1998). History of psychology: Commemorating E. L. Thorndike. *American Psychologist*, *53*, 1121–1152.
Edited by comparative psychologist and historian Don Dewsbury; includes a reprinting of a portion of Thorndike's 1898 paper along with papers on Thorndike's, life, his influence on comparative psychology, and his influence on educational psychology.

FURUMOTO, L. (1988). Shared knowledge: The Experimentalists, 1904–1929. In J. G. Morawski (Ed.), *The rise of experimentation in American psychology* (pp. 94–113). New Haven, CT: Yale University Press.
Examines the origins and development of Titchener's Experimentalists with a focus on the consequences for female psychologists, who were excluded from the group during Titchener's lifetime and only marginally included after his death.

HEIDBREDER, E. (1933). *Seven psychologies*. New York: Appleton-Century-Crofts.
A well-known early history of psychology that gives an especially strong description of the functionalism found at Columbia, written by a woman with firsthand experience as a student of Woodworth.

WINSTON, A. S. (1990). Robert Sessions Woodworth and the "Columbia bible": How the psychological experiment was redefined. *American Journal of Psychology*, *103*, 391–401.
Documents the development and impact of Woodworth's text in experimental psychology, emphasizing how the impact of his distinction between experimental and correlational research consigned the latter to second-class status in psychology.

CHAPTER 8

APPLYING THE NEW PSYCHOLOGY

Unless our laboratory results are to give us artificialities, mere scientific curiosities, they must be subjected to interpretation by gradual approximation to the conditions of life.

—John Dewey, 1900

PREVIEW AND CHAPTER OBJECTIVES

In the discussion of historiography in Chapter 1, I pointed out that E. G. Boring's famous 1929 text, A *History of Experimental Psychology*, was written in part as a way for him to return laboratory research to what he saw as its rightful place at the forefront of American psychology. Boring's concern about the threat to "pure science" was justified—American psychologists in the 1920s seemed to be obsessed with finding new ways to apply psychological principles to everyday life. Actually, interest in application existed from the earliest days of psychology in America, and this chapter explores both the roots and the development of applied psychology. Its origins lie deeply embedded in the American character and in the economic, political, and institutional contexts of the late 19th and early 20th centuries.

This chapter examines several examples of applied psychology, starting with the mental testing movement. We will learn how Galton's approach (Chapter 5) was replaced by the strategy of Alfred Binet of France, how Binet's methods were brought to America, and how a hereditarian view of mental ability colored interpretations of intelligence. The major American mental testers discussed are James McKeen Cattell, who brought the Galton tradition to America where it quickly failed; Henry Goddard, who brought Binet's test to America where it quickly succeeded; Lewis Terman, developer of the Stanford-Binet test that institutionalized the concept of IQ; and Robert Yerkes, a comparative psychologist at heart, whose development of the Army testing program was a major reason for Boring's fear that the spread of applied psychology was a direct threat to "pure" experimental psychology.

A second major application of psychology took place in the area of business or industrial psychology. This part of the chapter features the work of Hugo Münsterberg. He earned a doctorate with Wundt, but became known for his applied work. Münsterberg also made contributions to other applied areas, especially forensic psychology. The chapter also includes briefer descriptions of the work of several other prominent industrial psychologists—Walter Dill Scott, Walter Van Dyke Bingham, Lillian Gilbreth, and Harry Hollingworth. (Clinical psychology, another major area of application, is considered in Chapters 12 and 13.) After you finish this chapter, you should be able to:

■ Understand why it was important for early American psychologists to show that their New Psychology had practical applications

- Describe Cattell's approach to mental testing and, after the Wissler study, explain why it disappeared
- Contrast Binet's individual psychology with a more "general" psychology
- Describe the origins, content, and original purpose of the Binet-Simon scales
- Describe how Binet's beliefs about mental testing and intelligence differed from those of most American psychologists
- Describe Goddard's classification scheme for the different levels of feeblemindedness
- Describe and critically analyze the Kallikak study
- Describe and critically analyze Goddard's work at Ellis Island
- Explain the differences between the original Binet-Simon scale and Terman's revision, the Stanford-Binet
- Explain how Terman's belief in meritocracy led him to investigate gifted children, and describe the findings of his research
- Describe the contributions of Leta Hollingworth to (a) gifted education and (b) understanding gender differences in ability
- Describe the origins of the Army testing program, distinguish between Alpha and Beta, and explain why the program was controversial
- Describe the contributions made by Hugo Münsterberg to applied psychology
- Distinguish between the two general strategies used by Münsterberg to improve the employee selection process
- Describe the contributions to applied psychology of Walter Dill Scott, Walter Van Dyke Bingham, Lillian Gilbreth, and Harry Hollingworth

THE DESIRE FOR APPLICATION

In 1895, Yale psychologist E. W. Scripture published *Thinking, Feeling, Doing*, a book intended to explain the new experimental psychology to the general public. He wrote in the preface that he hoped his effort would "be taken as evidence of the attitude of the science in its desire to serve humanity" (Scripture, 1895, p. iii). Perhaps to hold the reader's interest, he included 209 photos and drawings in the 295 pages of text. Most of the book described the basic laboratory procedures in vogue at the time—psychophysics, reaction time, basic sensory processes, and so on. What was unusual, however, was Scripture's attempt to convince readers that basic laboratory methods could improve everyday life. For example, after describing reaction-time research, Scripture pointed out that the method could be used to study the "psychological elements involved in sports, gymnastics, and all sorts of athletic work" (p. 57). He then proceeded to illustrate the point by adapting the reaction procedures to measure the reaction times involved in such activities as boxing, track, and even fencing (Figure 8.1), thereby making him an early pioneer in what today is called sport psychology (Goodwin, 2009). He used a similar approach for other standard laboratory methods, as evident from these captions describing some of the photos found in the book:

> Recording a Sportsman's Unsteadiness
>
> Everyone is Somewhat Deaf. Finding the Threshold of Intensity
>
> Taking an Orchestra Leader's Record [of rhythmic action] with the Electric Baton

FIGURE 8.1   Photo from Scripture's *Thinking, Feeling, Doing* (1895) designed to show how reaction-time methodology can improve the performance of fencers.

That Scripture believed it necessary to convince the public of psychology's usefulness is just one example of the pressures for application felt by all of the early American psychologists. John Dewey (Chapter 7) recognized these pressures explicitly in an APA presidential address (1900), when he warned of the dangers inherent in emphasizing pure laboratory research. It could "give us artificialities, mere scientific curiosities [unless] subjected to interpretation by gradual approximation to the conditions of life" (p. 119). Four years later, in his own APA presidential address, entitled "Theory and Practice," William Lowe Bryan (1904) made a plea for the value of applying the results of theory-based psychological research to improve everyday life.

The interest in application was partly the consequence of American pragmatism, combined with the progressive drive for reform that infused the early 20th century. In an age of dramatic technological change, Americans were becoming accustomed to the idea that science should be used to improve their lives. In the last few decades of the 19th century, they had witnessed the arrival of such inventions as telephones, the telegraph, typewriters, electric lights (and chairs), skyscrapers, barbed wire, and the kinetoscope (for showing moving pictures). Railroads had expanded so dramatically that by 1900, virtually everyone in America lived within hearing distance of a train. The 35,000 miles of track that existed at the close of the Civil War had expanded to 193,000 miles by 1903 (Cashman, 1993). In the eyes of the public at that time, technology meant progress, and progress meant a better life. For psychology to gain public support, it needed to produce useful results.

In addition to the public expectation that science ought to be practical, psychologists at the turn of the century faced institutional pressures for application. Most psychologists still taught within larger departments of philosophy, for instance, and while the philosophers needed little more than an adequate library budget and space for a decent office with a comfortable armchair, the psychologists among them needed funds for equipment and physical space for their laboratories. To justify the costs to skeptical administrators, psychologists had to show that their new science would bring credit to the university by being helpful to society.

The stress on application created strong internal conflicts for many laboratory psychologists. Most had been trained to do basic laboratory research, conditioned to value the pursuit of knowledge for its own sake. They were also aware of the dangers inherent in promising more than they could hope to deliver. Yet reality forced them to adjust their activities toward application. For one thing, while laboratories proliferated in the decades before and after 1900, those with doctorates in laboratory psychology grew at an even faster rate. Historian John O'Donnell (1985) pointed out that in 1894 the number of psychology PhDs just about matched the number of available American laboratories, thus providing adequate employment opportunities for psychological scientists. By 1900, however, the number of PhDs outnumbered labs by three to one (90 to 33 by O'Donnell's count). Thus not everyone was going to find the ideal job—directing the university's psychology laboratory. Developing expertise as an applied psychologist enhanced one's résumé and put bread on the table.

Some psychologists embraced the idea of using their laboratory training for applied ends, but others were torn by the belief that by engaging in applied work, they were somehow "selling out" their "pure laboratory" principles. For many, the selling was literal because low academic salaries forced them to supplement their income. Taking on extra courses and teaching in the summer were shortcuts to burnout, however, and only minimally useful in easing the financial burden. Hence, many psychologists adjusted their priorities and engaged in the more remunerative activities associated with applied psychology. The experience of Harry Hollingworth illustrates the dilemma. Although he became known as a leading applied psychologist, near the end of his life he wrote that he became one only to earn a living. His "real interest, now and always, has been in the purely theoretical and descriptive problems of my science, and the books, among the twenty I have written, of which I am the proudest, are the . . . ones which nobody reads" (quoted in Poffenberger, 1957, p. 138).

Applied psychologists contributed their expertise to the areas of education, business, medicine, and the law. One activity common to all of these areas is mental testing. Because psychological testing, especially intelligence testing, is a controversial issue even today, the early history of this movement is worth examining in some detail.

THE MENTAL TESTING MOVEMENT

Mental testing has its origins in the attempts by Galton to measure individual differences. As you recall from Chapter 5, one of his goals was to create measures that could identify those best able to further his eugenic vision. He believed that mental ability was inherited and that it was important to encourage procreation among the able and discourage it among those less capable. Galton's attitudes were shared by many American psychologists and later caused controversy that continues to the present day. The strongest American supporter of Galton in the 19th century was Cattell.

James McKeen Cattell (1860–1944): An American Galton

You met James McKeen Cattell briefly in Chapter 4. His research on reaction time in Wundt's laboratory was representative of the technique of estimating the duration of mental events by "complicating" the reaction-time procedure. Cattell earned a doctorate from Wundt, although as you recall from the Chapter 4 Close-Up, he did not hold a high opinion of Wundt's research operation. Instead, Cattell was enthusiastic about Galton's work in mental testing and the study of individual differences, and he imported the Briton's ideas to America.

FIGURE 8.2   James McKeen Cattell as an intense young professor at Columbia. From Popplestone and McPherson (1994).

Cattell (Figure 8.2) was raised in an academic environment similar to James Angell's—both had college presidents for fathers. Cattell's father presided over Lafayette College in Pennsylvania. Young Cattell was schooled at home and then sent to Lafayette at age 16. There he found the type of education mentioned at the outset of Chapter 6—an emphasis on shaping students to reflect Protestant values (Presbyterian, in this case) and a curriculum based in Scottish Realist philosophy, with its focus on strengthening the productive and moral faculties. Cattell breezed through, graduating with honors in 1880. One lasting impact of this education resulted from courses taught by Francis Marsh, a well-known philologist (i.e., studied the nature and history of language). Marsh was a dyed-in-the-wool Baconian inductivist who believed in the importance of collecting data exhaustively and assumed that when sufficient data were at hand, significant patterns and general conclusions would emerge (Sokal, 1987). Cattell embraced this strategy, which prepared him to be awed by another Baconian, Francis Galton.

After graduating from Lafayette, Cattell traveled in Europe for a time and then spent a year (1882–1883) with Hall at Johns Hopkins, where he began the reaction-time research that he would continue at Leipzig. In one of his studies, he measured the times taken to identify different letters, which led him to make the practical suggestion that the shapes of those letters taking the longest time to recognize should be altered to improve their legibility. Using himself as the only subject, Cattell also studied the effects of various drugs on behavior and consciousness and later wrote that the amounts of caffeine, morphine, hashish, and opium he ingested were "perhaps the largest doses ever taken without suicidal intent" (quoted in Sokal, 1971, p. 623).

Cattell planned to stay in Baltimore and complete a doctorate with Hall, but after a year his fellowship was not renewed; instead, it was given to another promising student, John Dewey (Chapter 7). A rather miffed Cattell left Johns Hopkins, returned to Europe, entered studies with Wundt, and completed his doctorate in 1886. While at Leipzig, he continued his reaction-time research—in keeping with his Baconian principles, he compiled extensive data on the effects of such factors as attention, practice, and fatigue on reaction time (Sokal, 1987).

After completing the doctorate, Cattell went to England and briefly studied medicine at Cambridge. There he was exposed to Galton's anthropometric testing, and his life was changed. Cattell never studied formally with Galton, but the two met, and for some time after they exchanged correspondence. Cattell later wrote that Galton was the greatest man he had ever known. The two shared the fundamental inductive belief that the more one could measure, the more one would know.

Cattell returned to America in 1889, after being appointed professor of psychology at the University of Pennsylvania. The title was unusual at a time when most psychologists were still considered professors of philosophy, and it indicated the changes just starting to occur within departments of philosophy. Cattell quickly established a laboratory and set out to continue his reaction-time studies and bring Galton's testing approach to America. In an 1890 article in the British journal *Mind*, he summarized the results of testing Penn students on 10 different tests (Cattell, 1890/1948b). Some were borrowed from Galton, but Cattell eliminated the strictly physical measurements (e.g., height, weight, length of arm span), which led him to call his article "Mental Tests and Measurements." With this article, Cattell coined the term **mental test**.

The article's opening sentence revealed Cattell's inductivism: "Psychology cannot attain the certainty and exactness of the physical sciences, unless it rests on a foundation of experiment and measurement" (Cattell, 1890/1948b, p. 347). He did not propose any specific purpose for the tests, merely indicating in vague terms that people might "find their tests interesting" (p. 347) and that the results might somehow be "useful in regard to training, mode of life or indication of disease" (p. 347). The 10 tests, which Cattell estimated to take an hour, are summarized briefly in Table 8.1.

TABLE 8.1   Cattell's Mental Tests

In his article on mental tests, Cattell (1890/1948b) described these procedures.

1. *Dynamometer pressure.* A measure of grip strength, which Cattell believed to be more than just a physical measure; mental effort and concentration were involved.

2. *Rate of movement.* How quickly one's hand could move across a 50-cm interval was determined; Cattell believed that mental effort and concentration also contributed to this measure.

3. *Sensation-areas.* Two-point thresholds on the back of the right hand were measured.

4. *Pressure causing pain.* The narrow (5 mm in radius) tip of hard rubber pressed into forehead until pain was reported.

5. *Least noticeable difference in weight.* Traditional psychophysics procedure involving the lifting of small boxes that differed slightly in weight.

6. *Reaction time for sound.* For Cattell, the most reliable variety of reaction time.

7. *Time for naming colors.* 10 colored papers pasted adjacent to each other, to be named as quickly as possible.

8. *Bisection of a 50-cm line.* A movable line vertically adjusted until it was at a perceived midpoint of a horizontal line.

9. *Judgment of 10-sec time.* Experimenter tapped a pencil twice, with 10 sec between; those being tested had to repeat the task.

10. *Number of letters repeated on once hearing.* This was an early version of a short-term memory test, to determine how many letters could be repeated verbatim.

Cattell spent just 2 years at Penn before accepting (at a still youthful age of 31) an offer to head the psychology program at Columbia, where he remained until being fired in 1917. At Columbia, his testing plans became even more ambitious as he expanded the number of tests and reinstated some of Galton's physical measurements. Within a few years, he was lobbying the authorities for permission to test every incoming Columbia freshman, suggesting that the results could be useful "to determine the condition and progress of students, the relative value of different courses of study, etc." (quoted in Sokal, 1987, p. 32).

For the remaining years of the 1890s, Cattell and his students accumulated masses of data, but the project collapsed shortly after the turn of the century. Cattell, who was mathematically inept, had learned of Galton's correlational procedures and their development by Karl Pearson into the "coefficient of correlation" (Pearson's r). He asked one of his graduate students, Clark Wissler, to apply the new technique to the testing results, hoping to reveal strong mathematical relationships between the measures and to relate them to academic performance. Wissler completed the correlations, and the outcome was devastating for Cattell—the tests were unrelated to each other (e.g., the correlation between reaction-time color naming was a meager +.15) and, more critically, they did not correlate with academic performance (e.g., a correlation of +.02 between reaction time and "college standing"). A student's performance in class (including gym!) correlated more highly with overall academic performance than did any of Cattell's tests. If the mental tests were unrelated to academics, which presumably reflected mental ability, then how could the tests be said to measure such ability? Wissler (1901/1965 concluded:

> In general it appears that correlations in any of the foregoing tests are not of a degree sufficient for practical purposes. We do not learn much of an individual by any one or any group of them. It appears that we are dealing here with special and quite independent abilities and that the importance attributed to such measurements of elementary processes by many investigators is not justified in this case. (p. 444)

It is worth noting that Wissler might not have had to make his conclusion so dire. The famous British statistician Charles Spearman (1863–1945) completed his own studies of sensory ability and school performance, and found correlations close to +.40—modest, but much stronger than anything found by Wissler. Spearman knew of Wissler's results and concluded that Wissler's measurements were not high in reliability, in part because of problems with the methods used to collect the data (Spearman, 1904). Spearman was the first to show that unreliable measures result in correlations that underestimate the true strength of a relationship. He also developed a statistical technique (a "correction for attenuation") to estimate the true correlation if the exact reliability coefficients are known (Fancher, 1985).

After the Wissler debacle, Cattell turned his attention away from mental testing research and toward another of his interests, the professionalizing of psychology. A charter member of the American Psychological Association, he was an active participant and, in 1895, its fourth president. In 1894, he helped to launch what would become one of psychology's more prestigious journals, *Psychological Review*, and a year later he took over the editorship of the financially ailing journal *Science* and rejuvenated it. By 1910, he had transformed *Science* into the most important scientific journal published in America (Sokal, 1981a).

After the turn of the century, Cattell devoted most of his time to editorial and departmental administrative work. Always outspoken, he regularly irritated the Columbia administration by arguing for greater faculty participation in academic decision making and for increased academic freedom (i.e., a faculty member's right to investigate and teach about controversial topics). In 1917, he finally pushed the administration over the edge by publicly protesting the government's policy of sending conscientious objectors into combat in World War I. Columbia's president accused him of treason and fired him. Cattell also had alienated many of his peers over the years, so he received little faculty support (Sokal, 2009). Cattell sued Columbia for libel and won a large settlement, but his academic career was over. He continued his editorial work, though, and returned to applied psychology by founding the Psychological Corporation in 1921. Designed to be an organization of psychologist-consultants, it began at a time when American psychologists had high expectations for the applicability of their knowledge. Cattell proved to be a poor administrator, however, and although the Psychological Corporation exists today as a profitable subsidiary of a major publishing house, it barely survived the 1920s under Cattell's leadership (Sokal, 1981b).

Alfred Binet (1857–1911): The Birth of Modern Intelligence Testing

The Galton-Cattell strategy for assessing individual differences relied on physical measurements and the results of simple sensory and perceptual tasks. A completely different approach, which focused on more complex mental phenomena and used children rather than college students or adults as subjects, developed in Europe. One pioneer was Hermann Ebbinghaus, the famous memory researcher (Chapter 4), who developed a **completion test** in the mid-1890s as a way to assess the effects of mental fatigue in schoolchildren. He was responding to a practical problem—authorities in the German city of Breslau believed that the 5-hour uninterrupted morning school session was producing "fatigue and nervous irritability" (Ebbinghaus, 1897/1965, p. 433). City leaders appointed a commission to study how this 5-hour school day affected children. Some research in the Galtonian tradition used two-point thresholds as a measure, finding that changes in the thresholds occurred during the course of the school day. Ebbinghaus was unimpressed with the method, however, questioning the connection between skin sensitivity and school performance: "Are children who show a deterioration [in sensitivity] also to be regarded as mentally exhausted in other respects, or have they merely become incapable of performing that fixed, relatively insignificant task to which they are not accustomed?" (p. 435). If the goal was to assess mental fatigue, he argued, then the measures ought to be of cognitive activities, not sensory ones. Assuming that an important aspect of intellectual ability involves taking incomplete information and forming it into a comprehensible whole, Ebbinghaus came up with the idea of giving students incomplete prose passages—they were shown sentences that had syllables missing from words and words missing from sentences and asked to fill in the gaps to make the sentences complete and meaningful. Ebbinghaus found that his completion tests distinguished between strong and weak students, but he found no consistent differences in performance over the 5-hour school day, which remained intact.

Ebbinghaus did not develop his testing program further, but another European, Alfred Binet of France, took the same approach. Like Ebbinghaus, Binet was responding to an educational dilemma. Compulsory education had arrived in France, but some children lacked the ability to succeed in normal classes. By the turn of the century, school officials in Paris were faced with the problem of how to identify these children so they could be placed in

FIGURE 8.3 Alfred Binet, with his wife and the two daughters whose development he studied. From Popplestone and McPherson (1994).

what would later be called special education classes. In 1904, a commission was formed to study the problem; it included Binet, one of France's leading psychologists.

Binet's status among his peers was not always so high. In the mid-1880s, he published some dubious research on hypnosis, claiming that hysteric symptoms displayed in that state could be transferred from one side of the body to another by reversing the polarity of a magnet held next to the patient. More sober researchers demonstrated that the effects were the result of suggestion, and an embarrassed Binet was forced to retract his claim in print. He gradually resurrected his reputation, however, after becoming a research assistant at the Laboratory of Physiological Psychology at the Sorbonne in Paris in 1891 and eventually being named director, a position he held until his premature death in 1911 at the age of 54.

Even before starting his work at the Sorbonne, Binet had begun making careful observations of his two young daughters (Figure 8.3). The work shaped his belief in the value of conducting detailed case studies, and it contributed to his lifelong interest in studying and measuring individual differences. Binet was aware of Galton's work and used some of Galton's sensory tests on his daughters. He was surprised to discover that there didn't seem to be much difference between his daughters' scores and the scores reported for adults. Adults appeared to be superior only on tasks that involved mental processing that went beyond sensory capacity. For example, compared with adults, his daughters did quite poorly on color naming, a task requiring memory and language, but very well on color matching, a purely perceptual task. These and other similar results led Binet to conclude that Galton's sensory measures were inadequate to assess age differences in mental ability.[1] He concluded that differences between the intellects of children and adults could be determined only by examining the more complex higher mental processes (Fancher, 1985).

---

[1]Cattell, during the time he was deeply immersed in his Galtonian program of testing at Columbia in the 1890s, knew about Binet's work but rejected the new tests of "higher" mental processes as poorly defined and not capable of sufficient quantification (Sokal, 1987).

During his years at the Sorbonne, Binet developed a research program centered on studying individual differences. In an important paper coauthored with his assistant Victor Henri, he contrasted this **individual psychology** with a more general psychology. The latter is concerned with the discovery of general laws that apply to some degree to everyone (e.g., repetition strengthens memory), while individual psychology "studies the properties of psychic processes that vary from individual to individual—it has to determine the various properties and then study how much and in what ways they vary with the individuals" (Binet & Henri, 1895/1965, p. 428). Studying these differences required being able to measure them, of course, and that problem led Binet directly to his attempts to develop tests of mental processes. By 1904, when Paris school officials needed a way to identify students with low ability for special classes, Binet already had some definite ideas about what kinds of tests to use.

The term *retarded* did not exist as a category of mental disability in Binet's time. Instead, children with limited capacity were divided into three overlapping and poorly defined categories. *Idiots* were severely handicapped and not capable of caring for themselves; *imbeciles* were somewhat more capable but still not able to be independent; the third level included children capable of learning, but not in normal school classes. These were the children to be identified for special education, and Binet labeled them *débiles*, or "weak ones." He was appalled at the manner in which existing diagnostic labels were applied (three doctors examining the same child would often produce three diagnoses—idiot, imbecile, or débile) and determined to develop a more reliable way of differentiating these "weak" children from normal schoolchildren. He drew on a dozen years of his research into individual psychology, and the result was the first intelligence test.

The Binet-Simon Scales   Along with his research assistant Theodore Simon, Binet published the first version of his test in 1905. They revised it 3 years later and again in 1911, just before Binet's death. Rather than starting with a preconceived definition of intelligence, they developed the test empirically by identifying two groups of students, one normal and one impaired, and then giving each group a series of tests that appeared to be conceptually related to intelligence, looking for tests that differentiated between the groups. They eventually produced a series of 30 tests of increasing difficulty for their original 1905 test. By the 1908 revision, the number of tests grew to 58, and Binet and Simon incorporated age levels between 3 and 13. Table 8.2 lists some of the tests at different ages (note the contrast with Cattell's tests in Table 8.1).

Creating average performance at different age levels was Binet's way of solving the diagnosis problem. He believed that subnormal children could be defined in terms of how far behind they were in years. Thus a normal 5-year-old could solve the tasks at the 5-year level, but a subnormal 5-year-old might be able to score only at the 4-year level. The child's score identified what Binet called a **mental level**. He believed that children scoring at a mental level 2 years behind their actual age, a group he estimated to include 7% of the population, should be considered débiles and placed in special classes (Fancher, 1985). In general, Binet defined mental ability in functional terms as the faculty of "judgment, otherwise called good sense, practical sense, initiative, the faculty of adapting one's self to circumstances. To judge well, to understand well, to reason well—these are the essential wellsprings of intelligence" (Binet & Simon, 1916, p. 44).

TABLE 8.2 A Sample of Binet and Simon's Tests of Mental Levels

The 1908 revision of the Binet-Simon scale contained 58 different tests, arranged within 11 different age levels (3–13). Here are some of the tests.

Three Years
show eyes, nose, mouth
repeat 6-syllable sentence
name objects in picture

Five Years
copy a square
compare 2 boxes, different wts.
repeat 10-syllable sentence

Seven Years
copy written sentence
repeat five digits
indicate omissions in drawings

Nine Years
name days of week
retain 6 memories after reading
arrange five weights in order

Eleven Years
criticize absurd sentences*
place 3 given words in a sentence
give abstract definitions

Thirteen Years
differentiate word meanings
solve reversed triangle problem
solve paper cutting problem

*For example: The body of an unfortunate girl was found, cut into 18 pieces. It is thought that she killed herself.
Source: Dennis (1948).

In light of how the concept of IQ evolved over the years, it is worth noting Binet's attitudes about intelligence and its measurement. First, he believed that intelligence was multifaceted, composed of a variety of skills. Thus, while he reduced the outcome of the tests to a single unit—mental level—he did so reluctantly. Had he lived, he would have been disturbed at how the concept of IQ came to connote a unitary concept of intelligence. Second, he believed that within broad limits, mental levels could increase with training, and he developed a set of mental "orthopedics" to help children improve their mental levels. Binet was scornful of the prevailing opinion of his day, derived from evolutionary thinking, that intelligence was a fixed and unchangeable trait. Third, Binet believed that his scale was useful only within the narrow educational context of identifying weak students. He would have been surprised at how quickly the tool became much more widely used, as we are about to see.

Henry H. Goddard (1866–1957): Binet's Test Comes to America

Henry Goddard (Figure 8.4) was a product of Hall's genetic psychology at Clark University, earning a doctorate there in 1899. After a few years of teaching, he accepted an invitation from the Vineland Training School for the Feeble-Minded in southern New Jersey to develop a research program there. His initial efforts reflected his training—he set up a laboratory in imitation of the one he knew at Clark and began testing the children using standard laboratory tasks similar to the ones being used by Cattell. Goddard quickly learned that in his new nonacademic environment, using basic sensory tasks was easier said than done. His notes contain entries such as this: "A boy frightened at an insignificant thing so that it took six men to hold him could not squeeze a pound on the Dynamometer tho he clearly understood what was wanted" (quoted in Popplestone & McPherson, 1984, p. 242).

In search of better methods, Goddard discovered Binet's work while on a European tour of institutions for the feebleminded in 1908. He brought back the Binet-Simon scale, translated it into English, and began administering it to the Vineland children. When the results matched the expectations based on other observations of the children, Goddard became a convert. At a 1910 meeting of the American Association of the Feeble-Minded, he reported the results of testing 400 Vineland children and proposed a classification system based on Binet's mental level concept, which was now being called **mental age**. Idiots would now be defined as those scoring at mental ages 1 to 2 on the scale, and imbeciles would be those with mental ages between 3 and 7. As for the third category, Binet's débile, Goddard proposed a new name. These children had sometimes been called feebleminded, but that term was also used to describe the entire spectrum of mental retardation. Yet it was important to have a clearly defined category for these children, Goddard argued, "to help the general public

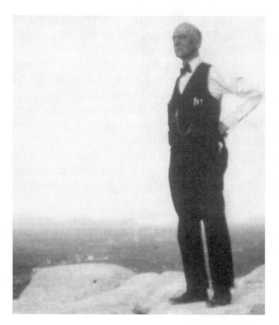

FIGURE 8.4 Henry Goddard, atop one of the pyramids of Egypt. From Popplestone and McPherson (1994).

understand that they are a special group and require special treatment,—in institutions where possible" (Goddard, 1910, p. 395). Goddard proposed the term **moron**, from the Greek word *moronia*, which means "foolish." These would be people with mental ages between 8 and 12.[2] Goddard's creation of the term and his promotion of its use helped to legitimize psychology as a professional discipline. Morons were believed to be responsible for many of society's ills, but to the average person they appeared to be normal, Goddard argued. To identify them, therefore, society needed the help of highly trained experts. Psychologists such as Goddard made it clear that they were the ones best prepared for the role, and mental tests were the proper tools to make the diagnoses.

Over the next few years, Goddard championed the Binet-Simon tests, and many others were soon using it to identify and classify those with limited mental capacity. Vineland distributed about 20,000 copies of Goddard's translated Binet-Simon test between 1910 and 1914 (Watson & Evans, 1991). Goddard's ultimate goals, however, were very different from Binet's. Unlike Binet, Goddard was a strong believer in the notion that intelligence was inherited and represented a fixed quantity. Well aware of the recent rediscovery of Mendel's work on genetics, Goddard came to believe that most feeblemindedness was caused by a single recessive gene. To support his hereditarian case, he published the results of a seemingly conclusive study of the family roots of one of the Vineland children.

The Kallikaks   Goddard made his case that feeblemindedness had a genetic basis in a brief 117-page book published in 1912 called *The Kallikak Family: A Study in the Heredity of Feeblemindedness*. In it he described a genealogical study of one of his wards at Vineland. "Deborah Kallikak" (Figure 8.5) was 22 at the time and had lived at Vineland for 14 years.

FIGURE 8.5   Deborah Kallikak at Vineland.

---

[2]Clearly, a 12-year-old with a mental age of 12 would be normal. In assigning mental ages for his classification scheme, Goddard (1910) asked readers to assume the subjects involved were about age 20. Thus a 20-year-old with a mental age of 12 or below would definitely be subnormal.

She had been referred to Vineland when she was 8, supposedly because she "did not get along well at school and might possibly be feebleminded" (Goddard, 1912, p. 1). In reality, the refusal of her mother's third husband to provide support for several of the woman's younger children, including Deborah, contributed to the placement. At Vineland, Deborah was tested periodically with the Binet-Simon scales, never achieving a mental age greater than 9 years. Goddard considered her to be an illustration of the person ideally suited for Vineland. Although she had learned to sew, cook, and do competent woodworking, she struggled to read or do math. If Deborah were to leave the safe and controlled environment of Vineland, Goddard believed,

> she would at once become a prey to the designs of evil men or women and would lead a life that would be vicious, immoral, and criminal, though because of her mentality she herself would not be responsible. There is nothing that she might not be led into, because she has no power of control, and all her instincts and appetites are in the direction that would lead to vice. (p. 12)

How could one account for such an individual? For Goddard the answer was simple: "'Heredity'—bad stock. We must recognize that the human family shows varying stocks or strains that are as marked and breed as true as anything in plant or animal life" (Goddard, 1912, p. 12).

Goddard routinely sent workers into the field to gather information about the backgrounds of those referred to Vineland. In Deborah's case, it soon became clear that many relatives lived close by and that the family was "notorious for the number of defectives and delinquents it had produced" (Goddard, 1912, p. 16). Goddard's diligent assistants were able to trace back several generations and "an appalling amount of defectiveness was everywhere found" (p. 16). On the other hand, field-workers occasionally found themselves among relatives who were highly educated and living in comfortable environments—doctors, lawyers, and educators. Further digging yielded a tale of a family that had branched in two decidedly different directions.

It seemed that a distant relative, a soldier in the Revolutionary War, behaved like soldiers sometimes do and had a brief affair with a young "feebleminded" girl that he met in a tavern. The result was a feebleminded son, Deborah's great-great grandfather, and the start of a long line of mental deficiency, the "bad" Kallikaks. Meanwhile, the soldier, unaware of the havoc he had created by sowing his wild oats, settled down, married "a respectable girl of good family" (p. 29), and began producing the "good" Kallikaks. Because the unfortunate girl at the tavern gave her young son the father's name, both sides of family bore the same surname.

Upon examining the Kallikaks, Goddard uncovered a stark contrast in the fates of those representing the two sides of the family. On the "bad" side, Goddard's field-workers identified 480 descendants and, on the basis of historical records, family histories, and some direct testing of living relatives, classified 189 of them; 143 were found to be feebleminded while only 46 were normal. On the other hand, the descendants of the soldier and his respectable bride tended to be pillars of the community: doctors, lawyers, educators, and so on. Of 496 descendants, only three were found to be "somewhat degenerate, but . . . not [mentally] defective" (p. 29).

Despite the thoroughness of the Kallikak study, it was seriously flawed. The most critical problem was Goddard's failure to recognize environmental effects. Nutritional and health care differences alone could have accounted for the large differences between the groups in infant mortality: 82 (bad side) versus just 15 (good side). Rather than a case study of the genetics of feeblemindedness, then, the Kallikak study could just as easily represent a case study of the differential effects of poverty and privilege. Goddard himself was of course highly intelligent; his inability to believe that the environment was important in the Kallikak family histories says more about the powerful influence of the contemporary historical context than it does about his individual shortcomings. Indeed, the strong belief that intelligence level was a consequence of heredity, taken for granted by most turn-of-the-century psychologists, even led Goddard to argue that the environments of the two groups were about the same.

Goddard's bias also affected the way he interpreted his data. Much of the information about family members was secondhand and sketchy, and ambiguous events were interpreted according to whether the person was on one side of the family or the other. Also, any Kallikak from the "bad" side with questionable morals or a criminal record, but without other evidence of feeblemindedness, was nonetheless classified as moronic by Goddard and his assistants. And at the very beginning of the story, Goddard merely assumed that the girl in the tavern was feebleminded, apparently on the questionable grounds that she was in a tavern and let herself be seduced by a soldier! Goddard claimed that he had independent evidence of the girl's feeblemindedness, but meticulous archival work by his biographer failed to substantiate the claim (Zenderland, 1998). In short, the Kallikak study, rather than being good science, is a classic illustration of how preconception can influence the both collection and the interpretation of data.

The name Kallikak was a pseudonym, of course, constructed by Goddard to protect Deborah's identity. He chose the name from two Greek words—*kalos*, meaning "good," and *kakos*, meaning "bad." He thought the name nicely captured the two sides of the unfortunate Deborah's family.

Goddard's conviction about the cause of mental defectiveness led him to an obvious solution to the problem—eliminate the gene. Hence, Goddard became a confirmed eugenicist, arguing that the mentally defective should be prevented from breeding. If this social engineering could be accomplished, then feeblemindedness would be eliminated in just a few generations. Goddard's main recommendation was that states build more institutions like Vineland, so that idiots, imbeciles, and morons could be properly diagnosed, removed from society, and prevented from having children by being carefully monitored. He also supported other prominent psychologists, including Thorndike, Terman, and Yerkes, in recommending the sterilization of the mentally unfit, pointing out that "the operation itself is almost as simple in males as having a tooth pulled. In females it is not much more serious" (Goddard, 1912, p. 108). Sterilization was a relatively new procedure, however, so Goddard advised caution until its long-term effects were better known.[3]

Thus Goddard had a plan for dealing with feeblemindedness in America. But what about the importation of mental deficiency? In the early years of the new century, there was growing concern about an apparent threat to the American gene pool—rampant immigration. Goddard had a solution to this problem also.

---

[3]The Kallikak study came under fire in the 1920s for its neglect of environmental factors, but the book (translated as *Die Familie Kallikak*) was quite influential in Nazi Germany in the 1930s. The Nazis, of course, were enthusiastic about eugenics; when they started killing people, they started with the so-called feebleminded, not with the Jews.

Goddard and the Immigrants   The United States has always been a nation of immigrants, but a regular feature of American political life is that immigrants who have lived in America for a few generations often seek to restrict new immigration. This was true at the turn of the century when the number of immigrants increased dramatically, and these "new" immigrants seemed to be decidedly inferior to "old" immigrants. Throughout most of the 19th century, the majority of immigrants came from western and northern Europe. For instance, 788,992 hopeful men, women, and children arrived in 1882; of these 87% were from Germany, Great Britain, and Scandinavia, whereas a mere 13% were from southern and eastern European countries such as Italy, Poland, and Russia. By 1907, however, when the total number of arrivals grew to 1,285,349, the proportions had reversed—just over 80% now came from southern and eastern Europe (data from Cashman, 1993). Most of the immigrants settled in, and began to influence the nature of, urban areas—by 1910, at least 70% of the populations of several large cities (e.g., Boston, Chicago, Detroit, New York) were immigrants and their children (Pegram, 1998). With this shift came increased fears among those whose ancestors had arrived earlier about the "quality" of the new immigrants. The old immigrants, generally Anglo-Saxon, Protestant, and at least moderately well-educated, contrasted strongly with the new immigrants, who were generally poor and uneducated, had larger families, were more culturally diverse, and were likely to be Catholic or Jewish. Most Americans simply disagreed with the sentiments of the poet Emma Lazarus, who wrote that the Statue of Liberty, unveiled in 1886, symbolized a welcome to "your tired, your poor, your huddled masses yearning to breathe free."

New York was the main entry point for European immigrants. To handle the growing numbers of huddled masses, the federal government in 1892 built a large immigration station on Ellis Island, a mile southwest of Manhattan and within sight of the Statue of Liberty. Immigrants arriving there, as many as 10,000 a day in the early 1900s, had to go through a series of evaluations before being allowed to enter the country.[4] Most immigrants passed through the Ellis Island inspections in a few hours, but about 20% were held for more detailed evaluations, and 1 to 2% were not allowed into the country (Schlereth, 1991). To be admitted, immigrants had to show that they were free from contagious diseases and mental illness, physically capable of working, not completely destitute, and not mentally defective. This latter criterion was difficult to measure, however, and Ellis Island examiners were concerned that "high-grade" defectives were slipping through the system.

In this context Goddard, anxious to demonstrate the diagnostic usefulness of the Binet tests, appeared on the scene. He first visited Ellis Island in 1911 and then returned with two research assistants in 1912. By assigning one of his assistants to pick out immigrants who "looked" defective and a second to administer some of the Binet tests, Goddard contended that his team could quickly identify mental defectives with about 90% accuracy. In one instance, Goddard's workers selected a young boy suspected of being defective and gave him the test with the aid of an interpreter. The boy scored an 8 on the Binet-Simon scale. Goddard reported that the "interpreter said 'I could not have done that when I came to this country,' and seemed to think the test unfair. We convinced him that the boy was defective" (Goddard, 1913, p. 105). Clearly, because of his faith in the technology of testing, Goddard

---

[4]When ships carrying immigrants arrived in New York harbor, only those passengers traveling in "steerage" (i.e., poor) were transported to Ellis Island for examination. Immigrants traveling first or second class were briefly examined in their cabins on the ship and then allowed to enter the city (Richardson, 2003).

FIGURE 8.6   Perplexed immigrants being processed at Ellis Island.

failed to consider that the immigrants were undoubtedly intimidated and confused by the entire Ellis Island experience (Figure 8.6 seems to capture this) and that they probably failed to understand why they were being asked to complete these odd tests.

Some physicians working at Ellis Island objected that the Binet tests, being highly verbal, were inadequate for detecting feeblemindedness (Richardson, 2003). Nonetheless, officials at Ellis Island were impressed enough to invite Goddard to expand his operation. In 1913, two female assistants spent 2-1/2 months at Ellis Island. Through interpreters, they tested 165 Russian, Hungarian, Jewish, and Italian immigrants on the Binet-Simon and several other tests. Goddard found that a disturbingly large proportion, about 80%, scored at a mental level of 12 or below (i.e., morons). Even after readjusting the scores to take cultural factors into account, he estimated that about 40% of the sample was feebleminded and concluded that "one can hardly escape the conviction that the intelligence of the average 'third class' immigrant is low, perhaps of moron grade" (Goddard, 1917, p. 243).

As a result of Goddard's work, mental testing became a part of the screening process at Ellis Island, perhaps contributing to an increase in the percentage of deportations over the next few years. In 1913, for example, 555 people were deported on the grounds of being feebleminded—triple the number deported in each of the previous 5 years (Richardson, 2003). No accurate estimate exists, but it is safe to say that during the second decade of the 20th century, hundreds of hopeful immigrants, yearning to breathe free, were nonetheless sent back to Europe because they performed poorly on the Binet-Simon tests.

As for Goddard, he remained at Vineland for only a few more years. In 1918, the state of Ohio hired him to direct its Bureau of Juvenile Research, which had just been established to deal with the problem of juvenile delinquency. Four years later, he became professor of abnormal and clinical psychology at The Ohio State University, where he remained until his retirement in 1938. While there, Goddard broadened his interests by studying children at the other end of the spectrum from those at Vineland—gifted students. These later experiences led him to write a remarkable paper in 1928, in which he reversed many of his earlier views. He decided that a mental age of 12 did not necessarily mean feeblemindedness, that many of those diagnosed as morons could function in society and did not need to be institutionalized, and that the danger of them producing feebleminded offspring had been overstated. He considered the problem of the moron to be primarily one of education and argued that "when we get an education that is entirely right there will be no morons who cannot manage themselves and their affairs and compete in the struggle for existence" (Goddard, 1928, p. 224). By the end of his career, then, Goddard had moved closer to Binet's original vision for educating those of marginal ability.

Lewis M. Terman (1877–1956): Institutionalizing IQ

Like Goddard, Lewis Terman was a product of Hall's psychology program at Clark University. He arrived there in 1903, just after finishing a master's degree at Indiana University, not far from his boyhood home on a large farm in the Hoosier State. Indiana was rather like a Midwestern branch of Clark University—its philosophy department featured three psychologists, William Lowe Bryan, Ernest Lindley, and John Bergström, who were all Clark graduates. In their classes, young Terman "became fired with the ambition to become a professor of psychology and to contribute something myself to the science" (Terman, 1932, p. 310). Lindley was especially influential and in a seminar with him, Terman wrote extensive papers on "degeneracy" and "great men." The projects, which brought him in contact with the writings of Binet and Galton, began to foreshadow his life's work (Minton, 1988). At Clark, his interests in intelligence and its testing deepened, and his doctoral dissertation compared the mental and physical abilities of 14 preadolescent boys, "seven bright and seven dull" (Terman, 1906, p. 314). The former group outperformed the latter on all of the mental tests, which included Binet-like procedures such as problem solving and memory, whereas the dull group did better on some motor coordination tasks. Perhaps influenced by his strong attraction to Galton's hereditarian ideas, Terman believed that his study supported "the relatively greater importance of endowment over training, as a determinant of an individual's intellectual rank" (p. 372). Terman never publicly wavered in his belief that heredity was the prime determiner of intelligence.

Terman suffered from periodic bouts with tuberculosis, leading him to search for employment in a warm climate after completing his doctorate in 1905. After spending a year as a school superintendent in San Bernardino, California, he landed an academic position, teaching child psychology and pedagogy at Los Angeles State Normal School (which later became UCLA). His big break came in 1910, when he was asked to move north to Palo Alto and join the faculty at Stanford University. The opening was sudden and unexpected—Terman replaced his former Indiana teacher, John Bergström, who had gone to Stanford in 1908 but died 2 years later (Capshew & Hearst, 1980). Within 12 years, Terman was chairing the psychology department, which he built into one of the premier departments in the country. Terman (Figure 8.7), three of his faculty recruits, and four of the doctoral students there during his tenure became APA presidents (Hilgard, 1957). He was much admired as a teacher, especially for the stimulating Monday evening seminars held at his home, where he recreated the atmosphere he had experienced as a student in Hall's famous Monday seminars. Terman retired from Stanford in 1941 but remained professionally active until his death in 1956,

FIGURE 8.7 Lewis Terman in his office at Stanford.

just a few weeks before his 80th birthday. His legacy to psychology includes (a) developing one of the world's best-known IQ tests, and (b) conducting the longest-running psychology research project of all time.

The Stanford-Binet IQ Test Goddard translated the Binet-Simon scales into English and first introduced them to America. Terman, however, went beyond translation by accomplishing a revision and the first real standardization of the test. Terman added new tests (including some of the ones created for his dissertation), revised others, and eliminated a few. Between 1910 and 1914, he standardized the test. He used about 2,300 participants, mostly children and adolescents from middle-class environments, but also about 400 adults. He eventually arrived at a series of 90 test items, compared with 54 in Binet's final (1911) version. Along with a complete set of norms that resulted from his standardization effort, Terman published in 1916 what he called the Stanford Revision of the Binet-Simon test. It became known as the Stanford-Binet, and it quickly dominated the market and earned Terman a healthy income in royalties. Terman completely revised and restandardized it again in 1937. In a more recent version, it remains perhaps the best-known individual test of intelligence.

The 1916 Stanford-Binet included a concept that Binet would have found disturbing—IQ. Terman borrowed it from a leader of the testing movement in Germany, William Stern. Stern had pointed out that an average 5-year-old should score at a mental level of 5, while a very bright 5-year-old might achieve a mental level of 6 or higher, and a slow 5-year-old would score lower than 5—perhaps 4. He suggested that mental ability be capsulized in a "mental quotient" that represented the relationship between mental age and chronological age, found by dividing the former by the latter. For Terman, the idea meshed nicely with his norming procedures and with his growing belief that intelligence was a unitary trait. He changed Stern's "mental quotient" to **intelligence quotient** or IQ, multiplied the ratio by 100 to lose the decimal point, and built it into the revision. With the 1916 Stanford-Binet, then, IQ was born. Three 5-year-olds with mental ages of 4, 5, and 6 would have IQs of 80, 100, and 120, respectively. The message was clear—mental capacity could be represented in a single number.

Terman Studies the Gifted Binet's original purpose in developing his test was to identify children in need of special training. Terman went beyond this vision, however, and believed that his IQ test could identify special children at both ends of the continuum. His long-standing interest in students at the upper end of the scale led him to design his best-known research, a study of giftedness. His original intent was to identify a group of talented children and then follow up on their lives at some later time to see if their promise had been fulfilled. Instead, the project took on a life of its own, continuing long after Terman himself died. It became psychology's longest-running longitudinal study.

In formulating his plans for the study, Terman was motivated by his hereditarian ideas about intelligence and his strong belief that America should be a **meritocracy**. That is, he believed its leaders should be those capable of leading. IQ testing, he suggested, would be a good way to identify such people. With the possible exception of one's morals, he once wrote, "nothing about an individual [was] as important as his IQ" (quoted in Minton, 1988, p. 99). Terman's vision of a true democracy meant equal opportunity, but only for those with some minimum level of mental ability. Those with low IQs, which Terman referred to as "democracy's ballast" (p. 99), could also reach fulfillment in life if properly identified, trained, and placed in jobs suitable for them. Thus large-scale IQ testing could produce a classification system that would result in different types of education for different levels of ability. Terman believed this system would "go far toward insuring that every pupil, whether mentally superior, average, or inferior, shall have a chance to make the most of whatever abilities nature has given to him" (quoted in Minton, 1987, p. 102).

With this ideal meritocracy in mind, Terman set out to identify gifted children in 1921. His aim was to select the top 1% of all California schoolchildren. Because of logistical and financial problems, however, his team of field-workers concentrated on just a few large and medium-sized urban areas. Teachers were asked to identify the three smartest children and the youngest child in their classes. These children were then tested with a brief version of the Stanford-Binet. Those scoring highest were given the full Stanford-Binet.

The outcome was a group of 1,470 children that included 824 boys and 646 girls. Most were in elementary school, but the group included 444 from junior or senior high school (sample size data from Minton, 1988, pp. 114–115). The average IQ was 151 for the younger children and 143 for the high schoolers. The sampling procedures appeared to be reasonable, but the resulting sample was not representative. Students tended to be middle- to upper-class, Protestant, and white, and their fathers tended to hold professional rather than working-class occupations. Jewish children were also overrepresented, while nonwhites and the poor were underrepresented (Cravens, 1992). The bias occurred in a number of subtle ways, from teacher selections to the reluctance of field-workers, concerned for their safety, to go to some schools in urban areas. For example, one of Terman's workers omitted 14 Los Angeles schools that had been set aside by authorities "to handle children who had been found guilty of minor offenses" (Minton, 1988, p. 114).

Having selected a sample, Terman's team compiled considerable information for each child, the result being the 600-page *Genetic Studies of Genius: Mental and Physical Traits of a Thousand Gifted Children* (Terman, 1925). Terman retested the group in the late 1920s and conducted major follow-ups 25 (Terman & Oden, 1947) and 35 years (Terman & Oden, 1959) after the original testing. When Terman died, Robert Sears, a member of the gifted group and by then a distinguished research psychologist himself, took over the project. He produced five additional follow-ups between 1960 and 1986 and was preparing *The Later Maturity of the Gifted* when he died in 1989 (Cronbach, Hastorf, Hilgard, & Maccoby, 1990).

The traditional view of gifted children is that although they are intellectually superior, they are physically weak, socially inferior, and burn out at a young age, never quite fulfilling their childhood promise. Terman's research questioned all aspects of this stereotype, however. In follow-up after follow-up, his group appeared to be not just smarter than others but more successful, productive, well adjusted, and physically healthy. Most entered professional life, but this was less likely to occur for the females in the group. Although more likely to be in a career and less likely to be married than their non-gifted peers, the women of Terman's group tended to be frustrated by the lack of opportunities for women in America at mid-20th century (Minton, 1988).

One final aspect of the study worth noting is Terman's devotion to the group and the corresponding loyalty of those who came to call themselves "Termites." A typical problem in longitudinal research is **attrition**—as time goes by, subjects drop out of the study for various reasons. Attrition was not a problem for Terman, however. Of those subjects who were alive for the follow-up studies done after 10, 25, and 35 years, the percentages of those participating were 92, 98, and 93%, respectively (Minton, 1988). Terman corresponded regularly with hundreds of his Termites and cared very much about the progress of their lives. This is not surprising, of course, for in Terman's mind, these were the meritorious people holding the key to America's future.

Terman is often credited with being the pioneer in the study of gifted children, and with reason. But others were interested in the topic—Goddard for instance, and a woman whose work on the gifted preceded Terman's. She might not have studied them as systematically as Terman did, but a case can be made that Leta Hollingworth was the first advocate for specialized education for gifted children. This chapter's Close-Up examines her work on behalf of gifted children and describes her research debunking the idea that women were intellectually inferior to men.

CLOSE-UP

LETA HOLLINGWORTH: ADVOCATING FOR GIFTED CHILDREN AND DEBUNKING MYTHS ABOUT WOMEN

At the end of this chapter, you will learn about the applied psychology of Harry Hollingworth. He was just half of one of psychology's dynamic duos, however, and his wife Leta (Figure 8.8) made contributions at least as important as her husband's. At a time when women faced the obstacles you learned about in Chapter 6, Leta Hollingworth (1886–1939) managed to earn a doctorate from Columbia, become the "mother of gifted education," in her biographer's words, and directly attack the belief that men were superior to women intellectually (Klein, 2002).

Like her husband, Leta Stetter Hollingworth was a native Nebraskan, born and raised in rugged frontier conditions and taught in the proverbial (and in

FIGURE 8.8 Leta Hollingworth, debunker of the variability hypothesis, and early promoter of special educational opportunities for gifted children.

this case literal) one-room schoolhouse. She graduated from the University of Nebraska in 1906 and then taught for 2 years before marrying Harry and following him to New York, where he was in his second year of graduate studies at Columbia. She immediately encountered one of the gender biases described in Chapter 6—the choice between marriage and career. Her plan was to teach in the New York school system, thereby supporting Harry in graduate school. Upon discovering a Board of Education policy prohibiting married women from being teachers (Hollingworth, 1943/1990), she started taking graduate courses and enrolled full-time after Harry finished his doctorate. She earned a PhD from Columbia's Teachers College in 1916, under Thorndike's direction, and was immediately hired there as an instructor.

In the spring semester of the academic year 1918–1919, Leta Hollingworth began offering a new course, Education 254, designed to examine "fortunate variants, the generally and specifically gifted" (quoted in Klein, 2002, p. 120). It is believed to be the first course ever designed to study gifted children, and it marked the official beginning of Hollingworth's devotion to this population. The work culminated with her widely cited *Gifted Children: Their Nature and Nurture* (1926), the first textbook of gifted education. Although the primary means of treating gifted children at that time was acceleration in grade, Hollingworth argued that such a path could damage children who would not spend much of their time with age-related peers.

Instead, she advocated for a full immersion enrichment approach. Gifted children, she argued, should be placed in classes with their gifted peers and given a curriculum that included the normal curricular topics as well as a level of enrichment that went far beyond what was taught to non-gifted children.

Gifted education was her life's passion, but Hollingworth was also a determined feminist and active in several groups advocating for, among other things, the right of women to vote (which came in 1920). In 1912, for instance, she was a founding member of the "Heterodoxy Club," a group of women who met weekly to discuss women's issues. Hollingworth's feminist beliefs were informed by data. In particular, two of her early studies challenged two widely held beliefs described in Chapter 6. First was the *variability hypothesis*, the evolution-based idea that women showed less variation in traits than men and were therefore less suited for highly intellectual tasks and for careers requiring exceptional mental ability. Second was the idea that sex differences were due in part to the *periodic function*—women were intellectually incapacitated during menstruation (Poffenberger, 1940).

Hollingworth published several studies questioning both beliefs, and summarized her work in a chapter ("The Vocational Aptitudes of Women") she wrote for her husband's *Vocational Psychology: Its Problems and Methods* (Hollingworth, 1916). Concerning the variability hypothesis, Hollingworth discovered that the belief rested on very little empirical data, and what information did exist was ambiguous. One study, which showed no differences among adult men and women in variability in physical traits, had been criticized by proponents of the variability hypothesis on the grounds that young children should have been investigated to get at "inherent or original differences in variability" (Hollingworth, 1916, p. 230). This prompted Leta and a pediatrician friend, Helen Montague, to study 2,000 newborns, half male and half female. After collecting a variety of physical measurements, they found that the boys were slightly larger than girls, but that the amount of *variability* in physical size was the same for both boys and girls (Montague & Hollingworth, 1914). Hollingworth was particularly incensed at the argument that the variability hypothesis accounted for the fact that relatively few women had achieved eminence—the simple reason for that, she argued, was lack of opportunity in a male-dominated world (Shields, 1982).

As for periodic function, it was the subject of Hollingworth's doctoral dissertation. Prevailing opinion was that men and women were inherently unequal, and an important factor was that while men were capable "of sustained and regular hard labor, [a woman], for one quarter of each month, during the best years of life, is more or less sick and unfit for hard work" (Maudsley; quoted in Klein, 2002, p. 91). This apparently irritated Hollingworth's social conscience, prompting her to reply:

It is positively stated that women are on this account unfitted to pursue professional and commercial life; yet it is not proposed that cooks, scrub women, mothers, nursemaids, housekeepers, or dancers should be periodically relieved from their labors and responsibilities. (Hollingworth, 1916, p. 235)

In her dissertation, Hollingworth carefully studied 23 women and examined their performance on tests for "speed and accuracy of perception, controlled association, steadiness, speed of voluntary movement, fatigability, and rate of learning" (Hollingworth, 1916,

p. 236) during all phases of the menstrual cycle. Data from several male "control" subjects were also collected. On all the tests she found no gender differences, and for the women, no differences traceable to periodic function.

Hollingworth recognized that at the time she wrote her chapter on women in her husband's book, little actual research had been done on sex differences. As she put it:

All we can say is that up to the present time experimental psychology has disclosed no sex differences in mental traits which would imply a division of labor on psychological grounds....So far as is...known, women are as competent intellectually as men are, to undertake any and all human vocations. (Hollingworth, 1916, p. 244)

Leta Hollingworth's research on gifted education and on gender would have been even more substantial had she not become desperately ill with abdominal cancer during the last 10 years of her brief, 53-year life.

Robert M. Yerkes (1876–1956): The Army Testing Program

Yerkes (Figure 8.9) began his academic career as a promising comparative psychologist at Harvard; his love of animals was rooted in his childhood on a farm (Carmichael, 1957). But Harvard's interest in comparative psychology was never great—research in the topic was expensive, the laboratory smelled, and it didn't seem especially relevant or useful (Reed, 1987). Thus Yerkes was pressured to produce more on the "human side" if he expected to advance through the ranks. Although comparative psychology remained his first love, he compromised by writing a mainstream introductory textbook that centered on the study of consciousness and even included introspective exercises at the end of each chapter (Yerkes, 1911). He further broadened his credentials by working part-time in the Psychopathic Department of Boston State Hospital from 1913 to 1917, where he first became familiar with intelligence testing by administering Binet tests to patients and improving the scoring system. Harvard still did not promote him, however, even though his reputation among peers was sufficient to get him elected to the presidency of the American Psychological Association in 1917. In that same year, perhaps tired of waiting for Harvard to promote him, he accepted an offer to chair the psychology department at the University of Minnesota. Fate intervened, however, and Yerkes never made it to the upper Midwest.

In April 1917, while Yerkes was cohosting a meeting of Titchener's Experimentalists at Harvard, the United States declared war on Germany and entered World War I. The group

FIGURE 8.9 Robert Yerkes, in a photo reflecting his first love, comparative psychology.

held an impromptu meeting to discuss how psychology might help the war effort and, as APA president, Yerkes took the lead. He later said that he had no real desire to take on the Army project, but did so out of a sense of duty (Dewsbury, 1996). Nonetheless, he quickly demonstrated superb organizational and persuasive skills, convincing the Army that psychological testing could aid the war effort.

By August of 1917, the Army had commissioned Yerkes as a major and placed him in charge of an elite group of psychologists (including Terman) tasked with preparing mental tests. Their task was daunting. For one thing, the sheer number of people to be examined meant that traditional Binet-style testing, in which examiners tested one person at a time, had to be replaced by group testing procedures. Second, although part of the goal was in the Binet tradition of identifying those who were unfit—in this case for Army service rather than for normal schooling—Yerkes also had more ambitious plans. He hoped to create tests that would enable the Army to identify those with special skills so they could be placed where they could serve best. For instance, he hoped to be able to select candidates for officer training. Pilot tests were conducted at four Army camps in October, and by the end of December 1917, the Surgeon General decreed that psychological testing would be extended to all new recruits. The program was in full swing in early 1918, and by the time the war ended in November of that year, Yerkes and his team had tested 1,726,966 soldiers (Yoakum & Yerkes, 1920).

Army Alpha and Army Beta Because nearly 30% of recruits could not "read and understand newspapers and write letters home" (Yoakum & Yerkes, 1920, p. 12), Yerkes developed two versions of his test. Recruits literate enough to read and follow written directions were given the **Army Alpha** test, and **Army Beta** test was created for those with

TABLE 8.3 Subtests for Army Alpha and Army Beta

Army Alpha Subtests	Army Beta Subtests
Commands Test	Maze Test
Arithmetic Problems	Cube Analysis
Practical Judgment	X-O Series
Synonym–Antonym	Digit-Symbol
Disarranged Sentences	Number Checking
Number Series Completion	Pictorial Completion
Analogies	Geometrical Construction
Information	

reduced literacy. Each test took just under an hour to administer. Any soldier failing Alpha was to be given Beta, and those failing Beta were supposed to be tested individually. Logistical problems and time pressures usually eliminated both levels of retesting, however. Army Alpha comprised eight different tests, whereas Army Beta had seven (Table 8.3). Soldiers given Army Alpha were told at the outset that the purpose of the test was to

> see how well you can remember, think, and carry out what you are told to do. We are not looking for crazy people. The aim is to help find out what you are best fitted to do in the Army. (Yoakum & Yerkes, 1920, p. 53)

By contrast, those taking Army Beta were simply told to follow instructions and "ask no questions" (p. 82); they were not told why they were taking the exam.

To get an idea of what confronted soldiers, consider the first test in Army Alpha: the directions or commands test. Soldiers had the score sheet in Figure 8.10 in front of them and were told that in the Army, it was important to be able to follow orders. The test would determine how well they could do so. For each of the 12 items, they were ordered to make specific marks on the page. Here are three of the commands:

> 4. Attention! Look at 4. When I say "go" make a figure 1 in the space which is in the circle but not in the triangle or square, and also make a figure 2 in the space which is in the triangle and circle, but not in the square.—Go! (Allow not over 10 seconds)
>
> 7. Attention! Look at 7. When I say "go" cross out the letter just before C and also draw a line under the second letter before H—Go! (Allow not over 10 seconds)
>
> 11. Attention! Look at 11. When I say "go" draw a line through every even number that is not in a square, and also through every odd number that is in a square with a letter.—Go! (Allow not over 25 seconds) (Yoakum & Yerkes, 1920, pp. 55–56)

Three of the Army Beta subtests can be found in Figure 8.11. In the maze test, recruits had to draw a line to negotiate the maze accurately—the dashed lines are the correct answers. In test 4, digit-symbol, the symbols paired with each number had to be written into the blank spaces. In test 6, recruits were instructed to identify the missing elements of each picture. They had 2 minutes to complete as many mazes and digit-symbols as they could, and 3 minutes to do the picture completion test.

Even though almost 2 million soldiers took the tests, the war ended before the Army could use them effectively. Indeed, most historians conclude that the Army derived little if

KEY DATE –1917

This year marked the origins of the Army testing program during World War I that gave great impetus to applied psychology in the United States.

These events also occurred that year:

- The Iowa Children Welfare Research Station was established in affiliation with the University of Iowa; it became a major center for research in child development; Kurt Lewin (Chapter 9) worked there for nine years, starting in 1935
- A 100-in. reflecting telescope was installed at Mount Wilson, California
- Four women were arrested for picketing the White House on behalf of women's suffrage, and sentenced to six months in jail
- The actor Charlie Chaplin's annual salary reached $1 million
- The Allies executed dancer Mata Hari as a German spy
- Revolution in Russia brought the Bolsheviks to power, eventually resulting in the formation of the Union of Soviet Socialist Republics (U.S.S.R.)

- Literacy requirements for U.S. citizenship were passed, over President Wilson's veto
- In World War I, German forces withdrew on the Western Front, a February revolution occurred in Russia, and Pershing arrived in Paris to lead American troops

These persons were born:

- John Fitzgerald Kennedy, U.S. President
- M. Pei, Chinese-American architect (e.g., designed John F. Kennedy library in Boston and the "pyramid" at the Louve)
- Andrew Wyeth, American artist (e.g., *Christina's World*)

These people died:

- William F. ("Buffalo Bill") Cody, American cowboy and entrepreneur
- Auguste Rodin, French sculptor (e.g., *The Thinker*)

any benefit from the enterprise (e.g., Kevles, 1968). During the war, many within the military welcomed the tests as more efficient than traditional methods for placing soldiers. Yet others stubbornly refused to use the test results, some local commanders didn't cooperate with the examiners giving the tests, and testing conditions were often so poor as to render the results meaningless. At one point the Secretary of War polled camp commanders about the value of the testing program, and most of the 100 responses were negative (Gould, 1981). That the Army discontinued the testing shortly after the war ended suggests that its top brass were less than impressed with the program's utility. On the other hand, the testing program laid the groundwork for a scientific approach to Army personnel work, and a number of younger officers saw its potential benefits. And the program certainly gave psychology a boost. As one historian put it, "While testing may not have made a significant contribution to the war, the war had made a significant contribution to testing and as a by-product to psychology in general" (Minton, 1988, p. 74).

Yerkes believed the project showed that mental testing could be applied on a large scale, and after the war he spared no effort to propagandize the benefits of mass testing. Other psychologists soon joined in. Terman, for instance, claimed that testing had "brought psychology down from the clouds and...transformed the 'science of trivialities' into the 'science of human engineering'" (Terman, 1924, p. 106). Yerkes and Terman joined with other prominent psychologists (e.g., Thorndike) to create the widely used "National Intelligence Tests" in 1920. Advertisements for the test used the alleged success of the

FORM 5   GROUP EXAMINATION ALPHA   GROUP NO. ....

Name .... Rank .... Age ....
Company .... Regiment................... Arm .... Division ....
In what country or state born?.......................... Years in U.S.?......... Race ....
Occupation .... Weekly Wages ....
Schooling: Grades, 1.2.3.4.5.6.7.8:   High or Prep. School, Year 1.2.3.4: College, Year 1.2.3.4.

TEST 1

FIGURE 8.10 Test on following orders; a part of Army Alpha. From Yoakum and Yerkes (1920).

FIGURE 8.11 Subtests of Army Beta included (a) mazes, (b) digit-symbol, and (c) picture completion. From Yoakum and Yerkes (1920).

Army program to promote group testing in schools—one portion of a widely circulated advertisement read:

> These tests are the direct result of the application of the Army testing methods to school needs.... The effectiveness of the Army intelligence tests in problems of classification and diagnosis is a measure of the success that may be expected to attend the use of the National Intelligence Tests. (Quoted in Gould, 1981, p. 179).

The 1920s soon became known as "the heyday of the testing movement" (Goodenough, 1949; quoted in Dennis, 1984, p. 23), as mental testing spread into schools, clinics, business, and industry. Universities began using test scores to screen applicants, and informal tests of character, personality, and ability began appearing in popular magazines. A writer in *Harper's Magazine*, referring to the mental test as "this bright little device," noted wryly that "in practically every walk of life . . . [it was] being introduced as a means of finding out what people don't know, and for what particular business they are specially unfitted" (quoted in Dennis, 1984, pp. 23–24). The glow soon faded, though, as the proponents and detractors of testing launched an acrimonious debate about the nature of intelligence and IQ that remains with us today. Before proceeding with the controversies over testing, however, let us close the book on Robert Yerkes.

After the war, Yerkes turned down the prewar offer from Minnesota and remained in Washington as an administrator in the National Research Council, which had just been organized to provide federal support for science. In 1924, he returned to academia when his good friend, fellow "Harvard man," and now university president, James Angell, recruited him for the newly created Institute of Psychology at Yale (Dewsbury, 1996). There he returned to his first love, the study of animal behavior, and began a campaign to create a research center to study primate behavior. The eventual result was the "Anthropoid Experiment Station of Yale University," which opened in 1930 in Orange Park, Florida, near Jacksonville. When Yerkes retired in 1941 (succeeded by Karl Lashley), the center was renamed the Yerkes Laboratories of Primate Biology. It moved to Atlanta in 1965, and today the Yerkes Primate Center is among the leading centers of primate research in the world (Dewsbury, 2006).

The Controversy Over Intelligence

As leaders of the mental testing movement, Goddard, Terman, and Yerkes shared the beliefs that (a) mental capacity was primarily the result of genetic inheritance; (b) the environment had little if any effect on this overall ability; (c) intelligence might be composed of a variety of skills, but underlying all of them was a single, unitary capability;[5] and (d) this capability was what intelligence tests measured. In the 1920s, the tests were at the forefront of the heyday of mental testing. By the middle of the decade, however, mental testing was under assault from several directions; Anne Anastasi, author of the best-known modern textbook on testing, would later write that "the testing boom of the 1920s probably did more to retard than to advance the progress of testing" (Anastasi, 1993, p. 17). What happened?

An early sign of trouble was in Yerkes's 1921 report summarizing the Army testing program. Buried in the 890-page mass of detail was this statement: "It appears that the

---

[5]In this regard, most Americans agreed with the British psychologist-statistician Charles Spearman, who argued that although separate intellectual skills might exist, underlying all of them was a unitary intellectual ability, which he called "g," for "general" intelligence.

intelligence of the principal sample of the white draft, when transmuted from Alpha and Beta exams into terms of mental age, is about 13 years" (Yerkes, 1921, p. 785). Combining the widely held belief that the mental age of an average adult should be 16 and the Goddard scale of deficiency that considered those scoring between 8 and 12 to be morons, this was disturbing news. If the Army testing program was valid and the sample representative (at 1.7 million, it was certainly big enough), then it appeared that the United States was becoming a nation of morons. Even though critics later pointed out that problems like the abysmal testing conditions and the failure to implement the retesting scheme made the results virtually impossible to interpret, the report reinforced existing biases and created alarm. Could the fears of the eugenicists be coming true? Could all those years of unrestricted immigration and the failure to control the breeding of feebleminded people be reducing the overall intelligence of America? To add fuel to the fire, Yerkes observed in the *Atlantic Monthly* that on the basis of the Army tests, no more than 10% of Americans "are intellectually capable of meeting the requirements for a bachelor's degree" (quoted in Degler, 1991, p. 168).

Yerkes also presented data on intelligence as a function of national origin and found higher scores for native-born Americans. And in support of prevailing fears about the new immigrants, he reported that for soldiers of northern European origin, mental age was higher than for those with roots in southern or eastern Europe. The average mental age for this latter group was about 11. Carl Brigham, who participated in the Army project, highlighted the immigrant findings in his *A Study of American Intelligence* (1923) and warned that continued mass immigration from southern and eastern Europe, combined with the tendency of these groups to have large families, would threaten the national IQ. In a theme that was to echo ominously in Germany in the 1930s, Brigham suggested that the fair-haired Nordic races were intellectually superior to others.

All of this was happening at a time when the general political climate was characterized by an increasing **nativism**, a defensive nationalism that viewed outsiders with suspicion and alarm. It was exacerbated in the 1920s by several factors. Immigration, which had declined during the war years, was surging again. The new immigrants, already disliked, seemed increasingly unwilling to join into the mythical American melting pot. They retained their own communities and language, and a large proportion had no intention of remaining in America—their goal was to make a sufficient amount of money to return home. In addition, as the 1917 Bolshevik revolution in Russia created headlines, the 1920s witnessed the first "Red Scare," and many Americans viewed immigrants from Russia as subversives rather than refugees from the harsh new Soviet regime. Thus it came as no surprise when Congress passed the National Origins Act of 1924, which established immigration quotas with reference to 1890 data (i.e., before the shift from old to new immigration patterns). The American psychologists who led the mental testing movement have sometimes been portrayed as leading the charge for restrictive immigration, but they reflected the context of their times as much as they contributed to it.

While fears about immigration were widespread, not everyone was willing to accept the beliefs about IQ held by Goddard, Terman, Yerkes, Thorndike, and others. Although the popular press generated a continuous flow of articles about the dangers of immigration that suggested unity among social scientists, there was in fact considerable disagreement within the professional community (Satariano, 1979). Noted anthropologist Franz Boas, for instance, was a strong critic of the hereditarian view, arguing instead for the effect of culture on mental abilities (Degler, 1991). Within psychology, behaviorism (Chapters 10 and 11), with its emphasis on the powerful effects of conditioning, was beginning to have a moderating effect, shifting opinion from nature to nurture. Furthermore, numerous psychologists (e.g., Freeman, 1922) urged caution when interpreting the Army data, pointing out that mental testing was still in its infancy and that the effects of upbringing on IQ scores could not be ignored when interpreting IQ data. In general, before behaviorism began shifting psychologists toward the nurture side of the issue, psychologists and biologists tended toward hereditarian explanations of mental capacity, whereas anthropologists and sociologists leaned toward an environmental emphasis (Hilgard, 1987).

The most visible debate about intelligence and IQ testing in the 1920s resulted from a series of six articles in the *New Republic*, by its founder, the noted columnist Walter Lippmann, and replies in the same magazine from Terman. Neither Lippmann nor Terman minced words. Conceding that the tests might have some value in placing students or selecting employees, Lippmann ridiculed the notion that the tests were measuring innate general "intelligence," arguing that "we cannot measure intelligence when we have never defined it, and we cannot speak of its hereditary basis after it has been indistinguishably fused with a thousand educational and environmental influences from the time of conception to school age" (Lippmann, 1922b, p. 10). Also, Lippmann was outraged at the possibility that testing could forever doom a child who happened not to perform very well for one 50-minute segment of his or her life. With the implications of Terman's meritocracy firmly in mind, he wrote that the result could be "an intellectual caste system in which the task of education had given way to the doctrine of predestination and infant damnation" (Lippmann, 1922a, p. 298). Terman, who Lippmann mentioned by name when likening testing to other "fads" such as phrenology and palm reading, responded in an article that did not really answer Lippmann but merely dismissed him as a rank amateur who should mind his own business and let the professionals deal with these complex issues. It was not one of Terman's better moments, and he later regretted writing the article (Minton, 1988).

Terman was one of the most vocal proponents of the hereditarian view of intelligence, but near the end of his life he had some second thoughts. In an autobiographical chapter for the series *A History of Psychology in Autobiography*, Terman wrote that differences in IQ could never be completely accounted for by environmental factors—heredity was the key. However, in Terman's personal copy of the volume, this section of his essay is circled, and he wrote in the margin on two occasions: "I am less sure of this now (1951)! And still less sure in 1955!—L. M. T." (quoted in Hilgard, 1957, p. 478). Today questions continue to be debated about the relative influence of nature and nurture on intelligence, whether the IQ is a useful measure of intelligence, and the very nature of intelligence.

APPLYING PSYCHOLOGY TO BUSINESS

Calvin Coolidge, U.S. president from 1923 to 1929, once said that the business of America was business. That being the case, and with psychologists desiring to be relevant to American life, it is not surprising that psychologists became interested in applying their knowledge to the business world. As early as 1895, in *Thinking, Feeling, Doing*, Scripture pointed out that advertisers could benefit from what psychologists knew about attention and memory. Shortly after the turn of the 20th century, Walter Dill Scott (1869–1955), a young professor at Northwestern University in Chicago who had been trained by Wundt at Leipzig, was asked by the head of a local advertising company to write a series of articles on the psychology of advertising. This must have seemed like just an interesting diversion to the young experimentalist, but instead it became the start of a distinguished career in what eventually came to be called industrial psychology. In 1903, Scott collected his magazine articles into a book, *The Theory of Advertising* (1903), and followed it 5 years later with *The Psychology of Advertising* (1908). Scott also wrote *Increasing Human Efficiency in Business* (1911), in which he applied psychological principles to suggest ways of increasing worker productivity. A main theme in Scott's work on advertising was that consumers were not rational decision makers and could be influenced by suggestion and appeals to emotion. He also applied what was known about memory—for instance, although he did not use the terms *primacy* and *recency*, he argued that "the first and last advertisement in a magazine are the most effective. Likewise the first and last parts of any particular advertisement (unless very short) are the parts we remember best" (Scott, 1908, p. 16).

During this same period, Hugo Münsterberg, a young German psychologist, who was also a product of Wundt's laboratory and now at Harvard, began to be involved in what he called "economic psychology." Although he became one of the most reviled public figures in America at the time of his sudden death in 1916, he was psychology's most visible applied psychologist in the first 15 years of the new century.

Hugo Münsterberg (1863–1916): The Diversity of Applied Psychology

As one of Germany's rising stars in the new experimental psychology, Hugo Münsterberg (Figure 8.12) attracted the attention of William James at a time when America's premier psychologist was shifting his interests from psychology to philosophy and desiring to distance

FIGURE 8.12 Hugo Münsterberg.

himself from the laboratory. Young Münsterberg had earned both a PhD with Wundt at Leipzig and an MD from Heidelberg, and he had established a productive laboratory of experimental psychology at Freiburg in the late 1880s. James was impressed with Münsterberg's research, citing it frequently in his *Principles of Psychology*. With promises of a well-equipped laboratory and minimal teaching demands, James lured Münsterberg to Harvard in 1892 (the same year that Titchener arrived at Cornell). Münsterberg stayed for 3 years while on leave from Freiburg and then returned home to Germany hoping to secure a professorship there. This was not forthcoming, however, and he went back to Harvard for good in 1897. There his career was nothing short of remarkable, including presidencies of both APAs (Psychological and Philosophical), a major position at Harvard as chair of the Philosophy Department, and status as a friend of the rich, the powerful, and the famous.

Although he could barely understand English when he arrived in Cambridge, and it took him several years before he could lecture comfortably in it, Münsterberg managed to write more than 20 books in the period between his arrival in America and his death. He also became a well-known public figure by writing extensively in popular magazines (e.g., *Harper's*, *Atlantic Monthly*) on such topics as hypnosis, gambling, lie detection, coeducation, and communicating with the dead (Benjamin, 2000). And he was a controversial figure. One of his goals was to explain the American temperament and personality to a German audience, and to an American audience, all the good qualities of Germans. His motives might have been pure, a simple desire to enhance intercultural understanding, and for a time his reputation as an ambassador of goodwill even earned him dinner at the White House with Teddy Roosevelt (Moskowitz, 1977). As World War I approached, however, his defense of German culture and his attacks on what he saw as anti-German propaganda, changed public opinion about him. He was editorially condemned, hated by the general public, and even accused of being a spy (Landy, 1992). After an editorial in the *London Times* labeled Harvard a center for pro-German agitation, Münsterberg became an outcast even among his colleagues, and former Harvard president Eliot questioned his sanity (Spillman & Spillman, 1993). The effects of this vilification can only be guessed at, but the resulting stress probably contributed to the cerebral hemorrhage that killed the 53-year-old Münsterberg in the midst of a lecture on December 16, 1916.[6]

During his productive years at Harvard, Münsterberg contributed substantially to the growth of experimental psychology in America. His research interests were eclectic, and his students found him willing to direct research on a wide range of topics. He welcomed anyone with an interest in research—even students like Mary Calkins (Chapter 6), whose sex prevented them from being there officially. Shortly after his arrival, he lobbied successfully for the construction of a new building to house a state-of-the-art, 24-room laboratory. It included facilities for both human and animal research, and Robert Yerkes was in charge of the latter. By the turn of the century, however, Münsterberg was spending less time in the laboratory and more time developing his interests in applied psychology. One of these interests was in forensic psychology, which examines how psychology applies to legal issues. His celebrated and best-selling *On the Witness Stand* (1908) included detailed descriptions of the reasons that eyewitness testimony often fails; modern research has confirmed many

---

[6] After Münsterberg's passing, psychology went into a decline at Harvard. Titchener was offered Münsterberg's position but declined, and Cattell sought the job but was rejected. Harvard brought the British psychologist William McDougall to America, but he quickly became isolated and left. The department began to recover only after E. G. Boring was induced to leave Clark and come to Cambridge in 1922 (Hilgard, 1987).

of Münsterberg's points. He also warned against the use of hypnosis in the courtroom as a means of determining guilt or innocence, and in his final chapter on "The Prevention of Crime," he argued against the prevailing hereditarian view of human behavior and promoted the idea that the "prevention of crime is more important than the treatment of crime" (p. 233). For Münsterberg, criminals were made, not born.

In addition to writing about the law, Münsterberg contributed to abnormal psychology; his approach to the treatment of insanity was based on suggestion. In essence, his strategy was to assume that if he suggested to patients how they should behave and think, the power of his authority would lead them to obey and be cured. In his *Psychotherapy* (1909), he was also critical of the newly popular Freudianism, with its belief in the importance of the unconscious. Münsterberg, often ahead of his times but behind them in this case, wrote that the subconscious mind had little if any impact on behavior. He did recognize the importance of Freud's emphasis on the early childhood determinants of later pathology, however.

Münsterberg and Employee Selection

Münsterberg had his greatest impact as an applied psychologist in the area of industrial, or "economic" psychology, as he called it. This influence resulted primarily from a book that he compiled from a set of lectures; it was published in German in 1912 and then in English a year later, with the title *Psychology and Industrial Efficiency* (Münsterberg, 1913). After some introductory chapters on applied psychology and its value, Münsterberg divided his book into three broad topics (Table 8.4 lists the full Table of Contents):

- "The Best Possible Man": chapters on how to select the best employees for the job
- "The Best Possible Work": chapters on training, the effects of working conditions (e.g., fatigue), and worker productivity
- "The Best Possible Effect": chapters on advertising and marketing

The first section of the book is the best known—here Münsterberg tried to show how psychological methods could help select workers. He argued for the importance of efficient selection of human resources by drawing an interesting parallel to the threats then existing to natural resources (which would soon lead to the creation of the National Park System). Just as the country was beginning to recognize "how the richness of the forests and the mines and the rivers had been recklessly squandered without any thought of the future" (1913, p. 38), so too were economists coming to believe that "no waste of valuable possessions is so reckless as that which results from the distribution of living force by chance methods instead of examining carefully how work and workmen can fit one another" (p. 38).

To show how psychology could contribute to the process of fitting work and workers together, Münsterberg described several examples. The first involved hiring driver-operators ("motormen") for the electric railways that provided the primary means of public transportation found in cities in those days; today, people go to San Francisco to experience anything comparable. The job was not easy, for the motorman had to stay on schedule while watching out for the carriages, motorcars, and pedestrians that filled the typical city street and often crossed in front of the rail car (no stoplights in those days). Mishaps were common—Münsterberg wrote that railway companies reported "up to fifty thousand accident indemnity cases a year" (1913, p. 64)! Because some operators had better records than others, the Boston Elevated Railway Company asked Münsterberg to develop a way to

TABLE 8.4 Table of Contents for Münsterberg's
Psychology and Industrial Efficiency **(1913)**

I.	Applied Psychology
II.	The Demands of Practical Life
III.	Means and Ends

The Best Possible Man

IV.	Vocation and Fitness
V.	Scientific Vocational Guidance
VI.	Scientific Management
VII.	The Methods of Experimental Psychology
VIII.	Experiments in the Interest of Electric Railway Service
IX.	Experiments in the Interest of Ship Service
X.	Experiments in the Interest of Telephone Service
XI.	Contributions from Men of Affairs
XII.	Individuals and Groups

The Best Possible Work

XIII.	Learning and Training
XIV.	The Adjustment of Technical to Psychological Conditions
XV.	The Economy of Movement
XVI.	Experiments on the Problem of Monotony
XVII.	Attention and Fatigue
XVIII.	Physical and Social Influences on the Working Power

The Best Possible Effect

XIX.	The Satisfaction of Economic Demands
XX.	Experiments on the Effects of Advertisements
XXI.	The Effect of Display
XXII.	Experiments with Reference to Illegal Imitation
XXIII.	Buying and Selling
XXIV.	The Future Development of Economic Psychology

distinguish between competent and accident-prone drivers. If he was able to do so, then the initial selection process could be improved.

Münsterberg believed there were two ways to proceed: (a) by simulating, as a whole, the essential processes involved in successful work (driving in this case); or (b) by breaking down the work into subprocesses and developing tests for each process. Regarding the motormen, Münsterberg first considered using the second, more analytic approach. Competent workers might be expected to have faster reaction times, for instance. But when he tested drivers working for the company, he quickly discovered a ceiling effect: No differences in reaction time could be found between drivers with spotless records and those who had experienced some accidents—all were fast. As Münsterberg (1913) put it, "the slow individuals do not remain in the service" (p. 65). Having rejecting the analytical approach, Münsterberg turned to his other method, simulation. After observing several motormen in action, he identified what he thought to be the critical process—an ability to attend simultaneously to an array of stimuli (e.g., pedestrians, horses, carriages, autos, etc.) while making a continual series of decisions about whether these stimuli would affect the progress of the electric trolley. The situation, he believed, could produce two types of ineffective drivers:

> There are men whose impulses are almost inhibited and who instinctively desire to wait for the movement of the nearest objects; they would evidently be unfit for the service, as they would drive the electric car too slowly. There are others who, even with the car at high speed, can adjust themselves for a time to the complex moving situation, but whose attention soon lapses, and while they are fixating a rather distant carriage, may overlook a pedestrian who carelessly crosses the track immediately in front of the car. (p. 66)

To simulate the process, Münsterberg developed a clever procedure. He created cards 4.5 inches wide and 13 inches long, divided into half-inch squares. Two parallel lines ran down the middle, representing tracks. In the squares to either side of the "tracks" were a random array of numbers representing people, horses, and automobiles, moving at different speeds and moving either in parallel with or perpendicular to the electric trolleys. Münsterberg rigged an apparatus so that the card was covered except for an area the width of the card and 2.5 inches long. By turning a crank, the motormen would successively expose various portions of the card and would be asked to identify objects that could end up being on the track and therefore be dangerous. Figure 8.13 shows a sketch of the apparatus.

Münsterberg tested each motorman on 12 different cards, and then combined time and errors into a weighted measure when describing the results. Unfortunately, his description of the outcome is not clear. For example, the reader never learns how many men were tested, only that the company supplied "a number of the best motormen in its service," others "who had only just escaped dismissal," and a third group "neither especially good nor especially bad" (p. 74). Despite identifying these main groups, Münsterberg failed to report exactly how the groups differed in their performance on the simulation. That the simulation had

FIGURE 8.13 Sketch of Münsterberg's simulation to test the skills of "motormen" of the Boston Elevated Railway Company. From Viteles (1932).

some validity to it, however, was evident from (a) reports from the drivers that the procedure did indeed involve the kinds of decisions made while driving; and (b) some data showing that all the motormen, even the poor drivers, outperformed a group of Harvard students. Münsterberg (1913) considered the simulation a success and made a series of (arbitrary) recommendations about what score should be obtained before a potential motorman could be considered competent. He concluded by claiming that "an experimental investigation of this kind which demands from each individual hardly 10 minutes would be sufficient to exclude perhaps one fourth of those who are nowadays accepted into the service as motormen" (p. 81).

A study involving telephone operators illustrates Münsterberg's second research strategy—analyzing the job into specific subtasks and developing tests for each. These underpaid and overworked women handled up to 300 calls per hour, resulting in fatigue, errors, and what today we call burnout. The Bell Telephone Company spent a lot of time and money on training, so they were looking for a way to screen out those most likely to have difficulty. Enter Münsterberg.

After observing operators for a time, Münsterberg (1913) was impressed with the complexity of their task. After identifying 14 different "psychophysical processes" (p. 97), he selected several of them and developed tests. For example, memory was tested by having operators recall lists of numbers, and attention was tested by having them examine a page of newspaper and cross out every example of a specific letter. They were also tested on word association, card sorting, and accuracy in touching a pencil to crosses drawn on a page (i.e., similar to hitting the correct hole in the switchboard). As with the motormen, Münsterberg failed to describe the results in any detail. A sly move on the part of Bell Telephone, however, provided some unexpected validation—they inserted some veterans into what Münsterberg thought was a class of 30 novices:

> The skeptical telephone company had mixed with the class a number of women who had been in the service for a long while and had even been selected as teachers in the telephone school. I did not know, in figuring out the results, which of the participants . . . these particularly gifted outsiders were. . . . The results showed . . . that these women who had proved most able in practical service stood at the top of our list. (pp. 108–109)

The motorman and the telephone operator selection examples are the best known of the studies reported in Münsterberg's book, but there are dozens more. Other projects examined such topics as the effects of monotony and fatigue on productivity, whether magazines should place ads together in one section or spread them throughout the magazine, and the effects of the size of ads on memory for products.

Other Leading Industrial Psychologists

Münsterberg was far from alone in his involvement with business and industry. The commercial world provided fruitful opportunities for many psychologists needing to supplement meager academic incomes. This part of the chapter began by mentioning one of them, Walter Dill Scott. Other prominent industrial psychologists included Walter Van Dyke Bingham, Lillian Gilbreth, and Harry Hollingworth.

Walter Van Dyke Bingham (1880–1952)   Bingham's career found him in direct contact with many of the psychologists who are or soon will be familiar to you. He was a graduate student at functionalist Chicago from 1905 to 1908, where he completed a dissertation on the perception of tones under James Angell and worked as John Watson's student assistant. In 1907 he traveled briefly in Europe, where he met the gestaltists Köhler and Koffka; he then spent some time at Harvard getting to know James and Münsterberg while acquiring a minor in philosophy. His shift to applied psychology began to occur after he went to Columbia in 1908 to start his academic career. There he encountered Cattell and Thorndike, who sparked his interests in mental testing and educational psychology, respectively. After 2 years he moved to Dartmouth College, where he remained until 1915. For the next 9 years, he presided over a unique academic enterprise, the Division of Applied Psychology at the Carnegie Institute of Technology, a school founded 10 years earlier and now known as Carnegie-Mellon University.

In Pittsburgh, Bingham established his reputation for applying psychological principles to business. With the aid of generous funding from local business executives (e.g., Westinghouse, Heinz), he established units within his division specifically oriented to business psychology. One example was the Bureau of Salesmanship Research, and Bingham recruited Walter Dill Scott to direct it. On temporary leave from Northwestern University, Scott is believed to be the first person ever given the title of Professor of Applied Psychology (Landy, 1993). The bureau produced a useful guide for personnel directors called *Aids in the Selection of Salesmen*, which included a standardized application form, a set of questions for interviewers, and recommendations for tests to be given to applicants (Bingham, 1952). The sales bureau soon spawned a related enterprise, the Research Bureau for Retail Training. It was also generously underwritten, this time by department store magnate Edgar Kaufmann.[7] The bureau "prepared employment tests, training manuals, merchandise manuals, and specific procedures for correcting defects of sales personality and of supervision" (Bingham, 1952, pp. 15–16). A third Bingham innovation was the School of Life Insurance Salesmanship, which trained a legion of sales reps to convince people that they were underinsured. Many of the staff and students that Bingham attracted to Carnegie became leaders in the field of industrial-organizational psychology (Vinchur, 2007).

In addition to his work at Carnegie from 1915 to 1924, Bingham was a key player in establishing the credibility of the Psychological Corporation. He replaced Cattell in 1926 when the temperamental founder was ousted as president of the corporation by its board (Sokal, 1981b). He also served with Yerkes in World War I, helping with the Army testing program, and he played a similar but even larger role in World War II. Given the title of Chief Psychologist by the War Department, he chaired a committee that produced the Army General Classification Test (AGCT), which was eventually given to 10 million soldiers (Hilgard, 1987). From the mid-1920s through the end of World War II, Bingham consistently promoted industrial psychology, making him the discipline's most visible advocate.

Lillian Moller Gilbreth (1878–1972)

The career of Lillian Gilbreth (Figure 8.14) can be divided into two segments by the early death of her husband, Frank. Before this unfortunate event, she was able to combine the roles of mother and professional in ways seldom seen before or since. Frank Gilbreth, a former bricklayer without the benefit of a

---

[7]Kaufmann is also known for hiring Frank Lloyd Wright to design a house, outside of Pittsburgh, that could be used as a getaway from the hustle and bustle (and pollution from wall-to-wall steel mills) of Pittsburgh. The result was one of Wright's best-known creations—Fallingwater.

FIGURE 8.14 Lillian Gilbreth, mother of 12 and pioneer in ergonomics and industrial psychology.

college education, was a pioneer in the new field of time-and-motion study. By carefully observing bricklayers, for instance, he identified wasteful motions and recommended more efficient ones, thereby increasing worker productivity. Lillian collaborated with this work, contributing equally to their successful consulting business, Gilbreth, Inc. In the process, she completed the requirements for a doctorate at Berkeley by writing a dissertation called "The Psychology of Management," but was not given the degree because she could not meet residency requirements. After the Gilbreths moved to Rhode Island, she finished a second doctorate at Brown University with a dissertation on how worker efficiency principles could be applied to the teaching profession. Her PhD, awarded in 1915, is the first ever granted in industrial psychology (Perloff & Naman, 1996). During this time she also published her initial dissertation in book form, after reluctantly bowing to pressure from her publisher to disguise her gender by having the book attributed to "L. M. Gilbreth." Together, the Gilbreths published books on ways to eliminate fatigue (Gilbreth & Gilbreth, 1916) and on the uses of time-and-motion study (Gilbreth & Gilbreth, 1917).

These achievements, remarkable by any measure, approach the incredible when one realizes that during the 20 years of their marriage, Frank and Lillian Gilbreth had a dozen children (six boys and six girls). You might be familiar with this part of the story from the book or the movie *Cheaper by the Dozen*; two of the children wrote the book (Gilbreth & Carey, 1949). It is a marvelous tale about living in a large family run by principles of worker efficiency (e.g., "shave" a few seconds off the morning's whisker removal by using two blades, one in each hand). Their family also became the focus of a paper written by one of Terman's students in 1923 and called "IQ Farming." Both parents and all the children tested in the "gifted" range, so the Gilbreths were the prototypical example of the kind of family destined to lead Terman's meritocracy (Minton, 1988).

After her husband's fatal heart attack in 1924, Lillian Gilbreth's accomplishments increased, even though she was now raising 11 children on her own (one of the dozen died in infancy) while continuing to run the consulting business and teaching part-time. She became a pioneer in the field of **ergonomics**, the study of how systems and products can be made efficient for human use. Her ideas included the redesign of household tasks, based on her own ample experiences. For instance, she became largely responsible for modern kitchen design, and pop-up trash cans and side-door shelves for refrigerators are among her innovations (Perloff & Naman, 1996). She was also a major force in helping people with physical handicaps become productive citizens—she considered this her most important work. When she died in 1972 at age 94, Gilbreth had added 16 honorary doctorates to her 2 earned ones.

Harry Hollingworth (1880–1956)   You have already met Hollingworth, the psychologist who confessed to being involved with applied psychology only to put food on the table. Regardless of his motives, however, he is justly recognized as a leader in the field of industrial psychology. As an undergraduate at the University of Nebraska, Hollingworth encountered the new psychology in a laboratory course taken with T. L. Bolton, a student of Hall's at Clark University. He left Nebraska in 1907 to pursue graduate studies at Columbia, where he studied with Cattell, Thorndike, and Woodworth. After a year, Hollingworth married fellow Nebraskan Leta Stetter, who you met in this chapter's Close-Up.

Hollingworth finished his doctorate in 1908 and then took a position as instructor at nearby Barnard College, but he barely managed on his $1,000 annual salary. Salvation came in the form of an offer from the Coca-Cola Company, which hired both Hollingworths in 1911 to conduct research on the effects of caffeine. The company had been charged by the government with adding an element to its formula (caffeine) that had what were believed to be unhealthy stimulant properties. The Hollingworths completed a series of studies, using careful double-blind procedures, and Harry was able to testify in court that the amount of caffeine in the cola had no discernible adverse effects except that relatively large amounts taken late in the evening could interfere with sleep (Benjamin, Rogers, & Rosenbaum, 1991).

The Coca-Cola project was lucrative for this financially strapped young couple. It provided enough money to finance 3 years of graduate education at Columbia's Teachers College for Leta, enabled the couple to spend the summer of 1912 touring Europe, and launched Harry onto the path of applied psychology (Benjamin, 2003). He became inundated with consulting opportunities from businesses that ranged from railroads, which wanted to know what color to paint their cars, to city planners, who wanted to know how to improve the legibility of traffic signs, to chewing gum manufacturers, who wanted some evidence that gum chewing provides useful relaxation (Benjamin, 1996). He took advantage of many of these requests, and he made a name for himself as a prominent applied psychologist. But he claimed that he did the work reluctantly, seeing himself first as a "psychologist," and only secondarily as an applied psychologist, writing that "it has been my sad fate to have established early in my career a reputation for interests that with me were only superficial" (quoted in Benjamin, 1996, p. 134).

IN PERSPECTIVE: APPLIED PSYCHOLOGY

Research methods textbooks typically make a distinction between basic and applied research. Basic research is normally done in a laboratory setting and investigates fundamental psychological processes (e.g., memory, perception, conditioning). Applied research, on the other hand, normally (but not necessarily) occurs outside of the laboratory and is focused on solving real-world problems (e.g., how to improve worker productivity). The texts will point out that both forms of research are necessary and that they complement each other. In reality, however, basic research in its purest form, the kind of research that would make Titchener smile, is a hard sell. Modern-day psychologists, for example, often find it difficult to win grants for basic research unless they can somehow show that the results can be applied in some way. In an interview after being elected president of the APS (Association for Psychological Science), for example, noted experimental psychologist Richard F. Thompson noted, "Many of us who have been basic scientists have come to feel that to justify our existence we, too, have really got to try to develop applications to the problems of society" (Kent, 1994, p. 10).

After reading this chapter, you now know that Thompson's concern is not a new one. Right from the start, many psychologists, even though they had been trained for the laboratory, believed it was necessary to make their work relevant. Indeed, in the United States at least, this focus on application existed even before the advent of the New Psychology. Consider the popularity of phrenology (Chapter 3), for example, which can be considered a form of applied psychology.

Although this chapter focuses on applied psychology in the United States, and application certainly fits with the American national character, it is important to note that applied psychology flourished in other countries as well. A thorough analysis is beyond the scope of this chapter, but important efforts at applying psychology occurred in a number of other countries, especially in Europe and especially during World War I (e.g., developing tests to select pilots for the brand new air forces in Germany and England) and in the period between the two world wars. A good summary can be found in Warr (2007).

Harry Hollingworth was typical of the kind of psychologist who was trained to be a "pure" researcher, but found himself immersed in applied work. Benjamin (2003) has argued that Hollingworth might have been protesting too much when he claimed that all he really wanted to be was a laboratory psychologist—he never seemed interested in abandoning the applied work that made his life comfortable. And for the most part, Hollingworth's nonapplied research has been forgotten. His doctoral dissertation on motor accuracy in reaching, however, which emphasized the importance of the overall environment within which the reaching behavior occurred, did catch the notice of at least one prominent figure. The Gestalt psychologist Kurt Koffka once told Hollingworth that the study had been a "cornerstone" of the Gestalt psychology movement, the topic of our next chapter. As we shall see, the gestaltists had an important impact on American psychology, especially in the areas of perception and thinking. Yet their influence was never as strong as they would have wished, in part because they never appreciated the lesson of this chapter—the importance of application.

SUMMARY

The Desire for Application

• Since the New Psychology first appeared in America in the late 19th century, psychologists have been concerned with how psychological knowledge could be put to good use. The concern over application was partly a natural consequence of traditional American pragmatism and the belief that scientific progress should result in beneficial technology.

• Psychologists also experienced institutional pressures to justify their existence within departments of philosophy and their needs for fully equipped laboratories.

The Mental Testing Movement

• Galton's approach to mental testing, which emphasized physical and sensory measures, was imported to America by James McKeen Cattell, who created the term *mental test* and developed an elaborate testing program at Columbia. The program failed when the measurements could not be correlated with academic performance, however. Cattell played an important role in the professionalization of psychology in America, primarily through his editorial work in rejuvenating (*Science*) or helping to found (*Psychological Review, Psychological Bulletin*) scientific journals.

- Modern intelligence testing, with its emphasis on measuring cognitive rather than sensory processes, originated with the Ebbinghaus completion tests and the creation of the Binet-Simon tests. Binet's goal was to identify students who were academically weak (*débiles*), so that special programs could be developed for them. The test was scored in terms of mental level (later called mental age), and children in need were considered to be those scoring two levels below their actual age. Binet's approach to psychology, which he called individual psychology, was to emphasize the study of individual differences rather than the search for general laws.

- The Binet tests came to America when they were translated by Henry Goddard of Vineland Training School. Goddard used the tests to classify degrees of feeblemindedness in terms of mental age and created the term *moron* to identify those with mental ages between 8 and 12. He believed that mental deficiency was inherited and supported his case with the methodologically flawed and biased Kallikak study, which traced the lineage of one of the Vineland children. Goddard also used the tests to help officials at the Ellis Island immigration center try to identify the mentally unfit. His results added to the perception that immigrants from southern and eastern Europe were inferior to those from northern and western Europe.

- Lewis Terman institutionalized intelligence testing by revising and standardizing the Binet tests, thereby creating the Stanford-Binet, one of the best-known modern tests of intelligence. The test was scored in terms of William Stern's concept of IQ, a ratio of mental age to chronological age. To support his belief in a meritocracy, Terman conducted an extended study of gifted children and found that they broke the stereotype that such children are intellectually superior but socially and physically inferior.

- Robert Yerkes, a comparative psychologist at heart, became involved in mental testing in World War I by organizing the Army testing program. He and his team developed two group intelligence tests, one for literate soldiers (Army Alpha) and one for illiterates (Army Beta). The program was minimally useful to the Army, but it launched intelligence testing as big business and made testing a popular enterprise in the 1920s. After the war, Yerkes's report on the program, which suggested that the typical American soldier scored barely higher than moron level, generated much controversy over mental testing, IQ, and the question of how much intelligence resulted from nature and nurture.

Applying Psychology to Business

- The first psychologists to apply psychological principles to business were Walter Dill Scott, who wrote pioneering books on advertising and how to improve business practices, and Hugo Münsterberg, who came from Germany to run the laboratory at Harvard but soon developed interests in several applied areas including forensic psychology, psychotherapy, and industrial ("economic") psychology.

- Münsterberg's *Psychology and Industrial Efficiency* included several examples of how psychological principles could be used to select employees. He recommended two approaches to measurement: simulations of critical features of the worker's task, as in driving an electric trolley car, and analysis into component skills, as in being a telephone operator. The book also included research-based advice on improving the workplace and marketing.

- Other pioneering industrial psychologists include Walter Van Dyke Bingham, whose Division of Applied Psychology at the Carnegie Institute developed programs for training people in sales and retailing; Lillian Moller Gilbreth, an efficiency expert and one of the first to study ergonomics; and Harry Hollingworth, a reluctant applied psychologist, but an effective one who applied sophisticated experimental design to applied problems such as the effects of caffeine on performance.

STUDY QUESTIONS

1. What was the significance of Scripture's *Thinking, Feeling, Doing*, which included numerous examples of how laboratory methods had a wider use?

2. Why was it important for advocates of the New Psychology to show that their work had applications?

3. Explain how Cattell's approach to mental testing was influenced by Galton, and describe any 5 of Cattell's original 10 mental tests.

4. Describe the Wissler study and explain its significance for the Galton-Cattell approach to mental testing.

5. When testing for fatigue in schoolchildren, what was the approach taken by Ebbinghaus? Explain.

6. Binet's approach to psychology has been referred to as "individual" psychology. Explain and contrast his approach with an alternative research strategy.

7. What was Binet's idea about the reason for developing mental tests, and what did he conclude about the placement of schoolchildren?

8. Had Binet learned of the subsequent history of IQ testing after his death, he might have turned over in his grave. Explain why.

9. According to Goddard, define the term *moron*, and explain why Goddard thought it was crucial to study and be able to identify this type of person.

10. Describe and criticize the Kallikak study. Explain why it is an example of how preconceived bias can influence research.

11. Describe and criticize Goddard's work at Ellis Island.

12. Describe the origins of the term *intelligence quotient*.

13. What was Terman's contribution to the measurement of intelligence?

14. Explain how the concept of a meritocracy led Terman to complete psychology's longest longitudinal study. Based on his research, what did Terman conclude about gifted children?

15. According to Leta Hollingworth, what was the best strategy for educating gifted children?

16. Describe the research reported by Leta Hollingworth that raised questions about gender differences in intellect.

17. Describe the Army testing program, being sure to distinguish between the two forms of the test. Why were the results controversial?

18. Use specific examples to illustrate the two primary methods Münsterberg used to accomplish employee selection.

19. In Münsterberg's study of telephone operators, an unexpected validation procedure occurred. Explain.

20. Aside from his work in industrial psychology, what other contributions did Münsterberg make to applied psychology?

21. Describe the contributions to applied psychology made by Walter Bingham and Lillian Gilbreth.

22. Using the Coco-Cola study as the example, describe how research psychologists brought special expertise to the area of applied psychology.

FOR FURTHER READING

BENJAMIN, L. T., Jr., ROGERS, A. M., & ROSENBAUM, A. (1991). Coca-Cola, caffeine, and mental deficiency: Harry Hollingworth and the Chattanooga trial. *Journal of the History of the Behavioral Sciences*, *27*, 42–55.

A description of Hollingworth's research on the effects of caffeine, set nicely into its historical context; shows how Hollingworth was reluctantly drawn into the project, how he tried to protect his scientific integrity while doing the research, and how his experiments, still cited today, were models of experimental design.

FANCHER, R. E. (1985). *The intelligence men: Makers of the IQ controversy.* New York: W. W. Norton.

An excellent history of the testing movement, with detailed descriptions of the work of Galton, Cattell, Binet, Goddard, Terman, and Yerkes; brings the controversy up to date by examining modern descendants of the hereditarian side of the

issue—Burt, Eysenck, and Jensen—and the debate over the alleged fabrication of twin study data by Burt.

Green, C. D., & Benjamin, L. T., Jr. (Eds.) (2009). *Psychology gets in the game: Sport, mind, and behavior, 1880–1960.* Lincoln: University of Nebraska Press.

A series of chapters on how psychologists have applied their science to exercise and athletics; includes chapters on E. W. Scripture and fencing, Walter Miles and football, Karl Lashley and archery, Norman Triplett and competition, Hugh Fullerton and Babe Ruth, and Coleman Griffith (considered the "father" of sports psychology) and the Chicago Cubs.

Sokal, M. M. (Ed.). (1987). *Psychological testing and American society.* New Brunswick, NJ: Rutgers University Press.

A collection of essays written by leading experts on the history of testing; includes chapters about Cattell, Goddard, Yerkes, Terman, and the origins of the multiple-choice testing format.

CHAPTER 9

GESTALT PSYCHOLOGY

There are wholes, the behaviour of which is not determined by that of their individual elements, but where the part-processes are themselves determined by the intrinsic nature of the whole.

—Max Wertheimer, 1924

PREVIEW AND CHAPTER OBJECTIVES

Advocates of a new way of thinking often find that they must speak loudly to be heard. Such was the case for those who became known as gestalt psychologists. With missionary zeal, these German psychologists promoted an approach to psychology that objected deeply to the prevailing analytical strategy that characterized certain aspects of other German psychologies, Titchenerian structuralism, American behaviorism, and any theory derived from British associationist principles. The gestaltists argued that understanding mind and behavior could not be achieved by trying to dissect conscious experience into its sensory elements, or by reducing complex behavior to elementary stimulus–response units. Rather, their emphasis was on phenomenologically whole experiences, and before long their movement came to be identified with this catchphrase: The whole of an experience is greater than the sum of its individual parts. The first section of this chapter highlights the work of three Germans who established the gestalt movement in the early years of the 20th century: Max Wertheimer, normally considered the founder by virtue of his elegant yet simple demonstrations of apparent motion; Kurt Koffka, who introduced gestalt concepts to an American audience and extended gestalt ideas into developmental psychology; and Wolfgang Köhler, whose research on learning and problem solving in apes challenged behaviorism.

All three gestalt pioneers emigrated from Europe to the United States, two of them (Wertheimer and Köhler) as a consequence of Hitler's dismantling of the German academic environment in the 1930s. The Gestalt psychology that arrived in America was sometimes associated only with the study of perception, but the gestaltists also made important contributions to the psychology of thinking and problem solving, and their ideas influenced the later development of cognitive psychology.

The final portion of the chapter describes the life and work of Kurt Lewin. He was for a time associated with the gestaltists in Germany, and like Wertheimer and Köhler, he came to the United States to escape the Nazi menace. Lewin went beyond Gestalt psychology, however, and developed a complex theory of human behavior that led him to make important contributions to developmental, social, and industrial-organizational psychology. Impatient with abstract laboratory studies, he developed "action research," aimed at making a direct impact on people's lives and solving social problems. After you finish this chapter, you should be able to:

279

- See the connection between Gestalt psychology and the issue of atomism versus wholism raised in Chapter 2
- Describe the immediate antecedents of Gestalt psychology, in the ideas of Brentano, Mach, and von Ehrenfels
- Describe Wertheimer's apparent motion study, show how he ruled out traditional explanations, and explain the significance of the study
- Summarize Koffka's contributions to Gestalt psychology
- Describe and apply the gestalt perceptual organizing principles
- Distinguish between geographical and behavioral environments, and describe the implications of the distinction for understanding behavior
- Describe Köhler's research on problem solving in apes and contrast his conclusions with those of Thorndike
- Describe Wertheimer's ideas about productive thinking and the general gestalt approach to thinking and problem solving
- Describe the essentials of Lewin's field theory
- Explain the Zeigarnik effect and show how it fits into Lewin's notion of equilibrium
- Describe the contributions made by Lewin to developmental and social psychology
- Describe the overall impact of Gestalt psychology on American psychology and explain why it did not become a dominant system in the United States

THE ORIGINS AND EARLY DEVELOPMENT OF GESTALT PSYCHOLOGY

The starting date for Gestalt psychology is normally thought to be somewhere between 1910 and 1912, the years when German psychologist Max Wertheimer looked at a common perceptual phenomenon from a new perspective. Like all intellectual movements, however, this one had roots. The gestaltists were influenced indirectly by the German philosophical tradition of Kant, with its emphasis on how a priori perceptual and cognitive categories shape our experiences (see Chapter 2), and by the late 19th-century phenomenology of Edmund Husserl, which stressed the importance of relying on direct descriptions of our experiences over the artificial introspective accounts that attempted dissection when trying to understand the nature of these experiences. The gestaltists were also influenced by contemporary physics, especially the studies of Max Planck, an important pioneer of field theory in physics, whose work emphasized how overall fields of force determined the nature of the relationships among components of the field. A magnetic field, for instance, represents a force that produces an overall pattern of interrelations among elements that cannot be understood by analyzing each of the elements within the total field.

Four direct influences on the creation of Gestalt psychology were the physicist Ernst Mach, and the philosopher-psychologists Christian von Ehrenfels, Franz Brentano, and Carl Stumpf. In a book on sensation written in 1886, Mach (1886/1914) argued that certain "space-forms" resisted analysis into basic elements. For example, a square has the essential spatial feature of "squareness" that cannot be further reduced. The four lines that compose it can change in size, but the relationship among the four lines must stay the same for squareness to occur. The overall relationship is what counts when identifying squares, not the individual components. The Austrian philosopher Christian von Ehrenfels came to a similar conclusion.

Certain qualities of experience, he contended, go beyond sensory elements and persist even if the elements are altered. A talented musician, von Ehrenfels used melody as an example. By playing a song in a different key or with a different instrument, the physical properties of every single note (element) might change, yet the melody itself does not change—it has a **form-quality** (German: *gestaltqualitat*) different from the sum of the individual notes.

At about the same time that Wundt was publishing his *Physiological Psychology*, proclaiming the founding of a new science, the Viennese philosopher Franz Brentano (1838–1917) published *Psychology from an Empirical Standpoint* (Brentano, 1874/1995). The title may be misleading to the modern reader, because the word *empirical* seems to imply the collection of data. The book, however, is more of a philosophical treatise, but it has important implications for psychology. In using the term *empirical*, Brentano simply meant acquiring knowledge through direct phenomenological experience and reflection on that experience. In the book, he argued that the important thing about studying the mind was not to examine its contents, or even to understand the underlying physiology, but to understand how the mind *operates* to create our experiences. When studying perception, for example, the important thing is not a detailed description of the sensations, images, and affects, as would occur in Titchener's lab, for example (Chapter 7). Rather, from an empirical standpoint, the important thing is the act of perceiving, how the individual perceives the event, and what the event means to the individual. Brentano's system has been called an **act psychology**, because of the emphasis on the mind as an active entity. Brentano had a direct influence on von Ehrenfels and Husserl, both students of his.

Like von Ehrenfels, Carl Stumpf (1848–1936; Figure 9.1) was a talented musician capable of playing six different instruments (Sprung, 1997). As an experimentalist, Stumpf was noted for his work on the auditory perception of tones. This expertise led him into a spirited debate with Wundt over who was best qualified to be an "observer" in experiments

FIGURE 9.1 Carl Stumpf.

about judging musical tones. At issue was an auditory phenomenon with a distinct gestalt theme. When listening to two pure tones simultaneously, the experience is of a unique new tone that does not seem to be a combination of its two components. Wundt believed that suitably trained laboratory workers would be capable of analyzing the phenomenon into its component tones, but Stumpf contended that skilled musicians were better observers and that the phenomenon resisted analysis. If a laboratory analysis contradicted the phenomenal experience of a trained musician, Stumpf argued, then the analysis was in error. While not denying the importance of laboratory work, Stumpf and his followers urged the primacy of direct experience over abstract reductionism (Ash, 1985).

Stumpf was named professor at Berlin in 1894, where he soon helped found Berlin's Psychological Institute. Two of the original three gestaltists you are about to meet took their doctorates with Stumpf in Berlin, and the third studied with him for a time.

Max Wertheimer (1880–1943): Founding Gestalt Psychology

Max Wertheimer (Figure 9.2) was born in Prague and initially studied law at its university, before his broad interests led him to switch to philosophy. He took courses with von Ehrenfels, where he learned of his teacher's concept of gestaltqualitat; he studied in Berlin for three semesters, where he encountered Stumpf; and he then went to Würzburg, where he completed a doctorate with Oswald Külpe (Chapter 4) in 1904. His dissertation reflected an interest in criminal law and used a word association technique to discern characteristic patterns of thinking (Newman, 1944). The next few years following 1904 are not well documented, but family wealth apparently made it possible for Wertheimer to indulge his varied interests.

FIGURE 9.2   Max Wertheimer, founder of Gestalt psychology.

Somewhere around 1910, Wertheimer became fascinated by the perceptual problem of **apparent motion**. The phenomenon was well known at the time and the basis for the newly created motion picture industry. It can be illustrated with a simple example. In a darkened room, two adjacent small circles are flashed on and off in sequence. If the interval between the flashing of the two lights is just right (about 60 milliseconds), the perception is not of two lights, each flashing on and off, but of a single light that moves from side to side. Thus two separate sensory events occur, but the perception is that of a single continuous event.[1] In the space between the lights, the circle is perceived even though there is no sensory basis for this perception. How could this occur?

Traditional explanations for apparent motion centered on sensory-motor events or higher cognitive inferences. The first idea was that as the circles flashed alternately, the person would shift the eyes (without awareness) from left to right, over and over. Sensory stimulation resulting from the eye movements was said to produce the perceptual "fusion" that was experienced as movement. The second explanation, in the spirit of Helmholtz, was that the individual made an unconscious logical inference that if a light was in position A then in position B, it must have moved there. The perception, held to be illusory, was the result of this "reasonable" inference.

With the cooperation of Friedrich Schumann, laboratory director at the University of Frankfurt (and coinventor, with G. E. Müller, of the memory drum), Wertheimer acquired laboratory space and equipment to develop his ideas about apparent motion into a program of research. He was aided by two young psychologists then working in Schumann's lab, Wolfgang Köhler and Kurt Koffka (Figure 9.3), who served as participants in the experiments (as

FIGURE 9.3 Kurt Koffka (left) and Wolfgang Köhler at 9th International Congress of Psychology, held at Yale University, 1929. From Popplestone and McPherson (1994).

[1]If the interval between the flashing of the lights is too short, about 30 msec or less, the perception is that both lights are on at the same time and neither is moving. If the interval is longer than 200 msec, two separate flashing lights will be seen. Producing the phi phenomenon reliably also depends on the intensity of the lights and the distance between them (Goldstein, 1996).

did Koffka's wife). The outcome was a 1912 paper, "Experimental Studies on the Perception of Movement" (Wertheimer, 1912/1965), often considered the founding event of Gestalt psychology. In the research, Wertheimer and his colleagues demonstrated the phenomenon under a variety of conditions and raised serious questions about prevailing explanations. In one of their studies, for example, three lights in a straight line, A, B, and C, were used. If lights A and C were flashed on and off simultaneously, then B was flashed after 60 msec, the perception was that two lights (A and C) had moved at the same time to the center point. This demonstration eliminated the eye movement explanation, because the eyes cannot move in two directions at the same time. The inference explanation was rejected on the grounds that the movement perception occurred too quickly to involve such a complicated sequence of mental events and that the perception of motion was real, not illusory. Instead, Wertheimer argued that the phenomenon must stand on its own as a valid example of an immediately given phenomenological experience that does not require any analysis into constituent parts. Indeed, because perception occurred in areas devoid of any sensory information (i.e., the space between the flashing lights), analysis into sensory elements could not possibly explain the phenomenon. Wertheimer referred to the perceived motion as the **phi phenomenon**; he disliked the term *apparent* motion because it implied that the motion was not really perceived (Henle, 1980). As he later concluded, we perceive whole, meaningful figures, not elements that somehow combine to form wholes. Not only is the whole different from the sum of its parts, but "the part-processes are themselves determined by the intrinsic nature of the whole" (Wertheimer, 1924/1967a, p. 2). The assault on elementism had begun.

Wertheimer lectured and continued doing research at Frankfurt until 1916 and then went to Berlin, where he became a central figure at the Berlin Psychological Institute until 1929.[2] In that year Schumann retired from Frankfurt, and Wertheimer returned there to chair the department. He probably would have remained at Frankfurt until his own retirement, but world events intervened with the rise of Nazi Germany. After Hitler came to power in 1933, academic freedom in German universities quickly disappeared; Jewish professors, including such luminaries as Wertheimer's close friend, Albert Einstein, began to be dismissed from their positions. In response to the argument that Germany would be losing an invaluable resource, Hitler is said to have replied: "If the dismissal of Jewish scientists means the annihilation of contemporary German science, then we shall do without science for a few years!" (quoted in Henle, 1986, p. 226). At least with regard to psychology, Hitler was correct. The effects of his reign crippled psychology in Germany for years.

Shortly after Hitler came to power, Wertheimer, who was Jewish and could see the writing on the wall, gathered up his wife and three children and emigrated to the United States, settling in New York.[3] There he joined a number of other German refugee-scientists at the recently created New School for Social Research. For the remaining 10 years of his life, he continued to work on perception and expanded an earlier interest in problem solving. The outcome was *Productive Thinking* (1945/1982), published posthumously, which is described later in the section on the gestalt approach to cognition and learning.

---

[2]For a sense of the geography, refer again to the map of Germany in Chapter 4 (Figure 4.1).

[3]One of the children, Michael Wertheimer, is professor emeritus of psychology at the University of Colorado at Boulder. He is a prominent historian of psychology, nationally recognized as a master teacher by the APA, and a leader in Psi Chi, psychology's national honor society for students.

Koffka (1886–1941) and Köhler (1887–1967): Cofounders

Kurt Koffka was born in Berlin and, except for a year spent at the University of Edinburgh in Scotland, educated there as well. He earned a PhD from Carl Stumpf at the University of Berlin in 1908. Under Stumpf, Koffka completed research in the perceptual topics of color contrast and auditory rhythm that would prepare the way for his acceptance of Gestalt psychology (Harrower-Erickson, 1942).

After completing his doctorate, Koffka studied physiology. He then went to Würzburg for several years and worked in Külpe's laboratory, investigating imagery. Starting in 1910, he spent three semesters working in Schumann's lab at Frankfurt; during this time he encountered Wertheimer, participated in the famous apparent motion studies along with Köhler, and became a convert to gestaltist thinking. As he later wrote, the three young researchers "liked each other, had the same kind of enthusiasms, same kind of backgrounds, and saw each other daily discussing everything under the sun" (quoted in Ash, 1995, p. 120). Koffka left Frankfurt in 1911 to begin his first professorial job at the University of Giessen. He remained there until 1924, producing a modest but steady flow of experimental papers on such topics as sound localization and memory. During World War I, he studied the cognitive consequences of severe brain injury in soldiers. In 1921, he extended gestalt ideas into the realm of developmental psychology by writing *The Growth of the Mind*.

Of the three early gestaltists, Koffka was primarily responsible for introducing the movement to the United States. He accomplished this first by writing an article in 1922 for *Psychological Bulletin* called "Perception: An Introduction to Gestalt-Theorie" (Koffka, 1922). It was an unfortunate choice of a title, however. Although the gestaltists thought of their movement as a new theory applicable to all psychology, the article implied that Gestalt psychology was merely a new approach to the study of perception. This "misperception" lingers today—in modern introductory texts, discussion of Gestalt psychology occurs almost exclusively in the perception chapter.

Koffka also spread the gestalt word in person starting in 1924, in a 30-campus lecture tour, in an invited address to the annual meeting of the APA in 1925, and in a pair of visiting professor appointments at Cornell and Wisconsin (Sokal, 1984). In 1927 he accepted a full-time academic position at Smith College in western Massachusetts, a private liberal arts college for women, where he remained until his death in 1941. At Smith, the absence of a graduate program curtailed Koffka's research productivity. He influenced the careers of several talented women psychologists, however, including Eleanor Gibson (look ahead to Figure 15.1), who later invented the visual cliff as a means of studying the development of depth perception in infants. In 1935, Koffka wrote his most important book, *Principles of Gestalt Psychology*. It established his reputation as Gestalt psychology's major theorist but also contributed to a growing impression among Americans that the gestaltists were more interested in theory than data. At a time when most American psychologists were firmly committed to active programs of experimental research, this tendency was seen as a weakness. Koffka's arguments in his highly abstract book were also somewhat difficult to follow. The works of his more erudite gestalt colleague, Köhler, were more widely read.

Wolfgang Köhler was just a year younger than Koffka and 7 years younger than Wertheimer, but he outlived his peers by 25 years and 23 years, respectively. This longevity, combined with his deliberate promotion of gestalt ideas, made him the best-known gestaltist of the three originators, especially in America. In 1958, he became the only one of them to be elected president of the APA. His early career was not unlike Koffka's—he earned a doctorate from Stumpf in 1909. He then became Schumann's assistant at Frankfurt, just in time for the arrival of Wertheimer and Koffka and their fateful collaboration (Asch, 1968).

In 1913, an intriguing opportunity came Köhler's way in the form of an invitation to direct the research at a primate colony that the Prussian Academy of Sciences had created at Tenerife, largest of the Canary Islands, which lie off the northwest coast of Africa.[4] He accepted, arriving just before the outbreak of World War I and consequently being marooned on the island with his family and his small colony of apes. As this chapter's Close-Up relates, though, research might not have been his only activity during these years—some think he could have been a German spy. Regardless of the espionage claims, the Tenerife years made Köhler's reputation as a scientist. There he produced his most famous research, the studies of problem solving in apes. This research, chronicled in *The Mentality of Apes* (1917/1926), is examined in more detail later in this chapter.

CLOSE-UP

A CASE OF ESPIONAGE?

Wolfgang Köhler's research on Tenerife during World War I established his scientific reputation. The insight studies he completed there are widely cited even today, and not just in history texts. But was research into the mental capabilities of apes Köhler's only interest during these years? No, according to psychologist Ronald Ley. During a visit to the island in 1975, while attempting to locate the original site of Köhler's Research Station, Ley happened to meet 87-year-old Manuel González y García, who was none other than the animal handler and caretaker during Köhler's years on Tenerife! Despite the passage of years, González y García's memory of the work done at the Research Station and of the behavior of the apes appeared to be intact. For instance, his recollections of the apes were not all fond. Köhler's most famous ape, Sultan, almost bit off Manuel's finger, and he showed Ley the scars from encounters with other apes in the colony. Concerning Köhler, he indicated that the German scientist seemed to enjoy working with the animals, but that he never went into the animal enclosures alone; he made most of his observations from outside the cages.

And the old man noted one other thing—Köhler was a German spy.

Naturally, the espionage claim astounded the initially skeptical Ley, who eventually wrote *A Whisper of Espionage: Wolfgang Köhler and the Apes of Tenerife* (Ley, 1990), a scientific detective story that describes his search for information to verify the assertion by González y García. It took him from Tenerife to archival collections throughout Europe to the homes of Köhler's wife and son. Ley failed to find direct evidence that Köhler was a spy, but he was able to piece together some circumstantial evidence suggesting that Köhler might have contributed to the German war effort. Located close to allied shipping lanes, the mountainous Canary Islands had strategic importance. Observers could easily spot allied shipping and convey information about it to German U-boats. Throughout the war, the British, who had numerous ships sunk in the area, made repeated claims to Spain that German spies on the island were doing just that. The islands were owned by Spain, supposedly a neutral country. Nonetheless, the British claimed that German scientists on the island had the means (wireless telegraph)

---

[4]Tenerife was chosen mainly because the climate would be favorable to the apes, but also because it was not too far from the African nation of Cameroon (a German colony at the time), where the animals could be captured (Teuber, 1994).

to conduct espionage. According to Ley, Köhler, who kept a wireless radio at the Research Station, was one of those scientists.

Ley's espionage claim is intriguing, but it has been criticized. According to Pastore (1990), the radio might simply have been for general communication with the mainland, Köhler's research and writing output would not have left much time for active spying, and the whole story might be nothing more than a rumor that eventually turned into a "fact" in an old man's mind. Köhler himself referred to such a rumor in some of his correspondence: "Certain Englishmen...take us for German spies, and are even so kind as to spread the rumors that the animals are just a pretext" (quoted in Pastore, 1990, p. 369). On the other hand, it would not be unusual for any young patriotic scientist, given the opportunity, to pass along information that might be of use to the homeland.

Ley's claim might be debatable, but his research uncovered interesting details about Köhler's years on Tenerife, including the role played by his first wife Thekla. While raising two young children, she managed to contribute substantially to the research. She was apparently more at ease with the apes than Köhler was and, according to her daughter, "the one who pressed to continue the work during times when things were going poorly" (quoted in Ley, 1990, p. 226). A talented artist, she drew the profile sketch of one of the apes that appeared as the frontispiece for *The*

Mentality of Apes (Figure 9.4), and she filmed the research. Köhler recognized her value, writing to German authorities that Thekla was capable of running the Research Station herself, and indicating that he wished her to be a coauthor of the book that summarized the research. He apparently changed his mind on the latter point, however. Thekla's initials below the sketch in the frontispiece are the only tangible sign of her contribution to the book.

FIGURE 9.4 This sketch of one of Köhler's apes was drawn by his first wife, Thekla, and appeared as the frontispiece to *The Mentality of Apes* (Köhler, 1917/1926).

Köhler returned to a war-ravaged Germany in 1920; within 2 years his status as a rising star in academia was confirmed when he was named to succeed the venerable Stumpf, his former mentor, as director of the Psychological Institute at the University of Berlin. Wertheimer was also there, as was a young Kurt Lewin (later in this chapter). Along with a talented group of students, the gestaltists created a "golden age" for their movement that lasted for about a decade (Henle, 1986). They produced important research, founded the journal *Psychologische Forschung* (*Psychological Research*) to promote their work, and sent their students throughout Germany to expand their base of operations. Then the Nazis came to power.

Of the three founding gestaltists, Köhler was the last to leave Germany when he emigrated in 1935. Because he was not Jewish, he did not face the kind of threat encountered by Wertheimer (and Lewin). Nonetheless, he was appalled by the Nazi interference in academia, and he spoke out publicly. In April 1933, for instance, he wrote the last anti-Nazi article published during the Hitler years, denouncing the dismissal of Jewish professors. In the article, he argued that "only the quality of a human being should determine his worth, that intellectual achievement, character, and obvious contributions to German culture retain their significance whether a person is Jewish or not" (quoted in Henle, 1986, p. 228). Although Köhler was not arrested for writing the article (to his surprise), his situation at the Institute deteriorated. He was forced to open lectures with a Nazi salute (which he did with notable sarcasm), Nazi sympathizer students began to "monitor" his lectures, and some of Köhler's students (e.g., Karl Duncker, whose problem-solving research is described later) were denounced as Communists. By early 1935, after refusing to sign a loyalty oath to Hitler, Köhler had had enough. He resigned his beloved directorship and accepted a position at Swarthmore College in eastern Pennsylvania, where he remained until his retirement in 1958. In addition to his ape book, Köhler wrote *Gestalt Psychology* in 1929. It was shorter, easier to read, and more popular than Koffka's book. It is notable for its assault on American behaviorism. Just as the structuralists and associationists had faltered by trying to analyze consciousness into its elements, Köhler argued, so would behaviorism fail because of its similar atomistic strategy of reducing behavior to artificial stimulus–response units.

GESTALT PSYCHOLOGY AND PERCEPTION

Wertheimer launched Gestalt psychology with his research on a perceptual phenomenon, apparent motion, and the study of perception became an important part of the gestalt program. Much of the effort went into describing the basic rules determining how phenomena become organized into whole, meaningful figures. These so-called **gestalt organizing principles**, first articulated by Wertheimer (1923/1967b), are now familiar fixtures in the perception chapters of general psychology texts. Here are some of the more important ones.

Principles of Perceptual Organization

One of our most basic perceptual tendencies is to separate whole figures from their backgrounds—it provides the foundation for all object perception (Goldstein, 1996). This **figure-ground** segregation was first described in detail in 1915 by Edgar Rubin, a Danish psychologist who studied with G. E. Müller at Göttingen (Prentice, 1951). Rubin was not a gestalt psychologist, but the gestaltists used his figure-ground phenomenon to support their cause. According to Rubin's description, figures have distinct features that enable them to be isolated from backgrounds. The border seems to "belong" to the figure, for example, while the ground seems to extend behind the figure, and this perceptual impression is a strong one, even though we "know" otherwise. Also, the figure is more memorable than the ground and seems to have a substance that is lacking in the ground (Rubin, 1915/1958). In Figure 9.5a, for instance, observers usually perceive the segments with the straight, radiating lines as a figure against a background of concentric circles. The result is an overall perception of a type of cross that covers the circles. With effort, it is possible to reverse the figure-ground relations in Figure 9.5a, making a cross with each arm composed of arcs. This reversal is more easily accomplished in Figure 9.5b, the most famous part of Rubin's 1915 paper. By changing the focus of attention, the viewer can see either a vase or two faces in profile. Note that only one of these perceptions can occur at a time. When the vase is the figure, the black area cannot be perceived as anything but an unformed background.

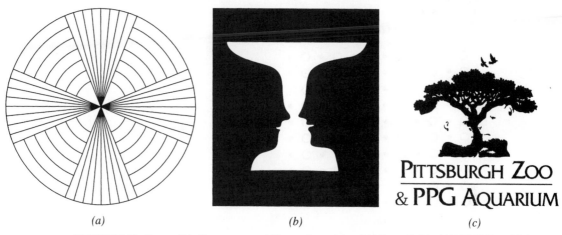

(a) *(b)* *(c)*

FIGURE 9.5 Reversible figure-ground illustrations. (*a* and *b*) From Rubin (1915/1958) and (*c*) a modern application of a figure-ground reversal.

When the faces are figures, the reverse happens. If you stare at Figure 9.5b, you will find your perception switching rapidly from one "whole" to another. One creative contemporary application of a figure-ground reversal is to be found in the logo for the Pittsburgh Zoo and Aquarium (Figure 9.5c); another is the FedEx logo (the next time you see it, look for the arrow).

Three other organizing principles are illustrated in Figure 9.6, taken from Wertheimer's 1923 paper on "Laws of Organization in Perceptual Forms" (Wertheimer, 1923/1967b). In Figure 9.6a, the first two dots seem to belong together, as do the next two, and so on. They are organized by the principle of **proximity**. Wertheimer demonstrated the power of this simple principle by challenging readers to perceive the first dot as a unit, the second and third as another unit, and so on; he considered the task impossible. If proximity is held constant, then stimuli might be organized according to **similarity**, as shown in Figure 9.6b, and we are compelled to perceive alternating vertical columns of open and closed dots. The third principle, **good continuation**, is a tendency to organize our perceptions in smoothly flowing directions. Thus we perceive Figure 9.6c as two wavy lines a–d and b–c. It is difficult to perceive the figure as two lines that sharply change direction, a–b or c–d.

All of the organizing principles have in common what is sometimes called the law of simplicity, or what the gestaltists called **prägnanz** (rough translation: "simplest good figure"). It refers to the basic tendency for our perceptions to mirror reality as closely as possible. When the situation is ambiguous, the organizational principles work to provide the most reasonable guess about the nature of what is being perceived. Thus, even though Figure 9.7 could have been created in several different ways, we tend to perceive the figure as being composed of a rectangle and a triangle, the simplest and most likely hypothesis. Similarly, when we encounter incomplete figures, we often construct a "good figure" by filling in the gaps; this phenomenon is called **closure**.

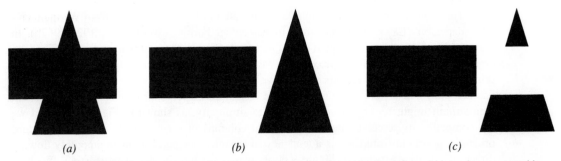

FIGURE 9.6 Gestalt perceptual organizing principles of (*a*) proximity, (*b*) similarity, and (*c*) good continuation. From Wertheimer (1923/1967b).

FIGURE 9.7 The gestalt principle of prägnanz. The figure on the left could have been created in several ways. We tend to perceive it as being composed of a rectangle and a triangle, the simpler of the two possibilities shown on the right.

One final point about these organizing principles is that psychologists have often referred to them when making the claim that the gestaltists were nativists with regard to perception. On the contrary, the gestaltists argued that the organizing principles had nothing to do with the nature–nurture issue. Rather, these principles were considered to be inherent in the nature of objects in the world; our perceptual systems are designed to make the best guess about what is out there. As Wertheimer (1923/1967b) put it, "one recognizes a resultant 'good Gestalt' simply by its own 'inner necessity'" (p. 83).

Behavioral Versus Geographical Environments

The organizing principles might be designed to help us perceive the world as it is, but that is not to say that our perceptions mirror physical reality. The gestaltists—most notably Koffka in his *Principles of Gestalt Psychology* (1935)—made an important distinction between the world as it is in reality, what he called the **geographical environment**, and the world as we perceive it, the **behavioral environment**. The latter perception determines how we act. Koffka used an old German folktale to drive home the point. It concerned a weary traveler in the dead of winter who reached an inn after riding on horseback for hours over what seemed to be an open, snow-covered plain. When he arrived, the innkeeper asked from which direction he had come. The rider pointed to the plain and the innkeeper, "in a tone of awe and wonder, said: 'Do you know that you have ridden across the Lake of Constance?' At which the rider dropped stone dead" (p. 28). Apparently, realizing that the behavioral environment ("this seems to be a wide open plain") does not match the geographical environment ("a frozen lake that could easily crack under the weight of a horse—I could have drowned!") can be rather stressful.

This distinction between physical reality and reality as perceived led Koffka to a point that would soon be elaborated by Kurt Lewin, with his concept of "life space" (described later). If the behavioral and geographic environments differ, then two people in the same geographic environment are likely to perceive it differently. For instance, the descriptions of a walk in the woods by a geologist and a botanist will vary considerably.

THE GESTALT APPROACH TO COGNITION AND LEARNING

Although the title of Koffka's 1922 landmark article in *Psychological Bulletin* gave the impression that Gestalt psychology was concerned only with perception, such was not the case. Rather, the gestaltists conceived of their system as a general psychology, and they made specific contributions to the study of thinking, problem solving, and learning. The two best-known examples are Köhler's research on problem solving in apes and Wertheimer's posthumous book, *Productive Thinking* (1945/1982). Köhler's *The Mentality of Apes* (1917/1926) was first published in German in 1917 and then translated into English and expanded slightly in 1924.

Köhler on Insight in Apes

Köhler and his family lived on Tenerife from 1913 to 1920, but most of the research reported in *The Mentality of Apes* was completed within the first full year on the island. Early in the book, Köhler took dead aim at Thorndike's puzzle box experiments. As you recall from Chapter 7, Thorndike concluded that learning and problem solving involve a process of trial and "accidental success," by which unsuccessful behaviors are gradually eliminated in favor of behaviors that work. Köhler, however, disagreed that problem solving was such a mechanical, step-by-step process. Instead, in keeping with his gestalt orientation, he argued that solutions to problems occur when individuals can view the entire problem field and rearrange the elements of the problem into a new configuration. Solutions have a perceptual quality to them, and they occur quickly, once the components have been reconfigured. Köhler used the term **insight** to label such a process. The main procedural problem with Thorndike's research, according to Köhler, was that the animals could never perceive the entire field. Hence, they were unable to see how the components of the apparatus related to each other in an overall configuration.[5] Regarding Thorndike's studies, Köhler (1917/1926) wrote:

> Cats . . . were frequently placed in cages containing the *extreme end* only of one or the other mechanism, or allowing a view of ropes or other parts of the mechanism, but from which a survey over the *whole* arrangement was not possible. (p. 23; emphasis in the original).

Köhler was determined not to make the same "mistake" in his research. His animals would have the entire field in front of them, and all of the elements needed to solve the problems would be in full view.

Perhaps the most famous problem-solving experiment appearing in *The Mentality of Apes* appears in a chapter called "The Making of Implements." Two hollow bamboo sticks with slightly different diameters were available, each too short to reach a banana just out of reach. Köhler wondered if one of his smartest chimpanzees, Sultan, could solve the problem by joining the sticks. Traditional accounts of this famous experiment portray a thoughtful animal carefully examining the problem and suddenly hitting upon an insightful solution. Sultan's "solution" was not witnessed by Köhler, but by the ape's keeper (the same Manuel González y García mentioned in the Close-Up). The keeper's dramatic account is one of psychology's most quoted passages:

> Sultan first of all squats indifferently on the box, which has been left standing a little back from the railings; then he gets up, picks up the two sticks, sits down again on the box and plays carelessly with them. While doing this, it happens that he finds himself holding one rod in either hand in such a way that they lie in a straight line; he pushes the thinner one a little way into the opening of the thicker, jumps up and is already on the run towards the railings, to which he has up to now half turned his back, and begins to draw a banana towards him with the double stick. (Köhler 1917/1926, p. 132)

This description has all the components of Köhler's definition of insight—the solution occurs quickly, and it occurs when Sultan perceives the elements of the problem in a new configuration. But a close reading of the book, in the pages preceding the famous quote, reveals that Sultan was in fact rather slow in figuring out the solution, and tried several strategies that failed. For example, he tried dragging a box to the side of the cage, apparently because of his experience in a box-stacking experiment, completed before the two-stick experiment. Another doomed strategy was to drop one stick outside the cage, and then push it with the other stick. Sultan was unable to take the hint even when an observer (probably Köhler) took the larger stick and pushed his finger into the open end, while Sultan was watching. In short, although Sultan might have displayed some degree of insight when eventually solving the problem, he also behaved in a way that would make sense to Thorndike—through trial and error.

Köhler's insight explanation was challenged by American psychologists, who questioned the methodological sophistication of Köhler's demonstrations and pointed out the trial-and-error evidence just described. Some attempts to replicate the research produced

---

[5] Köhler criticized maze-learning studies for the same reason, complaining that "American animal psychology makes animals (or people) seek their way out of mazes, over the whole of which there is no general survey from any point inside" (p. 18).

ambiguous results and suggested that the more prior experience the animal had with similar problems, the more likely a "quick" (i.e., insightful) solution would appear (Windholz & Lamal, 1985). On the other hand, Köhler's research introduced a new way of thinking into the debate about learning and problem solving and extended animal methodology beyond simple puzzle boxes and mazes.

Wertheimer on Productive Thinking

Köhler was not the only gestaltist studying cognition. Max Wertheimer had a long-standing interest in thinking and problem solving that culminated in *Productive Thinking* (1945/1982), which he sent to the publisher just before his death in 1943. Its topics ranged from how children learn arithmetic to how Einstein developed his theory of relativity. A good example of his use of gestalt principles can be found in his description of how to teach children about geometry. Wertheimer deplored the traditional approach to teaching math, which relied heavily on asking students to memorize rules and formulas without giving them insight into the concepts behind the symbols.

Early in the book, Wertheimer described his visit to a class in which the teacher was explaining how to find the area of parallelograms. Using the example in Figure 9.8a, the teacher explained the rules:

> "I drop one perpendicular line from the upper left corner and another perpendicular from the upper right corner."
> "I extend the baseline to the right."
> "I label the two new points *e* and *f*." (Wertheimer, 1945/1982, p. 14)

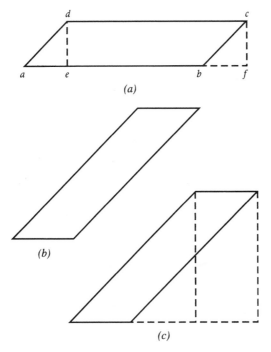

(a)

(b)

(c)

FIGURE 9.8 The area of a parallelogram: (*a*) diagram used to teach by formula; (*b*) problem presented by Wertheimer that caused difficulty for students taught by formula; (*c*) one solution attempt from students taught by formula. From Wertheimer (1945/1982).

Because students had already memorized the rule for finding the area of rectangles, they could now determine the area of the parallelogram by multiplying its base (e–f) by its height (d–e). The teacher then gave the students several more problems, which they solved by going through the same steps.

The next day, Wertheimer again visited the class, and with the teacher's permission, gave students a slightly different parallelogram—the one in Figure 9.8b. Most students could not find its area. Some gave up immediately—"Teacher, we haven't had that yet" (Wertheimer, 1945/1982, p. 15)—while others tried applying the rules they had been taught, producing drawings like Figure 9.8c, but being unsure of how to proceed from that point. A few rotated the parallelogram 90°, and then applied their rules successfully. The teacher was not amused, claiming that Wertheimer had given his students "a queer figure. Naturally they are unable to deal with it" (p. 16).

Wertheimer believed that children would be more productive thinkers if they truly understood the concept of area. He suggested that teachers start with simple concrete examples. For instance, students could easily grasp the idea that two equivalent square fields would produce the same amount of some crop. Next, rectangular surfaces could be understood as combinations of square fields. With that knowledge, students could be shown that any parallelogram could be transformed into a rectangle by chopping off one end and attaching it to the other. He demonstrated that children with such an insightful understanding had no trouble solving area problems like those on the left in Figure 9.9, what he called A-Figures, while at the same time recognizing instantly that the procedure would fail for the problems on the right, the B-Figures.

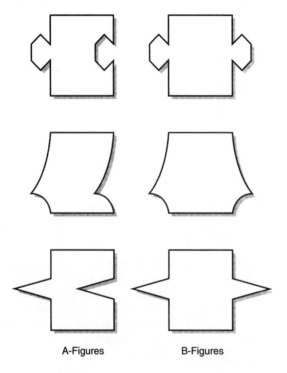

A-Figures   B-Figures

FIGURE 9.9 Sketches used by Wertheimer to illustrate productive thinking. Students with productive knowledge of area solve A-Figures and recognize the problem with B-Figures. For students who have learned area by rote, both types of figures seem unsolvable. From Wertheimer (1945/1982).

For Wertheimer, then, productive thinking in the classroom went far beyond memorizing rules and formulas for "correct" solutions. True understanding involved restructuring the problem to gain insight into its solution. By moving a portion of the parallelogram from one end to the other, children accomplished this "restructuring" and thereby created a "good gestalt," a simpler figure (rectangle) from which their understanding of squares and rectangles could be used to calculate area.

Other Gestalt Research on Cognition

As mentioned earlier, while at Berlin in the 1920s, the gestaltists attracted a talented group of students. Among them were Hedwig von Restorff and George Katona, who made important contributions to the study of memory, and Karl Duncker, whose studies of problem solving and insight are routinely found in general psychology texts today.

Hedwig von Restorff (1906–1962) discovered that if people learned lists with a 3-digit number embedded in a series of nonsense syllables, the number would almost always be recalled better than the syllables. In good gestaltist fashion, she interpreted the result as an illustration of the figure-ground relationship—the number provided a sharp figure against the background of nonsense syllables (Baddeley, 1990). Today, her result is called the **Von Restorff effect**. Anytime a stimulus in an information array stands out in some fashion, it will be recalled more easily than the remaining information. George Katona (1901–1981) had a long and distinguished career. His contribution to memory research came in the form of his 1940 book, *Organizing and Memorizing*, in which he applied gestalt organizational principles to memory. Like Wertheimer, he considered rote learning to be useless. Instead, he argued that memory would be enhanced if the information could be organized in meaningful patterns. The importance of organization in memory would be rediscovered by cognitive psychologists in the 1960s, most of whom were unaware of Katona's pioneering effort.

Karl Duncker (1903–1941) was a student of Köhler's in Berlin who followed his mentor to Swarthmore College during the Nazi years. Although he died young (suicide), he managed to produce a major work on thinking, extending his teacher's ideas about insight into the area of human problem-solving behavior. His innovative *Psychology of Productive Thought* appeared in German in 1935 and was translated into English 10 years later (Duncker, 1935/1945). It has been called "the most careful and analytical account of insight ever published" (Hilgard, 1987, p. 233). Duncker studied the cognitive processes of college students by asking them to think out loud while they were trying to solve problems. He then analyzed the transcripts of their protocols, searching for patterns of thinking and problem-solving strategies. He discovered, for instance, that students often solved problems creatively if they were able to imagine uses for objects that differed from typical uses. Duncker's famous candle problem illustrates the point. Subjects must mount a candle vertically on a wall so that it won't scorch the wall. They are given several objects, including a box of tacks. The correct solution involves seeing the box not as serving its normal function as a container, but as a platform on which to mount the candle. Subjects who failed to solve the problem were said by Duncker to show **functional fixedness**, an inability to think beyond the typical function of an object. Similarly, in his "tumor" problem, he asked subjects to figure out how to destroy an inoperable stomach tumor using radiation. The difficulty was that radiation of sufficient intensity to destroy the tumor would also destroy surrounding tissue. The solution was to expose the tumor to several rays from different directions that would focus on the tumor.

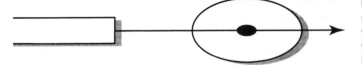

FIGURE 9.10 Diagram used by Duncker to induce functional fixedness in the tumor problem. From Duncker (1945).

Each individual ray would be relatively weak, leaving healthy tissue intact; but when the rays combined at the point of the tumor, they would be strong enough to kill it. Duncker found that when he showed students the diagram in Figure 9.10, only 9% solved the problem. On the other hand, 37% arrived at the solution when the diagram was not shown (Mayer, 1992). Duncker concluded that the diagram induced functional fixedness by making subjects think about using a single direction for the radiation.

KURT LEWIN (1890–1947): EXPANDING THE GESTALT VISION

Kurt Lewin[6] (Figure 9.11) was a contemporary of Gestalt psychology's "big three," Wertheimer, Koffka, and Köhler. Although he did not consider himself a gestalt psychologist per se, he recognized his debt to "these outstanding personalities.... The fundamental ideas of gestalt theory are the foundation of all our investigations in the field of the will, of affect, and of the personality" (quoted in Marrow, 1969, p. 76). Like the gestaltists, Lewin built his theory around concepts taken from field theory, and he borrowed freely from gestalt ideas. While the gestaltists tended to focus on perception, learning, and cognition, however, Lewin was more interested in motivation, emotion, personality and its development, and the influence of social forces on human action. Researchers investigating those topics today, especially developmental and social psychologists, typically claim Lewin as a pioneer in their fields.

Early Life and Career

Lewin was born in 1890 in the small Prussian village of Mogilno, now a part of Poland. The son of a merchant, he was raised in an environment that combined the relative comfort of the middle class with pervasive and state-approved anti-Semitism. Being on the receiving end of sanctioned discrimination created in Lewin a strong sense of social justice that guided his career. The Lewins moved to Berlin in 1905, where Kurt blossomed intellectually. As a university student, Lewin spent a semester each at Freiburg and Munich, studying medicine and biology but unsure of a vocation. At some point, he decided to emulate his professors and be one himself; he returned to Berlin and completed a doctorate on association with this chapter's most recognizable mentor—Carl Stumpf. That Lewin thought highly of his teacher is clear from an obituary that he later wrote, in which he placed Stumpf and

---

[6]The correct German pronunciation of Lewin is "LA-veen," but he began pronouncing it "LOO-in" after arriving in America. Apparently, his children's peers and schoolmates used the latter Americanized pronunciation, and Lewin decided to save his children the aggravation of continually "explaining to their friends why the family name was spelled 'Lewin' but pronounced 'Laveen'" (Marrow, 1969, p. 177).

FIGURE 9.11 Kurt Lewin.

G. E. Müller (Chapter 4) at "the highest rank . . . within the pyramid of psychologists participating in research" in Germany (Lewin, 1937, p. 189). Stumpf earned Lewin's high regard even though they had little personal contact. During the years spent on his doctoral research, for example, Lewin did not recall discussing his thesis with Stumpf until he defended it! Lewin generously characterized this aloofness as an indication of Stumpf's willingness to give his students considerable leeway in their own work. Lewin greatly admired Stumpf, but he was just the opposite in this regard, always taking a very active role in directing his students' research (Marrow, 1969).

Lewin finished his dissertation at a momentous time—the outbreak of World War I. As a loyal German, he enlisted in the Army in 1914 and spent the next several years trying to survive the brutal trench warfare that decimated a generation of European men. He entered as a lowly private and left as an officer; he was wounded once and earned Germany's Iron Cross. While on furlough to recover from his wounds in 1917, he reflected on his experiences and wrote "The War Landscape," an article containing the seeds of many of his later concepts. In a distinction similar to the one made later by Koffka between geographical and behavioral environments, Lewin pointed out that the same objects in the environment can be phenomenologically different, depending on whether they are part of the war landscape or the peace landscape. A narrow path in the woods, which might produce enjoyment and relaxation under peaceful circumstances, can be deadly in the war landscape because it can provide cover for the enemy.

Lewin returned to Berlin's Psychological Institute at the end of the war (1918), became an instructor in 1921, and remained there until 1933. During these years, he developed his ideas and his research program, attracted talented graduate students, and began establishing an international reputation. He also befriended his Berlin colleagues Wertheimer and Köhler, and he got to know Koffka. As his biographer wrote, although "he was never a completely orthodox Gestaltist, he did become a vital force in the new movement and contributed to it his own special insights" (Marrow, 1969, p. 13).

Lewin remained in Berlin until 1933, when his status as war hero was not sufficient to overcome the liabilities of his Jewish heritage.[7] He was already well known in the United States, after giving a stirring address at the 1929 International Congress at Yale and spending a 6-month leave as visiting professor in Terman's department at Stanford. Cornell's Robert Ogden, an early convert to the gestalt vision and as responsible as anyone for bringing the gestaltists to America (Freeman, 1977), arranged for Lewin to spend two academic years at Cornell. In 1935, he and his family moved from New York to Iowa, where Lewin joined the Child Welfare Research Station, a research institute connected to the University of Iowa but separate from the psychology department. The institute had been created in 1917 to study the development of normal children and train child development researchers (Ash, 1992). Lewin remained there for 9 years and then moved back east to Boston in 1944 after successfully lobbying for funding to create a Research Center for Group Dynamics, to be housed at the Massachusetts Institute of Technology. His work there had just begun when he died suddenly of a heart attack in February 1947.

Field Theory

Lewin contributed more empirical research than the three gestalt founders combined, but like them he was first and foremost a theorist—in response to the criticism that theories are sometimes far removed from useful applications, he once said that "there is nothing as practical as a good theory" (quoted in Marrow, 1969, p. 128). Lewin called his theory a **field theory** because he believed that understanding a person's behavior required knowing about all the forces acting on a person at a given moment. Lewin named the particular field within which the person operates the **life space**. It is the pivotal concept in his theory, and he defined it as a psychological field that includes the "totality of facts which determine the behavior (B) of an individual at a certain moment.... [It] includes the person (P) and the environment (E)" (Lewin, 1936, p. 216). Person factors include such things as personality variables, needs, goals, and beliefs; environmental factors include things external to the person that directly affect him or her. Furthermore, it is not simply the physical environment, but the environment as perceived by the individual that influences behavior. Thus all behavior is a joint function of the characteristics of the person behaving and the features of the psychological environment in which the person is behaving. Lewin summarized his idea in a now-famous formula: $B = f(P, E)$.

Lewin symbolized the life space concept by borrowing from **topology**, a nonquantitative spatial geometry. He represented life spaces with various ovals, which contained symbols of features influencing the individual. Life space included everything within an oval (i.e., the person, P, and the environment as perceived, E). Outside the oval, which Lewin referred to as the **foreign hull**, could be found all the events, circumstances, and stimuli that had no effect on a person at a particular moment.

A major difference between the original gestaltists and Lewin was the latter's emphasis on motivational constructs and goal-directed behavior. He believed that people were complex energy systems in which individual actions can be predicted with reference to "tension" in the

---

[7]While in America, and with the Nazi menace becoming more evident, Lewin desperately tried to arrange for his mother's emigration, first to the United States and then to Cuba, but was unsuccessful. Sometime in 1943 she perished in a Nazi death camp (Marrow, 1969).

FIGURE 9.12 An example of a Lewin "egg," depicting a child desiring an out-of-reach cookie.

system, which in turn is the consequence of the predominant needs being felt, the strengths of those needs, and the various obstacles in the life space. When all needs are satisfied, the individual is said to be in a state of **equilibrium**. The creation of a need produces disequilibrium, and a person is motivated to return to a steady state. Consider Figure 9.12 as an illustration. It represents a situation in which a hungry child desires a cookie, which resides in an out-of-reach jar. The desire has created a tension in the life space. The cookie is the desired object, or in Lewin's terms, it has a positive **valence** (symbolized by the plus signs). The arrow pointing from the child (P) is a **vector**—these arrows symbolize a push that is directed toward a specific desired goal, (i.e., an approach tendency), or away from a goal to be avoided, (an avoidance tendency). The arrow's length is proportional to the strength of the need. The vertical bar is a barrier (the cookie jar), which has a negative valence.

Lewin used his topological system to analyze conflicts, one of his best-known contributions. He described three common situations in which a conflict between needs occurs. In Lewin's scheme, a conflict exists whenever at least two vectors are exerting pressure in different directions. In an **approach-approach conflict**, there are two desirable goals of equal strength from which to choose. For instance, a diner might have to decide between steak and lobster. Two equally undesirable goals characterize **avoidance-avoidance conflicts**, as when a student might be faced with the choice of studying one of two disliked topics. Third, in an **approach-avoidance conflict**, the person experiences simultaneous approach and avoidance tendencies with reference to a single goal. Thus a person's decision about whether to order the hot fudge sundae is influenced by both approach (it's good) and avoidance (it's fattening) tendencies.

The Zeigarnik Effect

Lewin's system was highly theoretical, and it was criticized for being merely descriptive. That is, the diagrams might be able to describe virtually any event, but they were said to be of little use in predicting behavior (Frank, 1978). Yet Lewin and his students did conduct considerable research, and their studies produced results consistent with the theory. One famous example is a series of studies completed by one of Lewin's first students, the Russian psychologist Bluma Zeigarnik (1927/1967).[8]

[8]Bluma Zeigarnik (1901–1998) earned her doctorate with Lewin in Berlin in 1927. She then returned to Russia and had a long and productive career in the Soviet Union, specializing in abnormal psychology. Part of her time was spent working with the famed Russian psychologists Lev Vygotsky and Alexander Luria, researching the cognitive effects of brain injury (Luria, 1979). In 1983 she received the Kurt Lewin Award, given annually by the Society for the Psychological Study of Social Issues (SPSSI).

KEY DATE—1929

This year marked the convening of the Ninth International Congress of Psychology at Yale University, which included important talks by Köhler and Lewin that helped advance the gestalt cause.

These events also occurred that year:

- Psi Chi, the national honor society for students in psychology, was founded
- The term "apartheid" was used for the first time
- The German Graf Zeppelin airship circled the globe in 20 days
- The U.S. stock market crashed on October 28 ("Black Friday"), signaling the start of the Great Depression
- Kodak introduced 16 mm color movie film
- Herbert Hoover was inaugurated as thirty-first U.S. president

- Six notorious Chicago gangsters were machine-gunned by a rival gang in the "St. Valentine's Day Massacre"

These people were born:

- Martin Luther King, Jr., American civil rights leader
- Arnold Palmer, American golfer
- Jacqueline Bouvier Kennedy Onassis, wife of John Kennedy, U.S. President

These people died:

- Thorstein Verblen, American social scientist
- Katherine Lee Bates, American author and composer (e.g. *America the Beautiful*)
- Wyatt Earp, legendary figure of the American West

Ideas for research often come from everyday observation, and that happened for Zeigarnik's research. In Berlin, Lewin gathered a team of active graduate students around him. From about 1924 on, his group typically consisted of 12 to 15 doctoral candidates (Marrow, 1969). Lewin's research group often met informally for hours at a time at a café across the street from the Institute, keeping their table by occasionally ordering refills on coffee and pieces of cake. In that setting, Lewin was impressed by a waiter who seemed to be able to keep track of what each student had ordered without writing anything down. Soon after the bill was settled, however, the waiter had no memory of it. To Lewin the explanation was simple. As long as the bill was unpaid and the students remained at the café, the waiter's life space had a tension to it and needed to keep it in memory. Once the bill was paid, the tension resolved, closure had been achieved, and equilibrium had occurred—no need to remember the order any more.

Zeigarnik's study assessed Lewin's interpretation directly. In her main experiment, she tested 164 teachers, students, and children by giving them between 18 and 22 simple tasks, each requiring a few minutes to finish. They included such things as constructing a cardboard box, making a clay figure, completing puzzles, and performing arithmetic and other mental tasks. Each subject was allowed to complete half of the tasks, but was interrupted and not allowed to finish the other half. To ensure that the interruption was clearly felt to be a disruption, Zeigarnik "always chose a time when the subject was most engrossed in his work" (1927/1967, p. 303). What she found was that the interrupted tasks were 1.9 times as likely to be recalled as the uninterrupted ones. In Lewinian terms, the enhanced memory was the result of the unrelieved tension of the incomplete task. This phenomenon, that memory is better for incomplete rather than complete tasks, is today called the **Zeigarnik effect**.

Lewin as Developmental Psychologist

Lewin arrived in New York in the fall of 1933, when the United States was in the depths of the economic crisis of the Great Depression. His position at Cornell, made possible through limited funds from a committee to help displaced European scholars, was not in the psychology department but in the School of Home Economics, and it was not a faculty appointment. This might not seem very impressive, in light of Lewin's growing international status, but it must be seen in light of the academic job market in the 1930s. One effect of the Depression was that few families could afford college and, with low enrollments, few colleges could afford new faculty. As a result, finding an academic position was virtually impossible. The extent of the problem was revealed in an APA survey which found that in 1932, there were 32 positions available for 100 new psychology PhDs; the prospects looked even worse in 1933—46 jobs and 146 newly minted PhDs competing for them (Napoli, 1981). In this context, Lewin's appointment is perhaps an indication of his elevated stature rather than a puzzling loss of status.

When Lewin arrived in the United States, American psychologists thought of him as a developmental psychologist whose approach contrasted sharply with (a) the evolving behaviorist movement and (b) an increasing tendency to study groups of children and take statistical averages of their behavior (Ash, 1992). In contrast, Lewin believed that the behaviorists overemphasized the environment at the expense of personality factors. That is, in contrast to his balanced $B = f(P,E)$, the behaviorists had too much E and not enough P. Methodologically, Lewin criticized the strategy of trying to identify some mythical average child; he preferred nonstatistical in-depth case studies of individual children.

The impression of Lewin as a developmentalist was based on his much-discussed presentation at the Yale International Congress in 1929 and a chapter on developmental psychology that he wrote for the first edition of the *Handbook of Child Psychology* (Lewin, 1931). In the latter, he introduced his $B = f(P,E)$ formulation to the American audience. His Yale talk was highlighted by a film that he showed of an 18-month-old girl trying to sit on a rock. She apparently thought that she would miss the target if she took her eyes off the stone, so she circled the rock several times trying to figure out how to sit on it accurately without removing her eyes from it. She finally devised the creative solution of putting her head between her knees and slowly backing up to the stone before sitting. In that way she could watch the stone while depositing herself on it. In his talk, Lewin described this simple event in terms of field forces, vectors, and valances, and tied it to other research on reaching goals by making detours. Older children solve detour problems, according to Lewin, because they perceive the problem as a whole and recognize that the first step, a movement away from a goal (to get around the detour), is part of the overall structure of the solution. Thus a solution can be achieved even if the initial vector points away from a goal. An older child would solve the rock-sitting problem as a detour problem, by recognizing that taking one's eyes off the rock, while seeming to be a step away from the goal, could be organized as part of the solution. The 18-month-old could not make that detour step, however, and was forced to rely on maintaining a simple goal-directed vector by not letting the rock out of sight. The difference between the younger and older child, according to Lewin, was that the older child had a greater degree of **differentiation**. For this older child, the life space has become more complex (differentiated) over time.

Lewin's 2 years at Cornell were busy ones. In addition to acclimating himself to a new environment and polishing his English, Lewin plunged into a research program on how social pressure affected the eating habits of children; with the help of translators, he published a collection of essays on personality theory (Lewin, 1935) and a book on his topological theory (Lewin, 1936). He also organized a loose confederation of former and current students and colleagues into the "Topology Group." It first met in 1933 as a reunion of sorts, hosted by Koffka at Smith College. Its success produced its replication, and except for a few years during the World War II era, it met annually until 1965. In a manner reminiscent of Titchener's meetings of experimental psychologists, the sessions were marked by informality, camaraderie, and discussions of work in progress. Unlike Titchener's group, the Topology Group welcomed women to its meetings.

It was not until he moved to Iowa, however, and developed a research team at the Iowa Child Welfare Station, that Lewin was able to recreate an environment that reminded him of Berlin. He even found a substitute for the Berlin café where his observation of a waiter's memory inspired Zeigarnik's research. In Iowa City, Lewin and his students congregated at the Round Window Restaurant, where they dubbed their group the "Hot-Air Club" (Marrow, 1969). Lewin's research on children continued at Iowa and yielded one of his better-known studies—"Frustration and Regression: An Experiment with Young Children" (Barker, Dembo, & Lewin, 1941). Roger Barker came to Iowa from Stanford, where he had been a student during Lewin's brief time there as visiting professor. Tamara Dembo, from Russia, was one of Lewin's most loyal students and was with him at Berlin, Cornell, and Iowa. The experiment evolved from some earlier research by Dembo in which children in detour problems sometimes became frustrated at not being able to reach the goal and gave up trying. Barker, Dembo, and Lewin decided to study the problem more systematically, the goal being to determine the effects of frustration on the quality of play for children just under 4 years of age.

Each of the 30 children in the study first encountered a "free play" period in a room where they could play with some simple toys. After 30 minutes, a partition was raised to reveal a much richer play environment that included a large dollhouse and "toy lake" complete with real water and boats. Each child spent up to 15 minutes in this enriched environment and then was led back to the front of the room; then a wire mesh partition was lowered (and secured with a padlock) between them and the enriched environment. The child next spent a second 30-minute session with the same toys found in the original free-play session. Unlike the first session, however, in this session the children could now see what they were missing. In Lewinian terms, the toys on the other side of the room had a much higher valence than the ones now available to them; the barrier had a negative valence and was producing tension. And the children's behavior reflected their frustration. They tried to get around the barrier or out of the room entirely. Failing that, their play deteriorated significantly from that of the original free-play situation. They became destructive, easily distracted by what they could see across the room, and more emotionally upset. Under high frustration, then, their behavior regressed to less constructive patterns.[9] Although increased age produces differentiation, Lewin pointed out that under stress, a temporary shift in the opposite direction, what he called **dedifferentiation**, could occur. The Barker, Dembo, and Lewin study became a classic in the developmental psychology literature, and it still appears in modern developmental psychology textbooks.

Lewin as Social Psychologist

Lewin's American colleagues might have identified him as a developmental psychologist, but his self-identity was much broader, as reflected in his general theory and research on such

---

[9]Although the experiment occurred long before the APA adopted an ethics code, Lewin was sensitive to the emotional states of his young subjects. After they finished the final 30 minutes of observation, the barrier was again raised, and the children were allowed to play with the high-valence toys for as long as they wished.

topics as prejudice, group influence, and leadership. These latter studies are the reason he is considered one of the pioneers of modern social psychology. His leadership research, still frequently cited, grew out of his reflections on the state of the world in the mid-1930s. Mindful of the contrast between the democracy of his new home and the increasingly dictatorial environment of his old one, Lewin became interested in the consequences of different leadership styles. Along with Ronald Lippitt and Ralph White, he completed several experiments on the problem (Lewin, Lippitt, & White, 1939; Lippitt & White, 1943).

The basic procedure was to create different environments for five-person groups of boys (age 10) who were given various craft-making projects (e.g., making masks) to complete. The main experiment contrasted three different leadership styles—authoritarian, democratic, and laissez-faire. Table 9.1, taken from Lippitt and White (1943), describes the three approaches. Each group of boys experienced all three styles, and their behavior was dramatically influenced by their leaders. When led by an autocratic leader, the boys quickly became submissive, failed to take any initiative, did not produce high-quality products, and showed little interest in the tasks. They also tended to be aggressive when the leader was out of the room, and they often made fun of disliked group members, a form of scapegoating. Those in the laissez-faire group did not do much better. Because they were in an "unstructured field," they spent a great deal of time unsuccessfully trying to decide what to do. The lack of adult direction often led to

TABLE 9.1 Leadership Styles Compared by Lewin's Research Group

Authoritarian	Democratic	Laissez-faire
1. All determination of policy by the leader.	1. All policies a matter of group discussion and decision, encouraged and assisted by the leader.	1. Complete freedom for group or individual decision, with a minimum of leader participation.
2. Techniques and activity steps dictated by the authority, one at a time, so that future steps were always uncertain to a large degree.	2. Activity perspective gained during discussion period. General steps to group goal sketched, and where...advice was needed, the leader suggested...alternative procedures from which choice could be made.	2. Various materials supplied by the leader, who made it clear that he would supply information when asked. He took no other part in work discussion.
3. The leader...dictated the particular work task and work companion of each member.	3. The members were free to work with whomever they chose, and the division of tasks was left up to the group.	3. Complete nonparticipation of the leader.
4. The dominator tended to be too "personal" in his praise and criticism of each member; remained aloof from active group participation except when demonstrating.	4. The leader was "objective" or "fact-minded" in his praise and criticism and tried to be a regular group member in spirit without doing too much of the work.	4. Infrequent spontaneous comments on member activities unless questioned and no attempt to appraise or regulate the course of events.

Source: Lippitt & White (1943, p. 487).

confusion, frustration, and hostility. Under this form of leadership, nothing was accomplished. On the other hand, under a more democratic leader, the group became cohesive, task-oriented, and motivated; they also produced more high-quality products. One disturbing finding was that when the boys switched from a democratic to an authoritarian environment, they quickly and with minimal protest succumbed to the tyranny. As Lewin later described it:

> There have been few experiences for me as impressive as seeing the expression on children's faces during the first day under an autocratic leader. The group that had formerly been friendly, open, cooperative, and full of life, became within a short half-hour a rather apathetic-looking gathering without initiative. (quoted in Marrow, 1969, p. 127)

On the other hand, and equally troubling, those shifting from authoritarian to democratic settings had a difficult time overcoming the effects of being told what to do.

The broader implications of the leadership studies were obvious to Lewin. Although he recognized the problem of generalizing beyond the experimental setting, he saw the results as a strong endorsement of the democratic form of government and an indictment of anything short of it. They also reinforced his belief that scientists needed to be "in the arena" rather than confined to the rarified atmosphere of their laboratories. To that end, he became the prototype of the scientist-activist. He became a committed Zionist, vigorously advocating the creation of an independent Jewish state in Palestine, as a place for Jews to establish their own democratic system.[10] He also lobbied (unsuccessfully) for the creation of a psychological research institute at Hebrew University in Jerusalem. Third, Lewin became an early leader in the APA-affiliated Society for the Psychological Study of Social Issues (SPSSI), founded in 1936 and concerned with applying psychological knowledge to the solution of social problems. Activism pervaded his work, and much of his research was designed specifically to solve some real-world problems (Heims, 1978). He called this work "action research."

Action Research The leadership research is just one example of a theme in Lewin's work—using science as a means of bringing about social change. Psychology must do more than just explain behavior, Lewin argued; it must "be equally concerned with discovering how people can change their ways so that they learn to behave better" (quoted in Marrow, 1969, p. 158). During his Iowa years, which extended into the World War II era, he was involved in several studies designed to solve immediate real-world problems, several of which involved group processes. During World War II, for instance, in a project with anthropologist Margaret Mead, Lewin looked at the effects of group processes on convincing people to include more visceral meats (e.g., liver, kidney) in their diets. Such a change would help the war effort—by expanding the variety of foods eaten, shortages in more preferred foods could be avoided. Lewin and Mead found that people were more likely to change following group discussions than after hearing lectures on nutrition.

Much of Lewin's group research occurred in work settings, and for this reason he is an important historical figure for industrial psychologists. For example, in a series of studies designed to increase worker productivity in an industrial setting, Lewin showed that letting workers set production goals after meeting in groups had the twofold effect of improving morale and increasing worker output. Group processes could also be used effectively to train managers and to overcome male prejudice against women workers.

---

[10]The state of Israel was created in 1948, a year after Lewin's death.

- Describe Pavlov's relationship with the Soviets and explain why the Soviets valued his work
- Describe Pavlov's influence on American psychologists
- Describe Watson's research on animal behavior, from mazes to natural environments, and explain the significance of the work
- Explain Watson's analysis of contemporary structural and functional psychology, and what he proposed instead, in his Behaviorist Manifesto
- Describe the conditioning research reported by Watson in his APA presidential address and show its connection to the work of Pavlov and of another Russian, Bekhterev
- Describe Watson's research on basic emotions and the stimuli producing them
- Describe and critically analyze Watson and Rayner's demonstration of conditioned fear
- Show how Mary Cover Jones successfully eliminated a fear response and how her work relates to modern behavior therapy
- Show how Watson brought his behaviorist ideas and scientific training to the world of advertising
- Describe Watson's attempts to popularize the science of behavior

BEHAVIORISM'S ANTECEDENTS

American behaviorists often trace their roots to John B. Watson, and in particular to his so-called **Behaviorist Manifesto**, a paper he tried out in a talk at Columbia University in February 1913 and soon published (Watson, 1913). Yet history seldom turns dramatically on such events—they are usually individual chapters of a more complex narrative. Long before Watson saw the inside of the psychology laboratory at the University of Chicago, forces were at work paving the way for behaviorist thinking to become accepted as the norm by American psychologists. Furthermore, the psychological world did not convert to behaviorism just because of Watson's "revolutionary" pronouncements. Rather, Watson contributed a strong voice to the growing dissatisfaction with introspective psychology. Few psychologists, however, were immediately converted to Watsonian behaviorism (Samelson, 1981). Indeed, Watson was far removed from the academic scene by the time behaviorism became the central force in experimental psychology in the United States.

Behaviorism has a clear affinity with several of the philosophical movements described in Chapters 2 and 3. For example, the behaviorist's belief in the importance of the environment in shaping behavior resonates with the British empiricist-associationist dictum that experience is the all-important determiner of one's mind and character. There are also parallels between the behaviorist's stimulus–response connections and the concept of association. In Chapter 3, you learned about the influence of 19th-century mechanistic and materialist thinking on physiologists; these philosophies are also congenial to behaviorist thinking. During the 19th century **positivism** also emerged; it was associated with the French philosopher Auguste Comte (1798–1857) and eventually taken as an article of faith by behaviorists. Comte argued that we could be certain only of knowledge that results from publicly observable events. *Positive* knowledge was said to be the result of *objective* observations using the systematic methods of science, to be made by unbiased observers. Truth, then, amounted to agreement among these scientific observers. Metaphysical speculation about the fundamental nature of events (including behavioral ones) in the universe was considered to be a worthless exercise, according to the positivists, because such speculations could never be verified objectively. Positivists also valued "practical" knowledge, believing that an intimate connection existed between understanding nature and controlling it. Indeed, Comte argued that the ability to control nature was evidence that nature was understood—creating an effective steam engine, for instance, demonstrated an understanding of several principles of physics. Comte's faith in science even led him to recommend the deliberate redesign of society. This theme of controlling nature, virtually identical to arguments made 200 years earlier by Sir Francis Bacon (Chapter 2), later became a centerpiece of behaviorist thinking and was evident in such works as Skinner's *Walden Two* (1948), a description of an ideal community based on principles of behavioral control. John Watson's prescriptions about child rearing, which you will encounter near the end of this chapter, also fall under the heading of using science to exert control over nature.

At the start of the 20th century, psychologists were beginning to turn toward increased objectivity in their measures of psychological phenomena. One important influence was the rapid acceptance of evolutionary thinking among scientists and the resulting growth of animal psychology, as documented in Chapter 5. Animals cannot introspect, of course, so studying the relationship between human and animal consciousness required behavioral measures. Most 19th-century descriptions of animal behavior were unduly anthropomorphic, but, as we have seen, Morgan established the principle that simpler explanations for animal behaviors were to be favored over unnecessarily complex ones. Explaining a dog's ability to open a gate in terms of trial-and-error learning, rather than by means of intelligence and planning, moved comparative psychology from anecdotes to more objective descriptions of stimuli and responses. Thorndike's puzzle box research in the late 1890s (Chapter 7) is perhaps the clearest manifestation in America of this movement toward increased objectivity in animal psychology. In Czarist Russia at the same time, however, an even greater level of precision could be found in the laboratories of Ivan Pavlov and Vladimir Bekhterev. American psychologists did not immediately realize the value of the Russians' research for their own growing desire for an objective science, but the Russian conditioning approach to research eventually became a model that many American behaviorists emulated.

As the new century unfolded, the trend toward greater objectivity led a number of American psychologists to become disillusioned with the state of experimental psychology, especially its reliance on introspective procedures. The imageless thought controversy (Chapters 4 and 7) is a good illustration of this developing uneasiness. It came as no surprise to some American psychologists that an observer at Würzburg would experience imageless thoughts, while another at Cornell would fail to find them. Because introspective data were ultimately subjective, no independent way of evaluating each claim existed. In an address delivered at the 1904 World's Fair in St. Louis and later published in *Popular Science Monthly*, James McKeen Cattell declared that psychology should not be limited to the study of conscious experience and that introspection need not be the dominant method used by psychologists. In his words:

> The rather widespread notion that there is no psychology apart from introspection is refuted by the brute argument of accomplished fact.

> It seems to me that most of the research work that has been done by me or in my laboratory is nearly as independent of introspection as work in physics or in zoology. The time of mental processes, . . . individual differences, the behavior of animals and of children, these and other topics I have investigated without requiring the slightest introspection on the part of the subject. . . .
>
> It is certainly difficult to penetrate by analogy into the consciousness of the lower animals . . . and of children, but the study of their behavior has already yielded much and promises much more. (Cattell, 1904; quoted in Woodworth, 1931, pp. 48–49)

And reflecting the positivist thinking just described, Cattell said that he saw "no reason why the application of systematized knowledge to the *control of human nature* may not in the course of the present century accomplish results commensurate with the nineteenth century applications of physical science to the material world" (p. 49, emphasis added).

In the same year that Cattell addressed the St. Louis World's Fair, another event marked a milestone in a career that was shifting from a fascination with the digestive system to a passion for discovering how the brain works. The event was the awarding of a Nobel Prize for physiology to the Russian scientist Ivan Petrovich Pavlov.

PAVLOV'S LIFE AND WORK

Pavlov earned the Nobel Prize for his painstaking and ingenious investigations of the physiology of digestion. In particular, he was known for inventing or perfecting a number of surgical techniques to facilitate this research. Yet when the 54-year-old scientist delivered his acceptance address in December of 1904 at the Nobel awards ceremony in Stockholm, Sweden, he did not have much to say about the work that won him the prize. Rather, in an address entitled "The First Sure Steps along the Path of a New Investigation" (Babkin, 1949), Pavlov described the research that had interested him for the past several years and would occupy the rest of his life. This research is familiar to you, and it probably brings to mind images of salivating dogs. Pavlov's conditioning research eventually provided a model for American behavioral scientists, although Pavlov himself always insisted that he was a physiologist, not a psychologist, and his regard for psychology was not high. He once pointed out that while the study of reflexes had been dominated historically by those taking a psychological (by which he meant introspective) approach, his more objective strategy offered the hope of these investigations of the reflex "being liberated from such evil influences" (Pavlov, 1906, p. 618).

The Development of a Physiologist

Ivan Petrovich Pavlov (1849–1936) was born into relative poverty in the small farming village of Ryazan in west central Russia. His father was a priest, and his mother was the daughter of a priest; despite their resulting social status, both parents had to work as farmers to feed a large family. Ivan was the firstborn of 11 children, 6 of whom died in childhood. His early schooling was geared toward following in his father's clerical footsteps. While studying at the Ryazan Ecclesiastical Seminary, however, an interest in science blossomed from his discovery of (a) Darwin's *Origin of Species* and (b) *Reflexes of the Brain*, published in 1863 by Russia's leading 19th-century physiologist, Ivan Sechenov (1829–1905). Sechenov argued that all cortical processes involved complex relationships between excitatory and inhibitory processes in the nervous system and that "psychical" (psychological) events could be reduced to and explained by reflex action in the cortex. It was a model very much in tune with the mechanistic and materialistic climate of 19th-century science, and it was influenced by Sechenov's contact with some of Europe's leading physiologists. These ideas eventually became the cornerstone of Pavlov's model of nervous system functioning.

Pavlov left the seminary and enrolled as a student of physiology at the University of St. Petersburg in 1870, thereby trading a simple rural life for the glamour of Russia's most important city.[1] St. Petersburg, located in northwest Russia near the Gulf of Finland, was the cultural, political, and intellectual center of Russia in the late 19th century. It was also Russia's capital city until it was replaced by Moscow in 1918, following the Soviet Revolution. In this high-powered environment, Pavlov completed a degree in medicine in 1883 and became a research physiologist. After additional years of study, several low-level research positions, and financial hardship, he was named director of the physiology division of St. Petersburg's Imperial Institute of Experimental Medicine in 1891. During the 1890s he systematically investigated the physiology of the digestive system, and this research led to his winning the Nobel Prize.

Pavlov studied digestion by isolating various parts of the digestive system and extracting digestive fluids. The quantities of the various fluids secreted were measured as a function of the type of substance fed to the animal. The research was noted for its precision and for the development of surgical techniques to isolate and collect digestive secretions in dogs that were otherwise functioning normally. The best-known technique was the "Pavlov pouch." He created it by segregating a small section of stomach and redesigning it as a miniature stomach. It was situated so that food could not enter when it reached the stomach from the esophagus. A small tube or fistula led from the pouch to the exterior, thereby providing a means to collect the fluids secreted by the mini-stomach. Uncontaminated by food, these fluids could be analyzed with precision (Gray, 1979).

In addition to investigating gastric secretions, Pavlov studied salivary responses, relating them to the type of substance placed in the dog's mouth. He measured salivation with another fistula, this time a small tube directly connected to a salivary duct. Inevitably, as all dog owners know, the dogs would begin to salivate before food reached their mouths. One of Pavlov's students, S. G. Vul'fson, examined the phenomenon in a study comparing salivation to moist versus dry foods. The main finding was that dogs salivated more to dry foods (less saliva needed for moist foods), but a secondary finding was that after a number of trials, the dogs salivated before the food arrived (Windholz, 1997). The outcome presented Pavlov with a dilemma. On the one hand, these "psychic" secretions were a nuisance, reducing the accuracy of Pavlov's attempts to measure an exact amount of saliva in response to a specific amount of food. On the other hand, the animal's behavior was predictable, suggesting to Pavlov an objective way to study those "reflexes of the brain" that he had read about in Sechenov's book. Whereas a less creative scientist might have tried to control the secretions to focus on the problem at hand, the basic physiology of digestion, Pavlov chose to examine this new phenomenon directly. After the turn of the century, it became his life's work.

---

[1] After Lenin's death in 1924, the Soviets renamed the city Leningrad; in 1991, following the collapse of the Soviet Union, it was rechristened St. Petersburg.

Working in Pavlov's Laboratory

In a biography of Pavlov, Babkin (1949) sketched a fascinating account of life within Pavlov's laboratory. As a student of Pavlov's at the turn of the 20th century, Babkin was present during the early years of the research on conditioning. The Imperial Institute of Experimental Medicine was about a dozen years old, and although it was prestigious within Russia, it was not very impressive to the international visitor in those early years. As Babkin noted, "Compared with the palatial American laboratories, [Pavlov's] was a mere hovel" (p. 68). Although its budget was generous by Russian standards, Pavlov found it necessary to raise additional money through the sale of gastric juices taken from the dogs during "sham feeding" experiments. Dogs would eat normally, but a fistula connected to the esophagus redirected the food to a collection tube. The dog would eat and swallow, but the food never made it to the stomach, which nonetheless secreted gastric fluids in anticipation of the food's arrival. Another tube in the stomach collected the juices. Pavlov marketed the vile-tasting fluid as an elixir for those suffering from various digestive ailments, especially those resulting from "an insufficient flow of the [their] own gastric juice" (p. 69). It was also sold to laboratories throughout Europe for research purposes.

Despite the difficult conditions, Pavlov established rigorous controls in the laboratory and gradually created a highly professional research environment. He was especially careful about creating an antiseptic environment for his surgical procedures. That, combined with his skill as a surgeon, produced an environment that dramatically reduced infection and ensured the postoperative survival of virtually all of the animals in Pavlov's care. He also developed an efficient way to train the dozens of research assistants who passed through his laboratory.[2] Most of the assistants were already qualified as physicians and were looking to add a doctorate in physiology to their medical degree (Todes, 1997a). Whenever a new worker entered the lab, Pavlov would assign an experienced worker to guide the newcomer through the standard procedures and then give this person a problem that had already been investigated. Thus the student would learn experimental procedures without being under pressure to produce new findings while also providing an ongoing program of **replication**. Once the earlier research had been replicated successfully, the worker was given a new problem to investigate. A failure to replicate would trigger additional research to clear up the contradiction. Replication, of course, is a cornerstone of sound scientific research—results that cannot be repeated are of no value.

Beginning in 1910 (but not fully equipped until 1925), the Institute built a special laboratory for Pavlov's conditioning research. Later known as the Tower of Silence, it featured extensive soundproofing techniques to ensure that the dogs were responding only to the stimulus being studied at the time and not to any extraneous stimuli. As Figure 10.1 shows, there were eight experimental chambers, four on each of two floors that were separated by an intermediate floor. Each research chamber was fully insulated and separated from other chambers by a corridor. Experimenters were separated from the dogs by the double wall that is evident in Figure 10.2, although they occasionally joined the dogs for photo opportunities (Figure 10.3).

---

[2] According to Windholz (1990), no fewer than 146 researchers worked in Pavlov's laboratories between 1897 and 1936.

FIGURE 10.1 Cross-section and floor plan of Pavlov's laboratory at St. Petersburg. From Pavlov (1928).

FIGURE 10.2 Apparatus arrangement in Pavlov's laboratory, around 1915. From Pavlov (1928).

Pavlov's Classical Conditioning Research

In the spring of 1924, Pavlov organized a series of lectures that summarized about 25 years of his work on conditioning. He gave the lectures at the Military Medical Academy in St. Petersburg and then rewrote them for publication. Translated into English by G. V. Anrep, a British researcher and another former student of Pavlov's, they were published as *Conditioned Reflexes: An Investigation of the Physiological Activity of the Cerebral Cortex* by the British Royal Society in 1927 (Pavlov, 1927/1960).

FIGURE 10.3 Pavlov (right center) and students in the conditioning lab.

In his opening lecture, Pavlov acknowledged his debt to Sechenov and Darwin, credited Thorndike (Chapter 7) with doing pioneering research on the relationship between "visual and tactile stimuli on the one hand and the locomotor apparatus on the other" (p. 6), and then described the start of his own inquiries and his recognition that the problem had to be attacked from a physiological rather than a psychological standpoint. Pavlov believed that restricting the investigation to specific external stimuli and measurable physiological responses was the only scientifically defensible strategy to use. The "psychological approach," on the other hand, implied a dualism of mental and physical processes that Pavlov was not willing to accept. He often referred to an episode from the early years of his laboratory when one of his students, Anton Snarskii, investigated the effects of severing the facial nerves on the development of a conditioned response. Despite opposition from Pavlov (or so Pavlov later claimed), Snarskii interpreted his results in mentalistic terms and referred to such processes as "visual association" and "recognition" (Windholz, 1986). Pavlov believed such an approach to be unnecessarily speculative.[3]

[3]Pavlov often told the Snarskii story, using it as an illustration of the failure of a purely "psychological approach." Todes (1997a) examined the original episode carefully, however, and discovered that Pavlov's memory became altered over the years. At the time of the Snarskii research (1901), Pavlov was actually the one thinking in more subjective terms, whereas Snarskii was proposing a more mechanistic and associationistic model. As the years went by, Pavlov apparently felt the need to distance himself from his earlier psychological theorizing. In reorganizing memory to make it consistent with his later beliefs (a common feature of autobiographical memory), Pavlov convinced himself that he had been the objective one and Snarskii had been subjective, when the reverse was closer to the truth. The interesting historiographic point here is that you cannot always rely on the accuracy of autobiographical accounts.

After a detailed description of basic reflex action, Pavlov concluded his opening lecture by referring to the accidental discovery of salivary conditioning that launched him into his 25 years of research:

> Let us return now to the simplest reflex from which our investigations started. If food...finds its way into the mouth, a secretion of saliva is produced. The purpose of this secretion is...to alter [the food] chemically....But, in addition to this, a similar reflex secretion is evoked when these substances are placed at a distance from the dog and the receptor organs affected are only those of smell and sight. Even the vessel from which the food has been given is sufficient to evoke [a reflex] complete in all its details; and, further, the secretion may be provoked even by the sight of the person who brought the vessel, or by the sound of his footsteps. (Pavlov, 1927/1960, p. 13)

In his second lecture, Pavlov began by describing some of the technical details of his procedures and the measures taken to control experimental conditions. He explained that the dog presented with food shows both secretory (i.e., salivary) reflexes and motor reflexes. It drools, but it also turns its head, moves its mouth, and so on. That Pavlov decided to study the secretory reflex and ignore the motor reflexes is another indication of his concern over precise measurement and a desire to avoid anthropomorphic speculation about what the animal might be "trying" to do.

Conditioning and Extinction   Having set the stage, Pavlov described the basic procedure for acquiring a conditioned reflex. The essence of the technique is to pair a stimulus known to produce a particular response (i.e., salivation) with a neutral stimulus, such as a tone or a metronome.[4] During acquisition, then, the starting point is an already-existing reflex. For Pavlov, this reflex was the **unconditioned reflex (UCR)** of salivating when food (the **unconditioned stimulus, UCS**) was presented to the animal. Conditioning involved presenting first a neutral stimulus and then the UCS. This neutral stimulus Pavlov called a **conditional stimulus (CS)**—later translated as conditioned stimulus—because the resulting reflex depended on (was "conditional" on) the CS-UCS pairing. This resulting reflex was called a **conditioned reflex (CR)**.

After describing acquisition, Pavlov showed how a CR could undergo **extinction** if the metronome (the CS) was sounded without being accompanied by food (the UCS). Pavlov let the metronome run for 30-second intervals every 2 minutes, recording the amount of saliva secreted and what he called the "latent period"—the amount of time between the starting of the metronome and the beginning of salivation. As Pavlov described it, the "weakening of the reflex to a conditional stimulus which is repeated a certain number of times without reinforcement may appropriately be termed experimental extinction of conditioned reflexes" (Pavlov, 1927/1960, pp. 48–49). With successive extinction trials, it took longer (i.e., greater latency) for the animal to begin salivating, and the amount of salivation steadily declined.

Generalization and Differentiation   Pavlov's subsequent lectures describe his procedures for demonstrating a wide range of conditioning phenomena, including many of the ones you learned about in your general psychology course. Two of the most familiar

---

[4]Ironically, although most students think that Pavlov's typical CS was a bell, Pavlov reported that "the violent ringing of a bell" was seldom effective as a CS, because the dog tended to be startled by it (Pavlov, 1906, p. 616).

are generalization and discrimination (the latter referred to as differentiation by Pavlov). **Generalization** is in evidence when a response conditioned to stimulus A also occurs, to some degree at least, in response to stimuli that are similar to stimulus A. So if the CS of a tone of 60 cycles per second (CPS) produces 8 drops of saliva, the animal will also respond to a 70-CPS tone, perhaps with 6 drops. A generalization gradient also exists—the amount of saliva secreted is proportional to the similarity of the CS and the tested stimulus. **Differentiation** results from pairing the 60-CPS tone with food, while presenting the 70-CPS tone without the food. Eventually, the dog salivates only to the 60-CPS tone.

Pavlov also went to great lengths to incorporate Sechenov's constructs of cortical excitation and inhibition into his descriptions. For example, excitatory processes were said to be involved in acquisition and generalization, whereas inhibitory cortical processes contributed to extinction and differentiation. In general, Pavlov was not interested in the conditioning phenomena per se, but only in terms of the light they shed on how the brain operated.

Experimental Neurosis   One interesting outgrowth of Pavlov's research on generalization and differentiation was his discovery of how a breakdown in differentiation could produce **experimental neurosis** or "pathological disturbance," as he put it in the title of his Lecture 17. He first projected a circle onto a screen in front of the dog's face, pairing its presentation with food. Soon, the circle became a normal CS for the CR of salivation. After creating this conditioned reflex, Pavlov then trained the dog to make an easy differentiation between the circle and an ellipse that had a 4:3 ratio between its two axes. The shape of the ellipse was then changed until it reached a 9:8 ratio; that is, the ellipse was made to look more and more like the circle. The dog showed the ability to discriminate at first, but it then failed, and eventually its behavior reached the point where it even had difficulty distinguishing an easy 2:1 ellipse from the circle. For Pavlov, then, neurotic behavior meant a breakdown in the ability to make normal differentiations. The neurosis also manifested itself in other ways. As Pavlov described it,

> At the same time the whole behavior of the animal underwent an abrupt change. The hitherto quiet dog began to squeal in its stand, kept wriggling about, tore off with its teeth the apparatus for mechanical stimulation of the skin, and bit through the tubes connecting the animal's room with the observer, a behavior which never happened before. On being taken into the experimental room the dog now barked violently, which was also contrary to its usual custom; in short it presented all the symptoms of an acute neurosis. (Pavlov, 1927/1960, p. 291)

During the course of his research on experimental neurosis, Pavlov noticed that although all the dogs were adversely affected, they differed in how they displayed their pathology. Furthermore, these variations seemed to reflect individual differences in the temperaments of the dogs. Thus some dogs were generally more excitable than others—they tended to respond to the experimental neurosis procedure like the dog just described. Others, however, who were ordinarily of a more placid temperament, reacted to the procedure by becoming even more withdrawn. As he did with all of his results, Pavlov interpreted these outcomes in terms of excitatory and inhibitory cortical processes. He believed that the individual differences in temperament related to whether excitatory or inhibitory processes were more dominant.

A Program of Research Pavlov's research is a classic example of how experiments seldom occur in isolation but are embedded in an ongoing, systematic program of research. The outcome of one study has interest in itself, but it also raises new questions and leads invariably to the next study. For instance, the acquisition research led naturally to the question of the precise timing of the CS and UCS, and Pavlov and his students completed dozens of studies that carefully varied the timing and the sequencing of the CS-UCS interval. Similarly, research developed over the years on such topics as (a) higher order conditioning, which involved pairing a new CS with an already-conditioned one; (b) the durability of extinction, in which it was found that if a dog was returned to the laboratory several days after extinction, the CR would occur to some degree (i.e., so-called spontaneous recovery occurred); and (c) the effectiveness of various types of conditional stimuli in terms of how quickly conditioning could be established.

The sheer size and relentless productivity of Pavlov's lab made it easy to overlook other experimental demonstrations of the same type of conditioning that occurred at the time of or before Pavlov's initial studies. Both the American psychologist E. B. Twitmyer and the Viennese physiologist Alois Kreidl produced conditioning in their labs (Logan, 2002). However, neither Twitmyer, who studied the knee-jerk reflex, nor Kreidl, who was studying sensory capacity in fish, developed anything like Pavlov's research program.

Pavlov and the Soviets

Pavlov was the prototype of the scientist whose life was his work, a philosophy reflected in an article he wrote near the end of his life for a Soviet youth organization. He told them that scientists must be systematic, modest, and passionate about their work, and that "science demands of a man his whole life. And even if you could have two lives, they would not be sufficient. Science calls for tremendous effort and great passion" (quoted in Babkin, 1949, p. 110). While in the laboratory—and from September through May, he was there virtually every day—Pavlov was completely absorbed in the research at hand, and he expected everyone else to share his passion. Thus he was occasionally a stern taskmaster and was known for his frequent but short-lived outbursts of temper when mistakes were made. Nonetheless, his workers were intensely devoted to him; they knew that his anger passed quickly and was not directed at them personally.

One famous story about Pavlov emphasizes his single-minded devotion to his work. Although the story might be more mythical than real, it illustrates Pavlov's priorities. Pavlov is said to have admonished a worker for being late during the height of the 1917 Russian Revolution. When the worker told of bloody skirmishes in the streets of St. Petersburg that had caused him to take a more circuitous route to the laboratory, Pavlov was not impressed. After all, he had made his customary 3-mile walk to the lab, arriving safely and promptly at 9 o'clock. Pavlov made it clear to the worker that a mere revolution was not to interfere with the important work of the laboratory. The assistant was told to leave home earlier during the next revolution (Babkin, 1949).

Of course, the revolution of 1917 profoundly affected everything in Russia, including Pavlov's work. Pavlov was initially hostile to the winners of the Soviet Revolution, Lenin's Bolsheviks; he once said publicly that if "that which the Bolsheviks are doing with Russia is an experiment, for such an experiment I should regret giving even a frog" (quoted in Babkin, 1949, p. 161). He also protested directly to Stalin in the late 1920s about a policy to admit only Communist professors to the Russian Academy of Science, telling the Russian leader, "On account of what you are doing I am ashamed to be called a Russian" (quoted in Gantt, 1973). Pavlov's ambivalent attitude was not hard to understand—the Soviets confiscated his Nobel Prize money and, when he requested permission to emigrate in the early 1920s, they refused.[5] Yet by the end of his life, Pavlov had come to accept the reality of the Soviet Union. According to Babkin, Pavlov's change of heart came about primarily because of the developing threat of the Nazis in Germany, who came to power in 1933. Fiercely patriotic, Pavlov recalled the huge Russian losses at the hands of Germany in World War I and feared (accurately) that the Nazis would bring more suffering to his beloved homeland. In that context, the Soviets clearly appeared to be the lesser of two evils.

Pavlov's gradual accommodation to the reality of the Soviet state also was aided by the government's strong backing of his work. As early as 1921, when Russia was immersed in civil war, conditions were generally chaotic, and Pavlov's laboratory was in dire straits, the Soviets saw to it that Pavlov's research continued with as much support as they could provide. For example, it was officially decreed that a special committee be formed "to create as soon as possible the most favorable conditions for safeguarding the scientific work of Academician Pavlov and his collaborators" (quoted in Babkin, 1949, p. 165). These conditions included extra rations and a guarantee to fully equip Pavlov's laboratory.

It is easy to see why the Soviets were enamored of Pavlov. A major theme of his research was that controlling the environment could change behavior—actions could be "conditioned." That, of course, was exactly what the Soviets hoped to do on a broad scale, conditioning citizens to be comfortable with the Marxist-Leninist ideal whereby each should produce according to one's abilities and receive according to one's needs. Thus, although Pavlov had no interests beyond understanding the physiology of the brain, his research had great propaganda value for the Soviets. This tolerance by the Soviets is shown in a brief notice in *Time* magazine, which the American psychologist Walter Miles cut out and pasted into his diary in late 1929. It said that Pavlov had

> refused an official celebration of his 80th birthday.... Said he: "I deplore the destruction of cultural values by illiterate Communists." Mindful that upon his research rests the behavioristic "Science of Marxism"..., the Soviet tolerates his slaps gently and without reproach, babies him. Birthday gifts from the Soviet to him include $50,000 endowment of his laboratory and an assurance that traffic would be diverted from the street near it so as not to disturb the conditioned reflexes of some six score dogs, kept there for experimental purposes. (Miles, 1929)

After Pavlov's death from pneumonia in 1936, the Soviets treated him like a war hero. A monument to him was erected in St. Petersburg (at that time renamed Leningrad), the Medical Institute was renamed the Pavlov Institute, his wife was given a generous pension, and his brain was preserved.

---

[5]It is important to keep in mind that Pavlov was 71 years old in 1920. He had many influential international physiologist colleagues, who tried in various ways to support him during the hard times of the Russian civil war (e.g., fund-raising, arranging food shipments for his dogs). According to Todes (1995), however, his friends could not arrange an academic appointment for him, mainly because of his age; so emigration would have meant retirement, an outcome that Pavlov would have found unpalatable. Todes argued that Pavlov's talk of emigration was primarily a negotiating tool designed to improve conditions in his lab.

Pavlov and the Americans

Western scientists knew about Pavlov because of the Nobel Prize, but the impact of his conditioning research was slow in being felt. Most American psychologists were introduced to Pavlov through an article published in the *Psychological Bulletin* in 1909 by Robert Yerkes, whose interests at that time were mainly in comparative psychology (see Chapter 8), and Sergius Morgulis, a Russian student. One feature of the article was a series of apparatus sketches that eventually resulted in mistaken portrayals of Pavlov's apparatus that continue to this day in textbooks. See the Close-Up for this story.

CLOSE-UP

MISPORTRAYING PAVLOV'S APPARATUS

You probably recognize the sketch in Figure 10.4a. It shows up in one form or another in most general psychology texts, probably including the one you used, and it is usually identified as Pavlov's conditioning apparatus. It wasn't. Rather, it was devised by a German physiologist, G. F. Nicolai, who briefly worked in Pavlov's laboratory (Goodwin, 1991a). Nicolai wished to improve on how the saliva was recorded in the early years in Pavlov's lab, when the drops of saliva were simply counted as they fell into the graduated cylinder portrayed in Figure 10.4b. The early apparatus was cumbersome—a problem recognized by Pavlov,

who eventually developed the more sophisticated setup shown in Figure 10.2. How did the mistaken attribution of Nicolai's apparatus occur?

The article by Yerkes and Morgulis (1909), which introduced Pavlov's research to American psychologists, included both the sketches in Figure 10.4. Neither was labeled, but the text of the article described Figure 10.4b as showing a dog prepared for conditioning research in Pavlov's lab, whereas Figure 10.4a was described as showing "the modification of experimental technique *which has been devised by Nicolai in Berlin*" (p. 259, emphasis added).

(a)   (b)

FIGURE 10.4   (a) Conditioning setup developed by German physiologist Nicolai, but usually attributed to Pavlov; (b) Early device used by Pavlov for recording salivary responses. Both from Nicolai (1907).

The distinction between Nicolai's and Pavlov's procedures was recognized by John Watson, who reproduced and correctly labeled both drawings in his well-known comparative psychology text of 1914. The first erroneous attribution seems to have been in a popular introductory textbook by Walter Hunter (1919); it included only Figure 10.4a, referred to it as Pavlov's apparatus, and cited the Yerkes and Morgulis article. From this point on, the sketch of Nicolai's experimental setup became the standard depiction of Pavlov's apparatus, partly because it is consistent with Pavlov's eventual separation of dog and experimenter into two separate rooms, but also because it is simply a more interesting sketch than Figure 10.4b.

The perpetuation of this error over the years provides an important lesson for any writer—that is, beware of relying too heavily on secondary sources. Many subsequent writers probably included the wrong drawing simply because it had become so widely used by other textbook writers. When seeing the same drawing over and over, it is easy to assume it must be accurate.

Despite the Yerkes and Morgulis (1909) article, Pavlov's research had little immediate impact on American psychologists. The work was of interest to those studying animal behavior, but at a time when American psychology was still the science of human conscious experience, salivating dogs did not seem especially relevant. Most introductory psychology textbooks before 1920 either failed to mention Pavlov at all (including a 1911 text by Yerkes) or mentioned his work just briefly (Goodwin, 1991a). Even John Watson, whose proclamation of behaviorism you will read about shortly, did not see the immediate relevance of Pavlov's work for his model of learning. Instead, he was initially more influenced by the conditioning work of another Russian physiologist and rival of Pavlov's, Vladimir Bekhterev (Skinner, 1981). Bekhterev investigated motor rather than salivary conditioning, in which muscle movements were conditioned to various stimuli. This lent itself more readily to Watson's interests in overt behavior, which of course relies on muscle action.

Pavlov's major impact on American psychology began in the 1920s, when much of his work was translated into English for the first time (the lecture series described earlier). Pavlov also visited the United States twice, once in 1923 for a conference and lecture series at Rockefeller Institute in New York and again in 1929 for the Ninth International Congress of Psychology at Yale University. There he delivered one of the major addresses (Duncan, 1980), an impassioned description (in Russian) of his research on conditioning to a large audience of American and international psychologists. As one observer noted, "The audience was spellbound, and the following standing ovation brought little smiles and bows of appreciation from the Guest of Honor of the Congress" (Withington, quoted in Duncan, 1980).

American psychologists, especially behaviorists, eventually understood the importance of Pavlov's research for their own theories of learning. A passage from Ernest Hilgard's well-known *Theories of Learning* (1948) shows that Pavlov's importance was taken for granted by the late 1940s. Hilgard pointed out that research on "conditioned salivary responses in dogs was carried out systematically by Pavlov over many years, and he discovered most of the relationships which later studies have more fully explored. The translations of his terms have become common in the literature of learning" (Hilgard, 1948, p. 55).

Finally, Pavlov had a direct impact on the career choice of a young B. F. Skinner (Chapter 11), whose decision to pursue behavioral research was strongly influenced by reading Pavlov's *Conditioned Reflexes* (1927/1960). Skinner once wrote that a guiding principle in his scientific life was Pavlov's simple dictum that if you "control your conditions...you will see order" (Skinner, 1956, p. 223). Skinner was also excited by the writings of an American psychologist who shared with Pavlov a passion for systematic research grounded in measurable behavior. This person was John B. Watson, usually considered to be the founder of the American school of thought that came to be known as behaviorism.

JOHN B. WATSON AND THE FOUNDING OF BEHAVIORISM

Near the beginning of the chapter, I mentioned that at the start of the 20th century, a number of American psychologists argued that psychology should adopt a more "objective" methodology than introspection. One example was the address by Cattell at the 1904 St. Louis World's Fair. Also at St. Louis and probably in the audience for Cattell's address was John B. Watson, a young psychologist with a brand new PhD from the University of Chicago. The developing trends toward objectivity in psychology were beginning to crystallize in the thinking and writing of this young man, and he would shortly become the mouthpiece for the movement that came to be called behaviorism.

The Young Functionalist at Chicago

Watson was born in 1878 in a rural area just outside Greenville, South Carolina, into a family that would earn the label "dysfunctional" today. His father was a marginally successful farmer whose interests included consuming large amounts of alcohol, brawling, and committing adultery. Watson's mother was fiercely religious, enough so to name her son after a well-known Baptist preacher, John Broadus, and to insist that her son aspire to the ministry. Growing up in this environment, Watson understandably developed behavior problems of his own; by mid-adolescence he was a known troublemaker and had been arrested at least twice. Nonetheless, he was known to be an intelligent young man when he entered Furman University in Greenville at the age of 16. He graduated with a master's degree in 1900.

Watson's mother died during his final year at Furman, releasing him from any obligation to pursue the ministry. Instead, influenced by one of his Furman professors, he applied to and was accepted at the University of Chicago. Eight years old in 1900, the university was established with Rockefeller oil money and presided over by William Rainey Harper. As you recall from Chapter 7's discussion of functionalism, Harper envisioned a "practical" university that would produce leaders for an emerging class in America—the professional elite, experts who would manage society's improvement and industry's productivity. Watson's initial intention was to study philosophy and psychology, which coexisted in the philosophy department at Chicago. He quickly discovered that neither philosophy nor introspective psychology appealed to him (he had no talent for introspection), but he was comfortable with the functionalist psychology prevalent at Chicago. He was especially attracted to comparative psychology—not a surprise considering his rural background and familiarity with animals. Many years later, Watson's son rather painfully recalled that his father "preferred the company of animals to people most of the time" (Hannush, 1987, p. 150).

Watson's interests in animal behavior began to shape his beliefs about psychology in general. When reflecting on his Chicago years, he later wrote that he was always uncomfortable with introspective methods and human subjects but that with animals, he was "at home.... More and more the thought presented itself: Can't I find out by watching their behavior everything that the other students are finding out by using [human subjects]?" (Watson, 1936, p. 279). This belief was reinforced by Watson's contacts with Jacques Loeb and Henry Donaldson. Loeb was a German physiologist who studied **tropisms**, movements of plants or animals that are forced automatically by some aspect of the environment. For example, a flower that always faces the sun is said to be showing a positive heliotropism (*helio* = sun). Loeb was an uncompromising materialist and mechanist who believed that organic life could be understood as a series of automatic responses to stimuli. Donaldson was a neurologist specializing in the nervous system of white rats.

Watson's doctoral dissertation, codirected by Donaldson and James Angell, was a study of the relationship between cortical development and learning in young white rats. It was an important study; at the time, many leading physiologists believed that rats were incapable of true "associative learning" because their brains contained few if any "medullated" fibers.[6] Through a painstaking series of studies that showcased his talents as a careful scientist, Watson demonstrated that rats showed minimal learning ability for approximately the first 3 weeks of their lives, but that their ability to form associations improved dramatically in their fourth week. Furthermore, during this same time, the number of medullated fibers increased significantly. Thus Watson concluded that associations could be formed in young white rats and that these associations were correlated with cortical development. Watson borrowed $350 from Donaldson and had his results published as *Animal Education: An Experimental Study of the Psychical Development of the White Rat, Correlated with the Growth of Its Nervous System* (Watson, 1903). It earned him the doctorate and an offer to remain at Chicago as an instructor. Watson accepted.

The Watson-Carr Maze Studies

Watson remained on the Chicago faculty from 1903 to 1908, building a reputation as a good teacher and a careful scientist. His most important research during this time involved studying rats in mazes; the studies were completed with Harvey Carr, then a graduate student at Chicago, later an important leader in the functionalist movement, and eventually chair of Chicago's psychology department (Chapter 7).

The goal of the Watson-Carr studies (Carr & Watson, 1908; Watson, 1907) was to determine which senses were needed for a rat to learn a maze. Watson was intrigued by the maze studies done at Clark by Willard Small (Close-Up—Chapter 6) but believed that Small had not been very systematic when trying to identify the factors contributing to the rat's ability to learn a maze. For example, Small's willingness to let the rats live in the maze at night made it impossible to evaluate how the learning occurred. Watson and Carr remedied that problem and others, producing a methodologically brilliant series of studies that established (at least for a time) the importance of the kinesthetic (muscle) sense for maze learning.

In their first study (Watson, 1907), Watson and Carr eliminated the ability of rats to use their senses when solving a modified version of the Hampton Court maze. Displaying skillful surgical techniques, Watson removed the eyes from some rats, the middle ears from others, and the olfactory bulbs from a third group. Deprived of their various senses, the rats nonetheless learned the maze with ease. Watson and Carr also found that learning ability was not markedly hindered by removing the rats' whiskers, or by anesthetizing the

---

[6]Today such fibers would be called "myelinated axons."

rats' feet. By a process of elimination (literally), they concluded that the only important factors in the formation of learned associations were "the kinesthetic impressions coupled with certain other intra-organic impressions" (Watson, 1907, p. 84). That is, the animals were learning to associate sequences of muscle movements with the various turns in the maze. In essence, they learned to take seven steps, then turn right for another five steps, then turn left, and so on.

Having ruled out one sense after another, Watson and Carr set out to provide direct evidence of their remaining hypothesis about the kinesthetic sense. In their second study (Carr & Watson, 1908), they hit on the clever idea of shortening or lengthening the maze that their rats had already learned. Figure 10.5 shows the maze they used, in its full-length version; the piece that could be removed is shaded. The effects were dramatic—rats initially trained in the full-length maze literally ran into the walls of the shortened maze. For example, according to Watson's lab notes, one rat "ran into [the wall] with all her strength. Was badly staggered and did not recover normal conduct until she had gone 9 feet" (Carr & Watson, 1908, p. 39).

FIGURE 10.5 Maze used by Watson and Carr to test their kinesthetic model of maze learning; shaded piece could be removed to produce a shorter version of the maze. From Carr and Watson (1908).

FIGURE 10.6 Satirical antivivisectionist cartoon of Watson, after the Watson-Carr studies were publicized. From Dewsbury (1990a).

Similarly, rats trained in the shortened maze and tested in the long version often started to turn at the point where the correct turn used to be.

The Watson-Carr studies are models of scientific research, arriving at a data-based conclusion by eliminating one alternative hypothesis after another and then producing a direct demonstration of the viability of the remaining (kinesthetic) hypothesis. They also are a good illustration of the naiveté of scientists about how their research will be accepted in the public eye. Watson might have thought he was simply pursuing an important question about learning, but in the public eye he became a target for antivivisectionists[7] and was portrayed in the *New York Times* on December 30, 1906, as a butcher of helpless white rats, chopping out bits and pieces of them to satisfy some idle scientific curiosity (Figure 10.6).

Opportunity Knocks at Johns Hopkins

By 1908, Watson (Figure 10.7) was known among his professional colleagues as an up-and-coming star in the world of experimental psychology. He was also beginning to feel unappreciated at Chicago, where he still held the low academic rank of instructor after 5 years. Thus, when offered a full professor position, control of a laboratory, and more than double his salary from Johns Hopkins University, he could hardly refuse. Furthermore, within a year of his arrival in Baltimore, the head of the psychology department, James Mark Baldwin (Chapter 6), was fired for moral reasons (when arrested in a police raid on a house of prostitution, Baldwin claimed he was doing research). Barely into his third decade, Watson found himself in charge of psychology at Johns Hopkins University. Over the next 12 years, before he also would be fired for moral reasons, he would (a) cement his reputation

---

[7]Like today's animal rights activists, antivivisectionists protested the use of animals for research purposes; their influence on early comparative psychology has been documented nicely by Dewsbury (1990a).

FIGURE 10.7 John B. Watson in 1908, at age 30.

as a leading researcher in the world of animal psychology, (b) proclaim behaviorism, and (c) develop a program of research in developmental psychology with an emphasis on the study of emotional development.

Watson and Animal Behavior Once settled into his new position at Johns Hopkins, Watson launched a wide-ranging program of research in animal behavior. Like his dissertation and the maze studies with Carr at Chicago, some of the research was of the basic laboratory variety and included work in animal psychophysics. For example, he studied the visual abilities of several species by training them to make choices between pairs of slightly different stimuli (e.g., Watson, 1909) and by using the motor conditioning procedures of Pavlov's Russian colleague Bekhterev (Watson, 1916). The logic of Watson's psychophysics research was simple—if an animal could be trained or conditioned to respond correctly to one stimulus (e.g., light red) while not responding to another (e.g., a darker shade of red), then the animal must be able to perceive the difference between the two.

Outside the laboratory, Watson continued a series of naturalistic studies begun while he was still at the University of Chicago. He spent several summers on a small island near the Florida Keys (Bird Key, one of the Dry Tortugas) observing the behavior of several species of terns. In contrast with Watson's later writings, which downplayed the importance of the instinctive control of behavior, especially human behavior, this research reads like an early version of the kind of ethological research later associated with names like Konrad Lorenz and Niko Tinbergen; in it, Watson emphasized the importance of instinctive behavior for species survival (Dewsbury, 1994). Watson carefully documented the mating behaviors of the terns on Bird Key, their nest building and territoriality, and their behavior relating to the care of offspring before and after their hatching (Todd & Morris, 1986). He also observed that recently hatched birds would often persistently follow him around the island. This of course is the same behavior studied by Spalding (Close-Up—Chapter 5) and later called imprinting by Lorenz.

Watson's Behaviorist Manifesto In 1913, Watson accepted an invitation from Cattell to speak at Columbia University. By then he believed he had sufficient stature to proclaim what he had believed for at least 10 years—that it was time for the field to move away from an introspective psychology that studied consciousness and toward a psychology of behavior. His Columbia lecture, published later that year with the provocative title "Psychology as the Behaviorist Views It" (Watson, 1913), has come to be called the Behaviorist Manifesto. What did Watson proclaim? The opening sentences set the tone:

> Psychology as the behaviorist views it is a purely objective experimental branch of natural science. Its theoretical goal is the prediction and control of behavior. Introspection forms no essential part of its methods, nor is the scientific value of its data dependent upon the readiness with which they lend themselves to interpretation in terms of consciousness. (p. 158)

This is one of psychology's most quoted passages. In these first three sentences, Watson (a) firmly assigned psychology to the natural sciences, (b) articulated a set of goals for a scientific psychology, and (c) rejected the introspection-based research of his peers.

Watson quickly elaborated on his theme of discarding introspection and consciousness, pointing out the absurdity of a method that produced results that could never be independently verified (i.e., could never be objective) and where a failure to replicate some introspective result would be blamed on the inadequate training of introspectors. Concerning the introspective analysis of sensation, for example, he doubted whether "any one psychologist [could] draw up a set of statements describing what he means by sensation that would be agreed to by three other psychologists of different training" (Watson, 1913, p. 164). Consequently, Watson believed the time had come "when psychology must discard all reference to consciousness" (p. 163) and turn to behavior as the data to be observed. His attack was most clearly directed at the Titchenerian structuralists, but he was also critical of his mentors, the functionalists. Although the functionalist approach had increased the diversity and scope of psychological research, it nonetheless had failed to reject introspection and the study of consciousness. The functionalists might be studying consciousness in a way that differed from the structuralists, Watson pointed out, but they were still studying it.

In place of psychology as the study of consciousness, Watson proposed that psychology become the science of behavior. Just as behavioral methods had increased our understanding of animals, he argued, so could they enhance our knowledge of humans. He set as a goal for psychology the prediction and control of behavior and boldly proclaimed that in a mature stimulus–response (S-R) system, "given the response the stimuli can be predicted; given the stimuli the response can be predicted" (Watson, 1913, p. 167). Even such activities as thinking could be reduced to stimuli and responses. According to Watson, thinking was in essence nothing more than **subvocal speech**, and the subject of this thinking would be determined by habits that he referred to as "laryngeal habits." He argued that as children, we talk to ourselves "out loud," but that as we get older, the talk eventually becomes silent. Thinking, then, might involve central (i.e., brain) processes, but it also manifests itself in peripheral actions that could be measured. Hence, even something as apparently nonbehavioral as thinking could in fact be measured as a behavior. Watson (1919) admitted that "the experimental evidence for this view is slight" (p. 362) but reported that several studies had attempted to measure the behavioral manifestations of thinking, by attaching a device for recording vibrations to a subject's neck in the region of the larynx and then asking the subjects to read

KEY DATE—1913

This year marked the publication of Watson's behaviorist manifesto, "Psychology as the Behaviorist Views It."

These events also occurred that year:

- After several years of controversy over the direction of psychoanalysis, and after Carl Jung and Alfred Adler had abandoned him, Sigmund Freud (Chapter 12) consolidated his loyal followers into a special committee (e.g., Ernest Jones, who became Freud's hand-picked biographer), giving members rings to cement their loyalty
- Niels Bohr formulated his theory of atomic structure
- Albert Schweitzer opened his hospital in the French Congo
- Henry Ford pioneered new assembly line procedures in his car factory
- Grand Central Station opened in New York

- Federal income tax was introduced via the 16th Amendment to the Constitution
- Mahatma Ghandi, leader of Indian passive resistance movement, was arrested

These people were born:

- Richard Nixon and Gerald Ford, U.S. presidents
- Albert Camus, French author and existentialist philosopher (e.g., *The Plague*)
- Rosa Parks, pioneer in the American civil rights movement

These people died:

- Harriet Tubman, American abolitionist and reformer
- J. Pierpont Morgan, wealthy American industrialist

silently, do a math problem to themselves, or recall a poem. He reported some correlation between laryngeal movements and thinking, "but occasionally such records fail to appear even when a subvocal problem in arithmetic is worked out and the proper answer returned" (p. 326). Watson believed that better evidence would arrive when recording technology improved.[8] In an article written for the popular press, he later suggested (Watson, 1926), perhaps half-seriously, that some evidence in support of his position was the observation that our thinking tends to suffer when we experience a sore throat.

One thing that eventually made behaviorism popular among American psychologists was its insistence that behavioral principles must have applications to real life. Watson made the point in his manifesto as a way of contrasting his approach with introspective psychology, which seemed to him to be devoid of application. A behavioral strategy, he argued, was already making contributions to such applied topics as advertising, drug effects, the law, and education.

Watson's Behaviorist Manifesto was a powerful statement, sometimes seen as the starting point for a behaviorist "revolution" in psychology and as the vehicle that catapulted Watson to the presidency of the American Psychological Association (APA) in 1915. Yet Samelson (1981) has shown that the immediate effect of the manifesto was that most psychologists ignored it or saw it as just one more instance of a growing number of assaults on introspection. Only two psychologists— Titchener (1914) and Calkins (1913)—responded in print to it, and both were highly critical.[9] As for Watson's APA presidency, it was more

[8] In later years, the technology did improve and Watson's argument about thinking collapsed. Studies showed, for example, showed that normal thinking could occur even when laryngeal muscles were paralyzed or had been removed surgically.

[9] Despite the obvious contrast between the psychologies of Titchener and Watson, they maintained a mutual respect for each other—both were "laboratory men." They corresponded with some regularity, and when Watson hosted a

likely the outcome of his already-existing status among his peers, earned by virtue of a decade of solid research, as well as his friendships with influential APA members, his position as chair at Johns Hopkins, and his editorship of *Psychological Review*. Also, his nomination for the APA presidency occurred before the manifesto had been delivered (Samelson, 1981). On the other hand, while the manifesto might not have been a revolutionary event, it certainly energized Watson. For the remainder of the decade, he vigorously advocated behaviorism and eventually elaborated the manifesto into a book-length treatise—*Psychology from the Standpoint of a Behaviorist* (Watson, 1919). This book and Watson's promotional efforts in the 1920s, more than the earlier manifesto, were responsible for the increased influence of behaviorism among American psychologists as the 1920s drew to a close (Todd, 1994).

Watson's APA Presidential Address   Between the time of the 1913 manifesto and his 1915 APA presidency, Watson worked hard to provide evidence to support his strong beliefs. As he put it in the opening paragraph of his presidential address, "It is one thing to condemn a long-established practice, but quite another thing to suggest anything in its place" (Watson, 1916, p. 89). The method that Watson was eager to describe to his peers was the conditioning of two varieties of reflex. The first type was the salivary reflex, which Watson appropriately attributed to Pavlov's work. However, because of the need for surgery and the limitation (at that point) to research in dogs, Watson thought that the method had "no very wide sphere of usefulness or applicability" with humans (Watson, 1916, p. 93). To remedy the issue, Watson described a device for human salivary conditioning being developed by Karl Lashley (Chapter 3), who at the time was a zoology graduate student at Johns Hopkins but also worked as a volunteer in Watson's lab (Bruce, 1986). The device was designed to extract saliva from the inside of the cheek of humans by means of a suction principle. It never worked very well, however.

The second type of conditioning was of greater interest to Watson because it converged with his interests in measuring directly observable behavior. It was the motor reflex, a form of conditioning pioneered in Russia by the neurologist Vladimir Bekhterev (1857–1927), a rival of Pavlov's. A typical Bekhterev experiment consisted of using a mild electric shock to the heel of a subject's foot to produce withdrawal and then pairing the shock with a neutral stimulus (e.g., tone). Soon the tone would produce the withdrawal of the foot. In his presidential address, Watson (1916) indicated that "our own work has centered around the conditioned motor reflex of [Bekhterev], since we find for his method an immediate and widespread usefulness," p. 94). Watson then described several experiments on the conditioned motor reflex under way in the Hopkins lab and using animals as well as humans. Watson made much of this research in his 1915 APA address, but it appears that the results were not always clear and that the conditioning procedure was abandoned after little more than a year (Rilling, 2000).

Studying Emotional Development   In both his manifesto and presidential address, Watson made substantial claims about the ability of behaviorism to deliver applications that would improve the quality of life, based on conditioning. Yet by 1915, with a few exceptions, Watson's own research had been limited to animals. Thus, when an opportunity arose to

meeting of Titchener's Experimentalists in 1910, Titchener was Watson's houseguest. When Watson was fired from Johns Hopkins in 1920, Titchener was one of the few psychologists who publicly supported his colleague (Larson & Sullivan, 1965).

study infants, Watson saw this as a chance to apply behaviorism in a way that would convince skeptics and, more important, secure Watson's position as a leader in the application of psychological principles to improve society. Furthermore, Watson was feeling some of the same pressure felt by other comparative psychologists who were finding it increasingly difficult to maintain institutional support for their basic research in animal behavior. University administrators were becoming reluctant to supply budgetary support for research that seemed esoteric, of little practical value, and required facilities with strong, unpleasant odors (Buckley, 1989).

The opportunity came to Watson in the form of an invitation from Adolf Meyer, a well-known psychiatrist, to set up a human laboratory in Meyer's clinic at the Johns Hopkins Medical School. The new lab was adjacent to the medical school's obstetrical ward, thereby providing Watson with a supply of infants for his research. The result was a series of studies investigating reflexes, basic emotions, and conditioned emotional responses.

The work on basic emotions was coauthored with J. J. B. Morgan. They set out to identify the most fundamental human emotional responses and the stimuli that produced these responses. They identified three: fear, rage, and love. According to Watson and Morgan (1917), the fear response, defined behaviorally as "a sudden catching of the breath, clutching randomly with the hands, . . . blinking of the eye lids, puckering of the lips, then crying" (p. 166), occurred in response to either of two classes of stimuli, sudden loud noises (producing by banging a steel bar with a hammer, right behind the baby's head) or a loss of support (produced by dropping the infant or pulling out the infant's blanket just as the infant is falling asleep). The second emotion, rage, resulted from hindering the infant's movements: "If the face or head is held crying results, quickly followed by screaming. The body stiffens and fairly well coordinated slashing or striking movements of the hands and arms result" (pp. 166–167). The third emotion, love, defined as smiling, gurgling, or cooing, resulted from gently stroking the infant's skin or gently rocking or patting the child.

The Zenith and the Nadir of a Career: Little Albert

From the infant research, then, Watson concluded that only a few stimuli would elicit the three instinctive emotions of fear, rage, and love. Then why do older children show these emotional responses to a much wider range of stimuli? For Watson, the answer was simple—conditioning. His attempt to demonstrate this produced the well-known Little Albert study. It was published as "Conditioned Emotional Reactions" in the *Journal of Experimental Psychology* in 1920 and coauthored by Watson and Rosalie Rayner, a graduate student at Johns Hopkins. As will be seen shortly, she played a pivotal role in another important event for Watson in 1920—his forced resignation from Johns Hopkins.

Watson and Rayner (1920) opened the article by stating their belief that emotional reactions develop through conditioning but that "direct experimental evidence in support of such a view has been lacking" (p. 1). Hence, the goal of their study was to provide just such evidence, using an 11-month-old infant given the pseudonym of "Albert B." Albert was chosen for the study because "he was on the whole stolid and unemotional. His stability was one of the principal reasons for using him as a subject in this test. We felt that we could do him relatively little harm" (pp. 1–2). Watson and Rayner evidently felt some ethical concern over the effect of the experiment on the young boy, but "we decided finally to make the attempt, comforting ourselves by the reflection that such [fears] would arise anyway as soon as the child left the sheltered environment of the nursery for the rough and tumble of the home" (p. 3).

Before the experiment began, Albert was put through a series of tests—the same ones used in Watson's earlier infant research with Morgan. Albert showed no fear when presented "with a white rat, a rabbit, a dog, a monkey, with masks with and without hair, cotton wool, burning newspapers, etc." (p. 2). Unlike other infants, Albert did not show a fear response to the stimulus of a loss of support. Like the others, however, he was afraid of a loud, unexpected noise, so Watson decided to use that stimulus (produced by striking a metal bar with a hammer) to produce the fear. Watson and Rayner's first session only lasted two trials:

1. White rat suddenly taken from the basket and presented to Albert. He began to reach for rat with left hand. Just as his hand touched the animal the bar was struck immediately behind his head. The infant jumped violently and fell forward, burying his face in the mattress. He did not cry, however.

2. Just as the right hand touched the rat the bar was again struck. Again the infant jumped violently, fell forward and began to whimper.
   In order not to disturb the child too seriously no further tests were given for one week. (Watson & Rayner, 1920, p. 4)

One week later, Albert experienced, in succession, the rat, three trials of the rat combined with the loud noise, the rat alone, two more "joint stimulations," and the rat alone again. On this last trial, this happened:

Rat alone. *The instant the rat was shown the baby began to cry. Almost instantly he turned sharply to the left, fell over on one side, raised himself on all fours and began to crawl away so rapidly that he was caught with difficulty before reaching the edge of the table.* (p. 5, emphasis in the original)

Modern textbook accounts of the Albert study often describe it as a human example of classical conditioning, labeling the loud noise an unconditioned stimulus (UCS) and the fear of the noise an unconditioned response (UCR). The rat is the conditioned stimulus (CS) that comes to produce the conditioned response (CR) of fear through the pairing of CS and UCS. A close reading of Watson and Rayner's lab notes, however, suggests that elements of operant punishment were also involved, at least on the first two trials. The baby's behavior of reaching for the rat resulted in the immediate consequence of the loud noise. Whether the same sequence of events occurred on other trials that are simply labeled "joint stimulation" is not clear. What is clear is that Albert's behavior changed, but the ambiguity over precisely what happened is one reason the study has been criticized (Harris, 1979).

After conditioning (apparently) Albert to fear the rat, Watson and Rayner's second goal was to see if the response would "transfer" to other stimuli (or "generalize," as Pavlov would say). Five days after the famous trials just described, Albert was returned to the lab and tested first with blocks and the rat. He played with the former and continued to avoid the latter. After showing that the conditioned response still existed, Watson and Rayner presented other stimuli, alternating them with occasions for the child to play with his blocks. Albert showed some degree of fear with a rabbit, a dog, and a fur coat. Also, in a trial that suggests Albert's primary fear might have been of the experimenter, Watson "put his head down to see if Albert would play with his hair. Albert was completely negative. Two other observers did the same thing. He began immediately to play with their hair" (Watson & Rayner, 1920, p. 7).

Believing that transfer had been demonstrated, Watson and Rayner moved to a third research question: Would the response be retained for a significant period of time? The retention interval was limited to a month by a practical consideration—Albert was about to be removed from the hospital (no details provided by Watson and Rayner). During the interval, Albert was tested in other ways (e.g., in some research on handedness) and at the end of the month, he was once again shown the rat and some of the other stimuli used for generalization. He again showed fear responses, although they were not as strong as they had been a month earlier. Watson and Rayner (1920) concluded:

> These experiments would seem to show conclusively that directly conditioned emotional responses as well as those conditioned by transfer persist, although with a certain loss in the intensity of the reaction, for a longer period than one month. Our view is that they persist and modify personality throughout life. (pp. 10–12)

In the final section of their paper, Watson and Rayner addressed the question of how Albert's fear might have been alleviated, if additional time had been available. Although they gave the impression that they wished they could have had more time with Albert, it is clear that they knew of his forthcoming departure a month ahead of time and chose to test the persistence of the fear rather than to attempt its reversal. Nonetheless, they did make several suggestions about how the fear might be "unlearned."

> (1) Constantly confronting the child with those stimuli which called out the responses in the hopes that habituation would come in corresponding to "fatigue" of reflex when differential reactions are to be set up. (2) By trying to "recondition" by showing objects calling out fear responses (visual) and simultaneously stimulating the erogenous zones (tactual). We should try first the lips, then the nipples and as a final resort the sex organs. (3) By trying to "recondition" by feeding the subject candy or other food just as the animal is shown. This method calls for the food control of the subject. (4) By building up "constructive" activities around the object by imitation and by putting the hand through the motions of manipulation. (pp. 12–13)

Although Watson and Rayner made no attempt to alleviate Albert's fear, Watson later redeemed himself to some extent by supervising the research of Mary Cover Jones (Figure 10.8). Watson was out of academia by then and working in advertising (discussed

FIGURE 10.8 Mary Cover Jones of Columbia, during the time of her studies on the unlearning of fears.

later), but his research with children inspired Jones, a young Columbia graduate student and friend of Rosalie Rayner. Working with several children who feared various objects, Jones tried a number of methods (1924b), most of them unsuccessful. For example, fears were not reduced (a) simply through the passage of time, (b) through the method of verbal appeal (i.e., trying to convince the child that the fear was groundless), or (c) by having peers ridicule the child. What did work, however, was the third method that had been suggested in the Watson and Rayner paper. In a study that is often cited as a pioneering example of a behavior therapy technique that eventually became known as **systematic desensitization**, Jones (1924a) reduced a young boy's fear of rabbits by placing the animal at some distance from the boy while he was eating and then gradually moving the rabbit closer. The pleasurable responses associated with eating apparently replaced the fear response associated with the rabbit.

The Little Albert study can be found in the chapters on learning in virtually all modern introductory psychology texts. The study is often thought of as a "classic," displaying the power of behavioral principles to condition our emotions. If learning is a change in behavior brought about by experience (the typical textbook definition), then clearly the study illustrated learning of some kind. Albert was certainly affected by his encounter with Watson and Rayner. Yet the study had some serious flaws. First, there is some question about whether the initial procedure actually produced a strong fear of animals in Albert (Harris, 1979). Films of Albert made by Watson show the infant a bit hesitant about the animals even before testing began; after testing, while he appears to be concerned about the animals, he does not seem to be in a panic. Second, during the start of generalization testing ("transfer"), his reactions were often so weak that they needed to be "freshened up" with additional pairings of the animal with the loud noise. These additional pairings constituted further learning trials, thus rendering the generalization test hard to interpret. Third, even if one concedes that the child developed a fear, just what he was afraid of is not clear. As mentioned earlier, it is conceivable that Albert became afraid not of the animals, but of Watson himself. One gets an impression of some relatively rough treatment of infants on the part of Watson when viewing the films. Fourth, it is inappropriate to draw a general conclusion about fear conditioning based on a study using a single baby. Research limited to individual subjects is acceptable, and it represents an important tradition in psychological research, but confidence in the generality of results comes only with replication of the basic finding. Several attempts to produce conditioned emotional responses in the 1920s and 1930s produced ambiguous results, however. For instance, English (1929) failed to condition a 14-month-old to fear a wooden duck, primarily because the child did not react adversely to the loud noise. Also, Valentine (1930) failed to condition a child to fear opera glasses, but apparently succeeded with a caterpillar. Similarly, Bregman (1934) failed to condition fear to biologically neutral stimuli, including a curtain and some wooden blocks. Both the Valentine and Bregman studies were seriously flawed methodologically, however, making it difficult to determine whether replication occurred (Todd, 1994).

In summary, then, the Little Albert study cannot be considered a conclusive demonstration of the widespread applicability of conditioning principles. Why has it become so famous? One reason is political. For behaviorism to become recognized as an important force in American scientific psychology, it needed examples of the power of conditioning. It was one thing for Watson to proclaim behaviorism, but proof of its viability was needed. The Little Albert study seemed to fit the bill, and in subsequent descriptions of it by Watson and others sympathetic to behaviorism, the methodological weaknesses were ignored and it eventually achieved the status of an unambiguous case of "conditioning in action" (Prytula, Oster, &

Davis, 1977). A second reason for the study's popularity, related to the first, is that it has a certain dramatic appeal and applicability to one of life's importance tasks—how we raise our children. If their lives can be affected so strikingly by the experiences they encounter, then managing the child's environment becomes an important way to shape the child's future.

Thus the Little Albert study served the important function of legitimizing the new behavioral approach that within a decade would become a dominant force in American psychology. Watson was not destined to be a major player during that decade of the 1920s, however. The year the Little Albert study was published, 1920, was also the year that Watson was fired from Johns Hopkins.[10]

A New Life in Advertising

While a young bachelor instructor at the University of Chicago, Watson fell in love with Mary Ickes, a student in his introductory psychology class; he eventually married her. As an established experimental psychologist at Johns Hopkins, he had a similar experience with two major differences. This time the student was a graduate student (Rosalie Rayner) rather than an undergraduate; more important, this time Watson was already married—to the same woman who had been that undergraduate some 17 years earlier. The details of this unhappy situation can be found elsewhere (e.g., Buckley, 1989). It is enough to say that Watson's love for Rayner led to (a) his highly publicized divorce from Mary Ickes Watson, which featured the publication of love letters written by Watson to Rosalie and discovered by Mary; (b) his forced resignation from Johns Hopkins; and (c) his marriage to Rosalie.[11]

The exile from Johns Hopkins was devastating to Watson. Furthermore, the attendant publicity ruined any chance that he would secure another academic position. Instead, through the intercession of a friend, he entered the business world by joining the J. Walter Thompson advertising agency in New York City. After an apprenticeship, during which Watson (Figure 10.9) served in all departments of the agency, he rose to the position of vice president within 4 years (Buckley, 1989).

As an advertising executive, Watson had the opportunity to put into practice some of his claims about the applicability of behaviorism. For instance, he developed a number of advertising campaigns around themes derived from his research on the three basic emotions of fear, rage, and love. To sell a product to a consumer, Watson suggested, one must "tell him something that will tie [him] up with fear, something that will stir up a mild rage, that will call out an affectionate or love response, or strike at a deep psychological or habit need" (quoted in Buckley, 1989, p. 137). For example, an ad campaign for Johnson & Johnson baby powder sent a clear message designed to scare young parents into buying the product: If they failed to use baby powder, they risked exposing their children to serious infection. Watson

---

[10]Recently, a team of researchers attempted to track down the infant who was the real Albert, and his mother. After an exhaustive study, Beck, Levinson, and Irons (2009) concluded that his real name was Douglas Merritte, and he died at age 6 of hydrocephalus. This conclusion has been challenged, however, by psychologist-historian Ben Harris (2010), who argued that the infant's serious medical condition was at odds with Watson's description of the boy as robust and healthy. Harris also was unconvinced about the use of census data to trace the mother.

[11]Even Watson's love letters identify him as a behaviorist, interested only in measurable stimuli and responses. An example: "Every cell I have is yours, individually and collectively. My total reactions are positive and towards you. So likewise each and every heart reaction" (quoted in Buckley, 1989, p. 112).

FIGURE 10.9 John B. Watson as an advertising executive.

also relied heavily on the use of testimonials by well-known personalities and experts to sell products. The baby powder campaign used testimony by doctors, for example.

Watson brought to his new career the same passion for scientific method that characterized his life in academia. In an autobiographical statement, for example, he claimed that "it can be just as thrilling to watch the growth of a sales curve of a new product as to watch the learning curve of animals or man" (Watson, 1936, p. 280). Indeed, his major contribution to consumer psychology was not the introduction of new advertising techniques—historian Deborah Coon has shown that he merely adopted strategies in use at the time and described much earlier by Walter Dill Scott (Chapter 8). Rather, his more lasting impact was in the application of scientific thinking to the areas of marketing (e.g., using demographic data to target certain consumers) and in the development of training programs and productivity evaluations for sales personnel (Coon, 1994).

Advertising did not occupy all of Watson's time during the 1920s, however. He lectured on behaviorism in New York at the New School for Social Research, joined the board of directors of Cattell's Psychological Corporation, and renewed his work on infants by supervising research financed through a grant from the Laura Spelman Rockefeller Memorial Fund (Buckley, 1989). The fund provided $15,000 to Columbia University to continue the research begun at Johns Hopkins, and the experiments funded by the grant included the famous study mentioned earlier by Mary Cover Jones that successfully eliminated a learned fear in a young boy. Watson also continued writing about behaviorism during the 1920s, securing his reputation as behaviorism's popular voice.

Popularizing Behaviorism

Watson began communicating with the general public early in his academic career. He published articles in popular magazines (e.g., *Harper's Monthly*) with titles like "The New Science of Animal Behavior" (Watson, 1910), but this activity blossomed in the 1920s with additional magazine articles, radio broadcasts, a highly publicized debate ("The Battle of Behaviorism") in 1924 with British psychologist William McDougall, and two books: *Behaviorism* (1924/1930) and *Psychological Care of Infant and Child* (1928). The former became the most widely known statement of Watson's ideas. Although Columbia's Robert Wood-worth (1931) aptly described it as "certainly not one of [Watson's] most scientific books from the psychologist's point of view" (p. 91), the *New York Times* said that it would begin "a new epoch in the intellectual history of man" (quoted in Buckley, 1989, p. 173). It was the book (along with Pavlov's translated lectures) that first interested a young B. F. Skinner in behaviorism. The book included one of Watson's most famous quotations, a reflection of his belief in the importance of the environment in shaping our lives:

> Our conclusion, then, is that we have no real evidence of the inheritance of traits. I would feel perfectly confident in the ultimately favorable outcome of careful upbringing of a healthy, well-formed baby born of a long line of crooks, murderers and thieves, and prostitutes....
>
> I should like to go one step further now and say "Give me a dozen healthy infants, well-formed, and my own specified world to bring them up in and I'll guarantee to take any one at random and train him to become any type of specialist I might select—doctor, lawyer, artist, merchant-chief and, yes, even beggar-man and thief, regardless of his talents, penchants, tendencies, abilities, vocations, and race of his ancestors." (Watson, 1924/1930, pp. 103–104)

Watson admitted that he was going beyond the data in making his "dozen infants" claim; he was probably overstating the case to contrast his views with those psychologists, including most of the mental testers (see Chapter 8), who were promoting the role of inherited traits in individual behavior. Although Watson always recognized the interaction of nature and nurture in the production of behavior, his "dozen infants" quote has become a regular feature of introductory textbooks in psychology, and Watson is routinely but inaccurately portrayed as someone who completely denied the significance of the nature side of the nature–nurture dichotomy (Todd, 1994).

Watson's reputation as an extreme environmentalist was enhanced by some of the recommendations in his *Psychological Care of Infant and Child* (1928), written "with the assistance of Rosalie Rayner Watson" (frontispiece). The book contains Watson's strongest statements about how the technology of behavior could be brought to bear on that most important of tasks, the raising of children. He dedicated it to "the first mother who brings up a happy child" and began by stating the urgency of the task: Healthy babies can overcome the short-term effects of physiological deprivation, but "once a child's character has been spoiled by bad handling which can be done in a few days, who can say that the damage is ever repaired?" (p. 3).

Although Morris and Bigelow (2007) have shown that most of the recommendations in the book were innocuous and in line with other contemporary guides to raising children (e.g., avoiding physical punishment), one part of the book quickly became controversial. In a chapter entitled "The Dangers of Too Much Mother Love," Watson warned against being overly affectionate with children.[12] The result would be "invalidism"—a failure of the child to become responsible, independent, and ultimately successful in life. He warned that there were "serious rocks ahead for the over-kissed child" (p. 71). What to do instead?

---

[12] In the opening paragraph of this chapter in Watson's book, he described how a woman approached him after hearing him lecture, saying to him, "Thank God, my children are grown—and that I had the chance to enjoy them before I met you" (Watson, 1928, p. 69).

> There is a sensible way of treating children. Treat them as though they were young adults. Dress them, bathe them with care and circumspection. Let your behavior always be objective and kindly firm. Never hug or kiss them, never let them sit in your lap. If you must, kiss them once on the forehead when they say goodnight. Shake hands with them in the morning. Give them a pat on the head if they have made an extraordinarily good job of a difficult task. Try it out. In a week's time you will find how easy it is to be perfectly objective with your child and at the same time kindly. You will be utterly ashamed of the mawkish, sentimental way you have been handling it. (Watson, 1928, pp. 81–82)

Watson (1936) later said that he regretted writing the child-rearing book, that it was not sufficiently supported by data. Yet it stands as a perfect example of the faith that he had in the ability of behaviorism to affect daily living. More broadly, it illustrates the positivist belief that understanding and control go hand in hand.

Evaluating Watsonian Behaviorism

In a certain sense, Watsonian behaviorism was a magnificent failure. The grand scheme of being able to predict all responses, given the stimulus, was never realized. Most of Watson's proclamations went far beyond the available empirical evidence—the data never caught up with the excessive claims. What, then, was the impact of Watson's system?

Watson's lasting importance for psychology derives from his propagandizing on behalf of his strong beliefs. As mentioned previously, behaviorism certainly did not take hold immediately. Indeed, the initial reaction in academia was decidedly mixed. But Watson's forceful and repeated arguments started a process that by the mid-1930s brought behaviorism to the center of American experimental psychology. Thus he deserves the title "founder" of behaviorism.

Second, by attacking introspective psychology directly and exposing its Achilles' heel, its lack of objectivity, Watson contributed to the gradual shift from psychology as the study of immediate conscious experience to psychology as the study of behavior. By making observable and measurable behavior the dependent variable, rather than an introspective report, Watson ultimately helped place the field of psychology on firmer scientific ground.

Third, Watson's popularity with the general public suggests that his ideas struck a responsive chord with Americans. His belief that the environment could be arranged to shape someone's future development was consistent with the American ideal that through proper child rearing and education, people could aspire to any goal. As we have seen before (Chapter 3), this optimistic attitude helped maintain the popularity of phrenology long after the scientists had given up on it. It was an especially appealing message in the 1920s, when America prospered and average Americans were optimistic about their futures and had no comprehension that the Great Depression of the 1930s was just around the corner. Watson himself was a living example of this attitude, a poor farm boy who rose to the top of his profession twice—once in psychology and again in the business world. This message was much more inviting for average Americans than the one they were receiving from the mental testers. As you recall from Chapter 8, Terman and others were agitating for a meritocracy based on an IQ that was assumed to be largely innate.

Finally, Watson's behaviorism effectively bridged the gap between basic and applied psychology. Laboratory work in areas like conditioning and maze learning gradually became scientifically rigorous, thereby fulfilling the promise of a scientific psychology. At the same time, the possibilities for application, repeatedly stressed by Watson, also bore fruit as behaviorist ideas eventually influenced child rearing, education, industry, and even psychotherapy.

And what of Watson himself? His productivity as an advertising executive and as a popularizer of psychology declined precipitously in 1935 with the sudden death of Rosalie, the great love of his life. In that same year, he left J. Walter Thompson for a similar position with the William Esty Company and retired 10 years later. In his remaining years he became increasingly reclusive. In 1957, a year before his death, the APA honored Watson at their annual convention; and although he traveled to the meeting in New York from his home in Connecticut, he backed out at the last moment and did not attend the ceremony, sending his son in his place. According to his biographer, "Watson was afraid that in that moment his emotions would overwhelm him, that the apostle of behavior control would break down and weep" (Buckley, 1989, p. 182).

IN PERSPECTIVE: BEHAVIORISM'S ORIGINS

In Chapter 1's discussion of old versus new history, I introduced the concept of an eponym. Boring described these as historical periods or movements with labels referring to the names of people whose impact is thought to have had a determining influence on history—Darwinian biology is an example. In an article entitled "Eponym as Placebo," Boring (1963a) cautioned that overusing eponyms might lead us to oversimplify history by ignoring the importance of the zeitgeist. He argued that eponyms occur frequently, in part because we have limited cognitive abilities. History is enormously complex, so, for example, attributing crucial events in the 19th century to Darwinism simplifies matters cognitively, bringing "the historical subject matter within the range of comprehension and memory" (p. 21). The danger, of course, is that eponymy "magnifies those persons who are found above the threshold and diminishes those below it" (p. 24).

For the writer of a history of psychology (me) there is a special challenge, especially in chapters like this one (and in Chapter 5, for instance, which has an eponymous title). Pavlov and Watson are unquestionably important in psychology's history, and psychology students cannot take a history course without learning about their work. Yet there is a danger that the student will leave the history course with some general understanding of "Pavlovian conditioning" or "Watsonian behaviorism" and little else about the roots and early development of behaviorist thinking. My hope is that after reading this chapter, and perhaps after hearing more about the issue from your instructor, you will emerge from this chapter (and others) with an appreciation for the complexity of history and an understanding that historical context is inevitably intertwined with biography. Yes, Pavlov was a crucial figure, but the support of his work by the Soviets, hoping to reshape human behavior to their Communist ideal, made some of his work possible. Yes, Pavlov was initially skeptical of the Soviets, but his ultimate accommodation (and hence the continuance of his work) requires knowing about how Russians historically distrusted and feared Germans. Yes, Watson was a charismatic figure, but he also came along at a time when the problems with introspection were evident to an increasing number of psychologists, and his ideas found a receptive audience in a country where pragmatism ("What good is this?") was a value taken for granted and where the idea that the environment was an important force (anyone could become president) was part of the national psyche. Biography is important to history, but history is more than biography.

SUMMARY

Behaviorism's Antecedents

• Before Watson entered the picture, many psychologists were becoming concerned about the objectivity of their measures. One influence was evolutionary theory, which led to the study of animal behavior. Studying animals meant developing behavioral measures, and American psychologists did just that (e.g., Thorndike's puzzle box studies).

• The philosophies of empiricism and associationism, which both emphasize the importance of experience, provided a foundation for behavioral thinking. Positivism, which argued that the only valid knowledge is obtained through inductive, systematic observations, also contributed.

• Many psychologists became interested in more objective measures of psychological phenomena because they were becoming increasingly critical of introspection.

Pavlov's Life and Work

• Pavlov thought of himself more as a physiologist than a psychologist, and his 1904 Nobel Prize was for research on the physiology of digestion. He was especially known for developing surgical procedures (e.g., the Pavlov pouch) that allowed the digestive processes of live, intact animals to be studied.

• Pavlov's work on conditioning developed out of the digestion research, when he decided to investigate why his dogs often salivated before food reached their mouths. He investigated a large number of conditioning phenomena, including acquisition, extinction, generalization, differentiation, and experimental neurosis (a breakdown in the ability to differentiate stimuli). He interpreted these phenomena in terms of the reciprocal brain processes of excitation and inhibition.

• Although initially hostile to the Soviet government, Pavlov accommodated when the threat from Nazi Germany developed. The Soviets saw Pavlovian conditioning as a foundation for shaping the modern Communist citizen; consequently, the government heavily subsidized Pavlov's research.

• Pavlov's work was generally known to American psychologists from the early years of the 20th century, but not widely known and appreciated until his research was translated into English in the 1920s.

John B. Watson and the Founding of Behaviorism

• Watson was trained at the functionalist University of Chicago, where he developed a dislike for introspection and a love of animal research. His dissertation on the relationship between cortical development and the learning abilities of rats was followed by several important studies on how rats learned mazes by relying on their kinesthetic sense.

• After teaching at Chicago for several years following his doctorate, Watson moved to Johns Hopkins in 1908, where he stayed until 1920. His 1913 "Behaviorist Manifesto" proclaimed that introspective psychology, inherently subjective, should be replaced by a more objective behavioral psychology that specified the relationships between stimuli and responses. In his APA presidential address (1915), he showed how behaviors could be conditioned by using procedures similar to Pavlov's and (especially) Bekhterev's.

• In his final years at Johns Hopkins, Watson studied newborns and young children, especially their emotional development. He argued that fear, rage, and love were the three fundamental emotions, each resulting from specific stimuli. More elaborate emotional responses resulted from conditioning.

• Watson attempted to demonstrate the conditioning of emotional responses in the famous Little Albert experiment. By pairing a loud noise with a white rat, Watson and Rayner created a fear of the latter. The fear generalized to similar stimuli (e.g., rabbits) and lasted at least a month. Later, Mary Cover Jones (with Watson as consultant) demonstrated that fears could be unlearned.

• Watson spent his final professional years as an advertising executive, applying behavioral principles to marketing. During this time, he also became a popularizer of behaviorist philosophy, especially in the area of child rearing.

STUDY QUESTIONS

1. What are the similarities between John Locke's empiricist ideas and John Watson's behaviorist ideas?

2. What was positivism, and what was its significance for American psychology?

3. What was the influence of comparative psychology on the development of behaviorist thinking?

4. While being trained for the ministry, what influenced Pavlov to switch to science?

5. Describe the work that won Pavlov the Nobel Prize.

6. Describe the operation and organization of Pavlov's lab.

7. What important point about history is made in footnote 3?

8. How did Pavlov demonstrate the basic phenomena of conditioning, extinction, generalization, and differentiation?

9. What did Pavlov mean by experimental neurosis, and how did he demonstrate its existence?

10. Explain why Pavlov's ideas were valued by the Soviets, and explain why Pavlov initially disliked the Soviets but later made an accommodation.

11. How were Pavlov's ideas made known to American psychologists, and what was Pavlov's influence on American psychology?

12. What important point about historiography is made in the chapter's Close-Up?

13. Describe the factors that turned Watson into a behaviorist while at Chicago.

14. Describe the Watson-Carr maze studies from the standpoint of (a) methodology and (b) ethics.

15. On the Dry Tortugas, what did Watson learn about the behavior of birds?

16. In the Behaviorist Manifesto, what was the nature of Watson's criticism of structuralism and functionalism, and what did he propose instead?

17. In his manifesto, Watson described what could be called an S-R approach to psychology. Explain.

18. Describe the content of Watson's APA presidential address. Why did Watson prefer Bekhterev's model of conditioning to Pavlov's?

19. Describe how Watson determined that three fundamental emotions existed. What were the emotions, and what stimuli elicited them?

20. Describe and critically analyze the Little Albert study.

21. Watson and Rayner didn't even try to remove Albert's fear, but Jones showed that fear could be removed. How did she do it?

22. Describe how Watson influenced the world of advertising with his (a) general scientific attitude and (b) behaviorist ideas.

23. Describe a Watsonian approach to parenting.

24. Overall, how would you evaluate Watson's contribution to psychology?

FOR FURTHER READING

Babkin, B. P. (1949). *Pavlov: A biography.* Chicago: University of Chicago Press.
Provides a unique glimpse into Pavlov's life and his research, through the eyes of a former student. It is especially effective in portraying life inside Pavlov's laboratory during the early years of the 20th century.

Buckley, K. W. (1989). *Mechanical man: John Broadus Watson and the beginnings of behaviorism.* New York: Guilford.
The only existing scholarly biography of Watson; a thorough and critical analysis of how his ideas were shaped and how they in turn influenced American psychological thought. A good example of a biography that fits its central character into the social, cultural, and institutional context of the times.

Harris, B. (1979). Whatever happened to Little Albert? *American Psychologist, 34*, 151–160.

A critical examination of how the Little Albert study became a "classic study" of the application of conditioning principles, even though the study was seriously flawed and replication efforts were unsuccessful. Textbook descriptions of the experiment are often inaccurate, mainly because writers rely on secondary sources rather than the original article.

O'Donnell, J. M. (1985). *The origins of behaviorism: American psychology, 1870–1920.* New York: New York University Press.
Scholarly yet highly readable description and analysis of American psychology's formative years and the factors leading to the development of behaviorism; excellent example of an external, historicist, contextual history.

CHAPTER 11

THE EVOLUTION OF BEHAVIORISM

> I believe that everything important in psychology . . . can be investigated in essence through the continued experimental and theoretical analysis of the determiners of rat behavior at a choice-point in a maze.
>
> —Edward Chace Tolman, 1938

PREVIEW AND CHAPTER OBJECTIVES

This chapter continues to describe the development of behaviorist thinking by focusing on the work of three research psychologists (among many) who followed in Watson's footsteps—Edward Tolman, Clark Hull, and B. F. Skinner. But first it opens by examining the fate of Watsonian behaviorism and describes several trends (e.g., operationism) that prepared the way for behaviorism to become a major force in psychology in the 1930s through the 1950s, at least in the United States. You will also learn, however, that not all prominent American psychologists were behaviorists during this time, and that behaviorism was largely an American phenomenon.

  The learning theories to be considered here differed from each other substantially—concerning the definition and role of reinforcement in learning, for instance. All were grounded in research using animals as subjects, however, and all focused their research efforts on discovering the essential laws of conditioning. Although not discounting the importance of biological factors, the neobehaviorists, in the tradition of the British empiricists, believed that understanding human action largely meant discovering how life's experiences (i.e., conditioning history) shaped the individual. After you finish this chapter, you should be able to:

■ Distinguish between the myth of the behaviorist revolution and what really happened between Watson's 1913 manifesto and behaviorism's rise in the 1930s

■ Describe how the relationship between logical positivism and operationism paved the way for the theorizing of the neobehaviorists Tolman and Hull

■ Explain the importance of using operational definitions in psychology

■ Describe the beliefs held in common by neobehaviorists

■ Describe the major features of Tolman's theory of learning

■ Describe and explain the significance of Tolman's research on latent learning, place learning, and cognitive maps

■ Describe Hull's contributions to psychology before the development of his learning theory

343

■ Describe the major features of Hull's hypothetico-deductive theory of learning, especially postulate 4

■ Describe how Skinner's approach to psychology differed from that of Tolman and Hull

■ Describe the essential components of an experimental analysis of behavior, according to Skinner

■ Explain the influence of Sir Francis Bacon on Skinner's ideas

■ Describe examples of Skinner's attempts to apply his operant principles to real-life concerns

■ Describe the work of the Brelands, which showed that operant conditioning could be profitable but also showed that it had its (biological) limits

■ Evaluate the influence of neobehaviorism on the history of psychology

POST-WATSONIAN BEHAVIORISM

Traditional accounts of psychology's history often refer to Watsonian behaviorism as revolutionary. The bedtime story goes something like this: Before Watson, there was the darkness of introspective psychology. Because of its intensely subjective nature, introspectionism prevented psychology from being a truly "objective" science. Then came the hero—Watson and his 1913 "Behaviorist Manifesto." Except for a few narrow-minded holdouts, psychologists everywhere saw the light, and psychology dramatically changed from the quasi-science of consciousness to the true science of behavior. After Watson, behaviorism quickly became the only serious way of thinking among experimental psychologists. It is a dramatic plot, but not what happened. The actual story is infinitely more complex and considerably at odds with the myth.

As mentioned in Chapter 10, Watson's behaviorism did not catch on immediately; the initial response to his 1913 manifesto was most likely to have been indifference, criticism, or "here's yet another critique of introspection" (Samelson, 1981). Most American psychologists simply went about their business: If they were interested in imageless thoughts, they continued to study them by combining cognitive tasks with introspection; if they were interested in the functioning of the visual system, they continued to study phenomena like afterimages and illusions; if they were interested in comparative psychology, they continued to study animal behavior. And after World War I, of course, many psychologists became very interested in mental testing and other areas of "applied" psychology (Chapter 8). Furthermore, nonbehavioral approaches to psychology did not simply disappear after Watson's manifesto and during the 1920s. At least a dozen varieties of psychology were examined in Carl Murchison's *Psychologies of 1925* (1926) and *Psychologies of 1930* (1930), and Gestalt psychology (Chapter 9) attracted as much attention as behaviorism. As late as 1931, Robert Woodworth's widely read *Contemporary Schools of Psychology* preceded the chapter on behaviorism with one on introspective psychology and included chapters on Gestalt psychology, Freudian psychoanalysis, and "hormic" (i.e., focused on instincts) psychology. Woodworth (1931) correctly predicted that after 50 years, historians would assign much significance to the behaviorist movement, but he was "puzzled to guess exactly where [the historians] will find its significance to lie" (p. 89). He granted that behaviorism had an appeal to some of the younger psychologists, but he also pointed out that advocating objective methods was not unique to Watson and that, despite his arguments, introspective studies were still being carried out.

Beginning in the decade of the 1930s, however, behaviorism did begin to take hold in American experimental psychology. Watson certainly played a role, especially with his consistent proselytizing on behalf of behaviorism, even after leaving academia. During the 1920s, his child-rearing advice, his numerous articles in popular magazines (e.g., in a 1926 issue of *Harper's Monthly*, "How We Think: A Behaviorist's View"), and his *Behaviorism* (1924/1930), while "not one of his most scientific books from the psychologist's point of view" (Woodworth, 1931, p. 91), made great claims about shaping future generations during a decade of great optimism in America. In the Roaring Twenties, the United States had emerged from World War I as a new world power, and it was not until the end of the decade that its confidence was shaken by the stock market crash that brought on the Great Depression. The *New York Times* said Watson's *Behaviorism* "marks an epoch in the intellectual history of man" (quoted in Woodworth, 1931, p. 92). Woodworth believed that behaviorism's significance would lie primarily in its appeal to those who believed that science could be used to improve the common good. To some extent, then, the development of behaviorism as a force in American psychology derived from an optimistic public's belief that a way had been found to raise their children efficiently, to improve their marriages, their businesses, their education, and in general to help them lead more productive lives.

Public enthusiasm for behaviorism cannot account for the whole story of its rise to power, however. Other events in the 1920s played important roles in bringing behaviorism to the forefront of American psychology. First, as pointed out in Chapter 10, a substantial amount of Pavlov's research was translated into English for the first time. Americans knew about Pavlov, but before the 1920s, most experimental psychologists had little idea about the scope of his work, its precision, and its implications. If American psychologists were looking for a model of a systematic research program focusing on overt, measurable behavior, this was it. As discussed in Chapter 10, by the time of the International Congress at Yale in 1929, Pavlov was widely recognized by American psychologists as a major figure, and the term *Pavlovian* had become an eponym.

Another event that paved the way for behaviorism was the publication of a book by a Harvard physicist. In *The Logic of Modern Physics* (1927), Percy Bridgman introduced American psychologists to operationism. Along with its close relation, logical positivism, operationism provided the intellectual foundation for neobehaviorism.

Logical Positivism and Operationism

Operationism appeared at about the same time a small group of philosophers, mathematicians, and scientists began meeting Thursday evenings in a Viennese coffee house to discuss the logic and philosophy of science. Known as the Vienna Circle, they promoted a version of positivist thinking that came to be known as **logical positivism** (Gillies, 1993). Since the 19th century, positivists had taken a strictly empiricist stance, maintaining that certain knowledge about natural phenomena could result only from the public observation of measurable events. This philosophy suited Watson just fine, because it was consistent with his belief that psychology ought to be the study of observable behavior rather than subjective introspections. The difficulty was that even by focusing on observables, it is difficult if not impossible to avoid discussing unobservable concepts when developing a theory. For example, if you believe that human behavior can be motivated by the need to reduce a strong drive such as hunger, you are forced to address the question of just what is meant by hunger and how it functions to motivate us. Yet hunger is an unobservable event, seemingly limited to an introspective description ("my stomach just feels empty and I feel a bit light-headed"). The logical positivists, dealing with this problem in the context of physics—magnetism or gravity as forces also are not observed directly—resolved the issue to their satisfaction by distinguishing between observable and theoretical events and insisting that the two be closely tied to each other. Specifically, they admitted the use of abstract concepts into a scientific theory, as long as these concepts were closely tied to some observable events. Thus magnetism could be proposed as a theoretical force having specific properties if certain objects (e.g., metal filings) behaved in a predictable fashion and could be observed and measured objectively. Similarly, hunger could be used in a theory of motivation if it could be tied to observable behaviors. Operationism provided the link.

The essential idea of **operationism** was that scientific concepts were to be defined not in absolute terms, but with reference to the operations used to measure them. The concept of length, for instance, would be defined by agreed-upon procedures. As Bridgman put it in his *The Logic of Modern Physics* (1927), the "concept of length is . . . fixed when the operations by which length is measured are fixed; that is, the concept of length involves as much as and nothing more than a set of operations" (p. 5). Bridgman also discussed what he called *pseudoproblems*, questions that might be interesting but were unanswerable by means of scientific observations. Whether or not time has a beginning or an end is an example.

A Harvard colleague of Bridgman's, experimental psychologist S. S. Stevens, was the most vocal promoter of operationism within psychology. Stevens was a doctoral student of E. G. Boring in the early 1930s and became the best-known 20th-century researcher in psychophysics. He also developed the classification scheme for measurement scales (nominal, ordinal, interval, ratio) recognized by all those who have survived a statistics course. His 1935 paper, "The Operational Definition of Concepts," was the first of several attempts to convince psychologists to adopt an operational strategy. For Stevens, operationism provided an answer to the problem confronted by the logical positivists—how to define scientific concepts that could not be observed directly. By using **operational definitions**, that is, definitions involving precise descriptions of procedures for measurement and for specifying the variables in an experiment, psychologists could study such seemingly invisible concepts as hunger, anxiety, aggression, and memory while remaining faithful to the dictates of a positivist philosophy. Researchers could now define a motivational state like hunger or a perceptual quality like loudness in terms of the set of operations that were assumed to bring them about. Thus hunger could be defined as the outcome of a certain number of hours without food, perceived loudness could be defined as a series of discriminations of quantitatively different tones made by research participants, and so on.

Stevens also saw the relevance of Bridgman's pseudoproblems for experimental psychology. One of Bridgman's examples was the problem of whether person A's sensation of blue is the same as person B's sensation of blue. That can never be known for certain—the issue is a pseudoproblem. All that can be done is to determine if two persons make similar discriminations to a series of visual stimuli of measurable wavelengths. Thus one outcome of operational thinking was to raise additional questions about the validity of introspective observations and to argue that they should be replaced with behavioral observations (i.e., discriminations between stimuli).

Operational definitions continue to be widely used among psychological scientists today, a fact known to every student who has taken a research methods course, but a rigid operationism did not last long in psychology. Bridgman's original conception of the operational definition is that the meaning of a concept does not go beyond the operations used to measure it (Green, 1992). Thus hunger is *nothing more than* 24 hours without food. The problem was that researchers often disagreed on the "best" operational definition of a term. The idea that one definition could be better than another necessarily meant that researchers believed that the meaning of terms like *hunger* went beyond a mere set of operations (a belief not shared by Bridgman). To complicate matters further, many of psychology's concepts resisted simple operational definitions. For instance, researchers studying aggression have created operational definitions ranging from the delivery of shocks from one subject to another to horn honking among drivers at intersections. Is aggression being studied in both examples? Do widely different measures of a phenomenon measure the same thing? A strict operationist would have to argue that different operations measure different phenomena. Consequently, either all researchers would have to agree on a single definition of aggression, or all would have to agree that they are investigating different phenomena when using different measures.

Hilgard (1987) has argued that the effect of operationism in psychology was simply to force experimental psychologists to define their terms more precisely. The chief advantage is **replication**. If terms are defined clearly enough, other researchers can repeat a particular study. Successful replications produce increased confidence in some research outcome; unsuccessful replications generate additional research to clear up the inconsistency. Furthermore, if researchers using slightly different operational definitions of terms nonetheless produce the same outcome (e.g., frustration tends to be followed by aggression), the generality of the outcome is increased. The phrase **converging operations** refers to this idea that our understanding of some psychological phenomenon is enhanced when several studies, each using different operational definitions, "converge" on the same basic conclusion. According to Hilgard, metaphysical arguments over the "real" meaning of phenomena in the world could be left to philosophers. Thus he contended that the debate over the merits of operationism, and its philosophical cousin, logical positivism, was largely ignored by psychologists (Hilgard, 1987, p. 779). For them, the take-home message was simply that variables needed to be defined with precision.

Neobehaviorism

Public enthusiasm for the promise of behaviorism, recognition of the importance of Pavlov's long series of conditioning studies, and the general acceptance of operationism and logical positivism, along with the emergence of several hardworking and highly creative experimental psychologists, converged in the late 1920s and early 1930s to produce a movement in psychology called **neobehaviorism**. This movement became central to American experimental psychology and lasted roughly from 1930 to 1960.

Neobehaviorism was not a unified school of thought by any means; large differences existed among the psychologists that you are about to study. Nonetheless, there was a certain consensus among the neobehaviorists. First, all the neobehaviorists took for granted the evolutionary assumption of continuity among species. Laws of behavior that apply to one species should apply, at least to a degree that can be calibrated, to other species as well. Consequently, phenomena relevant for human behavior could be examined by using nonhuman subjects in research. Furthermore, Woodworth's famous text, the "Columbia bible" (Chapter 7), contributed to the increase in studies of animal behavior (Winston, 1990). Using the experimental method required having strict control over the variables of the study, often making animal studies more ethically and practically feasible than human studies (e.g., 24 hours without food, in a study of the effect of hunger on learning, is acceptable with rats but not with children). In experimental psychology, then, there was a substantial increase in the use of animal subjects for basic research on conditioning during the period 1930–1960. Although said partly tongue-in-cheek during his APA presidential address, Edward Tolman's comment—"I believe that everything important in psychology ... can be investigated in essence through the continued experimental and theoretical analysis of the determiners of rat behavior at a choice-point in a maze" (Tolman, 1938, p. 34)—reflected the neobehaviorist faith in the lessons to be learned by studying animal behavior. Tolman (1932) even dedicated his most important book to "M.N.A." (*Mus norvegicus albinus*—the white rat), and his bookplate further reflected his passion for animal research (Figure 11.1).

The second belief neobehaviorists held in common was that learning (conditioning) was central to understanding behavior. In simple terms, neobehaviorists leaned heavily toward the nurture end of the nature–nurture continuum, arguing that knowing why people do what they do requires a thorough analysis of the basic principles of how things are learned. This, of course, was one of Watson's guiding principles and the motivation for the Little Albert experiment. The emphasis on learning also provided a bridge between behaviorism and British empiricist thought. When John Locke resurrected the Aristotelian concept of the mind as a blank slate and proclaimed that "experience" was the writer, he was arguing the same point made by Watson when he claimed that fears were the result of learning. For the neobehaviorists, the world in which we live—that is, the environment—shapes our characteristic ways of behaving.

An emphasis on learning was also consistent with American psychology's fixation on practical applications. Watson's appeal with the general public was a result of his genius in showing how the principles of learning could be applied to improve education, child rearing, and sales figures. If we are what we learn, and if learning is the result of specific experiences

FIGURE 11.1   Tolman's bookplate.

in certain environments, then by arranging environments in certain ways, behavior can be shaped in any number of productive directions.

It is one thing to herald the importance of learning; it is quite another to know precisely how such learning comes about. Thus, during the era of neobehaviorism, the focus of research and theory was on the manner in which learning occurred. This fundamental issue produced the sharpest divisions among the neobehaviorists, but eventually yielded important knowledge about a variety of learning phenomena. We will examine the ideas of the three most prominent neobehaviorists: Edward Tolman, Clark Hull, and B. F. Skinner.

EDWARD C. TOLMAN (1886–1959):
A PURPOSIVE BEHAVIORISM

Edward Chace Tolman was born into an upper-middle-class environment near Boston. As a youth, he learned the virtues of perseverance and hard work from his father, a successful business executive, and the need for a reflective life with a strong moral foundation from his mother, a Quaker. He graduated from the Massachusetts Institute of Technology (MIT) 1911 with a degree in electrochemistry but did not pursue a career in this field, apparently to avoid competing with his talented older brother, Richard, also an MIT grad (Crutchfield, 1961). Richard Tolman became a well-known physicist who contributed to the development of the atomic bomb during World War II. Another reason for Edward's shift away from physics and chemistry was his discovery of William James (who else?) during his senior year. *The Principles* gave Tolman's life a new direction.

Immediately following graduation from MIT, Tolman enrolled in two summer classes at Harvard: a philosophy course and an introductory psychology course taught by Robert Yerkes. Yerkes sold him for good on psychology, and he entered graduate school at Harvard, earning his doctorate in 1915. While taking a second course from Yerkes, he worked his way through Watson's *Behavior: An Introduction to Comparative Psychology* (1914), and although he did not become immediately converted to the behaviorist point of view, Tolman saw behaviorism as an attractive alternative to the traditional introspective psychology he was encountering in Hugo Münsterberg's laboratory. As he later put it, he was troubled by the problems with introspection, and the "introduction in Yerkes' course to Watson's behaviorism came as a tremendous stimulus and relief" (Tolman, 1952, p. 326). During his graduate school years, while visiting Germany to prepare for his foreign language competency examination, Tolman met Kurt Koffka and was introduced to Gestalt psychology (Chapter 9). The gestalt concept of "wholes" would come to play an important role in his version of neobehaviorism (Figure 11.2 shows Tolman with Lewin and Koffka at a 1935 meeting of Lewin's Topology group.) A final important influence on Tolman during his Harvard years was another of his teachers, psychologist Edwin Holt (1873–1946), whose leanings toward behaviorism were infused with the notions of goals and purpose. Holt believed that Watsonian behaviorism was too reductionistic, that behavior could not be meaningfully reduced to simple physical stimuli and muscular or glandular responses. He argued instead that behavior should be defined more broadly as actions that serve some purpose. That is, behavior is goal directed. These ideas would become part of the core of Tolman's theory of learning.

Tolman taught for 3 years at Northwestern University during World War I. He was dismissed in 1918, allegedly for a lack of teaching skills but more likely because of his

FIGURE 11.2 Tolman (center) at a meeting of the Topology Group, with Lewin (left) and Koffka. From Marrow (1969).

visible antiwar stance (Tolman, 1952). It would not be the only time that his moral convictions, reflecting his mother's Quaker influence, would affect his career.

Tolman joined the faculty at Berkeley in 1918 and remained there for the rest of his academic career. When given an opportunity to develop a new course shortly after his arrival, he remembered "Yerkes' course and Watson's textbook [and] proposed 'comparative psychology.' And it was this that finally launched [him] down the behavioristic slope' (Tolman, 1952, p. 329). The course led to some research in animal maze learning, and Tolman was soon attracting talented graduate students to his lab. He began developing his unique form of behaviorism in the early 1920s, publishing articles with titles like "A New Formula for Behaviorism" (Tolman, 1922). His major work, *Purposive Behavior in Animals and Men*, appeared in 1932. For the remainder of his career at Berkeley, Tolman continued to develop and revise his system and to generate research support for it.

Tolman's System

Tolman's writings illustrate the complex interplay between empirical research and theorizing in the tradition of logical positivism. A theory makes testable predictions that lead to research, the outcome of which supports or reshapes the theory, which leads to more research, and so on. Because such theories evolve as a consequence of research outcomes, Tolman's theory of learning in 1932, when he produced *Purposive Behavior in Animals and Men*, was different from his theory in 1959, when he contributed a chapter ("Principles of Purposive Behavior") to Sigmund Koch's seven-volume series, *Psychology: A Study of a Science*. Nevertheless, there are some constant themes in Tolman's writings. His theories emphasized (a) molar over molecular behavior, (b) the purposiveness or goal-directedness of behavior, and (c) the use of intervening variables.

Molar Versus Molecular Behavior Taking cues from his gestalt friends and one of his Harvard mentors, Holt, Tolman argued that the unit of study had to be larger than the "molecular" muscle movements or glandular responses emphasized by Watson. One of Tolman's students, for example, showed that rats taught to swim through a maze were later able to run through it accurately (Macfarlane, 1930). Hence, what was learned could not be simply a series of individual kinesthetic responses. Rather, the animal must come to some general understanding of the pattern of the maze and the response needed to be understood in terms of whole behavior patterns that had meaning beyond the component movements. As a gestaltist would say, the whole behavior is more than the sum of its stimulus–response units. **Molar behavior**, then, referred to broad patterns of behavior directed at some goal. Tolman provided several examples:

> A rat running a maze; a cat getting out of a puzzle box; a man driving home to dinner; a child hiding from a stranger; a woman doing her washing...; a psychologist reciting a list of nonsense syllables; my friend and I telling one another our thoughts and feelings—*these are behaviors* (qua *molar*). And it must be noted that in mentioning no one of them have we referred to, or, we blush to confess it, for the most part have known, what were the exact muscles and glands, sensory nerves, and motor nerves involved. (Tolman, 1932, p. 8; emphasis in the original)

Tolman called his theory a **field theory** to distinguish it from the more molecular stimulus–response approach, which he likened to a telephone switchboard. Learning did not involve the mere strengthening and weakening of connections between incoming calls (stimulus information) and outgoing ones (motor responses), he argued. Instead, he proposed that the brain is more like a "map control room than it is like an old-fashioned telephone exchange" and that during learning, the animal develops a "field map of the environment" (Tolman, 1948, p. 192).

Goal-Directedness

The preceding examples of molar behavior all have another feature: They are directed toward some goal. For Tolman, goal-directedness or **purposiveness** was a universal feature of the behavior that we learn. Although the term *purpose* might seem like a return to a subjective, even introspective, psychology, Tolman merely meant that behavior

> always seems to have the character of getting-to or getting-from a specific goal-object.... Thus, for example, the rat's behavior of "running the maze" has as its first and perhaps most important identifying feature the fact that it is getting to food. (1932, p. 10)

Tolman was obviously influenced by evolutionary thinking here; goal-directed behavior is adaptive and therefore has survival value for the species. As a term, Tolman used *purposiveness* as descriptive, not causal. That is, it is merely a label for that which can be inferred from observing behavior, as when a hungry rat consistently worked its way through a maze until finding food. The causes of such behavior are to be found elsewhere, in the animal's specific learning history and its instinctive behaviors.

Intervening Variables

Tolman is credited with introducing a concept that has been widely used in psychology: the intervening variable. Stimulus conditions, or independent variables, are under the direct control of the experimenter; behaviors, or dependent variables, can be measured with precision by the experimenter. **Intervening variables** are hypothetical factors that are not seen directly but are inferred from the manner in which independent and dependent variables are operationally defined. They are assumed to "intervene" between stimulus and behavior, in such a way as to influence learning. For instance, "thirst" is an intervening variable. It is never seen directly but can be inferred to exist as a consequence of (a) creating some stimulus condition, such as not allowing an animal to drink water for 12 hours; or (b) measuring the completion of some behavior that leads to water, which is consumed by the animal. As you might guess from the discussion earlier in the chapter, Tolman's intervening variables reflect the influence of logical positivism, with its insistence that abstract, theoretical terms (i.e., intervening variables) be closely tied to observable events (i.e., stimuli and responses).

Tolman's intervening variables were usually cognitive in nature and followed from his field theory. For example, when exploring a maze, Tolman believed that the rat gradually learned a set of "expectancies" about the maze. As it encountered various parts of the maze, it learned that certain environmental cues (visual, olfactory, tactile, etc.) were associated with certain outcomes. Tolman used the term **sign-gestalt** to refer to learned relationships between these cues and the animal's expectations about what would happen if it chose path A instead of path B. Eventually, the rat developed an overall field map or "cognitive map" of the maze that directed its future goal-oriented behavior. Sign-gestalts, expectancies, and maps are all examples of cognitive intervening variables that decorate Tolman's theory. Behavior, for Tolman (1932), "reeks of purpose and of cognition. And such purposes and such cognitions are just as evident...if this behavior be that of a rat as if it be that of a human being" (p. 12).

Just as the term *purposiveness* strongly implies a subjectivity that seems foreign to behaviorist thinking, so do terms like *expectancy* and *cognitive map*. Tolman, however, again reflecting the dictates of logical positivism, carefully tied these cognitive intervening variables to operationally defined stimulus situations and behaviors. That is, he did not believe nor was he interested in whether a rat somehow had a map in its brain. Rather, he inferred the existence of this hypothetical map from the specific stimulus conditions he created and the subsequent behaviors that he observed and measured.

As an example, consider the cognitive intervening variable of *expectancy*. Tolman believed that one result of learning was that certain expectations were created. Rats finding food at the end of a maze expect to find food there in the future. Furthermore, it is reasonable to assume that they come to expect a particular type of food, an assumption tested in a clever study in Tolman's lab by Elliott (1928). Using the 14-unit T-maze shown in Figure 11.3a, Elliott taught two groups of rats the maze. The experimental group found bran mash in the goal box, whereas the control group found sunflower seeds. Over the first 9 days of the study (i.e., nine trials, one per day), both groups improved, although performance was better for the group fed with bran mash. On day 10, Elliott changed the reward for rats in the experimental group—they now found sunflower seeds at the goal instead of bran mash. As Figure 11.3b shows, their behavior was disrupted (errors increased). In Tolman's terms, they had come to expect bran mash; when that expectancy was violated, their behavior changed. In short, expectancy is a process intervening between stimulus and response, but closely tied to the stimulus features of the experiment and the observed behaviors.

Tolman's Research Program

Tolman and his students completed dozens of important studies of rats learning mazes. These were reported in a series of *University of California Publications in Psychology* during the 1920s and 1930s, in the *Purposive Behavior* book (1932), and in a famous *Psychological Review* paper entitled "Cognitive Maps in Rats and Men" (Tolman, 1948). The bulk of the

FIGURE 11.3 (*a*) Fourteen-unit multiple T-maze, used by Elliott to study expectancy; (*b*) Results of Elliott's study of expectancy. From Tolman (1932).

research was theory-related, but Tolman also spent considerable time and effort standardizing maze-learning procedures.

In the early 1920s, psychologists were beginning to question the **reliability** of the maze as a research tool. Any measurement is reliable to the extent that repeated measures yield approximately the same results, and the issue was a vital one. Mazes had evolved into a wide variety of shapes and sizes since the days of Willard Small and his Hampton Court design (Chapter 6—Close-Up). Different mazes often produced different outcomes, however, and sometimes even the same maze yielded inconsistent data. In a series of studies, Tolman and his students (e.g., Tolman & Nyswander, 1927) set out to examine the issue, identify the factors that reduced reliability, and develop a standardized procedure for maze learning that would ensure optimal reliability. Based on their research, they recommended that error scores be used rather than time-to-completion scores (some rats just run faster than others), that mazes have uniform choice points (e.g., a left–right choice at a T), numerous choice points rather than few (e.g., a 14-unit T-maze), and gates that closed once an animal had made a correct choice (to prevent retracing). They even developed an automated system for delivering animals from their home cages to the start points of mazes and removing them from the end points, thus eliminating human handling of the rats (Tolman, Tryon, & Jeffress, 1929). Having established procedures for improving the reliability of maze-learning data, Tolman and his students focused their attention on the meatier issues related to their evolving learning theory.

Latent Learning   One important issue was the role of reinforcement in learning. Tolman believed that food discovered by the rat at the end of the maze did not affect learning directly; it merely influenced the animal's motivation to complete the maze as quickly and accurately as possible. That is, learning needed to be distinguished from performance, and reinforcement affected the latter but not the former. Learning the overall layout of the maze occurred more or less automatically whenever the animal was experiencing the maze, even if no food was to be found in the goal box. Tolman termed the phenomenon **latent learning** because it occurred "below the surface," that is, without being immediately apparent in the animal's performance.

Testing for latent learning required showing that learning occurred even if reinforcement didn't, and Tolman and Honzik (1930) accomplished this by testing three groups of rats (one trial per day) in the same 14-unit T-maze shown in Figure 11.3a. The first group of rats (no reward, or NR) was never given food reward after completing the maze. The second group (R) was always rewarded with food. As you can see from Figure 11.4, the error scores for these two groups during the course of just over 2 weeks were about what you would expect—lots of errors for NR and steady improvement in performance for R. The third group was the key one, however. As suggested by their label—NR-R—rats in this group were not rewarded initially (i.e., during the first 10 days), but starting on day 11, they found food in the goal box. Tolman reasoned that if reinforcement was necessary for learning, then no learning would occur on days 1–10. Learning would start on day 11, presumably, and only then would performance gradually begin to improve. That pattern did not happen, though, as is clear from the graph. Instead, performance improved *immediately* after day 11. For Tolman, the evidence was clear—the maze was being learned during those first 10 days, even though the learning was not reflected in performance. That is, the learning on days 1–10

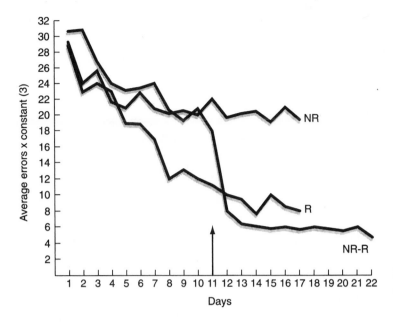

FIGURE 11.4 Results of Tolman and Honzik's study of latent learning. From Tolman (1932).

was "latent," and reinforcement was not needed for the learning to occur. As Tolman (1948) put it:

> Interpreting these results anthropomorphically, we would say that as long as the animals were not getting any food at the end of the maze they continued to take their time in going through it—they continued to enter many blinds. Once, however, they knew they were to get food, they demonstrated that during these preceding non-rewarded trials they had learned where many of the blinds were. They had been building up a "map," and could utilize the latter as soon as they were motivated to do so. (pp. 194–195)

Cognitive Maps As mentioned earlier, Tolman did not believe that rats learned stimulus–response connections when learning a maze. Rather, he argued that they created a **cognitive map** of the maze—an overall knowledge of the maze's structure and spatial pattern that gave them a general sense of where to go in the maze. A clever pair of studies demonstrated the operation of these maps.[1] In one study (Tolman, Ritchie, & Kalish, 1946b), rats encountered the maze found in Figure 11.5 and were started at either S_1 or S_2. Some rats, the "response learning" group, always found food by turning to the right. Others, the "place learning" group, always found food in the same place, F_1. Tolman, Ritchie, and Kalish (1946b) found that rats in the place-learning group learned faster, a result that is

---

[1]Tolman's ideas about cognitive maps were similar to those of Karl Lashley (Chapter 3), and in his "Cognitive Maps in Rats and Men" paper, Tolman referred to Lashley's observation about "a couple of his rats who, after having learned an alley maze, pushed back the cover near the starting box, climbed out and ran directly across the top to the goal-box where they climbed down in again and ate" (Tolman, 1948, p. 203).

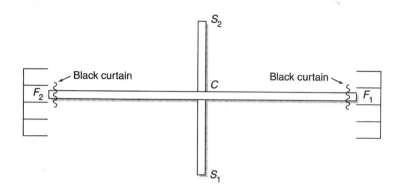

FIGURE 11.5 Maze used in place-learning experiment by Tolman, Ritchie, and Kalish (1946b).

of course congenial with Tolman's theory that the rats learn a cognitive map rather than a series of responses to specific stimuli.[2]

In the second study (Tolman, Ritchie, & Kalish 1946a), rats first learned to run the simple maze in Figure 11.6a. Starting at A, they ran across an open circular table to C, the only part of the maze with sidewalls, and then eventually to the goal box, G. A light was on at H. There were no errors to be made, so the rats soon learned to move quickly from A to G. After 12 trials, the simple maze was replaced with the one in Figure 11.6b. Now the path down C was blocked, and the rats had to choose another route to the food. An S-R behaviorist might expect the rats to choose either 9 or 10, the routes most similar to the original path at C; but Tolman, Ritchie, and Kalish reported that path 6, the best choice to get to the general location of the food, was the most frequently chosen. Tolman (1948) argued that

> the rats had . . . acquired not merely a strip-map to the effect that the original specifically trained-on path led to food but, rather, a wider comprehensive map to the effect that food was located in such and such a direction in the room. (p. 204)

Tolman elaborated on this distinction between narrow "strip-maps" and wider "comprehensive maps" in the last section of his 1948 "Cognitive Maps in Rats and Men" paper and tried to show how all of this had relevance for human behavior. According to Tolman, narrow strip-maps, which are maladaptive in the long run, result from too much mindless repetition on the original path, an environment too limited to see the whole picture, and levels of motivation or frustration that are too high. Comprehensive maps are to be preferred. Revealing the idealism and moral sensitivity that were never far from his thoughts, as well as his penchant for viewing the world as a large maze, Tolman (1948) closed his paper with an appeal to the

> child-trainers and world-planners [to] see to it that nobody's children are too over-motivated or too frustrated. Only then can these children learn to look before and after, learn to see that there are often round-about and safer paths to their quite proper goals—learn, that is, to realize that the well-beings of White and of Negro, of Catholic

[2]"Place" versus "response" learning became a contentious issue; Tolman's outcome was not always replicated, especially by those supportive of Clark Hull's learning theory. Restle (1957) eventually concluded that both types of learning are possible; the outcome depends on whether place or response cues are more dominant in a particular situation.

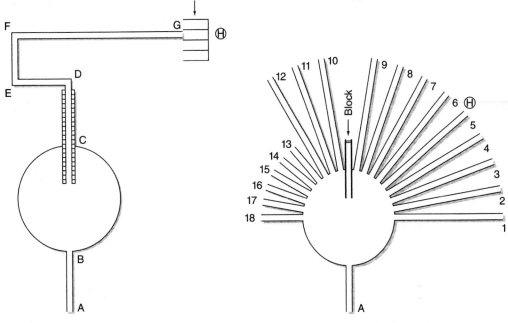

(*a*) Apparatus used in preliminary training   (*b*) Apparatus used in the test trial

FIGURE 11.6 (*a*) Apparatus used in the first phase of Tolman, Ritchie, and Kalish's experiment on the spatial abilities of rats; (*b*) "Sunburst" apparatus for studying spatial learning. From Tolman (1948).

and of Protestant, of Christian and of Jew, of American and of Russian (and even of males and females) are mutually interdependent. . . .

We must, in short, subject our children and ourselves (as the kindly experimenter would his rats) to the optimal conditions of moderate motivation and of an absence of unnecessary frustrations, whenever we put them and ourselves before that great God-given maze which is our human world. (p. 208)

Evaluating Tolman

During the heyday of neobehaviorism, Tolman's research and his theorizing commanded attention, especially from the followers of Clark Hull (discussed later), with whom Tolman disagreed on practically everything except the usefulness of intervening variables and the general precepts of logical positivism. The complexity of his theory contributed to its lack of lasting influence, but Tolman's research program was creative and helped to institutionalize the maze as standard research apparatus. His students were intensely loyal to him, and he in turn treated them as equals. On the other hand, despite their loyalty and devotion, few of Tolman's students continued doing research in "the Tolman tradition" when they left Berkeley. While academia in the 1940s, 1950s, and 1960s became crowded with Hullians and Skinnerians, the "Tolmanian" was a rare creature. Furthermore, Tolman's research with rats in mazes did not produce much in the way of practical application. His plea for training children to have broad cognitive maps, for instance, gave little explicit guidance to parents. Instead of demonstrating the applicability of Tolman's work for everyday problems, the example seemed more like a good illustration of the dangers inherent in extrapolating far beyond one's data.

Tolman's emphasis on purposiveness and his heavy use of mentalistic variables were both criticized by his contemporaries. Tolman was careful to tie these terms operationally to stimulus conditions and responses, but some critics saw his use of such subjective terms as a step backward. One learning theorist, Edwin Guthrie, complained that Tolman's theory proposed so many intervening cognitive factors that a rat faced with a choice in a maze would be overwhelmed: "In his concern with what goes on in the rat's mind, Tolman has neglected to predict what the rat will do. So far as the theory is concerned the rat is left buried in thought" (Guthrie, 1935, p. 172). The criticism is unfair—Tolman's writings are full of data showing rats doing quite a bit of behaving—but it illustrates the preference of many neobehaviorists for observable action over hypothesized internal states. On the other hand, Tolman's willingness to propose cognitive intervening variables makes him an important link between behaviorism and cognitive psychology (Chapter 14). More specifically, among those studying animal behavior, Tolman's cognitive theory resonates with recent interest in animal cognition. Olton's research on spatial behavior and short-term memory in rats (e.g., Olton, 1979), using a radial maze reminiscent of Tolman's sunburst maze, is an example.

Perhaps Tolman's lasting importance results not from his specific theory of learning but from a set of attitudes and values that he displayed. As a researcher, he was serious about his work and careful in executing it. He was persistent and passionate about developing and supporting his theory. Yet he also had a remarkable sense of perspective that enabled him to be fully absorbed in his research while not taking himself too seriously. He knew that better theories than his were bound to come along and that newer research would supersede his. As he said in one of the last pieces he wrote, published the year he died:

> The system may well not stand up. . . . But I do not much care. I have liked to think about psychology in ways that have proved congenial to me. Since . . . psychology [is] still immersed in such tremendous realms of the uncertain and the unknown, the best that any individual scientist . . . can do seems to be to follow his own gleam and his own bent, however inadequate they may be. In fact, I suppose that actually this is what we all do. In the end, the only sure criterion is to have fun. And I have had fun. (Tolman, 1959, p. 152)

In addition to his healthy sense of perspective, Tolman had one other enduring trait—his strong sense of morality. It led him to protest the U.S. involvement in World War I, thus contributing to his dismissal from Northwestern in 1918. In the midst of World War II, his strong feelings about war resurfaced, this time motivating him to write *Drives Toward War* (1942), in which he combined some of his ideas with those of Freud to explain what leads to warfare and to make some recommendations to eliminate the problem. One of his suggestions, which he granted was unlikely to occur, was the creation of a "World-Federation" that would replace nationalist boundaries and encourage cooperation among the peoples of the world rather than competition. The histories of the League of Nations and of the United Nations have made it clear just how difficult it is to overcome nationalist sentiment.

Near the end of his active career, Tolman's convictions faced a final test. In the early 1950s, America was at the beginning the so-called Cold War, its long ideological struggle with the Soviet Union. The Soviets' expressed desire to spread the gospel of Marxist-Leninist doctrine created images of one country after another being subverted and falling (like dominoes) into Communist hands. Holding the line against Communism meant defending South Korea in the 1950s and South Vietnam in the 1960s.

It was also feared that Communists would infiltrate the United States, corrupt its youth, and eventually take over the country. These fears were fueled by a previously obscure Wisconsin senator, Joseph McCarthy, who claimed to know of Communists who had infiltrated the government. Senate hearings, laced with rumor and innuendo, ruined the careers of anyone who was merely accused of being a "Red." McCarthy also hinted that Communists were infiltrating the film industry (dangerous because movies influence attitudes) and higher education (even greater influence—our children!).

In this climate, professors at California universities were told by those running the university system to sign oaths of loyalty to the United States and to declare that they were not members of the Communist Party. Professors were told to sign or resign. As a senior faculty member at Berkeley and by then one of America's leading psychologists, Tolman, offended by the demand, could easily have left Berkeley and been welcomed anywhere. Yet he stayed, and courageously refused to sign the oath, on the general principle that it violated the First Amendment's right of free speech. Also, not content with just his individual action, he led a fight that successfully repealed the oath in California and preserved the concept of academic freedom. In 1957, Tolman received the Distinguished Scientific Contribution Award from the APA; just before his death in 1959, the Board of Regents of the University of California recognized the significance of his fight for academic freedom by awarding him an honorary degree (Crutchfield, 1961).

CLARK HULL (1884–1952): A HYPOTHETICO-DEDUCTIVE SYSTEM

The life and career of Clark Leonard Hull is a case study in how perseverance and hard work can overcome seemingly insurmountable odds. Born into poverty on a farm in New York, raised on a "good but unimproved" farm in Michigan, and educated in a one-room schoolhouse, Hull grew up under "pioneer conditions" (Hull, 1952b, p. 143). In addition to these trying circumstances, he almost died from typhoid fever just before starting college; after his second year at Alma College in Michigan, he contracted polio, which left him partially paralyzed at age 24. At the time, he was aiming for a life as a mining engineer, but the polio made it impossible for him to meet the physical demands of that career.

After spending a year at home, during which time his health improved, Hull decided on a career in psychology. Why psychology? In his words, he was searching for a field related to philosophy that would involve theoretical work, and

> one which was new enough to permit rapid growth so that a young man would not need to wait for his predecessors to die before his work could find recognition, and...would provide an opportunity to design and work with automatic apparatus. (Hull, 1952b, p. 145)

The quote reveals two of Hull's enduring features: his strong ambition and his talent with the design and construction of experimental apparatus. The latter first manifested itself during the polio episode, when Hull designed his own leg brace.

Following 2 years of high school teaching and a marriage, Hull entered the University of Michigan to finish college. His most memorable experience was a yearlong course in experimental psychology, taught jointly by John Shepard, who had studied briefly with Watson, and Walter Pillsbury, a doctoral student of Titchener's. More teaching followed graduation, this time at a Normal School in Kentucky. Hull then applied to graduate school and was rejected at Cornell and Yale but taken in at the University of Wisconsin, where he earned a PhD under the tutelage of Joseph Jastrow, a former Johns Hopkins student of G. Stanley Hall's.

Doctoral dissertations often find their way into the far reaches of filing cabinets, but Hull's (1920) eventually became a well-known study of the processes involved in learning new concepts.[3] For stimuli, Hull used Chinese characters, including those in Figure 11.7. Notice that the characters in each row have a common feature, called a radical. Hull's subjects had to learn to associate a nonsense sound with each radical (e.g., "oo" for the radical that looks like a large check mark). Over the course of several sets ("packs") of stimuli, subjects learned to look at a character and give the correct nonsense sound; eventually they could identify stimuli they had not seen before. The study resulted in a number of findings, but the one that impressed Hull the most was the shape of the learning curve—performance improved gradually but steadily. The idea of learning being the result of a gradual increase in "habit strength" eventually became a salient feature of Hull's learning theory.

Hull completed the doctorate in 1918 at age 34, and he remained at Wisconsin for another decade. While there he developed two very different interests, both resulting from courses he taught. Early in his career, he was asked to teach a course in psychological testing.

Four of the Chinese radicals that Hull used are shown here. First, the subject was shown a Chinese character and guessed its "name" (for example, oo), then the experimenter gave the correct name, and so on. Characters with the same radicals always were given the same name so that after going through several packs of characters, the subjects improved their performances and were eventually able to correctly name characters they had never seen before.

Name	Concept	Pack I	Pack II	Pack III	Pack IV	Pack V	Pack VI
oo							
yer							
li							
ta							

From Hull (1920)

FIGURE 11.7 Chinese characters used as stimulus materials in Hull's doctoral dissertation on concepts learning. From Hull (1920).

[3]The study was initially ignored by other researchers, which discouraged Hull greatly. However, a brief description of it appeared in a popular general psychology text in the late 1920s, and due to the tendencies of textbook authors to borrow from each other, it became increasingly cited thereafter (Hilgard, 1987).

Although he knew little about testing, the subject interested him, especially the correlational math involved in test validation. He immersed himself in the literature of testing, and within a few years produced an authoritative text called *Aptitude Testing* (Hull, 1928). Displaying mechanical aptitude again, he built a machine to automatically calculate correlations. This saved him the tedium of calculating by hand the numerous correlations (e.g., between test scores and some measure of performance) needed to validate tests. The machine was delicate, however, a problem that prevented its widespread use.[4]

Shortly after Hull began teaching the testing course, he was assigned a section of introductory psychology being taught to premedical students. Because he believed that suggestion and physician authority influenced the outcome of many medical treatments, he decided to incorporate the topic into his lectures. This led him to hypnosis, and to the understatement that "the subject has largely tended to attract experimenters with a peculiarly unscientific type of approach" (Hull, 1952b, p. 152). Determined to correct the problem, Hull spent about 10 years examining the phenomenon systematically and eventually produced *Hypnosis and Suggestibility: An Experimental Approach* (Hull, 1933). He concluded that hypnosis was a state of hypersuggestibility and a reduction in analytical thought, brought on by hypnotically induced relaxation. He believed that hypnosis was not qualitatively different from normal consciousness, but only differed in degree. Thus, given the proper instructions, the various hypnotic phenomena (e.g., pain reduction) could be demonstrated in nonhypnotized subjects. Hull also believed that the medical community overestimated the therapeutic value of hypnosis. For example, he found that contrary to the medical community's widely held belief, memory was not notably improved by hypnosis.

Although working primarily on aptitude testing and hypnosis in the 1920s, Hull did not lose sight of his dissertation topic of learning. Indeed, while Hull's interests in aptitude testing, hypnosis, and learning are often portrayed as three distinct periods in his life, they were intertwined and all three reflected Hull's systematic, analytic approach to research (Triplett, 1982). During the 1920s, Hull was well aware of Watson's writings and was familiar with the research being done by Tolman. Learning became the primary focus of his life, however, after he read the translations of Pavlov's research in the late 1920s. The topic captured his full attention soon after 1929, the year he left Wisconsin to undertake (at age 45) a new challenge at Yale University.

When he arrived as president of Yale University in 1921, James Angell, one of the leaders of the Chicago functionalists (Chapter 7), found that psychology at Yale could only be described as moribund. The psychologists were still part of the philosophy department, virtually no research was being done, and only 8 psychology doctorates had been awarded between 1903 and 1921, compared with 46 at Columbia and 51 at Chicago (Morawski, 1986). With the aid of Robert Yerkes, Angell established the Institute of Psychology in 1924. Generous funding from the Laura Spelman Rockefeller Memorial, headed by a psychologist with close ties to both Yerkes and Angell, enabled the institute to recruit first-class researchers and equip laboratories. In 1929, the Institute expanded into the multidisciplinary Institute of Human Relations (IHR), which had as its lofty goal "to correlate knowledge and coordinate technique in related fields that greater progress may be made in the understanding of human life"

---

[4]In a diary entry after traveling by train with Hull to a conference in 1928, Walter Miles of Stanford reported that Hull had built three of the machines but "they are hard to keep in shape and [he] will not send one far away." Consequently, an order that Miles had placed for one had to be canceled (Miles, 1928).

(Angell, 1929; quoted in Morawski, 1986, p. 219). It was composed of professors taken from a range of disciplines, including psychology, law, sociology, anthropology, and economics; their teaching duties at Yale were reduced to a minimum for them to devote the bulk of their time to the institute and research. One of the psychologists assigned to IHR was Clark Hull, who had just been recruited from Wisconsin. Hull spent the rest of his career at Yale; he died of a second heart attack just 3 weeks from retirement. While there, he developed his theory of learning, tested it extensively in the laboratory, and created a small army of Hullians, students and colleagues who extended the research program far beyond New Haven. The best known was Kenneth Spence (1907–1967), who got to know Hull while studying at Yale with Yerkes. Spence made contributions significant enough for Hull's theory to become known as the Hull-Spence theory among devotees. At the University of Iowa, Spence perpetuated the Hullian legacy by producing no fewer than 73 PhD students between 1940 and 1963 (Hilgard, 1967).

Hull's System

One of Hull's heroes was Sir Isaac Newton. He kept a copy of Newton's *Principia Mathematica* on his desk, and he urged graduate students to read it so they would understand that Hull's approach to research mirrored Newton's. Newton viewed the universe as a giant machine controlled by precise mathematical laws; Hull thought of humans in the same mechanical fashion. Indeed, he believed that an ultimate understanding of human behavior could occur only if a machine were built that was indistinguishable from a human. The attitude was undoubtedly influenced by Hull's own highly developed skill as a machine builder.

Newton also influenced Hull's beliefs about progress in science and the importance of theory. For Hull, science advanced by developing sophisticated theories and then testing them, modifying them, testing the revisions, and so on. This system, also used by Tolman and consistent with the dictates of logical positivism, is called a **hypothetico-deductive system**. At the core of this type of theory of human behavior is a set of postulates, statements about behavior based on accumulated knowledge from research and logic. From these postulates specific hypotheses can be logically deduced, and these lead directly to experiments. The results of these experiments support or fail to support the postulates and, by extension, the theory. Over time, the theory evolves as a function of empirical support or nonsupport.

In addition to emulating Newton, Hull was motivated to develop his theory by what he saw as a relative absence of theory building among American psychologists, compared to the extensive work on theory compiled by the gestaltists (Mills, 1988). It was time for American psychology to catch up. As Hull put it:

> these Gestalt people are so terrifyingly articulate. Practically every one of them writes several books. The result is that whereas they constitute a rather small proportion of the psychological population of this country, they have written ten times as much in the field of theory as Americans have. (Hull, 1942; quoted in Mills, 1988, p. 393)

Hull worked on the theory right up to his death, and the final account of it, *A Behavior System* (1952a), appeared posthumously. The best-known version of the system, however, can be found in *Principles of Behavior* (1943); it includes a set of 16 postulates, presented both verbally and mathematically, along with descriptions of research supporting the theory. A complete description of Hull's theory is well beyond the scope of this chapter segment, but some insight can be gained by examining his most famous postulate, number 4.

Postulate 4: Habit Strength   Postulate 4 reveals the core of Hull's belief about the conditions necessary for learning to occur. It also illustrates the extent to which Hull aimed for theoretical precision and formality—*Principles of Behavior* was not meant to be light reading. Here is just a portion of the fourth postulate:

> Whenever an effector activity ($r \rightarrow R$) and a receptor activity ($S \rightarrow s$) occur in close temporal contiguity ($_sC_r$), and this $_sC_r$ is closely associated with the diminution of a need (G) or with a stimulus which has been closely and consistently associated with the diminution of a need (G), there will result an increment to a tendency (Δ_sH_R) for that afferent impulse on later occasions to evoke that reaction. The increments from successive reinforcements summate in a manner which yields a combined habit strength ($_sH_R$) which is a simple positive growth function of the number of reinforcements (N). (Hull, 1943, p. 178)

The key elements here are contiguity and reinforcement. According to Hull, learning occurs when there is a close contiguity between stimulus and response. A rat learns to associate a location X in a maze, for instance, with the response "turn right." This contiguity is necessary, but it is not sufficient. In addition, reinforcement must be present for learning to occur. Reinforcers for Hull were stimuli that reduce drives; food reduces hunger, for example. Together, S-R contiguity and reinforcement gradually increase $_sH_R$, or **habit strength**. Thus, by repeatedly reaching X, turning right, and finding food, the rat accumulates habit strength with each reinforced trial. To learn is to increase $_sH_R$. That learning is incremental ("a simple positive growth function") rather than sudden echoes the results of Hull's dissertation on concept learning. The importance to Hull of the ideas in postulate 4 may be inferred from Figure 11.8, a portrait completed late in Hull's career. The graph in the background is a theoretical learning curve—notice that habit strength increases gradually as a function of the number of reinforced trials.

For Hull, then, reinforcement was defined in terms of drive reduction ("diminution of a need") and as a result, his theory is sometimes known as a **drive reduction** theory. Primary drives are those connected directly with survival, and they can be reduced with **primary reinforcers** like food and water. But Hull also described **secondary reinforcers**, stimuli he

FIGURE 11.8   Portrait of Clark Hull.
From Popplestone and McPherson (1994).

described in postulate 4 as those that have been associated with primary reinforcers. A tone that has been paired with the primary reinforcer of food can itself become a reinforcer, for instance.

Reaction Potential   Although Hull rejected the type of intervening variables used by Tolman, he acknowledged that he borrowed the concept from his fellow neobehaviorist (Hull, 1943, p. 31). An important intervening variable for Hull was what he called **reaction potential**, or $_sE_R$. Introduced in postulate 7, $_sE_R$ refers to the probability ("potential") that a response ("reaction") will occur at a given time and can be inferred from several kinds of measurable behaviors (e.g., response latency, how long it takes an animal to respond in a particular situation—when reaction potential was high, latency was brief). Hull believed that $_sE_R$ was influenced by several factors, and drive and habit strength are the most important. That is, a response is most likely to occur if both habit strength and drive are high. And Hull argued that the relationship was multiplicative ($_sE_R = D \times {}_sH_R$) rather than additive. As he put it in postulate 7:

> Any effective habit strength ($_sH_R$) is sensitized into reaction potentiality ($_sE_R$) by all primary drives active within the organism at a given time, the magnitude of this potentiality being a product obtained by multiplying an increasing function of $_sH_R$ by an increasing function of D. (Hull, 1943, p. 253)

Thus, if either drive or habit strength is zero, the response won't occur. Rats will run a maze correctly only if they are motivated (e.g., hungry) and if they have a sufficient number of reinforced trials under their belts. Figure 11.9a shows how Hull envisioned the theoretical effects of drive and habit strength (i.e., number of reinforced trials) on reaction potential. For some empirical support, Hull included data from two studies (Perin, 1942; Williams, 1938) and combined them to form Figure 11.9b.

Evaluating Hull

Throughout the 1940s and into the early 1950s, Clark Hull was arguably the leading research psychologist in America. His work was cited more often than that of any other psychologist (far more frequently than Tolman's work), and his students (and their students) spread the Hullian gospel far and wide. Between 1941 and 1950, for example, approximately 70% of all research articles published in the areas of learning and motivation referred to and referenced Hull's work (Spence, 1952). For the psychologists of Hull's era, his theory met the need for a clear direction into the future. Introspective psychology had met its demise in the 1920s, but there was nothing to replace it. Watsonian behaviorism appeared, but so did Gestalt psychology, Freudianism, mental testing, and a host of other variants. Searching for maturity and respectability as a science, psychologists seized on what appeared to be just the kind of formalized theory that characterized the older sciences, especially physics.

Paradoxically, today's college students not only fail to appreciate Hull's stature, they seldom even recognize his name. Hull's rise and abrupt fall is illustrated by an analysis done by Guttman (1977). He examined the reference sections of all of the articles published in the *Journal of Experimental Psychology* in 1940, 1950, 1960, and 1970, counting up the number of references to the work of Hull or his best-known collaborator, Spence. For those four years, respectively, the percentages of articles citing Hull and/or Spence were 4%, 39%, 24%, and 4%.

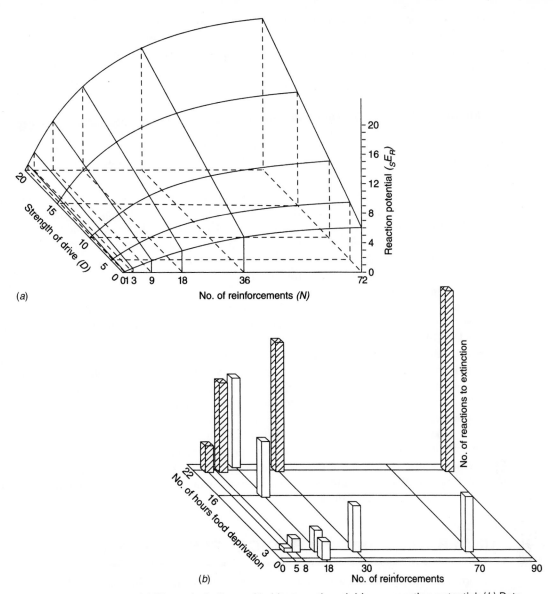

FIGURE 11.9 (*a*) Theoretical effects of habit strength and drive on reaction potential; (*b*) Data from studies research showing the effects of habit strength and drive on reaction potential. From Hull (1943).

There are several reasons for the collapse of Hull's theory. For one thing, it was overambitious, attempting to build a theory of extraordinary complexity and mathematical precision on what turned out to be a very narrow empirical base—the behavior of simple organisms (usually rats) in artificial, highly controlled, simple environments (a typical apparatus was a "straight maze"—no turns, no dead ends, and the time to run from one end to the other was the usual dependent variable). Hullians countered that other sciences do the same thing;

biologists, for instance, use isolated tissue cultures to study cellular processes, even though those cultures are "artificial" relative to real-life biological environments. Also, Hull was planning a major work that extended his system to complex human behavior, but was never able to get very far with it before his death. On the other hand, several of his students, along with other members of Yale's IHR, did manage to combine Hullian and Freudian ideas into a testable theory of human aggression. In *Frustration and Aggression* (Dollard, Doob, Miller, Mowrer, & Sears, 1939), Hull's students developed the well-known frustration-aggression hypothesis and tested it with both animal subjects and children. The same group later produced *Social Learning and Imitation* (Miller & Dollard, 1941), which launched modern social learning theory, best known through the work of Albert Bandura (e.g., Bobo dolls and imitative aggression).

Another criticism of Hull's theory was that it overlooked the very human nature of research. Consistent with his underlying Newtonian assumption of human as machine, Hull took it for granted that disputes over the empirical support for the theory would be resolved by dispassionate and objective scientists listening to their data. There was faith that "crucial experiments" would decide the "truth" of some issue, but contentious issues never seemed to go away. For example, Hull and Tolman engaged in a series of skirmishes over the nature of learning. Tolman's group would produce a study that seemed to question some aspect of Hull's theory; Hull's group would then rush to the barricades and produce some data that seemed to explain away Tolman's results while simultaneously maintaining the Hullian model. Tolman would then respond. And so on. Followers of each theorist felt they had the data on their side, but to those outside both camps, it appeared that little was being resolved. Furthermore, the failure to settle these disputes about learning contributed to the growing suspicion that behaviorism might be flawed as a system, and questions about the adequacy of behaviorism contributed to the development of cognitive psychology in the 1960s (Segal & Lachman, 1972), as will be seen in Chapter 14.

One final problem for Hull was shared by Tolman and was perhaps the most important reason that both men faded into relative obscurity in the latter half of the 20th century. The problem was the rising star of B. F. Skinner, who combined the brashness and entrepreneurial spirit of John Watson with the scientific creativity, work ethic, and ability to attract talented students to match Tolman or Hull.

B. F. SKINNER (1904–1990): A RADICAL BEHAVIORISM

Burrhus Frederick Skinner was a product of small-town America (Susquehanna, Pennsylvania) during the Progressive era. He grew up at a time when optimism within the emerging white middle class was high in America—the country had just emerged from difficult economic times in the 1890s, and it had just beaten the overmatched Spanish in the Spanish-American War. The president, Theodore Roosevelt, was the dashing hero of the war and the youngest man ever to hold the office at that time. Parents, unless poor and/or nonwhite, had every reason to expect endless opportunity for their children. Skinner's father was a moderately successful lawyer; his mother stayed at home and cultivated in young Fred the Protestant values of hard work and a constant concern about "what other people might think."

Hard work indeed characterized Skinner's life, but concern about what others thought did not become one of his enduring features. On the contrary, independent thinking and an unwillingness to accept the "wisdom of elders" unless accompanied by sound evidence was more his style. It emerged early—his high school principal wrote him a strong recommendation to New York's Hamilton College, but cautioned that young Fred was "passionately fond of arguing with his teachers. He is quite a reader and although I do not think he actually supposes himself wiser than his teachers, I have found him [to give] that impression" (quoted in Bjork, 1993, p. 28).

Skinner was initially unhappy in the fraternity/sorority-dominated atmosphere of Hamilton, but he soon found his niche and developed a passion for creative writing. He even sent some short stories to the poet Robert Frost, whom he had met at a writers' conference. Frost's praise led to a career decision. Determined to be a famous writer, Skinner informed his parents that he wished to take a year off after his 1926 graduation and simply write. This of course created problems for Skinner's parents, who were naturally concerned about what people would think of the new college graduate who was living at home but did not seem to have an actual job. It's not hard to imagine the pressure he felt from his parents to be productive ("And what did you write today, Fred?"), and as the year passed he also had a growing sense that he would never match the achievements of the famous writers whose works he was reading. Although Skinner later referred to this time as his "Dark Year," some of what he read started a sequence of events that eventually led to graduate studies in psychology at Harvard. For instance, during this time he read a number of popular articles on behaviorism, and this led him to Watson and Pavlov. He became intrigued by behaviorism and, in the fall of 1928, he was off to Cambridge, Massachusetts. Figure 11.10 shows Skinner working in the Harvard laboratory 2 years later.

Skinner developed his system of behaviorism while at Harvard, first as a graduate student and then as a prestigious University Fellow. There was no noticeable change in

FIGURE 11.10 B. F. Skinner as a graduate student at Harvard in 1930. From Malone (1991).

his general attitude toward authority. He was not impressed by the work of E. G. Boring, the head of the laboratory and, of course, Titchener's best-known student. He referred to Boring's perception course as "simply painful" (Skinner, 1979, p. 47) and lamented that Boring spent three entire lectures explaining a single visual illusion.[5] Boring, in turn, was not inclined toward behaviorism and removed himself from Skinner's doctoral committee. During the defense of his doctoral dissertation, when the noted personality theorist Gordon Allport (Chapter 14) asked him to describe what he thought to be the shortcomings of behaviorism, Skinner replied that he could not think of any (p. 75).

Skinner's first book, *The Behavior of Organisms* (1938), summarized his 8 years of research at Harvard. After 9 years at the University of Minnesota and another 3 chairing the psychology department at Indiana University, Skinner returned to Harvard in 1948, where he remained active, even after his retirement in 1974. Just 8 days before his death from leukemia in 1990, he addressed the opening session of the APA's annual meeting in Boston. I was in the audience that evening and recall that he needed assistance from his daughter getting on stage and walking to the podium (you can just see the top of her head in Figure 11.11),

FIGURE 11.11 Skinner's final public appearance, at APA's annual meeting in Boston, August 1990. Photo courtesy of Kathleen Davis.

[5]Skinner did not elaborate, but the illusion in question was probably the moon illusion—a full moon looks huge on the horizon, but smaller when high in the sky. Research on this illusion was probably Boring's most important contribution to experimental psychology, and in the 1930s he completed several studies attempting to explain the illusion (e.g., Holway & Boring, 1940).

but once there he barely glanced at his notes while delivering an articulate and impassioned plea for his brand of behaviorism and an attack on what he viewed as the misguided efforts of cognitive psychologists. The talk was published shortly after Skinner's death as "Can Psychology Be a Science of the Mind?" (Skinner, 1990).

The Experimental Analysis of Behavior

Do you still have your introductory psychology text? If you examine the chapter on learning, I guarantee that you will find a major section on "classical" or Pavlovian conditioning (probably accompanied by the wrong picture of Pavlov's apparatus), followed by an equally large section on "operant" conditioning. The relationship between the two is complex and beyond the scope of this chapter, but Skinner is responsible for making the distinction, and operant conditioning is sometimes referred to as Skinnerian conditioning.

In *The Behavior of Organisms* (1938), Skinner distinguished between Type S and Type R conditioning. **Type S conditioning** is the Pavlovian model: An identifiable stimulus elicits an identifiable response through the procedure of pairing two *stimuli*, one that initially elicits the response (e.g., food) and one that doesn't (e.g., a tone). It is called Type S because in this case an association is formed between two stimuli (food, the UCS, and tone, the CS), and both stimuli eventually produce the same response (drooling). Type S conditioning accounts for a certain type of behavior, but Skinner argued that it cannot explain a great deal of behavior that seems to have no easily identifiable stimulus. That is, some behavior is *emitted* by the organism and is controlled by the immediate consequences of the behavior, not by an eliciting stimulus. In **Type R conditioning**, or **operant conditioning**, a behavior is emitted, it is followed by some consequence, and the future chances of that behavior occurring are determined by those consequences. If the consequences are positive, a behavior being rewarded, for example, the behavior is strengthened. If the consequences are negative (e.g., punishment following some behavior), on the other hand, the behavior is weakened. Skinner called operant conditioning Type R because in this case a consequence (e.g., a child getting a toy) is associated with the emitted *response* that preceded it (e.g., a child throwing a tantrum in a toy store). Skinner chose the term **operant** to describe this form of behavior because the behavior "operates" on the environment—when the behavior happens, it produces a predictable outcome.

Skinner, like Watson, believed that psychology should have but two goals—the prediction and control of behavior, both nonhuman and human. This would be accomplished through an "experimental analysis of behavior," that is, through a full description of operant behaviors, the environments in which these behaviors occurred, and the immediate consequences of the behaviors. While recognizing that behaviors are influenced by an individual's innate behavioral tendencies and capabilities, Skinner focused on how behaviors were shaped by the environment. In that sense, then, he made contact with the British empiricists, the environmentalism of Watson, and he provided a clear example of neobehaviorism's emphasis on learning.

Operant Conditioning: A Primer   Skinner spent his life fleshing out the fine details of operant conditioning. The best full description can be found in his 1953 book, *Science and Human Behavior*, and reasonably thorough descriptions appear in textbooks on the psychology of learning. Here are some of the basics.

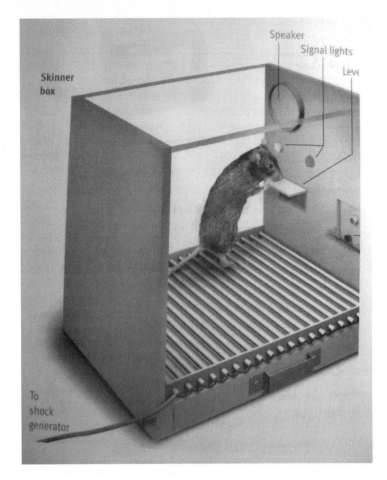

Speaker

Signal lights

Leve

Skinner
box

To
shock
generator

FIGURE 11.12   A typical Skinner box for rats.

Skinner investigated operant conditioning by creating a highly structured environment that enabled him to follow what he considered the good advice of Pavlov. As he put it: "I had the clue from Pavlov: Control your conditions and you will see order" (Skinner, 1956, p. 223). Figure 11.12 shows this controlled environment, as designed for rats. It consists of a chamber with a small lever on one wall that can be pressed by the rat, a small food trough for the delivery of positive consequences (food), devices for the presentation of visual and/or auditory stimuli, and a set of parallel bars as a floor, through which electrical current can pass for the delivery of negative consequences (mild shock). A similar apparatus exists for pigeons, but a circular disk to be pecked substitutes for the lever. Skinner called the apparatus an operant chamber, but Clark Hull referred to it as a Skinner box, and the name stuck. Behavior in a Skinner box is recorded by means of a cumulative recorder. As paper is fed out at a constant rate, thereby producing time on an x-axis, a pen moves across the paper by a small distance every time the bar is pressed (or key is pecked). Rate of response, which for Skinner was the only important measure of behavior, can be determined by looking at the slope of the line. Whenever a specific behavior is reinforced (e.g., followed by food), the pen

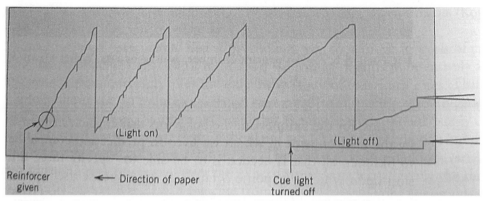

FIGURE 11.13 A sample cumulative record, initially showing a high rate of response, then a decline to no responding (perhaps the result of an extinction procedure).

makes a short downward vertical line. When the pen reaches the top of the paper, it quickly returns to the baseline to start over. Figure 11.13 shows an example of a cumulative record.

With an operant chamber and a cumulative recorder, Skinner was in a position to examine operant conditioning in depth. Just as Pavlov was able to demonstrate such phenomena as extinction in his classical conditioning paradigm, so Skinner was able to demonstrate them with an operant procedure. With a rat that had been conditioned to bar-press for food, for instance, Skinner could demonstrate *extinction* by withholding the reinforcer. In fact, Skinner's initial demonstration of extinction appeared by accident. In his words (which also reveal something about Skinner's passion for his work):

> My first extinction curve showed up by accident. A rat was pressing the lever in an experiment on satiation when the pellet dispenser jammed. I was not there at the time, and when I returned I found a beautiful curve....
>
> The change was more orderly than the extinction of a salivary reflex in Pavlov's setting, and I was terribly excited. It was a Friday afternoon and there was no one in the laboratory who I could tell. All that weekend I crossed streets with particular care and avoided all unnecessary risks to protect my discovery from loss through my accidental death. (Skinner, 1979, p. 95)

The extinction curve that Skinner found would have looked something like Figure 11.13—a high rate of response while the rat was being reinforced for bar pressing, followed by a gradual lessening of the response rate, eventually resulting in no responses.

In addition to extinction, Skinner demonstrated a variety of other conditioning phenomena. For example, while a rat was being conditioned to bar-press, a light would typically be on in the operant chamber. Dimming the light slowed the rate of response. This was *generalization*—behavior occurring in one environment also occurred in a similar environment. By reinforcing bar presses with the light on, but not when the light was off, Skinner eventually conditioned the rat to bar-press only when the light was on—this was what Pavlov called *differentiation* (Skinner called it *discrimination*, the term used today). Together, these phenomena illustrated what Skinner called **stimulus control**. In operant conditioning, the environment in which a behavior is reinforced (i.e., a Skinner box with the light on) comes to exert control over the rat's behavior. In an experimental analysis, then, understanding behavior involves being able to specify the behavior being studied, the immediate consequences of that behavior, and the environment where the behavior occurs. Notice that Skinner's two main goals are thereby accomplished—behavior can now be predicted, knowing the environment and the reinforcement history of the organism, and it also can be controlled (e.g., by turning a light on and off).

Skinner and Theory

Skinner's philosophy of science differed fundamentally from that of Hull and Tolman. Rather than deducing hypotheses from theoretical statements, designing studies to test these hypotheses, and then adjusting the theory depending on the research outcome, Skinner preferred an inductive approach to research that involved studying samples of behavior and looking for regularities that could become general principles. His reference to Pavlov and the search for orderly behavior hints at the strategy. This freedom from the dictates of theory is also evident in his recommendation to researchers that "when you find something fascinating, drop everything else and study it" (Skinner, 1956, p. 223).

Skinner's modus operandi was to study behavior intensively under a variety of circumstances and then draw general conclusions. His research on so-called reinforcement schedules is a classic illustration of this inductive strategy. Starting from the observation that in real life, reinforcers may occur sporadically rather than after every response, he set out to examine how different **schedules of reinforcement** could produce different patterns of behavior. For example, in a fixed ratio schedule for a bar-pressing rat, reinforcement might follow every 20th bar press instead of every bar press (i.e., an FR20 schedule). In a fixed interval schedule, affected more by time than by responses per se, reinforcement might follow the first response after 20 seconds had passed (an FI20 schedule). Skinner and his student, Charles Ferster, examined dozens of different reinforcement schedules, and the result was *Schedules of Reinforcement* (Ferster & Skinner, 1957). The book is massive (739 pages) and filled with over 900 different cumulative records of reinforcement schedules and the characteristic behaviors each produces (e.g., higher rates of responding for FR than for FI schedules). Something of Skinner's work ethic can be seen from his description of the process of compiling the book:

> Thousands of hours of data meant thousands of feet of cumulative records.... We worked systematically. We would take a protocol and a batch of cumulative records, dictate an account of the experiment, select illustrative records, and cut and nest them in a few figures. In the end, we had more than 1,000 figures, 921 of which went into the book. (Skinner, 1984, p. 109)

As you might guess from this description, the book is not much fun to read. But for Skinnerians, it became an indispensable reference source for information about how behavior can be predicted from knowledge of various reinforcement schedules.

Skinner and the Problem of Explanation

We have learned that both Tolman and Hull proposed the existence of intervening variables to help account for learned behavior, and these variables were carefully tied to stimuli and responses via operational definitions. Skinner avoided intervening variables, however, mainly because he thought it opened the

KEY DATE—1953

This year marked the publication date of Skinner's influential *Science and Human Behavior*.

These events also occurred that year:

- A revolution in the treatment of mental illness began with the approval of the tranquilizer drug Serpasil by the Food and Drug Administration
- James Watson and Francis Crick created the first accurate model of the DNA molecule
- General Dwight Eisenhower, American hero of World War II, began the first of two terms as President
- The reign of Marshall Tito of Yugoslavia began
- Queen Elizabeth II was crowned queen of England
- The Rosenbergs, having been found guilty of spying for the Soviet Union, were executed
- Sir Edmund Hillary became the first person to climb Mt. Everest
- Research reports first suggested a link between lung cancer and smoking

- The Boston Braves moved to Milwaukee and became the Milwaukee Braves, while the St. Louis Browns moved east and became the Baltimore Orioles (the Yankees won their fifth World Series in a row)

These people were born:

- Tony Blair, former Prime Minister of England
- Pierce Brosnan, American actor (e.g., James Bond films)
- Ken Burns, American filmmaker (e.g., *The Civil War*)

These people died:

- E. P. Hubble, American astronomer (orbiting telescope named for him)
- Jim Thorpe, native American athlete, who won Olympic gold medals in both the pentathlon and decathlon in 1912
- Eugene O'Neill, Nobel Prize winning American playwright (e.g., *Long Day's Journey into Night*)

door to what he called **explanatory fictions**. These refer to a tendency to propose some hypothetical internal factor mediating between observable stimuli and measurable behaviors and then later to use the factor as a pseudo-explanation for the behavior. It is something that we do all the time, at least informally. For example, suppose your new roommate stays up late at night studying and seems to spend more time in the library than anyone else you know. You ask his friends about him. They say that he has a high need for achievement. According to Skinner, at this point we might make the mistake of thinking that we have explained the studying behavior by attributing it to the high need for achievement. In fact, however, this "need for achievement" is an explanatory fiction, merely a label that summarizes the studying and library-going behaviors and adds nothing to our understanding of what causes the behavior. The explanation, Skinner would contend, lies in the person's overall learning history and the specific reinforcement contingencies in place when the behavior occurs.

The problem with explanatory fictions led Skinner to be critical of physiological psychologists, who sought to explain behavior by reducing it, in his view, to nervous system activity. Although Skinner recognized the importance of studying brain function and nervous system activity, he was certain that a thorough experimental analysis of behavior was possible without reference to the nervous system. In this regard, Skinner mirrored the attitude of the Harvard physiologist W. J. Crozier, with whom Skinner studied.[6]

[6]W. J. Crozier (1892–1955) was a professor of physiology at Harvard and follower of Loeb, who had a strong influence on Watson (Chapter 10). Crozier (like Loeb) believed that behavior could be interpreted in purely mechanical terms and without reference to the nervous system. Skinner (1956) once wrote that it "had been said of Loeb, and might have been said of Crozier, that he 'resented the nervous system.' Whether this was true or not, the fact was that both these men talked about animal behavior without mentioning the nervous system and with surprising success" (pp. 222–223).

Similarly, he rejected most of contemporary cognitive psychology, on the grounds that it also resorted to explanatory fictions (e.g., attributing memory failures to short-term memory capacity limits).

This is not to say that Skinner denied the obvious fact that thinking, memory, and language occur. He rejected the idea that there was a qualitative distinction between public and private events and, as some behaviorists argued, that private events could not be studied scientifically. He argued instead that both public and private events can be understood through an experimental analysis of them (Skinner, 1953). Running is a public event, and problem solving is a private event, but they are both things that humans do and are therefore subject to the contingencies of reinforcement and stimulus control. A Skinnerian analysis of problem solving, for instance, would focus on how different problem-solving behaviors occur in different environments and how these behaviors have been reinforced in the individual's learning history. Skinner first outlined his views about public and private events in a 1945 paper called "The Operational Analysis of Psychological Terms." In that paper, he explicitly labeled his approach a "radical behaviorism," a label that continues to be associated with his version of neobehaviorism.

A Technology of Behavior

Skinner's inductive strategy was in the tradition of Sir Francis Bacon, and Skinner often referred to Bacon as his model (Smith, 1996b). As you recall from Chapter 2, Bacon argued that understanding nature required making systematic observations of it without a preconceived theoretical framework. General principles would emerge out of these systematic observations. Bacon also believed that the control of nature was an important goal for science.

Bacon provided the prototype of what psychologist-historian Laurence Smith (1992) has referred to as the *technological ideal*—a scientist who desires not merely to understand nature but to control it. In fact, Bacon argued that true understanding occurred only if one could demonstrate control over some phenomenon, either by manipulating some aspect of the environment and observing a predicted outcome or by creating some technology that worked reliably. Thus a thorough understanding of physics can be demonstrated by creating machines that rely on various physical laws. For Skinner, the extrapolation to psychology was easy. He would show that behavior could be predicted, and he would create a technology of behavior, based on reinforcement principles, to show how behavior could be controlled.

Skinner's first attempt to develop a behavioral technology was known as Project Pigeon (Skinner, 1960) and was undertaken while he was at the University of Minnesota. During World War II, he obtained modest funding to pursue the development of a guidance system using pigeons to direct missiles toward targets. Along with a dedicated team of students, he was able to train pigeons to key-peck at a target screen. As they pecked at the target, the missile would change direction until the target remained in the crosshairs of the screen. As a backup measure, each nose cone was fitted with three pigeons, each with its own target. The pigeons, of course, would make just one trip. Skinner was able to build a sophisticated

CLOSE-UP

THE IQ ZOO AND THE "MISBEHAVIOR OF ORGANISMS"

Two of the Minnesota graduate students who worked with Skinner on Project Pigeon were Keller and Marian Breland. The experience changed their lives. Rather than following the normal path from graduate school to an academic career, they decided to make a life for themselves by using what they knew of operant conditioning to train animals. They created a business called Applied Behavior Enterprise (ABE) and quickly landed a contract with General Mills, Inc., which called for the training of chickens in advertisements for one of their products, Larro Farm Feed. The hens tap-danced and rolled wooden eggs down a chute and into a basket. Success with chickens led to bigger and better things, including "Priscilla the Fastidious Pig," who was able to turn on a radio, push around a vacuum cleaner, and select her favorite feed product

(Larro, naturally), among other things (Breland & Breland, 1951).

The Brelands moved ABE south to Arkansas in the early 1950s and, in 1955, opened the "IQ Zoo" in Hot Springs. It quickly attracted tourists, drawn by such acts as chickens walking tightropes, parrots riding bicycles, raccoons playing basketball, and rabbits playing pianos (Figure 11.14). The Brelands also became involved with dolphin training and, between 1955 and 1965, they consulted with Marineland of the Pacific (no longer exists, but was a model for today's Sea World). They wrote the first training manuals for conditioning dolphins, developed scripts for early dolphin shows, and trained others in basic operant principles (Gillaspy & Bailey, 2008).

(a)

(b)

FIGURE 11.14 (a) Keller and Marian Breland and a musical friend; (b) a poster for the IQ Zoo.

One belief held by ardent behaviorists was that conditioning principles, both the classical and operant variety, were so powerful that virtually any type of behavior could be conditioned. The Brelands were certainly convinced, at least early in their career. In 1951, for instance, they wrote an article called "A Field of Applied Animal Behavior" (Breland & Breland, 1951), in which they enthusiastically described their promising new business (ABE) and lamented that their new applied field was "so vast... that we cannot begin to develop one-tenth of the projects we have thought of" (p. 204). Ten years later, though, they were less convinced of the universality of conditioning principles; they wrote an article that represents their most important contribution to psychology's history.

The article was called "The Misbehavior of Organisms" (Breland & Breland, 1961), the first published description of what came to be referred to the "biological constraints on learning" or "biological preparedness." In the article, they described some occasional frustrations in training animals to do certain tricks and called the experience "a persistent pattern of discomforting failures" (p. 681). For example, they attempted to train a raccoon to pick up wooden coins and deposit them in a piggy bank. It was not difficult to shape the animal to pick up a coin by simply reinforcing the behavior. It was also not too difficult to train the raccoon to place a single coin in the bank. The big problem occurred when they introduced a second coin, training the raccoon to pick up and deposit both. As the Brelands described it:

> Now the raccoon really had problems (and so did we). Not only could he not let go of the coins, but he spent seconds, even minutes, rubbing them together (in a most miserly fashion),

and dipping them into the container. He carried on this behavior to such an extent that the practical application we had in mind—a display featuring a raccoon putting money in a piggy bank—simply was not feasible. The rubbing behavior became worse and worse as time went on, in spite of nonreinforcement. (p. 682)

The experience (and four similar ones described in the article) shook the Brelands' faith in the power of pure conditioning, but it led them to the important insight that conditioning principles could sometimes be trumped by instinct. That is, they discovered that if the animals were asked to behave in a way that reflected or interfered with any of their naturally occurring instinctive behaviors, then the instinct would take over. They referred to it as *instinctive drift*. So the raccoon was showing a "washing response," an instinctive tendency to wash or prepare food (e.g., raccoons apparently rub crayfish together to remove the exoskeletons). Animals, then, simply cannot be conditioned to produce any behavior a trainer wishes. What can be trained is limited by the animal's instinctive or species-specific behaviors.

Keller Breland (1915–1965) died suddenly in 1965, but Marian (1920–2001) carried on the work. Eleven years later she married Bob Bailey, a zoologist with a strong entrepreneurial spirit. Together they continued and expanded ABE, eventually developing behavioral exhibits with more than 150 species and gaining such clients as Opryland, Six Flags, Mobil Oil, and the U.S. Department of Defense (Gillaspy & Bihm, 2002). Perhaps the best known of the Breland-Bailey ABE programs was Bird Brain—a chicken who could play tic-tac-toe and *never* lost to a human. On one occasion, it even beat none other than B. F. Skinner.

prototype and demonstrate its effectiveness, but the military killed the project.[7] Many years later, though, operant conditioning did make its way into a missile project, although Skinner was not involved directly. On at least two of early flights during the NASA space program that began in the 1960s, chimpanzees spent their time in space learning various operant tasks. One psychologist involved in the project wrote that "every technique, schedule, and programming and recording device we used then and subsequently can be traced to [Skinner] or his students" (Rohles, 1992, p. 1533).

[7]One of the persons involved in killing Project Pigeon was Tolman's physicist brother, who was involved with the National Defense Research Committee. Skinner apparently believed that Richard Tolman's "lack of respect... for his brother's behavioral psychology" (Bjork, 1993, p. 123) contributed to the demise of the project.

Despite the military's lack of enthusiasm for guiding missiles with pigeons, the experience convinced Skinner that his brand of behaviorism was applicable outside the laboratory. At a 1947 symposium on current trends in psychology, he pointedly argued for "extending the practices of an experimental science to the world at large. We can do this as soon as we wish to do it" (quoted in Capshew, 1996, p. 144). Good to his word, Skinner would, in subsequent decades, (a) follow Watson's lead and delve into the areas of child development and parenting; (b) challenge educational practice and develop a programmed teaching machine to facilitate learning, long before the development of personal computers; and (c) satisfy his long-held desire to write fiction with *Walden Two* (Skinner, 1948), which described a utopian community based on operant principles. Other Skinnerians extended his ideas into the areas of psychotherapy and business. And applying Skinner's ideas to animal training not only yielded outcomes familiar to anyone who has been to Sea World but also demonstrated that operant conditioning has its limits.

Evaluating Skinner

Unlike Tolman and Hull, Skinner was never elected president of the American Psychological Association (perhaps the electorate got wind of his tic-tac-toe loss). His research is seldom referenced in mainstream APA journals like the *Journal of Experimental Psychology*. He attracted many enthusiastic graduate students and many remained devoted operant researchers, but their relative numbers (compared with cognitive psychologists, for instance) were small. Scattered across a number of universities there are still true believers and programs with a strong behavioral slant, and the two primary operant-based journals (*Journal of the Experimental Analysis of Behavior* and the *Journal of Applied Behavior Analysis*) remain vigorous, but Skinner's radical behaviorism was (and remains) outside of the mainstream of American psychology. Today, few psychology departments have more than a single "operant" person (Robinson & Woodward, 1996).[8] Skinner himself was concerned about the longevity of his brand of behaviorism, fearing that it would fade after his death. As early as 1974, he wrote about what he perceived to be "the lack of young operant conditioners" (quoted in Bjork, 1993, p. 224) and the difficulty they had in finding jobs during a time when cognitive psychology was "in." Yet it is clear that his impact on psychology surpasses that of Tolman and Hull, as well as most of the psychologists you have read about in this text. In a survey by Korn, Davis, and Davis (1991), for example, department chairs and historians were asked to rank order psychologists in terms of eminence. Two sets of rankings were obtained: one for the top 10 "contemporary" psychologists and another for an "all-time" top 10. Among contemporary psychologists, both chairpersons and historians ranked Skinner no. 1; on the all-time list, Skinner again ranked no. 1 among chairpersons, but dropped to no. 8 among historians. Although Skinner's rating might have been inflated by the proximity of the survey to his death in 1990, it is nonetheless clear that psychologists and historians alike consider him to be one of the discipline's premier figures. Incidentally, neither Tolman nor Hull made any of the final top 10 lists.

Throughout this history of modern psychology, we have seen that American psychologists have felt pressured to show that their systems could be applied to improve the general welfare. This is one reason for the failure of Titchenerian psychology and the general

---

[8]One Skinnerian even postponed retirement to ensure that operant work at a major research university continued—"On a personal note, rather than retire I feel compelled to retain my position at UCSD in order to keep the faculty line in behavior analysis and to insure that the undergraduate laboratory in operant psychology (a pigeon lab) that I have taught for 40 years can continue to be offered" (Fantino, 2008, p. 126).

success of functional and behavioral psychologies. In this regard, Skinner's contributions are unmatched in the history of psychology. His early research at Harvard, leading to *The Behavior of Organisms* (1938), and his work in the 1950s, which produced *Schedules of Reinforcement* (Ferster & Skinner, 1957), fall into the category of basic laboratory research. The bulk of his writing, however, was directed at convincing the world that an experimental analysis of behavior is the only hope for the future welfare of the human species. This, of course, makes Skinner the true heir to Watson, who also labored long and hard to spread the "good word" of behaviorism. His strong and consistent advocacy made Skinner a controversial figure,[9] but it also resulted in his ideas being applied in more ways than ever imagined by either Tolman or Hull.

IN PERSPECTIVE: NEOBEHAVIORISM

Behaviorism has been a powerful force in American psychology. It produced some of psychology's most famous persons (Watson, Skinner), it dominated the research scene for several decades in the middle of the 20th century, and its applications continue to have widespread use in business, education, psychotherapy, and even daily life. Yet it is important to make two qualifications. First, behaviorism has largely been an American phenomenon. Behaviorist thinking was not widely influential in Europe, for example. Despite the heritage of British empiricism, there was not much of a British community of committed behaviorists; in Europe, the movement has had little impact. We have already seen, in the discussion of Thorndike and his argument with Wells over laboratory methods (Chapter 7) for example, that European animal psychologists (e.g., Lorenz, Tinbergen) were much more inclined than Americans to study animal behavior in its natural environments than in the lab, and they were much more interested in instinctive than learned behavior. A key reason for behaviorism being more American centered has to do with its applicability. We have seen again and again that American pragmatism has played a strong role in shaping American psychology.

The second caveat is that although it is true that behaviorism dominated American experimental psychology in the '30s, '40s, and into the '50s, nonetheless a great deal of research was being done in American laboratories that had very little to do with behaviorism, and a substantial number of experimental psychologists were doing important research that had nothing to do with conditioning. During the years of behaviorist hegemony, the pages of the leading journals still contained numerous articles describing research on such cognitive topics as memory, perception, attention, language, and thinking. Among many others, they included, in 1935, one of psychology's most famous papers, a summary of three experiments by an obscure graduate student at George Peabody College in Tennessee—J. Ridley Stroop

---

[9]Skinner never wavered in his beliefs, and his strong advocacy led many to consider him to be arrogant, condescending, and out of touch with core American values. Yet, Rutherford (2003) has argued convincingly that Skinner's ideas for improving society occasionally meshed with contemporary cultural values and were applauded. His post–World War II attempt to build a market for an improvement on a baby's crib, for instance, was viewed favorably by many, in the context of a time when technological improvements to aid life at home were valued. Also, those who knew Skinner consistently described him as a warm, considerate, unassuming, and gentle man. He was also far from the narrow-minded scientist whose work occupied his every waking hour—he was widely read, a published poet, a big opera fan, and part of a Cambridge play-reading group (Smith, 1996a).

(1935/1992). The "Stroop effect," a problem in which color naming is hindered by interference from automatic reading processes (e.g., the word *RED* is printed in green ink, and the correct response to it is "green" not "red"), has been called psychology's most replicated finding (MacLeod, 1992). So not all the research during the heyday of behaviorism involved rats in mazes or pigeons in Skinner boxes.

In the opening paragraph of his book on the alleged mid-20th-century cognitive revolution in psychology, Baars (1986) made the observation that behaviorism "is often referred to in the past tense" (p. 1) and that not too many psychologists refer to themselves as behaviorists anymore. There is a grain of truth to this assertion—as we will learn in Chapter 14, behaviorism with a capital *B* has been on the wane for decades; and cognitive psychology, which returned the study of mental processes to scientific respectability, has to a certain extent replaced behaviorism as American psychology's predominant conceptual framework. Yet Baars's assertion overstates the case. It overlooks the fact that research on learning and conditioning continues to occur at virtually every major university in America and that behavioral principles continue to form the basis for many successful applications (e.g., behavior therapy). More important, and as an indication of just how influential behaviorism has been, the central message of behaviorism is now taken for granted by every research psychologist. That is, regardless of whether researchers consider themselves "behaviorists," they all are careful to operationally define psychological concepts in behavioral terms; and even if they are interested in internal, unobservable processes (e.g., insight in problem solving), they limit their evidence to behavioral phenomena (e.g., solutions to problems). Furthermore, I know of no introductory textbook that fails to include the term *behavior* in its definition of psychology. Baars recognized this himself in the preface to his book by writing that, in the sense just described, "we are all behaviorists" (1986, p. ix).

SUMMARY

Post-Watsonian Behaviorism

• Contrary to traditional historical accounts, American psychology did not become predominantly behaviorist as the immediate result of Watson's program. Behaviorism did begin to take hold in the 1930s, however, partly because of Watson's continued propagandizing but also because full translations of Pavlov's research became available for the first time.

• Logical positivism, which allowed for theories to include abstract concepts but insisted that these concepts be tied to observable events, created a fertile climate for the evolution of behaviorism. Operationism, originating in physics in the late 1920s, also helped to create an environment conducive to objective, behaviorist thinking. Operational definitions define concepts in terms of a set of operations, under the control of the researcher, that are assumed to bring about the concept in question

(e.g., 24 hours without food brings on hunger). Confidence in the generality of some research outcome increases when various studies, each using a slightly different operational definition, nonetheless converge on the same outcome.

• Nobehaviorists disagreed on a number of issues, but agreed that (a) continuity among species allowed for general rules of behavior to be derived from nonhuman species, (b) understanding behavior required a thorough knowledge of how the organism learns, and (c) research results should have practical applications.

Edward C. Tolman (1886–1959): A Purposive Behaviorism

• Much of Tolman's research used maze learning, and he investigated both the reliability of the maze as an apparatus and the manner in which rats learn mazes. According to Tolman, rats in a maze do not learn a series of S-R connections; rather, they learn an overall cognitive map of the maze. This spatial ability can be shown in latent learning studies, in which animals can be shown to be learning a maze even though the learning is not reflected in their performance until reinforcement is made available, and in place learning, in which animals learn to go to a location more quickly than they learn to make a specific response.

• Tolman believed that behavior was goal-directed or purposive and that molar rather than molecular behavior should be the unit of study. He did not think that reinforcement was necessary for learning to occur. He developed the concept of the intervening variable, a hypothetical factor internal to the organism that intervenes between stimulus and response and is defined operationally. Many of the intervening variables in Tolman's system (e.g., expectancy) were cognitive.

Clark Hull (1884–1952): A Hypothetico-Deductive Behaviorism

• Although known primarily for his theory of learning based on animal studies, Hull also studied the development of concept learning in humans, aptitude testing, and experimental hypnosis. He produced a doctoral dissertation on the first and books on the latter two topics.

• Modeled on Newtonian physics and consistent with the dictates of logical positivism, Hull's hypothetico-deductive system of behavior involved the development of a theory in which experiments were created to test hypotheses that were derived from highly formalized postulates. Research outcomes then strengthened faith in the postulates or brought about their revision.

• Hull's learning theory is a drive–reduction theory. Postulate 4 proposes that learning (i.e., an increase in habit strength) involves stimulus–response contiguity accompanied by reinforcement. Reinforcers are stimuli that reduce drives. They can be primary or biologically based (e.g., food), or secondary (learned through association with primary reinforcers).

• Hull used a large number of intervening variables. The most important one was reaction potential, $_sE_R$, the probability that a response will occur at a given time. It was said to be influenced by a number of factors, including drive (D) and habit strength ($_sH_R$), both of which Hull believed were necessary for learned behavior to occur.

B. F. Skinner (1904–1990): A Radical Behaviorism

• Skinner rejected the more formal theories of both Tolman and Hull and argued for a more inductive, descriptive behaviorism. He is best known for developing the distinction between classical and operant conditioning and for investigating the latter. To do so, he created the Skinner box, an experimental chamber in which the rate of some response (e.g., bar pressing) is recorded continuously by a cumulative recorder. Psychology's goals were to be the prediction and control of behavior; understanding behavior, according to Skinner, occurred through an experimental analysis of behavior. Operant conditioning occurs when behavior is shaped by its immediate consequences. If the consequences are positive, the behavior occurring in a specific environment is more likely to occur in that environment in the future; if they are negative, the behavior becomes less likely to occur. Patterns of behavior vary as a function of various reinforcement schedules.

• Skinner rejected the use of what he called explanatory fictions, hypothetical factors that appear to explain a phenomenon but actually do nothing more than relabel it. Hence, he was critical of nervous system explanations of behavior, and he never accepted the idea that explanations for behavior would be found by cognitive psychologists.

• Skinner called for a technology of behavior to improve child rearing, education, and society as a whole through the use of behavioral techniques. Two of his students, Keller and Marian Breland, became famous as animal trainers who used operant techniques. They also discovered that not all behaviors were equally conditionable—an animal's instinctive behaviors could limit the power of conditioning.

STUDY QUESTIONS

1. Describe the "myth" of the behaviorist revolution.

2. Describe the events of the 1920s that paved the way for neobehaviorism to become dominant in the 1930s.

3. Explain how logical positivism, combined with operationism, dealt with the issue of how to study abstract, nonobservable phenomena (e.g., hunger) objectively.

4. Give an example to show that you know what is meant by an operational definition, and explain the importance of using operational definitions in psychological research.

5. There was a degree of consensus among neobehaviorists on two important issues. Describe them.

6. Describe the influence of (a) Gestalt psychology and (b) Edwin Holt on Tolman's theory of learning.

7. Define intervening variable, and use examples to show how the concept was used by (a) Tolman and (b) Hull.

8. Describe Tolman's latent learning study, and explain what Tolman thought it demonstrated about the role of reinforcement in maze learning.

9. Describe Tolman's research on cognitive maps and show how it fits into his theory of learning.

10. Describe Tolman's place-learning experiment and explain its significance.

11. Describe Hull's doctoral dissertation on concept learning and show how it connected with his subsequent theory of learning.

12. Describe how research is conducted using a hypothetico-deductive approach.

13. Describe Hull's postulate 4.

14. What was the importance of reaction potential to Hull's theory, and what was the significance of the relationship between drive and habit strength being multiplicative rather than additive?

15. Explain why Hull was a leading figure in American psychology in the '40s and '50s and virtually forgotten today.

16. Describe the influence of Sir Francis Bacon on B. F. Skinner's ideas.

17. How did Skinner's approach to science differ from Hull's and Tolman's?

18. What is the distinction between Type S conditioning and Type R conditioning?

19. What did Skinner mean by an experimental analysis of behavior?

20. Describe the danger that Skinner saw with explanatory fictions. Use an example.

21. Write a brief essay that connects these concepts: technological ideal, Project Pigeon.

22. Describe the work of the Brelands and the significance of their 1961 paper on the "misbehavior of organisms."

23. In his book on the history of cognitive psychology, Baars concluded, "We are all behaviorists." Explain.

FOR FURTHER READING

BJORK, D. W. (1993). *B. F. Skinner: A life*. New York: Basic Books.

A brief and readable biography of Skinner. Not very detailed in treating Skinner's research or that of other operant scientists, but an excellent treatment of Skinner's early development as an operant scientist and his crusade for behavioral engineering.

BORING, E. G., LANGFELD, H. S., WERNER, H. & YERKES, R.M. (Eds.), *A history of psychology in autobiography* (Vol. 4). Worcester, MA: Clark University Press.

Part of a series of autobiographies. Volume 4 includes interesting autobiographical chapters written by Hull (pp. 143–162) and Tolman (pp. 323–339).

DELPRATO, D. J., & MIDGLEY, B. D. (1992). Some fundamentals of B. F. Skinner's behaviorism. *American Psychologist, 47*, 1507–1520.

A solid introduction to the essentials of Skinnerian psychology, designed to counter some of the misconceptions of his work.

This is just one of 25 articles on Skinner to be found in the November 1992 special issue of American Psychologist.

MALONE, J. C. (1991). *Theories of learning: A historical approach*. Belmont, CA: Wadsworth.

Provides thorough descriptions of the major theories of learning, written from a historical standpoint. In addition to Tolman, Hull, and Skinner, the book covers other important learning theories (i.e., Thorndike, Pavlov, Watson).

SMITH, L. D., & WOODWARD, W. R. (1996). *B. F. Skinner and behaviorism in American culture*. Bethlehem, PA: Lehigh University Press.

A volume edited by two noted historians of psychology that contains 14 different chapters, arranged under the topics of "Skinner as social philosopher," "Skinner as scientist," "Skinner's personal world," and "The diversification and extension of behaviorism."

CHAPTER 12

MENTAL ILLNESS AND ITS TREATMENT

Our hysterical patients suffer from reminiscences. Their symptoms are residues...of particular (traumatic) events.

—Sigmund Freud, 1909

PREVIEW AND CHAPTER OBJECTIVES

When students first begin to explore psychology, they typically identify the field with the diagnosis and treatment of "mental illness." Of course, they quickly discover that psychology is a much broader subject—in a normal introductory course, they must wade through a dozen or so chapters on such topics as the brain and behavior, perception, motivation, emotion, learning, and cognition before they get to the chapters on psychopathology and its treatment. Similarly, most histories of psychology, including this one, focus on how the discipline began applying scientific methods to age-old philosophical questions and how it developed as a "science" in the academic environment. Yet no history of psychology can be complete without describing, if briefly, the various ways that mental illness has been conceived of and treated over the years. Most of this chapter is devoted to Sigmund Freud's creation and his promotion of psychoanalysis—although trained as a physician, Freud pioneered the use of a nonmedical approach to treatment. We will explore the origins and evolution of some of his well-known concepts.

Before the detailed discussion of Freud, however, the chapter examines some early conceptions of mental illness and its treatment, beginning with the Enlightenment era "moral treatment" strategy pioneered by Phillipe Pinel in France and William Tuke in England, and a more biological approach taken by America's Benjamin Rush. This is followed by a brief history of the 19th-century asylum movement and the asylum reform efforts by Dorothea Dix and Clifford Beers. Leading directly into the discussion of Freud is a brief description of the use of hypnotism as a therapeutic tool, starting with the "magnetic personality" of Franz Anton Mesmer, and ending with the legendary Jean Charcot who, for a brief time, taught Freud. After you finish this chapter, you should be able to:

- ■ Show how Enlightenment thinking influenced reforms in the treatment of the mentally ill
- ■ Describe the features of the "moral treatment" approach, as used by Pinel in France and Tuke in England and then imported to the United States
- ■ Describe the medical approach to treatment that was pioneered by Rush

- Describe the development of the asylum movement and the influence of architecture (e.g., the Kirkbride model) on the philosophy of treatment for mental illness
- Describe the reform efforts of Dix and Beers, and the outcomes of their work
- Describe Kraepelin's early efforts at the classification and diagnosis of mental illness
- Describe Mesmer's approach to treating hysteria and explain why it was occasionally successful
- Contrast the theories of hypnosis posed by Liebeault and Bernheim and by Charcot
- Describe the Freudian myth and show how it was promoted
- Show how Freud's ideas were influenced by materialist and evolutionary thinking
- Describe and criticize the traditional description of the Anna O. case and explain what Freud believed he had learned from it
- Summarize the essential features of Freud's approach to therapy, in particular his strategies for accessing the unconscious
- Describe the general features of Freud's theory of personality
- Describe the alternatives to psychoanalytic theory proposed by Adler and Jung
- Critically analyze Freud's contributions to psychology

EARLY TREATMENT OF THE MENTALLY ILL

Every society has to deal with the needs of people whose thoughts, emotions, and behaviors mark them as deviant. For much of recorded history, such persons, so different from the rest of "us," have sometimes been a source of fear and loathing, their treatment less than humane. At times, they have been regarded as evil or possessed by the devil, to be punished by being tortured and put to death, perhaps by being burned at the stake or drowned as a "witch." Alternatively, they have been considered either morally deficient and dangerous to society because of their transgressions or as incurable nuisances in need of being locked away from decent folks, perhaps chained to a wall, with no hope of being freed. Out of sight, out of mind. On the other hand, the picture is not as uniformly bleak as is normally portrayed in standard histories of mental illness (e.g., Zilboorg, 1941). Treatises proposing reasonable biological causes for mental illness existed in medieval times, at the same time that demonology was a competing hypothesis, and there is accumulating evidence that the insane frequently were treated with compassion in their communities and through organized governmental intervention (Neugebauer, 1978; Kroll, 1973). As is true today, however, community size and socioeconomic status were important predictors of care. The mentally ill poor, especially those living in larger population areas, received the worst treatment, if they received any help at all.

"Enlightened" Reform: Pinel, Tuke, Rush

Several efforts at improving treatment of the mentally ill occurred in the late 18th and early 19th centuries as a product of the Enlightenment, a time of "spreading light into the dark corners of the human mind" (Appleby, Hunt, & Jacob, 1994, p. 36). As you recall from

Chapter 3, the hallmark of Enlightenment thinking was a belief in the ideas of progress and reform and a strong faith in the ability of science to improve society. It was the kind of thinking that helped produce political revolutions both in the United States and France, and it elevated "science," the engine of progress, to the status of religion. In that context, mental illness came to be viewed in naturalistic terms as being biologically based and amenable to treatment.

An important reformer during this era was the French physician Phillipe Pinel (1745–1826), who instituted humane reforms in Paris while working at both major hospitals there—the Bicêtre for men (1793) and the Salpêtrière for women (1795). Pinel's most dramatic action was to remove the chains from mentally ill patients who had been restrained, in some instances, for years. Although it has been shown (e.g., Weiner, 1979; cited in Micale, 1985) that the number of liberated patients was relatively small (about 15% of the total hospital populations), Pinel nonetheless deserves credit for bringing the concept of reform to institutions housing the mentally ill. He called his program *traitement moral* (**moral treatment**); it featured improvements in patient nutrition, hygiene, and general living conditions as well as an early form of behavior modification using rewards and punishments to bring some order into the lives of patients. Pinel's efforts, occurring in the context of the French Revolution, provide a clear example of the combined effects of an "enlightened" approach to insanity and an assault on institutions perceived to be repressing individual freedom. His reforms united the Enlightenment faith in progress and the revolutionary desire to liberate the oppressed.

At the same time that Pinel was effecting change in France, similar reforms were occurring in England, led by the work of William Tuke (1732–1822). As a Quaker, Tuke was predisposed to provide relief for the downtrodden (the Society of Friends also became leaders in the antislavery movement), and those suffering from mental illness were in special need of care. In 1792, a year before Pinel was named director of the Bicêtre, Tuke founded the York Retreat in the north of England and dedicated it to the benevolent treatment of the insane—the Retreat would be "a place in which the unhappy might obtain a refuge; a quiet haven in which the shattered bark might find the means of reparation and safety" (quoted in Beam, 2001, p. 11). Set in a rural environment and designed to resemble a working farm, the Retreat established a program of treatment similar in spirit to the one used by Pinel. Good nutrition and hygiene were priorities, and patients were given freedom of movement within the Retreat property, allowed regular visitors, and given opportunities for recreation and work, contingent on good behavior. The building was set on high ground, providing residents with a pleasant view of the surrounding countryside. The Retreat's origins in the Society of Friends meant that Quakers in other parts of the world who had similar reform motives would know about the York Retreat and its philosophy of treatment. According to Grob (1994), Tuke's York Retreat became the model for at least half of the private mental hospitals created in the United States in the first quarter of the 19th century (e.g., the Friends Asylum, just outside of Philadelphia, established in 1813).

In addition to the moral treatment approach, "enlightened" medical approaches to psychopathology developed during this time. The person credited with being the first in America to bring a medical approach to the treatment of the mentally ill was Benjamin Rush (1745–1813), a prominent signer of the Declaration of Independence and surgeon general to the Continental Army of the American Revolution. He has been called the "father" of modern psychiatry, largely on the basis of his *Medical Inquiries and Observations upon the Diseases of the Mind*, which went through five editions between 1812 and 1835. One of the few "doctors" of this era with actual university training in medicine,[1] Rush became a strong advocate of a contemporary belief that disease derived from abnormalities in the blood and circulatory system. Accordingly, a common remedy was to remove diseased or excess blood, and Rush became a promoter of **bloodletting** as a cure for a wide range of illnesses. These included mental ones, which Rush believed stemmed from "hypertension in the brain's blood vessels" (Bell, 1980, p. 9). Reducing the tension, then, involved opening veins and removing blood until the person reached a more tranquil state. This often worked rather well as a temporary means of calming violent patients, perhaps because these unfortunate individuals, down a few pints, were too weak to be hyperactive. Placebo effects may also have been involved. Rush reported one case in which a violent patient was given 47 different bleedings, involving a total loss of between 400 and 500 ounces of blood. He was eventually pronounced cured and was returned to the community. He wrote a glowing testimonial thanking Rush for the therapy, but then relapsed and tragically hung himself not long after his release (Bell, 1980).

In addition to bloodletting, Rush created several devices designed to calm or redistribute the blood. For example, the *tranquilizer*, shown in Figure 12.1, was a chair with straps for restraining arms and legs, and a boxlike device that fit tightly over the head. By restricting movement, the goal was to reduce pulse rate, thereby calming the patient. The chair and similar

FIGURE 12.1 The tranquilizer chair, devised by Benjamin Rush for restraining and "calming" agitated mental patients. From Bell (1980).

[1] His medical training included a stop at the university in Edinburgh, Scotland. As mentioned in Chapter 5, Edinburgh was Great Britain's foremost center for medical education, the locus of Darwin's unsuccessful attempt to become a doctor.

restraining devices became common forms of treatment in postrevolutionary America, and while they might seem cruel and unusual to us today, it is vital to recognize that they reflected an important new idea at the time—a belief that the mentally ill could benefit from therapy.

The 19th-Century Asylum Movement

In the United States, institutions created specifically for the mentally ill were rare before the 19th century. The first asylum built for housing the mentally ill was the Eastern State Hospital, completed in 1773 in Williamsburg, Virginia. It was concerned more with confinement and public safety than with care, however, since it was designed for "a poor unhappy set of people who are deprived of their senses and wander about the country, terrifying the rest of their fellow creatures" (quoted in Gamwell & Tomes, 1995, p. 20).

Other than at Williamsburg, however, the mentally ill in the late 18th and early 19th centuries typically would find themselves at home, hidden away from neighbors if possible; in prison, when their behavior seemed to threaten the community; in the back wards or cellars of hospitals, which began to appear in the United States in the mid-18th century; or in an "almshouse," originally planned as a refuse for the poor and/or elderly in a community (Grob, 1973). In virtually all cases, treatment was nonexistent.

In the 19th century, however, especially as the population of urban areas began to increase, the need for institutions devoted to the mentally ill became increasingly apparent. Private asylums began to appear—as mentioned earlier, many of them based on the York model and funded by Quakers. Yet private asylums could handle just a fraction of those in need. They were either too small (Philadelphia's Friends Asylum housed about 30 patients) or they were beyond the means of most Americans. Cost was a major consideration at the McLean Asylum, just outside of Boston (founded 1818), for instance. Populated largely by the affluent mentally ill, it housed a yearly average of around 50 patients during its first dozen years of existence and had a staff-to-patient ratio of approximately 2:1, compared with a ratio of (at best) 10:1 in public institutions (Beam, 2001). The need for publicly funded institutions for the mentally ill, which would have greater capacity and would be affordable, became increasingly evident as the 19th century unfolded.

An important pioneer in the design of these larger state-funded institutions was the physician Thomas Kirkbride (1809–1863). A Quaker and a firm believer in the principles of moral treatment, Kirkbride thought that architecture could be an important element of treatment. His ideas about the design of asylums, articulated in *On the Construction, Organization, and General Arrangements of Hospitals for the Insane with Some Remarks on Insanity and Its Treatment* (Kirkbride, 1854), established a standard that was widely copied in the second half of the 19th century (Grob, 1983). The "Kirkbride design" included these elements:

- Built in a rural environment, in imitation of the York plan, and placed on high ground, so as to provide patients with relaxing panoramic views of the countryside
- A central unit (called the "center main") to house administrative offices and "parlors" for family to visit patients
- A series of "pavilions" on either side of the center main, with males housed on one side and females on the other; each pavilion to have a relatively small number of rooms and common rooms for recreation
- The short pavilions set back from each other in a "shallow V," designed so that every room had a view of the countryside and was exposed to sunlight and fresh air

- Wide corridors in each pavilion, allowing space for patients to exercise when they could not go outside (e.g., in bad weather or in winter)[2]

- Three to four stories in height, with upper floors designated for the best-behaved patients (good behavior earned a better view)

- In some cases, separate smaller buildings for the most disruptive, noisiest, or more violent patients (better control, but also in response to pleas like this one: "Let her rooms be out of hearing of any shrieking you might have," quoted in Yanni, 2007, p. 39)

Figure 12.2 shows a classic example of a Kirkbride design, St. Elizabeths Hospital in Washington, DC. It dates from 1855 and was originally called the Government Hospital for the Insane. Kirkbride asylums were originally designed to hold 250 patients, which was considered small enough so that "the superintendent could visit all the male patients and his wife all the female patients daily" (Yanni, 2007, p. 52). By the end of the century, however, an association of asylum superintendents had approved expansion of the Kirkbride design to sprawling buildings holding 600 patients (no more daily visits by the superintendent and his wife). By the early 20th century, these buildings often housed considerably more than 600.

FIGURE 12.2   A Kirkbride design for St. Elizabeths Hospital, Washington, DC. Photo courtesy of Ludy T. Benjamin, Jr.

[2]This feature eventually had an unfortunate negative side effect—as asylums became overcrowded in the 20th century, these wide corridors provided space for additional beds.

Reforming Asylums: Dix and Beers

Kirkbride's contribution was substantial, but there were others whose advocacy for the mentally ill contributed to the creation, development, and reform of the 19th-century asylum. One such crusader was Dorothea Dix (1802–1887). Dix (Figure 12.3) was a New England educator whose general concern for the less fortunate led her to examine the conditions for treating those housed in public institutions. In Massachusetts in 1841, she began an 18-month tour of the state's jails, hospitals, and almshouses, and any other location that might house the mentally ill poor. She encountered an alarming level of abuse and neglect—instances where the mentally ill were chained to the walls of unheated closet-sized rooms filled with their excrement, poorly fed and clothed, sometimes beaten into submission, and generally abandoned. On her return home, she wrote a scathing indictment of the system and did not mince words when describing what she had seen. Her case was presented to the Massachusetts legislature and led to a series of reforms, including an increase of funds to improve the state's public asylum in Worcester.[3] This success prompted her to repeat her modus operandi in other states—a thorough tour of institutions followed by a lengthy and detailed exposé. By 1848, the Dix crusade had logged some 60,000 miles of travel, observing in the process "more than nine thousand idiots, epileptics, and insane . . . destitute of appropriate care and protection" (Dix, 1848; quoted in Viney, 1996, p. 22). Her efforts played a role in the creation of 47 mental hospitals (many using the Kirkbride design) and schools for the feebleminded (Viney &

FIGURE 12.3 Dorothea Dix, crusader for mental health reform. From Viney (1996).

[3]The Worcester asylum dated from the early 1830s. After the expansion following Dix's report, the asylum quickly became overcrowded and in the 1870s a major expansion was undertaken that adapted the Kirkbride design. This building burned in a massive fire in 1991.

Zorich, 1982). Although many of these institutions over the years grew to sizes that prevented effective care and led in the 20th century to a renewal of problems with overcrowding and abuse (e.g., increasing the capacity of the Kirkbride asylums from 250 to 600 and beyond), Dix's efforts on behalf of the mentally ill dramatically improved the living conditions of those powerless to help themselves. That she was able to accomplish what she did in the face of her own poor health (probably tuberculosis), difficult traveling conditions, and the generally accepted belief that women were not worth listening to is nothing less than extraordinary.

Another avenue for asylum reform came from within the asylum itself. It took the form of a remarkable book published in 1908 and written by a former mental patient, Clifford Beers (1876–1943). Beers was a graduate of Yale and had settled into a responsible position in a New York City insurance company when a suicide attempt, followed by a year of depression, landed him in the first of three mental institutions that he would inhabit for just over 3 years. After being released from the third one in 1903, Beers compiled his notes into a book describing what daily life was like for a hospitalized mental patient. *A Mind That Found Itself* appeared in 1908, complete with a prefatory letter from William James, who had read the manuscript and wished to support Beers's cause. Beers was critical of the doctors he had encountered, believing them to be generally incompetent and too willing to use punitive measures, but he saved his heaviest invective for the attendants in charge of the day-to-day operation of the wards. He documented the constant verbal and occasional physical abuse suffered at the hands of the staff, and called for improved conditions and professional training for attendants.

Because Beers had experienced mental institutions and lived to write about them, a second message of his book was that mental illness was curable. This was an important idea at a time when many in the medical community had come to believe that little hope existed for the institutionalized mentally ill. In 1909, Beers founded the National Committee for Mental Hygiene to further the cause of prevention, and he spent his remaining years informing the public of his beliefs about mental illness, promoting programs to enhance mental health, and lobbying for the creation of mental hygiene clinics (Williams, Bellis, & Wellington, 1980).

Progress in the treatment of mental illness necessarily implies improvements in the diagnosis of mental illness. You might know about the modern version of this, *DSM-IV*. This chapter's Close-Up provides some background and even yields a connection to Wundt.

CLOSE-UP

DIAGNOSING MENTAL ILLNESS

As you might recall from your general psychology course, or a course in abnormal psychology, one of the most valuable tools for psychiatrists and clinical psychologists is *DSM-IV*, short for *Diagnostic and Statistical Manual of Mental Disorders*, now in its fourth edition (APA, 1994); a fifth version is currently being produced. *DSM-IV* includes detailed descriptions of symptoms for the various disorders, based on the accumulated research of decades. It is encyclopedic, including more than 400 psychiatric diagnostic categories, arranged in 17 broad categories, and filling close to 900 pages. *DSM-IV* is just the most recent of a long line of attempts to categorize mental illness. A major advance in diagnosis was made by the German physician Emil Kraepelin (1856–1926), who appears to have used some of what he learned in Wundt's laboratory to provide the first clear insight into a disorder that he named *dementia praecox* and that we now call schizophrenia.

Kraepelin earned a medical degree from Würzburg in 1878, where he specialized in psychiatry. While working as a resident in Munich, he learned of the new laboratory psychology being developed at Leipzig, and he traveled there in 1882 to experience Wundt's laboratory firsthand. During his 2 years at Leipzig, Kraepelin was involved in several research projects but did not complete a doctoral degree with Wundt. After several brief appointments at asylums and universities in the 1880s, his big break arrived in 1890—a position as professor of psychiatry in the clinic at Heidelberg University. The prestigious clinic afforded Kraepelin a large patient base, enabling him to begin a process of sorting patients into discrete categories, based partly on symptoms but primarily on the kinds of outcomes (prognoses) that could be expected. He became known for his massive collections of individual note cards, one per patient, on which he recorded the details of each case, ranging from the information collected at the initial intake to the final outcome. Kraepelin remained at Heidelberg for 13 years and then finished his career in Munich as director of the university clinic there.

Kraepelin began his efforts at building a classification scheme for mental illness in 1883; his "textbook" went through nine editions, the last one appearing the year after his death. His first effort, published when he was only 27, was apparently completed for the main purpose of providing him money to get married. It has been described as a "slim *Compendium* of no particular merit" (Shorter, 1997, p. 102), but in fact it ran to 400 pages and began to establish Kraepelin's reputation. By the time he died, the ninth edition had expanded to two volumes and 2,425 pages (Menninger, 1963), longer than *DSM-IV*.

Kraepelin's sixth edition, appearing in 1899, is the best known. In it he identified 13 categories of mental illness, ranging from those that were relatively mild and had a promising prognosis (e.g., "fright neurosis") to the more serious disorders. Among the most debilitating were two that he labeled manic-depressive psychosis and dementia praecox (Havens, 1965). Mania and depression had been known for some time and "circular states" had been described

as well, but Kraepelin provided the first comprehensive description of the disorder that today is known as bipolar disorder. But his description of **dementia praecox** made Kraepelin famous. He used the name, which translates roughly as "premature dementia," to reflect the fact that this incapacitating mental disorder tended to appear relatively early in life, often during late adolescence. The symptoms included "disturbances in apprehension, . . . in orientation, . . . of attention, . . . of memory, . . . of the train of thought, . . . of judgment, . . . of the emotional field, . . . in the volitional field," and "hallucination" (Kraepelin, quoted in Sahakian, 1968, p. 323). Note that several of these symptoms reflect the kinds of cognitive processes that Kraepelin learned about as a student in Wundt's laboratory. Kraepelin believed that one of the defining attributes of dementia praecox was an inability to focus attention, and his theory is similar to modern attentional theories of the disorder. He argued that the thought processes of those with dementia praecox lack the normal apperceptive ability, and their attentional capacity is severely limited. While normal people can focus their attention and direct their mental activity along meaningful paths (i.e., they can apperceive, to use Wundt's term), those with dementia praecox cannot. Hence, their mental activity resembles random associations. This accounts for one of the common symptoms: the meaningless strings of phrases ("word salad") often emitted by those suffering from the disorder.

Kraepelin also believed that the prognosis was so poor for this form of dementia that any chance for recovery was virtually hopeless. It wasn't long before this fatalistic prognosis was challenged by psychiatrists who pointed to cases where improvement did occur. One such researcher was Eugene Blueler (1857–1939), who renamed the disorder *schizophrenia*, the name used today.

Dementia praecox was not the only form of mental deterioration that interested Kraepelin. He also investigated a form of dementia that mysteriously appeared in adults of late middle age and was similar in form to that shown by the very elderly. This premature dementia was later studied in greater depth by a close friend and research colleague of Kraepelin's at Heidelberg, Aloys Alzheimer (1864–1915), for whom this terrifying disease is named.

MESMERISM AND HYPNOSIS

Superintendents of asylums usually were psychiatrists, so treatment there tended to be based on a medical model of mental illness, although the moral treatment ideal had a psychological aspect to it (behave and you get a better room). Other strategies for treating mental illness based on a psychological strategy evolved through the years and, as will be seen shortly, one of them became very popular in the early 20th century, when Sigmund Freud invented psychoanalysis. First, though, it is necessary to set the stage for Freud by briefly describing the history of hypnosis, a technique that Freud learned about in Paris and tried before abandoning it for other methods. The origins of hypnosis lie with an eccentric Viennese physician who created an occasionally effective therapy based on the idea that illness, mental or otherwise, was the consequence of misaligned magnetic forces within the distressed person.

Mesmerism and Animal Magnetism

The start of Franz Anton Mesmer's (1734–1815) professional career was conventional enough. He earned a medical degree at the prestigious University of Vienna in 1766 and quickly established a thriving practice. Through a fortunate marriage, he entered into Vienna's highest social circles and counted the young composer Wolfgang Amadeus Mozart among his friends. As a scientist, Mesmer was aware of current developments and was especially intrigued by recent discoveries of such forces as electricity and magnetism. He became convinced that magnetism affected humans directly and that good health was the consequence of properly aligned internal magnetic forces. Were these forces to become misaligned, however, ill health (either physical or mental) would result. If you can imagine the effects of trying to push together the plus poles of two magnets, you can get an idea of Mesmer's disease concept. Illness resulted from the disharmony of forces opposing each other. The cure, then, involved straightening out these forces within the body. Thus Mesmer found that he could help many of his patients, especially those suffering from disorders with psychological roots, by giving them medicine containing heavy doses of iron and then passing magnets over their bodies. Patients would fall into a "crisis state," a type of trance, and when they emerged would find their health improved. He called his theory of illness and cure **animal magnetism**. He did not know it, but he had inadvertently demonstrated the power of suggestion on human behavior, and he had discovered what would later be renamed hypnosis.

Mesmer soon discovered that he could produce cures without the magnets. Convinced that he had magnetic powers himself, he discarded the magnets and began treating patients directly by passing his hands over them. He also massaged parts of a patient's body that were causing distress (e.g., an apparently paralyzed arm), following the path of the nerves and suggesting that things would improve (Winters, 1950). He also occasionally placed one hand on the patient's stomach and another on the small of the back, "in order to saturate the trunk with magnetic fluid" (Forrest, 1999, p. 19). Mesmer had some success and became convinced that he was quite special, but he aroused the ire of the generally conservative medical community in Vienna. The fact that most of his patients were women and his therapy was quite "hands on" contributed to the concern.[4] After becoming embroiled in several heated controversies over the effectiveness of his magnetic cures and the appropriateness of his technique, he found himself no longer welcome in Vienna. In May of 1777, he was expelled from the medical faculty of the University of Vienna and ordered to stop practicing medicine in the city (Hoffeld, 1980). It was time to move on.

Hoping to find a more open-minded environment, Mesmer moved his magnetic therapy to Paris in 1778. Aided by his promotional skills and his "magnetic" personality, he soon began attracting more patients than he could easily handle. His solution to the overcrowding was to create perhaps the first version of group therapy. In an expensively decorated clinic in one of the most fashionable neighborhoods in Paris, small groups of patients would congregate around Mesmer's famous *baquet*. This was a type of wooden tub that contained various chemicals and had iron rods protruding from it in all directions. Patients would encircle the baquet and grab hold of an iron rod while Mesmer, often dressed in a flowing lilac-colored robe, passed among them and encouraged them to enter the crisis state. There was much swooning and moaning, and many individuals undoubtedly were influenced by a kind of group contagion effect. Once the mass crisis passed, patients recovered their composure, pronounced themselves much better, and then left the clinic to spread the good word of its effectiveness. Indeed, many patients seemed to be cured, especially those suffering from a variety of what we would today call psychosomatic complaints (e.g., headaches, fainting spells, digestive problems). Although most of Mesmer's patients had the financial means to pay for treatment, others didn't. Mesmer responded by providing free magnetism—he magnetized a large oak tree in a Paris park, where those in need could go and receive some benefit by holding onto ropes attached to the tree (Forrest, 1999).

As in Vienna, however, the medical community was not impressed. Paris in the prerevolutionary years was a place of much uncertainty and flux, and it was full of faith healers and others promising simple answers to the anxieties of the day (Hoffeld, 1980). In this context, Mesmer seemed to be just another quack. The question of the validity of **mesmerism**, as Mesmer's technique was now called, was taken up by a distinguished commission of the French Royal Academy of Sciences, appointed by the king. At its head was the renowned Benjamin Franklin, the American ambassador to France and a distinguished scientist in his own right, a pioneer in the study of electricity and the inventor of a remarkable new device, the lightning rod (Cohen, 1995). The commission also included the eminent chemist Antoine Lavoisier, the discoverer of oxygen, and the physician Joseph Guillotin (who would soon give his name to a famous execution device).

The Franklin commission's 1784 report concluded that mesmerism had no foundation in science. It recognized that some patients indeed had been helped by Mesmer but shrewdly attributed any cures to the patient's beliefs rather than to Mesmer's "magnetizing" powers. As Franklin put it in a letter to a sick friend contemplating a visit to a mesmerist, if hypochondriacs who overuse medication "can be persuaded to forbear their drugs in expectation of being cured by only the physician's finger or an iron rod pointing at them, they may possibly find good effects tho' they mistake the cause" (quoted in Hoffeld, 1980, p. 380). Mesmer

---

[4]According to one account, Mesmer would "sit opposite his patient with his knees outside the patient's knees while he made long stroking movements (*grandes passes*) with his hands from the shoulders down the arms to the hands.... Sometimes the passes were continued to the feet, and they might be made in contact with the exposed skin and clothing or at a distance of a few inches" (Forrest, 1999, p. 19; emphasis in the original).

ignored the commission report and continued to practice for a time; he left Paris in 1792 and lived briefly both in London and Germany, where he practiced mesmerism until his death in 1815.

From Mesmerism to Hypnosis

Mesmer gradually faded from the scene after the Franklin commission's report, but mesmerism itself spread throughout Europe, mainly at the level of entertainment. Much like today's stage hypnotists, mesmerists toured the countryside giving dramatic demonstrations that awed the locals. Few scientists paid attention, but one who did was John Elliotson (1791–1868), a professor of medicine at University College, London, and senior physician at the teaching hospital affiliated with the college. He was intrigued by the demonstrations of apparent anesthesia, during which mesmerized people showed no signs of pain, even while being poked with sharp needles. Elliotson was one of those open-minded scientists who often antagonizes the establishment—he was already under suspicion for promoting a new contraption that other doctors refused to use, the stethoscope (Boring, 1950). Thus eyebrows were raised when he began mesmerizing patients. When Elliotson proposed researching the anesthetic effects of mesmerism in the late 1830s, the storm broke. He was denied permission by his hospital board, which also outlawed any use of mesmerism at the hospital. Elliotson resigned in protest and spent his remaining years promoting mesmerism.

Meanwhile, other physicians were starting to use mesmerism to reduce the pain of surgery. In the 1840s, for example, numerous cases were reported of amputations being done while the patient was in a trance. A witness to an 1842 case of an amputated leg reported:

> The placid look of his countenance never changed for an instant; his whole frame rested, uncontrolled, in perfect stillness and repose; not a muscle was seen to twitch. To the end of the operation, including the sawing of the bone, securing the arteries, and applying the bandages, occupying a period of upwards of twenty minutes, he lay like a statue. (quoted in Forrest, 1999, p. 180)

The largest study of mesmeric effects on pain was completed by James Esdaile (1808–1859), a Scottish surgeon working in India. In 1845, he summarized the results of several hundred surgeries using mesmerism-induced anesthesia. He reported a mortality rate of less than 5% as a result of the surgery, at a time when mortality was normally 40% (Gravitz, 1988). Keep in mind that these were the days before the existence of chemical anesthetics such as ether, and surgery was a brutal business that prized speed over precision and required screaming patients to be firmly secured to the operating table. Thus any procedure for pain reduction was a welcome development. Nonetheless, the medical community as usual was slow to change, and the prevailing medical wisdom was that pain, because it was a naturally occurring phenomenon, was good and even necessary for surgery to succeed. As one contemporary medical treatise put it, "Pain is a wise provision of nature, and patients ought to suffer pain while their surgeon is operating; they are all the better for it, and recover better" (quoted in Forrest, 1999, p. 181).

Mesmerism finally began to gain respectability in the late 1840s, in part by changing its name. The Scottish physician James Braid (1795–1860), a respected member of the conservative medical establishment, initially set out to demolish mesmerism but came to recognize the validity of some of its effects. Because he thought the trance state was similar to a state of sleep, he coined a new term for the phenomenon. **Neurypnology**, a contraction of "neuro-hypnology," combined Greek terms for nervous (*neuro*) and sleep (*hypnos*) and was defined by Braid as a "nervous sleep." Soon the initial part of the term began to be dropped, and the phenomenon came to be called hypnology or **hypnotism**. Braid discovered that the hypnotic trance could be induced by having patients stare fixedly at an object just above their line of vision, and he came to believe that a general fixation of attention was behind the phenomenon. He also emphasized the importance of suggestion in producing hypnotic effects, and he seemed to recognize that unconscious processing occurred, reporting that memories could persist from one hypnotic session to the next, even though the person had no recollection during the intervening periods of normal consciousness (Boring, 1950). By 1860, when the discovery of ether and chloroform rendered surgical use of hypnosis unnecessary, the phenomenon was recognized in the scientific community as legitimate and worthy of study. Further developments, and controversy, occurred in France.

The Hypnotism Controversies

Hypnotism achieved a degree of legitimacy with Braid, but little consensus existed over its explanation. Two opposing views about the nature of hypnotism developed in France: A pair of physicians working in the provincial city of Nancy (180 miles east of Paris) were on one side of the sometimes acrimonious debate, and the powerful director of the famous Salpêtrière Hospital in Paris was on the other.

The so-called Nancy School of hypnosis originated from the curiosity of Auguste Liebeault (1823–1904), an unassuming country doctor practicing just outside of Nancy, who decided to give hypnosis a try after being intrigued by an old book on animal magnetism. He recruited patients for hypnotic treatment by charging no fees for it, and his success produced a legendary local reputation. He soon attracted the attention of a nationally known physician living nearby in Nancy, Hippolyte Bernheim (1840–1919), who traveled to Liebeault's clinic expecting to discover and expose fakery. Instead, he became a convert.

The central feature of the Liebeault-Bernheim theory of hypnosis was **suggestion**, which they defined as the ability to uncritically accept an idea or a command suggested by a hypnotist and transform the suggestion into an action (Ellenberger, 1970). They considered suggestibility to be a personality trait that every person had to some degree. Hypnotic susceptibility was therefore considered to be a normal phenomenon experienced by different people with varying degrees of strength. In their medical practices, Liebeault and Bernheim induced hypnosis by having the patient stare into the doctor's eyes while being told to relax deeply. Once in a sleeplike trance, the doctor would suggest to the patient that the symptoms (e.g., headache) would go away. The symptoms often did just that.

Meanwhile, the sprawling Salpêtrière Hospital in Paris had become the European center for the study of hypnosis. Its director, Jean-Martin Charcot (1825–1893), was known throughout Europe for his pioneering work on epilepsy; he was the first to identify the features of grand mal seizures and distinguish them from petit mal seizures. Charcot was also an expert in the study of **hysteria**, a disorder characterized by a wide range of symptoms that appeared to indicate neurological malfunction, but without apparent damage to the nervous system. Some patients experienced epilepsy-like seizures, others developed paralyses that were neurologically impossible (e.g., only the hand), and still others had nervous tics, headaches, sensory loss (e.g., deafness), or severe memory lapses. Charcot's contribution was to take hysteria seriously as a disorder and search for its cause. Contemporary medical opinion, grounded in the materialistic belief that true disorders had a physical basis, was that hysterics were simply malingerers who made up their symptoms. Charcot's willingness to tackle the problem head on eventually earned him the title of "Napoleon of the Neuroses" (Ellenberger, 1970, p. 95).

Because Charcot observed that many of the symptoms of hysteria were the same as phenomena demonstrated under hypnosis, he came to believe that hysteria and the ability to be hypnotized shared the same underlying pathology. Thus, although the hypnotists at Nancy considered suggestibility a normal trait and therefore generally useful as a therapy tool, Charcot declared that hypnotism was dangerous if it was used indiscriminately. Furthermore, he argued, susceptibility to hypnosis was an indication of underlying hysteric tendencies, which Charcot believed were the result of an inherited nervous system disorder. Hypnotism, then, was an "innately predisposed reaction on the part of [hysterics] to stroking, fixations of the sensory apparatus, and various other means of hypnotic induction" (Sulloway, 1979, p. 46). Hypnotism could be useful, Charcot proclaimed, primarily as a means of investigating and influencing the symptoms of those suffering from hysteria. Furthermore, because some patients were indeed malingerers, hypnosis was the means of separating the true hysterics from the fakes. Only true hysterics could be hypnotized, Charcot believed.

At the Salpêtrière, Charcot was famous for his elaborate and spectacular clinical demonstrations of hysteria. He would pick his "best" hysteric patients, hypnotize them, and suggest various symptoms to them. Charcot's patients apparently competed with each other for the privilege of being "on stage." Predictably, they performed as expected. Figure 12.4 portrays Charcot giving a clinical demonstration of hypnosis on Blanche Wittman, whose dramatic performances earned her the title among her peers of "Queen of the Hysterics" (Fancher, 1990).

FIGURE 12.4 Painting of Charcot lecturing on hysteria at the Salpêtrière, with Blanche Wittman as the hypnotized patient (from Gay, 1988). Freud bought an engraving of the piece and hung it in his consulting room (look carefully at Figure 12.6).

Charcot also used hypnosis to suggest the removal of hysteric symptoms in his patients and claimed some success.[5]

The doctors from Nancy disagreed sharply with Charcot's beliefs about hypnosis, arguing that his dramatic clinical demonstrations merely showed the effects of suggestion. Charcot's patients knew exactly what was expected of them, it was argued, and they delivered. A fierce debate erupted in the mid-1880s; and between 1888 and 1893, one bibliography listed 801 publications in journals and magazines on the nature of hypnosis (Sulloway, 1979). By the mid-1890s, most observers had rejected Charcot's ideas about the connection between hysteria and hypnosis in favor of the Nancy model emphasizing suggestibility.

During the height of his fame, young physicians from all over Europe came to the Salpêtrière to experience Charcot and learn from his brilliant lectures and demonstrations. One such man was a young doctor from Vienna whose ideas reverberated through the 20th century.

SIGMUND FREUD (1856–1939): FOUNDING PSYCHOANALYSIS

Freud's profound influence on Western culture is widely recognized. Less well known is the manner in which his ideas evolved and the sources of influence on him. Indeed, students in introductory and personality courses often encounter a distorted description of Freud that perpetuates what science historian Frank Sulloway (1979) called the "myth of the hero." This Freudian myth encompasses two components, according to Sulloway. First, it includes the image of Freud as a solitary heroic figure fighting for his ideas against all odds, in a uniformly hostile environment. Second, it maintains the illusion that the hero's theories were original to him, without serious precedent. Both aspects of this Freudian myth have been brought into question by recent historical scholarship. As will be seen, (a) Freud was indeed controversial, but his ideas were not nearly as revolutionary as is normally portrayed; and (b) all of his major concepts have traceable origins to related or identical ideas in existence in the late 19th and early 20th centuries. Freud's genius was not in creation, but in synthesis and advocacy—in weaving ideas into a unified theory of human behavior and in vigorously promoting this theory in the medical community.

Interestingly enough, Freud played a role in creating his own myth. He did so in part by handpicking his first biographer, Ernest Jones, but also by destroying his papers and correspondence on at least two occasions (1885 and 1907), thereby making it difficult to trace the roots of his ideas. After the first of these events, Freud wrote this to his fiancée:

> One intention...I have almost finished carrying out, an intention which a number of as
> yet unborn and unfortunate people will one day resent...: my biographers. I have
> destroyed all my notes of the past fourteen years, as well as letters, scientific excerpts,
> and the manuscripts of my papers.... I couldn't have matured or died without worrying
> about who would get hold of those old papers.... As for the biographers, let them worry,

[5]Chapter 8 briefly describes some research on hypnosis that embarrassed a young Alfred Binet, in which his apparent success in producing effects with magnets was shown to be the result of suggestion. This study was conducted under Charcot's direction at the Salpêtrière, and the patient was none other than Blanche Wittman (Fancher, 1990).

we have no desire to make it too easy for them. Each one of them will be right in his opinion of "The Development of the Hero," and I am already looking forward to seeing them go astray. (quoted in Sulloway, 1979, p. 7)

This is a remarkable letter. Who was this young man, not yet 30 years old, who was certain that he would someday have biographies written about him?

Early Life and Education

Freud spent most of his life in Vienna, Austria. His father moved a growing family there in 1860, when young Sigmund was 4, and Freud left only when the Nazi threat to his personal safety took him to London in 1938, a year before his death. Freud's intellectual promise appeared early. He was a precocious young child in a large household of moderate means, the only one of his siblings given a room of his own for study. He was also given a generous book-buying allowance, and legend has it that when he once complained about the distractions of a younger sister's noisy piano lessons, they ended and the piano was banished from the house.

Freud was the first of eight children produced by the marriage of Jacob and Amalia Freud. Amalia was Jacob's third wife and half his age (20 versus 40). Freud developed a strong emotional attachment to his young mother, while his father was more distant and appeared more grandfatherly than fatherly; thus the family dynamics almost certainly played a role in Freud's later thinking about parent–child relationships, especially his advocacy of the Oedipus complex (Kramer, 2006). Although the Freud family was Jewish, religious practice was not at the center of family life, and Freud would later recall that his father "allowed [him] to grow up in complete ignorance of everything that concerned Judaism" (quoted in Gay, 1988, p. 6). One aspect of Judaism that Freud did manage to experience, however, was Vienna's pervasive anti-Semitism. The period of Freud's youth saw a steady rise in the Jewish population in Vienna: from 2% of the population in 1857 to 10% by 1880 (Gay, 1988). Reforms made life easier for Jews in the 1860s, but a serious economic depression in 1873 led to an all too familiar scapegoating scenario—Jews were blamed for Vienna's problems and became the objects of political (and physical) attack and discrimination. In that same year, Freud entered the University of Vienna's famed medical school, where he quickly became an academic star.

Although he was a medical student, Freud had no intention of practicing medicine—research was his passion. His mentor, one of the most important influences in his life, was Ernst Brücke, director of the university's Physiological Institute. Through Brücke, Freud became immersed in the 19th-century materialist-mechanist-determinist zeitgeist in physiology (see Chapter 3). Brücke had been a student of the great Johannes Müller, and together with Helmholtz and other students of Müller, he was a leader in the movement that sought to explain all living action by reducing it to physical, mechanical forces. Although Freud's interest in searching for the physiological mechanisms underlying psychological processes diminished over the years, he never wavered in his belief that all events have causes that can be identified through science. His later ideas that dreams were not random events, but had deep underlying meanings, and that even events seeming to be accidents (i.e., Freudian slips) are nonetheless meaningful, are just two examples of his strong faith in the essential orderliness and predictability of psychological events.

Freud's immersion in research was the main reason that it took him 8 years instead of the typical 5 to earn his medical degree. Working in Brücke's laboratory from 1876 to 1882, he published articles on the nervous systems of various species and the gonadal structure of eels; he also developed an important research technique for staining nerve fibers (similar to the stains developed by Golgi and Ramón y Cajal, described in Chapter 3). Much of his comparative neurological research carried with it strong evolutionary implications, for Darwin's monumental text was less than 20 years old and its ideas affected the thinking of all physiologists during the era. Indeed, Darwin's thinking would eventually influence Freud profoundly. First, Darwin's basic insight that human nature is rooted in its animal past provided support for Freud's beliefs about the importance of biological instincts in motivating behavior and about the fact that behavior is not always "rational." Second, Freud's belief in the importance of sexual motivation follows logically from the rather obvious point that sex, with the resulting perpetuation of the species, is at the core of evolutionary theory.

Meynert and Psychiatry   Freud had every intention of continuing as a researcher when he completed his medical degree in 1883, but by then he was also in love and faced with a financially uncertain future as a laboratory researcher. And as a Jew, he knew that few academic positions were open to him. If he wished to marry, establishing a medical practice would be necessary. Hence, on Brücke's advice, he reluctantly began to prepare for life as a practitioner by taking 3 years of instruction at Vienna's General Hospital.

For 5 months of this time, he came under the tutelage of Theodor Meynert (1833–1893), a famous brain anatomist and professor of psychiatry. Freud's earlier research with Brücke led him to be especially interested in disorders of the nervous system, and the time spent with Meynert confirmed in him the decision to specialize in that area. Patients with neurological problems also included hysterics, of course; through his experience with Meynert, Freud first began to encounter the type of patient who would soon become the focus of his life's work.

In 1885, Freud earned a 6-month travel grant to study with Charcot at the Salpêtrière. There he broadened his knowledge of hysteria and began to learn something about hypnosis. He later used hypnosis in the early years of his practice but eventually abandoned it as ineffective, for him at least.

Breuer and the Catharsis Method   Another important contact that Freud made while in medical school was with the eminent physician Joseph Breuer (1842–1925), known for his discovery of the role played by the semicircular canals of the inner ear in maintaining balance and equilibrium. From 1880 to 1882, while Freud was still finishing medical school, Breuer had treated a perplexing case of hysteria that was destined to become a defining event in the history of psychoanalysis—the **Anna O. case**. It is also just one example of how the story of psychoanalysis has become distorted over the years.

Anna O. (Figure 12.5) was the pseudonym that Breuer created for Bertha Pappenheim, an intelligent woman in her early twenties with a bewildering array of hysteric symptoms.[6] At various times her right (then her left) side appeared to be paralyzed and anesthetic, she had

---

[6]The family of Bertha Pappenheim (1859–1936) was not pleased when Ernest Jones revealed her true identity in the first volume of his biography of Freud (Jones, 1953). After recovering her health, Bertha became a leader in the women's movement in Germany and once wrote: "If there is any justice in the next world, women will make the laws and men will bear the children" (quoted in Sulloway, 1979, p. 57). The West German government issued a stamp in her honor in 1954.

FIGURE 12.5 Bertha Pappenheim (Anna O.) at the time of her therapy with Breuer. From Sulloway (1979).

a persistent nervous cough, experienced both visual and auditory deficits, developed bizarre eating habits (e.g., living solely on oranges for a period of several weeks), lost the ability to speak German for a time (while retaining the ability to speak English), and experienced dissociative states that she called "absences" (Sulloway, 1979). The problems appeared to be precipitated by the long-term nursing care she had given to her dying father, although Anna's general frustrations about her situation in life contributed as well. An intelligent young woman, Anna was raised in a family and cultural context that consistently stifled her intellect and ambition.

According to the traditional (and mythical) description of the case, Breuer found success with what he called the method of **catharsis**. He discovered that if Anna could be made to trace a particular symptom back to the occasion of its first appearance, she would experience an emotional release, which Breuer referred to as a catharsis, and she would gain relief from the symptom. Anna referred to it as her "talking cure." For example, for a time she was unable to drink water from a glass and thought the practice disgusting. Breuer got her to trace her hydrophobia back to a situation in which Anna had witnessed a woman who shared the same glass of water with her dog. Once the initial memory had been retrieved, she achieved a catharsis and the hydrophobia disappeared. In like manner, so the story goes, Breuer worked his way laboriously through Anna's remaining symptoms while seeing her almost every evening for more than a year.

The Anna O. case is a compelling story, but clever detective work by Ellenberger (1972) showed that the case was not as straightforward as it appears in most descriptions. Although the cathartic method had some success, relief of Anna's symptoms was often just temporary, and the initial diagnosis of hysteria was only a small part of her problem (she also had psychotic symptoms and possibly a dissociative disorder). She began to recover only after spending several lengthy confinements in a sanatorium after Breuer ended her treatment. Also, several of the events reported in traditional descriptions were factually wrong. For example, according to the account in the Jones biography of Freud, Breuer's wife was not happy about the amount of time he was spending with this attractive young woman, and when Anna developed a false pregnancy and named Breuer as the father, he did his catharsis magic to relieve the symptom and then terminated the therapy in a mild panic. The very next day he whisked his wife off to a second honeymoon to Venice where they conceived a daughter (and they all lived happily ever after). Ellenberger, however, showed that none of Breuer's case notes mentioned a false pregnancy, and the birth date of his daughter conflicts with the second honeymoon story.

Breuer told his younger colleague Freud about the case, and it eventually became featured as the first of several cases described in their coauthored *Studies on Hysteria* (Breuer & Freud, 1895/1955). This book is often considered the founding event for psychoanalysis. For Freud, the case demonstrated that (a) memory of a traumatic event might be actively repressed into the unconscious, but it will continue to influence the person's behavior as a hysteric symptom; (b) the form of a hysterical symptom bears a symbolic relationship to the traumatic event that caused it, as in the hydrophobia example; and (c) a symptom can be alleviated if the person gains insight into the originating event. As Freud would later say in the first of a series of lectures given at Clark University, "Our hysterical patients suffer from reminiscences. Their symptoms are residues . . . of particular (traumatic) events" (1909/1977, p. 16).

Freud also believed he detected a strong undercurrent of sexuality in the case. Anna seemed to be unusually attached to her father; and near the end of therapy, she developed a strong attachment to Breuer as well. Freud would eventually refer to this attachment for the therapist as **transference** and would consider it an important step on the road to recovery. Breuer, while recognizing that sexuality was involved in the case, rejected Freud's argument that hysteria had sexual origins. He split with Freud over the issue, thus ending a long friendship. It would not be the only time that Freud's insistence on the importance of sexual motivation cost him a colleague.

Creating Psychoanalysis

From the mid-1880s to the mid-1890s, Freud developed his clinical practice, specializing in the treatment of hysteria. He was not at a loss for patients. Vienna was like other European cities in the Victorian era—that is, sex in marriage was considered a necessary evil, good only for producing heirs, whereas sex for pleasure was confined to males visiting prostitutes. The results included frustrated sexual needs for the faithful wife, lingering guilt for the wandering husband, and good incomes for therapists like Freud. The picture was more complicated, of course, and historians continue to debate whether the Victorian female was sexually inhibited (e.g., Sterns, 1985). Nonetheless, neurotic symptoms seemed plentiful when Freud was establishing his practice. He tried everything with his patients; treatments ranged from hydrotherapy (i.e., similar to a modern whirlpool bath, presumably designed to soothe the nerves) to hypnosis to a procedure in which he pressed on a patient's forehead while insisting that they retrieve repressed memories. He eventually discovered a technique that became the centerpiece of psychoanalytic practice—**free association**. Patients were placed in a relaxed position (hence, the famous couch—Figure 12.6) and encouraged to say whatever came into their minds, without censoring anything. This often proved difficult for patients, who displayed what Freud called **resistance**—they would be unable or unwilling to mention some topics. Freud welcomed resistances, believing they were a sure sign that he was getting to the root of the patient's problem. For example, if a depressed female patient resisted telling the therapist that she was attracted to her brother-in-law, who looked a bit like her father and shared some of Dad's mannerisms, Freud would immediately begin thinking about how her problems might stem from unresolved feelings toward her father.

In addition to free association, Freud used **dream analysis** as a means to explore the unconscious. He went as far as to describe dreams as the "royal road" to the unconscious. He first hit upon the idea while searching for a way to perform psychoanalysis on himself, a task he undertook in the late 1890s. He could recall his dreams in great detail, and he discovered that they provided a rich source of information, both on their own and as a starting point for

FIGURE 12.6 Freud's couch.

further free association. He published what is widely considered his most important book, *The Interpretation of Dreams*, in 1900. Freud believed that dreams were disguised wishes, and he distinguished between the *manifest* content of a dream (our verbal description of it, what the dream appears to be about) from the *latent* content (its true unconscious meaning, usually having to do with sex and/or aggression). Through the process of *dream work*, latent content is transformed through symbolism into manifest content. A dream that is truly about a frustrated desire for sex, for example, might be disguised (thinly) as a dream about a model train set with lots of tunnels. By interpreting dreams, Freud argued, we could achieve insight into our genuine but unconscious wishes.

The Importance of Sex As Freud's experience with hysteria grew, he became convinced that unresolved sexual problems were at the heart of the matter for his troubled patients. Patients exploring their past by way of free associations and dream reports often seemed to have experienced some type of sexual trauma at a young age. By the mid-1890s, Freud had heard enough of this theme to propose what became known as his **seduction hypothesis**. Hysteria, he argued, was the result of childhood sexual abuse by a parent or other adult. Because the young child had no understanding of what was happening, Freud believed, the experience was forgotten, buried in the unconscious. Sometime after puberty, when the person began to understand about and experience mature sexuality, the long-buried memory would resurface in the form of one or more hysterical symptoms (Gleaves & Hernandez, 1999).

Freud first presented his seduction theory in public at an 1896 meeting of the Vienna Society for Psychiatry and Neurology, which was presided over by Richard von Krafft-Ebing, the era's leading authority on sexual pathology. The talk was not well received by the medical community, and Krafft-Ebing called Freud's theory a "scientific fairy tale" (Gay, 1988, p. 93). Freud himself soon began to doubt the strength of the abuse–hysteria connection, partly

---

KEY DATE—1900

This year marked the official publication date of Freud's *Interpretation of Dreams*. It appeared a year earlier, but Freud wanted the millennium publication date on his book.

These events also occurred that year:

- Philosophers and psychologists had formed an uncomfortable alliance in the American Psychological Association; the philosophers eventually formed their own formal association, which began in this year with the creation of the Western Philosophical Association in Kansas City
- Physicist Max Planck formulated quantum theory
- F. E. Dorn discovered radon
- The Commonwealth of Australia was created
- D. F. Davis was presented an international lawn tennis cup bearing his name

- Puccini's opera, *Tosca*, made its debut in Rome
- Boxer uprisings in China, protesting European influence, occurred

These people were born:

- Spencer Tracy, American actor (two Best Actor Academy Awards)
- Aaron Copeland, American composer (e.g., *Appalachian Spring*)

These people died:

- Oscar Wilde, English author (e.g., *The Importance of Being Earnest*)
- Friedrich Nietzsche, German philosopher (a widely quoted statement → "God is dead.")

because some of his patients' stories didn't seem to stand up to other evidence. Also, Freud was bothered by the idea that only sexual traumas in childhood led to later problems. What about all the other, nonsexual traumas (e.g., severe illness, bad falls) that children experience? Why didn't they lead to later hysteria? It seemed impossible, Freud later wrote, "to suppose that distressing sexual effects so greatly exceed all other unpleasurable effects in intensity. It must be another characteristic of sexual ideas that can explain how it is that sexual ideas are alone subjected to [pathological] repression" (quoted in Sulloway, 1979, p. 111).

Tradition has it that Freud's great intellectual breakthrough was to abandon his seduction theory and replace it with the idea that sexual events in childhood were not real but imagined and that sexuality did not begin in adolescence but existed in some form from infancy. This insight about universal childhood sexuality supposedly emerged from Freud's self-analysis in the late 1890s. There is probably some truth to Freud's "heroic" account of how, entirely on his own and without the influence of contemporary ideas, he came to abandon his seduction hypothesis and develop his famous Oedipus complex. However, the Freudian myth has also been at work in this area. Freud was not operating in an intellectual vacuum here, creating ideas that were unique. For instance, several other noted "sexologists" (e.g., Havelock Ellis) were also proposing that sexual strivings extended into infancy and that repressed sexuality was connected with later psychopathology. Indeed, the 1890s witnessed an outpouring of books on sex, childhood and otherwise, and Freud was fully aware of them (Sulloway, 1979). Hence, the origins of the concept of infantile sexuality include Freud's self-analysis but go much deeper to include the intellectual context of late 19th-century Europe.

Psychoanalysis Enters the 20th Century   By the turn of the 20th century, Freud was launched on his career as a psychoanalyst specializing in the treatment of hysteria. With *The Interpretation of Dreams*, he also began developing his general theory of behavior, which continued to evolve for the rest of his life. A year after the dream book, in 1901, he published *The Psychopathology of Everyday Life*, which featured the analysis of events that later came to be called Freudian slips.[7] In 1905, two books appeared: *Three Contributions to the Theory of Sex* and *Wit and Its Relation to the Unconscious*. With these publications (four books in 5 years), Freud's reputation grew, slowly but steadily, throughout the first decade of the 20th century. In America, his theories caught the enthusiastic attention of G. Stanley Hall of Clark University. As you recall from Chapter 6, Hall's enormous range of interests included the study of children and adolescents, including their sexual development. He described Breuer and Freud's work on hysteria in his two-volume book on adolescence, and he was offering courses on sexuality as early as 1904 (Rosenzweig, 1992).

In 1909, to celebrate the 20th anniversary of Clark University's founding, Hall invited Freud to Worcester to receive an honorary degree and to lecture on psychoanalysis. Several other prominent scientists also gave talks and were awarded degrees at the celebration, including Titchener, the noted anthropologist Franz Boas, and Carl Jung, who accompanied Freud on the transatlantic voyage. Still other psychologists came to hear the talks, including James, Cattell, and Goddard. It was Freud's only visit to the United States, and he returned

---

[7] *The Psychopathology of Everyday Life* is full of examples of Freudian slips. Here are two that Freud described. First, when a lecturer said "Freuer-Breudian" theory of hysteria instead of "Breuer-Freudian," in referring to their jointly authored hysteria book, Freud suggested that a hostile motive was behind the mistake. In second example, Freud described a patient who couldn't recall (i.e., had repressed) where a man had touched her but then quickly changed the subject to her summer home. When asked where it was located, she said "near the mountain loin" instead of "mountain lane."

with a healthy dislike of the country, especially its food. Nonetheless, he was forever grateful to Hall, crediting him with enhancing the international reputation of psychoanalysis and providing "the first official recognition of our endeavors" (quoted in Gay, 1988, p. 207).

The Evolution of Psychoanalytic Theory

Freud was already 54 years old when he delivered his lectures at Clark, but he was just beginning to develop his general theory of human behavior and mental processes. Over the next 20 years, this theory evolved considerably; indeed, many of the concepts most frequently associated with Freud did not appear until after World War I, when he was in his late sixties (for a more thorough description of the theory, refer to any textbook on personality). One major postwar change in Freud's theorizing was his conviction that destructive tendencies were just as powerful as sexual ones in motivating behavior.

Freud did not ignore aggression in the years before World War I. Male feelings of hostility toward the father were an integral part of the Oedipus complex, and the sex act itself contains elements of male aggression, he believed. Yet the war, with its seemingly unending brutality and appalling loss of life, deeply affected Freud's thinking (Gay, 1988). In 1920, he produced *Beyond the Pleasure Principle*, in which he proposed a distinction between **eros**, the life instinct, manifested in sexual motivation, and **thanatos**, a death instinct, which showed itself in the form of aggression and self-destruction. Hence, he came to believe that human behavior was jointly motivated by life-enhancing (sexual) and life-destroying (aggressive) instincts.

His reflections on the world war were the immediate stimulus for his proposal that we all have instinctive destructive tendencies. But the concept of a death instinct was also rooted in Freud's lifelong preoccupation with death, and his conviction of its reality was strengthened by events in his life during the 1920s. Shortly after he wrote *Beyond the Pleasure Principle*, for instance, one of his three daughters died during an influenza outbreak. Soon after that, a favorite grandson died and a niece committed suicide. Then in 1923, Freud, who smoked up to 20 cigars a day, was diagnosed with cancer of the mouth and saw his own demise coming. Over the next 16 years, he endured 33 painful surgeries and had to live with a series of increasingly bulky denturelike prostheses to replace parts of his palate and jaw. Freud saw all of these events as confirmation that death instincts go hand in hand with life instincts.

Other well-known Freudian concepts also developed in his later years. These include his structural analysis of personality and his description of the relationship between anxiety and ego defense mechanisms. Freud first wrote about his familiar tripartite structure of personality—id, ego, and superego—in *The Ego and the Id*, which appeared in 1923. The *ego*, partly conscious and partly unconscious, lies at the center of personality, Freud wrote, trying to maintain a balance between three conflicting forces: the id, the superego, and reality. The *id*, repository of the instinctive drives of sex and aggression, constantly demands that its needs be satisfied. On the other hand, the *superego*, the person's learned moral values, works to inhibit the free expression of the instincts. The ego must also take into account the environmental factors operating in the real world. For Freud, the properly functioning ego serves as a mediator, channeling id-based needs in directions that are both realistic and consistent with moral values.

The constant demands made on the ego produce anxiety. Freud distinguished three forms of it, one for each of the forces pressuring the ego. *Objective anxiety* (or "realistic" anxiety) is a normal reaction to a perceived threat from the external world, based on the person's memories of past situations of danger. Thus sailors observing a "red sky in the morning" know they must "take warning" because it means a storm is on the horizon. More interesting to the analyst, however, were the other two forms of anxiety, neurotic and moral. In *neurotic anxiety*, the person fears that id-based impulses will get out of control. In *moral anxiety*, feelings of guilt and shame arise from a sense that one is about to violate the strict moral code of the superego.

The feeling of anxiety serves as a signal to the ego that it is under attack, Freud reasoned, and it responds through defense. The response to objective anxiety is to deal with the situation realistically (e.g., the sailors prepare the ship for a storm). Because neurotic and moral anxieties are generated internally, however, the responses must also come from within, and they do so in the form of **ego defense mechanisms**. The most common form of defense is **repression**, accomplished by the unconscious portion of the ego. In repression, unwanted impulses are actively forced from awareness and into the unconscious. Repression is also an element in the other defenses. In *projection*, for example, personal faults cannot be accepted, so they are attributed to some other person. People who cannot accept the hostility within them, for example, might convince themselves that those around them are the hostile ones. That is, they repress their own hostility and project it onto others (Hall, 1954). *Sublimation* is a successful defense, Freud thought, for it channels instinctive urges into activities that have social value. Aggression is channeled into athletics, for example, and sex is channeled into art (both sex and art are "creative").

Freud's thinking about defense mechanisms was aided significantly by his daughter and fellow analyst, Anna Freud (1895–1982; Figure 12.7). Apparently oblivious to the risks, Freud psychoanalyzed Anna as part of her preparation for a career as analyst. Anna survived the analysis and went on to a distinguished career. She was a pioneer in extending psychoanalytic practice to children through the use of *play therapy*. Children lack the verbal fluency for normal analysis, of course, so Anna probed children's psyches by giving them various materials (e.g., Mommy and Daddy dolls) and asking them just to play. She also helped her father develop his own theory, especially the relationship between anxiety and defense. In fact, the lists of defense mechanisms (projection, etc.) normally found in introductory texts are more the result of her work than her father's. She articulated them in *The Ego and Mechanisms of Defense* (A. Freud, 1937). After Freud's death, Anna became a fierce protector of her father's reputation, and a collaborator in the "Freudian myth," according to Sulloway (1979).

FIGURE 12.7 Freud and his daughter Anna, in 1928, the year of Anna's book on child psychoanalysis. From Gay (1988).

Freud's Followers: Loyalty and Dissent

By the turn of the 20th century, Freud had begun attracting the interest of other physicians in Vienna. In 1902, he asked four of them to join him on Wednesday evenings to discuss issues related to psychoanalysis. The group expanded to about 20 by 1908 and began calling itself the Vienna Psychoanalytic Society. Discussions were spirited, but the authoritarian and dogmatic Freud dominated the meetings and made it clear that his word was to be law. As might be expected, while some members remained intensely loyal to Freud for years, others were not so compliant. The first major defector was one of the original five who met in 1902.

Alfred Adler (1870–1937) was trained in ophthalmology and general practice at the University of Vienna medical school; he graduated in 1895. He was apparently attracted to Freud's ideas on reading *The Interpretation of Dreams*, and he became an enthusiastic charter member of the Wednesday evening group. Soon, however, he began to question Freud's seeming obsession with sexual motivation. Instead, Adler drew on his own troubled childhood, which included illness and feelings of inferiority when compared to an older brother, and proposed the **inferiority complex** as the basis for an alternative theory. All infants are inherently inferior in their abilities, he argued, and life could be viewed as an attempt to compensate for this inferiority. He also pointed out that as we grow, the social environment places obstacles in our paths that also create feelings of inferiority to be overcome. Adler's emphasis on the importance of social factors over biological ones, along with his writings on inferiority and his belief that behavior was determined as much by conscious planning for the future as by the repressed events of one's past, alienated him from Freud. The official break came in 1911, when he was tossed out of the Vienna Psychoanalytic Society. Taking several followers with him, Adler went on to create a rival school of psychoanalysis that he called **individual psychology**. Adler and Freud never reconciled; indeed Gay (1988) described their subsequent relationship as one of mutual hate—when Adler died suddenly in 1937, Freud was evidently delighted to learn that he had outlived his rival.

An equally bitter split occurred between Freud and the Swiss psychiatrist Carl Jung (1875–1961), known for his pioneering work with schizophrenia. The two met in Vienna in 1907 after exchanging some earlier correspondence in which Jung's praise for Freud's dream theory was matched by Freud's enthusiasm for a **word association** task that Jung had developed. The procedure involved giving patients a prepared list of words and asking them to respond to each with the first word that came to mind. Also, their reactions were timed and some physiological measures were recorded (Watson & Evans, 1991). Jung assumed that longer reaction times and arousal (e.g., increased breathing) would indicate that a particular word had important emotional implications, a rationale similar to the one later used to justify the polygraph's validity as a lie detector.

Jung accompanied Freud to America and the Clark conference of 1909, where he lectured on his word association procedure. In 1911, Freud arranged to have Jung named the first president of the newly formed International Psychoanalytic Society, in part because Freud believed that naming Jung, who was neither Viennese nor Jewish, would make the association appear to be more international and broad based than it really was. Meanwhile, Freud began thinking of Jung in father–son terms, even writing to him as his "successor and crown prince" (quoted in McGuire, 1974, p. 218). But trouble was brewing; by 1913, Jung went the way of Adler and was expelled from the inner circle.

Like Adler, Jung questioned Freud's emphasis on sex, and he also had some ideas of his own. Over the rest of his career, Jung developed what came to be called **analytical**

psychology, to be distinguished from Freud's psychoanalysis. He went beyond Freud in some ways. For example, to the concept of a "personal" unconscious, similar to Freud's use of the term, Jung added the concept of the **collective unconscious**, said to include the collective experiences of our ancestors. He believed that the common themes found in mythology reflected a shared human legacy. Jung also contributed to personality theory with his distinction between what he saw as two major personality types: introverts and extroverts.

After the defections of Adler, Jung, and some others, Freud closed ranks. At the suggestion of Ernest Jones (pictured in Figure 6.7), destined to be Freud's handpicked biographer, Freud formed a secret group of eight called the "Committee." He even gave each member of his new inner sanctum a gold ring. Their task was to safeguard orthodox Freudianism, respond to critics, control the various psychoanalytic organizations, and as it turned out, perpetuate the Freudian myth (Sulloway, 1979).

Psychoanalysis in America

The 1909 Clark lectures put Freud on the intellectual map in America, but not all of those in attendance were impressed. An ailing William James, within a year of his death from heart disease, traveled to Worcester to hear one of Freud's lectures and the two men spent some time together in private. James later wrote to a colleague expressing the hope that Freud would push his interesting ideas to the limit because they "can't fail to throw light on human nature." On the other hand, James had to "confess that [Freud] made on me personally the impression of a man obsessed with fixed ideas. I can make nothing in my own case with his dream theories, and obviously 'symbolism' is a most dangerous method" (quoted in Rosenzweig, 1992, p. 174).

Over the next few years, American psychologists had the opportunity to learn more about Freud. Reviews of Freud's work and articles on psychoanalysis appeared in the *Journal of Abnormal Psychology* with some regularity, but many academic psychologists found psychoanalysis either tangential to their research interests or annoyingly "unscientific." Robert Woodworth of Columbia (Chapter 7), who might have been congenial to the Freudians because of his own interest in motivation and his general eclecticism, attacked psychoanalysis as being more religion than science (Woodworth, 1917). He was especially annoyed at a clever strategy used by analysts—whenever attacked, they would attribute the criticism to an unconscious resistance by the attacker, thereby providing pseudo-support for a key Freudian concept. It was a perfect catch-22: Analysts could claim support for Freud's ideas regardless of whether critics praised or condemned them. For Woodworth, this attitude was unconscionable. Equally galling to American psychologists was the analysts' claim that to truly understand psychoanalysis and to criticize it, one had to undergo a complete psychoanalysis oneself (Hornstein, 1992).

As mentioned in Chapter 11, in the late 1930s some behaviorally inclined psychologists (i.e., John Dollard and Neal Miller) tried to assimilate psychoanalysis by reinterpreting it in terms understandable to them. Repression, for instance, rather than being some mysterious force that wrestled with unacceptable ideas and shoved them into the deep void of the unconscious, could be considered "more rationally" as a response of nonthinking about certain events that were associated in one's learning history with negative emotions. It was simply a matter of avoidance conditioning—nonthinking about some event was reinforced by the elimination of anxiety associated with that event. Other psychologists tried to bring Freudian concepts into the laboratory and subject them to operational definitions. Repression, for example, could be defined in terms of whether or not people recognized "dirty words" that were flashed at threshold level (e.g., McGinnies, 1949). This research on perceptual defense was interesting in its own right, but whether it adequately tested Freud's ideas was another question.

Another substantial attempt to bring psychoanalytic concepts into the academic environment was made by Henry Murray (1893–1988) of Harvard, who became the second director of the Harvard Psychological Clinic in 1928 (it had been founded 2 years earlier). Murray had a background in medicine and a strong interest in the unconscious and in psychoanalysis—he studied briefly with Carl Jung. He brought to the Clinic a penchant for in-depth analyses of individual cases, and his *Explorations in Personality* (Murray, 1938), based on detailed analysis of 50 college-aged men, became a landmark study of a case-history approach to personality (Barenbaum, 2006). Along with Christiana Morgan, Murray also developed a projective personality assessment tool that remains widely used today—the Thematic Apperception Test, or TAT. Individuals taking the test see a series of ambiguous drawings (e.g., a young boy gazing at a violin) and are instructed to create stories that describe what they believe to be happening in the drawing. The test can be scored for such constructs as the need for achievement.

Murray was a charismatic figure. He attracted a number of young scholars to the clinic, and his abnormal psychology course was among the most popular at Harvard. However, he was often at odds with the more traditional academicians at Harvard, especially the legendary E. G. Boring, who lorded over the psychology department in the 1930s and, as you recall, favored a rigorous brand of experimental psychology. That Murray and Boring would clash was perhaps inevitable, given Murray's disdain for scientific psychology as it existed in the 1930s. In one often-quoted remark, Murray complained that contemporary psychology was misdirected—by studying such basic processes as sensation, perception, and memory in the laboratory, it had failed to understand real human beings:

> The truth which the informed are hesitant to reveal and the uninformed are amazed to discover is that academic psychology has contributed practically nothing to the knowledge of human nature. It has not only failed to bring light to the great, hauntingly recurrent problems, but it has no intention, one is shocked to realize, of attempting to investigate them. (Murray, 1935; quoted in Barenbaum, 2006, p. 170).

You will not be surprised to learn that such sentiments did not endear Murray to his more traditional colleagues, and his psychoanalytically based ideas never gained a strong foothold at Harvard.

Freudian psychoanalysis might not have played well within academia, but it had a strong impact on the medical practice of psychiatry, and it caught the imagination of the general public. Between 1912 and 1918, some 170 articles relating to psychoanalysis appeared in medical journals, and about 50 articles appeared in popular magazines ranging from *The Ladies' Home Journal* to *The New Republic* (Green & Reiber, 1980). By the 1920s, psychoanalysis was popular enough to be the subject of light satire. In "A Manual of the New Mentality," for example, Leacock (1924) noted that "in every direction one sees references to psychoanalysis, auto-suggestion, hypnosis, hopnoosis, psychiatry, inebriety, and things never thought of a little while ago" (p. 471). A more sarcastic tone was taken by Grace Adams, a former student of Titchener, in an *Atlantic Monthly* article. Referring to the Clark conference, she noted that the psychologists in the audience didn't realize they were listening to the wave of the future; rather, they thought "they were merely listening to a bearded foreigner make some altogether preposterous remarks" (1934, p. 85). Adams went on to lament the intrusion of psychoanalysis into everyday life, with "its majestic verbiage and high-minded meddlesomeness" (p. 88).

Despite the criticism and the satire, psychoanalysis persevered. It made significant inroads in the medical community and, by the 1930s, training in psychiatry and neurology typically included a strong dose of Freud (Hale, 1971). In addition, psychoanalytic institutes were created in urban areas, especially in the eastern United States, and catered to MDs who wished further certification as professional psychoanalysts. Over the years, reflecting differences in institutional contexts and the focus of their interests, academic psychologists and psychoanalysts have tended to go their separate ways.

Evaluating Freud

Near the end of his life, Freud was once again reminded of his Jewish heritage. Ominous signs occurred soon after the Nazis rose to power in 1933 when, as you recall from Chapter 9 (Gestalt Psychology), Jewish professors began to be fired. In addition, psychoanalysis was branded "Jewish science" and outlawed within Germany. Soon, Freud's writings were publicly burned, along with other books by Jews (e.g., Einstein). Freud wryly noted that the world seemed to be making progress: "In the Middle Ages they would have burnt me; nowadays they are content with burning my books" (quoted in Gay, 1988, pp. 592–593). Then, in March 1938, the Nazis occupied Austria; Vienna became a scene of beatings and even of cold-blooded murders of Jews on its streets. Freud was reluctant to leave Vienna, but he became convinced that it was time to go after Nazi sympathizers searched his home and the Gestapo briefly detained his daughter Anna.[8] He left Vienna with his family in June 1938 and resettled in London, where his cancer finally claimed him on September 23, 1939.

The value of Freud's contributions to psychology has been a matter of considerable debate. One critic went so far as to refer to psychoanalysis as "the most stupendous intellectual confidence trick of the twentieth century . . . [and] a vast structure of radically unsound design and with no posterity" (Medawar, 1975; quoted in Sulloway, 1979, p. 499). Scholars dissecting Freud's published case histories have found scant evidence of the effectiveness of psychoanalysis as therapy; indeed, there is considerable evidence that he bent the facts of his case histories to suit theories he had already decided upon (Kramer, 2006). He has also been chastised for missing the opportunity to expose widespread childhood sexual abuse when he abandoned his original seduction theory (Gay, 1988). Defenders, on the other hand, argue that Freud is responsible for some of the most important ideas of the 20th century and that his influence spreads beyond psychology and deeply into Western culture. This issue will not be resolved here, of course, nor anytime in the near future. What can be enumerated are some aspects of Freud's influence and some of the typical criticisms of his work.

Contributions   Modern scholars have uncovered many of the sources and antecedents of Freud's ideas. As a result, his ideas are recognized as considerably less than original (Sulloway, 1979). Nonetheless, any attempt to understand human nature must include serious consideration of his work. First, although Freud did not discover the unconscious, he popularized the concept, and components of unconscious thinking such as repression, defense, and the Freudian slip have become part of the psychological (and popular) lexicon. Freud's emphasis

---

[8]Freud never seemed to grasp the precariousness of his situation; and like most people living during that era, he had no idea of the extent of the evil to come. Four of his sisters were among the 6 million killed in the Nazi death camps (Fancher, 1990).

on unconscious motives also raised awareness of the general need to study motivational processes and of the fact that human behavior is not always rational. Second, we now take it for granted that the events of early childhood can significantly affect later development. We might take issue with the Freudian model of early development, especially the Oedipus complex and its ramifications, but there is no question that he made us more aware of the vulnerability of the young mind. Third, at a time when the medical community favored biological explanations of mental disorders and their treatment, Freud showed that some problems were psychological in origin and therefore could be treated with psychological means, through psychoanalysis.

Criticisms Many of Freud's conflicts with peers concerned the degree of emphasis he placed on sexual motivation. Breuer, Jung, and Adler all disagreed with him over the issue, and we now recognize that human behavior is too complex to be reduced to single broad motives. Psychoanalysts in the post-Freudian era have paid increasing attention to the roles of interpersonal relationships and the social environment in shaping personality (Pervin, 1991). The criticism of Freud's overemphasis on sex is part of a broader problem—he often overstated the case. Thus, while childhood is clearly an important determiner of later personality, it is an exaggeration to say, as Freud did, that the personality structure is essentially determined during the first 5 or 6 years of life. A third frequent criticism of Freud, often delivered by those accustomed to laboratory control over variables, concerns the "scientific status" of his work. Freud has been criticized for relying on a limited sample of case studies, for excessive bias in bending the data from his patients into shapes that suited him, and for defining terms too loosely for his theory to be adequately tested. Freud's dogmatic insistence on his point of view and his demands of loyalty from his followers have also been said to be at odds with the "objectivity" expected of scientists in the positivist tradition. Finally, Freud has been widely criticized for his theoretical views about female psychology, although one must be careful to recognize that few people can step away from the social context in which they live. Thus Freud was a typical Victorian male with a typical Victorian attitude about the second-class status of most women, and it showed in his work. He believed, for example, that superego development was never complete in women, that they envied the status of men ("penis envy"), and that a woman's best hope for fulfillment was to produce male children. Anatomy, Freud declared, was destiny. In fairness, Freud never hindered and even encouraged the development of competent female analysts, most obviously his daughter Anna. And he occasionally acknowledged his meager understanding of the female psyche, once asking plaintively, "What does a woman want?" (quoted in Gay, 1988, p. 501).

Freud's theory may not have held together over the years, but many of his insights have stood the test of time. As early as 1910, this conclusion about Freud was recognized by his contemporary, Havelock Ellis, and is a fitting way to close this section of the chapter: "But if . . . Freud sometimes selects a very thin thread, he seldom fails to string pearls on it, and these have value whether the thread snaps or not" (Ellis, 1910; quoted in Sulloway, 1979, p. 500).

IN PERSPECTIVE: TREATING MENTAL ILLNESS

This chapter has covered considerable ground, from early attempts to treat the mentally ill in a humane fashion through Freud's monumental effort to treat the mentally ill while simultaneously building a general theory of behavior. What you have read here is just a small part of a much larger story, a story that continues in the next chapter, when an early version of "clinical psychology" emerged from the laboratory of a late 19th-century American psychologist. Clinical psychology grew slowly and then dramatically changed its identity in the aftermath of World War II.

You might have been surprised to see that a relatively small proportion of this book has been devoted to the diagnosis and treatment of the mentally ill. After all, when most people think of psychology, they think of the psychologist-as-therapist stereotype, along with an image that might include a couch. By now, however, and perhaps through your other courses in psychology as well, you should know that psychology is a much wider endeavor. Its history, at least in the United States, has generally been a history of psychology becoming and establishing itself as a new scientific discipline, primarily in an academic environment. This in turn has meant that most psychologists have been engaged in the endeavor to increase our understanding of behavior and mental processes through scientific research, and through various applications, to improve society through this increased understanding. Treatment of the mentally ill, on the other hand, has a history that overlaps considerably with the history of medicine and, for the most part, has occurred outside of the academic environment (with a notable exception, as you will see in the next chapter). Most modern departments of psychology continue with this mission of research and application, so it is perhaps not surprising that your academic course in the history of psychology (and the text used for it) is a history that emphasizes the academic side.

SUMMARY

Early Treatment of the Mentally Ill

- Near the end of the 18th century, Enlightenment thinkers pressed for reform in the ways of treating the mentally ill. In France, Phillipe Pinel introduced the concept of moral treatment, in which institutional living conditions were improved, the tendency to rely exclusively on physical restraint of patients was reduced, and direct efforts were made to improve the behavior of patients. Similar reforms were undertaken at the York Retreat in England by William Tuke. His model was copied extensively in the United States in the 20th century. Benjamin Rush, considered the founder of modern psychiatry, introduced a medical model as a way of explaining mental illness and developed an approach to treatment that emphasized "improving" the condition of patients' blood and circulatory systems.

- In the middle of the 19th century, large-scale asylums were built to house the mentally ill, many following the Kirkbride design, which emphasized several architectural features (e.g., pleasant views from all rooms) that were thought to promote mental health. Dorothea Dix successfully urged the reform of asylums and better treatment for the mentally ill poor. At the turn of the 20th century, Clifford Beers, a former mental patient, agitated for similar reforms; he was also a pioneer in the mental hygiene movement, which emphasized prevention.

- The classification of mental illnesses took a major leap forward with the work of Emil Kraepelin, a psychiatrist who also studied with Wundt. Among other things, Kraepelin is known for his description of dementia praecox (later renamed schizophrenia) and his description of it in attentional terms.

Mesmerism and Hypnosis

- In the mid-1700s, Franz Anton Mesmer developed a procedure for treating hysteria (apparent nervous system disorders with no true organic damage), based on his belief that the disorder was the result of disturbed magnetic forces in the body. Believing that he had magnetic powers, he treated patients and effected some cures by "mesmerizing" them. Although he didn't know it, his successes were the result of the power of suggestion, and Mesmer had discovered a procedure that would eventually be known as hypnosis.

• Before the discovery of such drugs as ether in the 19th century, mesmerism was championed by the British doctor John Elliotson as an anesthetic for surgery and used extensively in India by another British doctor, James Esdaile. It gained further scientific credibility in the hands of James Braid, who renamed the procedure "neurypnology," which soon came to be called hypnology or hypnotism.

• In France in the mid-19th century, two schools of thought developed about the nature of hypnotism. According to Liebeault and Bernheim of the Nancy School, hypnotism was a normal phenomenon that had its effects through the power of suggestion; people differed in their levels of suggestibility. According to Charcot in Paris, however, hypnotic effects mirrored the symptoms of hypnosis and suggestibility was a sign of hysterical neurosis.

Sigmund Freud (1856–1939): Founding Psychoanalysis

• Freud is one of psychology's best-known figures. Over the years, a Freudian myth has developed, a false belief that Freud was the solitary hero fighting for his ideas against overwhelming opposition and that his ideas were original to him, without important antecedent. Recent scholarship has questioned both aspects of the myth.

• Freud was trained in neurology and influenced, through his contact with Ernst Brücke, by the prevailing materialism and determinism of 19th-century physiology. Financial problems led him to the private practice of neurology, where he became interested in the treatment of hysteria. In the 1880s, he studied with two of the leading experts in the problem, Meynert and Charcot. He was also greatly influenced by Darwin's work.

• Through his association with Josef Breuer, Freud learned of the Anna O. case, in which hysteric symptoms were shown to be related to repressed memories and successful treatment occurred (apparently) if the patient would retrieve memories of the events surrounding the first appearance of a symptom. The recall produced an emotional release or catharsis. With Breuer, Freud published *Studies on Hysteria* in 1895; this is normally considered the founding event for psychoanalysis.

• Freud believed that hysteria resulted from the repression of trauma, real or imagined, into the unconscious and that the purpose of psychoanalysis was to bring repressed memories back to the surface so that insight into the causes of the patient's problem could be gained. To explore the unconscious, Freud developed the procedures of free association, in which a person said whatever came to mind, and dream analysis, in which the surface or "manifest" content of a dream was examined to discover the underlying or "latent" content of the dream. All dreams reflected some disguised wish fulfillment, Freud argued. He also believed that all events have causes; even accidents or slips of the tongue (Freudian slips) can be traced to unconscious purposes.

• Freud believed that sexual problems were a critical determinant of hysteria. He initially believed that hysteria resulted from the effects of childhood sexual abuse, but he later abandoned this "seduction" hypothesis, arguing that the memories of abuse were actually the results of imagined sexual feelings originating in childhood. This led to his theory of infantile sexuality and the Oedipus complex.

• Freud cultivated an inner circle of followers loyal to psychoanalysis. Two early converts, Alfred Adler and Carl Jung, both broke with Freud over the issue of sex and established their own schools of thought: individual psychology (Adler) and analytical psychology (Jung). One of Freud's most loyal followers was his daughter Anna, known for extending psychoanalysis to the treatment of children.

• After World War I, Freud's theory evolved to include the proposals that (a) both life (sex) and death (aggression) instincts are part of human nature; (b) personality structure centers on the ego, which mediates between the instinctive demands of the id, the moral restrictions of the superego, and reality constraints; and (c) each of the three sources of pressure on the ego can create anxiety, and the ego reacts through defense mechanisms such as repression, projection, and sublimation.

• Freud's ideas were treated with some skepticism by academic psychologists (with some exceptions, including Henry Murray, who promoted individual case studies and created the TAT), and were more influential, at first, in the medical community and with the general public. His contributions include the concepts of the unconscious and repression, his emphasis on the importance of early childhood, and his insistence on the psychological nature of mental disorders. Critics have cited his overemphasis on sex, problems with the scientific status of psychoanalysis, and his description of female psychology.

STUDY QUESTIONS

1. Explain how Pinel was influenced by the general ideals of the Enlightenment.

2. Describe the practice of "moral treatment" as it appeared in the work of Pinel and Tuke.

3. Describe what it might be like to be a patient of Benjamin Rush.

4. Describe the Kirkbride plan for asylums, and explain how various aspects of the design were assumed to help the mentally ill.

5. As crusaders for mental health reform, describe the work of (a) Dorothea Dix and (b) Clifford Beers.

6. Describe the contribution of Emil Kraepelin to the classification of mental disorders.

7. What was the theory behind mesmerism? Why did the treatment sometimes "work"?

8. Describe the origins of the term *hypnotism*.

9. What was the theory of hypnotism developed by the Nancy School, and why did Charcot consider the theory dangerous? Which approach prevailed?

10. Describe the two main components of the so-called Freudian myth. What role did Freud play in perpetuating the myth?

11. How were Freud's ideas influenced by (a) 19th-century materialist thought and (b) Darwinian theory?

12. Describe the traditional version of the Anna O. case, what really happened, and what Freud learned from the case (or thought he learned).

13. Describe the methods used by Freud to probe the unconscious.

14. Freud's deterministic beliefs are evident in his dream theory and in his description of Freudian slips. Explain.

15. Describe Freud's seduction hypothesis and what happened to it.

16. Describe the evolution of Freud's theory after World War I.

17. What were Anna Freud's contributions to her father's theories?

18. What alternatives to Freudian psychoanalysis were proposed by (a) Alfred Adler and (b) Carl Jung?

19. What was the effect of Freudian psychoanalysis on America, both in the general public and in academic circles?

20. Describe the work of Henry Murray in attempting to bring a psychoanalytically based personality psychology into the academic environment at Harvard.

21. Write an analysis of the contributions of Freud to 20th-century psychology, and the ways in which he has been criticized.

FOR FURTHER READING

HORNSTEIN, G. A. (1992). The return of the repressed: Psychology's problematic relations with psychoanalysis, 1909–1960. *American Psychologist*, *47*, 254–263.

An excellent analysis (and for a scholarly article, witty) of how American psychologists reacted to psychoanalysis over the years; shows how the Americans first rejected analysis outright and then tried to incorporate it into mainstream experimental psychology.

KRAMER, P. D. (2006). *Freud: Inventor of the modern mind.* New York: HarperCollins.

A brief and highly readable biography of Freud that focuses on Freud's ambitions and his biased use of evidence. Rather than building his theories inductively from the accumulated database of his patient's cases, Kramer argues, Freud selected aspects of his cases to confirm his preconceived ideas about human nature and ignored information inconsistent with his ideas.

ROSENZWEIG, S. (1992). *The historic expedition to America (1909): Freud, Jung, and Hall the king-maker.* St. Louis: Rana House.

An authoritative source for information about Freud's trip to America; although it lacks contextual analysis, its extensive footnoting provides a wealth of detail; a translation of Freud's lectures gives the reader a chance to read Freud in the original and provides a good summary of Freud's thinking, circa 1909.

SULLOWAY, F. J. (1979). *Freud: Biologist of the mind.* New York: Basic Books.

One of several biographies of Freud, and an excellent one, focusing on an analysis of the Freudian myth; includes extensive treatment of the contemporary sources of ideas often thought to be original to Freud (e.g., infantile sexuality); more critical than another first-rate biography by Gay (1988).

CHAPTER 13

PSYCHOLOGY'S PRACTITIONERS

One brief way of describing the change which has taken place in me is to say that in my early professional years I was asking the question, How can I treat, cure, or change this person? Now I would phrase the question this way: How can I provide a relationship which this person may use for his own personal growth?

—Carl Rogers (1961a)

PREVIEW AND CHAPTER OBJECTIVES

The chapter opens with the history of clinical psychology in the United States. The story begins in an academic setting, the laboratory of experimentalist Lightner Witmer, who adapted existing laboratory procedures and created new ones to diagnose and treat children with various problems that were hindering their school performance. Clinical psychology took a dramatic turn after World War II, when psychiatrists were overwhelmed by the caseload. The war transformed clinical psychologists from psychiatric assistants, engaged mainly in administering psychological tests, into highly trained professionals, diagnosing and treating the full range of mental and behavioral disorders. Also after the war, traditional psychotherapy based on the Freudian psychoanalytic model came under fire for its questionable effectiveness, spawning alternative therapies. The alternatives to be considered here are behavior therapy, deriving from behaviorist conditioning principles, and therapies that derived from an approach called the third force. This "humanistic psychology" created its distinct identity by contrasting itself with psychology's other two forces, psychoanalysis and behaviorism. Its most visible advocates were Abraham Maslow and Carl Rogers, creator of client-centered therapy.

The professional practice of psychology extended beyond clinical psychology, of course. One major focus of application, as you recall from Chapter 8, was in business and industry. Modern industrial/organizational psychology continues the tradition begun by such pioneers as Scott, Münsterberg, and Bingham. The chapter continues Chapter 8's discussion of psychology as it applied to business and industry, highlighted by an examination of a famous series of studies at a plant that manufactured components for telephone systems in Hawthorne, Illinois. The chapter closes with a brief consideration of a fundamental but somewhat artificial division in modern psychology between psychological scientists and practitioners of psychology. After you finish this chapter, you should be able to:

■ Summarize Witmer's contribution to clinical psychology and explain why he is also considered a pioneer of school psychology

■ Describe the state of clinical psychology in the United States in the years before World War II

■ Describe the effect of World War II on the development of clinical psychology

■ Compare the Boulder and Vail models of graduate training for clinical psychologists, and describe the status of both approaches

■ Describe the Eysenck studies of psychotherapy effectiveness and their impact on clinical psychology

■ Describe the history of the lobotomy as a medical tool for treating severe mental illness

■ Describe behavior therapy, especially the history of systematic desensitization, and show its connection to behaviorist principles

■ Explain why humanistic psychology was called the "third force" in psychology

■ Describe the development of the concept of self-actualization and how it fit into the philosophy of humanistic psychology

■ Describe the essence of Carl Rogers's client-centered therapy, showing how the therapeutic atmosphere is crucial for personal growth of the client

■ Describe important developments in industrial psychology in the 1920s, the 1930s, and the postwar era

■ Describe the Hawthorne experiments and critically analyze them

■ Understand the reasons for the historical divide between psychological scientists and those who focus on the professional practice of psychology

CLINICAL PSYCHOLOGY BEFORE WORLD WAR II

Today, clinical psychologists specialize in the diagnosis and treatment of all types of mental disorders, and they are at the forefront of research concerning these problems. In contrast with psychiatrists, clinical psychologists train in graduate school rather than medical school and earn PhDs (or PsyDs) rather than MDs. Many have their own private practice, while others work in Veterans Administration (VA) hospitals or in private clinics. Some combine their practice with academic positions at colleges and universities. Some incorporate Freudian concepts into their practice, but most do not. Today, they comprise a highly influential group among those providing mental health services. This type of clinical psychologist began to emerge at the end of World War II, when the astounding number of psychological casualties created a need that the medical community (i.e., psychiatry) could not meet. In one sense, then, **clinical psychology** as we know it today is about 50 years old.

On the other hand, a portion of the American Psychological Association (APA) 1996 annual meeting was devoted to a celebration of clinical psychology's *centennial*. Much was made of a clinic created on the campus of the University of Pennsylvania in 1896 by Lightner Witmer, the director of the psychology laboratory there. The event was undoubtedly important, as elaborated shortly, and it set in motion circumstances that eventually led to modern clinical psychology. Yet the clinical psychology that existed before World War II was quite different from the discipline that emerged in the postwar era. The APA's centennial celebration is an interesting example of how the historical significance of some event can be created long after the event has occurred, through the decisions of historians and others (e.g., convention planners) who may be motivated by more than just a desire for historical truth. Thus, although the centennial of Witmer's clinic deserved a celebration on its own merits, it is probably no coincidence that it came at a time when clinicians were struggling to maintain their status in the face of cost-conscious health care providers who sometimes questioned the value of paying for clinical services. One hundred years as a profession looks more substantial than 50.

Lightner Witmer (1867–1956): Creating Psychology's First Clinic

Like a number of other American applied psychologists, Lightner Witmer (Figure 13.1) was trained in basic laboratory research but made his reputation by applying psychology to solve real-world problems. A native Philadelphian, Witmer stayed close to home for most of his life, earning a bachelor's degree at the nearby University of Pennsylvania in 1888 and then taking graduate courses there while teaching at a local college preparatory school. His shifting interests eventually settled on psychology, and for a time he served as the laboratory assistant for Penn's new psychology professor, James McKeen Cattell (Chapter 8). He then followed Cattell's example and went to Leipzig, completing a doctorate in Wundt's laboratory in 1892 (same year as his Leipzig classmate, E. B. Titchener). On his return to the United States, Witmer was named laboratory director at the University of Pennsylvania; Cattell had moved to Columbia the year before. Witmer became a vigorous advocate of the new laboratory psychology, revealing his passion for research in an amusing letter to Hugo Münsterberg in 1893 (quoted in the Chapter 7 Close-Up), in which he described a study on the psychology of memory and pain that he had undertaken on a very personal level, by deliberately letting a

FIGURE 13.1 Lightner Witmer.

horse throw him (Witmer, 1893). The episode apparently was in character—one friend later recalled that when on holiday in New York's Adirondacks, Witmer liked to ride his brakeless bicycle "down steep hills...with [his] legs on the handlebar" (Collins, 1931, p. 9).

Although fiercely committed to a scientific psychology, Witmer, like most American psychologists, believed that psychology should be able to improve people's lives. Thus he was intrigued when a local schoolteacher, who knew Witmer from taking a summer course with him, came into the laboratory in March of 1896. She brought along one of her students, a 14-year-old who couldn't spell very well, even though he was reasonably competent otherwise. The adventuresome Witmer, always willing to try something new, agreed to help and quickly discovered that part of the problem was poor eyesight; once it was corrected, the boy was able to undertake a training program and his spelling improved. This episode, and a second one involving a child with a speech disorder, turned a portion of Witmer's laboratory into a makeshift clinic and launched what came to be known as clinical psychology; the eventual outcome was several days of symposia and celebrations at the 1996 APA convention.

Word of the new clinic spread, and soon Witmer began seeing other cases of children with physiological, cognitive, and behavioral problems related to school performance—he saw about two dozen during the remainder of 1896 (McReynolds, 1987). In December of that year, he read a paper at the APA's annual meeting in Boston, in which he called for increased research on the kinds of problems he was encountering and the development of training programs to increase the number of experts able to solve such problems. In 1907 he founded the journal *The Psychological Clinic*, which included descriptions of case studies, research reports, and theoretical articles. The first issue contained a lead essay by Witmer; its title, "Clinical Psychology," gave a name to the emerging new specialty (Witmer, 1907/1931). In the article, he described the first 10 years of the clinic's development and again called for increased research and training. He urged the creation of "a new profession—that of the psychological expert, who should find his career in connection with the school system, through the examination and treatment of mentally and morally retarded children" (p. 346). Thus clinical psychology began with a relatively narrow focus—diagnosing and treating children with school-related problems. Today, that area of expertise is associated with **school psychology**. In fact, school psychologists also consider Witmer one of their pioneers, and the APA's Division for School Psychology gives an annual "Lightner Witmer Award" to a promising young school psychologist (Baker, 1988).

By 1909, Witmer's clinic had expanded and had developed a team approach. A child entering the program was given a thorough medical examination by a consulting physician, a social worker compiled a family and school history, and Witmer or one of his assistants did the mental testing, using a battery of tests for such things as memory, attention, and motor coordination (Fernberger, 1931). Witmer disliked paper-and-pencil tests of intelligence and, although he believed that Binet-style assessments could yield interesting information, he thought they were overused and he saw little value in IQ scores (McReynolds, 1996). After compiling all the information, Witmer's team classified the children as (a) experiencing some correctable medical condition (e.g., defective vision) but not needing special training, (b) possibly experiencing some medical problem but more clearly requiring some special program or other environmental intervention (e.g., improved nutrition), or (c) being severely retarded, untreatable, and requiring custodial care (Baker, 1988).

Unlike most of his contemporaries, Witmer was skeptical of the claims being made for the heritability of traits like mental defectiveness. He clearly recognized individual differences in ability in the students he saw, and he conceded that some degree of deficiency was inherent and unalterable. Severely retarded children, he believed, should be segregated from society in special institutions and prevented from having children. Yet the very existence of his clinic demonstrated his firm belief that some deficiencies could be corrected through proper training and/or control of the environment. Hence, Witmer shared with behaviorists the belief that the environment could shape behavior. He believed that if past environmental influences produced the problem behavior observed in the clinic, then future intervention could alter behavior and make the child more productive as a student. He considered his approach to be an optimistic one, arguing that to emphasize heredity is to give up hope of change: "To ascribe a condition to the environment, is a challenge to do something for its ameliorization or cure; to ascribe it to heredity often means that we fold our hands and do nothing" (Witmer, 1911, p. 232). Witmer introduced the term **orthogenics** to refer to this strategy of "investigat[ing] retardation and deviation and the *methods of restoring to normal condition* those who are found for one reason or another to be retarded or deviate" (Witmer, 1909, p. 122; emphasis added).

Witmer's clinic grew rapidly in the early decades of the 20th century; its total case files numbered just under 10,000 by 1931 (Fernberger, 1931). It also added several specialized functions to its general role of diagnosing and treating problems in school-aged children. One was a clinic for speech disorders, developed by E. B. Twitmyer in 1914.[1] Another was a vocational clinic where adolescents and adults could go for testing and advice about careers. It was created by Morris Viteles, who could be added to the Chapter 8 list of pioneers in industrial psychology (Figure 8.13, Münsterberg's simulation apparatus, is taken from the Viteles text). Witmer's clinics also spawned numerous copies and variants, about two dozen by the start of World War I (Sexton, 1965). Meanwhile other forces were at work that would eventually yield modern clinical psychology.

Clinical Psychology in the Prewar Years

Chapter 8 chronicled the evolution of the mental testing movement, Chapter 12 described the drive for mental hygiene that originated with the efforts of Clifford Beers, and this chapter just described Witmer's clinic. All of these events contributed to the history of clinical psychology. In addition, starting in the post–World War I era in the United States, several organizational efforts within the APA attempted to professionalize the work of the clinician. It was a difficult struggle. One problem was that psychology's increasing popularity and the apparent success of World War I's mental testing program prompted many unqualified people to claim that they could deliver psychological services. An illustration of the dilemma was the effect of a resolution the APA passed in 1915 requiring that testing be done only by those trained to do so. Most people administering the tests did not belong to APA, however, so the resolution had little effect (Napoli, 1981). And the issue of qualification was not resolved quickly—over 20 years later, Woodworth (1937) remained concerned that "unqualified practitioners will

---

[1]Twitmyer's dissertation, under Witmer's direction, was an examination of the knee-jerk reflex (Twitmyer, 1905). During the course of his investigation, he discovered that knee jerks could be elicited by stimuli associated with stimulation of the patellar tendon. That is, shortly after Pavlov discovered classical conditioning in Russia, Twitmyer was making the same discovery in the United States. Pavlov justifiably gets the credit, however, because of the massive research program that he undertook. Twitmyer, on the other hand, after being ignored when presenting his research at the 1904 APA meeting, abandoned conditioning and focused his efforts on Witmer's clinic.

continue to operate for some time and to besmirch the name of psychology by the harm they do to people" (p. 5). A second problem was that clinicians did not always feel welcome in an APA that was centered in the academic environment and maintained strict scholarly requirements for membership (this point is elaborated at the end of this chapter). A final problem for clinicians was that unless they worked in clinics like Witmer's, they generally had low status in their work environments, which were often hospitals or private clinics. They were usually limited to administering basic mental tests under close supervision while psychiatrists completed the major diagnostic and therapy work. And the medical community had no wish to yield its authority or status.

The first serious effort toward forming an identity for clinicians within APA was made at the 1917 annual convention, when J. E. Wallace Wallin organized a meeting "to consider the advisability of establishing a new association to 'encourage and advance professional service in the field of clinical psychology'" (Wallin, 1966, p. 107). The seven people (including Leta Hollingworth—see Chapter 8's Close-Up) who met that winter in Pittsburgh formed the American Association of Clinical Psychologists (AACP). APA's leadership was not amused, however, and feared the eventual disintegration of the APA. A compromise was reached in 1919 when the APA created a "section" for clinical psychology within the association, and the AACP members abandoned their new organization and joined it. During the 1920s, the Clinical section pursued a number of professional issues, including proper training, certification, and ethics; but little came of their efforts. The only major effect of the clinicians' growing presence was that the APA relaxed its membership requirements in the mid-1920s and created two categories: full member and associate member. By the end of the decade, associates outnumbered full members (Napoli, 1981).

During the 1930s, clinical psychologists (and other psychologists with applied interests) kept pushing for recognition in an APA that continued to be dominated by academic interests. Even the most firmly entrenched academician had to face the reality of the Great Depression, however. As you recall from the discussion of Lewin's experiences in the 1930s (Chapter 9), academic positions became increasingly difficult to find during the Depression years, making nonacademic employment a growing necessity for young psychologists. The APA created such committees as the Committee on the Social Utilization of Unemployed Psychologists and the Committee on Psychology and the Public Service. Despite these efforts, however, applied psychologists still felt the need for their own organization, and they created one in 1937—the American Association for Applied Psychology (AAAP). By 1940 it claimed more than 600 members, compared to approximately 4,000 in APA, and included sections in clinical, educational, consulting, and industrial psychology (Hilgard, 1987).

The AAAP remained in existence until the end of World War II, independent of the APA but not in deliberate competition with it—in fact, around 90% of AAAP members also belonged to the APA (Capshew, 1999). The organization made some progress on the issues of training and standards, but the advent of a second world war within a generation once more transformed psychology. The national spirit of unity and interdependence fostered a degree of cooperation between academicians and practitioners that had not existed before (and has not existed since). The outcome was a complete reorganization of the APA to incorporate both scientific and applied interests. It emerged from an "intersociety" convention held in New York in 1943, chaired by E. G. Boring, that brought together 25 delegates from several different organizations, but mainly APA and AAAP. The delegates approved a new structure for the APA, one that continues today. The structure was an umbrella organization that included special interest "Divisions" and a revised purpose. Whereas the original APA described its primary goal as the advancement of psychology as a "science," the expanded vision added advancement as a "profession" and as a "means of promoting human welfare" to its list of purposes (Napoli, 1981, p. 127). As you are about to learn, however, (a) the war-induced sense of unity in APA did not last long; and (b) the war brought about a significant transformation in the very nature of clinical psychology.

THE EMERGENCE OF MODERN CLINICAL PSYCHOLOGY

As we have seen, clinical psychologists struggled to establish their status as independent professionals before World War II. In the 1930s, for example, they tended to be employed in mental hospitals or clinics, under the supervision of psychiatrists; their "practice" was limited primarily to administering mental tests. Because virtually nothing in the way of formal clinical training was available to them, they developed their skills on the job or in internship-like arrangements (Capshew, 1999). The cruel circumstances of the war, however, created a permanent place for clinicians, who were among those providing professional services to the mentally wounded.[2] Organized psychiatry, which had controlled the delivery of therapeutic services to the mentally ill before the war, was overwhelmed by the need for therapy. As in the first world conflict, applied psychologists in the United States contributed their services through various testing programs; in the second war, they also gained experience treating those who were damaged psychologically by their war experiences. And the need was great. During the vicious Pacific battle for Guadalcanal in 1942, for example, 40% of the casualties that were serious enough to require evacuation were psychological breakdowns (Herman, 1995). Furthermore, of the first 1.5 million soldiers given medical discharges, about 675,000 (45%) were for psychiatric reasons (VandenBos, Cummings, & DeLeon, 1992). When the war ended, approximately 44,000 of the veterans who were in Veterans Administration hospitals suffered from various mental disorders resulting from the war, compared with 30,000 hospitalized with physical wounds (Sexton, 1965). Psychiatry simply could not cope with the caseload and was forced to abandon its therapeutic monopoly. In addition, the federal government, perceiving the increased need, launched an aggressive program to support the training of graduate students in clinical psychology. In the academic year 1946–1947, for instance, the VA funded training programs in 22 universities that enrolled 200 students (Capshew, 1999).

Out of these circumstances, the modern clinical psychologist emerged—no longer limited to testing, but gradually recognized as an expert diagnostician and therapist; no longer limited to children and juveniles in school settings, but now capable of delivering services to anyone in need of them; no longer restricted to a clinic setting, but now more likely to develop a private practice; no longer under the supervision of psychiatrists, but increasingly

---

[2]Battlefield casualties that are psychological rather than physical occur in all wars, of course, not just World War II. In the First World War, two British psychologists were instrumental in calling attention to the psychological toll of war (Hearnshaw, 1964). Charles S. Myers (1873–1946), who established the psychology laboratory at Cambridge, coined the term *shell shock* in 1915 to describe the psychological trauma experienced by front-line troops in the trenches of Europe; he argued that it was a true psychological disorder rather than cowardice (the military's position). William H. R. Rivers (1864–1922), a close colleague of Myers (they cofounded the British Psychological Society), treated shell-shocked British officers using a version of psychoanalysis. Rivers's work at the Craiglockhart War Hospital in England was featured in the 1997 film, *Behind the Lines*.

KEY DATE—1949

This was the year of the Boulder conference that established the scientist–practitioner model for the training of clinical psychologists.

These events also occurred that year:

- NIMH, the National Institute of Mental Health, was created in Washington
- In China, the Communist People's Republic was proclaimed, under the leadership of Mao Tse-tung
- The North Atlantic Treaty Organization (NATO) was created
- British House of Commons recognized the independence of the Republic of Ireland, with Dublin as capital, but confirmed the status of Northern Ireland as part of the United Kingdom
- Program of apartheid officially became established in South Africa
- Arthur Miller's *Death of a Salesman* won a Tony award and a Pulitzer Prize

- Rogers and Hammerstein launched the first production of *South Pacific*
- Soviet Union tested its first atomic weapon
- "Silly Putty" was invented

These people were born:

- George Foreman, world heavyweight champion from 1973 to 1974 (and later a grill master)
- John Belushi, comedian and actor (e.g., *Animal House*)

These people died:

- Margaret Mitchell, American author (e.g., *Gone with the Wind*)
- Solomon Guggenheim, U.S. art collector (Guggenheim Museum in NY, designed by Frank Lloyd Wright, named for him)

on a par with them. As this new clinician emerged, however, the needs for a standardized training program and an accreditation system became clear.

The Boulder Model

In 1947, with the financial support of the federal government, through the Veterans Administration and the U.S. Public Health Service, the APA formed a Committee on Training in Clinical Psychology (CTCP). It was chaired by David Shakow (1901–1981), who already had been quite active in promoting his ideas about the training of clinical psychologists. As chief psychologist at Worcester State Hospital in Massachusetts, Shakow (Figure 13.2) had been an active member of the original AAAP (American Association of Applied Psychologists) and, just before World War II, had served on its committee for the training of clinicians. Shakow's influence on the CTCP is evident from its committee report, which is usually referred to as the "Shakow Report" (Baker & Benjamin, 2000). It formed the backbone for deliberations about clinical training held during an intensive 15-day conference that attracted 71 clinical psychologists and other professionals to the University of Colorado in Boulder the late summer of 1949 (Figure 13.3).

Out of the Boulder conference came a blueprint for clinical training that was designed to balance what Shakow saw as the three primary types of expertise that any clinical psychologist should have—they should be experts in the diagnosis of mental disorders, they should be skilled psychotherapists, and they should be able to complete high-quality empirical research. The "Boulder model," because it combined training in the science and in the practice of psychology, came to be known as the **scientist–practitioner model** of clinical training. The

FIGURE 13.2 David Shakow, the person primarily responsible for the shape of the scientist–practitioner (Boulder) model for training in clinical psychology.

FIGURE 13.3 Participants in the historic 1949 Boulder conference.

training was to include a thorough grounding in basic knowledge of the principles of psychology and in the research methods for generating these principles; a thorough understanding of psychometrics (psychological testing), psychopathology, and psychotherapy; a data-based doctoral dissertation; and a yearlong internship at a professional clinic, VA hospital, or similar setting. Total preparation would take 4 to 5 years and lead to a PhD in clinical psychology. With this training model in place and a strong need for their services, clinical psychologists rapidly increased their numbers throughout the 1950s and 1960s.

The Eysenck Study: Problems for Psychotherapy

The conference at Boulder provided a new ideal for the training of clinical psychologists. At about the same time, the ability of clinicians to deliver effective therapy was enhanced by the development of new forms of psychotherapy. Two of these approaches, behavior therapy and client-centered therapy, are featured here. They developed and prospered in the context of a time when the effectiveness of traditional psychoanalytic and other "insight" therapies was being questioned. The doubts were magnified by a brief (six pages) article that appeared in 1952, written by a British psychologist, Hans Eysenck, and titled "The Effects of Psychotherapy: An Evaluation." In the article, Eysenck examined the efficacy of traditional insight approaches to psychotherapy by combining the results reported in 19 other studies: 5 of them evaluated psychoanalytic (Freudian) therapy, and the remaining 14 evaluated what he called "eclectic" therapy, which integrated a variety of theoretical approaches. In the absence of a control group not receiving therapy, Eysenck combined the results of two other studies that examined improvement among "neurotics" in the absence of formal psychotherapy (e.g., from insurance claims of disability). While recognizing problems with this comparison group, Eysenck claimed an improvement rate of about 72%, in the absence of therapy, over the course of 2 years. When he looked at the 2-year recovery rates for patients undergoing psychotherapy, however, he found that the reported percentage improved in Freudian psychoanalysis was a paltry 44%. A recovery rate of 64% for the eclectic therapy was better, but still less than the rate for those receiving *no therapy at all*. Eysenck (1952) concluded there "appears to be an inverse relationship between recovery and psychotherapy; the more psychotherapy, the smaller the recovery rate" (p. 322). Later research (e.g., Bergin, 1971) uncovered some methodological problems that moderated Eysenck's stark conclusion, but the damage was done. Throughout the 1950s and 1960s, psychologists proposing alternatives to traditional psychoanalysis often pointed to Eysenck's work as evidence that new strategies were needed. Two of those new approaches were therapies deriving from behaviorism and those based on what was called "humanistic" psychology. Before examining these therapeutic strategies, however, consider this chapter's Close-Up, which examines a well-known chapter in the history of medical procedures for the treatment of mental illness.

Behavior Therapy

We learned in Chapter 10 that one reason for the popularity of the behaviorist ideas of promoters like John Watson was the promise of their application to daily life through such things as the improvement of child-rearing practices. If behaviors are primarily the result of learning, then presumably dysfunctional behaviors could be unlearned and replaced with more adaptive ones. This rationale was part of Watson's thinking as he formulated the Little Albert study. As you recall from Chapter 10, although he and Rayner made no attempt to remove Albert's fear of rats, they made several suggestions about how to do so, based on conditioning principles. Furthermore, some of these ideas were tested in the 1920s, especially by Mary Cover Jones. She tried Watson's suggestions and several of her own ideas on a number of different children and is remembered for one particular case (Jones, 1924a) in which she removed a young boy's fear of rabbits by gradually moving the rabbit closer to the child while he was eating, using a procedure that she called "direct conditioning."

CLOSE-UP

THE MEDICAL STRATEGY—LOBOTOMIES, TRANSORBITAL AND OTHERWISE

In the late 19th century, the practice of psychiatry was centered on the asylum and the treatment of patients who were seriously mentally ill. As seen in Chapter 12, the Kirkbride design and moral treatment strategies attempted to improve the lives of those confined to asylums. Yet by the turn of the 20th century, it had become clear that architecture could not provide cures and that moral treatment, while laudatory, was not very effective with the severely mentally ill. Little could be done for these poor souls beyond custodial care, and "treatment" often amounted to restraint and sedation. With the advent of Freudian psychoanalysis, psychiatrists began to start private practices and to treat patients with less serious disorders (Shorter, 1997), shifting from medical treatment to a psychological analysis. Yet the seriously disturbed, their numbers steadily increasing in the 20th century, remained in asylums and hospitals and had little hope for improvement. In the 1920s and 1930s, however, several new medical treatments appeared on the scene and held some promise of providing help. As another lesson in the dangers of presentism, it is easy to dismiss some of these therapies as the misguided ideas of quack doctors. It is important to keep in mind, however, that the psychiatric community was honestly attempting to provide some relief to patients at a time when nothing else seemed to work and patients were clearly suffering. Also, especially during the Depression era of the 1930s, psychiatrists felt some pressure to justify their fees by showing that their procedures had some measurable effect (Grob, 1983). Nonetheless, some techniques seemed to come into fairly widespread practice even though there was a surprising lack of scientific basis for their implementation, and little if any evidence for their effectiveness. Consider, for example, the **lobotomy**.

The story begins with a paper presented at the Second International Congress on Neurology, held in London in 1935. It included some interesting research by two American scientists, Carlyle Jacobsen and John Fulton—they reported that surgical damage to the frontal lobes of chimpanzees could have a beneficial effect. Before the surgery, the animals had been quite aggressive; the aggression seemed to disappear after the surgery, however, and the animals' mental functions seemed otherwise unimpaired. By severing the connections between frontal lobes and lower brain centers affecting emotional behavior, the researchers seemed to have found a way to calm the easily agitated chimps. In the audience that day was a Portuguese neuropsychiatrist, António Egas Moniz. He was already well known and highly respected, having been nominated for a Nobel Prize for his discovery of methods to create images of cerebral blood flow. It occurred to Moniz that the Jacobsen-Fulton procedure could be applied to seriously disturbed (and agitated) psychotic patients (Grob, 1983).

With no science other than the Jacobsen and Fulton primate study for support, Moniz developed a procedure that he called a *prefrontal leucotomy* (roughly means a cutting of white matter in the prefrontal area of the cortex), carried out with a device he created called a *leucotone*. After a series of small holes were drilled in both sides of the skull, just above and in front of the temples, the thin leucotone was inserted successively into each hole to a fixed depth and moved side to side, thereby severing brain tissue that connected the frontal and prefronatal lobes with lower brain centers. By early 1936, Moniz had tried the procedure on 20 patients, those with manic-depressive or obsessive-compulsive disorders severe enough to make them suicidal or to show signs of being dangerous. Moniz reported (without substantial supporting data) that the procedure was mostly successful (14 of 20 "improved"; Shorter, 1997). Although many of the patients later became surprisingly listless, apathetic, and emotionally passive after recovering from the surgery, Moniz believed it was a small price to pay for the relief from their severe, even life-threatening symptoms. To his credit, Moniz urged that the procedure not be used except in extreme cases and only after all alternative methods of helping a patient had failed. For this work, he was awarded the Nobel Prize in 1949.

If Moniz was careful about the use of his new procedure, two American neurologists were not. Walter Freeman and James Watt thought that the Moniz procedure was a major breakthrough in the treatment of a wide range of psychiatric disorders, and they set about to spread the good news far and wide, while at the same time completing as many of these surgeries as they could. They renamed the procedure a *lobotomy* and, in 1946, Freeman invented a new technique called a *transorbital lobotomy*. It involved inserting a device similar in design to an ice pick through the eye sockets and into the prefrontal and frontal lobes. Compared with the Moniz technique, the new procedure could be completed more quickly, and it enabled a greater number of fibers to be cut (but it also increased the risk of severing a major artery). Freeman was undeterred by the occasional death (about 2.5% of patients), however, and vigorously promoted the new procedure, partly because of how quickly it could be done and partly because it could be completed on an outpatient basis (i.e., more lobotomy income per unit of time). Freeman's enthusiasm caused a split with Watt, who appeared increasingly nervous about Freeman's crusading zeal for the procedure. Freeman soldiered on, even traveling around the country doing "demonstrations" like the one pictured in Figure 13.4, in which he can be seen tapping his transorbital leucotone into

the eye of a patient while nurses hold onto the patient and onlookers carefully observe (and don't sneeze, one hopes). By himself, Freeman was responsible for just under 3,000 transorbital lobotomies.

FIGURE 13.4 A demonstration of a prefrontal transorbital lobotomy by Walter Freeman in 1949.

By 1951, despite growing uneasiness about the procedure, more than 18,000 patients had undergone various types of lobotomy, according to one estimate (Grob, 1991). A lobotomy was certainly effective in calming agitated patients, but it often resulted in permanent changes in personality and extreme lethargy. Also, the procedure was occasionally used simply to manage unruly or disagreeable patients, a situation portrayed disturbingly well in *One Flew Over the Cuckoo's Nest* (1962), a Ken Kesey novel that was made into a movie in 1975 and swept the Oscars the following year. Lobotomies quickly went out of fashion in the mid-1950s after the discovery of a number of effective antipsychotic drugs, especially thorazine, which was enthusiastically marketed as a "chemical" lobotomy, but without the mess.

During the 1920s and 1930s, there were several other demonstrations of how conditioning principles could be applied to alter behavior in a clinical setting. In Russia, for example, researchers applied Pavlovian principles to treat alcoholism by pairing alcohol (CS) with electric shock (UCS), and they treated hysteria by conditioning movement in limbs that appeared initially to be paralyzed (Kazdin, 1978). In the United States, O. Hobart and Willie M. Mowrer developed a treatment program for bed-wetting based on conditioning principles by creating a crib pad that rang a bell as soon as it became wet. The Mowrers used the success of their procedure to attack psychoanalytic concepts of bed-wetting, which relied on the usual deep-seated unconscious conflicts to explain the problem. Instead, the Mowrers argued, it is much simpler to assume that the problem results from a failure to recognize the stimulus cues connected with bladder tension. If conditioning is the problem, they believed, it is also the solution (Mowrer & Mowrer, 1938).

Behavior therapy gained impetus in the 1950s through (a) the work of Eysenck (Figure 13.5) and his colleagues in London, and (b) the development of an effective therapy technique similar to the method used by Mary Cover Jones. At Maudsley Hospital in London, Eysenck followed his 1952 critique of traditional psychotherapy by assembling a team of colleagues to examine the possibility of developing a new therapy approach, one based on the conditioning principles of Pavlov and Hull. By 1960, he and his group had accumulated a sufficient number of applications of conditioning principles to justify producing a book (Eysenck, 1960) that was the first to include the term *behavior therapy* in the title (Glass & Arnkoff, 1992). Three years later, Eysenck launched behavior therapy's first journal, *Behaviour Research and Therapy*, with a title that made clear Eysenck's belief that therapies should not be used unless they can be empirically validated.

In the 1950s, Joseph Wolpe, a South African at the University of Witwatersrand, created a procedure that he called **systematic desensitization** (Wolpe, 1958). It remains one of the best known and most effective behavior therapy techniques. Wolpe, a medical doctor, was trained in traditional psychoanalytic procedures but became dissatisfied with them. He began studying learning theory, especially Hull's, and benefited from the presence in South Africa of an American psychologist who had studied with Kenneth Spence, Hull's alter ego.

Wolpe began exploring behavioral techniques by studying the phobic reactions of cats. After creating fears by shocking the animals whenever they reached for food, he tried to eliminate the fear. Like Mary Cover Jones, he assumed that fear and eating were incompatible responses, so he tried to replace the fear responses by substituting eating responses. Wolpe accomplished this by feeding the animal first in a room that vaguely resembled the original room where the shock occurred, then in a room that more closely resembled the original room, and so on. That is, the fear response was gradually weakened, replaced by the approach to food (Kazdin, 1978).

Wolpe discovered a way to apply this procedure to phobic humans after reading a book by the Chicago physiologist Edmund Jacobson, who described a technique called **progressive**

FIGURE 13.5 British psychologist Hans Eysenck.

relaxation (Jacobson, 1929). Jacobson had been using relaxation to treat patients with nervous disorders; Wolpe viewed the procedure as a substitute for the eating response he had used with cats. In essence, Wolpe's systematic desensitization procedure involved relaxation training and then the creation of an "anxiety hierarchy," a list of situations that created increasing levels of anxiety. Patients would become relaxed and imagine the situation of least anxiety and then gradually ascend the hierarchy. Wolpe found that after just a few sessions, patients could remain relaxed in the presence of their most feared objects.

With additional modifications over the years, Wolpe's procedure has been shown to be highly effective for certain types of anxiety problems (Paul, 1966). A number of other behavior therapy techniques evolved over the years, ranging from token economy/reinforcement systems based on an operant model to cognitive-behavior therapy, which synthesizes learning theory and the insights from cognitive psychology. A good summary can be found in Kazdin (1978).

The Humanistic Approach to Psychotherapy

Humanistic psychology started as a revolt. It came to be known as psychology's third force, rejecting what it believed to be the "mechanistic, impersonal, hierarchical, elitist psycho-analytic establishment and [the] overly scientistic, cold, removed behaviorism" (Cushman, 1992, p. 55). Humanistic psychologists criticized the ideas that human behavior could be reduced to repressed biological instincts or simple conditioned reflexes, rejected the idea that individuals' past histories inevitably limited what their futures could be, and denied the deterministic assumptions of the other two "forces" in psychology, psychoanalysis and behaviorism. Instead, they proposed that the qualities best characterizing humans are free will and a sense of responsibility and purpose, a forward-looking lifelong search for meaning in one's life, and an innate tendency to grow toward what was called **self-actualization**. To become self-actualized meant to reach one's full potential in life.

The two American psychologists most closely associated with humanistic psychology were Abraham Maslow and Carl Rogers.

Abraham Maslow and Self-Actualization   Maslow (1908–1970; Figure 13.6) was trained as an experimental psychologist and researched dominance behavior in primates, but he later exchanged what he saw as a sterile and reductionist scientific approach for the more wholistic humanistic strategy. After completing a doctorate in 1934, he went to New York

FIGURE 13.6 Humanistic psychologist Abraham Maslow.

and eventually settled into a faculty position at Brooklyn College. He stayed until 1951, when he moved to Brandeis University (near Boston) and completed his career.[3] Maslow is known to all students in general psychology for his hierarchy of needs, a model that proposed a series of need systems, arranged in a pyramid, with lower-level and more primitive needs at the bottom and self-actualization at the top. Achieving self-actualization required satisfying all the needs below it—physiological needs, safety needs, the need for love and belonging, and the need for self-esteem, in that order. As he once wrote:

> Healthy people have sufficiently gratified their basic needs for safety, belongingness, love, respect, and self-esteem, so that they are motivated primarily by . . . self-actualization, defined as ongoing actualization of potentials, capacities and talents, as fulfillment of mission . . . , as a fuller knowledge of, and acceptance of, the person's own intrinsic nature, as an unceasing trend toward unity, integration or synergy within the person. (Maslow, 1971, p. 25)

Maslow argued that studying self-actualization, in contrast with a strategy focusing on psychological disorders (e.g., as Freud did), would produce a healthier psychology. As he put it in a famous quote, "The study of crippled, stunted, immature, and unhealthy specimens can yield only a cripple psychology. . . . The study of self-actualizing people must be the basis for a more universal science of psychology" (Maslow, 1954, p. 234). Maslow followed his own advice and examined the concept of self-actualization more closely, identifying real historical individuals who seemed to be self-actualized and then looking for commonalities among them. The work began informally with his reflections about two people that he had come to know in New York—the anthropologist Ruth Benedict and the gestalt psychologist Max Wertheimer (Chapter 9). He later reported that when studying Benedict and Wertheimer, he realized "their two patterns could be generalized. I was talking about a kind of person, not about two incomparable individuals. . . . I tried to see whether this pattern could be found elsewhere" (Maslow, 1971, pp. 41–42). It could. Through a variety of techniques, Maslow identified a number of people who seemed to share some of the attributes of Benedict and Wertheimer. Maslow found that self-actualizers perceived reality accurately, were highly independent and creative, were spontaneous and natural around others, thought of their work as a career or a calling rather than a job, had a strong moral code, and would occasionally have moments of intense enjoyment or satisfaction that Maslow called **peak experiences**. Maslow's work, and his unceasing optimism about the possibilities for human existence, foreshadowed today's *positive psychology*, a movement that emphasizes mental health rather than mental illness and examines such topics as happiness, optimism, and creativity.

Carl Rogers and Client-Centered Therapy

Humanistic psychology's second memorable character was Carl Rogers (1902–1987), the creator of **client-centered therapy**, an approach that appealed to a large number of clinicians in the 1960s and 1970s. Rogers

---

[3]Maslow influenced a number of students. One whose career he definitely affected was Elliot Aronson, a prominent social psychologist who was a doctoral student of Leon Festinger (featured in Chapter 14). As an undergraduate at Brandeis University, Aronson wandered into an introductory psychology lecture on prejudice being given by Maslow. The topic caught the attention of Aronson, who had been on the receiving end of the behavioral products of prejudice while growing up as a Jewish child in the tough working-class town of Revere, Massachusetts. Aronson immediately changed his major to psychology and developed a close and lasting friendship with Maslow. Aronson earned the APA's Award for Distinguished Scientific Contribution to psychology in 1999.

FIGURE 13.7 Carl Rogers, creator of client-centered therapy.

(Figure 13.7) was the product of a highly controlled environment, but he managed to build a career of his own despite his early experiences. The fourth of six children, he was raised in a Chicago suburb in an extremely conservative Protestant family that valued hard work and considered all pleasures sinful. As Rogers (1961b) later recalled, "Even carbonated beverages had a faintly sinful aroma, and I remember my slight feeling of wickedness when I had my first bottle of 'pop'" (p. 5). When Rogers was 12, his father moved the family to a Wisconsin farm, in part to remove his children from the evils of suburbia. He was determined to run the farm according to the principles of "scientific agriculture," and Carl developed a keen appreciation for science out of the experience. It led him to enroll in the college of agriculture at the University of Wisconsin, but the enthusiasm soon faded as the sheltered young man discovered a bright new world of people and ideas. He switched to studying history and, determined to be a minister, entered New York's Union Theological Seminary after graduating from Wisconsin in 1924. The theology students at Union were encouraged to think for themselves, and Rogers (1961b) "thought [himself] right out of religious work" (p. 8) and into psychology.

Rogers began taking courses across the street from Union at Columbia's Teachers College, where he came under the influence of Leta Hollingworth (Chapter 8—Close-Up). She sparked his interest in doing child guidance work, and he began for the first time to think about being a professional psychologist. He completed an internship at the Freudian-based Institute for Child Guidance in New York, where he gained some insights about unconscious processes but developed a distaste for psychoanalysis. He earned a doctorate from Columbia in 1931. Rogers then took a position as a staff psychologist at a child guidance clinic in Rochester, New York, where he began developing his unique brand of therapy. Professionally, he attended APA meetings, but he found them "full of papers on the learning processes of rats and laboratory experiments which seemed . . . to have no relation to what [he] was doing" (Rogers, 1961b, p. 12). When the American Association for Applied Psychology (AAAP) formed in 1937, he became an active member, and in 1939 he advocated a training model for clinicians that reduced the heavy emphasis on research and enhanced the opportunities for supervised practice in the craft of diagnosis and therapy. Academia ignored his proposal, but the idea was in essence identical to the one that emerged 30 years later at the University of Illinois in the form of the PsyD degree (Napoli, 1981).

Rogers entered academia himself in 1940, accepting a position at Ohio State University. There the stimulus provided by critically thinking graduate students sharpened his ideas about therapy and personality and resulted in his first book, *Counseling and Psychotherapy* (Rogers, 1942). Rogers went to the University of Chicago as a professor of psychology and director of the counseling center in 1945. In the following year, he was elected president of the APA; Rogers was the second president following the big postwar reorganization, and his election was a clear sign to research-oriented academicians that the APA had begun to shift in the practitioner direction. Rogers spent 12 years at Chicago and then 4 back at Wisconsin, where he had a joint appointment in psychology and psychiatry. The Wisconsin years were not happy ones—his client-centered therapy had come under attack as being relevant only for articulate people with mild problems, and Rogers wanted to show that more seriously disturbed clients could benefit as well. He launched an ambitious project to apply the therapy to schizophrenic patients at a local hospital, but the results were at best "equivocal" (Lakin, 1996). That outcome, combined with a cool reception from the experimentally oriented psychology department at Wisconsin, led Rogers to look for greener pastures. He found them in California in 1961, where he joined the staff at the Western Behavioral Sciences Institute at La Jolla. Several years later, he founded the Center for the Study of the Person in La Jolla, where he extended his client-centered therapy to a group therapy setting.

The essence of Rogers' client-centered therapy is not difficult to grasp. Consistent with one of humanistic psychology's cornerstone ideas, Rogers rejected the notion that it was important to delve into the client's past history for therapy to be effective. Rather, the formula for success was for the therapist to create the right kind of therapeutic environment; this, in turn, would allow the client to be able to take control of his or her life and begin to grow in the direction of self-actualization. This ideal therapeutic atmosphere included three fundamental components. First, the therapist must be "genuine" and honest with the client (Rogers avoided the word *patient*, with its medical overtones). As Rogers put it:

> This means that I need to be aware of my own feelings . . . rather than presenting an
> outward facade of one attitude, while actually holding another attitude at a
> deeper . . . level. Being genuine also involves the willingness to be and to express, in my
> words and my behavior, the various feelings and attitudes which exist in me. (Rogers,
> 1961a, p. 33)

Although Rogers didn't say it here, this genuineness also enables the therapist to act as a model for the kind of emotional health being sought in the client. Second, Rogers believed that the therapist must accept the client as a person, meaning "a warm regard for him as a person of unconditional worth—of value no matter what his condition, his behavior, or his feelings" (p. 34). This means accepting a person as having value simply by virtue of being a human being.

The third component of an effective therapist–client relationship is **empathy**, and it follows from the humanistic philosophy proposing that reality is the reality as perceived and experienced by a person. Hence, understanding someone else requires trying to understand how that person views things. Rogers recognized that completely understanding another person was impossible, but it was the effort that counted. This effort included a technique developed by Rogers called **reflection**. It meant taking something said by the client and rephrasing it in a way that leads the client to think, "This therapist understands what I'm saying."

If the therapist succeeded in establishing the proper therapeutic environment, good things would happen, according to Rogers. That is, the client "shows fewer of the characteristics which are usually termed neurotic or psychotic, and more of the characteristics of a healthy, well-functioning person" (Rogers, 1961a, p. 36). One final point is that Rogers believed that what he had to say about the therapeutic environment applied to *all* human relationships:

> Thus it seems reasonable to hypothesize that if the parent creates with his child a psychological climate such as we have described, then the child will become more self-directing, socialized, and mature. To the extent that the teacher creates such a relationship with his class, the student will become a self-initiated learner, more original, more self-disciplined, less anxious and other-directed. If the administrator, or military or industrial leader, creates such a climate within his organization, then his staff will become more self-responsible, more creative, better able to adapt to new problems, more . . . cooperative. (p. 37)

As an alternative to Freudian-based insight therapies, in which the therapist played the controlling role, client-centered therapy quickly became popular among clinical psychologists and counselors. In contrast with analytic approaches, it was easier to grasp conceptually and it actually seemed to help people. It was also based on a more optimistic assessment of human potential for change, reflecting Rogers's own ability to take control of his life and a general Midwestern faith that things can be improved if one works hard enough. Also, Rogers was able demonstrate the therapy's effectiveness. Perhaps stemming from his earlier experiences with scientific agriculture, Rogers took great pleasure in completing empirical research on therapy outcomes, complete with comparisons between those in treatment and those in waiting list control groups. He was able to show that his approach brought about measurable, positive changes in people's lives (e.g., Rogers, 1954).

Humanistic psychology enjoyed a period of great popularity in the 1960s and 1970s. A *Journal of Humanistic Psychology* was started in 1961, largely through Maslow's efforts; the American Association of Humanistic Psychologists was created a year later; Maslow was elected APA president in 1968; and the APA created a division for humanistic psychology (Division 32) in 1972. That it was popular during this period of American history is no surprise. As a rebellion against the forces of psychoanalysis and behaviorism, it fit well into the context of a time marked by numerous challenges to existing authority in the wider American culture. And as a philosophy centered on the individual person (e.g., *self*-actualization), it was consistent with some of the values of the 1970s, a period sometimes referred to as the "Me Decade" (Schulman, 2001). Despite its popularity, however, the humanistic movement has always been on the fringe of psychology. It has been faulted for overemphasizing the self at the expense of the importance of the community and for being clearer about what it was against than what it proposed as an alternative (e.g., Farson, 1978; Wertheimer, 1978). Nonetheless, it has had an important impact on the clinical practice of psychology, especially through the work of Rogers, and it provided some of the inspiration for today's *positive psychology* movement.

The Vail Conference and the PsyD Degree

Before leaving this section of the chapter on clinical psychology, it is worth noting how the Boulder model fared over the years and how a significant alternative to it developed. As you recall, the Boulder model was designed to produce a synthesis of scientist and practitioner, someone able to conduct high-quality research as well as be an effective clinician. Although the model continues to be the main approach to training, it is not clear that it always reached its ideal. In their analysis of Boulder's first 50 years, for example, Benjamin and Baker (2000) reported that it "is a model that has been much praised, much maligned, and according to some, rarely if ever tried" (p. 233). What were the problems?

First, because academic departments of psychology controlled the clinical training programs, in many cases the scientist side of the training received much greater emphasis than the practitioner side, despite Shakow's vision of a 50-50 split between research and practice training (Cautin, 2006). By the late 1950s, many PhD clinicians were complaining that they were unprepared for the actual practice of psychology and, because they were working in clinical settings for the most part, and not in academia, they were not getting much use out of their research skills. A second and related problem was that professors of clinical psychology, according to the Boulder recommendations, were expected to "maintain their clinical skills by continuing some clinical practice" (Raimy, 1950, p. 130). Most did so, but only to a limited extent. In the academic environment, professors of clinical psychology were under the usual pressure to publish, and that made it difficult for them to maintain their clinical skills. As a result, graduate students did not always get the best training in how to do clinical work. Many departments took the attitude that students would develop all the needed clinical skills when they did their yearlong internship, but the original Boulder model made it clear that training in clinical practice should occur throughout the 4- to 5-year program and that the internship should not be seen as a "repair shop" for a prior lack of experience (Stricker & Cummings, 1992).

Criticisms of the Boulder model led to considerations of an alternative, one that emphasized the practice of clinical psychology more than research. It was an idea that preceded Boulder. For example, in the mid-1920s, Crane (1925) wrote an article called "A Plea for the Training of Psychologists." Writing at a time when there were *no* doctoral training programs for clinical psychologists (Capshew, 1999), Crane argued that the typical PhD training in psychology, with its emphasis on basic research in traditional topic areas (e.g., perception, learning), was inappropriate. Instead, aspiring clinicians ought to be given much more instruction in the actual practice of psychology, and Crane suggested the creation of a new kind of degree that he called a "Doctor of Psychology" degree (Peterson, 1992). At that time, however, clinical psychologists had little status, so the proposal went nowhere. The same was true for a similar idea, mentioned earlier, and floated by Carl Rogers in 1939.

By the 1960s, however, dissatisfaction with the Boulder model was beginning to produce new proposals for the way in which clinicians should learn their craft. And the general atmosphere of dissent that permeated the 1960s led to several attempts to create a new direction for training. First, an APA committee on training recommended, in 1967, that alternatives to the scientist–practitioner model be explored, including one that would accentuate clinical practice and lead to a new degree, a doctor of psychology, or **PsyD**, degree. Second, the University of Illinois decided to implement the recommendation, thereby creating, in 1968, the first university-based PsyD program in the United States. The prestige of the

University of Illinois immediately gave the PsyD some respectability, and other universities soon began developing similar programs. Third, PsyD programs began developing at free-standing schools of professional psychology, not affiliated with universities. The first one was created in California—the California School of Professional Psychology. It opened with two campuses (San Francisco and Los Angeles) in 1970, and added two more (San Diego and Fresno) 2 years later.

Just as the need for training guidelines for the new postwar clinical psychologist led to the Boulder conference in 1949, the need for some degree of standardization in the training of the new PsyD clinician led to its own conference, held at Vail, Colorado, in 1973. The goal of the Vail conference was to legitimize the PsyD degree and provide a clear distinction between it and programs yielding a PhD in psychology. In essence, the PhD was designed to produce the traditional scientist–practitioner while the PsyD produced a practitioner-scientist who was knowledgeable about research but primarily trained to deliver psychological services. It took some time for PsyD programs to attain perceived legitimacy, and for many Boulder model clinicians, the quality of PsyD training remains an issue. PhD programs are considerably more selective, for instance; they typically accept about 10% of applicants, compared with up to 50% for PsyD programs (Norcross, Castle, Sayette, & Mayne, 2004). The APA provides full accreditation for both PhD Boulder model programs and PsyD Vail model programs, however.

A major part of the postwar story of clinical psychology has been its increased status in the community of mental health care providers. As you recall from Chapter 12, clinical psychologists before World War II had relatively low standing among health care professionals and were often under the direct supervision of psychiatrists. Since the war, however, organized psychiatry's hegemony has gradually diminished. Over the past half century, sometimes after intense legal battles, clinical psychologists have gained the rights to (a) admit and release patients from mental hospitals, (b) serve as expert witnesses in court (e.g., insanity and child custody cases), and (c) receive third-party payments from insurance companies. Today, organized psychology and psychiatry are skirmishing over prescription privileges, and a few states (e.g., New Mexico) already allow clinical psychologists to prescribe medicine. There is every indication that before too long, this major distinction between psychiatrists and clinical psychologists will disappear (Wiggins, 1994).

PSYCHOLOGY AND THE WORLD OF BUSINESS AND INDUSTRY

We have already seen (Chapter 8) that it did not take psychology long to become involved in the business world. Soon after the turn of the 20th century, Walter Dill Scott was writing on the application of psychology to advertising and how business could be made more efficient; Hugo Münsterberg was doing the consulting work that would produce his *Psychology and Industrial Efficiency* (1913); Walter Bingham was creating his Division of Applied Psychology at the Carnegie Institute in Pittsburgh and consulting with local businesses; the Gilbreths were establishing their successful industrial consulting business; and the Hollingworths were discovering that Coca-Cola could keep one awake at night.

During the 1920s, a period of growth, prosperity, and optimism in America (until the stock market crashed in 1929), these kinds of activities increased significantly. Following the highly visible Army testing program in World War I (Chapter 8), psychologists began developing tests as quickly as they could be printed, for applications in education as well as business. Numerous businesses and industries hired psychologists to revamp their personnel departments, primarily by developing tests for the selection and evaluation of workers. Many of these efforts produced tests of questionable quality and prompted Anne Anastasi, author of a legendary textbook on psychological testing (Anastasi, 1954), to conclude that the "testing boom of the 1920s probably did more to retard than to advance the progress of testing" (1993, p. 17). Problems with reliability and validity didn't slow the momentum of the testing boom until the late 1920s, and the apparent success of the enterprise spawned a new development in the 1920s—companies designed to provide psychological consulting services.

Walter Dill Scott created the first one, the Scott Company (see Figure 13.8), shortly after the end of World War I; it only lasted a few years, partly because Scott's leadership disappeared when he was named president of Northwestern University in 1920. A second attempt, although it floundered initially, was the Psychological Corporation. It was the brainchild of James McKeen Cattell, who, as you recall from earlier discussions (Chapters 4 and 8), was a doctoral student of Wundt, a promoter of the failed Galtonian approach to mental testing, and chair of the psychology department at Columbia when it became a leading graduate school in psychology (two of his students were Thorndike and Woodworth). In the early 1920s, Cattell no longer worked in academia, having been fired from Columbia for his antiwar views. He continued as editor-in-chief of the journal *Science*, but he was looking for a way to return to prominence among fellow psychologists. He was also concerned about the growing number of people fraudulently claiming expertise in psychology and cashing in on the widespread interest in psychological testing (Sokal, 1981b). His idea for the company was to create a nationwide network of PhD psychologists with recognized expertise in testing and experimental methodology. The Psychological Corporation would be a central

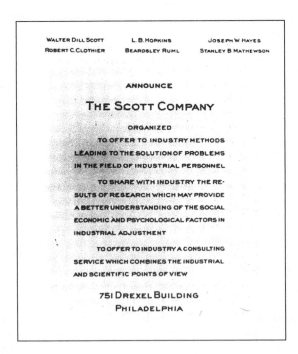

FIGURE 13.8 Announcement of the formation of the Scott Company, the first consulting company for business organized by psychologists.

clearinghouse—a business in St. Louis, for instance, in need of psychological assessment in its personnel department, would contact the Psychological Corporation in New York (or one of its planned branch offices) and would be referred to a local expert psychologist who had signed on with the Corporation. The psychologist would perform the service and collect a fee, half of which went back to the Corporation.

The Psychological Corporation began in 1921 with Cattell as its first president. It was a fine idea in principle, but almost immediately it ran into difficulty, primarily because of Cattell's leadership style. He was never very clear about precisely what services would be offered, thus making businesses hesitant to sign contracts. And he did not have a good head for business. As late as 1925, for instance, the Corporation's net income was $51.75 while renting offices in a prime New York location and paying $2,500 to the person in charge of day-to-day operations. To keep the operation afloat, Cattell had to contribute $5,000 of his own money (Sokal, 1981b). This wouldn't do—in 1926, Cattell was ousted by his board of directors. The new president was Walter Van Dyke Bingham, who had better connections in the business world because of his experiences running the applied psychology operation at the Carnegie Institute in Pittsburgh (Chapter 8). Like most businesses, the Psychological Corporation suffered during the Great Depression; but it survived and then flourished, especially after World War II. In 1969, when a publishing house purchased the corporation, it was worth $2.5 million in total assets and was selling about $5 million in psychological tests per year (Sokal, 1981b). It continues to be successful today.

The field of industrial psychology achieved an increase in perceived legitimacy with the publication of a large and important textbook with the simple title of *Industrial Psychology* (1932). Morris Viteles, Lightner Witmer's best-known doctoral student, wrote it. Viteles took his degree with Witmer at the University of Pennsylvania in 1921, completing a study (reminiscent of Münsterberg) on competency testing for streetcar employees (McReynolds, 1997). Two years later, Witmer named Viteles director of a new branch of the Psychological Clinic, called the Vocational Guidance Clinic. It offered testing and consulting services to businesses, but it was primarily for the purpose of helping high school and college students prepare for and enter the world of work. Viteles spent the rest of his career at the clinic while also working as a consultant to various businesses and industries in the Philadelphia area. His consulting work went far beyond the typical employee selection realm—Viteles conducted valuable studies on safety and accident prevention for the Yellow Cab Company, and he developed a program for the Bell Telephone Company to help managers develop leadership skills and participate more effectively in corporate decision making (Hilgard, 1987).

The Hawthorne Studies

An important event in the 1920s was the start of a series of applied research experiments that stretched into the 1930s. The research led to the naming of an effect that was (supposedly) demonstrated over and over in the studies and that today appears regularly in textbooks in industrial psychology, social psychology, and research methodology—the Hawthorne effect. The name derives from the Illinois city where the research occurred, the home of the Western Electric Plant. The plant manufactured communication equipment for the American Telephone and Telegraph Company (AT&T).

The experiments at Hawthorne began in 1924 with a series of studies, extending over 3 years, to examine the effects of lighting on worker productivity. The studies were sponsored in part by the electrical industry, which hoped to find evidence for its belief that there was a simple correlation between lighting and productivity—the more light in the workspace, the higher the productivity (Gillespie, 1991). Evidence for this, of course, would help sell light bulbs. Unfortunately for the industry, however, the research failed to show any consistent relationship between lighting and work output. Productivity remained about the same, regardless of lighting level, even when the lighting was poor. We now know that productivity is highly complex, influenced by a variety of factors. But at Hawthorne the outcome of the lighting study was the conclusion that the physical environment was not as important for productivity as the "human factor." Workers knew they were in a study and that the results were important, so their productivity remained high because they felt valued. At least that is the standard interpretation. What was not mentioned was that several other factors surely contributed to the high level of productivity—for instance, the level of direct supervision was increased during the lighting experiments (Gillespie, 1991).

The findings of the illumination experiments were confirmed and then some—or at least that is the standard line—in the most famous of the Hawthorne studies, the Relay Assembly Test Room (RATR) studies. In this experiment, six female workers were selected from a larger group in the plant. Their job was to assemble electrical relays for telephones. Five workers did the actual assembly, and the sixth kept them supplied with parts. Figure 13.9 shows the workroom from two angles. The assembly was a time-consuming, labor-intensive, repetitive job, requiring the assembly of some 35 parts per relay. Western Electric produced about 7 million relays a year (Gillespie, 1988), so naturally the firm wished to maximize worker productivity.

The first relay studies extended from May 1927 through September 1928. During that time, several workplace variables were studied. At various times there were changes in the scheduling of rest periods, total hours of work, and bonuses paid for certain levels of production. The standard account, similar to the outcome for the lighting studies, has it that productivity for this small group quickly reached high levels and stayed there even when working conditions were worsened. The example always mentioned concerned the infamous

FIGURE 13.9 The working arrangements in the Relay Assembly Test Room experiment at the Hawthorne plant. On the left can be seen the chutes that took the completed relays and counted them. On the right is the room as the workers saw it.

"12th test period" when workers were informed that the work week would increase from 42 to 48 hours per week, and that rest periods and free lunches would be discontinued (Gillespie, 1988). Virtually all research methods textbooks describe the results somewhat like this:

> With few exceptions, no matter what changes were made—whether there were many or few rest periods, whether the workday was made longer or shorter, and so on—the women tended to produce more and more telephone relays. (Elmes, Kantowitz, & Roediger, 2003, p. 138)

Supposedly, the workers remained productive because they believed they were a special group and the focus of attention—they were part of an experiment. This, along with the similar outcome of the lighting studies, is the origin of the concept called the **Hawthorne effect**, the tendency for performance to be affected because people know they are being studied in a research project.

The effect may be genuine in a research context, but whether it happened at Western Electric is uncertain. A close look at what actually happened reveals some interesting alternative explanations. First, although accounts of the RATR study typically emphasize how delighted the women were to be in this special testing room, the fact is that of the five original assemblers, two had to be removed from the room for insubordination and low output. One was said to have "gone Bolshevik" (Bramel & Friend, 1981). Remember, the Soviet Union was brand new then; the "red menace" was a threat to industrial America, resulting in things like a fear of labor unions by those in management. Of the two replacement workers, one was especially talented and enthusiastic and quickly became the group leader. She apparently was selected because she "held the record as the fastest relay-assembler in the regular department" (Gillespie, 1988, p. 122). Her efforts contributed greatly to the high level of productivity.

A second problem with interpreting the relay data is a simple statistical problem. In the famous 12th period, productivity was recorded as output per week rather than output per hour, yet workers were putting in an extra 6 hours per week compared to the previous test period. If the more appropriate output per hour is used, productivity actually *declined* slightly (Bramel & Friend, 1981). Also, the women were apparently angry about the change but afraid to complain lest they be removed from the test room, thereby losing bonus money (they got some not-so-subtle hints that such an outcome could occur if they failed to perform well). Last, it could have been that in the RATR, as well as in some of the other Hawthorne experiments, increased worker productivity could have been simply the result of feedback about performance, along with concrete rewards for productivity (Parsons, 1974).

As you know by now, historical events must be understood within their entire political, economic, and institutional context, and the Hawthorne studies are no exception. Painting a glossy picture of workers unaffected by specific working conditions and more concerned with being considered special ushered in a human relations movement in industry and led corporations to emphasize the humane management of employees to create the impression of one big happy family of labor and management. Paying attention to the well-being of workers was a significant advance, in the context of the long history of workers' needs being ignored by management. However, such a picture also helps maintain power at the level of management and impede efforts at unionization, which some historians (e.g., Bramel & Friend, 1981) believe were among the true motives behind the studies completed at Western Electric.

RESEARCHERS AND PRACTITIONERS

At the start of this chapter, after the discussion of Witmer, you learned about the first hints of a professional identity for clinical psychologists. They formed the short-lived American Association of Clinical Psychologists in 1917, then had a "section" created for them in the APA, and in 1937 joined other applied psychologists in forming a vigorous association, the American Association for Applied Psychology (AAAP). Near the end of World War II, they played a major role in the reorganization (recreation, actually) of APA. The new APA would no longer focus only on science; it would now have the additional stated goals of advancing psychology as a profession and promoting human welfare (Hilgard, 1987). Before World War II, academic psychology had dominated the APA; after the war, the power began to shift, and a turning point occurred in 1962, when psychologists working in nonacademic jobs outnumbered those working in colleges and universities for the first time (Tryon, 1963).

For research psychologists working in an academic environment, this shift represented a big change from the prewar years, when they held all the power, and the change was not a welcome one. But this was not the first time that academic–research psychologists had been unhappy with the APA. As early as 1898, none other than Lightner Witmer, at that time more interested in research than in his fledgling clinic, had proposed that researchers split from APA to form their own organization. G. Stanley Hall described the idea to Titchener this way:

> A line from Witmer says that he wants to join you, me, and others in forming a new Psychological organization which shall put the lab on a proper basis and exclude half-breeds and extremists. Do you want to consider it? (quoted in Goodwin, 1985, p. 386)

Witmer's revolt went nowhere, but as you know from Chapter 7, Titchener formed his "Experimentalists" group soon thereafter (in 1904). It evolved into the Society of Experimental Psychologists after Titchener's death in 1927 and continues to this day as an honorary society for distinguished psychological scientists (Goodwin, 2005).

Even before practitioners outnumbered researcher-academicians in 1962, the latter group had become distressed about the direction the reorganized APA was taking. They were especially concerned about the makeup of the annual meeting, which, after the war, seemed to be increasingly devoted to practice issues and was structured in a way that made presentation of research difficult. As one small example, in 1959 the APA decided not to allow slides to be shown during any of the presentations; this move infuriated experimentalists, who were accustomed to using slides to present their data (Dewsbury & Bolles, 1995). This seemingly trivial incident helped bring about a major defection of experimental psychologists, who formed the Psychonomic Society near the end of the 1950s. It held its first meeting in 1960, devoted to the presentation of research (including slides), and it continues today as an important organization for experimentalists.

Most members of the Psychonomic Society remained members of APA as well, and they continued to agitate for conditions favorable to the researcher-academician. APA, however, kept shifting its resources toward the practice of psychology and focused much of its energy on issues relevant for practitioners (e.g., whether clinical psychologists should gain the legal right to prescribe medicine). Researchers agitated for a new reorganization of APA in the mid-1980s that would restore some of their status, and when the effort failed, a group of prominent experimental psychologists banded together and formed the American Psychological Society (APS). Membership reached more than 5,000 within the first 6 months, indicating that the group had struck a chord, and APS quickly became a strong advocate for psychological research, created a group of high-quality journals (e.g., *Psychological Science*), and developed an annual convention entirely devoted to research. When it celebrated its 15th anniversary in 2003, it had reached a membership of just over 13,500. In 2006, the group retained its acronym but brought its mission into clearer focus by changing its name to the Association for Psychological Science.

This researcher–practitioner split, reflected in the histories of APA and APS, can easily be overstated. Many APS members also belong to APA; APA has a vigorous "Science Directorate"; most of the APA journals are devoted to research; and in 2001, APS launched a new journal, *Psychological Science in the Public Interest*, that includes research-based articles on topics of relevance for the practice of psychology. Yet the division between researcher-academicians and practitioners is a real one, representing different value systems and different interests. Gaining a clear understanding of psychology in the 21st century requires knowing about this division and its history.

IN PERSPECTIVE: PSYCHOLOGISTS AS PRACTITIONERS

We have seen that World War II was responsible for the creation of modern clinical psychology. The war also provided an impetus to other areas of applied psychology. As was the case during the first world conflict, psychologists were heavily involved in developing tests for such tasks as the selection of officers and the placement of soldiers into military jobs that suited them. The first war produced Army Alpha and Beta; the second war produced a much more sophisticated test, the Army General Classification Test (AGCT). It graded soldiers into five ability levels, had adequate reliability as a test, and had a degree of validity in that it correlated reasonably well with educational level (Capshew, 1999). The war also gave a boost to applied psychologists whose work examined the relationship between humans and machines, and the war produced a new specialty within psychology—**engineering psychology**. This field has as its goals the creation of machines that were designed for efficient human use. A well-engineered airplane cockpit, for example, has seats that reduce fatigue and instruments that avoid perceptual errors. As you recall from Chapter 8, an important pioneer in this field was Lillian Gilbreth.

The focus of this chapter has been on the application of psychology to the diagnosis and treatment of those with mental and behavioral disorders (clinical psychology) and the use of psychological principles to improve business (industrial psychology). It is important to note that applied psychology extends to other areas that have not been a part of this chapter, however. These include counseling, school, forensic, and educational psychology. A good historical analysis of these other applied areas can be found in Ludy Benjamin and David Baker's *From Séance to Science: A History of the Profession of Psychology in America* (2004).

The reorganization of the APA ushered in a period of tremendous growth for psychology in America. Applied psychology was the beneficiary of APA's new charter, which added advancing psychology as a profession to its original goal of advancing the science of psychology. As you now know, one outcome was a growing feeling of alienation among the scientists in APA. But the scientific side of psychology also prospered in the years after World War II, especially in the form of a major postwar movement called cognitive psychology. The story of cognitive psychology's postwar ascendance, along with discussion of other important historical landmarks in scientific psychology during this time, is told in the next chapter.

SUMMARY

Clinical Psychology before World War II

• Lightner Witmer is usually credited with establishing, in 1896, the first clinic for the treatment of psychological disorders in the United States. His clinic focused on "psycho-educational" problems similar to those encountered by modern school psychologists—physiological, cognitive, and behavioral problems related to school performance. He believed that the problems he studied could be cured, and he called his treatment program orthogenics.

• Before World War II, clinical psychologists for the most part provided mental testing services and did not have high status either in clinical settings, which were dominated by psychiatrists, or in the APA, which was controlled by academics. The American Association for Applied Psychology was formed in 1937 as a way of professionalizing the practice of psychology. The APA reorganized at the close of World War II and expanded its mission, beyond science, to include the professional practice of psychology.

The Emergence of Modern Clinical Psychology

• A Modern clinical psychology emerged from the terrible necessity of World War II. Psychiatry, up to then in control of treatment for mental illness, could not keep up with the caseload. Shortly after the war, a conference on the training of clinical psychologists was held at Boulder under the leadership of David Shakow. The outcome was a training model featuring a combination of scientific expertise along with expertise in the diagnosis and treatment of mental disorders. The clinical psychologist earned a PhD degree and had to complete a research-based doctoral dissertation.

• A study by Eysenck in 1952 questioned the effectiveness of traditional insight forms of psychotherapy (e.g., Freudian psychoanalysis) and focused attention on the need for high-quality research on therapy effectiveness. It led to the development of several new approaches to therapy, most notably behavior therapy and a variety of humanistic therapies.

• A controversial medical strategy for treating mental illness, the leucotomy (or lobotomy), was created in the 1930s by Egas Moniz. The procedure was based on the idea that severing the connections between the frontal lobe and lower brain centers would enable the person to exert better control over emotions. Walter Freeman developed a more efficient but controversial procedure, the transorbital lobotomy, by entering the brain through the eye socket. The procedure fell out of favor in the 1950s—it had limited effectiveness, it was sometimes used for questionable reasons, and better forms of treatment (drugs) appeared.

• Behavior therapy is based on the idea that many of life's problems are the result of learning and that experiences influence the kinds of disorders that develop. Therapies based on behaviorist principles existed well before World War II; after the war they came into their own, especially with the work of Joseph Wolpe, who developed a form of therapy called systematic desensitization.

• Humanistic psychology is sometimes called psychology's "third force," because it rejected the determinism of psychoanalysis and behaviorism and proposed that humans are free to develop and control their own lives, rather than being tied to their past. Humanistic psychologists believe that all humans have the potential for personal growth and self-actualization, a concept investigated by Abraham Maslow, who studied real-life exemplars of self-actualized people (e.g., Max Wertheimer). Self-actualizers perceive reality accurately; are independent, creative, spontaneous, moral, and natural; are devoted to a career; and have occasional peak experiences.

• Carl Rogers rejected traditional psychotherapy and developed a humanistic approach to treatment. The emphasis in client-centered therapy is on positive growth in a client, said to occur if the therapeutic atmosphere is healthy. The therapist's job is to create this atmosphere, which includes being a model of the self-actualized person ("genuine"), showing unconditional positive regard for the client, and displaying empathy. The therapeutic technique of reflection is designed to aid the process.

- In 1973, the Vail conference produced a new training model for clinicians, one that focused more on practice than on research and did not necessarily require a research-based dissertation. It resulted in a PsyD degree (doctorate of psychology) rather than the traditional PhD Today, APA accredits programs based on both the Boulder and the Vail model.

Psychology and the World of Business and Industry

- During the 1920s, many psychologists worked as consultants to business and industry, a development fueled in part by the great interest in testing in the 1920s. Psychologists also joined together to form consulting businesses that would provide a range of services. The Scott Company was the first, but it did not survive the 1920s. The Psychological Corporation, under the wayward leadership of James McKeen Cattell, did survive, and it eventually prospered, but not until Cattell was ousted.

- The Hawthorne studies, extending from 1924 to 1933, have traditionally been seen as providing evidence that productivity will be high if workers are cared for and given healthy work conditions. Productivity did not seem to be affected by such things as lighting conditions and changes in work breaks; what seemed to matter was that workers felt important because they were part of an experiment (i.e., the traditional Hawthorne effect). Historians have shown, however, that the traditional version of what happened at Hawthorne is questionable and that the Hawthorne studies had the effect of maintaining management control over the workplace.

- World War II contributed to the creation and growth of engineering psychology—a form of applied experimental psychology that examines the relationship between humans and machines, the goal being the development of machines that humans can use efficiently, comfortably, and safely.

Researchers and Practitioners

- One result of the reorganization of the APA in 1945 was increased visibility for professional practitioners of psychology. This did not sit well with academic psychologists, whose primary activities were teaching and research, and who had controlled the APA in the years between world wars.

- Believing the APA was becoming too focused on professional practice, psychological scientists formed the Psychonomic Society in 1960; in 1988, they formed the American Psychological Society (APS), which was renamed the Association for Psychological Science in 2006.

STUDY QUESTIONS

1. Lightner Witmer is sometimes considered the founder of clinical psychology in America. What is the basis for the claim? Why could he be considered the founder of school psychology instead?

2. Describe the typical work done by a clinician in the period before World War II.

3. How did the activities of clinical psychologists after World War II differ from their activities before the war? What brought about the change?

4. Compare the two major training models for clinicians. What were the problems with the Boulder model that led to the creation of the Vail model?

5. What was the scientific basis for the development of the lobotomy, and how did Freeman alter the procedure invented by Moniz? Why did lobotomies more or less disappear after the mid-1950s?

6. What did Hans Eysenck find in his analysis of studies that evaluated psychotherapy? What was the impact of the Eysenck study?

7. Describe Wolpe's systematic desensitization and show how it relates to behaviorist principles.

8. Why is humanistic psychology sometimes referred to as psychology's "third force"?

9. Briefly summarize the basic beliefs of humanistic psychologists.

10. Describe Maslow's work with self-actualization. What did he conclude were the attributes of a self-actualized person?

11. Describe the three necessary conditions for therapy to be effective, according to Rogers.

12. Describe the therapy technique of reflection, as used by Rogers, and explain its purpose.

13. In addition to creating client-centered therapy, Rogers is also known for being interested in research on therapy effectiveness. Explain how his personal history might have contributed to that interest.

14. Humanistic psychology was popular in the 1960s and 1970s but then faded. Explain.

15. Describe the origins of the Psychological Corporation, how it was designed to operate, and what happened to it.

16. What did Morris Viteles contribute to industrial psychology in the 1920s and 1930s?

17. What was the original purpose of the relay assembly test room at Hawthorne, what was the outcome, and what is the traditional interpretation of the results? What really happened in the relay assembly test room?

18. The Hawthorne studies were said to show that relationships with workers were the key to productivity, but historians have interpreted the Hawthorne studies differently. Explain.

19. What is the nature of the division between researcher-academicians and practitioners? What effect did the reorganization of APA have?

20. Describe the essential conflict between scientists and practitioners that led to the creation of the Psychonomic Society and the APS.

FOR FURTHER READING

GILLESPIE, R. (1991). *Manufacturing knowledge: A history of the Hawthorne experiments.* New York: Cambridge University Press.
A comprehensive description and analysis of all the Hawthorne studies, which extended from 1924 to 1933; shows how the results have been interpreted in ways congenial to the human relations movement in business, but that a close analysis questions the traditional interpretation of the so-called Hawthorne effect; a briefer analysis can be found in Gillespie (1988).

History of psychology: The Boulder conference. (2000). *American Psychologist*, *55*, 233–254.
A set of articles commemorating the 50th anniversary of the creation of the Boulder scientist-practitioner model for the training of clinical psychologists; includes articles on clinical training before Boulder, the impact of the Boulder conference, and a series of brief reflections on Boulder.

McREYNOLDS, P. (1997). *Lightner Witmer: His life and times.* Washington, DC: American Psychological Association.
The definitive biography of Witmer; includes detailed descriptions of the work of his clinic and the early cases that he treated, and covers the expansion of the clinic in later years.

ROGERS, C. R. (1961). *On becoming a person.* Boston: Houghton Mifflin.
A set of articles written and compiled by Rogers; includes an opening autobiographical essay, several essays on his basic philosophy, articles on therapy outcome research, and articles on client-centered therapy.

SOKAL, M. M. (1981). The origins of the Psychological Corporation. *Journal of the History of the Behavioral Sciences*, *17*, 54–67.
Describes the uneasy beginnings of one of psychology's most successful applied ventures; shows how Cattell's 19th-century vision of psychology made it impossible for him to lead effectively and fits the story nicely into the context of America in the 1920s and 1930s.

CHAPTER 14

PSYCHOLOGICAL SCIENCE IN THE POSTWAR ERA

The basic reason for studying cognitive processes has become as clear as the reason for studying anything else: because they are there.... Cognitive processes surely exist, so it can hardly be unscientific to study them.

—Ulric Neisser, 1967

PREVIEW AND CHAPTER OBJECTIVES

The most important development in academic psychology since World War II has been the advent and development of modern cognitive psychology. During the 1950s, and especially the 1960s, American psychologists began to shift their research and theoretical interests. Whereas in the 1930s and 1940s behaviorism and the search for basic laws of conditioning occupied the attention of most laboratory researchers, the postwar period saw a reemergence of interest in studying cognitive processes such as perception, memory, attention, imagery, and thinking. The shift was evolutionary rather than revolutionary, and not everyone joined in—behaviorists, especially Skinnerians, remained active and productive in the face of the shift toward cognitive psychology. Nonetheless, the academic psychology of 1970 was quite different from the 1950 version. Most of this chapter examines the rise of cognitive psychology and its influence on other subdisciplines of psychology.

After describing the evolution of cognitive psychology, the second half of the chapter examines five other prominent areas of research—physiological, perceptual, social, personality, and developmental psychology. For each of these specialty areas, the influence of one historically prominent researcher is highlighted—Donald Hebb, James Gibson, Leon Festinger, Gordon Allport, and Jean Piaget, respectively. After you finish this chapter, you should be able to:

▨ Describe examples of cognitive research that occurred during the era of neobehaviorism, especially the work of Sir Frederick Bartlett

▨ Describe the factors within psychology and in fields external to psychology that influenced the development of cognitive psychology

▨ Critically examine the issue of whether a "cognitive revolution" occurred in psychology

▨ Describe some of the landmark research (e.g., STM capacity) that established cognitive psychology

▨ Describe the influence of Neisser's first book on cognitive psychology and compare its emphasis with that of his second book, which advocated ecological validity

- Distinguish between cognitive psychology and cognitive science
- Critically examine the impact of cognitive psychology on psychology as a whole
- Describe the contributions of Donald Hebb to the study of the relationship between brain and behavior
- Describe the contributions of James Gibson to the study of perceptual psychology
- Describe the contributions of Leon Festinger to the study of social psychology
- Describe the contributions of Gordon Allport to the study of personality
- Describe the contributions of Jean Piaget to the study of developmental psychology

COGNITIVE PSYCHOLOGY ARRIVES (AGAIN)

When psychology began to identify itself as a separate discipline in the latter half of the 19th century, it aimed at a scientific understanding of human conscious experience; Ebbinghaus, Wundt, Külpe, Wertheimer, Titchener, and other pioneers studied such mental phenomena as memory, attention, perception, and thinking. Psychologists in America also took up these same topics, gave them a functional twist, and investigated them vigorously in the early years of the 20th century. Then Watson appeared and said that the study of mental life was unscientific and that everyone should be a behaviorist, studying the relationships between environmental stimuli and the individual's responses. Not everyone listened, of course; as we learned in Chapter 10, Watson's message took a long time to produce noteworthy effects. By the mid-1930s, however, behaviorism had become a force in American psychology, and the prototypical image of the psychology laboratory in those days included rats in mazes. After World War II, however, interests began to shift again, and the study of cognitive processes came once more to the forefront. This time the methods were different from those of Titchener's day, and the models were based on a new technological breakthrough—the computer. But the topics of interest were the same. Some psychologists began calling themselves cognitive psychologists, and a new movement, which was in a sense a return to an old one, was born. During the latter half of the 20th century, cognitive psychology became the dominant conceptual framework in American psychology.

The Roots of Modern Cognitive Psychology

Despite Watson's best efforts at promotion, American psychology did not become behaviorist overnight. Even when behaviorism was "in" among American psychologists, not everyone joined the party. In the 1920s, '30s, and '40s, the pages of the leading journals still contained numerous articles describing research on such cognitive topics as memory, perception, attention, language, and thinking. Among others, they included the famous "Stroop effect" study (Stroop, 1935/1992), which was mentioned briefly in Chapter 11, and a study by Jenkins and Dallenbach (1924) that still appears regularly in general psychology books. Their experiment examined the effect of cognitive interference on memory and showed that after studying verbal materials, recall could be improved if a period of sleep (i.e., minimal interference) intervened between study and recall. Books dealing with cognitive topics also appeared during behaviorism's heyday, even including one with the title *Cognitive Psychology* (Moore,

1939). Although its treatment of cognition was more of a look back to the earlier years of the century than a call for a new approach to cognition (Knapp, 1985), it dealt with many of the same topics that would concern cognitive psychologists two decades later. And on the theoretical front, the gestaltists (Chapter 9) promoted the study of cognition and argued with behaviorists throughout the 1930s and 1940s.

As you recall from Chapter 11, behaviorism was mostly an American phenomenon, and hence it is not surprising to learn that (a) several important European psychologists were doing cognitive work during behaviorism's glory years, and (b) most American experimental psychologists, focused intently on whether their rat was going to turn left or right at a choice point in a maze, paid little attention to this ongoing cognitive research. These Europeans included the famous Swiss developmental psychologist Jean Piaget, whose ideas about cognitive development first appeared in the 1920s (Piaget, 1923/1959) but weren't influential in the United States until the 1960s. Piaget and his work are profiled later in the chapter, in a section on research in developmental psychology. The second famous name was England's Sir Frederick Bartlett, who took memory research in a distinctly non-Ebbinghaus direction (Bartlett, 1932/1967).

Frederick C. Bartlett (1886–1969): Constructing Memory

In 1932, a brief book with the simple title of *Remembering: A Study in Experimental and Social Psychology* appeared. Its author was Frederick Bartlett, a psychologist from England's Cambridge University. In the United States, the book was ignored; an American psychologist, writing 3 years after its publication, concluded his generally dismissive review by saying that the book would "find a place upon the shelves of those who study remembering, but it will not be in the special section reserved for those investigators whose writings have become landmarks in the advance towards the comprehension of this important problem" (Jenkins, 1935, p. 715). The reviewer probably had Ebbinghaus in mind as a "landmark." Today, Bartlett's book is recognized as being equal to Ebbinghaus's in importance.

Frederick Bartlett was born and raised in the bucolic Cotswold region of England, northwest of London and near Oxford and Stratford-upon-Avon. Much of his early education was at home, and his first formal higher degree was by correspondence from London University. He then completed a more traditional undergraduate program at Saint John's College of Cambridge University in 1914. He remained at Cambridge for graduate studies and completed the research on memory as his doctoral thesis, shortly after World War I. Thus the studies described in *Remembering* were completed more than a decade before they were published (Oldfield, 1972). During the 1920s, Bartlett became head of the Psychology Laboratory at Cambridge and set about establishing one of the few centers of experimental psychology in Great Britain. He directed the laboratory until his retirement in 1952, producing, with his students, research on topics ranging from pilot fatigue to animal learning. He also adapted some of the methods used in his memory book to the study of thinking, the result being *Thinking: An Experimental and Social Study* (Bartlett, 1958b). It was the memory book that made his reputation, however.

Bartlett on Memory Bartlett opened his memory book by raising questions about the usefulness of research in the Ebbinghaus tradition, which emphasized the effects of rote repetition on memorizing highly artificial stimuli, the famous nonsense syllables.

> I endeavored, in this series of experiments, to avoid as far as possible the artificiality which hangs over laboratory experiments in psychology. I therefore discarded the use of nonsense syllables and throughout employed material a part of which, at least, might fairly be regarded as interesting and sufficiently normal. (Bartlett, 1932/1967, p. 47)

Also, in contrast with the meticulous Ebbinghaus, Bartlett described his results in narrative form, not as summary statistics, and his descriptions of methodology were often vague. As one reviewer pointed out, Bartlett's studies are better conceived of as "controlled demonstrations, rather than true experiments" (Roediger, 1997, p. 489).

Bartlett also argued that research on memory should focus more on the attributes of the memorizer and less on the nature of the stimulus materials. He believed that the memorizer, rather than passively accumulating associative strength as the result of practice and repetition, *actively* organizes the material into meaningful wholes that he referred to as **schemata** (plural form of *schema*). Bartlett defined these schemata as "active organisation[s] of past reactions, or of past experiences, which must always be supposed to be operating in any well-adapted organic response" (1932/1967, p. 201). For example, as a result of our experiences, we will develop a schema relating to the concept of death. This schema will in turn influence our current and future perceptions of death and dying and affect our memory of these experiences. People with different experiences and from different cultures will have different schemata about death.

To provide empirical support for his arguments, Bartlett developed a series of memory tasks, the most famous of which used what he called the "method of repeated reproduction." Participants were given a 328-word story to read through twice. The story was a Native American folk tale called *The War of the Ghosts*. Thus the story reflected a culture quite different from that of early 20th-century England, and the story had certain elements that would not seem to "make sense" from the standpoint of a typical Britisher. Here is the story:

> One night two young men from Egulac went down to the river to hunt seals, and while they were there it became foggy and calm. Then they heard war-cries, and they thought: "Maybe this is a war-party." They escaped to the shore, and hid behind a log. Now canoes came up, and they heard the noise of paddles, and saw one canoe coming up to them. There were five men in the canoe, and they said:
>
> "What do you think? We wish to take you along. We are going up the river to make war on the people."
>
> One of the young men said: "I have no arrows."
>
> "Arrows are in the canoe," they said.
>
> "I will not go along. I might be killed. My relatives do not know where I have gone. But you," he said, turning to the other, "may go with them."
>
> So one of the young men went, but the other returned home.
>
> And the warriors went on up the river to a town on the other side of Kalama. The people came down to the water, and they began to fight, and many were killed. But presently the young man heard one of the warriors say: "Quick, let us go home: that Indian has been hit." Now he thought: "Oh, they are ghosts." He did not feel sick, but they said he had been shot.
>
> So the canoes went back to Egulac, and the young man went ashore to his house, and made a fire. And he told everybody and said: "Behold I accompanied the ghosts, and we went to fight. Many of our fellows were killed, and many of those who attacked us were killed. They said I was hit, and I did not feel sick."

> He told it all, and then he became quiet. When the sun rose he fell down. Something black came out of his mouth. His face became contorted. The people jumped up and cried.
>
> He was dead. (Bartlett, 1932/1967, p. 65)

Unless you are a member of this particular culture, I suspect that you found the passage to be a bit odd. So did Bartlett's 20 participants (7 women, 13 men). Fifteen minutes after reading the story, they were asked to reproduce as much of it as they could. Additional reproductions were elicited at later intervals ranging from hours to months. Bartlett even found one former subject 6 *years* later and asked him to recall the story. Bartlett reported the results by reproducing dozens of the actual recalled stories and then summarizing the kinds of errors found. Total recall declined with the passage of time, of course, but what was more intriguing to Bartlett was the quality of the reproductions. Participants did not just recall less—what they recalled was shaped by their need to form a coherent, understandable story within the context of their own cultural knowledge system. Thus "something black coming out of his mouth" was transformed to "foaming at the mouth" for one participant and the soul leaving the body for another. Also, the ambiguity about the ghosts (if they are already ghosts, how can they be killed?) led one participant to decide that "Ghosts" was just a label for a particular tribe; that transformation (or *rationalisation*, as Bartlett called it) "made the whole thing more comprehensible" (p. 68). Others recalled erroneously, but logically for their death schema, that the "ghosts" appeared only after some Indians were killed in the battle. In all, then, subjects recalled the story within the framework of their own cultural schemata about battle and death and the afterlife. Thus memory was not merely an act of reproducing intact memory traces; rather, it was an active process of *construction*. As Bartlett put it:

> In the many thousands of cases of remembering which I collected, ... literal recall was very rare. With few exceptions, ... reexcitement of individual traces did not look to be in the least what was happening. ... In fact, if we consider the evidence rather than presupposition, remembering appears to be far more decisively an affair of construction rather than one of mere reproduction. ... [C]ondensation, elaboration and invention are common features of ordinary remembering, and these all very often involve the mingling of materials belonging originally to different "schemata." (Bartlett, 1932/1967, pp. 204–205)

Bartlett borrowed the term *schema* from a British neurologist, Henry Head. After saying that he did not like the term ("It is at once too definite and too sketchy," p. 201), Bartlett proceeded to rely on it for his theory. As described earlier, schemata can be thought of as general concepts that make up our understanding of the world, and memories are constructed with reference to them. So, for instance, when Bartlett's participant recalled "foaming at the mouth" instead of the more obscure "something black came out of his mouth," that person's schemata about illness and death contributed to the constructive memory. Perhaps because they appeared during the height of neobehaviorism, Bartlett's ideas about memory did not make much of a stir in the United States. It was only in the 1960s, after cognitive psychology had emerged from multiple sources, that the significance of the work began to be appreciated. His notion of memory as constructive is now widely accepted and central to the understanding of such phenomena as false memory (e.g., Roediger & McDermott, 1995) and eyewitness memory (e.g., Loftus, 1979).

KEY DATE—1932

This year marked the publication of Bartlett's classic study on memory, *Remembering: A Study in Experimental and Social Psychology*.

These events also occurred that year:

- A graduate student at Harvard, B. F. Skinner (Chapter 11) delivered his first professional convention talk; it was at the annual meeting of the American Psychological Association, held that year at Cornell
- Amelia Earhart became the first woman to fly solo across the Atlantic, traveling from Newfoundland to Ireland in 13.5 hours
- Work began on the Golden Gate Bridge in San Francisco (completed in 1937)
- Jack Sharkey (U.S.) defeated Max Schmeling (Germany) to capture the world heavyweight boxing crown
- Austrian-born Adolph Hitler was granted German citizenship
- Aldous Huxley published *Brave New World*
- Johnny Weissmuller made his first Tarzan movie and four-year-old Shirley Temple made her movie debut

These people were born:

- John Updike, American author (e.g., the five-volume Rabbit Angstrom series, starting with *Rabbit*, *Run*; two of the five won Pulitzer Prizes)
- Andrew Young, U.S. civil rights leader, politician, and diplomat
- Sylvia Plath, American author (e.g., *The Bell Jar*, semi-autobiographical novel about living with a bipolar disorder)

These people died:

- George Eastman, American inventor of photographic materials
- John Philip Sousa, American composer of marches (e.g., *Stars and Stripes Forever*)
- William Wrigley, American founder of chewing gum empire

A Convergence of Influences

The influences that produced modern cognitive psychology came both from within psychology, in the form of a growing suspicion about the widespread applicability of conditioning and associationist principles, and outside of psychology, through several disciplines that received their initial impetus in the context of World War II or developed after the end of the conflict (Segal & Lachman, 1972).

Influences Within Psychology Among psychologists during the 1940s and 1950s, there was growing concern that conditioning and associationist principles could not adequately account for all human behavior, especially language behavior. Although the radical behaviorists had either reduced mental events to subtle muscular responses to stimuli (Watson), or viewed them merely as internal behavior under the control of reinforcement contingencies (Skinner), Tolman and Hull had attempted to address the problem of "representation." That is, both recognized that individuals acted as if they were influenced by internal representations or conceptions of the external world (e.g., memories). Hull dealt with the issue by avoiding mentalistic concepts and proposing internal sequences of stimuli and responses that became chained together through reinforced learning trials. Tolman went further and proposed that such internal constructs as cognitive maps and expectancies served to guide behavior. Both approaches fell short when it came to explaining distinctly human behavior such as language, however, and attempts to force language into conditioning terms failed.

The adequacy of associationism's principles was also called into question, most notably by the neuropsychologist Karl Lashley (Chapter 3), a former research colleague of Watson's at Johns Hopkins but a longtime critic of simple Watsonian stimulus–response (S-R) formulations. In 1948, Lashley participated in the Hixon Symposium, an interdisciplinary meeting that brought together psychologists, mathematicians, neurologists, and psychiatrists to consider the general topic of the relationship between the cerebral cortex and behavior. Lashley's talk, published 3 years later in the collected symposium papers, dealt with the problem of serial order and the general failure of association theory to account for it (Lashley, 1951). Simply stated, the **serial order problem** concerns the question of how to explain, in terms of cerebral mechanisms, linear sequences of behavior, ranging from the series of finger movements while playing the violin to the memorization of a list of words to the production of language in sentences. A basic tenet of association theory was that adjacent elements in a sequence become associated or "chained" together because they are experienced together (i.e., contiguously). Lashley argued that such a formulation was inadequate. In complex motor skills such as playing the violin, for example, the sequence of behaviors occurs much too rapidly for one element to depend on the neurological analysis of the preceding element and be the stimulus for the next element. Also, the oral production of a sentence is more complex than a simple sequencing of words, as illustrated by the rules of syntax and slips of the tongue. Thus two sentences, one in the active voice and the other in the passive, have completely different sequences yet convey the same meaning. And certain errors of speech, called Spoonerisms, involve anticipations of words or word segments that were meant to occur later in the sentence.[1] Instead of a cortical model based on the concept of linear associative chains, Lashley argued that the brain was a more complex system that exercised organizational control over patterns of behavior.

Lashley's paper was well received. Like Bartlett's work, however, its significance for the development of cognitive psychology was not immediately recognized, as shown in a careful citation analysis by psychologist-historian Darryl Bruce (1994). References to the article accumulated at a leisurely pace throughout the 1950s and then increased dramatically in the mid-1960s, the decade when cognitive psychology achieved its greatest momentum. Thus the serial order paper was a bit ahead of its time. Nonetheless, it contributed to the critical mass that was developing in the postwar years that eventually led to the appearance of cognitive psychology.

Influences External to Psychology   One factor that influenced the cognitive movement included a dramatic increase in federal funding for research in psychology after the end of World War II, especially research related to cognition. By the end of the 1950s, for example, the federal government was funneling about $500 million to universities to fund research; within psychology, the topics being funded shifted from those primarily having to do with conditioning, to those concerning "cognition, memory, computing, and a broad range of nonlearning theory work on animal behavior" (Pickren, 2007, p. 283).

Developments in disciplines outside of psychology also profoundly affected the shift toward an interest in cognition. One of the most critical was the development of computer science, which was accelerated in the 1940s by the military needs of World War II and its demands for such things as automated radar-tracking systems (Baars, 1986). Of course,

---

[1] An example of a Spoonerism might be saying, "Let me sew you to your sheets" instead of the intended "Let me show you to your seats."

philosophers and psychologists have a long history of using contemporary technology as metaphors relating to human behavior. Examples range from Descartes's use of hydraulic garden figures in his model of the nervous system to Watson's belief that the telephone switchboard paralleled the S-R connections underlying the relationship between stimulus and action. In the postwar era, it wasn't long before scientists began to see parallels between the computer and the brain.

The computer is essentially a device for taking in information from the environment, processing it internally, and producing some output. By analogy, the brain could be seen as doing the same thing. The mathematician John von Neuman explicitly developed this metaphor in the opening address given at the Hixon Symposium in 1948. The analogy reappeared on occasion in the 1950s, and by the 1960s it was commonplace to hear cognitive phenomena described in computer language and its models portrayed as computer flowcharts. The best-known example, soon to be a regular feature in the memory chapters of introductory psychology books, was the model proposed by Atkinson and Shiffrin (1968). Some form of the flowchart in Figure 14.1, a simplified version of theirs, is probably familiar to you. It introduced the well-known distinctions between the limited capacity short-term memory system (STM), analogous to a computer's RAM, and the unlimited capacity long-term memory (LTM), likened to a computer's hard drive. And the Atkinson-Shiffrin model freely used computer jargon: Humans don't just memorize things, they "transfer information from STM to LTM," and they don't just remember things, they "retrieve information from LTM."

One advantage of the computer metaphor was that it provided a scientifically respectable way to discuss complex internal mental processes, thus muting behaviorism's criticisms that

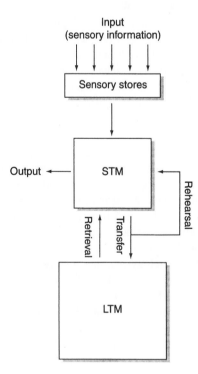

FIGURE 14.1 A typical example of the use of a flowchart to illustrate the two-stage model of memory like the Atkinson and Shiffrin (1968) model.

psychological scientists shouldn't be dealing with mysterious unobservable entities that intervene between stimulus and response as well as avoiding the old problems with introspection. As George Miller put it, "Computers give us an existence-proof of the complexity that is possible in information-processing systems. This made us all feel a lot freer" (quoted in Baars, 1986, p. 212). Further respectability came from a refinement in the way of describing the flow of information through the system. This occurred in 1949 with the publication of *The Mathematical Theory of Communication* by Claude Shannon and Warren Weaver, which introduced **information theory** and the concept of the **bit**, an abbreviation of *binary digit*. An electrical engineer, Shannon recognized a connection between the logical operators of true and false and the two states, on and off, of any electromagnetic relay. Working with Weaver, he defined the bit as the amount of information that would enable a decision between two equally likely alternatives. Thus information reduces uncertainty. A coin toss, for instance, contains one bit of information because it tells us which of two possible outcomes is true. Each time the number of alternatives doubles, one additional bit of information is added: With four alternatives, it takes two bits of information to reduce uncertainty, with eight alternatives, it takes three bits, and so on. The significance of the concept was that it provided a way of standardizing units of information, regardless of the form that the information took (e.g., coin toss, dice throw, numbers, letters, etc.). The bit wound up being more important for computer science than for cognitive psychology, but in the 1950s it added further legitimacy to the scientific study of the mind.

A third area of development outside of psychology, but relating to the assault on behaviorism within psychology, was linguistics. Led by Noam Chomsky (b. 1928) of the Massachusetts Institute of Technology (MIT), theories of language structure and language production began to proliferate in the 1950s, and they went beyond anything conceivable to behaviorists. Chomsky came to the attention of psychologists in 1959, when he wrote a highly critical review of *Verbal Behavior*, B. F. Skinner's (1957) creative attempt to put language into operant terms (Chomsky, 1959). Language development occurs too rapidly for conditioning to be relevant, Chomsky argued. Even if we could learn a sentence per second, there are not enough seconds in a lifetime to learn all the sentences that we are capable of producing. Furthermore, people routinely create and/or understand sentences they have never experienced before. Language was simply too complex for what Chomsky took to be an overly simplistic behaviorist explanation.

Through the work of Chomsky and other linguists, language came to be viewed not as verbal behavior that was the outcome of conditioning and associative learning, but as the result of the application of a hierarchical set of rules called a **grammar**. These rules allow the individual to generate a virtually infinite number of grammatical sentences while also immediately being able to identify nongrammatical sentences. For instance, to use one of Chomsky's favorite examples (Gardner, 1985), we easily recognize "Colorless green ideas sleep furiously" as perfectly grammatical, if silly, and we have no difficulty rejecting these same words in a different order, "Sleep ideas green colorless furiously," as ungrammatical. The sentences we use cannot be the result of simple learning, Chomsky argued, but must follow from the systematic application of a grammar. Furthermore, this ability to use grammar is instinctively human—Chomsky believed that language was the attribute that most clearly distinguished humans from other species. He believed that all languages shared common principles (he called them **linguistic universals**) and that the human brain is structured to be able to understand these universals quickly (Chomsky, 1966). Chomsky and other linguists supported their nativist arguments about language by pointing out that (a) as with other species-specific behaviors, there appears to be a critical period for language development; and (b) attempts to teach language skills to other species (e.g., through the use of sign language) have failed.[2]

Questions about behaviorism and associationism, along with developments in computer science, information theory, and linguistics, helped to change the intellectual climate among experimental psychologists. Then, during the 1950s and early 1960s, several landmark publications led to the recognition that experimental psychology had somehow changed. Some have referred to the events at this time as a *revolution* in psychology, an issue examined in this chapter's Close-Up. Whether revolutionary or evolutionary, however, it is clear that several events reflected a change in direction of experimental psychology.

Magical Numbers, Selective Filters, and TOTE Units

Perhaps the first psychologist to recognize the relevance of information theory to psychology was George A. Miller (b. 1920). As a research fellow in Harvard's Psycho-Acoustic Laboratory from 1944 to 1948, Miller (Figure 14.2) investigated speech perception, a problem that derived from a military context—the difficulty in hearing spoken messages while sitting in loud airplanes (Hilgard, 1987). Out of this research came a course offered to Harvard undergraduates called "The Psychology of Speech and Communication," and from the course came Miller's first book, *Language and Communication* (1951). Shortly after Shannon and Weaver produced their groundbreaking work (described earlier), Miller introduced information theory to psychologists in a *Psychological Review* article (Miller & Frick, 1949). Then, 7 years later,

FIGURE 14.2 George Miller, of 7 ± 2 fame.

[2]Chimpanzees and other primates have been quite successful at learning to use sign language and communicating their needs symbolically, but the general consensus among both linguists and cognitive psychologists is that their learning is imitative and does not show evidence of the use of a true rule-bound grammar (see Anderson, 1990, for a review).

WHAT REVOLUTION?

There is little doubt that more experimental psychologists in America were interested in studying cognitive processes in the 1960s than in the prior two decades and, except for diehard Skinnerian holdouts, behaviorism began to decline at the same time. Some have referred to the change as a revolution in psychology (e.g., Segal & Lachman, 1972; Sperry, 1993), and at least two books chronicling the shift to cognition include *cognitive revolution* in their titles (Baars, 1986; Gardner, 1985). On the other hand, psychologist-historian Thomas Leahey (1992) has argued that the development of cognitive psychology meets none of the accepted criteria for being a scientific revolution. Clearly, resolving the issue requires some understanding of what is meant by a revolution in science.

In 1962, a brief (172 pages) but momentous book entitled *The Structure of Scientific Revolutions* appeared on the academic scene, proposing a new way to look at progress in science. Its author, physicist-turned-historian Thomas Kuhn, argued against the traditional Enlightenment-based notion that scientific progress involves a gradual accumulation of objective knowledge over time. Rather, in Kuhn's view, science proceeds through history by establishing agreed-upon "paradigms" that guide scientists; then science shifts from one paradigm to another. When such a shift occurs, a revolution has happened.

According to Kuhn, all sciences begin in a "preparadigmatic stage." During this time there are competing schools of thought within a discipline, and their proponents argue over fundamental conceptual and definitional issues. Eventually, one of those schools gains a majority of adherents and becomes established as a **paradigm**. A Kuhnian paradigm is an all-embracing worldview within the scientific community that organizes what is known into a grand theory, determines how terms are defined and what problems are to be solved by scientists, and dictates appropriate research methods. Newtonian physics is the typical example. Once a paradigm has been established, there exists a period of **normal science** during which the paradigm guides research designed to provide empirical evidence for it. Because all paradigms have some truth to them, much of this research indeed supports the paradigm, but not all of it does. Anomalous findings can usually be ignored or explained away, but sometimes predictions keep failing and the science enters a "crisis" period during which confidence in the paradigm starts to wane. Eventually, a creative scientist or two comes up with a new idea that explains the anomalies along with everything else explained by the paradigm-in-crisis. If this new idea is sufficiently powerful and well promoted, it can become a new paradigm replacing the old one. If so, a revolution is said to have occurred. The replacement of Newtonian physics with Einsteinian physics is the typical example.

Kuhn's ideas have been applied to the history of psychology. Kirsch (1977), for example, claimed that psychology's first paradigm could be called "mentalism," and it encompassed Wundtian, structuralist, and functionalist thinking. Its guiding interest was the scientific study of human conscious experience. Methodological problems (i.e., introspection) led to a paradigm crisis, however, leading in turn to a behaviorist revolution. Similar arguments were made by Palermo (1971), who believed that psychology in the 1960s was in the midst of a second revolution moving from behaviorism to cognitive psychology. The shifts from mentalism to behaviorism and then to cognitive psychology have a certain intuitive appeal, and there is a degree of truth to the broad overview.

According to Leahey (1992), however, clothing psychology's history in Kuhnian garb can oversimplify complex events and perpetuate myths. Concerning the so-called cognitive revolution, for instance, he argued that (a) behaviorists disagreed on too many fundamental issues (e.g., the role of reinforcement) for behaviorism to be anything close to a Kuhnian paradigm; (b) any shift from behaviorism to cognition was too gradual for the term *revolutionary* to have any meaning; (c) the early research in cognition was not motivated by the perception of a "crisis" in behaviorism, but by a variety of other factors; and (d) cognitive psychologists themselves disagreed on too many fundamentals for cognitive psychology to resemble a Kuhnian paradigm.

Leahey (1992) also made the interesting suggestion that the 1962 appearance of Kuhn's book *by itself* helped to create the myth that a cognitive revolution was in progress. Reflecting on that era, researcher James Jenkins recalled it as a "tremendously exciting time. The basic assumption was that things were boiling over, and...a new day was coming. And of course, everyone toted around their little copy of Kuhn" (quoted in Baars, 1986, p. 249). Although not denying that changes were indeed occurring, Leahey concluded *there was no awareness of revolution until Kuhn's book suggested it*" (p. 315, emphasis in the original). It is worth noting that all of this was going on at a particularly turbulent time in American history. In the 1960s, protests against the war in Vietnam and the civil rights and women's movements produced a climate in which talk of overthrowing the existing order, not trusting anyone over 30, and rejecting institutional authority was commonplace on university campuses. As a graduate student in cognitive psychology myself at that time, I can recall how Kuhn's message of revolutionary change seemed to resonate with my professors and peers. For instance, the book was the first one we had to read in a seminar on "higher mental processes," and it colored the discussion for the whole semester. By formulating a new way of looking at the history of science, then, in a culture awash with calls for change, Kuhn's book might have helped to create the idea that a cognitive revolution was occurring.

he published an article with a title more whimsical than normally found in stuffy academic journals—"The Magical Number Seven, Plus or Minus Two: Some Limits on Our Capacity for Processing Information" (Miller, 1956). The conclusions of the paper were destined to become a standard feature in the memory chapters of introductory psychology textbooks, and the article itself became the most frequently cited paper in the first 100 years of the *Psychological Review* (Kintsch & Cacioppo, 1994).

In the article, Miller showed how information theory concepts such as bits and channel capacity could be used to describe limits on our ability to process information in several kinds of tasks. The last portion of the paper contains the most frequently cited information, Miller's analysis of the limited capacity of immediate memory. Depending on the type of information being memorized, he argued that people could process only between five (for monosyllabic words) and nine (for binary digits) items at a time. Recognizing that the amount of information in bits varies dramatically, depending on the type of material being studied, Miller introduced a new term, the **chunk**, to refer to the information being held in immediate memory. Hence, the capacity limit on short-term memory was identified as seven, plus or minus two, chunks of information, where the chunk is a small, meaningful unit of information. Further, Miller applied the information theory concept of **recoding** to take into account humans' ability to reorganize data, thereby squeezing in more information per chunk. In his words, because "the memory span is a fixed number of chunks, we can increase the number of bits of information that it contains simply by building larger and larger chunks, each chunk containing more information than before" (Miller, 1956, p. 349). Miller used the example of learning Morse code to drive home the point. The learner first hears each dot and dash as individual units. With experience, however, combinations of these sounds are recoded ("chunked") as whole letters, then words, then phrases, so that the experienced operator can, in effect, keep many more dots and dashes in immediate memory than the novice.

The mid-1950s also saw the publication of several works from England that applied information theory ideas to attention, a cognitive phenomenon largely neglected since Wundtian times. The prime mover was a student of Bartlett's at Cambridge, Donald Broadbent (1926–1993), who first became interested in psychology during World War II while being trained as a pilot in the Royal Air Force. Although impressed by the technical complexity of the aircraft he was flying, he was frustrated by the failure of engineers to take the human pilot into account when designing the cockpit instrumentation and controls. The similarity of gauges often induced perceptual and attentional errors—for instance, Broadbent recalled that while landing on one occasion, he thought he was flying at 2,000 feet, only to discover that he was attending to the wrong gauge and that he was actually flying at 2,000 rpm (Broadbent, 1980).

After the war, Broadbent went to Cambridge, studied with Bartlett, and was eventually named director of Bartlett's laboratory there, the Applied Psychology Unit. During the 1950s, he and Colin Cherry, a professor of telecommunications, pioneered modern research on attention by using a **dichotic listening** procedure: Research participants experienced two channels of information at the same time, one sent to each ear via headphones. They were able to document limits on the ability to use multiple communication channels and showed, for instance, that while attending to one message, very little of a second message could be recalled (e.g., Cherry, 1953). Broadbent summarized this research in *Perception and Communication* (1958) and proposed a simple **selective filter** model of attention. When confronted with two streams of information, he suggested, our limited-capacity system filters out one message and selects the other for attention and further processing. The problem of selective attention, which introductory textbooks soon began labeling the "cocktail party phenomenon" because the task resembled that of trying to listen to two conversations at once, remains an important and vigorous area of research in cognitive psychology.

A third example of the shift toward cognitive psychology in the 1950s took the form of a book. Entitled *Plans and the Structure of Behavior*, it appeared in 1960, the outcome of a collaboration between George Miller of 7 ± 2 fame, Eugene Galanter, a Harvard experimental psychologist with expertise in math and computers, and Karl Pribram, a well-known neuroscientist. The book centered on the idea of a *Plan*, defined as "any hierarchical process in the organism that can control the order in which a sequence of operations is to be performed" (Miller, Galanter, & Pribram, 1960, p. 16). In keeping with the computer metaphor that was rapidly coming into vogue, the authors explicitly likened these Plans to the program written for a computer. The second main concept was that of the *Image*, which the authors defined broadly as "all the accumulated, organized knowledge that the organism has about itself and its world" (p. 17). The main problem for the book was said to be to "explore the relationship between the Image and the Plan" (Miller, Galanter, & Pribram, 1960, p. 18).

The book is perhaps best remembered for borrowing the concept of feedback from the field of **cybernetics** (i.e., the study of the principles involved in controlling any living or nonliving system). In a radical departure from behaviorist-associationist tradition, they proposed that a feedback system could be substituted for the reflex arc as the basic unit of behavioral control. In a feedback system, the operation of one part of the system produces results that are fed back and monitored by the system, thereby affecting its future operation. The thermostat and furnace, for instance, operate together as a simple feedback system. On a cold day, the thermostat sends a signal to the furnace to start, which increases the air temperature, which is read by the thermostat, which eventually tells the furnace to stop. The temperature then drops, triggers another signal from the thermostat to restart the furnace, and so on. In the long run, the feedback system produces a "steady state," a temperature that does not vary much from the thermostat setting. For human feedback systems, Miller and his colleagues created the basic concept of the **TOTE unit** (TOTE is an acronym for Test-Operate-Test-Exit). The process begins with a Test phase that looks for incongruities

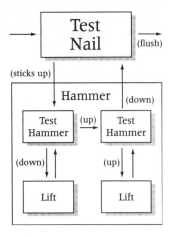

FIGURE 14.3 TOTE units arranged to illustrate a hierarchical plan for hammering nails. From Miller, Galanter, and Pribram (1960).

in the system (e.g., in the thermostat example, a difference between the desired temperature and the actual temperature). If there are no incongruities, nothing happens, but if there are, an operation occurs to reduce the incongruity. Another Test then occurs, and so on until no incongruity exists. For humans, these TOTE units are organized hierarchically, as in the example shown in Figure 14.3, which represents the authors' example of a two-level system for hammering a nail. The first Test is to see if the nail is sticking up. If not, no hammering is needed; if so, the second-level TOTE units engage to alter the state of the nail.

Neisser and the "Naming" of Cognitive Psychology

Miller's 7 ± 2 paper, the British work on attention, and the *Plans* book were just three prominent examples of numerous events that marked an important shift in experimental psychology during the 1950s, legitimizing the study of heretofore frowned-on mentalistic topics. The momentum continued to build in the 1960s, a tumultuous decade in which change from the existing order became a familiar theme (see this chapter's Close-Up). In addition, experimental psychology benefited from increased government funding of all scientific research, part of the attempt during the Cold War to reestablish American scientific supremacy in the wake of Soviet successes in space (e.g., launching the first satellite—Sputnik—into orbit in 1957). By the mid-1960s, sufficient research existed to warrant book-length summaries, and texts in cognitive psychology began to appear, most notably Ulric Neisser's *Cognitive Psychology* in 1967, which gave a specific name to the converging ideas of such people as Miller, Broadbent, and others. Neisser would later recall getting "letters from people saying that they were glad that I had given [the movement] a name, because they were interested in all the topics I considered, but the area had not had a theoretical identity" (quoted in Baars, 1986, p. 278). After Neisser, it did.

As an undergraduate at Harvard, Ulric Neisser (b. 1928) studied with George Miller, later recalling that Miller's course on speech and communication "covered some pretty unusual topics...[such as] linguistics, acoustics, articulatory physiology, and engineering mathematics" (Neisser, 1988, p. 82). Neisser's interest in cognition was aroused by the experience, and he followed his undergraduate degree with a master's degree from Swarthmore and further graduate study at MIT before earning a doctorate in psychoacoustics at Harvard in 1956. He subsequently taught at Brandeis, Cornell, and Emory before returning to Cornell, where he currently enjoys professor emeritus status.

In his opening chapter, Neisser (1967) began by pointing out that the times had changed in psychology:

> A generation ago, a book like this one would have needed at least a chapter of self-defense against the behaviorist position. Today, happily, the climate of opinion has changed, and little or no defense is necessary. Indeed, stimulus-response theorists themselves are inventing hypothetical mechanisms with vigor and enthusiasm and only faint twinges of conscience. The basic reason for studying cognitive processes has become as clear as the reason for studying anything else: because they are there. . . . Cognitive processes surely exist, so it can hardly be unscientific to study them. (p. 5)

As for the question of what cognitive psychology actually meant, Neisser considered it to be the experimental study of all cognitive process, and by cognition, he meant

> *all the processes by which the sensory input is transformed, reduced, elaborated, stored, recovered, and used*. It is concerned with these processes even when they operate in the absence of relevant stimulation, as in images and hallucinations. Such terms as sensation, perception, imagery, retention, recall, problem-solving, and thinking, among many others, refer to hypothetical stages or aspects of cognition. (p. 4, emphasis in the original)

The content chapters of Neisser's *Cognitive Psychology* are full of rich experimental detail about some of the ways that the human information processor can transform information. Reflecting the newness of cognitive psychology, about 60% of the book's 321 references are to research published in the decade of the 1960s (Weaver, 1998). The bulk of the book concerns the processing of visual and auditory information, but there are also chapters on memory, language, and a brief concluding chapter on the relationship between memory and thought.

The Evolution of Cognitive Psychology

Interest in cognitive psychology continued to grow rapidly after the publication of Neisser's 1967 book. Psychology departments rushed to create cognitive laboratories and hire cognitive psychologists; conferences on cognition were held, their contents later published in edited books (e.g., the Loyola Symposium; Solso, 1973); and informal networks such as Southeastern Workers in Memory (SWIM) were formed. Traditional journals such as the *Journal of Experimental Psychology* featured more cognitive research, and new journals appeared—*Cognitive Psychology* in 1970, *Cognition* in 1972, *Cognitive Science* in 1977, and *Memory and Cognition* in 1983. In addition, cognitive psychology spread to psychology's other subdisciplines, such as developmental, social, personality, and abnormal psychology. Even animal psychology was not immune—researchers began investigating "animal cognition" (e.g., Flaherty, 1985).

Within cognitive psychology itself, changes occurred in the 1970s, once again led by Neisser. In *Cognition and Reality* (1976), he argued that the laboratory tradition in cognitive psychology, while producing important results, nonetheless had failed to yield enough useful information about information processing in real-world contexts. He was even critical of his own 1967 text for being top-heavy with basic laboratory research. Instead, explicitly recognizing the influence of Bartlett and his close friend James Gibson (discussed later),

Neisser called for more research concerning what he called **ecological validity**—research with relevance for the everyday cognitive activities of people trying to adapt to their environment. Experimental psychologists, Neisser (1976) urged,

> must make a greater effort to understand cognition as it occurs in the ordinary environment and in the context of natural purposeful activity. This would not mean an end to laboratory experiments, but a commitment to the study of variables that are ecologically important rather than those that are easily manageable. (p. 7)

Neisser's call to arms was embraced by many cognitive researchers, and the 1980s and 1990s saw increased research in such topics as eyewitness memory (e.g., Loftus, 1979); the long-term recall of topics learned in school, such as Spanish (e.g., Bahrick, 1984); and autobiographical memory, the memory for one's lifetime (e.g. Kennedy, Mather, & Carstensen, 2004). This turn to everyday cognition should not be surprising, given what we know about the history of functionalist thinking in American psychology. Research that helps us understand how the individual adapts to the environment and has practical applications is the type of research that has always resonated with American psychology's functional and pragmatic spirit.

In addition to the interest in ecological validity, another aspect of the evolution of interests among research psychologists has been the creation of **cognitive science**, an interdisciplinary field that includes cognitive psychology, linguistics, computer science, cultural anthropology, and epistemology. Gardner (1985) defined the field broadly as an "empirically based effort to answer long-standing epistemological questions—particularly those concerned with the nature of knowledge, its components, its sources, its development, and its deployment" (p. 6). The term *cognitive science* began to appear in the mid-1970s and became institutionalized with the naming of a journal devoted to it in 1977. In the opening editorial for *Cognitive Science*, Collins (1977) pointed out that the discipline could have been called "applied epistemology or intelligence theory, but someone on high declared it should be cognitive science and so it shall" (p. 1).

It is worth noting, of course, that while the label is relatively new, cognitive science is not. The initial stirrings of the new discipline can be seen in the postwar era, when the above-mentioned "influences external to psychology" (information theory, computer science, linguistics) contributed to the emergence of what psychologists began calling cognitive psychology. From a broader perspective, however, it is clear that something more than a new type of psychology was developing back then, and that some of the key players were aware of it. George Miller, for instance, traced the origins of cognitive science to a 1956 symposium on information theory, held at MIT (Baars, 1986); in 1960, Miller and Jerome Bruner cofounded the Center for Cognitive Studies at Harvard, designed explicitly to foster the interdisciplinary study of cognition. Bruner later recalled that he and Miller decided "that psychology was too complicated a field to leave to the psychologists, [so] what we needed was an alliance with colleagues from other disciplines who were, each in his or her own context, concerned about how humans acquired and used knowledge" (Bruner, 1988, p. 92).

Artificial Intelligence One important focus of interest among cognitive scientists has been in the applied computer science area of **artificial intelligence (AI)**, which may be defined simply as the field that attempts to examine whether nonhuman, technological systems can act with intelligence. Workers in AI are interested in a variety of topics, but they generally fall into two broad categories. Some researchers are mainly interested in understanding human intelligence, studying it by attempting to write computer programs that simulate human cognitive processing. Consider human problem solving, for example. The idea is that if a computer can be made to solve problems in the same way that humans solve problems, then the problem-solving strategies built into the computer program can be seen as analogous to human strategies. This was the approach taken by two nonpsychologist pioneers in AI, Herbert Simon (b. 1916) and Alan Newell (1927–1992). Simon, whose work on decision making produced a Nobel Prize in economics in 1978, and Newell, a physicist, collaborated on computer simulations of thinking and problem solving in the 1950s and 1960s. Their first effort, the Logic Theorist (LT), was designed to solve problems in formal logic; their later and more ambitious project, the General Problem Solver (GPS), was aimed at a broader range of problems (Newell & Simon, 1972).

Both LT and GPS illustrate an important distinction in computer science between algorithms and heuristics. An **algorithm** is a set of rules guaranteed to produce a solution by working systematically through all possible steps. A **heuristic**, on the other hand, is a more creative strategy or "rule of thumb" that, while not guaranteeing a solution, is more efficient than an algorithm. A common anagram problem can illustrate the difference. When asked to rearrange the letters *LTEAGST* so that a real word is formed, an algorithmic approach would try every possible combination of letters until a solution was reached. This would not present a problem for a computer, which performs operations very quickly and does not get bored in the process. Humans, however, would probably attempt to solve the anagram by using heuristics, such as "do not consider uncommon combinations of pairs of letters." Thus the solver would try the combination *ST* but not *GT*, on the way toward solving the anagram (Hint: It's a word found throughout Chapter 9).

The primary heuristic built into Simon and Newell's GPS was called a **means-ends analysis**. A feedback system, it involved assessing the current state with the goal state, identifying a difference between the two, identifying and applying an operator (some behavior) to reduce the difference, reassessing the new state with the goal, and so on, until the current state became the goal state. Newell and Simon (1972) developed the program by giving problems (e.g., algebra problems) to people and asking them to externalize their thinking by describing their thought processes as they occurred—a procedure bearing an interesting similarity to introspection. They then wrote the GPS program in a way that attempted to simulate what their human subjects were doing. Hence, the goal was to understand human thinking, on the assumption that if they could simulate it, making the computer produce solutions just like human solutions, then they would increase their understanding of it. This simulation strategy was used in attempts to study cognitive processes ranging from pattern recognition to memory to thinking, although interest in such simulations reached its peak in the 1970s, in part because of the abandonment of GPS when it failed to be as "general" a problem solver as originally hoped (Gardner, 1985).

The second approach to AI, and the more dominant one since the 1980s, is to create a computer program that will perform some task in the most efficient way possible, regardless of how humans might approach the task. That is, the goal is to create expert systems that deal with problems intelligently. The outcome has been such things as computerized chess programs that can beat world-class human players, robots, interactive tutoring systems, and that voice in your car that bosses you around. This second usage of AI has raised the question of whether computers can be said to think, which in turn has led to debates on the nature of thinking and what it means to be human. That is, AI has perpetuated some of the issues that have always been of interest to psychologists.

The question of whether true intelligence can be found in computers was posed as early as 1950, in an article entitled "Computing Machinery and Intelligence," by Alan Turing (1912–1954), a brilliant English mathematician. Turing was instrumental in ensuring the allied victory in World War II by helping to break the Germans' supposedly unassailable "Enigma" code and thereby inform allied strategists of German troop movements, strategies, and the like. In his 1950 article, Turing described an "imitation game" that provided a set of criteria to determine whether computers could be said to think. This has since been called the **Turing test**. Imagine, wrote Turing, a situation in which a person in one room can ask a series of any questions to a human and a computer, both located in a second room. Based on the two sets of answers, the questioner must try to distinguish between the human and the machine. The human tries to convince the questioner that he or she is human, as does the computer. If the questioner cannot discriminate human from machine on the basis of the answers, according to Turing, then it must be concluded that no significant differences exist between computer intelligence and human intelligence; that is, computers can think like humans.

Your growing knowledge of psychology's history can help put the AI debates about thinking in some perspective, for the problem is not new, but merely an extension of the age-old mind–body (or mind–brain) problem. One of psychology's recurring issues has concerned whether purely mechanical explanations are sufficient for an understanding of human behavior and mental processes. From the time of Descartes's fascination with the hydraulically driven figures in the gardens of French royalty to the 19th-century physiologists who believed that all living function could be reduced to the movements of material objects to Watson's mechanistic S-R model that likened human functioning to a telephone switchboard, mechanical metaphors for human functioning have been commonplace. The AI debates are unlikely to resolve the issue.

Evaluating Cognitive Psychology

Although some have considered cognitive psychology to be an all-encompassing framework, even a paradigm for modern psychology, the movement has also been sharply criticized. Understandably, the most vocal critic was B. F. Skinner (Chapter 11), the leading behaviorist of the second half of the 20th century. Skinner objected to the creation of hypothetical mental mechanisms (e.g., short-term memory), which all too easily could become reified, he believed, into "explanatory fictions." That is, instead of looking for the causes of behavior in the environment and one's learning history, where they belonged (in Skinner's view), the cognitive psychologist turned these hypothetical mechanisms into real, causal entities. Attributing failures of recall to limited short-term memory capacity hardly explains the phenomenon, he argued. Skinner deplored the spread of cognitive ideas throughout the field of psychology, sarcastically observing that a graph showing the use of the term *cognitive* in psychology's literature would show exponential growth after 1960—"Is there any field of psychology today in which something does not seem to be gained by adding that charming adjective to the occasional noun?" (Skinner, 1987, p. 783).

A second general criticism of cognitive psychology derives from the computer metaphor, with its human-as-machine implication. Such a view ignores significant aspects of human behavior, critics charge, such as emotion and motivation (e.g., Zajonc, 1980) or intentionality (Searle, 1980). Hilgard (1980), referring to the 18th-century tripartite division of mental activities—the cognitive, the affective (emotional), and the conative (motivational/behavioral)—made a similar argument that cognitive psychology addresses only a portion of the whole. A related criticism has been that cognitive psychologists sometimes ignore neurological reality, building models of mental processing that contradict what is known about how the nervous system operates.

Despite the problems, the study of cognitive processes has worked its way into virtually every area of modern psychological investigation. The pervasiveness of cognitive factors is perhaps an indication of how important such processes have always been to psychology, even when prominent behaviorists may have questioned their importance, and how central they are to the very definition of what it means to be human.

OTHER RESEARCH AREAS

In Descartes' time, the first half of the 17th century, serious scholars believed that it was possible to gain a complete understanding of all scientific knowledge. Descartes himself made that his goal with the writing of his *The World* (completed in 1633 but not published until after his death), which included topics ranging from anatomy to meteorology. Today, of course, in an age of information explosion and specialization, nobody could hope to have a thorough knowledge of a single science, never mind all science. Even within a particular science such as psychology, comprehensive knowledge is impossible. The cognitive psychologist who studies eyewitness memory, for example, probably knows very little about developmental psychology's research on children's attachment behavior. In fact, the cognitive psychologist studying eyewitness memory almost certainly finds it impossible to keep up with the literature in other areas of cognitive psychology.

We have just seen that cognitive psychology came to dominate the interests of the typical researcher-academician in the second half of the 20th century. Concepts from cognitive psychology also had important influences on a variety of other subdisciplines in psychology. In social psychology, for example, a great deal of research on "social cognition" began appearing in the 1980s (e.g., Fiske & Taylor, 1984). These specialties have their own histories, and a comprehensive analysis of them is beyond the scope of this book. Instead, let us briefly examine some of the history of five research areas outside of cognitive psychology. Instead of attempting to string together a sentence or two about the long list of contributors to each of these areas (and the list is long for each), I will focus on one well-known person from each specialty area and look closely at that person's work and influence. The five areas to be considered involve the (a) study of the relationship between brain and behavior, which used to be called physiological psychology and is now usually referred to as neuroscience; (b) perceptual psychology, the experimental study of how we interpret sensory information in meaningful ways; (c) social psychology, the study of how behavior is influenced by social factors; (d) personality psychology, the study of individual differences in various personal traits; and (e) developmental psychology, the study of how behavior changes as we age.

The Brain and Behavior

One of psychology's enduring mysteries concerns the relationship between stimulus events that produce physical changes in the body, especially in the nervous system, and the psychological experience of those events. Research psychologists long ago gave up on the idea of solving the mind–body problem through science—it is a philosophical question. Thus, researchers can specify in extraordinary detail how the operation of certain combinations of neurons in the striate cortex is correlated with the perception of a line presented at a certain angle, but they cannot answer this question: How does the firing of these neurons actually result in the psychological experience of the tilted line? Recognizing this fundamental limitation, physiological psychologists have concentrated their attention on the search for relationships between physical and mental events by examining the functioning of the brain and nervous system and how the activity of these structures corresponds to experience and behavior.

Chapter 3 sketched the history of attempts to understand the brain, focusing on the past 200 years and ending with Karl Lashley. Lashley, you recall, investigated localization of function in the early years of the 20th century, agreeing with Pierre Flourens, the great French neurologist of a century before, that the brain operates more like an integrated system than a set of structures with different and independent functions. Ironically, Lashley's 1929 conclusions about mass action and equipotentiality had a dampening effect on brain research and encouraged behaviorists to think that the detailed study of conditioning could proceed without concern for the nervous system. Skinner (1938) reinforced the argument, explicitly rejecting the need for physiological explanations of behavior (Hilgard, 1987).

Donald O. Hebb (1904–1985)   Interest in the brain and behavior was rekindled by a student of Lashley's, Donald Hebb (Figure 14.4), the first Canadian psychologist elected to the presidency (in 1960) of the American Psychological Association (Hilgard, 1987).

FIGURE 14.4 Donald Hebb.

Hebb started slowly, barely graduating from college and being accepted into the graduate program at Montreal's McGill University because of personal connections. At McGill, he encountered two former students of Pavlov and learned Pavlovian conditioning techniques.[3] Like Pavlov, Hebb wondered about the relationship between brain and behavior but became skeptical of Pavlov's model of the cortex. After earning his master's degree in 1934, Hebb was encouraged to apply to Chicago and study with Lashley, who was at the height of his reputation. Lashley accepted the young Canadian, and when the mentor moved to Harvard the following year, he took Hebb with him. Hebb completed his doctorate there in 1938. Job prospects were bleak, however, a combination of the lingering effects of the Great Depression and the fact that "physiological psychology was in its long period of decline, between 1930 and 1950" (Hebb, 1980, p. 287).

Returning to his native Canada, Hebb was fortunate enough to land a job as research assistant to McGill University's Wilder Penfield, who was looking for someone to study the behavioral effects of brain surgery. Penfield was just beginning his famous research on the surgical treatment of epilepsy, in which some patients reported what appeared to be intact memories during electrical stimulation of the temporal lobe (Penfield & Perot, 1963). This research was also consistent with Lashley's equipotentiality idea—patients' mental capacities did not seem to deteriorate even after the loss of substantial portions of their frontal lobes. Hebb was right in the center of this research, and he was profoundly affected—it "set the main course for all my subsequent work, and I would not have met it anywhere else" (Hebb, 1980, p. 290). From this experience and his earlier research, Hebb came to the general conclusion that human intelligence develops during early childhood and that "injury to the infant brain interferes with that process, but the same injury at maturity does not reverse it" (p. 292). Thus, Hebb believed, early childhood experiences were crucial for the kind of cortical development related to intelligence.

Two fruitful years with Penfield were followed by 3 years of teaching at Ontario's Queen's University. In 1942, Hebb returned to Lashley, who had just been appointed director of the Yerkes Laboratory of Primate Biology in Florida, and studied primate behavior for 5 years. In 1947, his career came full circle when he was appointed to a professorship at McGill. Within a year, Hebb was named department chair, and he finished his distinguished career at McGill.

Hebb is best known for his 1949 book, *The Organization of Behavior*, which revived interest among American psychologists in the relationship between brain and behavior (Glickman, 1996). From the title, it is clear that the book is more than just a description of nervous system functioning. Rather, Hebb was aiming at a theory that would fully integrate physiology and psychology, not simply reduce the psychological to the physiological. As he later wrote, in criticism of such reductionist thinking, it was "not possible to substitute neurophysiological conceptions for psychological ones, either now or in the future, but it is possible to maintain liaison (translatability of terms) between the two universes of discourse" (Hebb, 1960, p. 744).

Hebb proposed that cortical organization occurs through the development of what he called cell assemblies and phase sequences. A **cell assembly** is the basic unit, referring to a set of neurons that become associated with each other because they have been activated together by repeated sensory experiences. Hebb (1949) recognized the associationist roots of

---

[3]One was Boris Babkin, whose 1949 biography of Pavlov included the description of Pavlov's lab that is featured in Chapter 10.

his construct, writing that the "general idea is an old one, that any two cells or systems of cells that are repeatedly active at the same time will tend to become 'associated,' so that activity in one facilitates activity in the other" (p. 70). **Phase sequences** are higher levels of organization involving the incorporation of several cell assemblies; for Hebb, they were the physiological equivalent of thinking. Taken together, cell assemblies and phase sequences accounted for the fact that stimuli do not simply produce responses, but are mediated by the brain. You will recognize this as similar to the *O* in the S-O-R formulation of Robert Woodworth (Chapter 7) and the intervening variables of the neobehaviorists Tolman and Hull (Chapter 11), but more explicitly physiological.

To account for the effects of experience and hence to provide a physiological account of learning, Hebb proposed that cell assemblies and phase sequences are formed because the repeated stimulation of adjacent cells produces structural changes at the synaptic level. Thus, according to Hebb (1949):

> When an axon of cell A is near enough to excite cell B and repeatedly... takes part in firing it, some growth process or metabolic change takes place in one or both cells such that A's efficiency, as one of the cells firing B, is increased. (p. 62)

This idea has come to be called "Hebb's rule," and synapses that change as the result of experience are often called **Hebb synapses**.

Hebb applied his theory to topics ranging from attention to emotion to mental illness; his book, combined with such technological advances as the electroencephalograph (EEG) for measuring brain waves, triggered a renewal of interest in the relationship between brain and behavior. The story is much too complex to be described here, but some of the more important developments in the 1950s and 1960s included (a) discovery of reinforcement centers in the brain, by Hebb's students James Olds and Peter Milner (1954); (b) the use of EEG to identify stages of sleep and the discovery of REM sleep by Eugene Aserinsky and Nathaniel Kleitman (1953); (c) the development of the split brain operation as a way to control epilepsy and to examine left and right hemisphere functions by Roger Sperry (1961); and (d) the identification of cortical cells ("feature detectors") that respond to specific events in the visual field by David Hubel and Torsten Wiesel (1963). Sperry, Hubel, and Wiesel all earned Nobel Prizes for their efforts.

In more recent years, the study of the brain–behavior interface has become increasingly interdisciplinary. Thus, just as cognitive science combines several disciplines, "neuropsychology," "behavioral neuroscience," "cognitive neuroscience," and even "social cognitive neuroscience" all refer to evolving specialties that cross disciplinary boundaries and involve graduate training in psychology, biology, and computer science.

The Psychology of Perception

How we come to perceive the world around us has long been a topic of interest to both philosophers and psychological scientists. To the British empiricists, as you recall, it was central to understanding how we accumulate our knowledge of the world—nothing in the mind not first in the senses, as they put it. For the early experimental psychologists, topics in sensation and perception were often a focus of attention; efforts ranged from Titchener's attempt to identify the elementary sensory attributes of perception to the gestaltist argument that an analytic approach necessarily fails (you'll recall their catchphrase—the whole is greater than the sum of its parts). For most 20th-century experimental psychologists, the study of perception centered on visual or auditory perception, and most research occurred in a laboratory environment. Concerning the study of vision, for instance, a great deal was learned about how we come to recognize objects in our world, how we perceive color, depth, motion, and so on. One of the most prominent of the 20th-century perceptual psychologists is James J. Gibson, whose ideas about perception as it occurred in the real world challenged many of the ideas about perception that had been developed over the years in a laboratory environment.

James J. Gibson (1904–1979) You might recall from Chapter 7 the story of Titchener's Experimentalists, the like-minded group of experimental psychologists who met every spring to discuss their current research. As a way to bring promising young scientists into the fold, Titchener encouraged his peers to bring their best graduate students to the meetings. One of them can be seen in the group photo in Figure 7.5, taken at the 1926 meeting at the University of Pennsylvania. He is in the back row on the far left, and hatless. This is James J. Gibson, and he was a Princeton doctoral student of H. S. Langfeld, one of the Experimentalist regulars. Gibson earned his PhD 2 years later, with a dissertation on form perception. He immediately landed a position at Smith College, a prominent women's college in western Massachusetts (alma mater of Mary Calkins), where he taught for just over 20 years. In 1949, he moved to Titchener's old stomping ground, Cornell, where he became legendary and was referred to in an obituary as the "seer of Ithaca" (Restle, 1980).

During World War II, on leave from Smith, Gibson served in the Army Air Corps, first developing standard paper-and-pencil selection tests for pilots and then creating films for training and selection purposes. The idea was to test pilots' abilities to judge distance and motion during simulated flight landings. The war experience began to change Gibson's ideas about how best to study perception (E. Gibson, 2002). Whereas traditional laboratory research typically used stationary participants perceiving various stationary stimuli, Gibson realized that in real-world perception, persons are usually in motion and objects in the environment seem to flow as the person moves through the environment. Out of this insight came a program of research and a theoretical stance that became known as **ecological perception** —perception while navigating through realistic environments and perception that emphasized environmental factors rather than the internal attributes of the perceiver. That is, instead of looking at perception from the standpoint of what was happening on the person's retina, the focus for Gibson shifted to what was happening in the environment (Reed, 1988). To illustrate the strength of Gibson's conviction, consider what he had to say about the tachistoscope. The "T-scope" has a long history and had become a standard apparatus in the perception laboratory; it is a device in which stationary participants peer into a box that presents simple stimuli to be judged in some way (e.g., compared for size or distance from the viewer). In a chapter of a well-known edited book, *A Century of Psychology as Science* (Koch & Leary, 1992), Gibson concluded that the results of a "century of research on perception are insignificant" (p. 229), and he singled out the T-scope for particular scorn:

> What experimenters have been trying to do is to impoverish the stimulation so as to allow the processes of perception to manifest themselves in purer form. . . . Hence the tachistoscope is used to reduce the flow of stimulation to a snapshot. Or a point stimulus is applied so as to reduce the stimulation even further. Is the tachistiscope an achievement? It seems to me to be a calamity. Far from reducing visual experience to its simplest form, it prevents the visual system from operating normally. (p. 228)

This quote hints strongly at Gibson's plan, which was to describe perception as it occurred in the complexity of the real world. The tone of the quote also helps you understand why his ideas were not always welcomed by more "traditional" perception researchers. Gibson's theories about perception reached their final form in the year he died, with the publication of *The Ecological Approach to Visual Perception* (J. Gibson, 1979). His ideas contributed significantly to Ulric Neisser's *Cognition and Reality* (1976)—as you recall from earlier in the chapter, Neisser called for a more ecological strategy when studying cognition.

Two examples will illustrate Gibson's ecological approach. First, he believed that perception was guided by environmental *invariances*. That is, some aspects of the environment will be constant and provide invaluable information directly to perceivers navigating the real world. One such invariance is produced by *texture gradients* in the environment. Imagine, for example, that you are standing at the end of a long corridor that has a floor with a checkerboard pattern, black and white tiles that are each 6 inches square. You look straight down and then you move your gaze down the corridor to the other end. At your feet, the texture is highly detailed (you can clearly make out the sharp edges of the squares); as your gaze moves down the corridor, however, your ability to detect that level of detail decreases. In Gibson's terms, the texture gradient changes as our gaze shifts from a near to a far distance. Now suppose you place a foot-tall cylinder midway down the corridor and an identical cylinder toward the far end of the corridor. The retinal image for the closer cylinder will be larger, but the two cylinders will appear to be the same size; one of them will just be farther away. They appear to be the same size, Gibson would say, because each cylinder covers exactly the same amount of texture (same number of tiles). So this phenomenon, size constancy, occurs because the relationship between the object and its surrounding texture remains the same (i.e., is invariant), and they will remain the same as you move along the corridor.

As a second example of Gibson's ecological approach, consider what happens when we move through an environment. Imagine running down the street, for example. As you move, your visual focus is normally on what is in front of you, and whatever that object happens to be remains relatively still, perceptually. Gibson called that object the *focus of expansion*. All the other information (left, right, above, and below) is moving past you, creating what Gibson called an *optic flow*. One basic principle is that there is a direct relationship between the distance between you and the objects moving toward you, and the speed of this optic flow. As objects get closer, the flow accelerates. That optic flow, then, and its relative speed, combined with the stability of the focus of expansion, yields information that keeps you from running off the path you are on.

One final point about Gibson is that his years at Smith College, in addition to giving him his start as a respected teacher and researcher, had one other life-changing outcome. While at Smith he met and fell in love with one of his students, eventually marrying her. Eleanor Jack became Eleanor Jack Gibson, and she was one of the 20th century's most prominent developmental psychologists, in some ways even surpassing her husband. As you will see in the next chapter, for instance, it was Eleanor, not James, standing in the Rose Garden of the White House and receiving the National Medal of Science from President Bush (look ahead to Figure 15.1).

Social Psychology

Social psychology began to develop as an identifiable subdiscipline of psychology through the efforts of Floyd Allport (1890–1978), whose brother Gordon is highlighted in this chapter's section on personality psychology. Floyd studied with Hugo Münsterberg at Harvard and earned a doctorate in 1919 (directed by Herbert Langfeld, who subsequently went to Princeton and mentored James Gibson). Allport's dissertation research was on social facilitation, the influence of others on the behavior of an individual, and this research set the tone for his approach to social psychology. It was behaviorist in spirit, and Allport deliberately contrasted his social psychology (with its emphasis on the behavior of the individual and its influence by the social environment) with a different version that evolved into modern sociology, which has more of an emphasis on group processes (Parkovnick, 2000). For example, when studying group problem solving, Allport insisted that the explanation for the behavior that occurred was to be found in the actions of the individuals making up the group. From a more group-oriented standpoint, emphasis might be on some "group process" that would influence the solution to the problem at hand. Allport criticized the tendency to explain behavior by referring to group processes as the group fallacy (Danziger, 2000). Allport promoted his view in his 1924 text, *Social Psychology* (F. Allport, 1924), a text said to have created social psychology as a course routinely found in psychology department course listings (Hilgard, 1987).

Leon Festinger (1919–1989)   Allport's emphasis on the individual in social psychology was challenged by the work of Kurt Lewin. We have already seen that in addition to his many other contributions, Lewin (Chapter 9) was an important pioneer in social psychology, through his studies of leadership and much of his action research. The gestalt influence was evident in Lewin's concepts of group processes—to relate the gestalt anthem to social psychology, one could say that group behavior is more than the sum of the behaviors of the group's individual members. Lewin's influence was widespread, and he had a direct effect on his most famous student, Leon Festinger (Figure 14.5), although Festinger's approach to methodology emphasized tighter experimental controls than Lewin's (Danziger, 2000).

FIGURE 14.5   Leon Festinger in the lab, expostulating.

Leon Festinger was born and raised in New York City, the son of Jewish immigrants from Eastern Europe. When he graduated from City College of New York in 1939, he already had a publication (with one of his college teachers) in the prestigious *Journal of Experimental Psychology* (Hertzman & Festinger, 1940). This professor was also responsible for introducing Festinger to Lewin's ideas, prompting Festinger to apply to graduate school at the University of Iowa to study with Lewin. Festinger earned a PhD under Lewin's direction after just 3 years, in 1942, and remained connected with Lewin until the latter's early death in 1947. During World War II, Festinger served as a statistician for the Committee on Selection and Training of Aircraft Pilots. Then, after the war, he rejoined Lewin at MIT in Boston, where Lewin had just inaugurated the Research Center for Group Dynamics. After Lewin's death, Festinger was part of the group that moved the Center to the University of Michigan. He went from Michigan to the University of Minnesota in 1951, to Stanford in 1955, and then returned home to New York in 1968, where he held the Staudinger Professorship at the New School for Social Research until his death (Zajonc, 1990). During his Stanford tenure, Festinger made his reputation and attracted students who became prominent social psychologists themselves (e.g., Elliott Aronson). Over the years, his students remained fiercely loyal to him, even though he could be a hard taskmaster and was not tolerant of imprecise thinking (Brehm, 1998).

Festinger completed important research in several social psychology topics, but he is remembered for developing what could be the most important theory that social psychology has yet seen: the theory of **cognitive dissonance**. Festinger drafted a version of it in 1954 and then produced the first thorough description in book form (Festinger, 1957). The theory's influence has been substantial. A social psychology text will give you a better description of the theory and its famous studies, but in general, the theory of cognitive dissonance can be summarized as follows:

- People are motivated to be consistent in their thoughts, feelings, and actions.
- Whenever people hold two or more thoughts that are inconsistent with each other, cognitive dissonance, a state of emotional and cognitive discomfort, occurs.
- Whenever people experience dissonance, they are motivated to reduce it and return to a state of internal consistency or balance.

To illustrate the theory, consider an example that Festinger frequently used, the intelligent person who smokes. Like everyone, the smoker desires to be consistent in thought and action. Yet two thoughts are inconsistent—"I am smoking" and "Research indicates that smoking will kill me." Assuming the person is not suicidal, these thoughts create dissonance, which the person is motivated to reduce. This can be accomplished in several ways: The person can stop smoking, might question the validity of the evidence, or might add other elements to the situation, saying, for instance, that everyone has to die and, while the smoking might not be ideal, it helps with weight control. One criterion of a good theory is that it produces research—by that measure, Festinger's dissonance theory has been exceptionally productive, generating literally hundreds of experiments and being applied to situations ranging from the consequences of decision making to the effects of hypocrisy (Harmon-Jones & Mills, 1999).

From a historical standpoint, Festinger's research is important because it created an experimental tradition in social psychology that was distinctive in its use of elaborately staged and deceptive research settings (Korn, 1997). These research environments were designed to involve research participants in the experiment so that their "true" reactions to dissonance-arousing situations could be measured and the theory given a strong test. Probably the most famous example was a study by Festinger and a Stanford undergraduate, Merrill Carlsmith (Festinger & Carlsmith, 1959). Students who signed up for the study first spent an hour completing a series of boring tasks; then, through an elaborate deception, they were induced to tell the person who seemed to be the next participant that the study was really interesting. Thus Carlsmith (who ran the study) convinced participants to lie, creating a situation that produced dissonance ("I am an honest person" is dissonant with "I just told someone that a very boring experiment was actually interesting"). As an incentive, participants were to be paid either $1 or $20 for their lie. Afterward, apparently as part of a survey being run by the psychology department (another deception), participants were asked what they *really* thought of the experiment. The results? Those paid $20 still thought the experiment was boring, but those paid just $1 shifted their attitude and decided the study was fairly interesting after all. Festinger and Carlsmith concluded that when faced with the dissonance about lying, participants in the $20 group justified it by saying it was a small lie and worth the money. Those paid $1, however, did not have sufficient justification for the lie, so they convinced themselves that they had not actually lied—the study really was kind of interesting after all.

The Festinger and Carlsmith (1959) study was typical of the research that emerged from Festinger's laboratory. They were intricately staged productions, often requiring many hours of rehearsal. Of Carlsmith's performance, for example, Aronson (1991) later wrote:

> One of the most vivid memories of my years as a graduate student in Leon's lab
> involves the exciting and tedious hours Leon and I spent prior to that experiment,
> coaching and directing the performance of a very precocious undergraduate named
> Merrill Carlsmith until he got it right. Initially, Merrill ... persisted in delivering his lines
> in a very stiff and wooden way; we kept walking him through the procedure, over and
> over again, until he eventually became extremely convincing. (p. 216)

The care with which these productions were choreographed resulted in what social psychologists call *experimental reality* (Aronson, 1999)—research participants were completely taken in by the research situations and reacted as if they were really involved in the situations being created. Of course, that meant participants in Festinger's studies were routinely deceived about the true purpose of the studies, which made Festinger's research the object of numerous discussions about the ethics of deception in research (e.g., Korn, 1997). Festinger later indicated that he stopped doing research in social psychology in 1964, mainly because he was looking for a new challenge (he found it in the study of archeology) but also because he found the increased concern about research ethics annoying. Festinger was not insensitive to the problem, harshly criticizing Army research that gave unwitting soldiers LSD to see their reactions (see Thomas, 1995, for more on this unfortunate episode). Compared to that, however, he saw little danger "in temporarily deceiving persons in order to study some important question" (Festinger, 1980, p. 249). Nonetheless, Festinger's procedures set the tone, and social psychological research in the 1960s and 1970s became infamous for its high level of deception.

Another legacy of the Festinger research program concerned research design. Festinger was clearly influenced by Lewin in the topics he studied, but Festinger thought Lewin's approach to research design was rather casual and in need of more precise control. Also, it was during the early 1950s that the analysis of variance (ANOVA), developed by British statistician Sir Ronald Fisher in the 1920s, became widely used as the way to analyze data (Rucci &

Tweney, 1980).[4] The ANOVA fit perfectly into Festinger's research designs, allowing for precise analyses of the main effects of "manipulated independent variables" (e.g., $1 vs. $20) as well as interactions among variables. Also, as Danziger (2000) observed, ANOVA was becoming widely used in the more traditional areas of experimental psychology in the 1950s. By applying ANOVA logic to his research, Festinger helped enhance the scientific reputation of social psychology, which was not always held in high esteem by experimentalists.

Festinger, a heavy smoker, died of liver cancer in 1989. Perhaps thinking of his often quoted dissonance example of the smoker, and perhaps reducing dissonance to the end, he is said to have announced during his illness, "Make sure everyone knows it wasn't lung cancer!" (quoted in Zajonc, 1990, p. 662).

Personality Psychology

For most of the research encountered in this chapter, the goal has been to understand some general principles about behavior or cognitive processes. Thus, when Miller declared a limit to the capacity of short-term memory, when Hebb detailed the actions of cell assemblies, when Gibson examined the effects of optic flow on perception, and when Festinger discussed dissonance reduction processes, they were describing principles that presumably affect humans in general. This approach to science is known as a **nomothetic** one. Another approach to science focuses on a detailed analysis of the unique individual and examines ways of determining how one individual differs from another. This kind of scientific strategy takes an **idiographic** approach. The nomothetic–idiographic distinction is usually associated with Gordon Allport, the featured psychologist in this section of the chapter, although he was not the first to use the terms (Hilgard, 1987). As will be seen, Allport championed an idiographic approach (as did Henry Murray, a colleague of Allport's at Harvard, as you might recall from Chapter 12).

The psychology of personality includes both nomothetic and idiographic elements. Personality researchers look for general principles (e.g., factors influencing shyness behavior), and they also examine individuals carefully, measure them with reference to their traits, and determine how one person's traits differ from another's (Fred's shyness level, compared to Ted's). The concept of "personality" is largely a 20th-century invention and the inventor, as you are about to learn, was Gordon Allport.

Gordon Allport (1897–1967)   Social psychology and personality psychology have important historical connections, including a family link. Gordon Allport (Figure 14.6) was born in Indiana and raised in Cleveland, Ohio, the last of his parents' four boys. He and his brothers were raised to value hard work, self-sacrifice, a strong moral code, and the kind of idealism that manifested itself in a duty to serve (Bruner, 1968). You just read about one of Gordon's older brothers—Floyd's 1924 social psychology text was an important step in the creation of social psychology as an identifiable subdiscipline of psychology. Gordon had

---

[4]Fisher developed the ANOVA in the context of agricultural research, in which he would examine, for instance, the effects of some type or some amount of fertilizer on corn production. He published his work on ANOVA in a general statistics text in the 1920s (Fisher, 1925), but his most elaborate description of the technique appeared a decade later (Fisher, 1935). If you are familiar with the technique from a statistics class, and remember calculating an F ratio or reading one from an SPSS printout, you have probably already guessed that the F stands for the test's inventor.

FIGURE 14.6 Gordon Allport in his office at Harvard.

exactly the same effect on personality psychology when he published a text in 1937 called *Personality: A Psychological Interpretation* (G. Allport, 1937).

Following his graduation from Harvard, Allport was unsure of his future; he spent a year reflecting on it while teaching English and sociology at an American-based men's school in Istanbul, Turkey. Following the urging of his brother, who was now an instructor at Harvard, Allport applied to graduate school there and was accepted, his financing assured by a fellowship. Following Floyd's suggestion, he chose the emerging topic of personality as his dissertation topic. That his topic was away from mainstream experimental psychology became evident to him in 1921, when Herbert Langfeld invited Allport to present his work on personality to a meeting of Titchener's Experimentalists at Clark University.[5] As Boring (1967) later reported in his history of the group:

[5]You have probably noticed that Herbert Langfeld appears several times in this chapter, directing the doctoral dissertations of three of the prominent psychologists featured—Gibson and both Allports. Langfeld (1879–1958) earned his PhD at Berlin in 1909 under Carl Stumpf (mentor to several gestaltists, as mentioned in Chapter 9 and pictured in Figure 9.1) and then joined the faculty at Harvard. He remained until 1924, when he moved to Princeton and became director of the laboratory there. He was APA president in 1930. With Boring and H. P.

There was a long discussion of David Katz's modes of appearance of colors, and after that Langfeld was asked for a report and he put up Gordon Allport to tell about his analysis of personality. Allport's communication was followed by a long silence, and then Titchener said: "As we were saying, the modes of appearance of colors are. . . ." Social psychology and personality were as much taboo at the Experimentalists as animal psychology. "What did you let him work on that for?" Titchener later asked Langfeld. (p. 323)

Undeterred, Allport completed his doctorate on personality traits in a mere 2 years, in 1922. He then toured Europe for 2 more years on a study grant before returning to Harvard as an instructor in the new department of Social Ethics. There he developed a course in personality that eventually led to his famous text of 1937 (Allport, 1937). Many years later, his mature views on personality appeared in *Pattern and Growth in Personality* (Allport, 1961). He stayed at Harvard for 2 years and went to Dartmouth for 4 years; then he was enticed to return to Harvard in 1930, where he finished his distinguished career.

Although he contributed research in the nomothetic tradition, Allport was a champion of the idiographic ideal that everyone was a unique personality and that much could be learned by the careful study of individuals. In Allport's conception of personality, the basic unit of individual personality was the **trait**, which for him meant a particular pattern of thinking, feeling, and behaving that was characteristic of a person and a means of distinguishing that person from others. A trait was "a kind of higher order habit, although it was much more generalized" (Nicholson, 2003, p. 154). Allport identified three varieties of traits that differed in level of generality and importance—cardinal, central, and secondary. **Cardinal traits**, not possessed by everyone, were attributes that were dominant in a person, to the point where describing a person's cardinal trait would identify that person to others, and most of what that person would do was related to the trait. Napoleon, for instance, might be described by a cardinal trait of a need for power. **Central traits** are those dozen or so attributes that provide a reasonably accurate summary description of an individual. For example, they are the kinds the terms typically found in letters of recommendation (Hilgard, 1987). **Secondary traits** are less obvious characteristics, manifested in relatively few behaviors, and perhaps known only to close friends of an individual.

In line with his idiographic sentiments, Allport advocated the **case study**, an in-depth analysis of a person, as a way to study personality.[6] As editor or associate editor of the *Journal of Abnormal and Social Psychology* from 1937 until his death in 1967, he was responsible for accepting many case study articles for inclusion in the journal (Pettigrew, 1969). Although he completed just one detailed case study himself, it was a famous one: *Letters from Jenny* (Allport, 1965). The book-length study described the personality of "Jenny Masterson" (a fictitious name), based on a close analysis of a series of 301 letters written over a 12-year period by a middle-aged woman to a young married couple (Hall & Lindzey, 1970). Allport was also involved in the development of a popular (for a time) personality test. With Philip

---

Weld, he published a successful introductory psychology text that went through several editions. And he developed a close friendship with another major character in this chapter, F. C. Bartlett—they often played golf together during Langfeld's frequent visits to England (Bartlett, 1958a).

[6]Allport was a Harvard colleague of Henry Murray (Chapter 12), who placed a similar emphasis on the in-depth study of individuals. Allport did not share Murray's enthusiasm for psychoanalysis. Yet when it appeared that Murray's contract might not be renewed in 1937 because of objections from the experimentalists at Harvard (e.g., Boring), Allport strongly supported Murray, whose contract was eventually renewed (Nicholson, 2003).

Vernon, a visiting professor from England who had been a student of Bartlett, Allport developed *A Study of Values* (Allport & Vernon, 1931), a test measuring the strength of a person's value systems and based on a theory of six "ideal types" developed by the German psychologist Eduard Spranger. The six types were theoretic, aesthetic, social, political, economic, and religious, and Allport and Vernon developed a popular self-report survey to measure the strength of each of them.

Allport came to prominence at a time when Freud's psychoanalytic theories were becoming very popular in America; unlike his Harvard colleague Henry Murray (Chapter 12), however, Allport was no fan of psychoanalytic theory. He did not reject the concept of the unconscious, but he simply did not think it was essential for understanding someone's personality. He also thought Freud's emphasis on sex was excessive, and he rejected the idea that our past history had an overwhelming effect on our present and future. He also was not impressed with the psychoanalytic strategy for measuring personality that came on the scene, the best example being the inkblot test developed by Hermann Rorschach in 1921, which was popular enough to have 38 articles written about it in the 1920s and about 230 more in the 1930s (Klopfer, 1973). Such "projective" tests (Murray's TAT was another example) assumed that people were not capable of giving an accurate description of their personality on a self-report, because much of the personality was said to be buried in the unconscious. After giving responses to ambiguous stimuli (inkblots), the "true" personality could be inferred through a process of interpretation, so the argument went. Allport did not buy it. Instead, perhaps because of his own calm rationality, he firmly believed people were capable of knowing themselves and therefore able to respond accurately to self-report personality inventories. The psychoanalytic strategy, Allport (1953; quoted in Hall & Lindzey, 1970) argued,

> seems to mark the culmination of a century-long era of irrationalism, and therefore of distrust. Has the subject no right to be believed?...The individual's conscious report is rejected as untrustworthy, and the contemporary thrust of his motives is disregarded in favor of a backward tracing of his conduct to earlier formative stages. The individual loses his right to be believed. And while he is busy leading his life in the present with a forward thrust into the future, most [psychoanalysts] have become busy tracing it backward into the past. (p. 280)

Allport's criticism of Freudian psychoanalysis was genuine and intellectually legitimate. However, his distaste might also have been influenced to a degree by a meeting that he had with Freud in Vienna while on his way back from the year in Turkey, just before he started graduate studies. After brashly making an appointment to see Freud and being ushered into the famous office, Allport found himself at a loss for a way to open the conversation in a way that might impress the great man. Hoping to get a quick Freudian interpretation, he described an incident he witnessed on a tram in which a small boy seemed to be overly concerned about dirt: "He kept saying to his mother, 'I don't want to sit there...don't let that dirty man sit beside me'" (Allport, 1967; quoted in Nicholson, 2003, p. 69). Allport apparently expected Freud to give an analysis of the relationship between mother and son, but instead, he "fixed his kindly therapeutic eyes upon me and said, 'And was that little boy you?'" (p. 69).

Allport is accurately considered the father of modern personality theory, and the title of a recent biography, *Inventing Personality* (Nicholson, 2003), is apt. Allport was primarily responsible for taking the 19th-century study of "character" and turning it into the 20th-century study of "personality." It is also worth noting that Allport made important contributions to his brother's area of social psychology (*The Nature of Prejudice*, 1954), and his deep spirituality led him to write on the psychology of religion (*The Individual and His Religion*, 1950).

For his contributions to personality psychology and his advocacy of an idiographic psychology, Gordon Allport earned numerous honors and awards during his career; his prized possession was a two-volume set of papers published by 55 of his former PhD students and presented to him near the end of his career. In his autobiography, Allport (1967) wrote that his students had "presented me with two handsomely bound volumes of their own writings with the following inscription: 'From his students—in appreciation of his respect for their individuality.' This is an intimate honor, and one I prize above all others" (p. 24).

Developmental Psychology

Interest in development has a long history that predates the creation of psychology. We have already seen that the nature–nurture issue is timeless. Since the creation of psychology as a discipline, interest in psychological development among psychologists has been high, from the child study movement initiated by G. Stanley Hall at the turn of the 20th century to the emphasis on the importance of the early years shown by both Freudians and behaviorists. During neobehaviorism's prominent years, a Swiss psychologist, soon to be among the 20th century's most famous psychologists, was carefully examining the cognitive development of young children, including his own.

Jean Piaget (1896–1980) All students who have taken a course in developmental psychology will recognize the name Jean Piaget and will probably recall seeing a photo in their text of a 6- or 7-year-old schoolchild staring at the water levels in two different-sized containers. Piaget was a master at creating simple demonstrations of complex cognitive phenomena, and his conservation of volume task, in which "preoperational" children typically fail to recognize that the volume of a liquid remains constant when it is transferred to a taller or shorter container, is among the better known of them.

Jean Piaget (Figure 14.7, in his office) was a native of Switzerland, and except for a few brief interludes, spent most of his life there. Much like John Stuart Mill and Francis Galton before him, he was a precocious child. He developed a strong interest in the biological sciences as a schoolboy and at age 10, he managed to publish a one-page description of an albino sparrow in a local natural history journal. He spent most of his adolescence collecting and classifying mollusks, publishing several articles about them and even being offered a job as curator of mollusks at a reputable museum in Geneva—he declined on the grounds that he had two years of high school remaining (Piaget, 1952). He completed his college degree at age 18. Within another 3 years, in 1918, he had earned a PhD in biology and had an international reputation as an expert on mollusks.

During his school years, Piaget also became interested in the philosophical problems of epistemology, especially the question of how we obtain our knowledge of the world. He read widely in philosophy and psychology (including William James and Sigmund Freud) and, after finishing his biology doctorate, decided to examine the problem more closely. An opportunity arose in 1919 when he met Théodore Simon, of Binet-Simon fame, who asked the young biologist to work on an intelligence-testing project in the Binet laboratory in Paris. Hence, Piaget spent the next few years studying verbal intelligence in school-aged children. His initial task was to standardize a reasoning test developed by British psychologist Cyril

FIGURE 14.7 Jean Piaget, Swiss development psychologist.

Burt, but while doing so, he discovered that he was less interested in whether the children answered questions correctly than in the thinking processes they used to answer the questions. Especially revealing were the cognitive processes involved when children got the wrong answers. To explore these strategies, Piaget began interviewing the children about how they solved the problems. From this experience, he concluded that children's cognition differs from adult cognition not just quantitatively, but qualitatively. That is, children do not just know less than adults, they think in an entirely different manner. Eventually, this insight led to Piaget's well-known stage theory of cognitive development.

Following the experience in the Binet lab and on the basis of the resulting publications, Piaget was offered a position as director at a research institute for the study of children in Geneva in 1921. During the 1920s, he also taught at the universities of Geneva and Neuchâtel (his hometown) and published numerous articles and five books. The first of the five, *The Language and Thought of the Child* (1923/1959), gave Piaget an international reputation while he was still in his late twenties (Brainerd, 1996).

Piaget and his wife also had three children during this time—daughters in 1925 and 1927, and a son in 1931. Piaget was not about to miss an opportunity, so he and his wife made systematic observations of their three children as they grew. One important lesson for Piaget was that the verbal interviews he used in the Binet laboratory were useless for preverbal infants—other observational procedures had to be used. For instance, he inferred that infants were learning about cause and effect by observing their tendency to systematically repeat their actions ("circular reactions"), and he developed his famous concept of "object permanence" by noting whether infants would search for objects that were out of sight. During these years, the decade of the 1930s, Piaget developed some of his most famous demonstrations of children's cognition and formulated his stage theory of cognitive development (Brainerd,

1996).[7] He referred to his approach as a **genetic epistemology**, using the term *genetic* to refer to developmental processes, not heredity (i.e., in the same way that G. Stanley Hall had used the term a generation earlier). That is, Piaget's focus was on determining precisely how knowledge, as represented by hypothetical mental structures that he called schemata, developed within the individual.[8] He believed that children were active formulators of their knowledge rather than passive recipients of their experiences, and he believed that knowledge structures formed "wholes" that could not be reduced to their elements. This latter point connects with Gestalt psychology (Chapter 9), of course, and Piaget was well aware of and generally appreciative of the gestaltists for showing him that he was not alone in formulating a theory based on "structures of the whole." As he put it:

> Contact with the work of Köhler and Wertheimer made [an] . . . impression on me. . . . I had the distinct pleasure of concluding that my previous research was not sheer folly, since one could design on such a central hypothesis of the subordination of the parts to the organizing whole not only a consistent theory, but also a splendid series of experiments. (Piaget, 1952, p. 248)

In the early 1950s, Piaget established a research institute of his own at the University of Geneva, the International Center for Genetic Epistemology, and was its director for all of his remaining years (Voyat, 1981). Despite his reputation in Europe, however, he was still relatively unknown in the United States, partly because not all of his work was being translated into English but also because of the American preoccupation with behaviorism. He was not completely unknown in America—he had been among the group of young international psychologists participating in the 1929 International Congress at Yale (others: Pavlov and Lewin), and Harvard had given him an honorary degree at a conference celebrating its 300th birthday in 1936 (Kessen, 1996). Also, as you might have noticed from the citation in the last paragraph, the editors of the prestigious *History of Psychology in Autobiography* series (including E. G. Boring) saw fit to include Piaget in their fourth edition, which appeared in 1952. Nonetheless, his work was not widely known in the United States until the 1960s, just when cognitive psychology was coming to the forefront of American experimental psychology. Following a 1960 conference devoted to his work in Dedham, Massachusetts, sponsored by the Social Science Research Council (Kessen & Kuhlman, 1962) and the publication of John Flavell's *The Developmental Psychology of Jean Piaget* (1963), Piaget's ideas exploded onto the scene, and he began accumulating the status he retains today as one of the century's most influential psychologists (Kessen, 1996).

IN PERSPECTIVE: PSYCHOLOGICAL SCIENCE

Chapter 13 closed with a description of a split in modern psychology between those who investigate the basic principles of psychology, the researcher-academicians, and those who apply these principles, the practitioners. Chapter 13 focused on the practitioners, and this chapter has concerned the researchers. For both chapters, it is important to note that the surface has barely

---

[7]As you may recall, the stages are sensorimotor (0–2), preoperational (2–7), concrete operational (7–11), and formal operational (11–adult). For details, refer to any textbook of developmental psychology.

[8]Thus, independently of Bartlett, Piaget arrived at a similar conclusion about cognitive structures and used the same term.

been scratched. Chapter 13 concentrated on clinical and industrial psychology, but left out other major areas of application: school psychology, community psychology, rehabilitation psychology, and forensic psychology, just to name a few. Similarly, this chapter concentrated on cognitive psychology and then sampled from physiological, perceptual, social, personality, and developmental psychology. A glimpse at any modern introductory text will tell you that much was omitted. But my goal was never to be comprehensive in my descriptions of psychology during the latter two thirds of the 20th century. Rather, my purpose is partly to give you a glimpse of the tremendous diversity of interests among psychologists, partly to show some of the interconnections among them, and partly to entice you to become interested in these topics and study them in more depth. The final chapter elaborates on the theme of diversity and ends by briefly discussing whether there is one psychology or many.

SUMMARY

Cognitive Psychology Arrives (Again)

• After World War II, psychologists became increasingly involved in studying mental processes, a topic that had been a key interest for psychology's earliest pioneers. This cognitive psychology movement in America developed gradually during the 1950s, 1960s, and 1970s, while behaviorism became a less powerful force. The change was more evolutionary than revolutionary.

• During the period when behaviorism dominated American psychology (the 1930s and 1940s), some American researchers (e.g., Stroop) still investigated cognitive topics; European psychologists, who never became as enamored of behaviorism as the Americans did, made important contributions to the understanding of mental processes. The British psychologist Frederick Bartlett is a prime example. He was critical of the laboratory-based, nonsense-syllable type of memory research and proposed instead that research on memory should emphasize real-life situations. He believed that memory was constructive and was influenced by schemata, that is, one's basic concepts about the phenomenal world. His "War of the Ghosts" research showed that memory is influenced by schemata influenced by one's culture.

• Within psychology, the cognitive movement gained momentum from problems that developed within the behaviorist-associationist tradition. At the Hixon Symposium in 1948, Lashley showed that associationist principles could not explain the problem of serial order, and behaviorism seemed incapable of explaining language behavior, which seemed to be more species specific than the outcome of conditioning.

• Outside of psychology, developments in the disciplines of computer science, information theory, and linguistics as well as a dramatic increase in federal funding for research contributed to the evolution of cognitive psychology. Researchers began to create models of cognitive processes that used the computer program as a metaphor and emphasized the concept of the individual as an information processor rather than a responder to stimuli. Chomsky argued that Skinnerian behaviorism was not relevant for the study of language and proposed a nativist account of language development.

• During the decade of the 1950s, several landmark papers and books appeared. These included Miller's paper on the limited capacity of information processing in immediate memory (7 ± 2), Broadbent's research on selective attention, and the book by Miller, Galanter, and Pribram (*Plans and the Structure of Behavior*), which featured the idea of information feedback in the form of TOTE units as a replacement for the reflex arc concept.

• The first major summary of laboratory research in cognitive psychology appeared in 1967 with Neisser's book; the book also produced a self-identification of the field as "cognitive psychology." About a decade later, Neisser questioned cognitive psychology's emphasis on basic laboratory research and, in the spirit of Bartlett, called for an increase in research on cognitive processes as they operate in the everyday world to help individuals adapt to their environments (i.e., research having ecological validity).

• Cognitive psychology has spread to other specialty areas within psychology. In addition, the interdisciplinary field of cognitive science evolved in parallel with cognitive psychology. Cognitive science includes psychology, computer science (e.g., artificial intelligence), linguistics, anthropology, and epistemology. The field of artificial intelligence includes the study of computer simulations of human cognitive processes and the development of expert systems in which the computer acts intelligently. Researchers disagree on the extent to which machine thinking resembles human thinking.

Other Research Areas

• In addition to the area of cognitive psychology, important developments emerged in other research topics of interest to psychologists. Advances were made in understanding (a) the relationship between the brain and behavior, (b) the nature of human perception, (c) the effect of the social environment on individual behavior, (d) the nature of human personality, and (e) the process of human development.

• Interest in studying the brain–behavior relationship accelerated in the second half of the 20th century. Technological breakthroughs (e.g., EEG) sparked this interest, but the research and theorizing of Donald Hebb were especially influential. Hebb's model of the brain centered on the cell assembly—an interrelated combination of associated neurons—and the phase sequence, an organization of cell assemblies and the neurological equivalent of thinking. Hebb synapses are synapses that have undergone structural change as a result of some learning process.

• For most of the history of research on the nature of human perception, the emphasis has been on the attributes of the perceiver. But James Gibson, promoting his ecological view of perception, argued that the important factors affecting human perception (e.g., perceptual invariances, optic flow) lie in the environment, not within the person.

• Floyd Allport and Kurt Lewin are important pioneers in social psychology, but Leon Festinger (a student of Lewin) developed the most important social psychological theory of the 20th century, the theory of cognitive dissonance. Festinger's experiments were known for the precision and elegance of their design, their use of complex statistical analysis (ANOVA), and their extensive use of deception.

• Gordon Allport was a champion of the idiographic tradition, which emphasizes the in-depth study of individuals, as opposed to the nomothetic tradition, the study of general principles. More than anyone, Allport is responsible for making personality psychology a topic of study in psychology. He believed that people could be characterized with reference to their cardinal, central, and secondary traits.

• In development psychology, the most important figure in the 20th century was the Swiss psychologist Jean Piaget, whose genetic epistemology (i.e., an interest in understanding the growth and development of knowledge within an individual) and stage theory of cognitive development eventually became influential in America, after American psychologists turned from behavior to an interest in cognitive processes.

STUDY QUESTIONS

1. Describe two examples of research that demonstrate an interest in cognitive psychology even during the heyday of behaviorism.

2. Describe Bartlett's criticism of the Ebbinghaus approach to memory. How did his methodology differ?

3. Describe the "War of the Ghosts" study, and use it to explain why Bartlett believed memory to be constructive. Be sure to work the term *schema* into your answer.

4. What was the serial order problem, and why did it create a problem for behaviorism?

5. Describe how the development of cognitive psychology was influenced by computer science and information theory.

6. Chomsky argued that behaviorism failed to explain language. What were his arguments?

7. Describe how scientific revolutions occur, according to Thomas Kuhn's model.

8. The Close-Up argues that a cognitive "revolution" did *not* really occur. Explain.

9. What did George Miller discover about the nature of STM?

10. Describe how Broadbent studied selective attention and what he concluded about it.

11. What was the influence of the "Plans" book on cognitive psychology?

12. Consider the two books by Neisser that are described in the chapter. What was the influence of each?

13. What is the difference between cognitive psychology and cognitive science?

14. Use an anagram problem to distinguish between an algorithm and a heuristic.

15. What is artificial intelligence, and how does it relate to the Turing test?

16. Donald Hebb is said to have revived interest in studying the relationship between brain and behavior. Explain.

17. Describe Hebb's ideas about cortical organization and the effects of experience on the brain.

18. How did Gibson's ecological approach to perception differ from traditional perception research?

19. What did Gibson mean by invariance? Give an example.

20. Floyd Allport and Kurt Lewin had different ways of conceptualizing social psychology. How did they differ?

21. Describe Festinger's theory of cognitive dissonance.

22. Describe Festinger's impact on the nature of research in social psychology.

23. Distinguish between nomothetic and idiographic approaches to psychology.

24. Describe Gordon Allport's influence on personality psychology. Why is he said to have "invented" personality?

25. Why did Piaget call himself a genetic epistemologist? Why was the importance of his work late in achieving recognition in the United States?

FOR FURTHER READING

BAARS, B. J. (1986). *The cognitive revolution in psychology.* New York: Guilford.

   A detailed description of the cognitive movement, taken from the standpoint that cognitive psychology represents a revolutionary shift away from behaviorism; noteworthy for containing extensive interviews with key figures, including B. F. Skinner, George Miller, Ulric Neisser, and Noam Chomsky.

BRUCE, D. (1994). Lashley and the problem of serial order. *American Psychologist, 49*, 93–103.

   A highly readable description of Lashley's paper on serial order, given at the Hixon Symposium; describes its impact at the time and later on different audiences; shows that Lashley's paper was not immediately recognized as a breakthrough for cognitive psychology, but its importance was eventually recognized once cognitive psychology became more established.

KORN, J. H. (1997). *Illusions of reality: A history of deception in social psychology.* Albany, NY: SUNY Press.

   A thorough and balanced analysis of the use of deception in social psychological research and the ethical implications of its use; includes whole chapters on the work of Lewin, Festinger, and Stanley Milgram, whose obedience studies in the 1960s and '70s always seem to be included in the ethics chapters of research methods textbooks.

LEAHEY, T. H. (1992). The mythical revolutions of American psychology. *American Psychologist, 47*, 308–318.

   A careful description of several models of the criteria necessary for there to be a "revolution" in science, followed by an analysis of why both behaviorism and cognitive psychology, while important developments in psychology's history, cannot be considered revolutionary.

NICHOLSON, I. A. M. (2003). *Inventing personality: Gordon Allport and the science of selfhood.* Washington, DC: American Psychological Association.

   An intellectual biography of Allport, focusing on the first half of his career and showing how he took the 19th-century study of character and transformed it into the 20th-century study of personality; emphasizes Allport's advocacy of an idiographic approach to psychology and places his work and his life into the contemporary social, political, and institutional context.

CHAPTER 15

LINKING PSYCHOLOGY'S PAST AND PRESENT

But there is a sense in which we are nothing if not our history. Our history is our binding force.

—Sigmund Koch, 1992

PREVIEW AND CHAPTER OBJECTIVES

Of necessity, this chapter is incomplete—the growth of psychology has been exponential in the last 40 to 50 years and would require its own book just to tell the story in broad outline (700-page introductory psychology texts barely scratch the surface). The more modest goal for the chapter is to examine some important trends that have developed in recent decades. One way that psychology has changed is in the area of diversity. Historically, women and minority group members found it difficult to make inroads into a field dominated by white males. Some improvements occurred in the post–World War II era, especially during the past 30 years, and especially for women. Other recent trends in psychology are sketched in the second part of the chapter and doing so highlights one of the book's themes—understanding the present requires understanding the past. The chapter closes with a discussion of whether psychology can be considered a unified discipline. After you finish this final chapter, you should be able to:

- Describe the indicators of increased diversity in psychology
- Describe the barriers to advancement in psychology faced by women and minorities
- Describe the career and contributions of Eleanor Gibson
- Describe the career and contributions of Kenneth and Mamie Clark, especially the effect of their work on the 1954 *Brown v. Board of Education* decision
- Summarize five current trends in psychology and show how their understanding requires knowing some history
- Understand why it can be argued that psychology is many disciplines, not just one
- Understand the role of history as a unifying force in psychology

THE GROWTH AND DIVERSITY OF PSYCHOLOGY

One indication of organized psychology's growth over the past 120 years lies in the membership data for its largest professional organization, the American Psychological Association. From its origins in G. Stanley Hall's study in 1892 until the mid-1920s, the APA showed steady but unspectacular expansion. The initial 31 charter members rose to about 125 by the turn of the century and to about 375 by the end of World War I (Fernberger, 1932, p. 5). With the creation of the associate member status in 1925, however, the growth curve changed direction. After World War II, the total membership stood at approximately 5,000 and has climbed steadily since that time, reaching the 70,000 mark by 1990 (Bulatao, Fulcher, & Evans, 1992). With the 21st century now under way, full APA membership has surpassed 100,000. And the future promises continued growth—psychology is among the most popular majors on campus, new graduate programs appear each year, and applications to graduate school far outnumber available places.

Along with the expansion reflected in APA membership rolls, psychology has also become more diverse over the years. One form of this diversity has been specialization. As you know from the last two chapters, psychologists are no longer just psychologists—they are developmental psychologists, social psychologists, industrial psychologists, clinical psychologists, and personality psychologists, among many others. Even these labels are far too broad. Developmental psychologists, to take just one example, cannot hope to be knowledgeable about their entire subfield but must specialize further within it, perhaps by establishing expertise in infant concept development, adolescent peer relations, or autobiographical memory in the elderly. A second form of psychology's increased diversity is in various types of persons who enter the field. After the 1980s, psychologists were more likely than ever to be female and/or nonwhite.

Women in Psychology's History

The problems for women in psychology have been examined several times in this book. From Chapter 6, you recall the difficulties experienced by such pioneering women as Mary Calkins, Margaret Washburn, and Christine Ladd-Franklin, who were either unable to secure full-time academic positions (Ladd-Franklin) or were limited to teaching at small women's colleges without graduate programs (Calkins and Washburn). This latter problem actually got worse in the 1920s, when many of these small colleges began replacing female professors with males to "enhance" their prestige (Diehl, 1992). Another long-standing barrier to advancement was that women were excluded from the all-important informal communication network of scientific psychologists, as described in Chapter 7. Although E. B. Titchener allowed women into his graduate program at Cornell, in part because of a university requirement, he kept them out of his Experimentalist "club." After Titchener's death in 1927, the group reorganized as the Society of Experimental Psychologists (SEP) and voted to include women, but the de facto obstacles remained. Two women, Washburn and June Downey of Wyoming (who died before attending any meetings), were made charter members of the new group, and Washburn even hosted an SEP meeting at Vassar in 1931.[1] Yet photos of the group in the 1940s and early 1950s simply don't include female faces, and no other woman was elected until 1958 (Furumoto, 1988). Although relatively small in number, the SEP constituted a closed network

---

[1] Walter Miles of Stanford attended the 1931 Vassar meeting and recorded an interesting comment made by Washburn about Titchener. Miles's diary for April 1, 1931, includes this entry: "Washburn's attitude toward T. He never discovered anything, he did not create any apparatus, or methods, he was simply not an experimenter. . . . His great points were his learning and his ability to give a lecture." Washburn apparently also believed that part of the reason Titchener "gave her but little" was that "they were too near the same age" (Miles, 1931).

that influenced academic hiring and advancement.[2] Hence, for many years, the exclusion of women from the group made it virtually impossible for them to fashion successful scientific careers. Some did, despite the odds, and a good postwar example is one of developmental psychology's most celebrated scientists.

Eleanor Gibson (1910–2002) In a Rose Garden ceremony in June of 1992, George H. W. Bush awarded the National Medal of Science, the highest honor a president can confer on a scientist, to Eleanor Gibson (Figure 15.1). The award was for a lifetime of research on topics ranging from the development of depth perception to the basic processes involved in reading. Only nine other psychologists had earned this award up to that time (Kent, 1992). Gibson is also the person referred to earlier as the first woman after Downey and Washburn to be elected to the SEP (in 1958). Today, students are most likely to recall Gibson as the creator of the "visual cliff" used to study depth perception in infants. Her career is a case study in perseverance.

Gibson first became interested in psychology at Smith College, a liberal arts college for women in western Massachusetts. There she learned to run rats in mazes from a student of Harvey Carr (Chapter 7) and studied psychology's history with a student of E. G. Boring (Chapter 1). In her senior year, she took a course from Smith's new German professor, Kurt Koffka (Chapter 9), but found the experience less than enthralling—the gestaltist did little more than read notes from his forthcoming book on Gestalt psychology (Koffka, 1935). She had better luck in a yearlong laboratory course taught by a newly minted experimental psychologist from Princeton—James Gibson, who you met in the last chapter. Eleanor fell in love with both the lab course and the professor. She remained at Smith for a year after graduation, earned a master's degree, and then married her favorite teacher in 1932. Smith hired her as an instructor, and the two Gibsons settled down to an academic life.

FIGURE 15.1 Eleanor Gibson receiving the National Medal of Science in 1992.

[2]The SEP exists today, primarily as an honor society for esteemed experimental psychologists. There are about 200 members, about 30 of them women. Most of the women members were elected in the 1990s (Goodwin, 2005).

Full of enthusiasm for research in psychology, Gibson wanted to earn a doctorate, so she went to Yale in 1935, eager to work in the primate lab of the famous Robert Yerkes (Chapter 8). There, however, she quickly encountered a world very different from Smith, where it was taken for granted that women could accomplish whatever they wished. She managed with some difficulty to get an appointment to see Yerkes, who seemed curious about why she was there. When she said that she wished to work for him, "he stood up, walked to the door, held it open, and said, 'I have no women in my laboratory'" (E. Gibson, 1980, p. 246). Although angered and somewhat disillusioned, Gibson stubbornly refused to leave Yale and eventually managed to convince the neobehaviorist Clark Hull (Chapter 11) of her abilities. She earned a doctorate under his direction in 1938 (she completed most of her doctoral work while still living in western Massachusetts and teaching part-time at Smith). She was then welcomed back to a full-time position at Smith, followed her husband around the country during the war years, and then moved to Ithaca, New York, when James was hired by Cornell University in 1949. Anti-nepotism rules, a major problem for many women psychologists married to professors, kept her from employment at Cornell, yet she persevered once again. For 16 years, she labored as an unpaid "research associate," earning her keep by winning a series of competitive and prestigious research grants. During these years, she created the visual cliff and completed the pioneering studies on depth perception with Richard Walk (e.g., Gibson & Walk, 1960). When Cornell removed its nepotism rules in 1966, Gibson was immediately made a full professor. In 1974, she was named the Susan Linn Sage Endowed Professor of Psychology and, while she never actually retired, she was named professor emeritus in 1980 (Pick, 1994). She continued to be an active scholar and, as late as 1994, addressed the question of psychology's future by vigorously arguing for a theory of organism–environmental interaction that was grounded in a developmental approach (E. Gibson, 1994). Shortly after her death in 2002, a former student wrote about her skills as a teacher:

> She was a very special mentor for her students. She excited our curiosity and engaged us as her collaborators in seeking knowledge about development right from the start. She was always available to talk, and eager to discuss one's ideas. She had an amazing knack for taking a student's most ill-formed idea, pondering it for a while, and then returning it—*and* the credit for it—barely recognizable, as it had been turned into a really good idea, elaborated, clarified, and often made precise as an elegant plan for a study. Her standards were very high and she taught us by example while generously sharing the credit. (Pick, 2003, p. 26)

Eleanor Gibson is just one example of a highly talented scientist who faced barriers to advancement simply because she was a woman. The situation improved somewhat in the 1960s and 1970s, when the women's movement emerged as part of the drive for civil rights. The Civil Rights Act of 1964 prohibited discrimination against women as well as minorities and, in 1972, Title IX specifically prohibited gender discrimination in higher education (Russo, 1988). Within APA, committees on the status of women were formed in the 1960s and 1970s, and in 1969 a group of activist women psychologists within APA formed the Association for Women in Psychology. This group applied enough pressure for APA for form a "Task Force on the Status of Women" in 1971, one outcome of which was the creation, in 1973, of a division for the psychology of women (Division 35—The Society for the Psychology of Women). Three years later, the division launched what has become a successful journal, *The Psychology of Women Quarterly*.

Today, women undergraduate majors in psychology outnumber men by about two to one, about three quarters of graduate students are female, and most of the doctorates in psychology are awarded to women. Although most senior faculty teaching in psychology departments continue to be male, changes are on the way—the proportion of women faculty in departments of psychology (with graduate programs) shifted from about 20% in the mid-1980s to 33% a decade later to 45% in 2009–10 ("Sex, Race/Ethnicity Data," 1995; Pagano, Wicherski, & Kohout, 2010).

Minorities in Psychology's History

Like women, members of minority groups have been on the outside looking in for most of psychology's history. Unlike the case for women, however, significant gains for blacks and most other minorities were not made in the years following World War II, and minorities continue to be underrepresented in psychology. In 1991, for example, only 14% of all bachelor's degrees, 11% of master's degrees, and 9% of doctoral degrees were granted to minorities ("Sex, Race/Ethnicity Data," 1995). Of these, about one half went to African American students, a quarter to Hispanic students, and the remainder to Asian Americans and Native Americans. In 2009–10, for psychology departments offering graduate programs, just 13% of faculty members were from minority groups. Change is coming, however—in 2009–10, minorities comprised 28% of the graduate student population (Finno, Wicherski, & Kohout, 2010).

Despite barriers at least as high as those confronting women, minority psychologists have made important contributions to psychology's history. We have already seen that displaced European Jewish psychologists such as Wertheimer and Lewin became major figures in American psychology. They did so in the face of an anti-Semitism that, though less virulent than the version found in Nazi Germany, occurred in subtle ways nonetheless. The gestaltists were already well enough known to secure positions, but job searches were not quite so easy for other Jewish psychologists, especially during the Great Depression when all jobs were scarce. As psychologist-historian Andrew Winston (1996) has shown, for example, letters of recommendation during the 1930s frequently reinforced the stereotype of Jewish persons as being shrewd and calculating, oversensitive to perceived slights, argumentative, clannish, and defensively aggressive. Candidates for academic positions could be doomed by a letter indicating that they possessed these attributes, and their chances were hardly improved if they were praised by saying, in effect, that while they might be Jewish, they were not like a "typical" Jew. In recommending one of his students, for example, Robert Woodworth wrote that "as his name indicates, [he is] a Jew, but I am sure you would find him a very satisfactory colleague . . . cooperative and eager to fit into the group" (quoted in Winston, 1996, p. 30).

The difficulties faced by Jews paled in comparison to those encountered by African Americans, however. At least nobody accused Jews of lacking intellectual ability. Blacks, on the other hand, have often had their basic abilities questioned; this was especially true during psychology's formative years. As you recall from Chapter 6, scholars such as Francis Sumner faced enormous obstacles when trying to obtain graduate education and then employment in academia. Sumner eventually found his way to Howard University in Washington, DC, where he established the best-known psychology program at a historically black university. Two of his most prominent students were the Clarks.

Kenneth B. (1914–2005) and Mamie Phipps (1917–1983) Clark   On May 17, 1954, the U.S. Supreme Court issued a ruling that has come to be recognized as possibly the most important court decision of the 20th century. Concerning a suit brought against the Board of Education in Topeka, Kansas, the Court declared, by a unanimous 7–0 vote, that "in the field of public education the doctrine of 'separate but equal' has no place. Separate educational facilities are inherently unequal" (quoted in Morison, 1965, p. 1086). The *Brown v. Board of Education* ruling reversed an earlier decision from another time—in 1896 the Court, in *Plessy v. Ferguson*, had ruled that it was legal for there to be separate public facilities (e.g., schools, restrooms) for whites and blacks, as long as the facilities reserved for blacks were of equal quality to those reserved for whites. By declaring the doctrine of "separate but equal" unconstitutional, the *Brown* decision helped pave the way for the civil rights movement of the 1960s and 1970s. Of importance for psychology's history, the *Brown* decision was notable because the Court's decision was influenced by, and made specific reference to, research by psychologists demonstrating the adverse effects of segregation on African American children. Although it was not the only research that contributed to the decision, studies on the self-esteem of black children, completed by Kenneth and Mamie Phipps Clark, have come to symbolize the contribution of psychology to a watershed moment in American history.[3]

Kenneth B. Clark (Figure 15.2) was born in the Panama Canal Zone, educated in the public school system of New York City, and went to college at Howard University in Washington, D.C. Mamie Phipps was a rarity—an African American raised in a comparatively affluent environment. Her father was a physician in Hot Springs, Arkansas, and although she "learned the things not to do" when growing up (quoted in Lal, 2002, p. 21), she was insulated from many of the daily indignities of being black and growing up in the South. Mamie also found her way to Howard University, where she planned to study math. That plan changed, however, when she met her future husband, who convinced her to join him as a psychology

FIGURE 15.2 Kenneth Clark.

[3]In its decision, the Supreme Court did not specifically cite the research completed by the Clarks but did cite Kenneth Clark's general summary of all the social scientific research relating to the issue of the effects of segregation on development (Keppel, 2002).

major. Together, they came under Sumner's influence. Kenneth and Mamie both completed bachelors and masters degrees at Howard (1935 and 1936 for Kenneth; 1938 and 1939 for Mamie), and both went on to earn doctorates from Columbia (1940 and 1943). They eloped a few months before Mamie's 1938 graduation from Howard.

The research for which the Clarks are best known originated in and grew out of Mamie's master's thesis in the late 1930s (Lal, 2002) and was summarized later as "Racial identification and preference in Negro children" (Clark & Clark, 1947). Eventually known as the "doll studies," the research tested early school-age black and white children from both the North and the South. They were shown four dolls, a female and a male with light-colored skin and a female and a male with dark skin, and asked a series of questions, including, "Show me the doll that you would like to play with," "Show me the doll that looks bad," and "Show me the doll that looks like you" (quoted in Phillips, 2000, p. 147). What they found was that black children showed a preference for the white dolls and tended to consider the black dolls "bad." In some cases, the children even thought they looked more like the white dolls than the black ones. In a slightly different procedure, children were given dolls and crayons and told to color in the dolls. Black children consistently colored the skins of the dolls lighter than their own (Herman, 1995). The Clarks concluded that one insidious effect of segregation was that the self-esteem of black children suffered. And if childhood shapes the adult, these effects would be lasting.

The legal strategy in *Brown v. Board of Education* evolved out of four different state court fights over the same basic issue—reversing the separate but equal doctrine. An architect of the legal strategy was Thurgood Marshall, who later became the first African American named to the Supreme Court. He explained it this way:

> If your car ran over my client, you'd have to pay up, and my function as an attorney would be to put experts on the stand to testify to how much damage was done. We needed exactly that kind of evidence in the school cases. When Bob Carter came to me with Ken Clark's doll test, I thought it was a promising way of showing injury to these segregated youngsters. (quoted in Kluger, 1987, p. 316)

Kenneth Clark testified in three of the four cases leading up to the Supreme Court case, even bringing the dolls with him to show jurors (Benjamin & Crouse, 2002). These cases culminated in the *Brown* decision, and although the "doll studies" were not cited in the text of the decision, Chief Justice Earl Warren's decision made specific reference to the importance of the expert testimony of social scientists who described the effects of segregation on black children (Jackson, 2000).

After earning her doctorate in 1943, Mamie Clark took a position at the Riverdale Home for Children, where she provided psychological services for homeless black children. In 1946, with her husband's support and some funds from her father, she established and became the executive director for the Northside Center for Child Development in Harlem. The center provided counseling and therapy for the youth of Harlem and their families and was a model of an interdisciplinary team approach to treatment—Clark's staff included "psychiatrists, psychologists, social workers, case workers, teachers, and consulting pediatricians" (Lal, 2002, p. 25). During this same time, Kenneth joined the faculty of City College of New York and began a distinguished academic career that culminated in his election to the presidency of the American Psychological Association in 1971. He was the first, and so far the only, African American to hold the office.

As noted earlier, minority group members are not as well represented in psychology today as they could be. Nonetheless, the APA has made a number of attempts over the years to create a climate of inclusiveness. As early as 1950, the APA Council passed a resolution that it would hold its annual meeting only in cities free from overt discriminatory practices. The 1957 meeting, for instance, was moved from Miami to New York after it was learned that some Miami hotels would not register blacks (Smith, 1992). And in 1963, APA created an Ad Hoc Committee on Equality of Opportunity in Psychology (CEOP) for the purpose of "explor[ing] the possible problems encountered in training and employment in psychology as a consequence of race" (quoted in Holliday, 2010, p. 1). Yet in the late 1960s, a survey of 398 African American psychologists found them dissatisfied with their status as professional psychologists (Wispe et al., 1969). This dissatisfaction led to the creation of the Association of Black Psychologists at the 1968 APA convention in San Francisco. Today this group has about 1,400 members and publishes the *Journal of Black Psychology*.

Mainly through the efforts of Kenneth Clark during his APA presidency, the APA followed up on the CEOP by creating the Board of Social and Ethical Responsibility for Psychology in 1972 (Pickren & Tomes, 2002); it in turn spawned today's Board of Ethnic Minority Affairs. The APA's Minority Fellows Program began awarding financial aid for graduate study in 1974; in 1987, Division 45, the Society for the Psychological Study of Ethnic Minority Issues, was created.

TRENDS IN CONTEMPORARY PSYCHOLOGY

Chapter 1 included the argument that understanding psychology's present requires knowing something of its past, a point made eloquently by E. G. Boring in that chapter's opening quote. I hope that what you have learned from your history of psychology course and from this book have combined with the knowledge accumulated in other psychology courses to enhance your understanding of psychology's present. This next-to-last segment of the book briefly identifies five contemporary trends in psychology, none of which can be properly understood without knowing something about psychology's history. As I see them, these trends are:

1. *The accelerated study of the relationship between the brain and behavior*, with the term *neuroscience* being added to an increasing number of subdisciplinary labels (e.g., cognitive neuroscience). Dramatic technological innovations have fueled this development, but our current understanding rests on a long history of studying the brain (Chapter 3), and the basic issues involved (e.g., the mind–body question; localization of function) remain deeply rooted in the histories of philosophy and physiology (Chapters 2 and 3).

2. *The vigorous return of evolutionary thinking*, accompanied by a shift toward the nature end of the nature–nurture issue. Chapter 5 told the story of Darwin and his influence during psychology's formative years. One aspect of that influence was the tendency to explain some behaviors with reference to evolutionary mechanisms and, consequently, to take the nature side of the nature–nurture issue. Evolutionary explanations went out of vogue in American psychology during the era of behaviorism, which produced a shift to the nurture side of the debate. In recent years, however, the balance seems to be shifting back again. Much attention is being given to behavior genetics, the study

of genetic influences on behavior and mental processes; evolutionary psychology has reached the status of a course in the psychology curriculum, and several textbooks are now available (e.g., Buss, 1999).

3. *Significant changes in research brought about by the capacities of modern computers.* The history of research methodology is a topic worthy of its own text, but you have encountered some elements of it—Titchener's Manuals (Chapter 7), Woodworth's text, the "Columbia bible" (Chapter 8), and the influence of ANOVA on Festinger's research designs in social psychology (Chapter 14). One effect of both the Woodworth text and ANOVA has been a relative neglect of correlational research designs, but they have become increasingly commonplace (and more sophisticated) in recent years with the development of statistical software capable of performing highly complex, multivariate analyses (e.g., multiple regression, factor analysis) quickly.

4. *The increased professionalization of psychological practitioners.* As you know from the closing paragraphs of Chapter 13, there is a long history of uneasiness between researcher-academicians and those who practice psychology professionally. Knowing something of that history helps understand tensions between these groups (e.g., APS and APA) and puts into perspective any attempts to bridge the gap between them.

5. *The increased fragmentation of psychology.* This trend requires a section of the chapter all its own, and one that closes the book.

THE FUTURE: PSYCHOLOGY OR PSYCHOLOGIES?

Clearly, psychology has demonstrated enormous growth and increased specialization over the past half century; it is therefore worth considering whether the field can be said to be unified in any way. A decade into the 21st century, it is reasonable to ask, is there a field of psychology, or are there multiple psychologies?

First, the question implies that psychology was once unified, yet it is unclear if psychology has *ever* been a coherent discipline. It may have approached unity in its early years, when it was trying to forge an identity separate from physiology and philosophy, but it is evident that strong disagreements existed even then. The conflicts between Titchener and others (e.g., Watson) over psychology's very definition illustrate the point, as do the long-standing squabbles within the APA among various constituencies. As discussed in Chapter 13, practitioners of psychology were dissatisfied with the APA in the two decades before World War II, but the 1945 reorganization made the APA more attractive to them. The wartime spirit of cooperation that reshaped the APA soon dissipated, however, and conflicts developed between those who wanted the APA to retain its traditional role as the promoter of scientific psychology and those who thought of the organization as a means to promote the practice of psychology. Frustration among scientific psychologists produced the Psychonomic Society in 1960; attempts to further reorganize the APA, including a failed one in the mid-1980s, led directly to the creation of the Association for Psychological Science (APS). In terms of its professional organizations, psychology seems to be characterized more by disunity than unity.

When addressing the issue of fragmentation at an APA symposium celebrating the centennial of Wundt's laboratory in 1979, George Miller, trained in the traditional experimental psychology of E. G. Boring, "discovered several other psychologies, all claiming proprietary rights to the label, all competing for disciples, and each contemptuous of the others. In short, I discovered that psychology is an intellectual zoo" (Miller, 1992, p. 40). Some understanding of the range of species in this zoo can be achieved by examining the specialties of just a few of the 56 divisions of the APA:

3	Experimental Psychology
14	Industrial/Organization Psychology
12	Clinical Psychology
16	School Psychology
25	Behavior Analysis
26	History of Psychology
28	Psychopharmacology and Substance Abuse
30	Psychological Hypnosis
36	Psychology of Religion
38	Health Psychology
47	Exercise and Sport Psychology
52	International Psychology
56	Trauma Psychology

Many psychologists belong to more than one division, but it is clear that widely divergent interests are represented under the APA's broad umbrella. Also, some of the experimental psychology areas represented by the APS extend the range of specialties even further. It is difficult to imagine a neuropsychologist studying the effects of neurotransmitter X on memory, a developmental psychologist studying parallel play in children, an industrial psychologist developing a performance evaluation procedure, and a counselor in a rape crisis center as having much in common.

As for modern psychology as an academic discipline, the field appears to have a fragile sense of unity, reflected in the standard definition found in all introductory textbooks (some version of "psychology is the science of behavior and mental processes") and manifested in the institutional organization of "psychology departments." Yet some academic psychologists have specialties that lead them to other departments. This phenomenon led Spence (1987) to worry about

> a decimation of institutional psychology as we know it. Human experimental
> psychologists desert to the emerging discipline of cognitive science; physiological
> psychologists go happily to departments of biology and neuroscience;
> industrial/organizational psychologists are snapped up by business schools; and
> psychopathologists find their home in medical schools. (p. 1053)

What concerned Spence in 1987 might have occurred to a degree, but it is worth noting that virtually all university campuses still have departments called psychology departments, and these departments employ the vast majority of academic psychologists (just as campuses have biology, chemistry, and physics departments, even though these disciplines have experienced even greater specialization than psychology, and over a longer period of time).

Perhaps it is most reasonable to assume that psychology is not a single discipline but a collection of them. One of psychology's foremost theoreticians, Sigmund Koch (1917–1996), argued this point for years, recommending that the term *psychology* be replaced with the more pluralistic label of *psychological studies* (Koch, 1993). He viewed this as a historical process similar to that found in other sciences—biology, for instance, encompasses a wide range of "biological studies" (e.g., botany, zoology). Similarly, memory researcher and former APS president Gordon Bower, in an APA symposium on "The Fragmentation of Psychology," suggested that a more positive connotation results from labeling the phenomenon *specialization* rather than *fragmentation* (Bower, 1993). Although the term *psychology* has not been replaced with *psychological studies*, most psychologists would agree with Koch and Bower's general point that psychology today is really a plurality of subdisciplines, each a specialty in its own right. Bower likened the growth and diversity of psychology to the growth process of a tree, which produces more and more branches as it ages. He compared the individual psychological scientist to a "small bug feeding on a succulent leaf at one end of a very tiny branch and perhaps talking to the other bugs feeding on the same leaf" (p. 905).

If there is any sense of a unifying force in modern psychology, other than the institutional one deriving from the academic category of "psychology department," and the definitional one found in general psychology texts, one could argue that it derives from psychology's history. As Koch (1992a) put it, "There is a sense in which we are nothing if not our history. Our history is our binding force" (p. 966). Regardless of one's modern specialty, there are common origins (to follow the tree metaphor, one trunk and one root system) and familiar themes, many of which have been discussed in this book. I hope that what you have read in those pages will entice you to learn more about what connects psychologists and will deepen your understanding of psychology's rich heritage.

SUMMARY

The Growth and Diversity of Psychology

• Psychology has shown vigorous growth during its 100-plus years of existence as an independent discipline; as it has grown, the interests of psychologists have become more specialized. Throughout most of psychology's history, leading psychologists were white and male, a situation that is now changing, especially as more women enter the field. Although women were excluded from psychology's inner circles throughout most of the 20th century, some made important contributions. Eleanor Gibson is a prime postwar example. She overcame negative stereotypes of "woman as scientist" and became a leading developmental psychologist known for her research on depth perception (visual cliff research) and reading.

• Minority groups, including Jews and African Americans, also have faced discrimination throughout psychology's history. Blacks in particular had to confront the prejudices deriving from the early 20th-century belief in the inherited racial superiority of white males and the social policy of separate but (not really) equal schools. Research on the self-esteem of black children, completed by Kenneth and Mamie Phipps Clark, was instrumental in helping to strike down the concept of separate but equal

education for blacks and whites in the *Brown v. the Board of Education* decision of 1954.

Trends in Contemporary Psychology

• Five major trends are evident in modern psychology—increased interest in neuroscience, the development of evolutionary psychology, the expanding impact of computers, an increased level of professionalization, and increased specialization. None of these trends can be thoroughly understood without knowing something about history.

The Future: Psychology or Psychologies?

• Psychology in the late 20th century is not a unified discipline; with its recurring debates over fundamental issues, it may never have been one. Modern psychology is marked by increased specialization, and it might be more appropriate to replace the idea of a single field of psychology with Koch's concept of there being a set of psychological studies. One unifying force in psychology lies in the discipline's history, however.

STUDY QUESTIONS

1. What barriers did Eleanor Gibson face on her way to a career as a prominent developmental psychologist?

2. What was the essence of the *Brown v. Board of Education* decision, what prior decision did it overcome, and what role did psychology play?

3. Describe the Clarks' doll studies and how they contributed to *Brown v. Board of Education*.

4. Describe five trends that are evident in modern psychology.

5. Explain why it might be better to use the term *psychologies* instead of *psychology*.

6. For which reasons can psychology be considered a unified discipline?

FOR FURTHER READING

GUTHRIE, R. V. (1976). *Even the rat was white: A historical view of psychology.* New York: Harper & Row.
A brief volume that documents the 19th- and early 20th-century research on psychology and race, including chapters on early research comparing the performance of blacks and whites on numerous measuring scales and the effects of eugenics-based legislation; includes chapter-length biographical information on Sumner and briefer sketches of the contributions of several other African American psychologists (e.g., the Clarks, Herman Canady).

History of psychology: The contributions of KENNETH B. and MAMIE PHIPPS CLARK. (2002). *American Psychologist*, *57*, 19–59.
A series of four articles (by Lal, Keppel, Benjamin & Crouse, and Pickren & Tomes) describing the life, work, and impact of the Clarks, from the Northside Center to the Brown *decision to the formation of the Board of Social and Ethical Responsibility.*

KOCH, S. (1992). Postscript: The second century of psychology at age 12 and the American Psychological Association at age 100. In S. Koch & D. E. Leary (Eds.), *A century of psychology as science* (pp. 951–968). Washington, DC: American Psychological Association.
The final section of a large set of chapters on developments in psychology over 100 years (plus 12); a reissuing and updating of a book first appearing in 1985 and based on a 1979 symposium celebrating 100 years since Wundt's lab; an eloquent description of Koch's beliefs about the disciplinary status of psychology.

Winston, A. S. (Ed.). (1996). *Defining difference: Race and racism in the history of psychology.* Washington, DC: American Psychological Association.
An edited volume including chapters on how the concept of race has changed over time, how racist ideas have affected psychology, how research on race has been used to further political ends, and how psychologists (e.g., the Clarks) have confronted racism.

REFERENCES

Adams, G. (1934, January). The rise and fall of psychology. *The Atlantic Monthly*, 82–92.

Albrecht, F. M. (1970). A reappraisal of faculty psychology. *Journal of the History of the Behavioral Sciences*, 6, 36–40.

Allport, F. H. (1924). *Social psychology*. Boston: Houghton-Mifflin.

Allport, G. W. (1937). *Personality; A psychological interpretation*. New York: Holt.

Allport, G. W. (1950). *The individual and his religion*. New York: Macmillan.

Allport, G. W. (1954). *The nature of prejudice*. Cambridge, MA: Addison-Wesley.

Allport, G. W. (1961). *Pattern and growth in personality*. New York: Holt, Rinehart, & Winston.

Allport, G. W. (1965). *Letters from Jenny*. New York: Harcourt, Brace, & World.

Allport, G. W. (1967). Gordon Allport. In E. G. Boring & G. Lindzey (Eds.), *A history of psychology in autobiography* (Vol. 5, pp. 3–25). New York: Appleton-Century-Crofts.

Allport, G. W., & Vernon, P. E. (1931). *A study of values*. Boston: Houghton.

American Psychiatric Association (APA). (1994). *Diagnostic and statistical manual of mental disorders* (4th ed.). Washington, DC: Author.

Anastasi, A. (1954). *Psychological testing*. New York: Macmillan.

Anastasi, A. (1993). A century of psychological testing: Origins, problems, and progress. In T. K. Fagan & G. R. VandenBos (Eds.), *Exploring applied psychology: Origins and critical analyses* (pp. 13–36). Washington, DC: American Psychological Association.

Anderson, J. R. (1990). *Cognitive psychology and its implications* (3rd ed.). New York: Freeman.

Angell, J. R. (1904). *Psychology*. New York: Holt.

Angell, J. R. (1948). The province of functional psychology. In W. Dennis (Ed.), *Readings in the history of psychology* (pp. 439–456). New York: Appleton-Century-Crofts. (Original article published 1907).

Angell, J. R., & Moore, A. W. (1896). Reaction time: A study in attention and habit. *Psychological Review*, 3, 245–258.

Appleby, J., Hunt, L., & Jacob, M. (1994). *Telling the truth about history*. New York: W. W. Norton.

Armstrong, P. (1993). An ethologist aboard the H.M.S. *Beagle*: The young Darwin's observations on animal behavior. *Journal of the History of the Behavioral Sciences*, 29, 339–344.

Aronson, E. (1991). Leon Festinger and the art of audacity. *Psychological Science*, 2, 213–217.

Aronson, E. (1999). *The social animal* (8th ed.). New York: W. H. Freeman.

Arnett, J. J., & Cravens, H. (2006). G. Stanley Hall's *Adolescence*: A centennial reappraisal. Introduction. *History of Psychology*, 9, 165–171.

Asch, S. E. (1968). Wolfgang Köhler: 1887–1967. *American Journal of Psychology*, 81, 110–119.

Aserinsky, E., & Kleitman, N. (1953). Regularly occurring periods of eye motility and concomitant phenomena during sleep. *Science*, 118, 273–274.

Ash, M. G. (1985). Gestalt psychology: Origins in Germany and reception in the United States. In C. E. Buxton (Ed.), *Points of view in the modern history of psychology* (pp. 295–344). New York: Academic Press.

Ash, M. G. (1992). Cultural contexts and scientific change in psychology: Kurt Lewin in Iowa. *American Psychologist*, 47, 198–207.

Ash, M. G. (1995). *Gestalt psychology in German culture, 1890–1967: Holism and the quest for objectivity*. Cambridge, UK: Cambridge University Press.

Atkinson, R. C., & Shiffrin, R. M. (1968). Human memory: A proposed system and its control processes. In K. W. Spence & J. T. Spence (Eds.), *The psychology of learning and motivation: Advances in research and theory* (pp. 89–195). New York: Academic Press.

Averill, L. A. (1982). Recollections of Clark's G. Stanley Hall. *Journal of the History of the Behavioral Sciences, 18*, 341–346.

Baars, B. J. (1986). *The cognitive revolution in psychology.* New York: Guilford.

Babkin, B. P. (1949). *Pavlov: A biography.* Chicago: University of Chicago Press.

Bache, R. M. (1895). Reaction time with reference to race. *Psychological Review, 2*, 475–486.

Baddeley, A. (1990). *Human memory: Theory and practice.* Boston: Allyn & Bacon.

Bahrick, H. P. (1984). Semantic memory content in permastore: 50 years of memory for Spanish learned in school. *Journal of Experimental Psychology: General, 113*, 1–29.

Bakan, D. (1966). The influence of phrenology on American psychology. *Journal of the History of the Behavioral Sciences, 2*, 200–220.

Baker, D. B. (1988). The psychology of Lightner Witmer. *Professional School Psychology, 3*, 109–121.

Baker, D. B., & Benjamin, L. T., Jr. (2000). The affirmation of the scientist-practitioner: A look back at Boulder. *American Psychologist, 55*, 241–247.

Balance, W. D. G., & Bringmann, W. G. (1987). Fechner's mysterious malady. *History of Psychology Newsletter, 19*(1, 2), 36–47.

Baldwin, J. M. (1895). *Mental development in the child and the race.* New York: Macmillan.

Baldwin, J. M. (1897). *Social and ethical interpretations in mental development.* New York: Macmillan.

Baldwin, J. M. (1913). *History of psychology: A sketch and an interpretation.* New York: Putnam.

Barenbaum, N. B. (2006). Henry A. Murray: Personology as biography, science, and art. In D. A. Dewsbury, L. T. Benjamin, Jr., & M. Wertheimer (Eds.), *Portraits of pioneers in psychology* (Vol. VI, pp. 169–187). Washington, DC: American Psychological Association.

Barker, R., Dembo, T., & Lewin, K. (1941). Frustration and regression: An experiment with young children. *University of Iowa Studies in Child Welfare, 18*(1), 1–314.

Barone, D. F. (1996). John Dewey: Psychologist, philosopher, and reformer. In G. A. Kimble,

C. A. Bonneau, & M. Wertheimer (Eds.), *Portraits of pioneers in psychology* (Vol. II, pp. 47–61). Washington, DC: American Psychological Association.

Bartlett, F. C. (1958a). Herbert Sidney Langfeld: 1879–1958. *American Journal of Psychology, 71*, 616–619.

Bartlett, F. C. (1958b). *Thinking: An experimental and social study.* London: Allen & Unwin.

Bartlett, F. C. (1967). *Remembering: A study in experimental and social psychology.* Cambridge, UK: Cambridge University Press. (Original work published 1932).

Bayton, J. A. (1975). Francis Sumner, Max Meenes, and the training of black psychologists. *American Psychologist, 30*, 185–186.

Beam, A. (2001). *Gracefully insane: The rise and fall of America's premier mental hospital.* New York: Perseus Books.

Beck, H. P., Levinson, S., & Irons, G. (2009). Finding Little Albert: A journey to John B. Watson's infant laboratory. *American Psychologist, 64*, 605–613.

Beers, C. W. (1908). *A mind that found itself.* New York: Longmans Green.

Bell, C. (1965). Bell on the specificity of sensory nerves, 1811. In R. J. Herrnstein & E. G. Boring (Eds.), *A sourcebook in the history of psychology* (pp. 23–26). Cambridge, MA: Harvard University Press. (Original work published 1811).

Bell, L. V. (1980). *Treating the mentally ill: From colonial times to the present.* New York: Praeger.

Benjamin, L. T., Jr. (1993). *A history of psychology in letters.* Dubuque, IA: Brown & Benchmark.

Benjamin, L. T., Jr. (1996). Harry Hollingworth: Portrait of a generalist. In G. A. Kimble, C. A. Bonneau, & M. Wertheimer (Eds.), *Portraits of pioneers in psychology* (Vol. II, pp. 119–135). Washington, DC: American Psychological Association.

Benjamin, L. T., Jr. (2000). Hugo Münsterberg: Portrait of an applied psychologist. In G. A. Kimble & M. Wertheimer (Eds.), *Portraits of pioneers in psychology* (Vol. IV, pp. 112–129). Washington, DC: American Psychological Association.

Benjamin, L. T., Jr. (2003). Harry Hollingworth and the shame of applied psychology. In D. B. Baker (Ed.), *Thick description and fine texture: Studies in the history of psychology* (pp. 38–56). Akron, OH: The University of Akron Press.

Benjamin, L. T., Jr., & Baker, D. B. (2000). Boulder at 50: Introduction to the section. *American Psychologist*, *55*, 233–236.

Benjamin, L. T., Jr., & Baker, D. B. (2004). *From séance to science: A history of the profession of psychology in America.* Belmont, CA: Wadsworth.

Benjamin, L. T., Jr., & Crouse, E. M. (2002). The American Psychological Association's response to *Brown v. Board of Education*. *American Psychologist*, *57*, 38–50.

Benjamin, L. T., Jr., Durkin, M., Link, M., Vestal, M., & Accord, J. (1992). Wundt's American doctoral students. *American Psychologist*, *47*, 123–131.

Benjamin, L. T., Jr., Rogers, A. M., & Rosenbaum, A. (1991). Coca-Cola, caffeine, and mental deficiency: Harry Hollingworth and the Chattanooga trial. *Journal of the History of the Behavioral Sciences*, *27*, 42–55.

Benjamin, L. T., Jr., & VandenBos, G. R. (2006). The window on psychology's literature: A history of *Psychological Abstracts*. *American Psychologist*, *61*, 941–954.

Bergin, A. E. (1971). The evaluation of therapeutic outcomes. In A. E. Bergin & S. L. Garfield (Eds.), *Handbook of psychotherapy and behavior change: An empirical analysis.* New York: Wiley.

Berkeley, G. (1948). An essay towards a new theory of vision. In A. A. Luce & T. E. Jessup (Eds.), *The works of George Berkeley, Bishop of Cloyne. Vol. 1.* London: Thomas Nelson & Sons. (Original work published 1709).

Berkeley, G. (1957). *Treatise concerning the principles of human knowledge.* Indianapolis: Bobbs-Merrill. (Original work published 1710).

Binet, A., & Henri, V. (1965). Alfred Binet (1857–1911) and Victor Henri (1872–1940) on the psychology of individual differences. In R. J. Herrnstein & E. G. Boring (Eds.), *A sourcebook in the history of psychology* (pp. 428–433). Cambridge, MA: Harvard University Press. (Original work published 1895).

Binet, A., & Simon, T. (1916). *The development of intelligence in children* (E. S. Kite, Trans.). Baltimore, MD: Williams and Wilkins.

Bingham, W. V. (1952). Walter Van Dyke Bingham. In E. G. Boring, H. S. Langfeld, H. Werner, & R. M. Yerkes (Eds.), *A history of psychology in autobiography* (Vol. 4, pp. 1–26). Worcester, MA: Clark University Press.

Bjork, D. W. (1983). *The compromised scientist: William James in the development of American psychology.* New York: Columbia University Press.

Bjork, D. W. (1993). *B. F. Skinner: A life.* New York: Basic Books.

Blum, D. (2006). *Ghost hunters: William James and the search for scientific proof of life after death.* New York: Penguin.

Blumenthal, A. L. (1975). A reappraisal of Wilhelm Wundt. *American Psychologist*, *30*, 1081–1088.

Blumenthal, A. L. (1980). Wilhelm Wundt and early American psychology: A clash of cultures. In R. W. Reiber & K. Salzinger (Eds.), *Psychology: Theoretical-historical perspectives* (pp. 25–42). New York: Academic Press.

Blumenthal, A. L. (2001). A Wundt primer: The operating characteristics of consciousness. In R. W. Reiber & D. K. Robinson (Eds.), *Wilhelm Wundt in history: The making of scientific psychology* (pp. 121–144). New York: Kluwer Academic.

Boakes, R. (1984). *From Darwin to behaviourism: Psychology and the minds of animals.* New York: Cambridge University Press.

Boorstin, D. J. (1971). *Democracy and its discontents: Reflections on everyday America.* New York: Random House.

Boorstin, D. J. (1983). *The discoverers.* New York: Vintage Books.

Boring, E. G. (1929). *A history of experimental psychology.* New York: Century.

Boring, E. G. (1942). *Sensation and perception in the history of experimental psychology.* New York: Appleton-Century-Crofts.

Boring, E. G. (1950). *A history of experimental psychology* (2nd ed.). Englewood Cliffs, NJ: Prentice-Hall.

Boring, E. G. (1961a). Edward Bradford Titchener, 1867–1927. In E. G. Boring (Ed.), *Psychologist at large: An autobiography and selected essays* (pp. 246–265). New York: Basic Books. (Original work published 1927).

Boring, E. G. (1961b). *Psychologist at large: An autobiography and selected essays.* New York: Basic Books.

Boring, E. G. (1963a). Eponym as placebo. In R. I. Watson & D. T. Campbell (Eds.), *History, psychology, and science: Selected papers by Edwin G. Boring, Harvard University* (pp. 5–25). New York: Wiley.

Boring, E. G. (1963b). Fechner: Inadvertent founder of psychophysics. In R. I. Watson & D. T. Campbell (Eds.), *History, psychology, and science: Selected papers by Edwin G. Boring, Harvard University* (pp. 126–131). New York: Wiley.

Boring, E. G. (1963c). The influence of evolutionary theory upon American psychological thought. In R. I. Watson & D. T. Campbell (Eds.), *History, psychology, and science: Selected papers by Edwin G. Boring, Harvard University* (pp. 159–184). New York: Wiley.

Boring, E. G. (1967). Titchener's Experimentalists. *Journal of the History of the Behavioral Sciences, 3*, 315–325.

Boring, E. G., Langfeld, H. S., & Weld, H. P. (1939). *Introduction to psychology.* New York: Wiley.

Bower, G. H. (1993). The fragmentation of psychology? *American Psychologist, 48*, 905–907.

Brainerd, C. J. (1996). Piaget: A centennial celebration. *Psychological Science, 7*, 191–195.

Bregman, E. O. (1934). An attempt to modify the emotional attitudes of infants by the conditioned response technique. *Journal of Genetic Psychology, 45*, 169–198.

Breland, K., & Breland, M. (1951). A field of applied animal psychology. *American Psychologist, 6*, 202–204.

Breland, K., & Breland, M. (1961). The misbehavior of organisms. *American Psychologist, 16*, 681–684.

Brentano, F. (1995). *Psychology from an empirical standpoint.* London: Routledge. (Original work published 1874).

Bramel, D., & Friend, R. (1981). Hawthorne, the myth of the docile worker, and class bias in psychology. *American Psychologist, 36*, 867–878.

Brands, H. W. (1995). *The reckless decade: America in the 1890s.* New York: St. Martin's Press.

Brehm, J. W. (1998). Leon Festinger: Beyond the obvious. In G. A. Kimble & M. Wertheimer (Eds.), *Portraits of pioneers in psychology* (Vol. III, pp. 329–344). Washington, DC: American Psychological Association.

Breuer, J., & Freud, S. (1955). *Studies on hysteria.* New York: Basic Books. (Original work published 1895).

Brewer, W. F., & Schommer-Aikins, M. (2006). Scientists are not deficient in mental imagery: Galton revised. *Review of General Psychology, 10*, 130–146.

Bridgman, P. W. (1927). *The logic of modern physics.* New York: Macmillan.

Brigham, C. C. (1923). *A study of American intelligence.* Princeton, NJ: Princeton University Press.

Bringmann, W. G., Balance, W. D. G., & Evans, R. B. (1975). Wilhelm Wundt 1832–1920: A brief biographical sketch. *Journal of the History of the Behavioral Sciences, 11*, 287–297.

Bringmann, W. G., Bringmann, N. J., & Balance, W. D. G. (1980). Wilhelm Maximilian Wundt 1832–1920: The formative years. In W. G. Bringmann & R. D. Tweney (Eds.), *Wundt studies: A centennial collection* (pp. 13–32). Toronto: C. J. Hogrefe.

Broadbent, D. E. (1958). *Perception and communication.* London: Pergamon Press.

Broadbent, D. E. (1980). Donald E. Broadbent. In G. Lindsey (Ed.), *A history of psychology in autobiography* (Vol. 7, pp. 39–73). San Francisco: Freeman.

Broca, P. (1965). Paul Broca (1824–1880) on the speech center, 1861. In R. J. Herrnstein & E. G. Boring (Eds.), *A sourcebook in the history of psychology* (pp. 223–229). Cambridge, MA: Harvard University Press. (Original work published 1861).

Brown, R., & McNeill, D. (1966). The tip of the tongue phenomenon. *Journal of Verbal Learning and Verbal Behavior, 5*, 325–327.

Browne, J. (1995). *Charles Darwin: Voyaging.* New York: Knopf.

Browne, J. (2002). *Charles Darwin: The power of place.* Princeton, NJ: Princeton University Press.

Brozek, J., Watson, R. I., & Ross, B. (1970). A summer institute on the history of psychology: Part II. *Journal of the History of the Behavioral Sciences, 6*, 25–35.

Brubacher, J. S., & Rudy, W. (1976). *Higher education in transition: A history of American colleges and universities, 1636–1976* (3rd ed.). New York: Harper and Row.

Bruce, D. B. (1986). Lashley's shift from bacteriology to neuropsychology, 1910–1917, and the influence of Jennings, Watson, and Franz. *Journal of the History of the Behavioral Sciences, 22*, 27–44.

Bruce, D. B. (1991). Integrations of Lashley. In G. A. Kimble, M. Wertheimer, & C. L. White (Eds.),

Portraits of pioneers in psychology (Vol. I, pp. 306–323). Washington, DC: American Psychological Association.

Bruce, D. B. (1994). Lashley and the problem of serial order. *American Psychologist*, *49*, 93–103.

Bruner, J. S. (1968). Gordon Willard Allport: 1897–1967. *American Journal of Psychology*, *81*, 279–284.

Bruner, J. S. (1988). Founding the Center for Cognitive Studies. In W. Hirst (Ed.), *The making of cognitive science: Essays in honor of George A. Miller* (pp. 90–99). New York: Cambridge University Press.

Bryan, W. L. (1904). Theory and practice. *Psychological Review*, *11*, 71–82.

Buckley, K. W. (1989). *Mechanical man: John Broadus Watson and the beginnings of behaviorism*. New York: Guilford.

Bulatao, E. Q., Fulcher, R., & Evans, R. B. (1992). Appendix: Statistical data on the American Psychological Association. In R. B. Evans, V. S. Sexton, & T. C. Cadwallader (Eds.), *The American Psychological Association: A historical perspective* (pp. 391–394). Washington, DC: American Psychological Association.

Burnham, J. C. (1972). Thorndike's puzzle boxes. *Journal of the History of the Behavioral Sciences*, *8*, 159–167.

Buss, D. M. (1999). *Evolutionary psychology: The new science of the mind*. Boston: Allyn & Bacon.

Buss, D. M. (2009). The great struggles of life: Darwin and the emergence of evolutionary psychology. *American Psychologist*, *64*, 140–148.

Cairns, R. B. (1994). The making of a developmental science: The contributions and intellectual heritage of James Mark Baldwin. In R. D. Parke, P. A. Ornstein, J. J. Reiser, & C. Zahn-Waxler (Eds.), *A century of developmental psychology* (pp. 127–143). Washington, DC: American Psychological Association.

Calkins, M. W. (1894). Association I. *Psychological Review*, *1*, 476–483.

Calkins, M. W. (1896). Association II. *Psychological Review*, *3*, 32–49.

Calkins, M. W. (1906). A reconciliation between structural and functional psychology. *Psychological Review*, *13*, 61–81.

Calkins, M. W. (1907). *The persistent problems of philosophy*. New York: Macmillan.

Calkins, M. W. (1913). Psychology and the behaviorist. *Psychological Bulletin*, *10*, 288–291.

Calkins, M. C. (1930). Mary Whiton Calkins. In C. Murchison (Ed.), *A history of psychology in autobiography* (Vol. 1, pp. 31–62). Worcester, MA: Clark University Press.

Camfield, T. M. (1973). The professionalization of American psychology, 1870–1917. *Journal of the History of the Behavioral Sciences*, *9*, 66–75.

Capaldi, N. (2004). *John Stuart Mill: A biography*. Cambridge, UK: Cambridge University Press.

Capshew, J. H. (1996). Engineering behavior: Project Pigeon, World War II, and the conditioning of B. F. Skinner. In L. D. Smith & W. R. Woodward (Eds.), *B. F. Skinner and behaviorism in American culture* (pp. 128–150). Bethlehem, PA: Lehigh University Press.

Capshew, J. H. (1999). *Psychologists on the march: Science, practice, and professional identity in America, 1929–1969*. New York: Cambridge University Press.

Capshew, J. H., & Hearst, E. (1980). Psychology at Indiana University: From Bryan to Skinner. *Psychological Record*, *30*, 319–342.

Carmichael, L. (1957). Robert Mearns Yerkes, 1876–1956. *Psychological Review*, *64*, 1–7.

Carr, E. H. (1961). *What is history?* New York: Vintage Books.

Carr, H. A. (1925). *Psychology: A study of mental activity*. New York: Longmans, Green.

Carr, H. A. (1935). *An introduction to space perception*. New York: Longmans, Green.

Carr, H. A., & Watson, J. B. (1908). Orientation in the white rat. *Journal of Comparative Neurology and Psychology*, *18*, 27–44.

Cashman, S. D. (1993). *America in the gilded age* (3rd ed.). New York: New York University Press.

Cattell, J. M. (1886). The time it takes to see and name objects. *Mind*, *11*, 63–65.

Cattell, J. M. (1895). Report of the Secretary and Treasurer for 1894. *Psychological Review*, *2*, 149–152.

Cattell, J. M. (1948a). The influence of the intensity of the stimulus on the length of the reaction time. In W. Dennis (Ed.), *Readings in the history of psychology* (pp. 323–325). New York: Appleton-Century-Crofts. (Original article published 1885).

Cattell, J. M. (1948b). Mental tests and measurements. In W. Dennis (Ed.), *Readings in the history of psychology* (pp. 347–354). New York: Appleton-Century-Crofts. (Original work published 1890).

Cautin, R. L. (2006). David Shakow: Architect of modern clinical psychology. In D. A. Dewsbury, L. T. Benjamin, Jr., & M. Wertheimer (Eds.), *Portraits of pioneers in psychology* (Vol. VI, pp. 207–221). Washington, DC: American Psychological Association.

Cherry, E. C. (1953). Some experiments on the recognition of speech with one and with two ears. *Journal of the Acoustical Society of America, 25,* 975–979.

Chomsky, N. (1959). Review of Skinner's *Verbal Behavior. Language, 35,* 26–58.

Chomsky, N. (1966). *Cartesian linguistics.* New York: Harper & Row.

Clark, K., & Clark, M. (1947). Racial identification and racial preferences in Negro children. In T. M. Newcomb & E. L. Hartley (Eds.), *Readings in social psychology* (pp. 169–178). New York: Holt.

Cohen, E. (1991, Fall). Psychology's attic. *Akron, 6*(1), 12–19.

Cohen, I. B. (1995). *Science and the founding fathers.* New York: W. W. Norton.

Collins, A. (1977). Why cognitive science? *Cognitive Science, 1,* 1–2.

Collins, J. (1931). Lightner Witmer: A biographical sketch. In R. A. Brotemarkle (Ed.), *Clinical psychology: Studies in honor of Lightner Witmer* (pp. 3–9). Philadelphia: University of Pennsylvania Press.

Colp, R., Jr. (1986). "Confessing a murder": Darwin's first revelations about transmutation. *Isis, 77,* 9–32.

Conley, J. J. (1984). Not Galton, but Shakespeare: A note on the origin of the term "nature and nurture." *Journal of the History of the Behavioral Sciences, 20,* 184–185.

Coon, D. J. (1992). Testing the limits of sense and science: American experimental psychologists combat spiritualism, 1880–1920. *American Psychologist, 47,* 143–151.

Coon, D. J. (1994). "Not a creature of reason": The alleged impact of Watsonian behaviorism on advertising in the 1920s. In J. T. Todd & E. K. Morris (Eds.), *Modern perspectives on John B. Watson and classical behaviorism* (pp. 37–63). Westport, CT: Greenwood Press.

Costall, A. (1993). How Lloyd Morgan's Canon backfired. *Journal of the History of the Behavioral Sciences, 29,* 113–122.

Cottingham, J. (1986). *Descartes.* New York: Basil Blackwell.

Crane, L. (1925). A plea for the training of psychologists. *Journal of Abnormal and Social Psychology, 20,* 228–233.

Cravens, H. (1992). A scientific project locked in time: The Terman genetic studies of genius, 1920s–1950s. *American Psychologist, 47,* 183–189.

Croce, P. J. (1995). *Science and religion in the era of William James: Eclipse of certainty, 1820–1880.* Chapel Hill: University of North Carolina Press.

Cronbach, L. J. (1957). The two disciplines of scientific psychology. *American Psychologist, 12,* 671–684.

Cronbach, L. J., Hastorf, A. H., Hilgard, E. R., & Maccoby, E. E. (1990). Robert R. Sears (1908–1989). *American Psychologist, 45,* 663–664.

Crutchfield, R. S. (1961). Edward Chace Tolman: 1886–1959. *American Journal of Psychology, 74,* 135–141.

Cushman, P. (1992). Psychotherapy to 1992: A historically situated interpretation. In D. K. Freedheim (Ed.), *History of psychotherapy: A century of change* (pp. 21–64). Washington, DC: American Psychological Association.

Dallenbach, K. M. (1913). The measurement of attention. *American Journal of Psychology, 24,* 465–507.

Danziger, K. (1980). The history of introspection reconsidered. *Journal of the History of the Behavioral Sciences, 16,* 241–262.

Danziger, K. (1988). A question of identity: Who participated in psychological experiments? In J. G. Morawski (Ed.), *The rise of experimentation in American psychology* (pp. 35–52). New Haven, CT: Yale University Press.

Danziger, K. (2000). Making social psychology experimental: A conceptual history, 1920–1970. *Journal of the History of the Behavioral Sciences, 36,* 329–347.

Darwin, C. (1839). *Journal of researches into the geology and natural history of the various countries visited by the* H.M.S. *Beagle.* London: Henry Colburn.

Darwin, C. (1871). *The descent of man, and selection in relation to sex.* London: Murray.

Darwin, C. (1872). *The expression of the emotions in man and animals.* London: Murray.

Darwin, C. (1877) A biographical sketch of an infant. *Mind*, *2*, 285–294.

Darwin, C. (1958a). Autobiography. In F. Darwin (Ed.), *The autobiography of Charles Darwin and selected letters* (pp. 5–58). New York: Dover. (Original work published 1892).

Darwin, C. (1958b). *On the origin of species by means of natural selection, or the preservation of favoured races in the struggle for life.* New York: Mentor Books. (Original work published 1859).

Degler, C. N. (1991). *In search of human nature: The decline and revival of Darwinism in American social thought.* New York: Oxford University Press.

Dennis, P. M. (1984). The Edison questionnaire. *Journal of the History of the Behavioral Sciences*, *20*, 23–37.

Dennis, W. (Ed.). (1948). *Readings in the history of psychology.* New York: Appleton-Century-Crofts.

Denny-Brown, D. (1952). Charles Scott Sherrington: 1857–1952. *American Journal of Psychology*, *65*, 474–477.

Descartes, R. (1960). *Discourse on method* (L. J. Lafleur, Trans.). Indianapolis: Bobbs-Merrill. (Original work published 1637).

Descartes, R. (1969). Passions of the soul. In E. S. Haldane & G. R. T. Ross (Trans.), *The philosophical works of Descartes, Volume I* (pp. 329–427). New York: Cambridge University Press. (Original work published 1649).

Desmond, A., & Moore, J. (1991). *Darwin: The life of a tormented evolutionist.* New York: W. W. Norton.

Desmond, A., & Moore, J. (2009). *Darwin's sacred cause: How a hatred of slavery shaped Darwin's views on human evolution.* Boston: Houghton-Mifflin.

Dewey, J. (1886). *Psychology.* New York: HarperCollins.

Dewey, J. (1899). *The school and society.* Chicago: University of Chicago Press.

Dewey, J. (1900). Psychology and social practice. *Psychological Review*, *7*, 105–124.

Dewey, J. (1948). The reflex arc concept in psychology. In W. Dennis (Ed.), *Readings in the history of psychology* (pp. 355–365). New York: Appleton-Century-Crofts. (Original work published 1896).

Dewsbury, D. A. (1984). *Comparative psychology in the twentieth century.* Stroudsburg, PA: Hutchinson Ross.

Dewsbury, D. A. (1990a). Early interactions between animal psychologists and animal activists and the founding of the APA committee on precautions in animal experimentation. *American Psychologist*, *45*, 315–327.

Dewsbury, D. A. (1990b). Whither the introductory course in the history of psychology? *Journal of the History of the Behavioral Sciences*, *26*, 371–377.

Dewsbury, D. A. (1992). Triumph and tribulation in the history of comparative psychology. *Journal of Comparative Psychology*, *106*, 3–19.

Dewsbury, D. A. (1994). John B. Watson: Profile of a comparative psychologist and proto-ethologist. In J. T. Todd & E. K. Morris (Eds.), *Modern perspectives on John B. Watson and classical behaviorism* (pp. 141–144). Westport, CT: Greenwood Press.

Dewsbury, D. A. (1996). Robert M. Yerkes: A psychobiologist with a plan. In G. A. Kimble, C. A. Bonneau, & M. Wertheimer (Eds.), *Portraits of pioneers in psychology* (Vol. II, pp. 87–105). Washington, DC: American Psychological Association.

Dewsbury, D. A. (2006). *Monkey farm: A history of the Yerkes laboratories of primate biology in Orange Park, Florida, 1930–1965.* Lewisburg, PA: Bucknell University Press.

Dewsbury, D. A., & Bolles, R. C. (1995). The founding of the Psychonomic Society. *Psychonomic Bulletin and Review*, *2*, 216–233.

Diamond, I. T. (1985). A history of the study of the cortex: Changes in the concept of the sensory pathway. In G. A. Kimble & K. Schlesinger (Eds.), *Topics in the history of psychology.* (Vol. 1, pp. 305–387). Hillsdale, NJ: Erlbaum.

Diehl, L. A. (1992). The discovering of Iva Lowther Peters: Transcending male bias in the history of psychology. In J. C. Christer & D. Howard (Eds.), *New directions in feminist psychology: Practice, theory, and research* (pp. 101–115). New York: Springer.

Dollard, J., Doob, L. W., Miller, N. E., Mowrer, O. H., & Sears, R. R. (1939). *Frustration and aggression.* New Haven: Yale University Press.

Donnelly, M. E. (Ed.). (1992). *Reinterpreting the legacy of William James.* Washington, DC: American Psychological Association.

Dorn, H. (1972). Ernst Heinrich Weber. In C. C. Gillespie (Ed.), *Dictionary of scientific biography* (Vol. XIV). New York: Scribner.

Douthat, R. (2006, December). They made America. *The Atlantic, 298,* 59–78.

Duncan, C. P. (1980). A note on the 1929 International Congress of Psychology. *Journal of the History of the Behavioral Sciences, 16,* 1–5.

Duncker, K. (1945). On problem solving. *Psychological Monographs, 58,* Whole No. 270. (Original work published 1935).

Ebbinghaus, H. (1908). *Psychology: An elementary textbook* (M. Meyer, Trans.). Boston: D. C. Heath.

Ebbinghaus, H. (1964). *Memory: A contribution to experimental psychology* (H. A. Ruger & C. A. Bussenius, Trans.). New York: Dover. (Original work published 1885).

Ebbinghaus, H. (1965). Hermann Ebbinghaus (1850–1909) on the completion test. In R. J. Herrnstein & E. G. Boring (Eds.), *A sourcebook in the history of psychology* (pp. 433–437). Cambridge, MA: Harvard University Press. (Original work published 1897).

Eiseley, L. (1958). *Darwin's century: Evolution and the men who discovered it.* New York: Doubleday.

Ellenberger, H. F. (1970). *The discovery of the unconsciousness.* New York: Basic Books.

Ellenberger, H. F. (1972). The story of "Anna O": A critical review with new data. *Journal of the History of the Behavioral Sciences, 8,* 267–279.

Elliott, M. H. (1928). The effect of change of reward on the maze performance of rats. *University of California Publications in Psychology, 4,* 19–30.

Elmes, D. G., Kantowitz, B. H., & Roediger, H. L. III. (2003). *Research methods in psychology* (7th ed.). St. Paul, MN: West.

Emde, R. N., Plomin, R., Robinson, J., Corley, R., DeFries, J., Fulker, D. W., Resnick, J. S., Campos, J., Kagan, J., & Zahn-Waxler, C. (1992). Temperament, emotion, and cognition at fourteen months: The MacArthur longitudinal twin study. *Child Development, 63,* 1437–1455.

English, H. B. (1929). Three cases of "conditioned fear response." *Journal of Abnormal and Social Psychology, 24,* 221–225.

Estes, W. K. (1981). The bible is out. *Contemporary Psychology, 26,* 327–330.

Evans, R. B. (1972). E. B. Titchener and his lost system. *Journal of the History of the Behavioral Sciences, 8,* 168–180.

Evans, R. B. (1984). The origins of American academic psychology. In J. Brozek (Ed.), *Explorations in the history of psychology in the United States* (pp. 17–60). Lewisburg, PA: Bucknell University Press.

Evans, R. B., & Koelsch, W. A. (1985). Psychoanalysis arrives in America: The 1909 psychology conference at Clark University. *American Psychologist, 40,* 942–948.

Evans, R. B., Sexton, V. S., & Cadwallader, T. C. (1992). *The American Psychological Association: A historical perspective.* Washington, DC: American Psychological Association.

Eysenck, H. J. (1952). The effects of psychotherapy: An evaluation. *Journal of Consulting Psychology, 16,* 319–324.

Eysenck, H. J. (Ed.). (1960). *Behaviour therapy and the neuroses.* London: Pergamon.

Fancher, R. E. (1983). Alphonse de Candolle, Francis Galton, and the early history of the nature-nurture controversy. *Journal of the History of the Behavioral Sciences, 19,* 341–352.

Fancher, R. E. (1985). *The intelligence men: Makers of the IQ controversy.* New York: W. W. Norton.

Fancher, R. E. (1987). Henry Goddard and the Kallikak family photographs: "Conscious skullduggery" or "Whig history"? *American Psychologist, 42,* 585–590.

Fancher, R. E. (1990). *Pioneers of psychology* (2nd ed.). New York: W. W. Norton.

Fancher, R. E. (2009). Scientific cousins: The relationship between Charles Darwin and Francis Galton. *American Psychologist, 64,* 84–92.

Fantino, E. (2008). Behavior analysis is thriving, but what about its future? *Journal of the Experimental Analysis of Behavior, 89,* 125–127.

Farr, R. M. (1983). Wilhelm Wundt (1832–1920) and the origins of psychology as an experimental and social science. *British Journal of Social Psychology, 22,* 289–301.

Farson, R. (1978). The technology of humanism. *Journal of Humanistic Psychology, 18,* 5–35.

Faust, D. G. (2008). *This republic of suffering.* New York: Knopf.

Fearing, F. (1930). *Reflex action: A study in the history of physiological psychology.* New York: Hafner.

Fernberger, S. W. (1931). The history of the psychological clinic. In R. A. Brotemarkle (Ed.), *Clinical psychology: Studies in honor of Lightner Witmer* (pp. 10–36). Philadelphia: University of Pennsylvania Press.

Fernberger, S. W. (1932). The American Psychological Association: A historical summary, 1892–1930. *Psychological Bulletin, 29*, 1–89.

Ferrier, D. (1876). *The functions of the brain.* New York: Putnam.

Ferster, C. B., & Skinner, B. F. (1957). *Schedules of reinforcement.* New York: Appleton-Century-Crofts.

Festinger, L. (1957). *A theory of cognitive dissonance.* Evanston, IL: Row, Peterson, & Co.

Festinger, L. (1980). Looking backward. In L. Festinger (Ed.), *Retrospections on social psychology* (pp. 236–254). New York: Oxford University Press.

Festinger, L., & Carlsmith, J. M. (1959). Cognitive consequences of forced compliance. *Journal of Abnormal and Social Psychology, 58*, 203–211.

Finger, S. (2000). *Minds behind the brain: A history of the pioneers and their discoveries.* New York: Oxford University Press.

Finno, A. A., Wicherski, M., & Kohout, J. L. (2010). *First-Year Students in U.S. and Canadian graduate departments of psychology: 2009–2010.* Washington, DC: Center for Workforce Studies, American Psychological Association.

Fisher, R. A. (1925). *Statistical methods for research workers.* London: Oliver & Boyd.

Fisher, R. A. (1935). *The design of experiments.* London: Oliver & Boyd.

Fiske, S. T., & Taylor, S. E. (1984). *Social cognition.* Reading, MA: Addison-Wesley.

Flaherty, F. C. (1985). *Animal learning and cognition.* New York: McGraw-Hill.

Flavell, J. H. (1963). *The developmental psychology of Jean Piaget.* Princeton, NJ: Van Nostrand Reinhold.

Flourens, P. (1978). Phrenology examined (C. D. Meigs, Trans.). In D. N. Robinson (Ed.), *Significant contributions to the history of psychology* (Series E, Volume II). Washington, DC: University Publications of America. (Original work published 1846).

Forrest, D. W. (1974). *Francis Galton: The life and work of a Victorian genius.* New York: Taplinger.

Forrest, D. W. (1999). *Hypnotism: A history.* New York: Penguin.

Frank, J. D. (1978). Kurt Lewin in retrospect— A psychiatrist's view. *Journal of the History of the Behavioral Sciences, 14*, 223–227.

Freeman, F. N. (1922). The mental age of adults. *Journal of Educational Research, 6*, 441–444.

Freeman, F. S. (1977). The beginnings of Gestalt psychology in the United States. *Journal of the History of the Behavioral Sciences, 13*, 352–353.

Freud, A. (1928). *Introduction to the technique of child analysis.* New York: Nervous and Mental Disease Publishing Co.

Freud, A. (1937). *The ego and mechanisms of defense.* New York: International Universities Press.

Freud, S. (1938a). *The interpretation of dreams.* In A. A. Brill (Ed. & Trans.), *The basic writings of Sigmund Freud* (pp. 179–549). New York: Random House. (Original work published 1900).

Freud, S. (1938b). *The psychopathology of everyday life.* In A. A. Brill (Ed. & Trans.), *The basic writings of Sigmund Freud* (pp. 33–178). New York: Random House. (Original work published 1901).

Freud, S. (1938c). *Three contributions to the theory of sex.* In A. A. Brill (Ed. & Trans.), *The basic writings of Sigmund Freud* (pp. 551–629). New York: Random House. (Original work published 1905).

Freud, S. (1938d). Wit and its relation to the unconscious. In A. A. Brill (Ed. & Trans.), *The basic writings of Sigmund Freud* (pp. 631–803). New York: Random House. (Original work published 1905).

Freud, S. (1959a). *Beyond the pleasure principle* (J. Strachey, Trans.). New York: Bantam Books. (Original work published 1920).

Freud, S. (1959b). *The ego and the id* (J. Strachey, Trans.). New York: Bantam Books. (Original work published 1923).

Freud, S. (1977). *Five lectures on psycho-analysis* (J. Strachey, Trans.). New York: W. W. Norton. (Original work published 1909).

Fritsch, G., & Hitzig, E. (1965). Gustav Fritsch (1838–1927) and Eduard Hitzig (1838–1907) on cerebral motor centers, 1870. In R. J. Herrnstein & E. G. Boring (Eds.), *A sourcebook in the history of psychology* (pp. 229–233). Cambridge, MA: Harvard University Press. (Original work published 1870).

Fuchs, A. H. (2000). Contributions of American mental philosophers to psychology in the United States. *History of Psychology, 3*, 3–19.

Fuchs, A. H., & Viney, W. (2002). The course in the history of psychology: Present status and future concerns. *Journal of the History of the Behavioral Sciences*, *5*, 3–15.

Furumoto, L. (1979). Mary Whiton Calkins (1863–1930): Fourteenth president of the American Psychological Association. *Journal of the History of the Behavioral Sciences*, *15*, 346–356.

Furumoto, L. (1988). Shared knowledge: The Experimentalists, 1904–1929. In J. G. Morawski (Ed.), *The rise of experimentation in American psychology* (pp. 94–113). New Haven, CT: Yale University Press.

Furumoto, L. (1989). The new history of psychology. In I. S. Cohen (Ed.), *The G. Stanley Hall lecture series: Vol. 9* (pp. 9–34). Washington, DC: American Psychological Association.

Furumoto, L. (1991). From "paired associates" to a psychology of self: The intellectual odyssey of Mary Whiton Calkins. In G. A. Kimble, M. Wertheimer, & C. L. White (Eds.), *Portraits of pioneers in psychology* (Vol. I, pp. 56–72). Washington, DC: American Psychological Association.

Furumoto, L. (1992). Joining separate spheres— Christine Ladd-Franklin, woman-scientist (1847–1930). *American Psychologist*, *47*, 175–182.

Galef, B. G., Jr. (1998). Edward Thorndike: revolutionary psychologist, ambiguous biologist. *American Psychologist*, *53*, 1128–1134.

Gall, F. J. (1965). Franz Joseph Gall (1758–1828) on phrenology, the localization of the functions of the brain, 1825. In R. J. Herrnstein & E. G. Boring (Eds.), *A sourcebook in the history of psychology* (pp. 211–220). Cambridge, MA: Harvard University Press. (Original work published 1825).

Gallistel, C. R. (1981). Bell, Magendie, and the proposals to restrict the use of animals in neurobehavioral research. *American Psychologist*, *36*, 357–360.

Galton, F. (1874). *English men of science: Their nature and nurture*. London: Macmillan.

Galton, F. (1883). *An inquiry into human faculty and its development*. London: Macmillan.

Galton, F. (1908). *Memories of my life*. London: Methuen.

Galton, F. (1950). *Hereditary genius: An inquiry into its laws and consequences*. London: Watts & Co. (Original work published 1869).

Galton, F. (1965). Galton on mental capacity, 1883. In R. J. Herrnstein & E. G. Boring (Eds.), *A sourcebook in the history of psychology* (pp. 421–423). Cambridge, MA: Harvard University Press. (Original work published 1883).

Gamwell, L., & Tomes, N. (1995). *Madness in America: Cultural and medical perceptions of mental illness before 1914*. Ithaca, NY: Cornell University Press.

Gantt, W. H. (1973). Reminiscences of Pavlov. *Journal of the Experimental Analysis of Behavior*, *20*, 131–136.

Gardner, H. (1985). *The mind's new science: A history of the cognitive revolution*. New York: Basic Books.

Garrett, H. E. (1951). *Great experiments in psychology* (3rd ed.). New York: Appleton-Century-Crofts.

Gay, P. (1988). *Freud: A life for our time*. New York: W. W. Norton.

Gibson, E. J. (1980). Eleanor Gibson. In G. Lindsey (Ed.), *A history of psychology in autobiography* (Vol. 7, pp. 239–271). San Francisco: Freeman.

Gibson, E. J. (1994). Has psychology a future? *Psychological Science*, *5*, 69–76.

Gibson, E. J. (2002). *Perceiving the affordances: A portrait of two psychologists*. Mahweh, NJ: Erlbaum.

Gibson, E. J., & Walk, R. D. (1960). The "visual cliff." *Scientific American*, *202*, 64–71.

Gibson, J. J. (1979). *The ecological approach to visual perception*. Boston: Houghton-Mifflin.

Gilbreth, F. B., Jr., & Carey, E. G. (1949). *Cheaper by the dozen*. New York: Bantam.

Gilbreth, F. B., & Gilbreth, L. M. (1916). *Fatigue study: The elimination of humanity's greatest unnecessary waste*. New York: Sturgis & Walton.

Gilbreth, F. B., & Gilbreth, L. M. (1917). *Applied motion study*. New York: Sturgis & Walton.

Gilderhus, M. T. (2000). *History and historians: A historiographic introduction* (4th ed.). Upper Saddle River, NJ: Prentice-Hall.

Gillaspy, J. A., & Bailey, R. E. (2008, August). *Expansion of operant psychology into animal training (1955–1965)*. Boston: American Psychological Association.

Gillaspy, J. A., & Bihm, E. M. (2002). Marian Breland Bailey (1920–2001). *American Psychologist*, *57*, 292–293.

Gillespie, R. (1988). The Hawthorne experiments and the politics of experimentation. In J. G. Morawski

(Ed.), *The rise of experimentation in American psychology* (pp. 114–137).

Gillespie, R. (1991). *Manufacturing knowledge: A history of the Hawthorne experiments.* New York: Cambridge University Press.

Gillies, D. (1993). *Philosophy of science in the twentieth century: Four central themes.* Oxford, UK: Blackwell Press.

Glass, C. R., & Arnkoff, D. B. (1992). Behavior therapy. In D. K. Freedheim (Ed.), *History of psychotherapy: A century of change* (pp. 587–628). Washington, DC: American Psychological Association.

Gleaves, D. H., & Hernandez, E. (1999). Recent formulations of Freud's development and abandonment of his seduction theory: Historical/scientific clarification or a continued assault on truth? *History of Psychology, 2,* 324–354.

Glickman, S. E. (1996). Donald Olding Hebb: Returning the nervous system to psychology. In G. A. Kimble, C. A. Bonneau, & M. Wertheimer (Eds.) *Portraits of pioneers in psychology. Vol. II* (pp. 227–244). Washington, DC: American Psychological Association.

Goddard, H. H. (1910). Four hundred feeble-minded children classified by the Binet method. *Journal of Genetic Psychology, 17,* 387–397.

Goddard, H. H. (1912). *The Kallikak family: A study in the heredity of feeble-mindedness.* New York: Macmillan.

Goddard, H. H. (1913). The Binet tests in relation to immigration. *Journal of Psycho-Asthenics, 18,* 105–107.

Goddard, H. H. (1917). Mental tests and the immigrant. *Journal of Delinquency, 2,* 243–277.

Goddard, H. H. (1928). Feeblemindedness: A question of definition. *Journal of Psycho-Asthenics, 33,* 219–227.

Goldstein, E. B. (1996). *Sensation and perception* (4th ed.). Pacific Grove, CA: Brooks/Cole.

Goodenough, F. L. (1950). Edward Lee Thorndike: 1874–1949. *American Journal of Psychology, 63,* 291–301.

Goodwin, C. J. (1985). On the origins of Titchener's Experimentalists. *Journal of the History of the Behavioral Sciences, 21,* 383–389.

Goodwin, C. J. (1987). In Hall's shadow: Edmund Clark Sanford (1859–1924). *Journal of the History of the Behavioral Sciences, 23,* 153–168.

Goodwin, C. J. (1991a). Misportraying Pavlov's apparatus. *American Journal of Psychology, 104,* 135–141.

Goodwin, C. J. (1991b). Using psychologists' letters to teach about introspection. *Teaching of Psychology, 18,* 237–238.

Goodwin, C. J. (2003). An insider's look at experimental psychology in America: The diaries of Walter Miles. In D. B. Baker (Ed.), *Thick description and fine texture: Studies in the history of psychology* (pp. 57–75). Akron, OH: The University of Akron Press.

Goodwin, C. J. (2005). Reorganizing Titchener's Experimentalists: The origins of the Society of Experimental Psychology. *History of Psychology, 8,* 347–361.

Goodwin, C. J. (2009). E. W. Scripture: The application of "new psychology" methodology to athletics. In C. D. Green & L. T. Benjamin, Jr. (Eds.), *Psychology gets in the game: Sport, mind, and behavior, 1880–1960* (pp. 78–97). Lincoln: University of Nebraska Press.

Goodwin, C. J., & Royer, L. (Eds.). (2010). *Walter Miles and his 1920 grand tour of European physiology and psychology laboratories.* Akron, OH: The University of Akron Press.

Gould, S. J. (1981). *The mismeasure of man.* New York: W. W. Norton.

Gravitz, M. A. (1988). Early uses of hypnosis as surgical anesthesia. *American Journal of Clinical Hypnosis, 30,* 201–208.

Gray, J. A. (1979). *Ivan Pavlov.* New York: Viking.

Gray, P. H. (1962). Douglas Alexander Spalding: The first experimental behaviorist. *Journal of General Psychology, 67,* 299–307.

Green, C. D. (1992). Of immortal mythological beasts: Operationism in psychology. *Theory and Psychology, 2,* 291–320.

Green, C. D. (2004). The hiring of James Mark Baldwin and James Gibson Hume at the University of Toronto in 1889. *History of Psychology, 7,* 130–153.

Green, C. D. (2009). Darwinian theory, functionalism, and the first American psychological revolution. *American Psychologist, 64,* 75–83.

Green, C. D., & Benjamin, L. T., Jr. (Eds.). (2009). *Psychology gets in the game: Sport, mind, and behavior, 1880–1960.* Lincoln: University of Nebraska Press.

Green, M., & Rieber, R. W. (1980). The assimilation of psychoanalysis in America. In R. W. Rieber & K. Salzinger (Eds.), *Psychology: Theoretical-historical perspectives* (pp. 263–304). New York: Academic Press.

Greenwood, J. D. (2003). Wundt, Volkerpsychologie, and experimental social psychology. *History of Psychology*, *6*, 70–88.

Grmek, M. D. (1972). François Magendie. In C. C. Gillespie (Ed.), *Dictionary of scientific biography* (Vol. IX). New York: Scribner.

Grob, G. N. (1973). *Mental institutions in America: Social policy to 1875.* New York: Free Press.

Grob, G. N. (1983). *Mental institutions and American society: 1875–1940.* Princeton, NJ: Princeton University Press.

Grob, G. N. (1991). *From asylum to community: Mental health policy in modern America.* Princeton, NJ: Princeton University Press.

Grob, G. N. (1994). *The mad among us: A history of the care of America's mentally ill.* New York: Free Press.

Gundlach, H. U. K. (1986). Ebbinghaus, nonsense syllables, and three-letter words. *Contemporary Psychology*, *31*, 469–470.

Guthrie, E. R. (1935). *The psychology of learning.* New York: Harper and Brothers.

Guthrie, R. V. (1976). *Even the rat was white: A historical view of psychology.* New York: Harper & Row.

Guttman, N. (1977). On Skinner and Hull: A reminiscence and projection. *American Psychologist*, *32*, 321–328.

Haldane, J. B. S. (1954). Introducing Douglas Spalding. *British Journal of Animal Behavior*, *2*, 1–11.

Hale, N. G., Jr. (1971). *Freud and the Americans: The beginnings of psychoanalysis in the United States, 1876–1917.* New York: Oxford University Press.

Hall, C. S. (1954). *A primer of Freudian psychology.* New York: World Publishing Company.

Hall, C. S., & Lindzey, G. (1970). *Theories of personality* (2nd ed.). New York: Wiley.

Hall, G. S. (1887). Editorial. *American Journal of Psychology*, *1*, 3–4.

Hall, G. S. (1890–1891). Review of "The Principles of Psychology." *American Journal of Psychology*, *3*, 578–591.

Hall, G. S. (1904). *Adolescence.* New York: Appleton.

Hall, G. S. (1922). *Senescence: The last half of life.* New York: Appleton.

Hall, G. S. (1923). *Life and confessions of a psychologist.* New York: Appleton.

Hall, G. S. (1948). The contents of children's minds. In W. Dennis (Ed.), *Readings in the history of psychology* (pp. 255–276). New York: Appleton-Century-Crofts. (Original work published 1883).

Hannush, M. J. (1987). John B. Watson remembered: An interview with James B. Watson. *Journal of the History of the Behavioral Sciences*, *23*, 137–152.

Harlow, J. M. (1868). *Recovery from the passage of an iron bar through the head.* Boston: Clapp.

Harmon-Jones, E., & Mills, J. (Eds.). (1999). *Cognitive dissonance: Progress on a pivotal theory in social psychology.* Washington, DC: American Psychological Association.

Harris, B. (1979). Whatever happened to Little Albert? *American Psychologist*, *34*, 151–160.

Harris, B. (2010). Letting go of Little Albert: Disciplinary memory, history, and the uses of myth. *Journal of the History of the Behavioral Sciences*, *47*, 1–17.

Harrower-Erickson, M. R. (1942). Kurt Koffka: 1886–1941. *American Journal of Psychology*, *55*, 278–281.

Hartley, D. (1971). *Observations on man, his frame, his duty, and his expectations. Volume I.* New York: Garland. (Original work published 1749).

Haupt, E. J. (1998). The origins of American psychology in the work of G. E. Müller: Classical psychophysics and serial learning. In R. W. Reiber & K. D. Salzinger (Eds.), *Psychology: Theoretical-historical perspectives* (2nd ed., pp. 17–75). Washington, DC: American Psychological Association.

Havens, L. L. (1965). Emil Kraepelin. *Journal of Nervous and Mental Disease*, *141*, 16–28.

Hawkins, H. (1960). *Pioneer: A history of the Johns Hopkins University, 1874–1899.* Ithaca, NY: Cornell University Press.

Hearnshaw, L. S. (1964). *A short history of British psychology, 1840–1940.* London: Butler and Tanner.

Hebb, D. O. (1949). *The organization of behavior.* New York: Wiley.

Hebb, D. O. (1959). Karl Spencer Lashley (1890–1958). *American Journal of Psychology*, *72*, 142–150.

Hebb, D. O. (1960). The American revolution. *American Psychologist*, *15*, 735–745.

Hebb, D. O. (1980). D. O. Hebb. In G. Lindsey (Ed.), *A history of psychology in autobiography* (Vol. 7, pp. 273–303). San Francisco: Freeman.

Heidbreder, E. (1933). *Seven psychologies*. New York: Appleton-Century-Crofts.

Heims, S. (1978). Kurt Lewin and social change. *Journal of the History of the Behavioral Sciences*, *14*, 238–241.

Helmholtz, H. (1965). Hermann Ludwig Ferdinand von Helmholtz (1821–1894) on the three-color theory of vision and visual specific nerve energies, 1860. In R. J. Herrnstein & E. G. Boring (Eds.), *A sourcebook in the history of psychology* (pp. 223–229). Cambridge, MA: Harvard University Press. (Original work published 1860).

Henle, M. (1974). E. B. Titchener and the case of the missing element. *Journal of the History of the Behavioral Sciences*, *10*, 227–237.

Henle, M. (1980). The influence of Gestalt psychology in America. In R. W. Rieber & K. Salzinger (Eds.), *Psychology: Theoretical-historical perspectives* (pp. 177–190). New York: Academic Press.

Henle, M. (1986). One man against the Nazis—Wolfgang Köhler. In M. Henle (Ed.), *1879 and all that: Essays in the theory and history of psychology* (pp. 225–237). New York: Columbia University Press.

Herman, E. (1995). *The romance of American psychology: Political culture in the age of experts*. Berkeley: University of California Press.

Hertzman, M., & Festinger, L. (1940). Shifts in explicit goals in a level of aspiration experiment. *Journal of Experimental Psychology*, *27*, 439–452.

Hess, U., & Thibault, P. (2009). Darwin and emotional expression. *American Psychologist*, *64*, 120–128.

Hicks, L. H., & Ridley, S. E. (1979). Black studies in psychology. *American Psychologist*, *34*, 597–602.

Hilgard, E. R. (1948). *Theories of learning*. New York: Appleton-Century-Crofts.

Hilgard, E. R. (1957). Lewis Madison Terman: 1877–1956. *American Journal of Psychology*, *70*, 472–479.

Hilgard, E. R. (1964). *Introduction to Dover Edition of "Memory: A contribution to experimental psychology."* New York: Dover.

Hilgard, E. R. (1967). Kenneth Wartinbee Spence: 1907–1967. *American Journal of Psychology*, *80*, 314–318.

Hilgard, E. R. (1980). The trilogy of mind: Cognition, affection, and conation. *Journal of the History of the Behavioral Sciences*, *16*, 107–117.

Hilgard, E. R. (1982). Robert I. Watson and the founding of Division 26 of the American Psychological Association. *Journal of the History of the Behavioral Sciences*, *18*, 308–311.

Hilgard, E. R. (1987). *Psychology in America: A historical survey*. San Diego, CA: Harcourt Brace Jovanovich.

Hindeland, M. J. (1971). Edward Bradford Titchener: A pioneer in perception. *Journal of the History of the Behavioral Sciences*, *7*, 23–28.

Hoffeld, D. R. (1980). Mesmer's failure: Sex, politics, personality, and the zeitgeist. *Journal of the History of the Behavioral Sciences*, *16*, 377–386.

Hofstadter, R., & Hardy, C. D. (1952). *The development and scope of higher education in the United States*. New York: Columbia University Press.

Holliday, B. G. (2010, April). *Communiqué: Ethnic minority recruitment, retention, and training*. Washington, DC: Office of Ethnic Minority Affairs, American Psychological Association.

Hollingworth, H. L. (1916). *Vocational psychology: Its problems and methods*. New York: D. Appleton and Company.

Hollingworth, H. L. (1990). *Leta Stetter Hollingworth: A biography*. Bolton, MA: Anker Publishing. (Original work published 1943).

Hollingworth, L. S. (1926). *Gifted children: Their nature and nurture*. New York: Macmillan.

Holway, A. H., & Boring, E. G. (1940). The moon illusion and the angle of regard. *American Journal of Psychology*, *53*, 109–116.

Horley, J. (2001). After "The Baltimore affair": James Mark Baldwin's life and work, 1908–1934. *History of Psychology*, *4*, 24–33.

Hornstein, G. A. (1992). The return of the repressed: Psychology's problematic relations with psychoanalysis, 1909–1960. *American Psychologist*, *47*, 254–263.

Hothersall, D. (1995). *History of psychology* (3rd ed.). New York: McGraw-Hill.

Hubel, D. H., & Wiesel, T. N. (1963). Receptive fields of cells in the striate cortex of very young, visually inexperienced kittens. *Journal of Neurophysiology*, *26*, 994–1002.

Hull, C. L. (1920). Quantitative aspects of the evolution of concepts. *Psychological Monographs*, *28*(123).

Hull, C. L. (1928). *Aptitude testing*. Yonkers-on-Hudson, NY: Word Book.

Hull, C. L. (1933). *Hypnosis and suggestibility: An experimental approach*. New York: Appleton-Century-Crofts.

Hull, C. L. (1943). *Principles of behavior*. New York: Appleton-Century-Crofts.

Hull, C. L. (1952a). *A behavior system*. New Haven, CT: Yale University Press.

Hull, C. L. (1952b). Clark L. Hull. In E. G. Boring, H. S. Langfeld, H. Werner, & R. M. Yerkes (Eds.), *A history of psychology in autobiography* (Vol. 4, pp. 143–162). Worcester, MA: Clark University Press.

Hume, D. (1969). *A treatise of human nature* (E. C. Mossner, Ed.). Baltimore: Penguin. (Original work published 1739–1740).

Hunter, W. S. (1919). *General psychology*. Chicago: University of Chicago Press.

Hunter, W. S. (1949). James Rowland Angell, 1869–1949. *American Journal of Psychology*, *62*, 439–450.

Izard, C. E. (1977). *Human emotions*. New York: Plenum.

Jackson, J. P., Jr. (2000). The triumph of the segregationalists? A historiographic inquiry into psychology and the *Brown* litigation. *History of Psychology*, *3*, 239–261.

Jacobson, E. (1929). *Progressive relaxation*. Chicago: University of Chicago Press.

James, W. (1891, December 20). *Letter to M. W. Calkins*. Wellesley, MA: Wellesley College, Calkins Papers.

James, W. (1950a). *Principles of psychology* (Vol. 1). New York: Dover. (Original work published 1890).

James, W. (1950b). *Principles of psychology* (Vol. 2). New York: Dover. (Original work published 1890).

James, W. (1892). *Psychology: The briefer course*. Boston: Henry Holt.

Jaynes, J. (1969a). Edwin Garrigues Boring: 1886–1968. *Journal of the History of the Behavioral Sciences*, *5*, 99–112.

Jaynes, J. (1969b). The historical origins of "ethology" and "comparative psychology." *Animal Behaviour*, *17*, 601–606.

Jeffreys, M. V. C. (1967). *John Locke: Prophet of common sense*. London: Methuen.

Jenkins, J. G. (1935). Review of *Remembering* by F. C. Bartlett. *American Journal of Psychology*, *47*, 712–715.

Jenkins, J. G., & Dallenbach, K. M. (1924). Minor studies from the psychological laboratory of Cornell University: Oblivescence during sleep and waking. *American Journal of Psychology*, *35*, 605–612.

Jenkins, K. (1991). *Re-thinking history*. London: Routledge.

Johnson, M. G., & Henley, T. B. (Eds.). (1990). *Reflections on "The Principles of Psychology."* Hillsdale, NJ: Erlbaum.

Johnston, T. D. (2003). Three pioneers of comparative psychology in America, 1843–1890. *History of Psychology*, *6*, 14–51.

Jonçich, G. (1968). *The sane positivist: A biography of Edward L. Thorndike*. Middletown, CT: Wesleyan University Press.

Jones, E. (1953, 1955, 1957). *The life and work of Sigmund Freud* (Vols. 1–3). New York: Basic Books.

Jones, M. C. (1924a). A laboratory study of fear: The case of Peter. *Pedagogical Seminary*, *31*, 308–315.

Jones, M. C. (1924b). The elimination of children's fears. *Journal of Experimental Psychology*, *7*, 382–390.

Joynt, R. J. (1973, October). Phrenology in New York State. *New York State Journal of Medicine*, 2382–2384.

Jung, C. G. (1919). *Studies in word association*. New York: Moffat-Yard.

Kant, I. (1952). *Critique of judgment* (J. C. Meredith, Trans.). Oxford: Oxford University Press. (Original work published 1790).

Kant, I. (1959). *Critique of practical reason*. (T. K. Abbott, Trans.). New York: Longmans, Green. (Original work published 1788).

Kant, I. (1965). *Critique of pure reason*. (N. K. Smith, Trans.). New York: St. Martin's. (Original work published 1781).

Katona, G. (1940). *Organizing and memorizing*. New York: Columbia University Press.

Kazdin, A. E. (1978). *History of behavior modification: Experimental foundations of contemporary research.* Baltimore, MD: University Park Press.

Kennedy, Q., Mather, M., & Carstensen, L. L. (2004). The role of motivation in the age-related positivity effect in autobiographical memory. *Psychological Science, 15,* 208–214.

Kent, D. (1992, September). E. Gibson, A. Newell receive National Medal of Science. *APS Observer, 5*(1), 14–15.

Kent, D. (1994, July/August). Interview with APS President-elect Richard F. Thompson. *APS Observer, 7*(4), 4, 10.

Keppel, B. (2002). Kenneth B. Clark in the patterns of American culture. *American Psychologist, 57,* 29–37.

Kessen, W. (1996). American psychology just before Piaget. *Psychological Science, 7,* 196–199.

Kessen, W., & Kuhlman, C. (Eds.). (1962). Thought in the young child: Report of a conference on intellective development with particular attention to the work of Jean Piaget. *Monographs of the Society for Research in Child Development, 27* (Serial No. 83).

Kevles, D. J. (1968). Testing the Army's intelligence: Psychologists and the military in World War I. *Journal of American History, 55,* 565–581.

King, D. B. (1992). Evolution and revision of the Principles. In M. E. Donnelly (Ed.), *Reinterpreting the legacy of William James* (pp. 67–75). Washington, DC: American Psychological Association.

King, H. (1955). *The history of the telescope.* London: Griffin.

Kinnaman, A. J. (1902). Mental life of two *Macacus rhesus* monkeys in captivity. II. *American Journal of Psychology, 13,* 173–218.

Kintsch, W. (1985). Reflections on Ebbinghaus. *Journal of Experimental Psychology: Learning, Memory, and Cognition, 11,* 461–463.

Kintsch, W., & Cacioppo, J. T. (1994). Introduction to the 100th anniversary issue of the *Psychological Review. Psychological Review, 101,* 195–199.

Kirkbride, T. S. (1854). *On the construction, organization, and general arrangements of hospitals for the insane with some remarks on insanity and its treatment.* Philadelphia: J. B. Lippincott.

Kirsch, I. (1977). Psychology's first paradigm. *Journal of the History of the Behavioral Sciences, 13,* 317–325.

Klein, A. G. (2002). *Forgotten voice: A biography of Leta Stetter Hollingworth.* Scottsdale, AZ: Great Potential Press.

Klein, D. B. (1970). *A history of scientific psychology: Its origins and philosophical background.* New York: Basic Books.

Kline, L. W. (1899). Suggestions toward a laboratory course in comparative psychology. *American Journal of Psychology, 10,* 399–430.

Klopfer, W. G. (1973). The short history of projective techniques. *Journal of the History of the Behavioral Sciences, 9,* 60–65.

Knapp, T. J. (1985). Contributions to the history of psychology: XXXIX. T. V. Moore and his cognitive psychology of 1939. *Psychological Reports, 57,* 1311–1316.

Koch, S. (1992). Postscript: The second century of psychology at age 12 and the American Psychological Association at age 100. In S. Koch & D. E. Leary (Eds.), *A century of psychology as science* (2nd ed., pp. 951–968). Washington, DC: American Psychological Association.

Koch, S. (1993). "Psychology" or "the psychological studies"? *American Psychologist, 48,* 902–904.

Koch, S., & Leary, D. E. (Eds.). (1992). *A century of psychology as a science* (2nd ed.). Washington, DC: APA.

Koffka, K. (1922). Perception: An introduction to Gestalt-theorie. *Psychological Bulletin, 19,* 531–585.

Koffka, K. (1924). *The growth of the mind: An introduction to child psychology* (R. M. Ogden, Trans.). New York: Harcourt, Brace. (Original work published 1921).

Koffka, K. (1935). *Principles of Gestalt psychology.* New York: Harcourt, Brace.

Köhler, W. (1926). *The mentality of apes* (E. Winter, Trans.). New York: Harcourt, Brace. (Original work published 1917).

Köhler, W. (1947). *Gestalt psychology.* New York: Liveright. (Original work published 1929).

Köhler, W. (1969). Gestalt psychology. In D. L. Krantz (Ed.), *Schools of psychology: A symposium* (pp. 69–85). New York: Appleton-Century-Crofts. (Original work published 1967).

Korn, J. H. (1997). *Illusions of reality: A history of deception in social psychology.* Albany, NY: SUNY Press.

Korn, J. H., Davis, R., & Davis, S. F. (1991). Historians' and chairpersons' judgments of eminence among psychologists. *American Psychologist*, *46*, 789–792.

Krantz, D. L. (1969). The Baldwin-Titchener controversy. In D. L. Krantz (Ed.), *Schools of psychology: A symposium* (pp. 1–19). New York: Appleton-Century-Crofts.

Kroll, J. (1973). A reappraisal of psychiatry in the Middle Ages. *Archives of General Psychiatry*, *29*, 276–283.

Kluger, R. (1987). *Simple justice: The history of* Brown v. Board of Education *and black America's struggle for equality*. New York: Knopf.

Kramer, P. D. (2006). *Freud: Inventor of the modern mind*. New York: HarperCollins.

Kuhn, T. S. (1962). *The structure of scientific revolutions*. Chicago: University of Chicago Press.

Ladd, G. T. (1887). *Elements of physiological psychology*. New York: Scribners.

Ladd, G. T., & Woodworth, R. S. (1911). *Elements of physiological psychology* (revised ed.). New York: Scribners.

Lakin, M. (1996). Carl Rogers and the culture of psychotherapy. *The General Psychologist*, *32*, 62–68.

Lal, S. (2002). Giving children security: Mamie Phipps Clark and the racialization of child psychology. *American Psychologist*, *57*, 20–28.

Landy, F. J. (1992). Hugo Münsterberg: Victim or visionary? *Journal of Applied Psychology*, *77*, 787–802.

Landy, F. J. (1993). Early influences on the development of industrial/organizational psychology. In T. K. Fagan & G. R. VandenBos (Eds.), *Exploring applied psychology: Origins and critical analyses* (pp. 83–118). Washington, DC: American Psychological Association.

Larson, C., & Sullivan, J. J. (1965). Watson's relation to Titchener. *Journal of the History of the Behavioral Sciences*, *1*, 338–354.

Lashley, K. S. (1929). *Brain mechanisms and intelligence*. Chicago: University of Chicago Press.

Lashley, K. S. (1951). The problem of serial order in behavior. In L. A. Jeffress (Ed.), *Cerebral mechanisms in behavior: The Hixon Symposium* (pp. 112–146). New York: Wiley.

Lathem, E. C. (1994). *Bernard Bailyn on the teaching and writing of history: Responses to a series of questions*. Hanover, NH: University Press of New England.

Leacock, S. (1924, March). A manual of the new mentality. *Harper's Monthly Magazine*, 47, 480.

Leahey, T. H. (1979). Something old, something new: Attention in Wundt and modern cognitive psychology. *Journal of the History of the Behavioral Sciences*, *15*, 242–252.

Leahey, T. H. (1981). The mistaken mirror: On Wundt's and Titchener's psychologies. *Journal of the History of the Behavioral Sciences*, *17*, 273–282.

Leahey, T. H. (1992). The mythical revolutions of American psychology. *American Psychologist*, *47*, 308–318.

Leary, D. E. (1992). William James and the art of human understanding. *American Psychologist*, *47*, 152–160.

Leary, D. E. (2006). G. Stanley Hall, a man of many words: The role of reading, speaking, and writing in his psychological work. *History of Psychology*, *9*, 198–223.

Leibniz, G. W. (1982). *New essays on human understanding* (P. Remnant & J. Bennett, Trans.). New York: Cambridge University Press. (Original work published 1765).

Lesch, J. E. (1972). George John Romanes. In C. C. Gillespie (Ed.), *Dictionary of scientific biography* (Vol. XI). New York: Scribner.

Lewin, K. (1931). Environmental forces in child behavior and development. In C. Murchison (Ed.), *Handbook of child psychology* (pp. 94–127). Worcester, MA: Clark University Press.

Lewin, K. (1935). *A dynamic theory of personality* (D. K. Adams & K. E. Zener, Trans.). New York: McGraw-Hill.

Lewin, K. (1936). *Principles of topological psychology* (F. Heider & G. M. Heider, Trans.). New York: McGraw-Hill.

Lewin, K. (1937). Cark Stumpf. *Psychological Review*, *44*, 189–194.

Lewin, K., Lippitt, R., & White, R. (1939). Patterns of aggressive behavior in experimentally created "social climates." *Journal of Social Psychology*, *10*, 271–299.

Lewis, R. W. B. (1991). *The Jameses: A family narrative*. New York: Farrar, Straus, & Giroux.

Ley, R. (1990). *A whisper of espionage*. Garden Park, NY: Avery Publishing Group.

Leys, R., & Evans, R. B. (1990). *Defining American psychology: The correspondence between Adolf Meyer and Edward Bradford Titchener*. Baltimore, MD: Johns Hopkins University Press.

Lippit, R., & White, R. K. (1943). The "social climate" of children's groups. In R. G. Barker, J. S. Kounin, & H. F. Wright (Eds.), *Child behavior and development* (pp. 485–508). New York: McGraw-Hill.

Lippmann, W. (1922a). The abuse of tests. *New Republic, 32*, 297–298.

Lippmann, W. (1922b). A future for tests. *New Republic, 33*, 9–10.

Lloyd, M. A., & Brewer, C. B. (1992). National conferences on undergraduate education. In A. E. Puente, J. R. Matthews, & C. B. Brewer (Eds.), *Teaching psychology in America: A history* (pp. 263–284). Washington, DC: American Psychological Association.

Locke, J. (1960). *Two treatises on government*. New York: Cambridge University Press. (Original work published 1690).

Locke, J. (1963a). *An essay concerning human understanding*. Germany: Scientia Verlag Aalen. (Original work published 1690).

Locke, J. (1963b). *Some thoughts concerning education*. Germany: Scientia Verlag Aalen. (Original work published 1693).

Loftus, E. F. (1979). *Eyewitness testimony*. Cambridge, MA: Harvard University Press.

Logan, C. A. (2002). When scientific knowledge becomes scientific discovery: The disappearance of classical conditioning before Pavlov. *Journal of the History of the Behavioral Sciences, 38*, 393–403.

Luria, A. R. (1979). *The making of mind: A personal account of Soviet psychology* (M. Cole & S. Cole, Eds.). Cambridge, MA: Harvard University Press.

Macfarlane, D. A. (1930). The role of kinesthesis in maze learning. *University of California Publications in Psychology, 4*, 277–305.

Mach, E. (1914). *Analysis of sensations*. La Salle, IL: Open Court. (Original work published 1886).

MacLeod, C. M. (1992). The Stroop task: The "gold standard" of attention measures. *Journal of Experimental Psychology: General, 121*, 12–14.

MacMillan, M. B. (1986). A wonderful journey through skull and brain: The travels of Mr. Gage's tamping iron. *Brain and Cognition, 5*, 67–107.

Madigan, S., & O'Hara, R. (1992). Short-term memory at the turn of the century: Mary Whiton Calkins's memory research. *American Psychologist, 47*, 170–174.

Magendie, F. (1965). François Magendie (1783–1855) on spinal nerve roots, 1822. In R. J. Herrnstein & E. G. Boring (Eds.), *A sourcebook in the history of psychology* (pp. 19–22). Cambridge, MA: Harvard University Press. (Original work published 1822).

Malone, J. C. (1991). *Theories of learning: A historical approach*. Belmont, CA: Wadsworth.

Marrow, A. J. (1969). *The practical theorist: The life and work of Kurt Lewin*. New York: Basic Books.

Maslow, A. H. (1954). *Motivation and personality*. New York: Harper.

Maslow, A. H. (1971). *The farther reaches of human nature*. New York: Viking.

Mayer, R. E. (1992). *Thinking, problem solving, cognition* (2nd ed.). New York: Freeman.

Mazlish, B. (1975). *James and John Stuart Mill: Father and son in the nineteenth century*. New York: Basic Books.

McCullough, D. (1992). *Brave companions: Portraits in history*. New York: Simon & Schuster.

McGinnies, E. (1949). Emotionality and perceptual defense. *Psychological Review, 56*, 244–251.

McGuire, W. (Ed.). (1974). *The Freud/Jung letters*. Princeton, NJ: Princeton University Press.

McReynolds, P. (1987). Lightner Witmer: Little-known founder of clinical psychology. *American Psychologist, 42*, 849–858.

McReynolds, P. (1996). Lightner Witmer: The father of clinical psychology. In G. A. Kimble, C. A. Bonneau, & M. Wertheimer (Eds.), *Portraits of pioneers in psychology* (Vol. II, pp. 63–71). Washington, DC: American Psychological Association.

McReynolds, P. (1997). *Lightner Witmer: His life and times*. Washington, DC: American Psychological Association.

Meischner-Metge, A., & Meischner, W. (1997). Fechner and Lotze. In W. G. Bringmann, H. E. Lück, R., Miller, & C. E. Early (Eds.), *A pictorial history of psychology* (pp. 101–106). Chicago: Quintessence Publishing.

Menninger, K. (1963). *The vital balance: The life process in mental health and illness*. New York: Viking Press.

Merton, R. K. (1961). Singletons and multiples in scientific discovery: A chapter in the sociology of science. *Proceedings of the American Philosophical Society*, *105*, 470–486.

Micale, M. S. (1985). The Salpêtrière in the age of Charcot: An institutional perspective on medical history in the late nineteenth century. *Journal of Contemporary History*, *20*, 703–731.

Miles, W. R. (1928, March 29). *Diary entry*. Akron, OH: The University of Akron, Archives of the History of American Psychology, Walter R. Miles Papers.

Miles, W. R. (1929). *Diary insertion* (Box 1165, Folder 4). Akron, OH: The University of Akron, Archives of the History of American Psychology, Walter R. Miles Papers.

Miles, W. R. (1930). On the history of research with rats and mazes: A collection of notes. *Journal of General Psychology*, *3*, 324–337.

Miles, W. R. (1931, April 1). *Diary entry*. Akron, OH: The University of Akron, Archives of the History of American Psychology, Walter R. Miles Papers.

Mill, J. (1948). Analysis of the phenomena of the human mind. Excerpt in W. Dennis (Ed.), *Readings in the history of psychology* (pp. 140–154). New York: Appleton-Century-Crofts. (Original work published 1829).

Mill, J. S. (1869). *The subjection of women*. London: Longmans, Green, Reader, and Dyer.

Mill, J. S. (1987). *The logic of the moral sciences*. LaSalle, IL: Open Court Classics. (A reprinting of the sixth book of Mill's *A system of logic, ratiocinative and inductive, being a connected view of the principles of evidence, and the methods of scientific investigation*; original work published 1843).

Mill, J. S. (1989). *Autobiography*. London: Penguin. (Original work published 1873).

Miller, G. A. (1951). *Language and communication*. New York: McGraw-Hill.

Miller, G. A. (1956). The magic number seven plus or minus two: Some limits on our capacity for processing information. *Psychological Review*, *63*, 81–97.

Miller, G. A. (1992). The constitutive problem of psychology. In S. Koch & D. E. Leary (Eds.), *A century of psychology as science* (pp. 40–45). Washington, DC: American Psychological Association.

Miller, G. A. (1956). The magical number seven, plus or minus two: Some limits on our capacity for processing information. *Psychological Review*, *63*, 81–97.

Miller, G. A., & Frick, F. C. (1949). Statistical behavioristics and sequences of responses. *Psychological Review*, *56*, 311–324.

Miller, G. A., Galanter, E., & Pribram, K. H. (1960). *Plans and the structure of behavior*. New York: Holt.

Miller, N. E., & Dollard, J. (1941). *Social learning and imitation*. New Haven, CT: Yale University Press.

Mills, E. S. (1974). George Trumbull Ladd: The great textbook writer. *Journal of the History of the Behavioral Sciences*, *10*, 299–303.

Mills, J. A. (1988). The genesis of Hull's *Principles of Behavior*. *Journal of the History of the Behavioral Sciences*, *24*, 392–401.

Mills, W. (1899). The nature of animal intelligence and the methods of investigating it. *Psychological Review*, *6*, 262–274.

Minton, H. L. (1987). Lewis M. Terman and mental testing: In search of the democratic ideal. In M. M. Sokal (Ed.), *Psychological testing and American society, 1890–1930* (pp. 95–112). New Brunswick, NJ: Rutgers University Press.

Minton, H. L. (1988). *Lewis M. Terman: Pioneer in psychological testing*. New York: New York University Press.

Monastersky, R. (1997, March 1). The call of catastrophes. *Science News*, *151*, 20.

Montague, H., & Hollingworth, L. S. (1914). The comparative variability of the sexes at birth. *American Journal of Sociology*, *20*, 342.

Moore, T. V. (1939). *Cognitive psychology*. Philadelphia: Lippincott.

Moorehead, A. (1969). *Darwin and the Beagle*. New York: Harper & Row.

Morawski, J. G. (1986). Organizing knowledge and behavior at Yale's Institute of Human Relations. *Isis*, *77*, 219–242.

Morgan, C. L. (1890). *Animal life and intelligence*. London: Edward Arnold.

Morgan, C. L. (1903). *An introduction to comparative psychology*. London: Walter Scott. (Original work published 1895).

Morgan, M. J. (1977). *Molyneux's question*. New York: Cambridge University Press.

Morison, S. E. (1965). *The Oxford history of the American people*. New York: Oxford University Press.

Morris, E. K., & Bigelow, K. M. (2007, July). *Childrearing as the behaviorist views it: John B. Watson's advice in perspective*. Dublin, Ireland: University College, Cheiron Society.

Moskowitz, M. J. (1977). Hugo Münsterberg: A study in the history of applied psychology. *American Psychologist, 32*, 824–842.

Mowrer, O. H., & Mowrer, W. M. (1938). Enuresis— a method for its study and treatment. *American Journal of Orthopsychiatry, 8*, 436–459.

Münsterberg, H. (1908). *On the witness stand*. New York: The McClure Company.

Münsterberg, H. (1909). *Psychotherapy*. New York: Moffat, Yard.

Münsterberg, H. (1913). *Psychology and industrial efficiency*. New York: Houghton Mifflin.

Murchison, C. (Ed.). (1926). *Psychologies of 1925*. Worcester, MA: Clark University Press.

Murchison, C. (Ed.). (1930). *Psychologies of 1930*. Worcester, MA: Clark University Press.

Murphy, G., & Ballou, R. O. (Eds.). (1960). *William James on psychical research*. New York: Viking.

Murray, H. A. (1938). *Explorations in personality: A clinical and experimental study of fifty men of college age*. New York: Oxford University Press.

Napoli, D. S. (1981). *Architects of adjustment: The history of the psychological profession in the United States*. Port Washington, NY: Kennikat Press.

Neisser, U. (1967). *Cognitive psychology*. New York: Appleton-Century-Crofts.

Neisser, U. (1976). *Cognition and reality*. San Francisco: Freeman.

Neisser, U. (1988). Cognitive reflections. In W. Hirst (Ed.), *The making of cognitive science: Essays in honor of George A. Miller* (pp. 81–88). New York: Cambridge University Press.

Neugebauer, R. (1978). Treatment of the mentally ill in medieval and early modern England: A reappraisal. *Journal of the History of the Behavioral Sciences, 14*, 158–169.

Newell, A., & Simon, H. A. (1972). *Human problem solving*. Englewood Cliffs, NJ: Prentice-Hall.

Newman, E. B. (1944). Max Wertheimer: 1880–1943. *American Journal of Psychology, 57*, 428–435.

Nicholson, I. A. M. (2003). *Inventing personality: Gordon Allport and the science of selfhood*. Washington, DC: American Psychological Association.

Nicolai, G. F. (1907). *Die physiologische methodik zur erforschung der tierpsyche, ihre möglichkeit und ihre anwendung* [The physiological method for research in animal psychology, its method and application]. *Journal für Psychologie und Neurologie, 10*, 1–27.

Norcross, J. C., Castle, P. H., Sayette, M. A., & Mayne, T. J. (2004). The PsyD: Heterogeneity in practitioner training. *Professional Psychology: Research and Practice, 35*, 412–419.

Ogden, R. M. (1951). Oswald Külpe and the Würzburg school. *American Journal of Psychology, 64*, 4–19.

Oldfield, R. C. (1972). Frederick Charles Bartlett: 1886–1969. *American Journal of Psychology, 85*, 133–140.

Olds, J., & Milner, P. (1954). Positive reinforcement produced by electrical stimulation of septal area and other regions of rat brain. *Journal of Comparative and Physiological Psychology, 47*, 419–427.

Olton, D. S. (1979). Mazes, maps, and memory. *American Psychologist, 34*, 583–596.

O'Donnell, J. M. (1979a). The clinical psychology of Lightner Witmer: A case study of institutional innovation and intellectual change. *Journal of the History of the Behavioral Sciences, 15*, 3–17.

O'Donnell, J. M. (1979b). The crisis of experimentalism in the 1920s: E. G. Boring and his uses of history. *American Psychologist, 34*, 289–295.

O'Donnell, J. M. (1985). *The origins of behaviorism: American psychology, 1870–1920*. New York: New York University Press.

Pagano, V., Wicherski, M., & Kohout, J. L. (2010). *Faculty in U.S. and Canadian graduate departments of psychology: 2009–2010*. Washington, DC: Center for Workforce Studies, American Psychological Association.

Palermo, D. (1971). Is a scientific revolution taking place in psychology? *Science Studies, 1*, 135–155.

Palmer, R. R. (1964). *A history of the modern world* (2nd ed.). New York: Alfred A. Knopf.

Parkovnick, S. (2000). Contextualizing Floyd Allport's *Social Psychology*. *Journal of the History of the Behavioral Sciences, 36*, 429–441.

Parsons, H. M. (1974). What happened at Hawthorne? *Science*, *183*, 922–932.

Pastore, N. (1990). Espionage. *Journal of the History of the Behavioral Sciences*, *26*, 366–371.

Paul, G. L. (1966). *Insight vs. desensitization in psychotherapy*. Palo Alto, CA: Stanford University Press.

Pavlov, I. P. (1906, November). The scientific investigation of the psychical faculties or processes in the higher animals. *Science*, *24*, 613–619.

Pavlov, I. P. (1928). *Lectures on conditioned reflexes* (W. H. Gantt, Trans.). New York: International Publications.

Pavlov, I. P. (1960). *Conditioned reflexes: An investigation of the physiological activity of the cerebral cortex* (G. V. Anrep, Trans.). New York: Dover. (Original work published by Oxford University Press in 1927).

Pegram, T. R. (1998). *Battling demon rum: The struggle for a dry America, 1800–1933*. Chicago: Irvin R. Dee.

Penfield, W., & Perot, P. (1963). The brain's record of auditory and visual experience. *Brain*, *86*, 595–696.

Perin, C. T. (1942). Behavior potentiality as a joint function of the amount of training and the degree of hunger at the time of extinction. *Journal of Experimental Psychology*, *30*, 93–113.

Perloff, R., & Naman, J. L. (1996). Lillian Gilbreth: Tireless advocate for a general psychology. In G. A. Kimble, C. A. Bonneau, & M. Wertheimer (Eds.), *Portraits of pioneers in psychology* (Vol. II, pp. 107–116). Washington, DC: American Psychological Association.

Perloff, R., & Perloff, L. S. (1977). The fair—an opportunity for depicting psychology and for conducting behavioral research. *American Psychologist*, *32*, 220–229.

Pervin, E. J. (1991). *Introduction to personality* (5th ed.). New York: HarperCollins.

Peterson, D. R. (1992). The doctor of psychology degree in professional psychology. In D. K. Freedheim (Ed.), *History of psychotherapy: A century of change* (pp. 829–849). Washington, DC: American Psychological Association.

Pettigrew, T. F. (1969). Gordon Willard Allport, 1897–1967. *Journal of Personality and Social Psychology*, *12*, 1–5.

Philbrick, N. (2006). *Mayflower*. New York: Viking.

Phillips, L. (2000). Recontextualizing Kenneth B. Clark: An Afrocentric perspective on the paradoxical legacy of a model psychologist-activist. *History of Psychology*, *3*, 142–167.

Piaget, J. (1952). Jean Piaget. In E. G. Boring, H. S. Langfeld, H. Werner, & R. M. Yerkes (Eds.), *A history of psychology in autobiography* (Vol. 4, pp. 237–256). New York: Russell & Russell.

Piaget, J. (1959). *The language and thought of the child*. London: Routledge and Kegan Paul. (Original work published 1923).

Pick, A. (2003). A role model for generations. *APS Observer*, *16*(4), 26.

Pick, H. L., Jr. (1994). Eleanor J. Gibson: Learning to perceive and perceiving to learn. In R. D. Parke, P. A. Ornstein, J. J. Rieser, & C. Zahn-Waxler (Eds.), *A century of developmental psychology* (pp. 527–544). Washington, DC: American Psychological Association.

Pickren, W. (2007). Tension and opportunity in post–World War II American psychology. *History of Psychology*, *10*, 279–299.

Pickren, W. E., & Tomes, H. (2002). The legacy of Kenneth B. Clark to the APA: The Board of Social and Ethical Responsibility for Psychology. *American Psychologist*, *57*, 51–59.

Pillsbury, W. B. (1955). Harvey A. Carr: 1873–1954. *American Journal of Psychology*, *67*, 149–151.

Poffenberger, A. T. (1940). Leta Stetter Hollingworth: 1886–1939. *American Journal of Psychology*, *53*, 299–301.

Poffenberger, A. T. (1957). Harry Levi Hollingworth: 1880–1956. *American Journal of Psychology*, *70*, 136–140.

Poffenberger, A. T. (1962). Robert Sessions Woodworth: 1869–1962. *American Journal of Psychology*, *75*, 677–689.

Popplestone, J. A. (1975). Retrieval of primary sources. *Journal of the History of the Behavioral Sciences*, *11*, 20–22.

Popplestone, J. A. (1987). *The legacy of memory in apparatus and methodology*. In W. Traxel (Ed.), *Ebbinghaus-Studien 2* (pp. 203–215). Passau, Germany: Passavia Universitätsverlag.

Popplestone, J. A., & McPherson, M. W. (1984). Pioneer psychology laboratories in clinical settings. In J. Brozek (Ed.) *Explorations in the history of psychology in the United States* (pp. 196–272). Lewisburg, PA: Bucknell University Press.

Popplestone, J. A., & McPherson, M. W. (1994). *An illustrated history of American psychology*. Dubuque, IA: Brown & Benchmark.

Porter, J. P. (1904). A preliminary study of the psychology of the English sparrow, *American Journal of Psychology*, *15*, 313–346.

Prentice, W. C. H. (1951). Edgar John Rubin: 1886–1951. *American Journal of Psychology*, *64*, 608–609.

Prytula, R. E., Oster, G. D., & Davis, S. F. (1977). The "rat rabbit" problem: What did John B. Watson really do? *Teaching of Psychology*, *4*, 44–46.

Radbill, S. X. (1972). Robert Whytt. In C. C. Gillespie (Ed.), *Dictionary of scientific biography* (Vol. XIV). New York: Scribner.

Raimy, V. C. (Ed.). (1950). *Training in clinical psychology*. Englewood Cliffs, NJ: Prentice-Hall.

Ramón y Cajal, S. (1999). *Advice for a young investigator* (N. Swanson & L. W. Swanson, Trans.). Cambridge, MA: MIT Press.

Raphelson, A. C. (1973). The pre-Chicago association of the early functionalists. *Journal of the History of the Behavioral Sciences*, *9*, 115–122.

Reed, E. S. (1988). *James J. Gibson and the psychology of perception*. New Haven, CT: Yale University Press.

Reed, J. (1987). Robert M. Yerkes and the mental testing movement. In M. M. Sokal (Ed.), *Psychological testing and American society, 1890–1930* (pp. 75–94). New Brunswick, NJ: Rutgers University Press.

Restak, R. (1984). *The brain*. Toronto: Bantam Books.

Restle, F. (1957). Discrimination of cues in mazes: A resolution of the "place-vs.-response" question. *Psychological Review*, *64*, 217–228.

Restle, F. (1980). The seer of Ithaca. *Contemporary Psychology*, *25*, 291–293.

Richards, R. J. (1983). Why Darwin delayed, or interesting problems and models in the history of science. *Journal of the History of the Behavioral Sciences*, *19*, 45–53.

Richardson, J. T. E. (2003). Howard Andrew Knox and the origins of performance testing on Ellis Island, 1912–1916. *History of Psychology*, *6*, 143–170.

Richardson, R. D. (2007). *William James: In the maelstrom of American modernism*. Boston: Houghton-Mifflin.

Rilling, M. (2000). How the challenge of explaining learning influenced the origins and development of John B. Watson's behaviorism. *American Journal of Psychology*, *113*, 275–301.

Robinson, D. N. (1981). *An intellectual history of psychology* (2nd ed.). New York: Macmillan.

Robinson, J. K., & Woodward, W. R. (1996). Experimental analysis of behavior at Harvard: From cumulative records to mathematical models. In L. D. Smith & W. R. Woodward (Eds.), *B. F. Skinner and behaviorism in American culture* (pp. 254–272). Bethlehem, PA: Lehigh University Press.

Roediger, H. L., III. (1985). Remembering Ebbinghaus. *Contemporary Psychology*, *30*, 519–523.

Roediger, H. L., III. (1997). Remembering. *Contemporary Psychology*, *42*, 488–492.

Roediger, H. L., III, & McDermott, K. B. (1995). Creating false memories: Remembering words not presented in lists. *Journal of Experimental Psychology: Learning Memory, and Cognition*, *21*, 803–814.

Rogers, C. R. (1942). *Counseling and psychotherapy*. Boston: Houghton-Mifflin.

Rogers, C. R. (1954). Changes in the maturity of behavior as related to therapy. In C. R. Rogers & J. A. Precker (Eds.), *Psychotherapy and personality change* (pp. 215–237). Chicago: University of Chicago Press.

Rogers, C. R. (1961a). Some hypotheses regarding the facilitation of personal growth. In C. R. Rogers (Ed.), *On becoming a person* (pp. 31–38). Boston: Houghton-Mifflin.

Rogers, C. R. (1961b). This is me. In C. R. Rogers (Ed.), *On becoming a person* (pp. 3–27). Boston: Houghton-Mifflin.

Rohles, F. H., Jr. (1992). Orbital bar pressing: A historical note on Skinner and the chimpanzees in space. *American Psychologist*, *47*, 1531–1533.

Romanes, G. J. (1886). *Animal intelligence*. New York: D. Appleton. (Original work published 1882).

Rosenzweig, S. (1992). *The historic expedition to America (1909): Freud, Jung, and Hall the king-maker*. St. Louis: Rana House.

Rosnow, R. L., & Rosenthal, R. (1993). *Beginning behavioral research*. New York: Macmillan.

Ross, D. (1969). The "zeitgeist" and American psychology. *Journal of the History of the Behavioral Sciences*, *5*, 256–262.

Ross, D. (1972). *G. Stanley Hall: The psychologist as prophet*. Chicago: University of Chicago Press.

Rubin, E. (1958). Figure and ground. In D. C. Beardslee & M. Wertheimer (Eds.), *Readings in perception* (pp. 194–203). Princeton, NJ: Van Nostrand. (Original work published 1915).

Rucci, A. J., & Tweney, R. D. (1980). Analysis of variance and the "second discipline" of scientific psychology: A historical account. *Psychological Bulletin*, *87*, 166–184.

Ruse, M. (1979). *The Darwinian revolution: Science red in tooth and claw*. Chicago: University of Chicago Press.

Russo, N. F. (1988). Women's participation in psychology: Reflecting and shaping the social context. In A. N. O'Connell & N. F. Russo (Eds.), *Models of achievement: Reflections of eminent women in psychology*. (Vol. 2, pp. 9–27). Hillsdale, NJ: Erlbaum.

Rutherford, A. (2003). B. F. Skinner's technology of behavior in American life: From consumer culture to counterculture. *Journal of the History of the Behavioral Sciences*, *39*, 1–23.

Ryan, W. C. (1939). *Studies in early graduate education*. New York: Carnegie Foundation.

Sahakian, W. S. (Ed.). (1968). *History of psychology: A source book in systematic psychology*. Itasca, IL: F. E. Peacock.

Sahakian, W. S. (1975). *History and systems of psychology*. New York: Wiley.

Samelson, F. (1981). Struggle for scientific authority: The reception of Watson's behaviorism in 1913. *Journal of the History of the Behavioral Sciences*, *17*, 399–425.

Sanford, E. C. (1910, August 8). *Letter to E. B. Titchener*. Ithaca, NY: Cornell University, Titchener Papers.

Satariano, W. A. (1979). Immigration and the popularization of social science, 1920 to 1930. *Journal of the History of the Behavioral Sciences*, *15*, 310–320.

Scarborough, E., & Furumoto, L. (1987). *Untold lives: The first generation of American women psychologists*. New York: Columbia University Press.

Schlereth, T. J. (1991). *Victorian America: Transformations in everyday life*. New York: HarperCollins.

Schulman, B. J. (2001). *The seventies: The great shift in American culture, society, and politics*. Cambridge, MA: Perseus.

Schultz, D. P. (1981). *A history of modern psychology* (3rd ed.). New York: Academic Press.

Schultz, D. P., & Schultz, S. E. (1987). *A history of modern psychology* (4th ed.). San Diego, CA: Harcourt, Brace, Jovanovich.

Scott, W. D. (1903). *The theory of advertising*. Boston: Small & Maynard.

Scott, W. D. (1908). *The psychology of advertising*. Boston: Small & Maynard.

Scott, W. D. (1911). *Increasing human efficiency in business*. New York: Macmillan.

Scott-Kakures, D., Castagnetto, S., Benson, H., Taschek, W., & Hurley, P. (1993). *History of philosophy*. New York: HarperCollins.

Scripture, E. W. (1895). *Thinking, feeling, doing*. New York: Chautauqua-Century Press.

Searle, J. R. (1980). Minds, brains, and programs. *Behavioral and Brain Sciences*, *3*, 417–424.

Sechenov, I. M. (1965). Reflexes of the brain. Cambridge, MA: MIT Press. (Original work published 1863).

Sechzer, J. A., (1983). The ethical dilemma of some classical animal experiments. *Annals of the New York Academy of Sciences*, *406*, 5–12.

Segal, E. M., & Lachman, R. (1972). Complex behavior or higher mental processes: Is there a paradigm shift? *American Psychologist*, *27*, 46–55.

Sex, race/ethnicity data available. (1995, Winter). *Trends in Education: APA Education Directorate News*, *2*(1), 2–3.

Sexton, V. S. (1965). Clinical psychology: An historical survey. *Genetic Psychology Monographs*, *72*, 401–434.

Shakow, D. (1930). Hermann Ebbinghaus. *American Journal of Psychology*, *42*, 505–518.

Shannon, C. E., & Weaver, W. (1949). *The mathematical theory of communication*. Urbana: University of Illinois Press.

Sherrington, C. S. (1906). *The integrative action of the nervous system*. New Haven, CT: Yale University Press.

Shields, S. A. (1982). The variability hypothesis: History of a biological model of sex differences in intelligence. *Signs: Journal of Women in Culture and Society*, *7*, 769–797.

Shorter, E. (1997). *A history of psychiatry: From the era of the asylum to the age of Prozac*. New York: Wiley.

Simon, L. (1998). *Genuine reality: A life of William James*. Chicago: University of Chicago Press.

Simonton, D. K. (1994). *Greatness: Who makes history and why*. New York: Guilford.

Singer, C. A. (1957). *A short history of anatomy and physiology from the Greeks to Harvey*. New York: Dover.

Skinner, B. F. (1938). *The behavior of organisms: An experimental analysis*. New York: Appleton-Century-Crofts.

Skinner, B. F. (1945). An operational analysis of psychological terms. *Psychological Review*, *52*, 270–277.

Skinner, B. F. (1948). *Walden two*. New York: Macmillan.

Skinner, B. F. (1953). *Science and human behavior*. New York: Macmillan.

Skinner, B. F. (1956). A case history in scientific method. *American Psychologist*, *11*, 221–223.

Skinner, B. F. (1957). *Verbal behavior*. New York: Appleton-Century-Crofts.

Skinner, B. F. (1960). Pigeons in a pelican. *American Psychologist*, *15*, 28–37.

Skinner, B. F. (1979). *The shaping of a behaviorist*. New York: Knopf.

Skinner, B. F. (1981). Pavlov's influence on psychology in America. *Journal of the History of the Behavioral Sciences*, *17*, 242–245.

Skinner, B. F. (1984). *A matter of consequences*. New York: NYU Press.

Skinner, B. F. (1987). Whatever happened to psychology as the science of behavior? *American Psychologist*, *42*, 780–786.

Skinner, B. F. (1990). Can psychology be a science of the mind? *American Psychologist*, *45*, 1206–1210.

Small, W. S. (1901). Experimental study of the mental processes of the rat. II. *American Journal of Psychology*, *12*, 206–239.

Smith, L. D. (1992). On prediction and control: B. F. Skinner and the technological ideal of science. *American Psychologist*, *47*, 216–223.

Smith, L. D. (1996a). Conclusion: Situating B. F. Skinner and behaviorism in American culture. In L.

D. Smith & W. R. Woodward (Eds.), *B. F. Skinner and behaviorism in American culture* (pp. 294–315). Bethlehem, PA: Lehigh University Press.

Smith, L. D. (1996b). Knowledge as power: The Baconian roots of Skinner's social meliorism. In L. D. Smith & W. R. Woodward (Eds.), *B. F. Skinner and behaviorism in American culture* (pp. 56–82). Bethlehem, PA: Lehigh University Press.

Sobel, D. (1995). *Longitude: The true story of a lone genius who solved the greatest scientific problem of his time*. New York: Walker.

Sobel, D. (2000). *Galileo's daughter: A historical memoir of science, faith, and love*. New York: Penguin.

Sokal, M. M. (1971). The unpublished autobiography of James McKeen Cattell. *American Psychologist*, *26*, 626–635.

Sokal, M. M. (1980). Biographical approach: The psychological career of Edward Wheeler Scripture. In J. Brozek & L. J. Pongratz (Eds.), *Historiography of modern psychology: Aims, resources, approaches* (pp. 255–278). Toronto: C. J. Hogrefe.

Sokal, M. M. (Ed.). (1981a). *An education in psychology: James McKeen Cattell's journal and letters from Germany and England, 1880–1888*. Cambridge, MA: MIT Press.

Sokal, M. M. (1981b). The origins of the Psychological Corporation. *Journal of the History of the Behavioral Sciences*, *17*, 54–67.

Sokal, M. M. (1984). The Gestalt psychologists in behaviorist America. *American Historical Review*, *89*, 1240–1263.

Sokal, M. M. (1987). James McKeen Cattell and mental anthropometry: Nineteenth-century science and reform and the origins of psychological testing. In M. M. Sokal (Ed.), *Psychological testing and American society* (pp. 21–45). New Brunswick, NJ: Rutgers University Press.

Sokal, M. M. (1992). Origins and early years of the American Psychological Association, 1890–1906. *American Psychologist*, *47*, 111–122.

Sokal, M. M. (2009). James McKeen Cattell, Nicholas Murray Butler, and academic freedom at Columbia University, 1902–1923. *History of Psychology*, *12*, 87–122.

Sokal, M. M., & Rafail, P. A. (1982). *A guide to manuscript collections in the history of psychology and selected areas*. Millwood, NY: Kraus International.

Solso, R. L. (Ed.). (1973). *Contemporary issues in cognitive psychology: The Loyola Symposium*. Washington, DC: V. H. Winston.

Spalding, D. A. (1873). Instinct, with original observations on young animals. *Macmillan's Magazine*, *27*, 282–293.

Spearman, C. (1904). "General intelligence," objectively determined and measured. *American Journal of Psychology*, *15*, 201–293.

Spence, J. T. (1987). Centrifugal versus centripetal tendencies in psychology: Will the center hold? *American Psychologist*, *42*, 1052–1054.

Spence, K. W. (1952). Clark Leonard Hull: 1884–1952. *American Journal of Psychology*, *65*, 639–646.

Sperry, R. W. (1961). Cerebral organization and behavior. *Science*, *133*, 1749–1757.

Sperry, R. W. (1993). The impact and promise of the cognitive revolution. *American Psychologist*, *48*, 878–885.

Spillman, J., & Spillman, L. (1993). The rise and fall of Hugo Münsterberg. *Journal of the History of the Behavioral Sciences*, *29*, 322–338.

Sprung, H. (1997). Carl Stumpf. In W. G. Bringmann, H. E. Lück, R., Miller, & C. E. Early (Eds.), *A pictorial history of psychology* (pp. 247–250). Chicago: Quintessence Publishing.

Spurzheim, J. G. (1978). Outlines of phrenology. In D. N. Robinson (Ed.), *Significant contributions to the history of psychology* (Series E, Volume II). Washington, DC: University Publications of America. (Original work published 1832).

A stash in the stacks. (1996, August/September). *Civilization*, *3*(4), 15.

Sterns, C. Z. (1985). Victorian sexuality: Can historians do it better? *Journal of Social History*, *18*, 625–634.

Stetson, G. R. (1897). Some memory tests of whites and blacks. *Psychological Review*, *4*, 285–289.

Steudel, J. (1972). Johannes Peter Müller. In C. C. Gillespie (Ed.), *Dictionary of scientific biography* (Vol. IX). New York: Scribner.

Stevens, S. S. (1935). The operational definition of concepts. *Psychological Review*, *42*, 517–527.

Stocking, G. W., Jr. (1965). On the limits of "presentism" and "historicism" in the historiography of the behavioral sciences. *Journal of the History of the Behavioral Sciences*, *1*, 211–217.

Stricker, G., & Cummings, N. A. (1992). The professional school movement. In D. K. Freedheim (Ed.), *History of psychotherapy: A century of change* (pp. 801–828). Washington, DC: American Psychological Association.

Stroop, J. R. (1992). Studies of interference in serial verbal reactions. *Journal of Experimental Psychology: General*, *121*, 15–23. (Original work published 1935).

Strunk, O., Jr. (1972). The self-psychology of Mary Whiton Calkins. *Journal of the History of the Behavioral Sciences*, *8*, 196–203.

Sulloway, F. J. (1979). *Freud: Biologist of the mind*. New York: Basic Books.

Sulloway, F. J. (1982). Darwin and his finches: The evolution of a legend. *Journal of the History of Biology*, *15*, 1–53.

Swazey, J. P. (1972). Charles Scott Sherrington. In C. C. Gillespie (Ed.), *Dictionary of scientific biography* (Vol. XII). New York: Scribner.

Taylor, D. W. (1972). Santiago Ramón y Cajal. In C. C. Gillespie (Ed.), *Dictionary of scientific biography* (Vol. XI). New York: Scribner.

Temkin, O. (1947). Gall and the phrenological movement. *Bulletin of the History of Medicine*, *21*, 275–321.

Terman, L. M. (1906). Genius and stupidity: A study of some of the intellectual processes of seven "bright" and seven "stupid" boys. *Pedagogical Seminary*, *13*, 307–373.

Terman, L. M. (1924). The mental test as a psychological method. *Psychological Review*, *31*, 93–117.

Terman, L. M. (1925). *Genetic studies of genius. Vol. 1. Mental and physical traits of a thousand gifted children*. Stanford, CA: Stanford University Press.

Terman, L. M. (1932). Trails to psychology. In C. Murchison (Ed.), *A history of psychology in autobiography* (Vol. 2, pp. 297–332). Worcester, MA: Clark University Press.

Terman, L. M., & Oden, M. H. (1947). *Genetic studies of genius. Vol. 4. The gifted child grows up: Twenty-five years' follow-up of a superior group*. Stanford, CA: Stanford University Press.

Terman, L. M., & Oden, M. H. (1959). *Genetic studies of genius. Vol. 5. The gifted group at mid-life: Thirty-five years' follow-up of the superior child*. Stanford, CA: Stanford University Press.

Teuber, M. L. (1994). The founding of the primate station, Tenerife, Canary Islands. *American Journal of Psychology*, *107*, 551–581.

Thomas, E. (1995). *The very best men*. New York: Simon & Schuster.

Thomson, K. S. (1975). HMS *Beagle*, 1820–1870. *American Scientist*, *63*, 664–672.

Thorndike, E. L. (1899). A reply to "The nature of animal intelligence and the methods of investigating it." *Psychological Review*, *6*, 412–420.

Thorndike, E. L. (1900). Comparative psychology. *Psychological Review*, *7*, 424–426.

Thorndike, E. L. (1913). *Educational psychology*. New York: Teacher's College.

Thorndike, E. L. (1914). *Educational psychology: The briefer course*. New York: Teacher's College.

Thorndike, E. L. (1936). Edward Lee Thorndike. In C. Murchison (Ed.), *A history of psychology in autobiography* (Vol. 3, pp. 263–270). Worcester, MA: Clark University Press.

Thorndike, E. L. (1948). Animal intelligence. In W. Dennis (Ed.), *Readings in the history of psychology* (pp. 377–387). New York: Appleton-Century-Crofts. (Original work published 1898).

Thorndike, E. L. (2000). *Animal intelligence: Experimental studies*. New Brunswick, NJ: Transaction Publishers. (Original work published 1911).

Thorndike, E. L., & Woodworth, R. S. (1901). The influence of improvement in one mental function upon the efficiency of other functions. I. *Psychological Review*, *8*, 247–261.

Thorndike, R. L. (1991). Edward L. Thorndike: A professional and personal appreciation. In G. A. Kimble, M. Wertheimer, & C. L. White (Eds.), *Portraits of pioneers in psychology* (Vol. I, pp. 139–151). Washington, DC: American Psychological Association.

Titchener, E. B. (1895). Note. *American Journal of Psychology*, *7*, 448–449.

Titchener, E. B. (1897, October 26). *Letter to Walter Pillsbury*, Ithaca, NY: Cornell University, Titchener Papers.

Titchener, E. B. (1898a). A psychological laboratory. *Mind (n.s.)*, *7*, 311–331.

Titchener, E. B. (1898b). Postulates of a structural psychology. *Psychological Review*, *7*, 449–465.

Titchener, E. B. (1899). *An outline of psychology*. New York: Macmillan. (Original work published 1896).

Titchener, E. B. (1901). *Experimental psychology: A manual of laboratory practice. Vol. 1: Qualitative experiments. Part 1: Student's manual; part 2: Instructor's manual*. New York: Macmillan.

Titchener, E. B. (1905a). *Experimental psychology: A manual of laboratory practice. Vol. 2: Quantitative experiments. Part 1: Student's manual; part 2: Instructor's manual*. New York: Macmillan.

Titchener, E. B. (1905b). Review [of Thorndike's Elements of Psychology]. *Mind*, *56*, 552–554.

Titchener, E. B. (1906, June 6). *Letter to L. N. Wilson*. Worcester, MA: Clark University, Wilson Papers.

Titchener, E. B. (1909). *A text-book of psychology*. New York: Macmillan.

Titchener, E. B. (1914). On "Psychology as the behaviorist views it." *Proceedings of the American Philosophical Society*, *53*, 1–17.

Titchener, E. B. (1921a). George Trumbull Ladd. *American Journal of Psychology*, *32*, 600–601.

Titchener, E. B. (1921b). Wilhelm Wundt. *American Journal of Psychology*, *32*, 161–178.

Titchener, E. B. (1929). *Systematic psychology: A prolegomena*. New York: Macmillan.

Todd, J. T. (1994). What psychology has to say about John B. Watson: Classical behaviorism in psychology textbooks, 1920–1989. In J. T. Todd & E. K. Morris (Eds.), *Modern perspectives on John B. Watson and classical behaviorism* (pp. 75–107). Westport, CT: Greenwood Press.

Todd, J. T., & Morris, E. K. (1986). The early research of John B. Watson: Before the behavioral revolution. *The Behavior Analyst*, *9*, 71–88.

Todes, D. P. (1995). Pavlov and the Bolsheviks. *History and Philosophy of the Life Sciences*, *17*, 379–418.

Todes, D. P. (1997a). From the machine to the ghost within: Pavlov's transition from digestive physiology to conditional reflexes. *American Psychologist*, *52*, 947–955.

Todes, D. P. (1997b). Pavlov's physiological factory. *Isis*, *88*, 205–246.

Tolman, E. C. (1922). A new formula for behaviorism. *Psychological Review*, *29*, 44–53.

Tolman, E. C. (1932). *Purposive behavior in animals and men*. New York: Appleton-Century-Crofts.

Tolman, E. C. (1938). The determiners of behavior at a choice point. *Psychological Review*, *45*, 1–41.

Tolman, E. C. (1942). *Drives toward war*. New York: D. Appleton-Century Company.

Tolman, E. C. (1948). Cognitive maps in rats and men. *Psychological Review*, *55*, 189–208.

Tolman, E. C. (1952). Edward Chace Tolman. In E. G. Boring, H. S. Langfeld, H. Werner, & R. M. Yerkes (Eds.), *A history of psychology in autobiography* (Vol. 4, pp. 323–339). Worcester, MA: Clark University Press.

Tolman, E. C. (1959). Principles of purposive behavior. In S. Koch (Ed.), *Psychology: A study of a science. Study 1.* (Vol. 2, pp. 92–157). New York: McGraw-Hill.

Tolman, E. C., & Honzik, C. H. (1930). Introduction and removal of reward, and maze performance in rats. *University of California Publications in Psychology*, *4*, 257–275.

Tolman, E. C., & Nyswander, D. B. (1927). The reliability and validity of maze-measures for rats. *Journal of Comparative Psychology*, *7*, 425–460.

Tolman, E. C., Ritchie, B. F., & Kalish, D. (1946a). Studies in spatial learning. I. Orientation and the short-cut. *Journal of Experimental Psychology*, *36*, 13–24.

Tolman, E. C., Ritchie, B. F., & Kalish, D. (1946b). Studies in spatial learning. II. Place learning versus response learning. *Journal of Experimental Psychology*, *36*, 221–229.

Tolman, E. C., Tryon, R. C., & Jeffress, L. A. (1929). A self-recording maze with an automatic delivery table. *University of California Publications in Psychology*, *4*, 99–112.

Tolstoy, L. (1942). *War and peace* (L. Maude and A. Maude, Trans.). New York: Simon and Schuster.

Triplett, R. G. (1982). The relationship of Clark L. Hull's hypnosis research to his later learning theory: The continuity of a life's work. *Journal of the History of the Behavioral Sciences*, *18*, 22–31.

Tryon, R. C. (1963). Psychology in flux: The academic-professional polarity. *American Psychologist*, *18*, 134–143.

Turing, A. M. (1950). Computing machinery and intelligence. *Mind*, *59*, 433–460.

Turner, R. S. (1972). Hermann von Helmholtz. In C. C. Gillespie (Ed.), *Dictionary of scientific biography* (Vol. VI). New York: Scribner.

Twitmyer, E. B. (1905). Knee-jerks without stimulation of the patellar tendon. *Psychological Bulletin*, *2*, 43–44.

Valentine, C. W. (1930). The innate bases of fear. *Journal of Genetic Psychology*, *37*, 394–420.

VandenBos, G. R., Cummings, N. A., & DeLeon, P. H. (1992). A century of psychotherapy: Economic and environmental influences. In D. K. Freedheim (Ed.), *History of psychotherapy: A century of change* (pp. 65–102). Washington, DC: American Psychological Association.

Veysey, L. R. (1965). *The emergence of the American university*. Chicago: University of Chicago Press.

Vinchur, A. J. (2007). Early contributions to the science and practice of industrial psychology. In L. L. Koppes (Ed.), *Historical perspectives in industrial and organizational psychology* (pp. 37–58). Mahwah, NJ: Erlbaum.

Viney, W. (1996). Dorothea Dix: An intellectual conscience for psychology. In G. A. Kimble, C. A. Bonneau, & M. Wertheimer (Eds.), *Portraits of pioneers in psychology* (Vol. II, pp. 15–31). Washington, DC: American Psychological Association.

Viney, W., & Zorich, S. (1982). Contributions to the history of psychology: XXIX. Dorothea Dix and the history of psychology. *Psychological Reports*, *50*, 211–218.

Viteles, M. S. (1932). *Industrial psychology*. New York: W. W. Norton.

Voyat, G. (1981). Jean Piaget: 1896–1980. *American Journal of Psychology*, *94*, 645–648.

Vrooman, J. R. (1970). *René Descartes: A biography*. New York: Putnam.

Wade, N. J. (1994). Hermann von Helmholtz. *Perception*, *23*, 981–989.

Wallin, J. E. W. (1966). A red-letter day in APA history. *Journal of General Psychology*, *75*, 107–114.

Warner, L. H., & Warden, C. J. (1927). The development of a standardized animal maze. *Archives of Psychology*, *15*(92).

Warr, P. (2007). Some historical developments in I-O psychology outside the United States. In L. L. Koppes (Ed.), *Historical perspectives in industrial and organizational psychology* (pp. 81–107). Mahwah, NJ: Erlbaum.

Warren, R. M. (1984). Helmholtz and his continuing influence. *Music Perception*, *1*, 253–275.

Washburn, M. F. (1908). *The animal mind*. New York: Macmillan.

Washburn, M. F. (1932). Margaret Floy Washburn. In C. Murchison (Ed.), *A history of psychology in autobiography* (Vol. 2, pp. 333–358). Worcester, MA: Clark University Press.

Washburn, M. F. (1935). James Mark Baldwin (1861–1934). *American Journal of Psychology*, *47*, 168–169.

Watson, J. B. (1903). *Animal education: An experimental study of the psychical development of the white rat, correlated with the growth of its nervous system*. Chicago: University of Chicago Press.

Watson, J. B. (1907). Kinesthetic and organic sensations: Their role in the reactions of the white rat to the maze. *Psychological Review Monograph Supplements*, *8*(33).

Watson, J. B. (1909). Some experiments bearing upon color vision in monkeys. *Journal of Comparative Neurology and Psychology*, *19*, 1–28.

Watson, J. B. (1910, February). The new science of animal behavior. *Harper's Monthly Magazine*, *120*, 346–353.

Watson, J. B. (1913). Psychology as the behaviorist views it. *Psychological Review*, *20*, 158–177.

Watson, J. B. (1914). *Behavior: An introduction to comparative psychology*. New York: Holt.

Watson, J. B. (1916). The place of the conditioned reflex in psychology. *Psychological Review*, *23*, 89–116.

Watson, J. B. (1919). *Psychology from the standpoint of the behaviorist*. Philadelphia: Lippincott.

Watson, J. B. (1926, June). How we think: A behaviorist's view. *Harper's Monthly Magazine*, *153*, 40–45.

Watson, J. B. (1928). *Psychological care of infant and child*. New York: W. W. Norton.

Watson, J. B. (1930). *Behaviorism* (2nd ed.). New York: W. W. Norton. (Original work published 1924).

Watson, J. B. (1936). Autobiography. In C. Murchison (Ed.), *A history of psychology in autobiography* (Vol. 3, pp. 271–281). Worcester, MA: Clark University Press.

Watson, J. B., & Morgan, J. J. B. (1917). Emotional reactions and psychological experimentation. *American Journal of Psychology*, *28*, 163–174.

Watson, J. B., & Rayner, R. (1920). Conditioned emotional reactions. *Journal of Experimental Psychology*, *3*, 1–14.

Watson, R. I. (1960). The history of psychology: A neglected area. *American Psychologist*, *15*, 251–255.

Watson, R. I., & Evans, R. B. (1991). *The great psychologists: A history of psychological thought* (5th ed.). New York: HarperCollins.

Weaver, K. A. (1998). Capturing the fervor of cognitive psychology's emergence. *Teaching of Psychology*, *25*, 136–138.

Webb, M. E. (1988). A new history of Hartley's "Observations on Man." *Journal of the History of the Behavioral Sciences*, *24*, 202–211.

Weiner, J. (1994). *The beak of the finch*. New York: Vintage Books.

Wertheimer, M. (1965). Experimental studies on the seeing of motion. In R. J. Herrnstein & E. G. Boring (Eds.), *A sourcebook in the history of psychology* (pp. 163–168). Cambridge, MA: Harvard University Press. (Original work published 1912).

Wertheimer, M. (1967a). Gestalt theory. In W. D. Ellis (Ed.), *A source book of Gestalt psychology* (pp. 1–11). London: Routledge and Kegan Paul. (Original talk delivered 1924).

Wertheimer, M. (1967b). Laws of organization in perceptual forms. In W. D. Ellis (Ed.), *A source book of Gestalt psychology* (pp. 71–88). London: Routledge and Kegan Paul. (Original work published 1923).

Wertheimer, M. (1978). Humanistic psychology and the humane but tough-minded psychologist. *American Psychologist*, *33*, 739–745.

Wertheimer, M. (1982). *Productive thinking*. Chicago: University of Chicago Press. (Original work published 1945).

White, M. (1997). *Isaac Newton: The last sorcerer*. Reading, MA: Perseus Books.

White, R. K. (1978). Has "field theory" been "tried and found wanting"? *Journal of the History of the Behavioral Sciences*, *14*, 242–246.

Wiggins, J. G., Jr. (1994). Would you want your child to be a psychologist? *American Psychologist*, *49*, 485–492.

Williams, D. H., Bellis, E. C., & Wellington, S. W. (1980). Deinstitutionalization and social policy: Historical perspectives and present dilemmas. *American Journal of Orthopsychiatry*, *50*, 54–64.

Williams, S. B. (1938). Resistance to extinction as a function of the number of reinforcements. *Journal of Experimental Psychology*, *23*, 506–521.

Windholz, G. (1986). A comparative analysis of the conditional reflex discoveries of Pavlov and Twitmyer, and the birth of a paradigm. *Pavlovian Journal of Biological Science*, *21*, 141–147.

Windholz, G. (1990). Pavlov and the Pavlovians in the laboratory. *Journal of the History of the Behavioral Sciences*, *26*, 64–74.

Windholz, G. (1997). Ivan P. Pavlov: An overview of his life and psychological work. *American Psychologist*, *52*, 941–946.

Windholz, G., & Lamal, P. A. (1985). Köhler's insight revisited. *Teaching of Psychology*, *12*, 165–167.

Winston, A. S. (1990). Robert Sessions Woodworth and the "Columbia Bible": How the psychological experiment was redefined. *American Journal of Psychology*, *103*, 391–401.

Winston, A. S. (1996). "As his name indicates": R. S. Woodworth's letters of reference and employment for Jewish psychologists in the 1930s. *Journal of the History of the Behavioral Sciences*, *32*, 30–43.

Winters, B. (1950). Franz Anton Mesmer: An inquiry into the antecedents of hypnosis. *Journal of General Psychology*, *43*, 63–75.

Wispe, L., Awkward, J., Hoffman, M., Ash, P., Hicks, L. H., & Porter, J. (1969). The Negro psychologist in America. *American Psychologist*, *24*, 142–150.

Wissler, C. (1965). Clark Wissler (1870–1947) on the inadequacy of mental tests. In R. J. Herrnstein & E. G. Boring (Eds.), *A sourcebook in the history of psychology* (pp. 442–445). Cambridge, MA: Harvard University Press. (Original work published 1901).

Witmer, L. (1893, July 14). *Letter to Hugo Münsterberg*. Boston: Boston Public Library, Münsterberg Papers.

Witmer, L. (1909). The study and treatment of retardation: A field of applied psychology. *Psychological Bulletin*, *6*, 121–127.

Witmer, L. (1911). Criminals in the making. *The Psychological Clinic*, *4*, 221–238.

Witmer, L. (1931). Clinical psychology. In R. A. Brotemarkle (Ed.), *Clinical psychology: Studies in honor of Lightner Witmer* (pp. 341–352). Philadelphia: University of Pennsylvania Press. (Original work published 1907).

Wolpe, J. (1958). *Psychotherapy by reciprocal inhibition*. Palo Alto, CA: Stanford University Press.

Woodward, W. R. (2010). Russian women émigrés in psychology: Informal Jewish networks. *History of Psychology*, *13*, 111–137.

Woodworth, R. S. (1917). Some criticisms of the Freudian psychology. *American Journal of Psychology*, *12*, 174–194.

Woodworth, R. S. (1918). *Dynamic psychology*. New York: Columbia University Press.

Woodworth, R. S. (1921). *Psychology*. New York: Holt.

Woodworth, R. S. (1931). *Contemporary schools of psychology*. New York: Ronald Press.

Woodworth, R. S. (1932). Robert S. Woodworth. In C. Murchison (Ed.), *A history of psychology in autobiography* (Vol. 2, pp. 359–380). Worcester, MA: Clark University Press.

Woodworth, R. S. (1937). The future of clinical psychology. *Journal of Consulting Psychology*, 1, 4–5.

Woodworth, R. S. (1938). *Experimental psychology*. New York: Holt.

Woodworth, R. S. (1958). *Dynamics of behavior*. New York: Holt.

Woodworth, R. S., & Schlosberg, H. (1954). *Experimental psychology* (2nd ed.) New York: Holt.

Wozniak, R. H. (2009). Consciousness, social heredity, and development: The evolutionary thought of James Mark Baldwin. *American Psychologist*, *64*, 93–101.

Wright, R. (1994). *The moral animal*. New York: Vintage Books.

Wundt, W. (1897). *Outlines of psychology* (C. H. Judd, Trans.). Leipzig Wilhelm Engelman.

Wundt, W. (1904). *Principles of physiological psychology* (5th ed.; E. B. Titchener, Trans.). New York: Macmillan. (Original work published 1873–1874).

Wundt, W. (1907). Lectures on human and animal psychology (J. Creighton & E. B. Titchener, Trans.). New York: Macmillan. (Original work published 1863).

Yanni, C. (2007). *The architecture of madness: Insane asylums in the United States*. Minneapolis: University of Minnesota Press.

Yerkes, R. M. (1911). *Introduction to psychology*. New York: Holt.

Yerkes, R. M. (Ed.). (1921). Psychological examining in the United States Army. *Memoirs of the National Academy of Sciences*, *15*, 1–890.

Yerkes, R. M., & Morgulis, S. (1909). The method of Pawlow in animal psychology. *Psychological Bulletin*, *6*, 257–273.

Yoakum, C. S., & Yerkes, R. M. (1920). *Army mental tests*. New York: Holt.

Young, R. M. (1972). Franz Joseph Gall. In C. C. Gillespie (Ed.), *Dictionary of scientific biography* (Vol. V). New York: Scribner.

Youniss, J. (2006). G. Stanley Hall and his times: Too much so, yet not enough. *History of Psychology*, *9*, 224–235.

Zajonc, R. B. (1980). Feeling and thinking: Preferences need no inferences. *American Psychologist*, *35*, 151–175.

Zajonc, R. B. (1990). Leon Festinger (1919–1989). *American Psychologist*, *45*, 661–662.

Zeigarnik, B. (1967). On finished and unfinished tasks. In W. D. Ellis (Ed.), *A source book of Gestalt psychology* (pp. 300–314). London: Routledge and Kegan Paul. (Original work published 1927).

Zenderland, L. (1998). Measuring mind: *Henry Herbert Goddard and the origins of American intelligence testing*. New York: Cambridge University Press.

Zilboorg, G. (1941). *A history of medical psychology*. New York: W. W. Norton.

GLOSSARY

Ablation Method of studying the brain, pioneered by Flourens, in which the function of some brain area is assessed after that portion of the brain has been destroyed.

Absolute threshold Point on the continuum of a physical dimension where an increase in physical stimulation results in the initial perception of a stimulus.

Accommodation Visual phenomenon described by Berkeley; the tendency of the lens of the eye to change shape as objects move toward and away from the person.

Act psychology Brentano's position that psychology should be the study of mental acts, not mental contents; with the perception of some event, for example, one should not analyze it into its elements, but examine the act of perception (how the individual perceives the event and what the event means to the individual).

Algorithm In math and computer science, a set of rules guaranteed to produce an eventual solution to a problem by exhaustively working through all possible solutions.

Analytical psychology Jung's theory of psychology, which differed from Freud's in a number of ways, including a decreased emphasis on sex.

Anecdotal evidence Research method in which evidence takes the form of an accumulation of examples supporting some principle or theory; associated with Romanes and the origins of comparative psychology; also used by phrenologists; heavy reliance on such evidence leads one to ignore counterinstances that might disprove a hypothesis.

Animal magnetism Belief held by Mesmer and contemporaries that living organisms were influenced by magnetic forces and that cures for illness could result from the proper use of magnets.

Animal spirits Hypothetical essence once believed (e.g., by Descartes) to inhabit the nervous system and to be the driving force behind muscle movement.

Anna O. case Famous case of hysteria treated by Breuer and reported by Breuer and Freud in *Studies on Hysteria*; gave Freud the insight that hysterics suffer from their memories of traumatic events; details distorted over the years.

Anthropomorphism Tendency to attribute human characteristics to nonhuman entities; associated with Romanes and the origins of comparative psychology.

Antithesis Darwin's principle of emotional expression, stating that some emotions that were the opposite of each other were reflected in expressions that were likewise opposed.

Apparent motion Phenomenon studied by Wertheimer in which stationary stimuli appear to move under certain circumstances.

Apperception A high level of awareness, in which we focus our full attention on some object and apprehend it fully; associated with Leibniz originally; central concept for Wundt's psychology.

Approach–approach conflict For Lewin, a situation in which a conflict exists within a person, resulting from having to make a choice between two goals with a positive valence.

Approach–avoidance conflict For Lewin, a situation in which a conflict exists within a person, occurring when a goal elicits both approach and avoidance tendencies.

Archive A repository of unpublished data of use to historians.

Argument from design Explained the great complexity in nature by arguing that it required a superior being (i.e., God) to produce it; associated with Reverend Paley.

Army Alpha Group intelligence test developed by Yerkes for testing the abilities of literate soldiers in World War I.

Army Beta Group intelligence test developed by Yerkes for testing the abilities of illiterate soldiers in World War I.

Artificial intelligence (AI) The study of whether nonhuman technological systems can be said to act with some degree of human-like intelligence.

Association For Locke, analogous to Newtonian gravity; a force that attracts ideas.

Associationism Philosophical school of thought, related to empiricism, that emphasizes the rules by which relationships between ideas and experiences are formed.

Atomism Belief that nature can be understood best by reducing complexity to its smallest, most fundamental elements (opposed to holism).

Attributes In Titchener's system, these were the ways of classifying the various elements of conscious experience; for example, the element of sensation had the attributes of quality, intensity, duration, and clarity.

Attrition Methodological problem in longitudinal research, when participants drop out of the study; notably low in Terman's longitudinal study of giftedness.

Avoidance–avoidance conflict For Lewin, a situation in which a conflict exists within a person, resulting from having to make a choice between two goals with a negative valence.

Behavioral environment For the gestaltists, this referred to the environment as perceived, as contrasted with the physical environment (the geographical environment).

Behaviorist Manifesto Watson's 1913 paper that argued for a behaviorist approach to psychology.

Bell-Magendie law A statement that the posterior roots of the spinal cord controlled sensation, while the anterior roots controlled motor movement; sometimes considered an example of a "multiple."

Binocular vision Vision involving the use of two eyes; aids in depth perception.

Bit Abbreviation of "binary digit"; the amount of information that enables a choice between two alternatives.

Bloodletting Medical technique promoted by Benjamin Rush; drawing blood was believed to relieve, among other things, mental disorders brought about by excessive tension in the circulatory system.

Brass instrument psychology Term used (sarcastically) by William James to describe the German reaction time and psychophysics research, which relied heavily on apparatus made of brass.

Cardinal trait For Allport, the most essential traits that characterize an individual.

Cartesian dichotomy From Descartes, the distinction between humans (mind + body) and animals (only a mechanical body).

Case study Research method involving an in-depth analysis of a single individual; advocated by Allport as a way to investigate personality.

Catastrophism Theory in geology that geological change occurred infrequently and as a consequence of such catastrophic events as the biblical flood.

Catharsis In Freudian psychoanalysis, an emotional release that occurs when one gains insight into the unconscious origins of some problem; key part of the Anna O. case.

Cause and effect One of Hume's laws of association; Hume argued that we cannot be certain of the fundamental causes of events, only that events occur together regularly.

Cell assembly For Hebb, a basic unit in the nervous system; a set of neurons that become associated with each other because they have been repeatedly activated together.

Central trait For Allport, a set of traits that sum up an individual's personality, aside from cardinal traits.

Chain of being Belief that all species on earth could be placed on a linear scale with reference to their level of complexity.

Chunk For Miller, a meaningful unit of information; short-term memory capacity said to be 7 ± 2 chunks of information.

Client-centered therapy Humanistic approach to psychotherapy created by Rogers; it assumed that responsibility for therapeutic change ultimately belonged to the client, and the therapist's responsibility was to create an atmosphere conducive to such change.

Clinical method Method of studying the brain, pioneered by Broca, in which existing behavioral or cognitive deficits are correlated with brain damage upon autopsy.

Clinical psychology Field of psychology concerned with the diagnosis and treatment of mental and behavioral disorders; named by Witmer.

Closure Gestalt organizing principle; a tendency to fill in missing gaps in our perception in order to perceive whole figures.

Cognitive dissonance In a theory proposed by Festinger, a state of cognitive discomfort resulting from the experience of holding two inconsistent thoughts simultaneously or behaving in a way that is inconsistent with one's beliefs.

Cognitive map For Tolman, a hypothetical spatial memory of a maze, acquired simply as a result of experiencing the maze (i.e., reinforcement not needed).

Cognitive science An interdisciplinary field that includes cognitive psychology, linguistics, computer science, cultural anthropology, and epistemology.

Collective unconscious Jung's concept that the unconscious included the collective experiences of our ancestors; reflected in the common themes that occur in the mythology of various cultures.

Comparative psychology Study of the similarities and differences among species; originated from the implication of Darwin's theory of evolution that continuity existed among species.

Completion test Mental test designed by Ebbinghaus to measure mental fatigue in schoolchildren; because it focused on higher mental activity, it anticipated the approach later taken by Binet.

Complex idea For Locke, ideas that were combinations of simple ideas.

Complication experiment A 19th-century reaction time experiment, typically using the Donders subtractive method, in which reaction times for simple tasks were subtracted from reaction times for more "complicated" tasks.

Concomitant variation From Mill's *Logic*, method that examines whether changes in event X are associated with changes in event Y.

Conditional stimulus (CS) Any stimulus in Pavlovian conditioning that will be paired with an unconditioned stimulus to produce a conditioned response (e.g., tone).

Conditioned reflex (CR) The outcome of Pavlovian conditioning; by pairing a conditioned (conditional) stimulus (e.g., tone) with an unconditioned stimulus (e.g., food), the conditioned stimulus eventually elicits a conditioned response or reflex.

Connectionism Thorndike's model of learning, emphasizing the development and strengthening of connections between stimulus situations and responses that became stronger with trial-and-error learning.

Conscious attitudes In the Würzburg school, this term referred to such mental processes as hesitation and doubt; occurred during the imageless thought studies.

Consciousness Sense of awareness; how to study it became a contentious issue in the late 19th and early 20th centuries.

Conservation of energy Associated with Helmholtz and used by him to combat vitalism; proposed that the total energy within a system remains constant, even if changes occur within the system.

Contiguity One of Hume's laws of association and Hartley's fundamental law; events experienced together, either simultaneously (spatial contiguity) or successively (temporal contiguity), become associated with each other.

Contralateral function The notion that each side of the brain controls the opposite side of the body.

Convergence Visual phenomenon described by Berkeley; the tendency of the eye muscles to make the eyes move in the direction of "crossing" as objects move closer to the person.

Converging operations Refers to a series of studies, each with different operational definitions of the main constructs, that nonetheless lead to the same general conclusion.

Correlation Statistical tool that assesses the degree of relationship between two variables; concept originated with Galton and his studies of intelligence.

Critical period Certain instinctive behaviors (e.g., imprinting) must develop within a limited time frame, if they are to develop at all; associated with Lorenz and other European ethologists, but also proposed by Spalding.

Cybernetics Study of principles (e.g., feedback) involved in controlling and maintaining any living or nonliving system; feedback loop borrowed by Miller, Galanter, and Pribram for their TOTE unit.

Dedifferentiation For Lewin, a process that occurs under stress, in which a person reverses the normal differentiation process and reverts to an earlier, more primitive way of behaving; similar to Freudian regression.

Dementia praecox Term used by Kraepelin that literally means a premature dementia, a disorder later named schizophrenia.

Dependent variable   Any variable in research that is measured as an outcome of an experimental study; this usage introduced by Woodworth.

Derived ideas   For Descartes, ideas that result from one's experiences in the world.

Determinism   Philosophical position that all events in the universe have prior causes.

Dichotic listening   A procedure in research on selective attention in which a person wearing headphones hears one message in one ear and a second message in the other ear.

Difference threshold   Point on the continuum of a physical dimension where a difference between two stimuli is first detected.

Differentiation   For Lewin, a developmental process in which a child's life space becomes more complex; for Pavlov, refers to discrimination, the ability to distinguish between two stimuli.

Direct action of the nervous system   Darwin's principle of emotional expression, stating that some expressions (e.g., blushing) are the side effects of the physiological arousal accompanying strongly felt emotions.

Doctrine of the skull   The phrenological belief that skull contour reflected brain shape; enabled measurement of faculties by measuring contour of the skull.

Dream analysis   A cornerstone of Freudian psychoanalysis; for Freud, dreams were the "royal road" to the unconscious; surface or manifest content of dreams needed to be analyzed for their deeper, or latent, content.

Drill courses   Instructional courses in basic laboratory techniques; predominant in American universities in the late 19th century.

Drive reduction   Central to Hull's theory of learning; learning required reinforcers, which were any stimuli (e.g., food) that reduced a strong drive (e.g., hunger).

Dualist   On the mind–body problem, someone (e.g., Descartes) who believes that mind and body are two separate and distinguishable essences.

Ecological memory   Study of memory as it occurs in everyday situations.

Ecological perception   Gibson's approach to the study of perception, which emphasized perception while navigating in realistic environments; the emphasis is on environmental factors guiding perception rather than the internal perceptual systems of the perceiver.

Ecological validity   In cognitive psychology, research that is relevant for understanding everyday cognitive activities is said to have ecological validity.

Ego defense mechanisms   In Freudian theory, ways of behaving or thinking that serve to defend the ego against anxiety.

Empathy   Ability to understand, both cognitively and emotionally, what another person is experiencing; important prerequisite for therapy success, according to Rogers.

Empiricist   Someone who believes that our knowledge of the world is constructed from our experiences in it; school of thought associated with such British philosophers as Locke, Berkeley, and Mill.

Engineering psychology   That branch of psychology concerned with the design of objects to improve their use by humans (e.g., by reducing perceptual errors or reducing fatigue).

Enlightenment   Historical period from mid-18th century to late 19th century, characterized by a belief that true knowledge could be found through the use of science and reason and that progress was inevitable and good.

Epistemology   Branch of philosophy concerned with studying the nature of and the origins of human knowledge.

Eponyms   Historical periods or movements named with reference to some important historical person (e.g., Darwinian biology).

Equilibrium   For Lewin, a steady state in which all needs have been satisfied for the moment.

Equipotentiality   Principle associated with Lashley; proposed that if some portion of the brain is destroyed, other areas will be able to serve the same function (to a degree).

Ergonomics   Study of how systems and equipment can be best designed to avoid human error; pioneered by Gilbreth.

Eros   In Freudian theory, the name given to the life instinct and manifested in the sex drive.

Ethology   The study of animal behavior in its natural surroundings; associated with Lorenz, but with roots in Spalding's work.

Eugenics   Term created by Galton; refers to a variety of methods (e.g., selective breeding) for enhancing the quality of a species, especially humans.

Evolutionary psychology   Late 20th century development in psychology, with roots in Darwinian thinking; proposes that virtually all human behavior, especially social behavior, must be understood in an evolutionary context, as the product of natural selection.

Experimental neurosis   In Pavlovian conditioning, an emotional response that occurs after training a discrimination between two stimuli and then making the stimuli too similar to be discriminated.

Explanatory fictions   For Skinner, hypothetical constructs proposed as mediators between stimuli and responses that erroneously become used as explanations for behavioral phenomena (e.g., recalling only a few words because of limited short-term memory).

External history   A history that examines factors external to a discipline (e.g., social, political, institutional, economic) that influence the history of that discipline.

Extinction   In Pavlovian conditioning, the gradual elimination of a conditioned response following the repeated presentation of a conditioned stimulus in the absence of an unconditioned stimulus.

Faculty psychology   Prevalent early and mid-19th-century approach to psychology, derived from Scottish Realism; emphasized real existence of mind, which they believed held a number of innate attributes ("faculties") such as intelligence and judgment.

Field theory   Associated with Lewin and Tolman; for Lewin, derived from his belief that to understand behavior requires knowing about all of the forces acting on a person at a particular time; for Tolman, reflected the extent to which his neobehaviorism was influenced by the gestaltists.

Figure-ground   Gestalt organizing principle stating that a fundamental perceptual tendency is to separate whole figures from their backgrounds.

Foreign hull   For Lewin, all events outside of the person's life space and therefore having no effect on the individual at a given moment.

Form-quality   As described by von Ehrenfels, the overall quality of some entity (e.g., a melody, a square) that exists over and above its individual components (e.g., notes, lines).

Fractionation   Procedure developed in Külpe's laboratory in Würzburg, in which complicated events were broken down into sections ("fractionated"); then separate introspections were accomplished for each section.

Free association   In Freudian psychoanalysis, a procedure to probe the unconscious; involves patients describing whatever occurs to them without internal censorship.

Functional fixedness   Failure to solve a problem because of an inability to think of using some object in a manner different from its normal function.

Functionalism   School of psychology favored by most early American psychologists; focused on the study of human conscious experience from an evolutionary perspective; concerned with studying the adaptive value of various mental and behavioral processes.

Generalization   The tendency for a response learned to one stimulus to occur after the presentation of a second stimulus similar to the first.

Genetic epistemology   Piagetian psychology that examined the manner in which knowledge developed within the individual.

Genetic psychology   Approach that emphasizes the evolution and development of the mind, including developmental psychology, comparative psychology, and abnormal psychology; associated with Hall.

Geocentric   Ancient astronomical viewpoint that placed earth at the center of the known universe.

Geographical environment   For the gestaltists, this referred to the physical environment, as contrasted with the environment as perceived (the behavioral environment).

Gestalt organizing principles   Perceptual principles described by the gestaltists that summarize the ways in which sensory phenomena become organized into a whole, meaningful figure.

Good continuation   Gestalt organizing principle; a tendency to organize perceptions in a smoothly flowing direction.

Grammar   Set of rules allowing for (a) the production of all possible sentences in a language, and (b) the recognition and rejection of nonsentences.

Habit strength   For Hull, an intervening variable influencing behavior that was a direct function of the number of reinforced trials ($_SH_R$).

Hawthorne effect   Tendency for the performance of subjects in an experiment to be influenced by their knowledge that they are under observation; based on the Hawthorne studies.

Hebb synapses   For Hebb, synapses that change their structure as a result of learning.

Heliocentric   Astronomical viewpoint proposed by Copernicus and elaborated by Galileo that placed the sun at the center of the known universe.

Heuristic   In math and computer science, a creative rule of thumb that, while not guaranteeing to produce a problem solution, is likely to produce one and will be more efficient than an algorithm (e.g., means-ends analysis).

Historicist   An interpretation of historical events made from the vantage point of the knowledge and values in place at the time of the events.

Historiography   The writing of history; historical methodology and theory.

Holism   The philosophical assumption underlying gestalt psychology; argues that wholes (e.g., complex ideas) are more than the sum of their constituent elements (e.g., sensations, simple ideas); opposed to atomism.

Humanistic psychology   Movement pioneered by Rogers, Maslow, and others as a reaction to the deterministic assumptions of behaviorism and psychoanalysis; assumed that humans are characterized by free will, a search for meaning, and the potential for self-actualization.

Hypnotism   State of heightened suggestibility; pioneered by Mesmer and Elliotson and named by Braid.

Hypothetico-deductive system   General approach taken by Hull in which hypotheses for research are deduced from the formal postulates of the theory, and the outcomes of research support the theory or lead to its modification.

Hysteria   Disorder in which a number of symptoms (e.g., paralysis) indicate neurological damage, but no such damage exists.

Ideas   For Hume, ideas were "faint copies" of sensory impressions.

Idiographic   A research tradition emphasizing an in-depth analysis of individual cases; also examines differences from one individual to another; contrasted with a nomothetic strategy.

Imageless thought   Any thought process that could not be further reduced to mental images; considered nonexistent by Titchener, who believed that all thought included images.

Impressions   For Hume, these were basic sensations, the raw data of experience.

Imprinting   Instinctive tendency for newly hatched ducklings (and other related species) to follow the first moving object they encounter; associated with Lorenz, but also observed by Spalding and Watson.

Independent variable   Any variable in research that can be directly manipulated by an experimenter; this usage introduced by Woodworth.

Individual differences   Originally referring to the individual variation among members of a particular species, became for psychology the more general study of the characteristics that differentiated one person from another (e.g., intelligence).

Individual psychology   Label used by both Binet and Adler; for Binet, psychology should focus on ways of identifying and measuring individual differences (e.g., mental testing) rather than on general laws; for Adler, individual psychology was his version of psychoanalysis, which emphasized social factors in the development of the individual.

Inductive   An approach to knowledge that emphasizes that general scientific principles are generalizations made after the collection of large amounts of data; associated with Sir Francis Bacon.

Inferiority complex   Concept associated with Adler, who believed that much of human behavior could be viewed as an attempt to compensate for feelings of inferiority.

Information theory   An influence external to psychology that helped develop cognitive psychology; concerns the manner in which information is structured (bits) and processed.

Inheritance of acquired characteristics   Theory that characteristics developed as a result of experience during one's lifetime could be passed on biologically to offspring; associated with Lamarck.

Innate idea   Idea that exists or can be deduced in the absence of direct experience, through reasoning (Descartes used the idea of a material object's "extension" in space as an example).

Insight   For the gestaltists, a sudden problem solution that occurred when the individual reorganized the elements of the problem situation into a new configuration.

Instinct   Behavior is said to be instinctive when alternative explanations in terms of learning or experience can be ruled out; pioneering work was done by early comparative psychologists, especially Spalding.

Intelligence quotient   Term invented by Stern and used by Terman in the Stanford-Binet tests; IQ equaled mental age divided by chronological age, the result multiplied by 100.

Interactionist   A dualist who believes that body and mind directly influence each other.

Internal history   A history of the ideas, theories, and findings of a discipline, without regard for the influence of external, contextual factors.

Internal perception   Wundt's version of introspection, in which "observers" would give brief verbal responses to controlled stimuli (e.g., in reaction time or psychophysics experiments).

Intervening variables   Used by Tolman and Hull; referred to hypothetical internal factors (e.g., cognitive map for Tolman; habit strength for Hull) that intervened between stimulus and response.

Introspection   Method of experiencing some phenomenon and then describing the conscious experience of the phenomenon.

Introspective habit   The result of extensive practice with introspection, this was a dissociative ability to make mental notes about an experience while the experience was occurring.

James-Lange theory of emotion   Theory holding that the strong emotions were in essence the physiological reaction that followed the perception of some emotion-eliciting event.

jnd   Or *just noticeable difference*; point where the difference (in weight, color, pitch, etc.) between two stimuli becomes just barely detectable.

Joint Method   J. S. Mill's combination of the methods of agreement and difference.

Jost's law   If two associations have equal strength, additional practice strengthens the older of the associations more than the younger.

Latent learning   For Tolman, learning that occurred but was not reflected in an animal's performance.

Law of Effect   Thorndike's principle that behaviors that were effective in problem solving would be strengthened (stamped in), while behaviors that were not effective would be weakened (stamped out).

Law of Exercise   Thorndike's principle that learned connections between stimuli and responses were strengthened with additional practice.

Life space   For Lewin, a field within which a person operates; includes all the factors that influence a person's behavior at a certain moment.

Linguistic universals   For Chomsky, common principles shared by all languages, the existence of which supports the notion that language is innate to the human species.

Lloyd Morgan's canon   Principle stating that the best explanation for some behavioral phenomenon was the one with the fewest unnecessary assumptions; Morgan did not deny the use of mental processing when explaining animal behavior, but argued that there was no need to propose mental capabilities beyond the level needed for survival in a given species.

Lobotomy   Surgical procedure pioneered by Moniz in the 1930s; it involves severing connections between the cortex and lower brain centers. The lobotomy was originally designed to treat severe mental illness but was abandoned when found to be marginally effective and often abused.

Localization of function   Concerns the issue of whether specific parts of the brain have specific functions.

Logical Positivism   Philosophical movement associated with the Vienna Circle that extended positivist thinking; distinguished between theoretical and observable events and described ways of connecting the two through operational definitions.

Mass action   Principle associated with Lashley, proposing a limit on equipotentiality; the greater the amount of brain destroyed, the greater the difficulty for remaining areas of the brain to take over brain function.

Materialism   Philosophical position that the only reality is physical reality and that living matter can be reduced to physical and chemical properties; held by most physiologists of the 19th century (opposed to vitalism).

Means-ends analysis   Primary heuristic used in GPS (General Problem Solver), a computer simulation of logic by Newell and Simon; involves a feedback system of recognizing a difference between present state and goal state and then applying a series of operations to reduce the difference until it disappears.

Mechanist   Someone who explains bodily actions in mechanical terms.

Memory drum   Device for presenting verbal stimuli in a memory experiment; invented by G. E. Müller.

Mental age   Mistranslation of Binet's mental level; indicated a child's level of mental ability, reported in terms of years.

Mental chronometry   Name given to 19th-century reaction time research, in which the goal was to measure the time taken for various mental events.

Mental level   Term used by Binet to indicate a child's level of mental functioning; those in need of remediation scored two levels below the norm for their chronological age.

Mental set   In the Würzburg laboratory, this term referred to the effect of giving observers some instructions that predispose them to think in certain ways; for the Gestaltists, a fixed, habitual way of thinking.

Mental test   Any test designed to measure mental activity or ability; term introduced in 1890 by Cattell.

Meritocracy   A model of society based on the idea that the most mentally competent should be the leaders; championed by most American mental testers, especially Terman.

Mesmerism   Early version of hypnotism, associated with Mesmer; held that hysteria and other disorders could be cured through the use of magnets.

Method of adjustment   Method of psychophysics, described by Fechner, in which the subject directly controls a physical stimulus, adjusting it until it is just barely detected.

Method of agreement   From Mill's *Logic*, a method in which a proposed cause is present whenever the effect is also present.

Method of constant stimuli   Method of psychophysics, described by Fechner, in which stimuli of varying physical intensities are presented in random order.

Method of difference   From Mill's *Logic*, a method in which the absence of a proposed effect is always accompanied by the absence of a proposed cause.

Method of limits   Method of psychophysics, described by Fechner, which alternates ascending trials (stimulus is first below threshold, then increased until detected) and descending trials (stimulus is first well above threshold, then decreased until no longer detected).

Molar behavior   For Tolman, broad patterns of behavior that were goal directed, in contrast with the molecular behavior that was the result of a reductionist model of behavior.

Monads   For Leibniz, the fundamental elements of both physical and mental reality.

Moral treatment   For Pinel and for Tuke, an approach to treating mental illness that included improved nutrition and living conditions, and rewards for productive behavior.

Moron   Term invented by Goddard as a label for adolescents or adults scoring at a mental age of 8 through 12.

Motor aphasia   Found in Broca's patient Tan; speech apparatus normal, intelligence normal, but a serious inability to express ideas verbally.

Multiple   The simultaneous or near simultaneous discovery of some phenomenon, used to support the importance of the zeitgeist and a naturalistic approach to history.

Nativism   An extreme nationalist tendency, in which outsiders are considered inferior and dangerous; characterized by United States in 1920s, contributing to restrictions placed on immigration.

Nativist   Someone who argues for the existence of innate ideas or, more generally, believes that some knowledge, faculties, or abilities are innate.

Naturalistic history   An approach to history that emphasizes the importance of environmental and situational forces in shaping history.

Natural selection   Central idea in Darwin's theory of evolution; held that in the struggle for existence, those organisms with adaptive variations would be most likely to survive (i.e., be selected by nature) and pass their attributes on to the next generation.

Neobehaviorism   Behaviorist movement that emerged in the 1930s; associated with Tolman, Hull, and others.

Neurypnology   Term created by Braid to reflect his belief that hypnotism was related to the state of sleep.

Nomothetic   A research strategy that focuses on discovering general principles that apply, to a calibrated degree, to all individuals; contrasted with an idiographic strategy.

Nonsense syllables Consonant-vowel-consonant combinations, invented by Ebbinghaus as stimulus materials in his studies on the formation and retention of associations.

Normal science In Kuhn's approach to the history of science, this is a period during which a paradigm is in control and a scientist's activities are shaped by the constraints of the paradigm.

Observer Label for someone participating in a psychological experiment in the late 19th and early 20th centuries; used because the primary activity was observing one's mental activities through introspection.

Operant Any behavior emitted by an organism and controlled by the immediate consequences of the behavior.

Operant conditioning Skinnerian conditioning in which a behavior occurs, and the immediate consequences of the behavior determine its future probability of occurrence.

Operational definition A definition in terms of a specific, observable set of operations (e.g., hunger = 24 hours without food); more generally, defining scientific terms with precision.

Operationism Philosophical position that scientific concepts were to be defined in terms of a set of operations used to measure those concepts.

Ophthalmoscope Device for examining the retina; invented by Helmholtz.

Opponent process theory Theory of color vision associated with Hering; proposed that color-sensitive cells are arranged in opponent pairs (e.g., red-green, blue-yellow).

Orthogenics Witmer's term for his therapeutic strategy of helping those with school-related problems (e.g., learning disabilities) to recover.

Paired-associate learning Popular learning procedure in which pairs of stimuli are presented; after a study time, stimuli are presented and the associated response must be given; invented by Calkins.

Paradigm In Kuhn's approach to the history of science, an all-encompassing theory that determines which problems are to be solved and the methods used to solve them.

Peak experience In humanistic psychology, a rare experience of extreme joy, pleasure, or accomplishment.

Periodic function Concept used in the early 20th century to refer to a women's alleged incapacity during the time of menstruation.

Personal equation Calibrating the reaction of one astronomer against another astronomer; needed because different reaction times among astronomers yielded different astronomical measurements.

Personalistic history An approach to history that emphasizes persons and their roles in shaping historical events.

Petites perceptions For Leibniz, perceptions below the level of awareness, but essential for higher levels of perception.

Phase sequences For Hebb, a higher level of cortical organization than the cell assembly, in which combinations of assemblies are formed.

Phi phenomenon Wertheimer's term for apparent motion, chosen to avoid the connotation that "apparent" motion was not really perceived, but was illusory.

Phrenology The first serious localization of function theory; proposed that "faculties" were located in specific brain locations, that the strength of a faculty was proportional to the amount of brain assigned to it, and that faculties could be assessed by measuring skull contours.

Pineal gland Portion of the brain selected by Descartes as the locus for mind–body interactions.

Positivism Philosophical position associated with Comte, who argued that the only certain knowledge is obtained through objective, publicly observable events.

Pragmatism Position taken by several late 19th-century American philosophers, most notably William James; judged the value of ideas by their usefulness in helping someone adapt to the environment.

Prägnanz Gestalt organizing principle of perception (translation—"good figure"); a tendency for our perceptions to mirror reality as closely as possible.

Presentist An interpretation of historical events made from the vantage point of present-day knowledge and values.

Primary qualities For Locke, attributes of some object that are inherent to that object that exist regardless of perception (e.g., extension in space).

Primary source Materials written or created at or near the time of some historical event, such as correspondence, diaries, speeches, minutes of meetings, university records.

Primary reinforcers For Hull, unlearned reinforcers (e.g., food).

Problem of perception For Helmholtz, the dilemma posed by the fact that human perception is extraordinary, while the mechanisms (e.g., eye, ear) appear to have design flaws.

Progressive education Associated with Dewey; an approach to education that emphasized making the student an active learner (learning by doing).

Progressive relaxation Technique of gradually and systematically relaxing major muscle groups; pioneered by Jacobson and used by Wolpe in systematic desensitization.

Proximity Gestalt organizing principle of perception, a tendency to perceive that objects in close proximity "belong" together.

Psychophysical Parallelism Dualistic position on the mind–body problem, associated with Hartley, Leibniz, and others; asserts that mind and body are separate and noninteracting, but in perfect harmony.

Psychophysics Study of the relationship between physical stimuli and the perception of those stimuli; pioneered by Weber and (especially) Fechner.

PsyD Degree given to clinical psychologists trained with reference to the Vail model, which places a heavier emphasis on practice and a lighter emphasis on research expertise than does the Boulder model of scientist-practitioner.

Purposiveness For Tolman, this term referred to goal-directedness; he believed it to be a universal feature of learned behavior.

Rationalist Philosophical tradition emphasizing the use of reason and logic to arrive at truth; associated with Descartes.

Reaction potential For Hull, the probability that a response will occur at a given time, depending on such factors as drive and habit strength ($_sE_R$).

Recapitulation Hall's theory, taken from a similar idea in biology, that the development of the individual mirrors the evolution of that individual's species.

Reciprocal innervation For Sherrington, the idea that muscles work in coordinated pairs under nervous system control—when one muscle flexes, a second, paired muscle, extends; the action allows complex and coordinated actions (e.g., walking).

Recoding For Miller, a process of reorganizing information to increase the amount of information per chunk.

Reflection Therapy technique used by Rogers to show that the therapist could empathize; involved rephrasing a client's comment to show understanding.

Reflex A biological process in which an automatic and involuntary response follows a stimulus.

Reflex arc Basic unit of behavior, reduced by physiologists into the stimulus producing sensation, the central processing producing an idea, and the motor response; analysis rejected by Dewey, who argued that the arc should be seen instead as a coordinated unit that adapted the individual to the environment.

Reliability The extent to which repeated measures yield the same outcome; some of Tolman's research on maze learning concerned the factors influencing the reliability of mazes.

Remote associations Indirect associations between list items separated by more than a single item; studied by Ebbinghaus.

Replication Process of repeating an experiment to judge its validity and generality.

Repression A Freudian defense mechanism in which unwanted impulses or traumatic memories are forced out of awareness and into the unconscious.

Resemblance One of Hume's laws of association; objects similar to each other become associated with each other.

Resistance In Freudian psychoanalysis, occurs when a person is unable to free associate; this indicates (to a Freudian) the presence of repressed material.

Resonance theory Theory of hearing associated with Helmholtz; proposed that different frequencies of sound stimulated receptors located in different places along the basilar membrane of the cochlear (found in the inner ear).

Retroactive inhibition Interference from some activity that intervenes between the learning of a list of stimulus items and its recall.

S-O-R model Proposed by Woodworth to recognize the importance of the organism intervening between stimulus and response.

Savings method Measure of memory used by Ebbinghaus, based on the difference between the amount of time to learn a list of nonsense syllables during original learning and the amount of time to relearn the list some time later.

Schedules of reinforcement   Specification of the relationship between the number or pattern of responses and the delivery of reinforcers, whenever reinforcement does not follow each behavior.

Schemata   Term used both by Piaget and Bartlett to refer to hypothetical mental structures that represent knowledge.

Scholasticism   Educational tradition combining the careful use of reason with the received wisdom of the Church and Aristotelian authority.

School psychology   Field of psychology concerned with the development of programs for treating children and adolescents with school-related problems (e.g., learning disabilities); pioneered by Witmer, although he did not use the term.

Scientist-practitioner model   Training model for PhD in clinical psychology that emphasizes a research dissertation; also called the Boulder model.

Secondary qualities   For Locke, attributes of some object that depend on perception for their existence (e.g., color).

Secondary reinforcers   For Hull, reinforcers that are learned through association with primary reinforcers (e.g., money).

Secondary source   Materials written or created some time after a historical event that serve to summarize or analyze that event.

Secondary trait   For Allport, part of an individual personality that is not often displayed.

Seduction hypothesis   Freud's original belief that hysteria originated from actual childhood sexual abuse.

Selective filter   For Broadbent, a model of selective attention emphasizing our tendency to separate information on the basis of physical characteristics (e.g., pitch) and then focus on one message while filtering out other ones.

Self-actualization   For humanistic psychologists, a state in which people have reached their full potential.

Self-psychology   Theoretical approach to psychology taken by Calkins, influenced by James; held that all consciousness is ultimately self-consciousness.

Sensory aphasia   A disorder characterized by the inability to comprehend speech; while there is no

difficulty in producing speech, the speech product is incoherent and/or illogical.

Serial learning   Procedure used by Ebbinghaus that involved memorizing a list of verbal stimuli (e.g., nonsense syllables) and then recalling them in the exact order of presentation.

Serial order problem   The problem of explaining sequences of behavioral events in neurological terms; posed by Lashley as a problem not solvable by traditional S-R behaviorist models.

Serviceable associated habits   Darwin's belief that emotional expressions were the product of evolutionary forces; certain expressions (e.g., sneer) originally had some survival function.

Sexual selection   Darwin's theory, expressed in his *Descent of Man*, that mate selection is influenced by factors (e.g., coloration), not necessarily relevant for natural selection, that favor one male over another in the competition for females.

Sign-gestalt   For Tolman, intervening variable referring to learned relationships between stimuli and an animal's expectation about the consequences of choosing path A over path B.

Similarity   Gestalt organizing principle of perception, a tendency to perceive that objects resembling each other "belong" together.

Simple ideas   For Locke, ideas resulting from sensory experience or simple reflection.

Social contract   Proposal that an implied contract exists between government, which provides for the common good, and the governed, which agrees to follow laws, pay taxes, and so on.

Social Darwinism   The belief that evolutionary forces were natural and inevitable and that any attempt to disrupt them (e.g., by creating programs for the poor) was misguided and doomed to failure; associated with Spencer.

Spatial contiguity   When a person experiences two events simultaneously, they become associated, according to Hartley.

Spatial summation   Process described by Sherrington; individual stimuli fail to elicit a response, but several stimuli simultaneously in close spatial proximity to each other will produce one; supported Sherrington's proposal of the synapse.

Species problem   Problem of the origin of species, addressed by Enlightenment thinkers faced with increasing uncertainty over Biblical accounts.

Specific energy of nerves   Doctrine proposed by Bell and Müller that different sensory nerves convey different qualities; pointed out that we perceive the world indirectly through the action of our nervous systems.

Spiritualism   Popular 19th-century belief in the afterlife and in the ability to communicate with the dead; William James was a strong believer that spiritualist claims needed to be evaluated seriously.

Stimulus control   In a stimulus environment in which a behavior is reinforced regularly, the stimulus is said to gain stimulus control over the behavior.

Stimulus error   To be avoided for proper introspection, according to Titchener, this was a tendency to report the products of conscious experience instead of the conscious experience itself.

Structuralism   School of psychology associated with Titchener; focused on identifying the structural elements of human conscious experience, primarily through basic laboratory and introspective methods.

Subjective idealism   For Berkeley, the philosophical position that the reality of the material world cannot be determined with certainty; we can be certain of the reality of our own perceptions, however.

Subtractive method   Method of measuring the duration of mental events, pioneered by Donders; reaction times for simple tasks were subtracted from reaction times for more "complicated" tasks.

Subvocal speech   Watson's definition of thinking.

Suggestion   The ability to uncritically accept an idea or command from another; underlies hypnosis and was central to the view of hypnosis held by Liebeault and Bernheim of the Nancy school.

Survey method   Research method that originated with Darwin's questionnaires on emotion and Galton's questionnaires on a variety of topics; Galton is normally credited with creating the survey method.

Synapse   physical space between neurons; first proposed by Sherrington.

Systematic desensitization   Behavior therapy procedure in which fear response is replaced by an incompatible response (e.g., relaxation); pioneered by Jones and Wolpe, who named it.

Systematic experimental introspection   Form of introspection, associated with Külpe and Titchener, in which the experience of complex mental events was followed by detailed introspective descriptions; a more elaborate form of introspection than Wundt's.

Temporal contiguity   When a person experiences two events in immediate succession, they become associated, according to Hartley.

Temporal summation   Process described by Sherrington; individual stimuli fail to elicit a response, but several stimuli in close temporal contiguity will produce one; supported Sherrington's proposal of the synapse.

Thanatos   In Freudian theory, the name given to the death instinct and manifested in aggression.

Thresholds   Points on a continuum of awareness where a person passes from no conscious awareness to some awareness (absolute threshold) or from an awareness that one stimulus is noticeably different from another stimulus (difference threshold); associated with Leibniz and begun as a topic in experimental psychology by Weber and Fechner.

Topology   Mathematical field of nonquantitative spatial geometry, used by Lewin as a basis for his field theory.

TOTE Unit   Feedback unit (Test-Operate-Test-Exit) to replace reflex arc; proposed by Miller, Galanter, and Pribram and influenced by developments in cybernetics.

Trait   A characteristic and distinctive attribute of a person.

Transfer   The effect of learning in one situation on learning in a second situation; could be positive or negative; pioneer studies by Woodworth and Thorndike.

Transference   In Freudian psychoanalysis, occurs when the patient develops a strong emotional attachment to the therapist.

Trial-and-error learning   Thorndike's explanation for the behavior of his cats in puzzle boxes—they escaped by trying various behaviors until hitting on one that worked; also used by Morgan as a parsimonious explanation for the behavior of dogs escaping from yards.

Trichromatic theory   The Young-Helmholtz theory of color vision, which proposed the existence of three different color-sensitive cells in the eye, one for each of the primary colors (red, green, blue); color vision was believed to result from various combinations of firings of these cells.

Tropisms   Forced movements; automatic responses to specific stimuli, as studied by Loeb.

Turing test In artificial intelligence, a thought problem posed by Turing to distinguish humans from computers.

Twin studies First suggested by Galton as a means of demonstrating the heritability of intelligence.

Two-point threshold Point where the perception of two points touching the skin changes from "one point perceived" to "two points perceived"; studied extensively by Weber.

Type R conditioning Skinner's term for operant conditioning, in which an association is formed between some behavior (R) and a consequence.

Type S conditioning Skinner's term for classical conditioning (Pavlov) in which two stimuli are associated and both produce the same response.

Unconditioned reflex (UCR) For Pavlov, any stimulus–response connection (e.g., food–salivate) that does not have to be learned.

Unconditioned stimulus (UCS) Any stimulus that will produce a specific reflex response (e.g., food elicits saliva).

Unconscious inference For Helmholtz, a process, outside of our awareness, by which our perceptions are influenced by past experiences.

Uniformitarianism Theory in geology, championed by Lyell, that geological change occurred gradually, over a long period of time, and as a consequence of such regular phenomena as erosion.

Valence For Lewin, term used to describe whether an object is valued by the person (positive valence) or not valued (negative valence).

Variability hypothesis The idea that men had a greater degree of variability in most traits, compared to women, and were therefore at a selective advantage in evolutionary terms.

Vector For Lewin, refers to the direction of a desired goal.

Vitalism Belief that a "life force" or vital force existed that went beyond the physical and chemical components of living organisms; opposed to materialism.

Voluntarism Wundt's system of psychology, so called because of his emphasis on the idea that the mind actively organizes information.

Von Restorff effect Increased recall of information that stands out in some manner from other to-be-learned information.

Weber's law As stimulus A increases in intensity, it takes progressively larger differences between stimulus A and stimulus B for a person to detect a difference between the two; the jnd divided by the size of the standard stimulus is a constant.

White paper Locke's term, borrowed from Aristotle, for the nature of the mind at birth; knowledge acquired through experience is analogous to writing on this white paper.

Word association test Procedure associated with both Galton and Jung to investigate the nature of associations in the mind; involves responding to a stimulus word with the first response word that comes to mind.

Zeigarnik effect Named for a student of Lewin; refers to a tendency to be more likely to recall unfinished tasks than finished tasks.

Zeitgeist The overall intellectual, political, and cultural climate of a particular historical era.

PHOTO AND ILLUSTRATION CREDITS

PHOTO CREDITS

Chapter 1 Figure 1.1 Rick Zaidan/Zaidan Photography. Figure 1.2 Robert M. Pringle/Harvard Alumni Bulletin (Now Harvard Magazine). Figure 1.3 C. James Goodwin.

Chapter 2 Figure 2.4 Copyright © Fabian von Poser/ AgeFotostock America, Inc. Figure 2.5 The Granger Collection. Figure 2.6 Copyright © Photodreams1/Alamy.

Chapter 3 Figure 3.1 Copyright © SSPL/The Image Works. Figure 3.4 C. James Goodwin. Figure 3.6 Courtesy of Musée de Dupuytren. Figure 3.9 Courtesy National Library of Medicine. Figure 3.10 The Granger Collection, New York. Figure 3.11 Archives of the History of American Psychology, The Center for the History of Psychology-The University of Akron.

Chapter 4 Figure 4.3 Science Source/Photo Researchers. Figure 4.4 Archives of the History of American Psychology, The Center for the History of Psychology-The University of Akron. Figure 4.5 Courtesy Clark University Archives. Figure 4.6 Copyright © Bettmann/Corbis Images. Figure 4.8 James Goodwin.

Chapter 5 Figure 5.1 Copyright © Everett Collection Inc/Alamy. Figure 5.3a Hulton Archive/Stringer/Getty Images. Figure 5.3b Mary Evans/Photo Researchers, Inc. Figure 5.4 Copyright © Image Asset Managemen/AgeFotostock America, Inc. Figure 5.5 The Granger Collection, New York. Figure 5.6. Photo from wikipedia: http://en.wikipedia.org/wiki/File:Alfred_Russel_Wallace_ 1862_-_Project_Gutenberg_eText_15997.png. Figures 5.7a and 5.7b Copyright © SSPL/The Image Works. Figure 5.8 Image from wikipedia: http://en.wikipedia.org/wiki/File: George_John_Romanes.jpg. Figure 5.9 University of Bristol, UK. Figure 5.10 Copyright © Corbis. Figure 5.11 Copyright © SSPL/The Image Works.

Chapter 6 Figure 6.1 Courtesy Clark University Archives. Figure 6.2 By permission of the Houghton Library, Harvard University. Figure 6.3 By permission of the Houghton Library, Harvard University. Figure 6.4 Clark University Archives. Figures 6.5a and 6.5b Courtesy Clark University Archives. Figure 6.7 Copyright © Corbis. Figure 6.8 Photo by Partridge, courtesy Wellesley College Archives.

Chapter 7 Figure 7.1 Archives of the History of American Psychology, The Center for the History of Psychology-The University of Akron. Figure 7.5 Courtesy of the Society of Experimental Psychologists. Figure 7.6 Image from wikipedia: http://en.wikipedia. org/wiki/File: James_Rowland_Angell.png. Figure 7.11 Copyright © Bettmann/Corbis Images. Figure 7.12 Archives of the History of American Psychology, The Center for the History of Psychology-The University of Akron.

Chapter 8 Figure 8.1 From Scripture, E. E. (1985), Thinking, Feeling, Doing. Meadville, PA: Chautauqua– Century Press. Figure 8.2 The Granger Collection, NYC- All rights reserved. Figure 8.3 Archives of the History of American Psychology, The Center for the History of Psychology-The University of Akron. Figure 8.4 Archives of the History of American Psychology, The Center for the History of Psychology-The University of Akron. Figure 8.5 Photo from wikipedia: http://commons.wikimedia.org/wiki/File: Kallikaks_deborah1.jpg. Figure 8.6 Copyright © Bettmann/CORBIS. Figure 8.7 Courtesy National Library of Medicine. Figure 8.8 Archives of the History of American Psychology, The Center for the History of Psychology-The University of Akron. Figure 8.9 Copyright © Bettmann/ Corbis Images. Figure 8.12 Picture History/NewsCom. Figure 8.14 UPI/Corbis–Bettmann.

Chapter 9 Figure 9.1 Image from wikipedia: http://en. wikipedia.org/wiki/File:Carlstumpf.jpg. Figure 9.2 UPI/ Bettmann/Copyright © Corbis. Figure 9.3 Archives of the

537

History of American Psychology, The Center for the History of Psychology-The University of Akron. Figure 9.11 Copyright © INTERFOTO/Alamy.

Chapter 10 Figure 10.3 The Granger Collection, New York. Figure 10.4b Nicolai, G. F. (1907). Die physiologische methodik zur erforschung der tierpsyche, ihre möglichkeit und ihre anwendung [The physiological method for research in animal psychology, its method and application]. *Journal für Psychologie und Neurologie, 10,* 1–27. Page 326, Figure 10.5 Carr, H. A., & Watson, J. B. (1908). Orientation in the white rat. *Journal of Comparative Neurology and Psychology, 18,* 27–44. Figure 10.6 Journal of Zoophily, 1907, 16(6), p.65. Figure 10.7 Archives of the History of American Psychology, The Center for the History of Psychology-The University of Akron. Figure 10.8 Archives of the History of American Psychology, The Center for the History of Psychology-The University of Akron. Figure 10.9 Archives of the History of American Psychology, The Center for the History of Psychology-The University of Akron.

Chapter 11 Figure 11.1 Archives of the History of American Psychology, The Center for the History of Psychology-The University of Akron. Figure 11.2 Archives of the History of American Psychology, The Center for the History of Psychology-The University of Akron. Figure 11.8 Archives of the History of American Psychology, The Center for the History of Psychology-The University of Akron. Figure 11.10 UPI/Bettmann/Copyright © Corbis–Bettmann. Figure 11.11 Photo courtesy of Kathleen Davis. Figure 11.12 Walter Dawn/Photo Researchers. Figures 11.14a and 11.14b Bob Bailey Animal Behavior Enterprises.

Chapter 12 Figure 12.1 Copyright © Corbis. Figure 12.2 Courtesy Ludy T. Benjamin. Figure 12.3 Copyright © Corbis. Figure 12.4 Courtesy National Library Medicine. Figure 12.5 Hulton Archive/Getty Images, Inc. Figure 12.6 Copyright © AP/Wide World Photos. Figure 12.7 Mary Evans Picture Library/Sigmund Freud Copyrights.

Chapter 13 Figure 13.1 Image from wikipedia: http://en.wikipedia.org/wiki/File: WitmerYoung.jpeg. Figure 13.2 Archives of the History of American Psychology, The Center for the History of Psychology-The University of Akron. Figure 13.3 Archives of the History of American Psychology, The Center for the History

of Psychology-The University of Akron. Figure 13.4 Bettmann/Copyright © Corbis. Figure 13.5 ANNA WIDOFF Agence France Presse/NewsCom. Figure 13.6 The Granger Collection, NYC. All rights reserved. Figure 13.7 Bettmann/Copyright © Corbis. Figure 13.9 (left) and (right) Women in the Relay Assembly Test Room, ca. 1930. Western Electric Company Hawthorne Studies Collection. Baker Library Historical Collections. Harvard Business School. Property of AT&T Archives. Reprinted with permission of AT&T.

Chapter 14 Figure 14.2 Archives of the History of American Psychology, The Center for the History of Psychology-The University of Akron. Figure 14.4 Chris F. Payne/McGill University Archives, PR041564. Figure 14.5 Copyright © Estate of Francis Bello/Photo Researchers. Figure 14.6 The Granger Collection, New York. Figure 14.7 Copyright © Tappe/ullstein bild/The Image Works.

Chapter 15 Figure 15.1 Courtesy George Bush Presidential Library & Museum. Figure 15.2 Copyright © Bettmann/Corbis Images.

ILLUSTRATION CREDITS

Chapter 2 Page 35, Figure 2.1 Fearing, F. (1930). *Reflex action: A study in the history of physiological psychology.* New York: Hafner. Figure 2.2 Finger, S. (2000). *Minds behind the brain: A history of the pioneers and their discoveries.* New York: Oxford University Press. Page 43, Figure 2.3 Berkeley, G. (1948). An essay towards a new theory of vision. In A. A. Luce & T. E. Jessup (Eds.), *The works of George Berkeley, Bishop of Cloyne. Vol. 1.* London: Thomas Nelson & Sons. (Original work published 1709).

Chapter 3 Page 69, Figure 3.2 Helmholtz, H. (1965). Hermann Ludwig Ferdinand von Helmholtz (1821–1894) on the three-color theory of vision and visual specific nerve energies, 1860. In R. J. Herrnstein & E. G. Boring (Eds.), *A sourcebook in the history of psychology* (pp. 223–229). Cambridge, MA: Harvard University Press. (Original work published 1860). Page 79, Figure 3.5 Harlow, J. M. (1868). *Recovery from the passage of an iron bar through the head.* Boston: Clapp. Page 82 Figure 3.7 Fritsch, G., & Hitzig, E. (1965). Gustav Fritsch (1838–1927) and Eduard Hitzig (1838–1907) on cerebral motor centers, 1870. In R. J. Herrnstein & E. G.

Boring (Eds.), *A sourcebook in the history of psychology* (pp. 229–233). Cambridge, MA: Harvard University Press. (Original work published 1870). Figure 3.8 Boring, E. G. (1950). *A history of experimental psychology* (2nd ed.). Englewood Cliffs, NJ: Prentice-Hall. Page 88, Figure 3.12 Lashley, K. S. (1929). *Brain mechanisms and intelligence.* Chicago: University of Chicago Press. Page 89, Figure 3.13 Lashley, K. S. (1929). *Brain mechanisms and intelligence.* Chicago: University of Chicago Press.

Chapter 4 Page 96, Figure 4.2 Boring, E. G. (1950). *A history of experimental psychology* (2nd ed.). Englewood Cliffs, NJ: Prentice-Hall. Page 118, Figure 4.7 Drawn by C. James Goodwin, from the original Ebbinghaus data that was presented in table form.

Chapter 6 Page 184, Figure 6.6 C. James Goodwin.

Chapter 7 Page 205, Figure 7.3 Titchener, E. B. (1901). *Experimental psychology: A manual of laboratory practice. Vol. 1: Qualitative experiments. Part 1: Student's manual; part 2: Instructor's manual.* New York: Macmillan. Page 206, Figure 7.4 Titchener, E. B. (1905a). *Experimental psychology: A manual of laboratory practice. Vol. 2: Quantitative experiments. Part 1: Student's manual; part 2: Instructor's manual.* New York: Macmillan. Page 222, Figure 7.7 C. James Goodwin. Page 224, Figure 7.8 Thorndike, E. L. (2000). *Animal intelligence: Experimental studies.* New Brunswick, NJ: Transaction Publishers. (Original work published 1911). Page 225, Figure 7.9 Burnham, J. C. (1972). Thorndike's puzzle boxes. *Journal of the History of the Behavioral Sciences, 8,* 159–167. Page 226, Figure 7.10 Thorndike, E. L. (2000). *Animal intelligence: Experimental studies.* New Brunswick, NJ: Transaction Publishers. (Original work published 1911).

Chapter 8 Page 262, Figure 8.10 Yoakum, C. S., & Yerkes, R. M. (1920). *Army mental tests.* New York: Holt. Page 263, Figure 8.11 Yoakum, C. S., & Yerkes, R. M. (1920). *Army mental tests.* New York: Holt. Page 271, Figure 8.13 Viteles, M. S. (1932). *Industrial psychology.* New York: Norton.

Chapter 9 Page 287, Figure 9.4 Köhler, W. (1926). *The mentality of apes* (E. Winter, Trans.). New York: Harcourt, Brace. (Original work published 1917). Page 289, Figure 9.5 Rubin, E. (1958). Figure and ground. In D. C. Beardslee & M. Wertheimer (Eds.), *Readings in perception* (pp. 194–203). Princeton, NJ: Van Nostrand.

(Original work published 1915). Page 290, Figure 9.6 Wertheimer, M. (1967b). Laws of organization in perceptual forms. In W. D. Ellis (Ed.), *A source book of Gestalt psychology* (pp. 71–88). London: Routledge and Kegan Paul. (Original work published 1923). Page 290, Figure 9.7 C. James Goodwin. Page 293, Figure 9.8 Wertheimer, M. (1982). *Productive thinking.* Chicago: University of Chicago Press. (Original work published 1945). Page 294, Figure 9.9 Wertheimer, M. (1982). *Productive thinking.* Chicago: University of Chicago Press. (Original work published 1945). Page 296, Figure 9.10 Duncker, K. (1945). On problem solving. *Psychological Monographs, 58, Whole No. 270.* (Original work published 1935). Page 299, Figure 9.12 C. James Goodwin.

Chapter 10 Page 316, Figures 10.1 and 10.2 Pavlov, I. P. (1928). *Lectures on conditioned reflexes* (W. H. Gantt, Trans.). New York: International Publications. Page 322, Figure 10.4 Nicolai, G. F. (1907). Die physiologische methodik zur erforschung der tierpsyche, ihre möglichkeit und ihre anwendung [The physiological method for research in animal psychology, its method and application]. *Journal für Psychologie und Neurologie, 10,* 1–27. Page 326, Figure 10.5 Carr, H. A., & Watson, J. B. (1908). Orientation in the white rat. *Journal of Comparative Neurology and Psychology, 18,* 27–44.

Chapter 11 Page 353, Figure 11.3 Tolman, E. C. (1932). *Purposive behavior in animals and men.* New York: Appleton-Century-Crofts. Page 355, Figure 11.4 Tolman, E. C. (1932). *Purposive behavior in animals and men.* New York: Appleton-Century-Crofts. Page 356, Figure 11.5 Tolman, E. C., Ritchie, B. F., & Kalish, D. (1946b). Studies in spatial learning. II. Place learning versus response learning. *Journal of Experimental Psychology, 36,* 221229. Page 357, Figure 11.6 Tolman, E. C. (1948). Cognitive maps in rats and men. *Psychological Review, 55,* 189–208. Page 360, Figure 11.7 Hull, C. L. (1920). Quantitative aspects of the evolution of concepts. *Psychological Monographs, 28, No. 123.* Page 365, Figure 11.9 Hull, C. L. (1943). *Principles of behavior.* New York: Appleton-Century-Crofts. Page 371, Figure 11.13 C. James Goodwin.

Chapter 14 Page 451, Figure 14.2 C. James Goodwin. Page 456, Figure 14.4 Miller, G. A., Galanter, E., & Pribram, K. H. (1960). *Plans and the structure of behavior.* New York: Holt.

AUTHOR INDEX

SUBJECT INDEX

Adorno, et al.: *The Authoritarian Personality*	**1950**	N. Korean forces invade S. Korea
Boulder model for clinical training	1949	Gilbreth and Cary: *Cheaper by the Dozen*
Skinner: *Walden Two*	1948	
	1947	Transistor invented in Bell Labs
Spock: *Baby and Child Care*	1946	Nobel Prize for physics: Percy Bridgman
Wertheimer: *Productive Thinking*	**1945**	Atom bombs dropped on Japan; WW II ends
	1944	D-Day landings in Normandy
Hull: *Principles of Behavior*	1943	Academy Award Best Picture: *Casablanca*
	1942	
	1941	Pearl Harbor attacked; U.S. enters WW II
Hilgard and Marquis: *Conditioning and Learning*	**1940**	Hemingway: *For Whom the Bell Tolls*
Freud dies in London	1939	Germany invades Poland; WW II begins
Woodworth's "Columbia Bible"	1938	
AAAP formed by applied psychologists	1937	Steinbeck: *Of Mice and Men*
	1936	Berlin Olympics; 4 gold medals for Jesse Owens
Koffka: *Principles of Gestalt Psychology*	**1935**	
	1934	Toynbee: *A Study of History*
	1933	Hitler appointed chancellor of Germany
Bartlett: *Remembering*	1932	
	1931	Al Capone arrested for tax evasion
Lewin introduces B $= f$(P,E)	**1930**	
International conference at Yale / Psi Chi formed	1929	U.S. stock market crashes
Sumner begins his tenure at Howard University	1928	Amelia Earhart, first woman to fly across the Atlantic
	1927	Babe Ruth hits 60 home runs
	1926	
Köhler: *Mentality of Apes*	**1925**	Scopes "monkey trial" in Tennessee
	1924	21-day protest fast in India by Gandhi
Freud: *The Ego and the Id*	1923	
	1922	James Joyce: *Ulysses*
National Institute for Industrial Psychology founded	1921	Sacco and Vanzetti found guilty of murder
Watson and Rayner's Little Albert study	**1920**	Wharton: *Age of Innocence*
	1919	WW I ends; first meeting League of Nations, Paris
The Army testing program (Alpha and Beta)	1918	Red Sox win 3rd World Series in 4 years
	1917	
Terman's Stanford-Binet IQ test	1916	National Park Service established
	1915	Einstein proposes general theory of relativity
	1914	WW I begins in Europe; Panama Canal opens
Watson's behaviorist manifesto	1913	
Wertheimer's apparent motion study	1912	S.S. *Titanic* sinks
	1911	
	1910	W. E. B. Dubois founds NAACP
Freud's Clark lectures	1909	Explorer Robert Peary reaches North Pole
Washburn: *Animal Mind*	1908	Foster: *A Room with a View*
	1907	Baden-Powell founds Boy Scouts
Angell's presidential address on functionalism	1906	
Calkins elected first female APA president	**1905**	
Nobel Prize to Pavlov	1904	Barrie: *Peter Pan*
Pavlov's first public talk on conditioning (Madrid)	1903	London: *The Call of the Wild*
	1902	Doyle: *Hound of the Baskervilles*
First of Titchener's lab manuals (second in 1905)	1901	J. P. Morgan organizes U.S. Steel corporation
Freud: *Interpretation of Dreams*	**1900**	Planck formulates quantum theory in physics